101 Speeches of the World

101 Speeches of the World

Om Books International

Reprinted in 2022 by

Om Books International

Corporate & Editorial Office
A-12, Sector 64, Noida 201 301
Uttar Pradesh, India
Phone: +91 120 477 4100
Email: editorial@ombooks.com
Website: www.ombooksinternational.com

Sales Office
107, Ansari Road, Darya Ganj,
New Delhi 110 002, India
Phone: +91 11 4000 9000
Fax: +91 11 2327 8091
Email: sales@ombooks.com
Website: www.ombooks.com

Speeches on pp. 348-349, 511-515, 516-520, 521-530, 536-539, 545-547 and 773-783 have been taken from www.nobelprize.org

Compiled by: Anukriti Singh

ISBN: 978-93-52767-05-2

Printed in India

10 9 8 7 6 5 4 3 2

Contents

Last Speech Before the Outbreak of the Peloponnesian War

Pericles

(451 BC)

Pericles was an Athenian general, orator and a politician under whose leadership Athens witnessed the Golden Age. He undertook several cultural projects such as building temples and other important forms of architecture. He also made fine arts accessible to the masses and promoted literature and works of playwrights such as Sophocles.

The policies and strategies of this great leader led to the devastating Peloponnesian War. Before the outbreak of the war, Pericles gave this speech in support of the war. The speech was recorded by historian Thucydides.

There is one principle, Athenians, which I hold to through everything, and that is the principle of no concession to the Peloponnesians. I know that the spirit which inspires men while they are being persuaded to make war is not always retained in action; that as circumstances change, resolutions change. Yet I see that now as before the same, almost literally the same, counsel is demanded of me; and I put it to those of you who are allowing yourselves to be persuaded, to support the national resolves even in the case of reverses, or to forfeit all credit for their wisdom in the event of success. For sometimes the course of things is as arbitrary as the plans of man; indeed this is why we usually blame chance for whatever does not happen as we expected. Now it was clear before that Lacedaemon entertained designs against us, it is still more clear now. The treaty provides that we shall mutually submit our differences to legal settlement, and that we shall meanwhile each keep what we have. Yet the Lacedaemonians never yet made us any such offer, never yet would accept from us any such offer; on the contrary, they wish complaints to be settled by war instead of by negotiation; and in the end we find them here dropping the tone of expostulation and adopting that of command. They order us to raise the siege of Potidaea, to let Aegina be independent, to revoke the Megara decree; and they conclude with an ultimatum warning us to leave the Hellenes independent. I hope that you will none of you think that we shall be going to war for a trifle if we refuse to revoke the Megara decree, which appears in front of their complaints, and the revocation of which is to save us from war, or let any feeling of self-reproach linger in your minds, as if you went to war for slight cause. Why, this trifle contains the whole seal and trial of your resolution. If you give way, you will instantly have to meet some greater demand, as having been frightened into obedience in the first instance; while a firm refusal will make them clearly understand that they must treat you more as equals. Make your decision therefore at once, either to submit before you are harmed, or if we are to go to war, as I for one think we ought, to do so without caring whether the ostensible cause be great or small, resolved against making concessions or consenting to a precarious tenure of our possessions. For all claims from an equal, urged upon a neighbour as commands before any attempt at legal settlement, be they great or be they small, have only one meaning, and that is slavery. As to the war and the resources of either party, a detailed comparison will not show you the inferiority of Athens. Personally engaged in the cultivation of their land, without funds either private or public, the Peloponnesians are also without experience in long wars across sea, from the strict limit which poverty imposes on their attacks upon each other. Powers of this description are quite incapable of often manning a fleet or often sending out an army: they cannot afford the absence from their homes, the expenditure from their own funds; and besides, they have not command of the sea. Capital, it must be remembered, maintains a war more than forced contributions. Farmers are a class of men that are always more ready to serve in person than in purse. Confident that the former will survive the dangers, they are by no means so sure that the latter will not be prematurely exhausted, especially if the war last longer than they expect, which it very likely will. In a single battle the Peloponnesians and their allies may be able to defy all Hellas, but they are incapacitated from carrying on a war against a power different in character from their own, by the want of the single council-chamber requisite to prompt and vigorous action, and the substitution of a diet composed of various races, in which every state possesses an equal vote, and each presses its own ends, a condition of things which generally results in no action at all. The great wish of some is to avenge themselves on some particular enemy, the great wish of others to save their own pocket. Slow in assembling, they devote a very small fraction of the time to the consideration of any public object, most of it to the prosecution of their own objects. Meanwhile each fancies that no harm will come of his neglect, that it is the business of somebody else to look after this or that for him; and so, by the same notion being entertained by all separately, the common cause imperceptibly decays. But the principal point is the hindrance that they will experience from want of money. The slowness with which it comes in will cause delay; but the opportunities of war wait for no man. Again, we need not be alarmed either at the possibility of their raising fortifications in Attica, or at their navy. It would be difficult for any system of fortifications to establish a rival city, even in time of peace, much more, surely, in an enemy's country, with Athens just as much fortified against it as it against Athens; while a mere post might be able to do some harm to the country by incursions and by the facilities which it would afford for desertion, but can never prevent our sailing into their country and raising fortifications there, and making reprisals with our powerful fleet. For our naval skill is of more use to us for service on land, than their military skill for service at sea. Familiarity with the sea they will not find an easy acquisition. If you who have been practicing at it ever since the Median invasion have not yet brought it to perfection, is there any chance of anything considerable being effected by an agricultural, un-seafaring population, who will besides be prevented from practicing by the constant presence of strong squadrons of observation from Athens? With a small squadron they might hazard an engagement, encouraging their ignorance by numbers; but the restraint of a strong force will prevent their moving, and through want of practice they will grow more clumsy, and consequently more timid. It must be kept in mind that seamanship, just like anything else, is a matter of art, and will not admit of being taken up occasionally as an occupation for times of leisure; on the contrary, it is so exacting as to leave leisure for nothing else. Even if they were to touch the moneys at Olympia or Delphi, and try to seduce our foreign sailors by the temptation of higher pay, that would only be a serious danger if we could not still be a match for them by embarking our own citizens and the aliens resident among us. But in fact by this means we are always a match for them; and, best of all, we have a larger and higher class of native coxswains and sailors among our own citizens than all the rest of Hellas. And to say nothing of the danger of such a step, none of our foreign sailors would consent to become an outlaw from his country, and to take service with them and their hopes, for the sake of a few days' high pay. This, I think, is a tolerably fair account of the position of the Peloponnesians; that of Athens is free from the defects that I have criticized in them, and has other advantages of its own, which they can show nothing to equal. If they march against our country we will sail against theirs, and it will then be found that the desolation of the whole of Attica is not the same as that of even a fraction of Peloponnese; for they will not be able to supply the deficiency except by a battle, while we have plenty of land both on the islands and the continent. The rule of the sea is indeed a great matter. Consider for a moment. Suppose that we were islanders; can you conceive a more impregnable position? Well, this in future should, as far as possible, be our conception of our position. Dismissing all thought of our land and houses, we must vigilantly guard the sea and the city. No 3 irritation that we may feel for the former must provoke us to a battle with the numerical superiority of the Peloponnesians. A victory would only be succeeded by another battle against the same superiority: a reverse involves the loss of our allies, the source of our strength, who will not remain quiet a day after we become unable to march against them. We must cry not over the loss of houses and land but of men's lives; since houses and land do not gain men, but men them. And if I had thought that I could persuade you, I would have bid you go out and lay them waste with your own hands, and show the Peloponnesians that this at any rate will not make you submit. I have many other reasons to hope for a favourable issue, if you can consent not to combine schemes of fresh conquest with the conduct of the war, and will abstain from willfully involving yourselves in other dangers; indeed, I am more afraid of our own blunders than of the enemy's devices. But these matters shall be explained in another speech, as events require; for the present dismiss these men with the answer that we will allow Megara the use of our market and harbours, when the Lacedaemonians suspend their alien acts in favour of us and our allies, there being nothing in the treaty to prevent either one or the other: that we will leave the cities independent, if independent we found them when we made the treaty, and when the Lacedaemonians grant to their cities an independence not involving subservience to Lacedaemonian interests, but such as each severally may desire: that we are willing to give the legal satisfaction which our agreements specify, and that we shall not commence hostilities, but shall resist those who do commence them. This is an answer agreeable at once to the rights and the dignity of Athens. It must be thoroughly understood that war is a necessity; but that the more readily we accept it, the less will be the ardour of our opponents, and that out of the greatest dangers communities and individuals acquire the greatest glory. Did not our fathers resist the Medes not only with resources far different from ours, but even when those resources had been abandoned; and more by wisdom than by fortune, more by daring than by strength, did not they beat off the barbarian and advance their affairs to their present height? We must not fall behind them, but must resist our enemies in any way and in every way, and attempt to hand down our power to our posterity unimpaired.

First Philippic

Demosthenes

(351 BC)

Demosthenes was an Athenian statesman widely regarded as the greatest orator of ancient Greece. Through his speeches, he roused the Athenians to oppose Philip of Macedon and his son, Alexander the Great.

Despite his failed attempts at public speaking at an early stage, he persevered and became a master of rhetoric. With the gift of oration, Demosthenes eventually became the leader of the democratic faction. He spoke against Philip of Macedon in his famous speeches that came to be known as 'Philippics'. 'Philippic 1' or the 'First Philippic' was his first oration against Philip of Macedon.

If some new subject were being brought before us, men of Athens, I would have waited until most of your ordinary advisers had declared their opinion; and if anything that they said were satisfactory to me, I would have remained silent, and only if it were not so, would I have attempted to express my own view. But since we find ourselves once more considering a question upon which they have often spoken, I think I may reasonably be pardoned for rising first of all. For if their advice to you in the past had been what it ought to have been, you would have had no occasion for the present debate.

In the first place, then, men of Athens, we must not be downhearted at our present situation, however wretched it may seem to be. For in the worst feature of the past lies our best hope for the future—in the fact, that is, that we are in our present plight because you are not doing your duty in any respect; for if you were doing all that you should do, and we were still in this evil case, we could not then even hope for any improvement. In the second place, you must bear in mind (what some of you have heard from others, and those who know can recollect for themselves), how powerful the Spartans were, not long ago, and yet how noble and patriotic your own conduct was, when instead of doing anything unworthy of your country you faced the war with Sparta in defense of the right. Now why do I remind you of these things? It is because, men of Athens, I wish you to see and to realize, that so long as you are on your guard you have nothing to fear; but that if you are indifferent, nothing can be as you would wish: for this is exemplified for you both by the power of Sparta in those days, to which you rose superior because you gave your minds to your affairs; and by the insolence of Philip today, which troubles us because we care nothing for the things which should concern us. If, however, any of you, men of Athens, when he considers the immense force now at Philip›s command, and the city›s loss of all her strongholds, thinks that Philip is a foe hard to conquer, I ask him (right though he is in his belief) to reflect also that there was a time when we possessed Pydna and Poteidaea and Methone; when all the surrounding country was our own, and many of the tribes which are now on his side were free and independent, and more inclined to be friendly to us than to him. Now if in those days Philip had made up his mind that it was a hard thing to fight against the Athenians, with all their fortified outposts on his own frontiers, while he was destitute of allies, he would have achieved none of his recent successes, nor acquired this great power. But Philip saw quite clearly, men of Athens, that all these strongholds were prizes of war, displayed for competition. He saw that in the nature of things the property of the absent belongs to those who are on the spot, and that of the negligent to those who are ready for toil and danger. It is, as you know, by acting upon this belief, that he has brought all those places under his power, and now holds them—some of them by right of capture in war, others in virtue of alliances and friendly understandings; for everyone is willing to grant alliance and to give attention to those whom they see to be prepared and ready to take action as is necessary. If then, men of Athens, you also will resolve to adopt this principle today—

the principle which you have never observed before—if each of you can henceforward be relied upon to throw aside all this pretence of incapacity, and to act where his duty bids him, and where his services can be of use to his country; if he who has money will contribute, and he who is of military age will join the campaign; if, in one plain word, you will resolve henceforth to depend absolutely on yourselves, each man no longer hoping that he will need to do nothing himself, and that his neighbour will do everything for him; then, God willing, you will recover your own; you will take back all that your indolence has lost, and you will have your revenge upon Philip. Do not imagine that his fortune is built to last forever, as if he were a God. He also has those who hate him and fear him, men of Athens, and envy him too, even among those who now seem to be his closest friends. All the feelings that exist in any other body of men must be supposed to exist in Philip's supporters. Now, however, all such feelings are cowed before him: your slothful apathy has taken away their only rallying point; and it is this apathy that I bid you put off today. Mark the situation, men of Athens: mark the pitch which the man's outrageous insolence has reached, when he does not even give you a choice between action and inaction, but threatens you, and utters (as we are told) haughty language: for he is not the man to rest content in possession of his conquests: he is always casting his net wider; and while we procrastinate and sit idle, he is setting his toils around us on every side. When, then, men of Athens, when, I say, will you take the action that is required? What are you waiting for? 'We are waiting,' you say, 'till it is necessary' But what must we think of all that is happening at this present time? Surely the strongest necessity that a free people can experience is the shame which they must feel at their position! What? Do you want to go round asking one another, 'Is there any news?' Could there be any stranger news than that a man of Macedonia is defeating Athenians in war, and ordering the affairs of the Hellenes? 'Is Philip dead?' 'No, but he is sick.' And what difference does it make to you? For if anything should happen to him, you will soon raise up for yourselves a second Philip, if it is thus that you attend to your interests. Indeed, Philip himself has not risen to this excessive height through his own strength, so much as through our neglect. I go even further. If anything happened to Philip—if the operation of Fortune, who always cares for us better than we care for ourselves, were to effect this too for us—you know that if you were at hand, you could descend upon the general confusion and order everything as you wished; but in your present condition, even if circumstances offered you Amphipolis, you could not take it; for your forces and your minds alike are far away.

Well, I say no more of the obligation which rests upon you all to be willing and ready to do your duty; I will assume that you are resolved and convinced. But the nature of the armament which, I believe, will set you free from such troubles as these, the numbers of the force, the source from which we must obtain funds, and the best and quickest way, as it seems to me, of making all further preparations—all this, men of Athens, I will at once endeavour to explain when I have made one request of you. Give your verdict on my proposal when you have heard the whole of it; do not prejudge it before I have done; and if at first the force which I propose appears unprecedented, do not think that I am merely creating delays. It is not those whose cry is, 'At once', 'Today', whose proposals will meet our need; for what has already happened cannot be prevented by any expedition now. It is rather he who can show the nature, the magnitude, and the financial possibility of a force which when provided will be able to continue in existence either until we are persuaded to break off the war, or until we have overcome the enemy; for thus only can we escape further calamity for the future. These things I believe I can show, though I would not stand in the way of any other speaker›s professions. It is no less a promise than this that I make; the event will soon test its fulfillment, and you will be the judges of it.

First then, men of Athens, I say that 50 warships must at once be got in readiness: and next, that you must be in such a frame of mind that, if any need arises, you will embark in person and sail. In addition, you must prepare transports for half our cavalry, and a sufficient number of boats. These, I think, should be in readiness to meet those sudden sallies of his from his own country against Thermopylae, the Chersonese, Olynthus, and any other place which he may select. For we must make him realize that there is a possibility of your rousing yourselves out of your excessive indifference, just as when once you went to Euboea, and before that (as we are told) to Haliartus, and finally, only the other day, to Thermopylae. Such a possibility, even if you are unlikely to make it a reality, as I think you ought to do, is not one which he can treat lightly; and you may thus secure one of two objects. On the one hand, he may know that you are on the alert—he will in fact know it well enough: there are only too many persons, I assure you, in Athens itself, who report to him all that happens here: and in that case his apprehensions will ensure his inactivity. But if, on the other hand, he neglects the warning, he may be taken off his guard; for there will be nothing to hinder you from sailing to his country, if he gives you the opportunity. These are the measures upon which I say you should all be resolved, and your preparations for them made. But before this, men of Athens, you must make ready a force which will fight without intermission, and do him damage. Do not speak to me of 10000 or 20000 mercenaries. I will have none of your paper-armies. Give me an army which will be the army of Athens, and will obey and follow the general whom you elect, be there one general or more, be he one particular individual, or be he who he may. You must also provide maintenance for this force. Now what is this force to be? How large is it to be? How is it to be maintained? How will it consent to act in this manner? I will answer these questions point by point. The number of mercenaries—but you must not repeat the mistake which has so often injured you, the mistake of, first, thinking any measures inadequate, and so voting for the largest proposal, and then, when the time for action comes, not even executing the smaller one; you must rather carry out and make provision for the smaller measure, and add to it, if it proves too small—the total number of soldiers, I say, must be two thousand, and of these five hundred must be Athenians, beginning from whatever age you think good: they must serve for a definite period—not a long one, but one to be fixed at your discretion—and in relays. The rest must be mercenaries. With these must be cavalry, 200 in number, of whom at least 50 must be Athenians, as with the infantry; and the conditions of service must be the same. You must also find transports for these. And what next? 10 swift ships of war.

For as he has a fleet, we need swift-sailing warships too, to secure the safe passage of the army. And how is maintenance to be provided for these? This also I will state and demonstrate, as soon as I have given you my reasons for thinking that a force of this size is sufficient, and for insisting that those who serve in it shall be citizens.

The size of the force, men of Athens, is determined by the fact that we cannot at present provide an army capable of meeting Philip in the open field; we must make plundering forays, and our warfare must at first be of a predatory nature. Consequently the force must not be over-big—we could then neither pay nor feed it—any more than it must be wholly insignificant. The presence of citizens in the force that sails I require for the following reasons. I am told that Athens once maintained a mercenary force in Corinth, under the command of Polystratus, Iphicrates, Chabrias and others, and that you yourselves joined in the campaign with them; and I remember hearing that these mercenaries, when they took the field with you, and you with them, were victorious over the Spartans. But even since your mercenary forces have gone to war alone, it is your friends and allies that they conquer, while your enemies have grown more powerful than they should be. After a casual glance at the war to which Athens has sent them, they sail off to Artabazus, or anywhere rather than to the war; and the general follows them naturally enough, for his power over them is gone when he can give them no pay. You ask what I bid you do. I bid you take away their excuses both from the general and the soldiers, by supplying pay and placing citizen-soldiers at their side as spectators of these mysteries of generalship; for our present methods are a mere mockery. Imagine the question to be put to you, men of Athens, whether you are at peace or no. 'At peace?' you would say; 'Of course not! We are at war with Philip.' Now have you not all along been electing from among your own countrymen 10 captains and generals, and cavalry-officers, and two masters-of-the-horse? And what are they doing? Except the one single individual whom you happen to send to the seat of war, they are all marshalling your processions for you with the commissioners of festivals. You are no better than men modelling puppets of clay. Your captains and your cavalry-officers are elected to be displayed in the streets, not to be sent to the war.

Surely, men of Athens, your captains should be elected from among yourselves, and your master-of-the-horse from among yourselves; your officers should be your own countrymen, if the force is to be really the army of Athens. As it is, the master-of-the-horse who is one of yourselves has to sail to Lemnos; while the master-of-the-horse with the army that is fighting to defend the possessions of Athens is Menelaus. I do not wish to disparage that gentleman; but whoever holds that office ought to have been elected by you.

Perhaps, however, while agreeing with all that I have said, you are mainly anxious to hear my financial proposals, which will tell you the amount and the sources of the funds required. I proceed, therefore, with these at once. First for the sum. The cost of the bare rations for the crews, with such a force, will be 90 talents and a little over—40 talents for ten swift ships, and 20 minae a month for each ship; and for the soldiers as much again, each soldier to receive rations to the value of 10 drachmae a month; and for the cavalry (two hundred in number, each to receive 30 drachmae a month) twelve talents. It may be said that the supply of bare rations to the members of the force is an insufficient initial provision; but this is a mistake. I am quite certain that, given so much, the army will provide everything else for itself from the proceeds of war, without injury to a single Hellene or ally of ours, and that the full pay will be made up by these means. I am ready to sail as a volunteer and to suffer the worst, if my words are untrue. The next question then is of ways and means, in so far as the funds are to come from yourselves. I will explain this at once.

[*A schedule of ways and means is read*.]

This, men of Athens, is what we have been able to devise; and when you put our proposals to the vote, you will pass them, if you approve of them; that so your war with Philip may be a war, not of resolutions and dispatches, but of actions.

I believe that the value of your deliberations about the war and the armament as a whole would be greatly enhanced, if you were to bear in mind the situation of the country against which you are fighting, remembering that most of Philip's plans are successfully carried out because he takes advantage of winds and seasons; for he waits for the Etesian winds or the winter-season, and only attacks when it would be impossible for us to effect a passage to the scene of action. Bearing this in mind, we must not carry on the war by means of isolated expeditions; we shall always be too late. We must have a permanent force and armament. As our winter-stations for the army we have Lemnos, Thasos, Sciathos, and the islands in that region, which have harbours and corn, and are well supplied with all that an army needs. And as to the time of year, whenever it is easy to approach the shore and the winds are not dangerous, our force can without difficulty lie close to the Macedonian coast itself, and block the mouths of the ports.

How and when he will employ the force is a matter to be determined, when the time comes, by the commander whom you put in control of it. What must be provided from Athens is described in the scheme which I have drafted. If, men of Athens, you first supply the sum I have mentioned, and then, after making ready the rest of the armament—soldiers, ships, cavalry—bind the whole force in its entirety, by law, to remain at the seat of war, if you become your own paymasters, your own commissioners of supply, but require your general to account for the actual operations; then there will be an end of these perpetual discussions of one and the same theme, which end in nothing but discussion: and in addition to this, men of Athens, you will, in the first place, deprive him of his chief source of supply. For what is this? Why, he carries on the war at the cost of your own allies, harrying and plundering those who sail the seas! And what will you gain besides this? You will place yourselves out of reach of disaster. It will not be as it was in the past, when he descended upon Lemnos and Imbros, and went off, with your fellow-citizens as his prisoners of war, or when he seized the vessels off Geraestus, and levied an enormous sum from them; or when (last of all) he landed at Marathon, seized the sacred trireme, and carried it off from the country; while all the time you can neither prevent these aggressions, nor yet send an expedition which will arrive when you intend it to arrive. But for what reason do you think, men of Athens, do the festival of the Panathenaea and the festival of the Dionysia always take place at the proper time, whether those to whom the charge of either festival is allotted are specially qualified persons or not—festivals upon which you spend larger sums of money than upon any armament whatsoever, and which involve an amount of trouble and preparation, which are unique, so far as I know, in the whole world— and yet your armaments are always behind the time—at Methone, at Pagasae, at Potidaea? It is because for the festivals all is arranged by law. Each of you knows long beforehand who is to supply the chorus, and who is to be steward of the games, for his tribe: he knows what he is to receive, and when, and from whom, and what he is to do with it. No detail is here neglected, nothing is left indefinite. But in all that concerns war and our preparation for it, there is no organization, no revision, no definiteness. Consequently it is not until the news comes that we appoint our trierarchs and institute exchanges of property for them, and inquire into ways and means. When that is done, we first resolve that the resident aliens and the independent freed men shall go on board; then we change our minds and say that citizens shall embark; then that we will send substitutes; and while all these delays are occurring, the object of the expedition is already lost. For we spend on preparation the time when we should be acting, and the opportunities which events afford will not wait for our slothful evasions; while as for the forces on which we think we can rely in the meantime, when the critical moment comes, they are tried and found wanting. And Philip's insolence has reached such a pitch, that he has sent such a letter as the following to the Euboeans.

[*The letter is read.*]

The greater part of the statements that have been read are true, men of Athens; and they ought not to be true! But I admit that they may possibly be unpleasant to hear; and if the course of future events would pass over all that a speaker passes over in his speech, to avoid giving pain, we should be right in speaking with a view to your pleasure. But if attractive words, spoken out of season, bring their punishment in actual reality, then it is disgraceful to blind our eyes to the truth, to put off everything that is unpleasant, to refuse to understand even so much as this, that those who conduct war rightly must not follow in the wake of events, but must be beforehand with them: for just as a general may be expected to lead his army, so those who debate must lead the course of affairs, in order that what they resolve upon may be done, and that they may not be forced to follow at the heels of events. You, men of Athens, have the greatest power in the world-warships, infantry, cavalry, revenue. But none of these elements of power have you used as you ought, down to this very day. The method of your warfare with Philip is just that of barbarians in a boxing-match. Hit one of them, and he hugs the place; hit him on the other side, and there go his hands; but as for guarding, or looking his opponent in the face, he neither can nor will do it. It is the same with you. If you hear that Philip is in the Chersonese, you resolve to make an expedition there; if he is at Thermopylae, you send one there; and wherever else he may be, you run up and down in his steps. It is he that leads your forces. You have never of yourselves come to any salutary decision in regard to the war. No single event do you ever discern before it occurs—before you have heard that something has happened or is happening. Perhaps there was room for this backwardness until now; but now we are at the very crisis, and such an attitude is possible no longer. Surely, men of Athens, it is one of the gods—one who blushes for Athens, as he sees the course which events are taking—that has inspired Philip with this restless activity. If he were content to remain at peace, in possession of all that he has won by conquest or by forestalling us—if he had no further plans—even then, the record against us as a people, a record of shame and cowardice and all that is most dishonourable, would, I think, seem complete enough to some of you. But now he is always making some new attempt, always grasping after something more; and unless your spirit has utterly departed, his conduct will perhaps bring you out into the field. It amazes me, men of Athens, that not one of you remembers with any indignation, that this war had its origin in our intention to punish Philip; and that now, at the end of it, the question is, how we are to escape disaster at his hands. But that he will not stay his progress until someone arrests it is plain enough. Are we then to wait for that? Do you think that all is right, when you dispatch nothing but empty ships and somebody's hopes? Shall we not embark? Shall we not now, if never before, go forth ourselves, and provide at least some small proportion of Athenian soldiers? Shall we not sail to the enemy's country? But I heard the question, 'At what point on his coast are we to anchor?' The war itself, men of

Athens, if you take it in hand, will discover his weak points: but if we sit at home listening to the mutual abuse and recriminations of our orators, you can never realize any of the results that you ought to realize. I believe that whenever any portion of Athens is sent with the forces, even if the whole city does not go, the favour of Heaven and of Fortune fights on our side. But whenever you dispatch anywhere a general with an empty resolution and some platform-hopes to support him, then you achieve nothing that you ought to achieve, your enemies laugh at you, and your allies are in deadly fear of all such armaments. It is impossible, utterly impossible, that any one man should be able to effect all that you wish for you. He can give undertakings and promises; he can accuse this man and that; and the result is that your fortunes are ruined. For when the general is at the head of wretched, unpaid mercenaries, and when there are those in Athens who lie to you light-heartedly about all that he does, and, on the strength of the tales that you hear, you pass decrees at random, what *must* you expect?

How then can this state of things be terminated? Only, men of Athens, when you expressly make the same men soldiers, witnesses of their general›s actions, and judges at his examination when they return home; for then the issue of your fortunes will not be a tale which you hear, but a thing which you will be on the spot to see. So shameful is the pass which matters have now reached, that each of your generals is tried for his life before you two or three times, but does not dare to fight in mortal combat with the enemy even once. They prefer the death of kidnappers and brigands to that of a general. For it is a felon›s death, to die by sentence of the court: the death of a general is to fall in battle with the enemy. Some of us go about saying that Philip is negotiating with Sparta for the overthrow of the Thebans and the breaking up of the free states; others, that he has sent ambassadors to the king; others, that he is fortifying cities in Illyria. We all go about inventing each his own tale. I quite believe, men of Athens, that he is intoxicated with the greatness of his successes, and entertains many such visions in his mind; for he sees that there are none to hinder him, and he is elated at his achievements. But I do not believe that he has chosen to act in such a way that the most foolish persons in Athens can know what he intends to do; for no persons are so foolish as newsmongers. But if we dismiss all such tales, and attend only to the certainty—that the man is our enemy, that he is robbing us of our own, that he has insulted us for a long time, that all that we ever expected any one to do for us has proved to be against us, that the future is in our own hands, that if we will not fight him now in his own country we shall perhaps be obliged to do so in ours—if, I say, we are assured of this, then we shall have made up our minds aright, and shall be quit of idle words. For you have not to speculate what the future may be: you have only to be assured that the future must be evil, unless you give heed and are ready to do your duty.

Well, I have never yet chosen to gratify you by saying anything which I have not felt certain would be for your good; and today I have spoken freely and without concealment, just what I believe. I could wish to be as sure of the good that a speaker will gain by giving you the best advice as of that which you will gain by listening to him. I should then have been far happier than I am. As it is, I do not know what will happen to me, for what I have said: but I have chosen to speak in the sure conviction that if you carry out my proposals, it will be for your good; and may the victory rest with that policy which will be for the good of all!

'Depart!'

Alexander the Great

(324 BC)

Alexander the Great, son of Philip of Macedon, established the largest empire of the ancient world, spanning from Greece to north-western India. Undefeated in battle, he remains one of the most successful military commanders in history.

Alexander the Great gave this speech when the Macedonians protested against his increasingly Persian style of dressing and the honorary posts assigned to the Persians. Angered at this mutiny, the king reproached the Macedonians and stripped some of them of honorary positions.

The speech which I am about to deliver will not be for the purpose of checking your start homeward, for, so far as I am concerned, you may depart wherever you wish. But for the purpose of making you understand when you take yourselves off, what kind of men you have been to us who have conferred such benefits upon you. In the first place, as is reasonable, I shall begin my speech from my father Philip. For he found you vagabonds and destitute of means, most of you clad in hides, feeding a few sheep up the mountain sides, for the protection of which you had to fight with small success against Illyrians, Triballians, and the border Thracians.

Instead of the hides he gave you cloaks to wear, and from the mountains he led you down into the plains, and made you capable of fighting the neighboring barbarians, so that you were no longer compelled to preserve yourselves by trusting rather to the inaccessible strongholds than to your own valor. He made you colonists of cities, which he adorned with useful laws and customs; and from being slaves and subjects, he made you rulers over those very barbarians by whom you yourselves, as well as your property, were previously liable to be carried off or ravaged.

He also added the greater part of Thrace to Macedonia, and by seizing the most conveniently situated places on the sea-coast, he spread abundance over the land from commerce, and made the working of the mines a secure employment. He made you rulers over the Thessalians, of whom you had formerly been in mortal fear; and by humbling the nation of the Phocians, he rendered the avenue into Greece broad and easy for you, instead of being narrow and difficult.

The Athenians and Thebans, who were always lying in wait to attack Macedonia, he humbled to such a degree, I also then rendering him my personal aid in the campaign, that instead of paying tribute to the former and being vassals to the latter, those states in their turn procure security to themselves by our assistance. He penetrated into the Peloponnese, and after regulating its affairs, was publicly declared commander-in-chief of all the rest of Greece in the expedition against the Persian, adding this glory not more to himself than to the commonwealth of the Macedonians.

These were the advantages which accrued to you from my father Philip; great indeed if looked at by themselves, but small if compared with those you have obtained from me. For though I inherited from my father only a few gold and silver goblets, and there were not even sixty talents in the treasury, and though I found myself charged with a debt of 500 talents owing by Philip, and I was obliged myself to borrow 800 talents in addition to these, I started from the country which could not decently support you, and forthwith laid open to you the passage of the Hellespont, though at that time the Persians held the sovereignty of the sea.

Having overpowered the satraps of Darius with my cavalry, I added to your empire the whole of Ionia, the whole of Aeolis, both Phrygias and Lydia, and I took Miletus by siege. All the other places I gained by voluntary surrender, and I granted you the privilege of appropriating the wealth found in them. The riches of Egypt and Cyrene, which I acquired without fighting a battle, have come to you. Coele-Syria, Palestine, and Mesopotamia are your property. Babylon, Bactra, and Susa are yours.

The wealth of the Lydians, the treasures of the Persians, and the riches of the Indians are yours; and so is the External Sea. You are viceroys, you are generals, you are captains. What then have I reserved to myself after all these labors, except this purple robe and this diadem? I have appropriated nothing myself, nor can any one point out my treasures, except these possessions of yours or the things which I am guarding on your behalf. Individually, however, I have no motive to guard them, since I feed on the same fare as you do, and I take only the same amount of sleep.

Nay, I do not think that my fare is as good as that of those among you who live luxuriously; and I know that I often sit up at night to watch for you, that you may be able to sleep.

But someone may say, that while you endured toil and fatigue, I have acquired these things as your leader without myself sharing the toil and fatigue. But who is there of you who knows that he has endured greater toil for me than I have for him? Come now, whoever of you has wounds, let him strip and show them, and I will show mine in turn; for there is no part of my body, in front at any rate, remaining free from wounds; nor is there any kind of weapon used either for close combat or for hurling at the enemy, the traces of which I do not bear on my person.

For I have been wounded with the sword in close fight, I have been shot with arrows, and I have been struck with missiles projected from engines of war; and though oftentimes I have been hit with stones and bolts of wood for the sake of your lives, your glory, and your wealth, I am still leading you as conquerors over all the land and sea, all rivers, mountains, and plains. I have celebrated your weddings with my own, and the children of many of you will be akin to my children.

Moreover I have liquidated of all those who had incurred them, without inquiring too closely for what purpose they were contracted, though you received such high pay, and carry off so much booty whenever there is booty to be got after a siege. Most of you have golden crowns, the eternal memorials of your valor and of the honor you receive from me. Whoever has been killed has met with a glorious end and has been honored with a splendid burial. Brazen statues of most of the slain have been erected at home, and their parents are held in honor) being released from all public service and from taxation. But no one of you has ever been killed in flight under my leadership. And now I was intending to send back those of you who are unfit for service, objects of envy to those at home; but since you all wish to depart, depart all of you!

Go back and report at home that your king Alexander, the conqueror of the Persians, Medes, Bactrians, and Sacians; the man who has subjugated the Uxians, Arachotians, and Drangians; who has also acquired the rule of the Parthians, Chorasmians, and Hyrcanians, as far as the Caspian Sea; who has marched over the Caucasus, through the Caspian Gates; who has crossed the rivers Oxus and Tanais, and the Indus besides, which has never been crossed by anyone else except Dionysus; who has also crossed the Hydaspes, Acesines, and Hydraotes, and who would have crossed the Hyphasis, if you had not shrunk back with alarm; who has penetrated into the Great Sea by both the mouths of the Indus; who has marched through the desert of Gadrosia, where no one ever before marched with an army; who on his route acquired possession of Carmania and the land of the Oritians, in addition to his other conquests, his fleet having in the meantime already sailed round the coast of the sea which extends from India to Persia— report that when you returned to Susa you deserted him and went away, handing him over to the protection of conquered foreigners.Perhaps this report of yours will be both glorious to you in the eyes of men and devout I ween in the eyes of the gods. Depart!

The First Oration Against Catiline

Cicero

Roman Senate (63 BC)

Marcus Tullius Cicero was a Roman statesman, lawyer and philosopher who was considered one of the greatest Roman orators. He was also a prolific writer and translator whose letters, notes and official dispatches were important sources that provided a glimpse into the society and politics of ancient Rome.

The Catiline Orations are one of the most famous orations by Cicero from the period when he was Consul. Through these orations, Cicero accused Senator Lucius Sergius Catilina of a plot to overthrow the Roman government.

When, O Catiline, do you mean to cease abusing our patience? How long is that madness of yours still to mock us? When is there to be an end of that unbridled audacity of yours, swaggering about as it does now? Do not the nightly guards placed on the Palatine Hill—do not the watches posted throughout the city—does not the alarm of the people, and the union of all good men—does not the precaution taken of assembling the senate in this most defensible place—do not the looks and countenances of this venerable body here present, have any effect upon you? Do you not feel that your plans are detected? Do you not see that your conspiracy is already arrested and rendered powerless by the knowledge which everyone here possesses of it? What is there that you did last night, what the night before—where is it that you were—who was there that you summoned to meet you—what design was there which was adopted by you, with which you think that any one of us is unacquainted?

Shame on the age and on its principles! The senate is aware of these things; the consul sees them; and yet this man lives. Lives! aye, he comes even into the senate. He takes a part in the public deliberations; he is watching and marking down and checking off for slaughter every individual among us. And we, gallant men that we are, think that we are doing our duty to the republic if we keep out of the way of his frenzied attacks.

You ought, O Catiline, long ago to have been led to execution by command of the consul. That destruction which you have been long plotting against us ought to have already fallen on your own head.

What? Did not that most illustrious man, Publius Scipio, the Pontifex Maximus, in his capacity of a private citizen, put to death Tiberius Gracchus, though but slightly undermining the constitution? And shall we, who are the consuls, tolerate Catiline, openly desirous to destroy the whole world with fire and slaughter? For I pass over older instances, such as how Caius Servilius Ahala with his own hand slew Spurius Maelius when plotting a revolution in the state. There was—there was once such virtue in this republic that brave men would repress mischievous citizens with severer chastisement than the most bitter enemy. For we have a resolution of the senate, a formidable and authoritative decree against you, O Catiline; the wisdom of the republic is not at fault, nor the dignity of this senatorial body. We, we alone—I say it openly, —we, the consuls, are wanting in our duty.

The senate once passed a decree that Lucius Opimius, the consul, should take care that the republic suffered no injury. Not one night elapsed. There was put to death, on some mere suspicion of disaffection, Caius Gracchus, a man whose family had borne the most unblemished reputation for many generations. There was slain Marcus Fulvius, a man of consular rank, and all his children. By a like decree of the senate the safety of the republic was entrusted to Caius Marius and Lucius Valerius, the consuls. Did not the vengeance of the republic, did not execution overtake Lucius Saturninus, a tribune of the people, and Caius Servilius, the pretor, without the delay of one single day? But we, for these twenty days, have been allowing the edge of the senate's authority to grow blunt, as it were. For we are in possession of a similar decree of the senate, but we keep it locked up in its parchment—buried, I may say, in the sheath; and according to this decree you ought, O Catiline, to be put to death this instant. You live,—and you live, not to lay aside, but to persist in your audacity.

I wish, O conscript fathers, to be merciful; I wish not to appear negligent amid such danger to the state; but I do now accuse myself of remissness and culpable inactivity. A camp is pitched in Italy, at the entrance of Etruria, in hostility to the republic; the number of the enemy increases every day; and yet the general of that camp, the leader of those enemies, we see within the walls—aye, and even in the senate—planning every day some internal injury to the republic. If, O Catiline, I should now order you to be arrested, to be put to death, I should, I suppose, have to fear lest all good men should say that I had acted tardily, rather than that any one should affirm that I acted cruelly. But yet this, which ought to have been done long since, I have good reason for not doing as yet; I will put you to death, then, when there shall be not one person possible to be found so wicked, so abandoned, so like yourself, as not to allow that it has been rightly done. As long as one person exists who can dare to defend you, you shall live; but you shall live as you do now, surrounded by my many and trusty guards, so that you shall not be able to stir one finger against the republic; many eyes and ears shall still observe and watch you, as they have hitherto done, though you shall not perceive them.

For what is there, O Catiline, that you can still expect, if night is not able to veil your nefarious meetings in darkness, and if private houses cannot conceal the voice of your conspiracy within their walls—if everything is seen and displayed? Change your mind: trust me: forget the slaughter and conflagration you are meditating. You are hemmed in on all sides; all your plans are clearer than the day to us; let me remind you of them. Do you recollect that on the 21st of October I said in the senate that on a certain day, which was to be the 27th of October, C. Manlius, the satellite and servant of your audacity, would be in arms? Was I mistaken, Catiline, not only in so important, so atrocious, so incredible a fact, but, what is much more remarkable, in the very day? I said also in the senate that you had fixed the massacre of the nobles for the 28th of October when many chief men of the senate had left Rome, not so much for the sake of saving themselves as of checking your designs. Can you deny that on that very day you were so hemmed in by my guards and my vigilance that you were unable to stir one finger against the republic; when you said that you would be content with the flight of the rest, and the slaughter of us who remained? What? When you made sure that you would be able to seize Praeneste on the 1st of November by a nocturnal attack, did you not find that that colony was fortified by my order, by my garrison, by my watchfulness and care? You do nothing, you plan nothing, you think of nothing which I not only do not hear, but which I do not see and know every particular of.

Listen while I speak of the night before. You shall now see that I watch far more actively for the safety than you do for the destruction of the republic. I say that you came the night before (I will say nothing obscurely) into the Scythe dealers' Street, to the house of Marcus Lecca; that many of your accomplices in the same insanity and wickedness came there, too. Do you dare to deny it? Why are you silent? I will prove it if you do deny it; for I see here in the senate some men who were there with you.

O ye immortal gods, where on earth are we? In what city are we living? What constitution is ours? There are here,—here in our body, O conscript fathers, in this the most holy and dignified assembly of the whole world, men who meditate my death, and the death of all of us, and the destruction of this city, and of the whole world. I, the consul, see them; I ask them their opinion about the republic, and I do not yet attack, even by words, those who ought to be put to death by the sword. You were, then, O Catiline, at Lecca's that night; you divided Italy into sections; you settled where everyone was to go; you fixed whom you were to leave at Rome, whom you were to take with you; you portioned out the divisions of the city for conflagration; you undertook that you yourself would at once leave the city, and said that there was then only this to delay you, —that I was still alive. Two Roman knights were found to deliver you from this anxiety, and to promise that very night, before daybreak, to slay me in my bed. All this I knew almost before your meeting had broken up. I strengthened and fortified my house with a stronger guard; I refused admittance, when they came, to those whom you sent in the morning to salute me, and of whom I had foretold to many eminent men that they would come to me at that time.

As, then, this is the case, O Catiline, continue as you have begun. Leave the city at least; the gates are open; depart. That Manlian camp of yours has been waiting too long for you as its general. And lead forth with you all your friends, or at least as many as you can; purge the city of your presence; you will deliver me from a great fear, when there is a wall between you and me. Among us you can dwell no longer—I will not bear it, I will not permit it, I will not tolerate it. Great thanks are due to the immortal gods, and to this very Jupiter Stator, in whose temple we are, the most ancient protector of this city, that we have already so often escaped so foul, so horrible, and so deadly an enemy to the republic. But the safety of the commonwealth must not be too often allowed to be risked on one man. As long as you, O Catiline, plotted against me while I was the consul-elect, I defended myself, not with a public guard, but by my own private diligence. When, in the next consular comitia, you wished to slay me when I was actually consul, and your competitors also, in the Campus Martius, I checked your nefarious attempt by the assistance and resources of my own friends, without exciting any disturbance publicly. In short, as often as you attacked me, I by myself opposed you, and that, too, though I saw that my ruin was connected with great disaster to the republic. But now you are openly attacking the entire republic.

You are summoning to destruction and devastation the temples of the immortal gods, the houses of the city, the lives of all the citizens—in short, all Italy. Wherefore, since I do not yet venture to do that which is the best thing, and which belongs to my office and to the discipline of our ancestors, I will do that which is more merciful if we regard its rigor, and more expedient for the State. For if I order you to be put to death, the rest of the conspirators will still remain in the republic; if, as I have long been exhorting you, you depart, your companions, those worthless dregs of the republic, will be drawn off from the city, too. What is the matter, Catiline? Do you hesitate to do that when I order you which you were already doing of your own accord? The consul orders an enemy to depart from the city. Do you ask me, Are you to go into banishment? I do not order it; but, if you consult me, I advise it.

For what is there, O Catiline, that can now afford you any pleasure in this city? For there is no one in it, except that band of profligate conspirators of yours, who does not fear you, —no one who does not hate you. What brand of domestic baseness is not stamped upon your life? What disgraceful circumstance is wanting to your infamy in your private affairs? From what licentiousness have your eyes, from what atrocity have your hands, from what iniquity has your whole body ever abstained? Is there one youth, when you have once entangled him in the temptations of your corruption, to whom you have not held out a sword for audacious crime, or a torch for licentious wickedness?

What? When lately by the death of your former wife you had made your house empty and ready for a new bridal, did you not even add another incredible wickedness to this wickedness? But I pass that over, and willingly allow it to be buried in silence, that so horrible a crime may not be seen to have existed in this city, and not to have been chastised. I pass over the ruin of your fortune, which you know is hanging over you against the ides of the very next month; I come to those things which relate not to the infamy of your private vices, not to your domestic difficulties and baseness, but to the welfare of the republic and to the lives and safety of us all.

Can the light of this life, O Catiline, can the breath of this atmosphere be pleasant to you, when you know that there is not one man of those here present who is ignorant that you, on the last day of the year, when Lepidus and Tullus were consuls, stood in the assembly armed; that you had prepared your hand for the slaughter of the consuls and chief men of the state, and that no reason or fear of yours hindered your crime and madness, but the fortune of the republic? And I say no more of these things, for they are not unknown to everyone. How often have you endeavored to slay me, both as consul elect and as actual consul? How many shots of yours, so aimed that they seemed impossible to be escaped, have I avoided by some slight stooping aside, and some dodging, as it were, of my body? You attempt nothing, you execute nothing, you devise nothing that can be kept hid from me at the proper time; and yet you do not cease to attempt and to contrive. How often already has that dagger of yours been wrested from your hands? How often has it slipped through them by some chance, and dropped down? And yet you cannot any longer do without it; and to what sacred mysteries it is consecrated and devoted by you I know not, that you think it necessary to plunge it in the body of the consul.

But now, what is that life of yours that you are leading? For I will speak to you not so as to seem influenced by the hatred I ought to feel, but by pity, nothing of which is due to you. You came a little while ago into the senate; in so numerous an assembly, who of so many friends and connections of yours saluted you? If this in the memory of man never happened to anyone else, are you waiting for insults by word of mouth, when you are overwhelmed by the most irresistible condemnation of silence? Is it nothing that at your arrival all those seats were vacated? That all the men of consular rank, who had often been marked out by you for slaughter, the very moment you sat down, left that part of the benches bare and vacant? With what feelings do you think you ought to bear this? On my honor, if my slaves feared me as all your fellow citizens fear you, I should think I must leave my house. Do not you think you should leave the city? If I say that I was even undeservedly so suspected and hated by my fellow citizens, I would rather flee from their sight than be gazed at by the hostile eyes of every one. And do you, who, from the consciousness of your wickedness, know that the hatred of all men is just and has been long due to you, hesitate to avoid the sight and presence of those men whose minds and senses you offend? If your parents feared and hated you, and if you could by no means pacify them, you would, I think, depart somewhere out of their sight. Now, your country, which is the common parent of all of us, hates and fears you, and has no other opinion of you, than that you are meditating parricide in her case; and will you neither feel awe of her authority, nor deference for her judgment, nor fear of her power?

And she, O Catiline, thus pleads with you, and after a manner silently speaks to you: There has now for many years been no crime committed but by you; no atrocity has taken place without you; you alone unpunished and unquestioned have murdered the citizens, have harassed and plundered the allies; you alone have had power not only to neglect all laws and investigations, but to overthrow and break through them. Your former actions, though they ought not to have been borne, yet I did bear as well as I could; but now that I should be wholly occupied with fear of you alone, that at every sound I should dread Catiline, that no design should seem possible to be entertained against me which does not proceed from your wickedness, this is no longer endurable. Depart, then, and deliver me from this fear—that, if it be a just one, I may not be destroyed; if an imaginary one, that at least I may at last cease to fear.

If, as I have said, your country were thus to address you, ought she not to obtain her request, even if she were not able to enforce it? What shall I say of your having given yourself into custody? What of your having said, for the sake of avoiding suspicion, that you were willing to dwell in the house of Marcus Lepidus? And when you were not received by him, you dared even to come to me, and begged me to keep you in my house; and when you had received answer from me that I could not possibly be safe in the same house with you, when I considered myself in great danger as long as we were in the same city, you came to Quintus Metellus, the pretor, and being rejected by him, you passed on to your associate, that most excellent man, Marcus Marcellus, who would be, I suppose you thought, most diligent in guarding you, most sagacious in suspecting you, and most bold in punishing you; but how far can we think that man ought to be from bonds and imprisonment who has already judged himself deserving of being given into custody.

Since, then, this is the case, do you hesitate, O Catiline, if you cannot remain here with tranquility, to depart to some distant land, and to trust your life, saved from just and deserved punishment, to flight and solitude? Make a motion, say you, to the senate (for that is what you demand), and if this body votes that you ought to go into banishment, you say that you will obey. I will not make such a motion—it is contrary to my principles, and yet I will let you see what these men think of you. Be gone from the city, O Catiline; deliver the republic from fear; depart into banishment, if that is the word you are waiting for. What now, O Catiline? Do you not perceive, do you not see the silence of these men; they permit it, they say nothing; why wait you for the authority of their words when you see their wishes in their silence?

But had I said the same to this excellent young man, Publius Sextius, or to that brave man, Marcus Marcellus, before this time the senate would deservedly have laid violent hands on me, consul though I be, in this very temple. But as to you, Catiline, while they are quiet they approve, while they permit me to speak they vote, while they are silent they are loud and eloquent. And not they alone, whose authority forsooth is dear to you, though their lives are unimportant, but the Roman knights, too, those most honorable and excellent men, and the other virtuous citizens who are now surrounding the senate, whose numbers you could see, whose desires you could know, and whose voices you a few minutes ago could hear, —aye, whose very hands and weapons I have for some time been scarcely able to keep off from you; but those, too, I will easily bring to attend you to the gates if you leave these places you have been long desiring to lay waste.

And yet, why am I speaking? That anything may change your purpose? That you may ever amend your life? That you may meditate flight or think of voluntary banishment? I wish the gods may give you such a mind; though I see, if alarmed at my words you bring your mind to go into banishment, what a storm of unpopularity hangs over me, if not at present, while the memory of your wickedness is fresh, at all events hereafter. But it is worthwhile to incur that, as long as that is but a private misfortune of my own, and is unconnected with the dangers of the republic. But we cannot expect that you should be concerned at your own vices, that you should fear the penalties of the laws, or that you should yield to the necessities of the republic, for you are not, O Catiline, one whom either shame can recall from infamy, or fear from danger, or reason from madness.

Wherefore, as I have said before, go forth, and if you wish to make me, your enemy as you call me, unpopular, go straight into banishment. I shall scarcely be able to endure all that will be said if you do so; I shall scarcely be able to support my load of unpopularity if you do go into banishment at the command of the consul; but if you wish to serve my credit and reputation, go forth with your ill-omened band of profligates; betake yourself to Manlius, rouse up the abandoned citizens, separate yourself from the good ones, wage war against your country, exult in your impious banditti, so that you may not seem to have been driven out by me and gone to strangers, but to have gone invited to your own friends.

Though why should I invite you, by whom I know men have been already sent on to wait in arms for you at the forum Aurelium; who I know has fixed and agreed with Manlius upon a settled day; by whom I know that that silver eagle, which I trust will be ruinous and fatal to you and to all your friends, and to which there was set up in your house a shrine as it were of your crimes, has been already sent forward. Need I fear that you can long do without that which you used to worship when going out to murder, and from whose altars you have often transferred your impious hand to the slaughter of citizens?

You will go at last where your unbridled and mad desire has been long hurrying you. And this causes you no grief, but an incredible pleasure. Nature has formed you, desire has trained you, fortune has preserved you for this insanity. Not only did you never desire quiet, but you never even desired any war but a criminal one; you have collected a band of profligates and worthless men, abandoned not only by all fortune but even by hope.

Then what happiness will you enjoy! With what delight will you exult! In what pleasure will you revel! When in so numerous a body of friends, you neither hear nor see one good man. All the toils you have gone through have always pointed to this sort of life; your lying on the ground not merely to lie in wait to gratify your unclean desires, but even to accomplish crimes; your vigilance, not only when plotting against the sleep of husbands, but also against the goods of your murdered victims, have all been preparations for this. Now you have an opportunity of displaying your splendid endurance of hunger, of cold, of want of everything; by which in a short time you will find yourself worn out. All this I effected when I procured your rejection from the consulship, that you should be reduced to make attempts on your country as an exile, instead of being able to distress it as consul, and that that which had been wickedly undertaken by you should be called piracy rather than war.

Now that I may remove and avert, O conscript fathers, any in the least reasonable complaint from myself, listen, I beseech you, carefully to what I say, and lay it up in your inmost hearts and minds. In truth, if my country, which is far dearer to me than my life—if all Italy—if the whole republic were to address me, 'Marcus Tullius, what are you doing?' Will you permit that man to depart whom you have ascertained to be an enemy? Whom you see ready to become the general of the war? Whom you know to be expected in the camp of the enemy as their chief, the author of all this wickedness, the head of the conspiracy, the instigator of the slaves and abandoned citizens, so that he shall seem not driven out of the city by you, but let loose by you against the city? Will you not order him to be thrown into prison, to be hurried off to execution, to be put to death with the most prompt severity? What hinders you? Is it the customs of our ancestors? But even private men have often in this republic slain mischievous citizens. Is it the laws which have been passed about the punishment of Roman citizens? But in this city those who have rebelled against the republic have never had the rights of citizens. Do you fear odium with posterity? You are showing fine gratitude to the Roman people which has raised you, a man known only by your own actions, of no ancestral renown, through all the degrees of honor at so early an age to the very highest office, if from fear of unpopularity or of any danger you neglect the safety of your fellow citizens. But if you have a fear of unpopularity, is that arising from the imputation of vigor and boldness, or that arising from that of inactivity and indecision most to be feared? When Italy is laid waste by war, when cities are attacked and houses in flames, do you not think that you will be then consumed by a perfect conflagration of hatred?

To this holy address of the republic, and to the feelings of those men who entertain the same opinion, I will make this short answer: If, O conscript fathers, I thought it best that Catiline should be punished with death, I would not have given the space of one hour to this gladiator to live in. If, forsooth, those excellent men and most illustrious cities not only did not pollute themselves, but even glorified themselves by the blood of Saturninus, and the Gracchi, and Flaccus, and many others of old time, surely I had no cause to fear lest for slaying this parricidal murderer of the citizens any unpopularity should accrue to me with posterity. And if it did threaten me to ever so great a degree, yet I have always been of the disposition to think unpopularity earned by virtue and glory not unpopularity.

Though there are some men in this body who either do not see what threatens, or dissemble what they do see; who have fed the hope of Catiline by mild sentiments, and have strengthened the rising conspiracy by not believing it; influenced by whose authority many, and they not wicked, but only ignorant, if I punished him would say that I had acted cruelly and tyrannically. But I know that if he arrives at the camp of Manlius to which he is going, there will be no one so stupid as not to see that there has been a conspiracy, no one so hardened as not to confess it. But if this man alone were put to death, I know that this disease of the republic would be only checked for a while, not eradicated forever. But if he banishes himself, and takes with him all his friends, and collects at one point all the ruined men from every quarter, then not only will this full-grown plague of the republic be extinguished and eradicated, but also the root and seed of all future evils.

We have now for a long time, O conscript fathers, lived among these dangers and machinations of conspiracy; but somehow or other, the ripeness of all wickedness, and of this long-standing madness and audacity, has come to a head at the time of my consulship. But if this man alone is removed from this piratical crew, we may appear, perhaps, for a short time relieved from fear and anxiety, but the danger will settle down and lie hid in the veins and bowels of the republic. As it often happens that men afflicted with a severe disease, when they are tortured with heat and fever, if they drink cold water, seem at first to be relieved, but afterward suffer more and more severely; so this disease which is in the republic, if relieved by the punishment of this man, will only get worse and worse, as the rest will be still alive.

Wherefore, O conscript fathers, let the worthless be gone,—let them separate themselves from the good,—let them collect in one place,—let them, as I have often said before, be separated from us by a wall; let them cease to plot against the consul in his own house,—

to surround the tribunal of the city praetor,—to besiege the senate-house with swords,—to prepare brands and torches to burn the city; let it, in short, be written on the brow of every citizen, what his sentiments are about the republic. I promise you, this, O conscript fathers, that there shall be so much diligence in us the consuls, so much authority in you, so much virtue in the Roman knights, so much unanimity in all good men that you shall see everything made plain and manifest by the departure of Catiline,—everything checked and punished.

With these omens, O Catiline, be gone to your impious and nefarious war, to the great safety of the republic, to your own misfortune and injury, and to the destruction of those who have joined themselves to you in every wickedness and atrocity. Then do you, O Jupiter, who were consecrated by Romulus with the same auspices as this city, whom we rightly call the stay of this city and empire, repel this man and his companions from your altars and from the other temples,—from the houses and walls of the city,—from the lives and fortunes of all the citizens; and overwhelm all the enemies of good men, the foes of the republic, the robbers of Italy, men bound together by a treaty and infamous alliance of crimes, dead and alive, with eternal punishments.

'With Such People I Want No Peace'

Acuera, Chief of the Timucua People

(1539)

Acuera was the chief of the Timucua people who lived in Northeast and North Central Florida as well as southeast Georgia. Once the largest indigenous group of people in the area, the tribe faced extinction with the onset of European colonialism.

In 1539, when the Spanish explorer Hernando de Soto reached Florida with an army and called for peace with the Timucua people, their chief, Acuera, retorted with this statement-speech, denouncing the Europeans for their violent acts and intolerance.

Others of your accursed race have, in years past, poisoned our peaceful shores. They have taught me what you are. What is your employment? To wander about like vagabonds from land to land, to rob the poor, to betray the confiding, to murder in cold blood the defenseless. No! With such a people i want no peace—no friendship. War, never ending War, exterminating War, is all the boon I ask.

You boast yourself valiant, and so you may be; but my faithful warriors are not less brave, and this too you shall one day prove; for I have sworn to maintain an upsparing conflict while one white man remains in my borders—not only in battle, though even thus we fear not to meet you, but by strategem, ambush, and midnight surprisal.

I am lord in my own land, and will never become a slave of a mortal like myself. Vile and coward is he who will submit to the yoke of another when he may be free. As for me and my people, we choose death—yes! a hundred deaths—before the loss of our liberty and the subjugation of our country.

Keep on, robbers and traitors: in Acuera and Apalachee we will treat you as you deserve. Every captive will we quarter and hang up to the highest tree along the road.

Speech to the Troops at Tilbury

Queen Elizabeth I

(19 August 1588)

Queen Elizabeth I was the queen of England during the Elizabethan Age (1558-1603) when England foregrounded itself as a major European power in the field of politics, commerce and art. Despite facing several contentions, both foreign and internal, the Queen with her sheer courage, cleverness and determination persevered to become a monarch.

She delivered this speech to the English forces gathered at Tilbury, Essex during the time of the Spanish Armada. The troops stood ready to repel the Spanish invasion and the Queen's words gave them fresh courage.

My loving people,

We have been persuaded by some that are careful of our safety, to take heed how we commit ourselves to armed multitudes, for fear of treachery; but I assure you I do not desire to live to distrust my faithful and loving people. Let tyrants fear. I have always so behaved myself that, under God, I have placed my chiefest strength and safeguard in the loyal hearts and goodwill of my subjects; and therefore I am come amongst you, as you see, at this time, not for my recreation and disport, but being resolved, in the midst and heat of the battle, to live and die amongst you all; to lay down for my God, and for my kingdom, and my people, my honour and my blood, even in the dust.

I know I have the body of a weak, feeble woman; but I have the heart and stomach of a king, and of a king of England too, and think foul scorn that Parma or Spain, or any prince of Europe, should dare to invade the borders of my realm; to which rather than any dishonour shall grow by me, I myself will take up arms, I myself will be your general, judge, and rewarder of every one of your virtues in the field.

I know already, for your forwardness you have deserved rewards and crowns; and We do assure you on a word of a prince, they shall be duly paid. In the mean time, my lieutenant general shall be in my stead, than whom never prince commanded a more noble or worthy subject; not doubting but by your obedience to my general, by your concord in the camp, and your valour in the field, we shall shortly have a famous victory over these enemies of my God, of my kingdom, and of my people.

Abolition Speech

William Wilberforce

(12 May 1789)

William Wilberforce was an English politician and philanthropist who played a crucial role in the abolishment of slavery in Britain and its colonies. An eloquent speaker, he introduced several resolutions in the House of Commons to end slave trade. The campaign which he led for complete abolition of slavery culminated in the Slavery Abolition Act 1833, which did away with slavery in most of the British Empire.

The 'Abolition Speech' of 12 May 1789 was delivered by Wilberforce in the House of Commons and is one of his most eloquent speeches on the issue.

When I consider the magnitude of the subject which I am to bring before the House—a subject, in which the interests, not of this country, nor of Europe alone, but of the whole world, and of posterity, are involved: and when I think, at the same time, on the weakness of the advocate who has undertaken this great cause—when these reflections press upon my mind, it is impossible for me not to feel both terrified and concerned at my own inadequacy to such a task. But when I reflect, however, on the encouragement which I have had, through the whole course of a long and laborious examination of this question, and how much candour I have experienced, and how conviction has increased within my own mind, in proportion as I have advanced in my labours;—when I reflect, especially, that however averse any gentleman may now be, yet we shall all be of one opinion in the end;—when I turn myself to these thoughts,

I take courage—I determine to forget all my other fears, and I march forward with a firmer step in the full assurance that my cause will bear me out, and that I shall be able to justify upon the clearest principles, every resolution in my hand, the avowed end of which is, the total abolition of the slave trade. I wish exceedingly, in the outset, to guard both myself and the House from entering into the subject with any sort of passion. It is not their passions I shall appeal to—I ask only for their cool and impartial reason; and I wish not to take them by surprise, but to deliberate, point by point, upon every part of this question. I mean not to accuse any one, but to take the shame upon myself, in common, indeed, with the whole parliament of Great Britain, for having suffered this horrid trade to be carried on under their authority. We are all guilty—we ought all to plead guilty, and not to exculpate ourselves by throwing the blame on others; and I therefore deprecate every kind of reflection against the various descriptions of people who are more immediately involved in this wretched business.

Having now disposed of the first part of this subject, I must speak of the transit of the slaves in the West Indies. This I confess, in my own opinion, is the most wretched part of the whole subject. So much misery condensed in so little room, is more than the human imagination had ever before conceived. I will not accuse the Liverpool merchants: I will allow them, nay, I will believe them to be men of humanity; and I will therefore believe, if it were not for the enormous magnitude and extent of the evil which distracts their attention from individual cases, and makes them think generally, and therefore less feelingly on the subject, they would never have persisted in the trade. I verily believe therefore, if the wretchedness of any one of the many hundred Negroes stowed in each ship could be brought before their view, and remain within the sight of the African Merchant, that there is no one among them whose heart would bear it. Let anyone imagine to himself six or 700 of these wretches chained two and two, surrounded with every object that is nauseous and disgusting, diseased, and struggling under every kind of wretchedness! How can we bear to think of such a scene as this? One would think it had been determined to heap upon them all the varieties of bodily pain, for the purpose of blunting the feelings of the mind; and yet, in this very point (to show the power of human prejudice) the situation of the slaves has been described by Mr. Norris, one of the Liverpool delegates, in a manner which, I am sure will convince the House how interest can draw a film across the eyes, so thick, that total blindness could do no more; and how it is our duty therefore to trust not to the reasonings of interested men, or to their way of colouring a transaction. 'Their apartments,' says Mr. Norris, 'are fitted up as much for their advantage as circumstances will admit. The right ankle of one, indeed is connected with the left ankle of another by a small iron fetter, and if they are turbulent, by another on their wrists. They have several meals a day; some of their own country provisions, with the best sauces of African cookery; and by way of variety, another meal of pulse, etc., according to European taste. After breakfast they have water to wash themselves, while their apartments are perfumed with frankincense and lime-juice. Before dinner, they are amused after the manner of their country. The song and dance are promoted,' and, as if the whole was really a scene of pleasure and dissipation it is added, that games of chance are furnished. 'The men play and sing, while the women and girls make fanciful ornaments with beads, which they are plentifully supplied with.' Such is the sort of strain in which the Liverpool delegates, and particularly Mr. Norris, gave evidence before the privy council. What will the House think when, by the concurring testimony of other witnesses, the true history is laid open. The slaves who are sometimes described as rejoicing at their captivity, are so wrung with misery at leaving their country, that it is the constant practice to set sail at night, lest they should be sensible of their departure. The pulse which Mr. Norris talks of are horse beans; and the scantiness, both of water and provision, was suggested by the very legislature of Jamaica in the report of their committee, to be a subject that called for the interference of parliament. Mr. Norris talks of frankincense and lime juice; when surgeons tell you the slaves are stowed so close, that there is not room to tread among them: and when you have it in evidence from Sir George Yonge, that even in a ship which wanted 200 of her complement, the stench was intolerable. The song and the dance, says Mr. Norris, are promoted. It had been more fair, perhaps, if he had explained that word promoted. The truth is, that for the sake of exercise, these miserable wretches, loaded with chains, oppressed with disease and wretchedness, are forced to dance by the terror of the lash, and sometimes by the actual use of it. 'I,' says one of the other evidences, 'was employed to dance the men, while another person danced the women.' Such, then is the meaning of the word promoted; and it may be observed too, with respect to food, that an instrument is sometimes carried out, in order to force them to eat which is the same sort of proof how much they enjoy themselves in that instance also. As to their singing, what shall we say when we are told that their songs are songs of lamentation upon their departure which, while they sing, are always in tears, insomuch that one captain (more humane as I should conceive him, therefore, than the rest) threatened one of the women with a flogging, because the mournfulness of her song was too painful for his feelings. In order, however, not to trust too much to any sort of description, I will call the attention of the House to one species of evidence which is absolutely infallible. Death, at least, is a sure ground of evidence, and the proportion of deaths will not only confirm, but if possible will even aggravate our suspicion of their misery in the transit. It will be found, upon an average of all the ships of which evidence has been given at the privy council, that exclusive of those who perish before they sail, not less than 12½ per cent perish in the passage. Besides these, the Jamaica report tells you, that not less than 4½ per cent die on shore before the day of sale, which is only a week or two from the time of landing. One third more die in the seasoning, and this in a country exactly like their own, where they are healthy and happy as some of the evidences would pretend. The diseases, however, which they contract on shipboard, the astringent washes which are to hide their wounds, and the mischievous tricks used to make them up for sale, are, as the Jamaica report says, (a most precious and valuable report, which I shall often have to advert to) one principle cause of this mortality. Upon the whole, however, here is a mortality of about 50 per cent, and this among negroes who are not bought unless (as the phrase is with cattle) they are sound in wind and limb. How then can the House refuse its belief to the multiplied testimonies before the privy council, of the savage treatment of the negroes in the middle passage? Nay, indeed, what need is there of any evidence? The number of deaths speaks for itself, and makes all such enquiry superfluous. As soon as ever I had arrived thus far in my investigation of the slave trade, I confess to you sir, so enormous so dreadful, so irremediable did its wickedness appear that my own mind was completely made up for the abolition. A trade founded in iniquity, and carried on as this was, must be abolished, let the policy be what it might, let the consequences be what they would, I from this time determined that I would never rest till I had effected its abolition.

Red Jacket Defends Native American Religion

Sagoyewatha (Red Jacket)

Buffalo Creek, New York (1805)

Red Jacket, originally named Otetiani or Sagoyewatha, was the chief of the Seneca people. His oratory skills helped preserve his self-interests in the face of American intervention in Indian matters. He made cunning manoeuvres which helped him retain his position as Chief of the Seneca people while making underhanded deals with the Americans.

However, he genuinely opposed American intervention in Seneca culture and practices. He delivered this speech in 1805 to the representatives of a Boston missionary society in order to vehemently defend the right to practice the culture and religion of the Seneca people.

Friend and brother; it was the will of the Great Spirit that we should meet together this day. He orders all things, and he has given us a fine day for our council. He has taken his garment from before the sun, and caused it to shine with brightness upon us; our eyes are opened, that we see clearly; our ears are unstopped, that we have been able to hear distinctly the words that you have spoken; for all these favors we thank the Great Spirit, and him only.

Brother, this council fire was kindled by you; it was at your request that we came together at this time; we have listened with attention to what you have said. You requested us to speak our minds freely; this gives us great joy, for we now consider that we stand upright before you, and can speak what we think; all have heard your voice, and all speak to you as one man; our minds are agreed.

Brother, you say you want an answer to your talk before you leave this place. It is right you should have one, as you are a great distance from home, and we do not wish to detain you; but we will first look back a little, and tell you what our fathers have told us, and what we have heard from the white people.

Brother, listen to what we say. There was a time when our forefathers owned this great island. Their seats extended from the rising to the setting sun. The Great Spirit had made it for the use of Indians. He had created the buffalo, the deer, and other animals for food. He made the bear and the beaver, and their skins served us for clothing. He had scattered them over the country, and taught us how to take them. He had caused the earth to produce corn for bread. All this he had done for his red children because he loved them. If we had any disputes about hunting grounds, they were generally settled without the shedding of much blood. But an evil day came upon us; your forefathers crossed the great waters, and landed on this island. Their numbers were small; they found friends, and not enemies; they told us they had fled from their own country for fear of wicked men, and come here to enjoy their religion. They asked for a small seat; we took pity on them, granted their request, and they sat down amongst us; we gave them corn and meat; they gave us poison in return. The white people had now found our country; tidings were carried back, and more came amongst us; yet we did not fear them, we took them to be friends; they called us brothers; we believed them, and gave them a larger seat. At length, their numbers had greatly increased; they wanted more land; they wanted our country. Our eyes were opened, and our minds became uneasy. Wars took place; Indians were hired to fight against Indians, and many of our people were destroyed. They also brought strong liquor among us; it was strong and powerful, and has slain thousands.

Brother, our seats were once large, and yours were very small; you have now become a great people, and we have scarcely a place left to spread our blankets; you have got our country, but are not satisfied; you want to force your religion upon us.

Brother, continue to listen. You say you are sent to instruct us how to worship the Great Spirit agreeably to his mind, and if we do not take hold of the religion which you white people teach, we shall be unhappy hereafter. You say that you are right, and we are lost; how do we know this to be true? We understand that your religion is written in a book; if it was intended for us as well as you, why has not the Great Spirit given it to us, and not only to us, but why did he not give to our forefathers the knowledge of that book, with the means of understanding it rightly? We only know what you tell us about it. How shall we know when to believe, being so often deceived by the white people?

Brother, you say there is but one way to worship and serve the Great Spirit; if there is but one religion, why do you white people differ so much about it? Why not all agree, as you can all read the book?

Brother, we do not understand these things. We are told that your religion was given to your forefathers, and has been handed down from father to son. We also have a religion which was given to our forefathers, and has been handed down to us their children. We worship that way. It teacheth us to be thankful for all the favors we receive; to love each other, and to be united. We never quarrel about religion.

Brother, the Great Spirit has made us all; but he has made a great difference between his white and red children; he has given us a different complexion, and different customs; to you he has given the arts; to these he has not opened our eyes; we know these things to be true. Since he has made so great a difference between us in other things, why may we not conclude that he has given us a different religion according to our understanding. The Great Spirit does right; he knows what is best for his children; we are satisfied.

Brother, we do not wish to destroy your religion, or take it from you; we only want to enjoy our own.

Brother, you say you have not come to get our land or our money, but to enlighten our minds. I will now tell you that I have been at your meetings, and saw you collecting money from the meeting I cannot tell what this money was intended for, but suppose it was for your minister; and if we should conform to your way of thinking, perhaps you may want some from us.

Brother, we are told that you have been preaching to the white people in this place. These people are our neighbors; we are acquainted with them; we will wait, a little while and see what effect your preaching has upon them. If we find it does them good, makes them honest and less disposed to cheat Indians, we will then consider again what you have said.

Brother, you have now heard our answer to your talk, and this is all we have to say at present. As we are going to part, we will come and take you by the hand, and hope the Great Spirit will protect you on your journey, and return you safe to your friends.

In Conference with Governor William Henry Harrison

Tecumseh (Shawnee war leader)

Vincennes, Indiana (1811)

Tecumseh was a Shawnee Indian chief, military leader and orator who strongly resisted white rule in the Ohio River Valley. During the War of 1812, he supported the British to fight the U.S. troops. However, Governor William Henry Harrison's U.S. troops defeated the British and killed Tecumseh in battle.

Before the war, in 1811, Tecumseh met Governor William Henry Harrison in order to negotiate terms and prevent the expansion of the Americans into native American lands. However, this negotiation failed and Tecumseh fled to Canada to join the British.

Brother: I wish you to listen to me well. As I think you do not clearly understand what I before said to you, I will explain it again. Brother, since the peace war made, you have killed some of the Shawnees, Winnebagoes, Delawares, and Miamis, and you have taken our land from us, and I do not see how we can remain at peace if you continue to do so. You try to force the red people to do some injury. It is you that are pushing them on to do mischief. You endeavor to make distinctions. You wish to prevent the Indians doing as we wish them—to unite, and let them consider their lands as the common property of the whole; you take tribes aside and advise them not to come into this measure; and until our design is accomplished we do not wish to accept of your invitation to go and see the President. The reason I tell you this, you want, by your distinctions of Indian tribes in allotting to each a particular tract of land, to make them to war with each other. You never see an Indian come and endeavor to make the white people do so. You are continually driving the red people; when, at last, you will drive them into the Great Lake, where they can't either stand or walk.

Brother, you ought to know what you are doing with the Indians. Perhaps it is by direction of the President to make those distinctions. It is a very bad thing, and we do not like it. Since my residence at Tippecanoe we have endeavored to level all distinctions—to destroy village chiefs, by whom all mischief is done. It is they who sell our lands to the Americans. Our object is to let our affairs be transacted by warriors.

Brother, this land that was sold and the goods that were given for it were only done by a few. The treaty was afterwards brought here, and the Weas were induced to give their consent because of their small numbers. The treaty at Fort Wayne was made through the threats of Winnemac; but in future we are prepared to punish those chiefs who may come forward to propose to sell the land. If you continue to purchase of them it will produce war among the different tribes, and at last, I do not know what will be the consequence to the white people.

Brother, I was glad to hear your speech. You said that if we could show that the land was sold by people that had no right to sell, you would restore it. Those that did sell did not own it. It was me. These tribes set up a claim, but the tribes with me will not agree with their claim. If the land is not restored to us you will see, when we return to our homes, how it will be settled. We shall have a great council, at which all the tribes will be present, when we shall show to those who sold that they had no right to the claim that they set up; and we will see what will be done to those chiefs that did sell the land to you. I am not alone in this determination; it is the determination of all the warriors and red people that listen to me. I now wish you to listen to me. If you do not, it will appear as if you wished me to kill all the chiefs that sold you the land. I tell you so because I am authorized by all the tribes to do so. I am the head of them all; I am a warrior, and all the warriors will meet together in two or three moons from this;

then I will call for those chiefs that sold you the land and shall know what to do with them. If you do not restore the land, you will have a hand in killing them.

Brother, do not believe that I came here to get presents from you. If you offer us any, we will not take. By taking goods from you, you will hereafter say that with them you purchased another piece of land from us... It has been the object of both myself and brother to prevent the lands being sold. Should you not return the land, it will occasion us to call a great council that will meet at the Huron village, where the council-fire has already been lighted, at which those who sold the lands shall be called, and shall suffer for their conduct.

Brother, I wish you would take pity on the red people and do what I have requested. If you will not give up the land and do cross the boundary of your present settlement, it will be very hard, and produce great troubles among us. How can we have confidence in the white people? When Jesus Christ came on earth, you killed him and nailed him on a cross. You thought he was dead, but you were mistaken. You have Shakers among you, and you laugh and make light of their worship. Everything I have said to you is the truth. The Great Spirit has inspired me, and I speak nothing but the truth to you.... Brother, I hope you will confess that you ought not to have listened to those bad birds who bring you bad news. I have declared myself freely to you, and if any explanation should be required from our town, send a man who can speak to us. If you think proper to give us any presents, and we can be convinced that they are given through friendship alone, we will accept them. As we intend to hold our council at the Huron village, that is near the British, we may probably make them a visit. Should they offer us any presents of goods, we will not take them; but should they offer us powder and the tomahawk, we will take the powder and refuse the tomahawk. I wish you, brother, to Consider everything I have said as true, and that it is the sentiment of all the red people that listen to me.

Farewell to the Old Guard

Napoleon Bonaparte

Paris, France (20 April 1814)

Napoleon Bonaparte, often called Napoleon I, was a French emperor and military leader who managed to build a French empire and conquer most of Europe in the 19th century. Though he was a shrewd and excellent military strategist, who was successful for most of his term, a devastating invasion of Russia in 1812 and the subsequent Battle of Leipzig (1813) led to his abdication in 1814.

He gave this farewell speech to the few loyal members of his Old Guard at Fontainebleau, France, before being exiled to Elba.

Soldiers of my Old Guard: I bid you farewell. For 20 years I have constantly accompanied you on the road to honor and glory. In these latter times, as in the days of our prosperity, you have invariably been models of courage and fidelity. With men such as you our cause could not be lost; but the war would have been interminable; it would have been civil war, and that would have entailed deeper misfortunes on France.

I have sacrificed all of my interests to those of the country.

I go, but you, my friends, will continue to serve France. Her happiness was my only thought. It will still be the object of my wishes. Do not regret my fate; if I have consented to survive, it is to serve your glory. I intend to write the history of the great achievements we have performed together. Adieu, my friends. Would I could press you all to my heart.

Ain't I a Woman?

Sojourner Truth

Women's Convention, Akron, Ohio (28 May 1851)

Sojourner Truth was a slave-turned-reformer whose experiences as a slave led her to denounce slavery and racism. After escaping from bondage, she engaged in social reform, preaching about women's experiences in slavery and the need for religious freedom. Her oratory skills made her very popular. She spoke extensively against racial segregation on public transport, women's suffrage, amongst other issues.

'Ain't I a Woman' is one of her most famous speeches, delivered during a Women's Convention in Akron, Ohio (1851). Brief and witty, she turns the argument against women's inferiority to their benefit and successfully puts the point across.

(Sojourner Truth spoke in a southern dialect that might be difficult for modern readers. This is the speech in modern English.)

Well, children, where there is so much racket there must be something out of kilter. I think that 'twixt the negroes of the South and the women at the North, all talking about rights, the white men will be in a fix pretty soon. But what's all this here talking about?

That man over there says that women need to be helped into carriages, and lifted over ditches, and to have the best place everywhere. Nobody ever helps me into carriages, or over mud-puddles, or gives me any best place! And ar'n't I a woman?

Look at me! Look at my arm! I have ploughed and planted, and gathered into barns, and no man could head me! And ar'n't I a woman?

I could work as much and eat as much as a man—when I could get it—and bear the lash as well! And ain't I a woman?

I have borne thirteen children, and seen most all sold off to slavery, and when I cried out with my mother's grief, none but Jesus heard me! And ain't I a woman?

Then they talk about this thing in the head; what's this they call it? [Member of audience whispers, 'intellect'.] That's it, honey. What's that got to do with women's rights or negroes' rights? If my cup won't hold but a pint, and yours holds a quart, wouldn't you be mean not to let me have my little half measure full?

Then that little man in black there, he says women can't have as much rights as men, 'cause Christ wasn't a woman! Where did your Christ come from? Where did your Christ come from? From God and a woman! Man had nothing to do with Him.

If the first woman God ever made was strong enough to turn the world upside down all alone, these women together ought to be able to turn it back and get it right side up again!

And now they is asking to do it, the men better let them. Obliged to you for hearing me, and now old Sojourner ain't got nothing more to say.

'What, to the Slave, Is the Fourth of July'

Frederick Douglass

Rochester Ladies' Anti-Slavery Society (5 July 1852)

Frederick Douglass was an escaped slave, author, orator and a prominent activist who became a leader of the abolitionist movement. He fought for equality and human rights throughout his life and penned several biographies to depict the devastating effects of slavery. The most poignant work penned by him is his autobiography, *Narrative of the Life of Frederick Douglass, an American Slave* (1845).

Besides being a persuasive writer, Douglass was an eloquent orator and 'What, to the Slave, is the Fourth of July' is one of his most famous speeches, delivered to the Rochester Ladies' Anti-Slavery Society in 1852.

Mr. President, Friends and Fellow Citizens: He who could address this audience without a quailing sensation, has stronger nerves than I have. I do not remember ever to have appeared as a speaker before any assembly more shrinkingly, nor with greater distrust of my ability, than I do this day. A feeling has crept over me, quite unfavorable to the exercise of my limited powers of speech. The task before me is one which requires much previous thought and study for its proper performance. I know that apologies of this sort are generally considered flat and unmeaning. I trust, however, that mine will not be so considered. Should I seem at ease, my appearance would much misrepresent me. The little experience I have had in addressing public meetings, in country schoolhouses, avails me nothing on the present occasion.

The papers and placards say, that I am to deliver a 4th [of] July oration. This certainly sounds large, and out of the common way, for it is true that I have often had the privilege to speak in this beautiful Hall, and to address many who now honor me with their presence. But neither their familiar faces, nor the perfect gage I think I have of Corinthian Hall, seems to free me from embarrassment.

The fact is, Ladies and Gentlemen, the distance between this platform and the slave plantation, from which I escaped, is considerable—and the difficulties to be overcome in getting from the latter to the former, are by no means slight. That I am here today is, to me, a matter of astonishment as well as of gratitude. You will not, therefore, be surprised, if in what I have to say, I evince no elaborate preparation, nor grace my speech with any high sounding exordium. With little experience and with less learning, I have been able to throw my thoughts hastily and imperfectly together; and trusting to your patient and generous indulgence, I will proceed to lay them before you.

This, for the purpose of this celebration, is the 4th of July. It is the birthday of your National Independence, and of your political freedom. This, to you, is what the Passover was to the emancipated people of God. It carries your minds back to the day, and to the act of your great deliverance; and to the signs, and to the wonders, associated with that act, and that day. This celebration also marks the beginning of another year of your national life; and reminds you that the Republic of America is now 76 years old. I am glad, fellow-citizens, that your nation is so young. 76 years, though a good old age for a man, is but a mere speck in the life of a nation. Three score years and 10 is the allotted time for individual men; but nations number their years by thousands. According to this fact, you are, even now, only in the beginning of your national career, still lingering in the period of childhood. I repeat, I am glad this is so. There is hope in the thought, and hope is much needed, under the dark clouds which lower above the horizon. The eye of the reformer is met with angry flashes, portending disastrous times; but his heart may well beat lighter at the thought that America is young, and that she is still in the impressible stage of her existence. May he not hope that high lessons of wisdom, of justice and of truth, will yet give direction to her destiny? Were the nation older, the patriot's heart might be sadder, and the reformer's brow heavier. Its future might be shrouded in gloom, and the hope of its prophets go out in sorrow. There is consolation in the thought that America is young. Great streams are not easily turned from channels, worn deep in the course of ages. They may sometimes rise in quiet and stately majesty, and inundate the land, refreshing and fertilizing the earth with their mysterious properties. They may also rise in wrath and fury, and bear away, on their angry waves, the accumulated wealth of years of toil and hardship. They, however, gradually flow back to the same old channel, and flow on as serenely as ever. But, while the river may not be turned aside, it may dry up, and leave nothing behind but the withered branch, and the unsightly rock, to howl in the abyss-sweeping wind, the sad tale of departed glory. As with rivers so with nations.

Fellow-citizens, I shall not presume to dwell at length on the associations that cluster about this day. The simple story of it is that, 76 years ago, the people of this country were British subjects. The style and title of your 'sovereign people' (in which you now glory) was not then born. You were under the British Crown . Your fathers esteemed the English Government as the home government; and England as the fatherland. This home government, you know, although a considerable distance from your home, did, in the exercise of its parental prerogatives, impose upon its colonial children, such restraints, burdens and limitations, as, in its mature judgment, it deemed wise, right and proper.

But, your fathers, who had not adopted the fashionable idea of this day, of the infallibility of government, and the absolute character of its acts, presumed to differ from the home government in respect to the wisdom and the justice of some of those burdens and restraints. They went so far in their excitement as to pronounce the measures of government unjust, unreasonable, and oppressive, and altogether such as ought not to be quietly submitted to. I scarcely need say, fellow citizens, that my opinion of those measures fully accords with that of your fathers. Such a declaration of agreement on my part would not be worth much to anybody. It would, certainly, prove nothing, as to what part I might have taken, had I lived during the great controversy of 1776. To say now that America was right, and England wrong, is exceedingly easy. Everybody can say it; the dastard, not less than the noble brave, can flippantly descant on the tyranny of England towards the American Colonies. It is fashionable to do so; but there was a time when to pronounce against England, and in favor of the cause of the colonies, tried men's souls. They who did so were accounted in their day, plotters of mischief, agitators and rebels, dangerous men. To side with the right, against the wrong, with the weak against the strong, and with the oppressed against the oppressor! Here lies the merit, and the one which, of all others, seems unfashionable in our day. The cause of liberty may be stabbed by the men who glory in the deeds of your fathers. But, to proceed.

Feeling themselves harshly and unjustly treated by the home government, your fathers, like men of honesty, and men of spirit, earnestly sought redress. They petitioned and remonstrated; they did so in a decorous, respectful, and loyal manner. Their conduct was wholly unexceptionable. This, however, did not answer the purpose. They saw themselves treated with sovereign indifference, coldness and scorn. Yet they persevered. They were not the men to look back.

As the sheet anchor takes a firmer hold, when the ship is tossed by the storm, so did the cause of your fathers grow stronger, as it breasted the chilling blasts of kingly displeasure. The greatest and best of British statesmen admitted its justice, and the loftiest eloquence of the British Senate came to its support. But, with that blindness which seems to be the unvarying characteristic of tyrants, since Pharaoh and his hosts were drowned in the Red Sea, the British Government persisted in the exactions complained of.

The madness of this course, we believe, is admitted now, even by England; but we fear the lesson is wholly lost on our present ruler.

Oppression makes a wise man mad. Your fathers were wise men, and if they did not go mad, they became restive under this treatment. They felt themselves the victims of grievous wrongs, wholly incurable in their colonial capacity. With brave men there is always a remedy for oppression. Just here, the idea of a total separation of the colonies from the crown was born! It was a startling idea, much more so, than we, at this distance of time, regard it. The timid and the prudent (as has been intimated) of that day, were, of course, shocked and alarmed by it. Such people lived then, had lived before, and will, probably, ever have a place on this planet; and their course, in respect to any great change, (no matter how great the good to be attained, or the wrong to be redressed by it), may be calculated with as much precision as can be the course of the stars. They hate all changes, but silver, gold and copper change! Of this sort of change they are always strongly in favor.

These people were called Tories in the days of your fathers; and the appellation, probably, conveyed the same idea that is meant by a more modern, though a somewhat less euphonious term, which we often find in our papers, applied to some of our old politicians.

Their opposition to the then dangerous thought was earnest and powerful; but, amid all their terror and affrighted vociferations against it, the alarming and revolutionary idea moved on, and the country with it.

On the second of July, 1776, the old Continental Congress, to the dismay of the lovers of ease, and the worshipers of property, clothed that dreadful idea with all the authority of national sanction. They did so in the form of a resolution; and as we seldom hit upon resolutions, drawn up in our day whose transparency is at all equal to this, it may refresh your minds and help my story if I read it.

[We] solemnly publish and declare, That these United Colonies are, and of right, ought to be free and Independent States; that they are Absolved from all Allegiance to the British Crown; and that all political connection between them and the State of Great Britain is and ought to be [totally] dissolved.

Citizens, your fathers made good that resolution. They succeeded; and to-day you reap the fruits of their success. The freedom gained is yours; and you, therefore, may properly celebrate this anniversary. The 4th of July is the first great fact in your nation's history—the very ring—bolt in the chain of your yet undeveloped destiny.

Pride and patriotism, not less than gratitude, prompt you to celebrate and to hold it in perpetual remembrance. I have said that the Declaration of Independence is the ring-bolt to the chain of your nation's destiny; so, indeed, I regard it. The principles contained in that instrument are saving principles. Stand by those principles, be true to them on all occasions, in all places, against all foes, and at whatever cost.

From the round top of your ship of state, dark and threatening clouds may be seen. Heavy billows, like mountains in the distance, disclose to the leeward huge forms of flinty rocks! That bolt drawn, that chain broken, and all is lost. Cling to this day—cling to it, and to its principles, with the grasp of a storm-tossed mariner to a spar at midnight.

The coming into being of a nation, in any circumstances, is an interesting event. But, besides general considerations, there were peculiar circumstances which make the advent of this republic an event of special attractiveness.

The whole scene, as I look back to it, was simple, dignified and sublime.

The population of the country, at the time, stood at the insignificant number of three millions. The country was poor in the munitions of war. The population was weak and scattered, and the country a wilderness unsubdued. There were then no means of concert and combination, such as exist now. Neither steam nor lightning had then been reduced to order and discipline. From the Potomac to the Delaware was a journey of many days. Under these, and innumerable other disadvantages, your fathers declared for liberty and independence and triumphed.

Fellow Citizens, I am not wanting in respect for the fathers of this republic. The signers of the Declaration of Independence were brave men. They were great men too—great enough to give fame to a great age. It does not often happen to a nation to raise, at one time, such a number of truly great men. The point from which I am compelled to view them is not, certainly, the most favorable; and yet I cannot contemplate their great deeds with less than admiration. They were statesmen, patriots and heroes, and for the good they did, and the principles they contended for, I will unite with you to honor their memory.

They loved their country better than their own private interests; and, though this is not the highest form of human excellence, all will concede that it is a rare virtue, and that when it is exhibited, it ought to command respect. He who will, intelligently, lay down his life for his country, is a man whom it is not in human nature to despise. Your fathers staked their lives, their fortunes, and their sacred honor, on the cause of their country. In their admiration of liberty, they lost sight of all other interests.

They were peace men; but they preferred revolution to peaceful submission to bondage. They were quiet men; but they did not shrink from agitating against oppression. They showed forbearance; but that they knew its limits. They believed in order; but not in the order of tyranny. With them, nothing was 'settled' that was not right. With them, justice, liberty and humanity were 'final;' not slavery and oppression. You may well cherish the memory of such men. They were great in their day and generation. Their solid manhood stands out the more as we contrast it with these degenerate times.

How circumspect, exact and proportionate were all their movements! How unlike the politicians of an hour! Their statesmanship looked beyond the passing moment, and stretched away in strength into the distant future. They seized upon eternal principles, and set a glorious example in their defense. Mark them!

Fully appreciating the hardship to be encountered, firmly believing in the right of their cause, honorably inviting the scrutiny of an on-looking world, reverently appealing to heaven to attest their sincerity, soundly comprehending the solemn responsibility they were about to assume, wisely measuring the terrible odds against them, your fathers, the fathers of this republic, did, most deliberately, under the inspiration of a glorious patriotism, and with a sublime faith in the great principles of justice and freedom, lay deep the cornerstone of the national superstructure, which has risen and still rises in grandeur around you.

Of this fundamental work, this day is the anniversary. Our eyes are met with demonstrations of joyous enthusiasm. Banners and pennants wave exultingly on the breeze. The din of business, too, is hushed. Even Mammon seems to have quitted his grasp on this day. The ear-piercing fife and the stirring drum unite their accents with the ascending peal of a thousand church bells. Prayers are made, hymns are sung, and sermons are preached in honor of this day; while the quick martial tramp of a great and multitudinous nation, echoed back by all the hills, valleys and mountains of a vast continent, bespeak the occasion one of thrilling and universal interests nation's jubilee.

Friends and citizens, I need not enter further into the causes which led to this anniversary. Many of you understand them better than I do. You could instruct me in regard to them. That is a branch of knowledge in which you feel, perhaps, a much deeper interest than your speaker. The causes which led to the separation of the colonies from the British crown have never lacked for a tongue. They have all been taught in your common schools, narrated at your firesides, unfolded from your pulpits, and thundered from your legislative halls, and are as familiar to you as household words. They form the staple of your national poetry and eloquence.

I remember also that as a people Americans are remarkably familiar with all facts which make in their own favor. This is esteemed by some as a national trait—perhaps a national weakness. It is a fact, that whatever makes for the wealth or for the reputation of Americans, and can be had cheap will be found by Americans. I shall not be charged with slandering Americans if I say I think the American side of any question may be safely left in American hands.

I leave, therefore, the great deeds of your fathers to other gentlemen whose claim to have been regularly descended will be less likely to be disputed than mine!

My business, if I have any here today, is with the present. The accepted time with God and his cause is the ever-living now.

Trust no future, however pleasant, Let the dead past bury its dead; Act, act in the living present, Heart within, and God overhead.

We have to do with the past only as we can make it useful to the present and to the future. To all inspiring motives, to noble deeds which can be gained from the past, we are welcome. But now is the time, the important time. Your fathers have lived, died, and have done their work, and have done much of it well. You live and must die, and you must do your work. You have no right to enjoy a child's share in the labor of your fathers, unless your children are to be blest by your labors. You have no right to wear out and waste the hard-earned fame of your fathers to cover your indolence. Sydney

Smith tells us that men seldom eulogize the wisdom and virtues of their fathers, but to excuse some folly or wickedness of their own. This truth is not a doubtful one. There are illustrations of it near and remote, ancient and modern. It was fashionable, hundreds of years ago, for the children of Jacob to boast, we have 'Abraham to our father,' when they had long lost Abraham's faith and spirit. That people contented themselves under the shadow of Abraham's great name, while they repudiated the deeds which made his name great. Need I remind you that a similar thing is being done all over this country today? Need I tell you that the Jews are not the only people who built the tombs of the prophets, and garnished the sepulchres of the righteous? Washington could not die till he had broken the chains of his slaves. Yet his monument is built up by the price of human blood, and the traders in the bodies and souls of men, shout—'We have Washington to our father'—Alas! That it should be so; yet so it is.

The evil that men do, lives after them, The good is oft' interred with their bones.

Fellow-citizens, pardon me, allow me to ask, why am I called upon to speak here today? What have I, or those I represent, to do with your national independence? Are the great principles of political freedom and of natural justice, embodied in that Declaration of Independence, extended to us? And am I, therefore, called upon to bring our humble offering to the national altar, and to confess the benefits and express devout gratitude for the blessings resulting from your independence to us?

Would to God, both for your sakes and ours, that an affirmative answer could be truthfully returned to these questions! Then would my task be light, and my burden easy and delightful. For who is there so cold, that a nation's sympathy could not warm him? Who so obdurate and dead to the claims of gratitude, that would not thankfully acknowledge such priceless benefits? Who so stolid and selfish, that would not give his voice to swell the hallelujahs of a nation's jubilee, when the chains of servitude had been tom from his limbs? I am not that man. In a case like that, the dumb might eloquently speak, and the 'lame man leap as an hart.'

But, such is not the state of the case. I say it with a sad sense of the disparity between us. I am not included within the pale of this glorious anniversary! Your high independence only reveals the immeasurable distance between us. The blessings in which you, this day, rejoice, are not enjoyed in common. The rich inheritance of justice, liberty, prosperity and independence, bequeathed by your fathers, is shared by you, not by me. The sunlight that brought life and healing to you, has brought stripes and death to me. This Fourth of July is yours, not mine. You may rejoice, I must mourn. To drag a man in fetters into the grand illuminated temple of liberty, and call upon him to join you in joyous anthems, were inhuman mockery and sacrilegious irony. Do you mean, citizens, to mock me, by asking me to speak today? If so, there is a parallel to your conduct. And let me warn you that it is dangerous to copy the example of a nation whose crimes, lowering up to heaven, were thrown down by the breath of the Almighty, burying that nation in irrecoverable ruin! I can today take up the plaintive lament of a peeled and woe-smitten people!

'By the rivers of Babylon, there we sat down. Yea! We wept when we remembered Zion. We hanged our harps upon the willows in the midst thereof. For there, they that carried us away captive, required of us a song; and they who wasted us required of us mirth, saying, Sing us one of the songs of Zion. How can we sing the Lord's song in a strange land? If I forget thee, O Jerusalem, let my right hand forget her cunning. If I do not remember thee, let my tongue cleave to the roof of my mouth.'

Fellow-citizens; above your national, tumultuous joy, I hear the mournful wail of millions! Whose chains, heavy and grievous yesterday, are, today, rendered more intolerable by the jubilee shouts that reach them. If I do forget, if I do not faithfully remember those bleeding children of sorrow this day, 'may my right hand forget her cunning, and may my tongue cleave to the roof of my mouth!' To forget them, to pass lightly over their wrongs, and to chime in with the popular theme, would be treason most scandalous and shocking, and would make me a reproach before God and the world. My subject, then fellow-citizens, is American slavery. I shall see, this day, and its popular characteristics, from the slave's point of view.

Standing, there, identified with the American bondman, making his wrongs mine, I do not hesitate to declare, with all my soul, that the character and conduct of this nation never looked blacker to me than on this 4th of July! Whether we turn to the declarations of the past, or to the professions of the present, the conduct of the nation seems equally hideous and revolting. America is false to the past, false to the present, and solemnly binds herself to be false to the future. Standing with God and the crushed and bleeding slave on this occasion, I will, in the name of humanity which is outraged, in the name of liberty which is fettered, in the name of the constitution and the Bible, which are disregarded and trampled upon, dare to call in question and to denounce, with all the emphasis I can command, everything that serves to perpetuate slavery—the great sin and shame of America! 'I will not equivocate; I will not excuse;' I will use the severest language I can command; and yet not one word shall escape me that any man, whose judgment is not blinded by prejudice, or who is not at heart a slaveholder, shall not confess to be fight and just. But I fancy I hear some one of my audience say, it is just in this circumstance that you and your brother abolitionists fail to make a favorable impression on the public mind. Would you argue more, and denounce less, would you persuade more, and rebuke less, your cause would be much more likely to succeed. But, I submit, where all is plain there is nothing to be argued. What point in the anti-slavery creed would you have me argue? On what branch of the subject do the people of this country need light? Must I undertake to prove that the slave is a man? That point is conceded already. Nobody doubts it. The slaveholders themselves acknowledge it in the enactment of laws for their government. They acknowledge it when they punish disobedience on the part of the slave. There are 72 crimes in the State of Virginia, which, if committed by a black man, (no matter how ignorant he be), subject him to the punishment of death; while only two of the same crimes will subject a white man to the like punishment. What is this but the acknowledgement that the slave is a moral, intellectual and responsible being? The manhood of the slave is conceded. It is admitted in the fact that Southern statute books are covered with enactments forbidding, under severe fines and penalties, the teaching of the slave to read or to write. When you can point to any such laws, in reference to the beasts of the field, then I may consent to argue the manhood of the slave. When the dogs in your streets, when the fowls of the air, when the cattle on your hills, when the fish of the sea, and the reptiles that crawl, shall be unable to distinguish the slave from a brute, their will I argue with you that the slave is a man!

For the present, it is enough to affirm the equal manhood of the Negro race. Is it not astonishing that, while we are ploughing, planting and reaping, using all kinds of mechanical tools, erecting houses, constructing bridges, building ships, working in metals of brass, iron, copper, silver and gold; that, while we are reading, writing and cyphering, acting as clerks, merchants and secretaries, having among us lawyers, doctors, ministers, poets, authors, editors, orators and teachers; that, while we are engaged in all manner of enterprises common to other men, digging gold in California, capturing the whale in the Pacific, feeding sheep and cattle on the hillside, living, moving, acting, thinking, planning, living in families as husbands, wives and children, and, above all, confessing and worshipping the Christian's God, and looking hopefully for life and immortality beyond the grave, we are called upon to prove that we are men!

Would you have me argue that man is entitled to liberty? That he is the rightful owner of his own body? You have already declared it. Must I argue the wrongfulness of slavery? Is that a question for Republicans? Is it to be settled by the rules of logic and argumentation, as a matter beset with great difficulty, involving a doubtful application of the principle of justice, hard to be understood? How should I look today, in the presence of Americans, dividing, and subdividing a discourse, to show that men have a natural right to freedom? Speaking of it relatively, and positively, negatively, and affirmatively. To do so, would be to make myself ridiculous, and to offer an insult to your understanding. There is not a man beneath the canopy of heaven, that does not know that slavery is wrong for him.

What, am I to argue that it is wrong to make men brutes, to rob them of their liberty, to work them without wages, to keep them ignorant of their relations to their fellow men, to beat them with sticks, to flay their flesh with the lash, to load their limbs with irons, to hunt them with dogs, to sell them at auction, to sunder their families, to knock out their teeth, to bum their flesh, to starve them into obedience and submission to their masters? Must I argue that a system thus marked with blood and stained with pollution is wrong? No! I will not. I have better employments for my time and strength than such arguments would imply.

What, then, remains to be argued? Is it that slavery is not divine; that God did not establish it; that our doctors of divinity are mistaken? There is blasphemy in the thought. That which is inhuman, cannot be divine! Who can reason on such a proposition? They that can, may; I cannot. The time for such argument is past.

At a time like this, scorching irony, not convincing argument, is needed. O! Had I the ability, and could I reach the nation's ear, I would, today, pour out a fiery stream of biting ridicule, blasting reproach, withering sarcasm, and stern rebuke. For it is not light that is needed, but fire; it is not the gentle shower, but thunder. We need the storm, the whirlwind, and the earthquake. The feeling of the nation must be quickened; the conscience of the nation must be roused; the propriety of the nation must be startled; the hypocrisy of the nation must be exposed; and its crimes against God and man must be proclaimed and denounced.

What, to the American slave, is your Fourth of July? I answer: a day that reveals to him, more than all other days in the year, the gross injustice and cruelly to which he is the constant victim. To him, your celebration is a sham; your boasted liberty, an unholy license; your national greatness, swelling vanity; your sounds of rejoicing are empty and heartless; your denunciations of tyrants, brass fronted impudence; your shouts of liberty and equality, hollow mockery; your prayers and hymns, your sermons and thanksgivings, with all your religious parade, and solemnity, are, to him, mere bombast, fraud, deception, impiety, and hypocrisy—a thin veil to cover up crimes which would disgrace a nation of savages. There is not a nation on the earth guilty of practices, more shocking and bloody, than are the people of these United States, at this very hour.

Go where you may, search where you will, roam through all the monarchies and despotisms of the old world, travel through South

America, search out every abuse, and when you have found the last, lay your facts by the side of the everyday practices of this nation, and you will say with me, that, for revolting barbarity and shameless hypocrisy, America reigns without a rival. Take the American slave-trade, which, we are told by the papers, is especially prosperous just now. Ex-Senator Benton tells us that the price of men was never higher than now. He mentions the fact to show that slavery is in no danger. This trade is one of the peculiarities of American institutions. It is carried on in all the large towns and cities in one-half of this confederacy; and millions are pocketed every year, by dealers in this horrid traffic. In several states, this trade is a chief source of wealth. It is called (in contradistinction to the foreign slave-trade) 'the internal slave trade.' It is, probably, called so, too, in order to divert from it the horror with which the foreign slave-trade is contemplated. That trade has long since been denounced by this government, as piracy. It has been denounced with burning words, from the high places of the nation, as an execrable traffic. To arrest it, to put an end to it, this nation keeps a squadron, at immense cost, on the coast of Africa. Everywhere, in this country, it is safe to speak of this foreign slave-trade, as a most inhuman traffic, opposed alike to the laws of God and of man. The duty to extirpate and destroy it, is admitted even by our doctors of divinity. In order to put an end to it, some of these last have consented that their colored brethren (nominally free) should leave this country, and establish themselves on the western coast of Africa! It is, however, a notable fact that, while so much execration is poured out by Americans upon those engaged in the foreign slave-trade, the men engaged in the slave-trade between the states pass without condemnation, and their business is deemed honorable.

Behold the practical operation of this internal slave-trade, the American slave-trade, sustained by American politics and America religion. Here you will see men and women reared like swine for the market. You know what is a swine-drover? I will show you a man-drover. They inhabit all our Southern States. They perambulate the country, and crowd the highways of the nation, with droves of human stock. You will see one of these human flesh-jobbers, armed with pistol, whip and bowie-knife, driving a company of a hundred men, women, and children, from the Potomac to the slave market at New Orleans. These wretched people are to be sold singly, or in lots, to suit purchasers. They are food for the cotton-field, and the deadly sugar-mill. Mark the sad procession, as it moves wearily along, and the inhuman wretch who drives them. Hear his savage yells and his blood-chilling oaths, as he hurries on his affrighted captives! There, see the old man, with locks thinned and gray. Cast one glance, if you please, upon that young mother, whose shoulders are bare to the scorching sun, her briny tears falling on the brow of the babe in her arms. See, too, that girl of thirteen, weeping, yes! Weeping, as she thinks of the mother from whom she has been torn! The drove moves tardily. Heat and sorrow have nearly consumed their strength; suddenly you hear a quick snap, like the discharge of a rifle; the fetters clank, and the chain rattles simultaneously; your ears are saluted with a scream, that seems to have torn its way to the center of your soul! The crack you heard, was the sound of the slave-whip; the scream you heard, was from the woman you saw with the babe. Her speed had faltered under the weight of her child and her chains! That gash on her shoulder tells her to move on. Follow the drove to New Orleans. Attend the auction; see men examined like horses; see the forms of women rudely and brutally exposed to the shocking gaze of American slave-buyers. See this drove sold and separated forever; and never forget the deep, sad sobs that arose from that scattered multitude. Tell me citizens, where, under the sun, you can witness a spectacle more fiendish and shocking. Yet this is but a glance at the American slave-trade, as it exists, at this moment, in the ruling part of the United States.

I was born amid such sights and scenes. To me the American slave-trade is a terrible reality. When a child, my soul was often pierced with a sense of its horrors. I lived on Philpot Street, Fell's Point, Baltimore, and have watched from the wharves, the slave ships in the Basin, anchored from the shore, with their cargoes of human flesh, waiting for favorable winds to waft them down the Chesapeake. There was, at that time, a grand slave mart kept at the head of Pratt Street, by Austin Woldfolk. His agents were sent into every town and county in Maryland, announcing their arrival, through the papers, and on flaming hand-bills headed 'Cash for

Negroes'. These men were generally well dressed men, and very captivating in their manners. Ever ready to drink, to treat, and to gamble. The fate of many a slave has depended upon the turn of a single card; and many a child has been snatched from the arms of its mother by bargains arranged in a state of brutal drunkenness.

The flesh-mongers gather up their victims by dozens, and drive them, chained, to the general depot at Baltimore. When a sufficient number have been collected here, a ship is chartered, for the purpose of conveying the forlorn crew to Mobile, or to New Orleans. From the slave prison to the ship, they are usually driven in the darkness of night; for since the antislavery agitation, a certain caution is observed.

In the deep, still darkness of midnight I have been often aroused by the dead heavy footsteps, and the piteous cries of the chained gangs that passed our door. The anguish of my boyish heart was intense; and I was often consoled, when speaking to my mistress in the morning, to hear her say that the custom was very wicked; that she hated to hear the rattle of the chains, and the heart-rending cries. I was glad to find one who sympathized with me in my horror. Fellow-citizens, this murderous traffic is, today, in active operation in this boasted republic. In the solitude of my spirit, I see clouds of dust raised on the highways of the South; I see the bleeding footsteps; I hear the doleful wail of fettered humanity, on the way to the slave markets, where the victims are to be sold like horses, sheep and swine, knocked off to the highest bidder. There I see the tenderest ties ruthlessly broken, to gratify the lust, caprice and rapacity of the buyers and sellers of men. My soul sickens at the sight.

Is this the land your Fathers loved, The freedom which they toiled to win? Is this the earth whereon they moved? Are these the graves they slumber in?

But a still more inhuman, disgraceful, and scandalous state of things remains to be presented. By an act of the American Congress, not yet two years old, slavery has been nationalized in its most horrible and revolting form. By that act, Mason & Dixon's line has been obliterated; New York has become as Virginia; and the power to hold, hunt, and sell men, women, and children as slaves remains no longer a mere state institution, but is now an institution of the whole United States. The power is co-extensive with the Star-Spangled Banner and American Christianity. Where these go, may also go the merciless slave-hunter. Where these are, man is not sacred. He is a bird for the sportsman's gun. By that most foul and fiendish of all human decrees, the liberty and person of every man are put in peril. Your broad republican domain is hunting ground for men. Not for thieves and robbers, enemies of society, merely, but for men guilty of no crime. Your lawmakers have commanded all good citizens to engage in this hellish sport. Your President, your Secretary of State, your lords, nobles and ecclesiastics enforce, as a duty you owe to your free and glorious country, and to your God, that you do this accursed thing. Not fewer than forty Americans have, within the past two years, been hunted down and, without a moment's warning, hurried away in chains, and consigned to slavery and excruciating torture. Some of these have had wives and children, dependent on them for bread; but of this, no account was made. The right of the hunter to his prey stands superior to the right of marriage, and to all rights in this republic, the rights of God included! For black men there are neither law, justice, humanity, not religion. The Fugitive Slave Law makes mercy to them a crime; and bribes the judge who tries them. An American judge gets ten dollars for every victim he consigns to slavery, and five, when he fails to do so. The oath of any two villains is sufficient, under this hell-black enactment, to send the most pious and exemplary black man into the remorseless jaws of slavery! His own testimony is nothing. He can bring no witnesses for himself. The minister of American justice is bound by the law to hear but one side; and that side, is the side of the oppressor. Let this damning fact be perpetually told. Let it be thundered around the world, that, in tyrant-killing, king-hating, people-loving, democratic, Christian America, the seats of justice are filled with judges, who hold their offices under an open and palpable bribe, and are bound, in deciding in the case of a man's liberty, to hear only his accusers!

In glaring violation of justice, in shameless disregard of the forms of administering law, in cunning arrangement to entrap the defenseless, and in diabolical intent, this Fugitive Slave Law stands alone in the annals of tyrannical legislation. I doubt if there be another nation on the globe, having the brass and the baseness to put such a law on the statute-book. If any man in this assembly thinks differently from me in this matter, and feels able to disprove my statements, I will gladly confront him at any suitable time and place he may select.

I take this law to be one of the grossest infringements of Christian Liberty, and, if the churches and ministers of our country were not stupidly blind, or most wickedly indifferent, they, too, would so regard it.

At the very moment that they are thanking God for the enjoyment of civil and religious liberty, and for the right to worship God according to the dictates of their own consciences, they are utterly silent in respect to a law which robs religion of its chief significance, and makes it utterly worthless to a world lying in wickedness. Did this law concern the 'mint, anise and cumin' — abridge the fight to sing psalms, to partake of the sacrament, or to engage in any of the ceremonies of religion, it would be smitten by the thunder of a thousand pulpits. A general shout would go up from the church, demanding repeal, repeal, instant repeal! And it would go hard with that politician who presumed to solicit the votes of the people without inscribing this motto on his banner. Further, if this demand were not complied with, another Scotland would be added to the history of religious liberty, and the stern old Covenanters would be thrown into the shade. A John Knox would be seen at every church door, and heard from every pulpit, and Fillmore would have no more quarter than was shown by Knox, to the beautiful, but treacherous queen Mary of Scotland. The fact that the church of our country, (with fractional exceptions), does not esteem 'the Fugitive Slave Law' as a declaration of war against religious liberty, implies that that church regards religion simply as a form of worship, an empty ceremony, and not a vital principle, requiring active benevolence, justice, love and good will towards man. It esteems sacrifice above mercy; psalm-singing above right doing; solemn meetings above practical righteousness. A worship that can be conducted by persons who refuse to give shelter to the houseless, to give bread to the hungry, clothing to the naked, and who enjoin obedience to a law forbidding these acts of mercy, is a curse, not a blessing to mankind. The Bible addresses all such persons as 'scribes, Pharisees, hypocrites, who pay tithe of mint, anise, and cumin, and have omitted the weightier matters of the law, judgment, mercy and faith.' But the church of this country is not only indifferent to the wrongs of die slave, it actually takes sides with the oppressors. It has made itself the bulwark of American slavery, and the shield of American slave-hunters. Many of its most eloquent Divines, who stand as the very lights of the church, have shamelessly given the sanction of religion and the Bible to the whole slave system. They have taught that man may, properly, be a slave; that the relation of master and slave is ordained of God; that to send back an escaped bondman to his master is clearly the duty of all the followers of the Lord Jesus Christ; and this horrible blasphemy is palmed off upon the world for Christianity.

For my part, I would say, Welcome infidelity! Welcome atheism! Welcome anything—in preference to the gospel, as preached by those divines. They convert the very name of religion into an engine of tyranny, and barbarous cruelty, and serve to confirm more infidels, in this age, than all the infidel writings of Thomas Paine, Voltaire, and Bolingbroke, put together, have done! These ministers make religion a cold and flinty-hearted thing, having neither principles of right action, nor bowels of compassion. They strip the love of God of its beauty, and leave the throng of religion a huge, horrible, repulsive form. It is a religion for oppressors, tyrants, man-stealers, and thugs. It is not that 'pure and undefiled religion' which is from above, and which is 'first pure, then peaceable, easy to be entreated, full of mercy and good fruits, without partiality and without hypocrisy.' But a religion which favors the rich against the poor; which exalts the proud above the humble; which divides mankind into two classes, tyrants and slaves; which says to the man in chains, stay there; and to the oppressor, oppress on; it is a religion which may be professed and enjoyed by all the robbers and enslavers of mankind; it makes God a respecter of persons, denies his fatherhood of the race, and tramples in the dust the great truth of the brotherhood of man. All this we affirm to be true of the popular church, and the popular worship of our land and nation—a religion, a church, and a worship which, on the authority of inspired wisdom, we pronounce to be an abomination in the sight of God. In the language of Isaiah, the American church might be well addressed, 'Bring no more vain ablations; incense is an abomination unto me: the new moons and Sabbaths, the calling of assemblies, I cannot away with; it is iniquity even the solemn meeting. Your new moons and your appointed feasts my soul hateth. They are a trouble to me; I am weary to bear them; and when ye spread forth your hands I will hide mine eyes from you. Yea! When ye make many prayers, I will not hear. Your hands are full of blood; cease to do evil, learn to do well; seek judgment; relieve the oppressed; judge for the fatherless; plead for the widow.'

The American church is guilty, when viewed in connection with what it is doing to uphold slavery; but it is superlatively guilty when viewed in connection with its ability to abolish slavery.

The sin of which it is guilty is one of omission as well as of commission. Albert Barnes but uttered what the common sense of every man at all observant of the actual state of the case will receive as truth, when he declared that 'There is no power out of the church that could sustain slavery an hour, if it were not sustained in it.'

Let the religious press, the pulpit, the Sunday school, the conference meeting, the great ecclesiastical, missionary, Bible and tract associations of the land array their immense powers against slavery and slave-holding; and the whole system of crime and blood would be scattered to the winds; and that they do not do this involves them in the most awful responsibility of which the mind can conceive.

In prosecuting the anti-slavery enterprise, we have been asked to spare the church, to spare the ministry; but how, we ask, could such a thing be done? We are met on the threshold of our efforts for the redemption of the slave, by the church and ministry of the country, in battle arrayed against us; and we are compelled to fight or flee. From what quarter, I beg to know, has proceeded a fire so deadly upon our ranks, during the last two years, as from the Northern pulpit? As the champions of oppressors, the chosen men of American theology have appeared—men, honored for their so-called piety, and their real learning. The Lords of Buffalo, the Springs of New York, the Lathrops of Auburn, the Coxes and Spencers of Brooklyn, the Gannets and Sharps of Boston, the Deweys of Washington, and other great religious lights of the land, have, in utter denial of the authority of Him, by whom the professed to he called to the ministry, deliberately taught us, against the example or the Hebrews and against the remonstrance of the Apostles, they teach 'that we ought to obey man's law before the law of God.'

My spirit wearies of such blasphemy; and how such men can be supported, as the 'standing types and representatives of Jesus Christ,' is a mystery which I leave others to penetrate. In speaking of the American church, however, let it be distinctly understood that I mean the great mass of the religious organizations of our land. There are exceptions, and I thank God that there are. Noble men may be found, scattered all over these Northern States, of whom Henry Ward Beecher of Brooklyn, Samuel J. May of Syracuse, and my esteemed friend [Rev. R. R. Raymond] on the platform, are shining examples; and let me say further, that upon these men lies the duty to inspire our ranks with high religious faith and zeal, and to cheer us on in the great mission of the slave's redemption from his chains.

One is struck with the difference between the attitude of the American church towards the anti-slavery movement, and that occupied by the churches in England towards a similar movement in that country. There, the church, true to its mission of ameliorating, elevating, and improving the condition of mankind, came forward promptly, bound up the wounds of the West Indian slave, and restored him to his liberty. There, the question of emancipation was a highly religious question. It was demanded, in the name of humanity, and according to the law of the living God. The Sharps, the Clarksons, the Wilberforces, the Buxtons, and Burchells and the Knibbs, were alike famous for their piety, and for their philanthropy. The anti-slavery movement there was not an anti-church movement, for the reason that the church took its full share in prosecuting that movement: and the anti-slavery movement in this country will cease to be an anti-church movement, when the church of this country shall assume a favorable instead or a hostile position towards that movement.

Americans! Your republican politics, not less than your republican religion, are flagrantly inconsistent. You boast of your love of liberty, your superior civilization, and your pure Christianity, while the whole political power of the nation (as embodied in the two great political parties) is solemnly pledged to support and perpetuate the enslavement of three millions of your countrymen. You hurl your anathemas at the crowned headed tyrants of Russia and Austria, and pride yourselves on your Democratic institutions, while you yourselves consent to be the mere tools and bodyguards of the tyrants of Virginia and Carolina. You invite to your shores fugitives of oppression from abroad, honor them with banquets, greet them with ovations, cheer them, toast them, salute them, protect them, and pour out your money to them like water; but the fugitives from your own land you advertise, hunt, arrest, shoot and kill. You glory in your refinement and your universal education yet you maintain a system as barbarous and dreadful as ever stained the character of a nation—a system begun in avarice, supported in pride, and perpetuated in cruelty. You shed tears over fallen Hungary, and make the sad story of her wrongs the theme of your poets, statesmen and orators, till your gallant sons are ready to fly to arms to vindicate her cause against her oppressors; but, in regard to the ten thousand wrongs of the American slave, you would enforce the strictest silence, and would hail him as an enemy of the nation who dares to make those wrongs the subject of public discourse! You are all on fire at the mention of liberty for France or for Ireland; but are as cold as an iceberg at the thought of liberty for the enslaved of America. You discourse eloquently on the dignity of labour; yet, you sustain a system which, in its very essence, casts a stigma upon labor. You can bare your bosom to the storm of British artillery to throw off a three penny tax on tea; and yet wring the last hard-earned farthing from the grasp of the black laborers of your country You profess to believe 'that, of one blood, God made all nations of men to dwell on the face of all the earth,' and hath commanded all men, everywhere to love one another; yet you notoriously hate, (and glory in your hatred), all men whose skins are not colored like your own. You declare, before the world, and are understood by the world to declare, that you 'hold these truths to be self evident, that all men are created equal; and are endowed by their Creator with certain inalienable rights; and that, among these are, life, liberty, and the pursuit of happiness;' and yet, you hold securely, in a bondage which, according to your own Thomas Jefferson, 'is worse than ages of that which your fathers rose in rebellion to oppose,' a seventh part of the inhabitants of your country.

Fellow-citizens! I will not enlarge further on your national inconsistencies. The existence of slavery in this country brands your republicanism as a sham, your humanity as a base pretence, and your Christianity as a lie. It destroys your moral power abroad; it corrupts your politicians at home. It saps the foundation of religion; it makes your name a hissing, and a by word to a mocking earth. It is the antagonistic force in your government, the only thing that seriously disturbs and endangers your Union. It fetters your progress; it is the enemy of improvement, the deadly foe of education; it fosters pride; it breeds insolence; it promotes vice; it shelters crime; it is a curse to the earth that supports it; and yet, you cling to it, as if it were the sheet anchor of all your hopes. Oh! Be warned! Be warned! A horrible reptile is coiled up in your nation's bosom; the venomous creature is nursing at the tender breast of your youthful republic; for the love of God, tear away, and fling from you the hideous monster, and let the weight of twenty millions crush and destroy it forever!

But it is answered in reply to all this, that precisely what I have now denounced is, in fact, guaranteed and sanctioned by the Constitution of the United States; that the right to hold and to hunt slaves is a part of that Constitution framed by the illustrious Fathers of this Republic. Then, I dare to affirm, notwithstanding all I have said before, your fathers stooped, basely stooped

To palter with us in a double sense: And keep the word of promise to the ear, But break it to the heart.

And instead of being the honest men I have before declared them to be, they were the veriest imposters that ever practiced on mankind. This is the inevitable conclusion, and from it there is no escape. But I differ from those who charge this baseness on the framers of the Constitution of the United States. It is a slander upon their memory, at least, so I believe. There is not time now to argue the constitutional question at length - nor have I the ability to discuss it as it ought to be discussed. The subject has been handled with masterly power by Lysander Spooner, Esq., by William Goodell, by Samuel E. Sewall, Esq., and last, though not least, by Gerritt Smith, Esq. These gentlemen have, as I think, fully and clearly vindicated the Constitution from any design to support slavery for an hour.

Fellow-citizens! There is no matter in respect to which, the people of the North have allowed themselves to be so ruinously imposed upon, as that of the pro-slavery character of the Constitution. In that instrument I hold there is neither warrant, license, nor sanction of the hateful thing; but, interpreted as it ought to be interpreted, the Constitution is a glorious liberty document. Read its preamble, consider its purposes. Is slavery among them? Is it at the gateway? Or is it in the temple? It is neither. While I do not intend to argue this question on the present occasion, let me ask, if it be not somewhat singular that, if the Constitution were intended to be, by its framers and adopters, a slave-holding instrument, why neither slavery, slave-holding, nor slave can anywhere be found in it. What would be thought of an instrument, drawn up, legally drawn up, for the purpose of entitling the city of Rochester to a track of land, in which no mention of land was made? Now, there are certain rules of interpretation, for the proper understanding of all legal instruments. These rules are well established. They are plain, common-sense rules, such as you and I, and all of us, can understand and apply, without having passed years in the study of law. I scout the idea that the question of the constitutionality or unconstitutionality of slavery is not a question for the people. I hold that every American citizen has a fight to form an opinion of the constitution, and to propagate that opinion, and to use all honorable means to make his opinion the prevailing one. Without this fight, the liberty of an American citizen would be as insecure as that of a Frenchman. Ex Vice President Dallas tells us that the constitution is an object to which no American mind can be too attentive, and no American heart too devoted. He further says, the constitution, in its words, is plain and intelligible, and is meant for the home-bred, unsophisticated understandings of our fellow-citizens. Senator Berrien tell us that the Constitution is the fundamental law, that which controls all others. The charter of our liberties, which every citizen has a personal interest in understanding thoroughly. The testimony of Senator Breese, Lewis Cass, and many others that might be named, who are everywhere esteemed as sound lawyers, so regard the constitution. I take it, therefore, that it is not presumption in a private citizen to form an opinion of that instrument.

Now, take the constitution according to its plain reading, and I defy the presentation of a single pro-slavery clause in it. On the other hand it will be found to contain principles and purposes, entirely hostile to the existence of slavery.

I have detained my audience entirely too long already. At some future period I will gladly avail myself of an opportunity to give this subject a full and fair discussion. Allow me to say, in conclusion, notwithstanding the dark picture I have this day presented of the state of the nation, I do not despair of this country.'

Allow me to say, in conclusion, notwithstanding the dark picture I have this day presented of the state of the nation, I do not despair of this country. There are forces in operation, which must inevitably work the downfall of slavery. 'The arm of the Lord is not shortened,' and the doom of slavery is certain. I, therefore, leave off where I began, with hope. While drawing encouragement from the Declaration of Independence, the great principles it contains, and the genius of American Institutions, my spirit is also cheered by the obvious tendencies of the age. Nations do not now stand in the same relation to each other that they did ages ago. No nation can now shut itself up from the surrounding world, and trot round in the same old path of its fathers without interference. The time was when such could be done. Long established customs of hurtful character could formerly fence themselves in, and do their evil work with social impunity. Knowledge was then confined and enjoyed by the privileged few, and the multitude walked on in mental darkness. But a change has now come over the affairs of mankind. Walled cities and empires have become unfashionable. The arm of commerce has borne away the gates of the strong city. Intelligence is penetrating the darkest corners of the globe. It makes its pathway over and under the sea, as well as on the earth. Wind, steam, and lightning are its chartered agents. Oceans no longer divide, but link nations together. From Boston to London is now a holiday excursion. Space is comparatively annihilated. Thoughts expressed on one side of the Atlantic are, distinctly heard on the other.

The far-off and almost fabulous Pacific rolls in grandeur at our feet. The Celestial Empire, the mystery of ages, is being solved. The fiat of the Almighty, 'Let there be Light,' has not yet spent its force. No abuse, no outrage whether in taste, sport or avarice, can now hide itself from the all-pervading light. The iron shoe, and crippled foot of China must be seen, in contrast with nature. Africa must rise and put on her yet unwoven garment. 'Ethiopia shall stretch out her hand unto God.' In the fervent aspirations of William Lloyd Garrison, I say, and let every heart join in saying it.

God speed the year of jubilee The wide world o'er When from their galling chains set free, Th' oppress'd shall vilely bend the knee, And wear the yoke of tyranny Like brutes no more. That year will come, and freedom's reign, To man his plundered fights again Restore.

God speed the day when human blood Shall cease to flow! In every clime be understood, The claims of human brotherhood, And each return for evil, good, Not blow for blow; That day will come all feuds to end. And change into a faithful friend Each foe.

God speed the hour, the glorious hour, When none on earth Shall exercise a lordly power, Nor in a tyrant's presence cower; But all to manhood's stature tower, By equal birth! That hour will com, to each, to all, And from his prison-house, the thrall Go forth.

Until that year, day, hour, arrive, With head, and heart, and hand I'll strive, To break the rod, and rend the gyve, The spoiler of his prey deprive- So witness Heaven! And never from my chosen post, Whate'er the peril or the cost, Be driven.

The Gettysburg Address

Abraham Lincoln

Soldiers' National Cemetery (19 November 1863)

Abraham Lincoln was the 16th President of the United States, a self-taught lawyer and a vocal opponent of slavery. He proved to be a shrewd military strategist during the Civil War and his Emancipation Proclamation paved the way for the abolition of slavery. Considered amongst the greatest Presidents of the United States, Lincoln was assassinated in April 1865 by a supporter of the Confederacy.

'The Gettysburg Address' is one of the most famous speeches in American history, delivered by Lincoln at the Soldiers' National Cemetery in Gettysburg, Pennsylvania on 19 November 1863.

Four score and seven years ago our fathers brought forth on this continent, a new nation, conceived in Liberty, and dedicated to the proposition that all men are created equal.

Now we are engaged in a great civil war, testing whether that nation, or any nation so conceived and so dedicated, can long endure. We are met on a great battlefield of that war. We have come to dedicate a portion of that field, as a final resting place for those who here gave their lives that that nation might live. It is altogether fitting and proper that we should do this.

But, in a larger sense, we cannot dedicate—we cannot consecrate—we cannot hallow—this ground. The brave men, living and dead, who struggled here, have consecrated it, far above our poor power to add or detract. The world will little note, nor long remember what we say here, but it can never forget what they did here. It is for us the living, rather, to be dedicated here to the unfinished work which they who fought here have thus far so nobly advanced. It is rather for us to be here dedicated to the great task remaining before us—that from these honored dead we take increased devotion to that cause for which they gave the last full measure of devotion—that we here highly resolve that these dead shall not have died in vain—that this nation, under God, shall have a new birth of freedom—and that government of the people, by the people, for the people, shall not perish from the earth.

On Women's Rights to Suffrage

Susan B. Anthony

Monroe County, New York (1873)

Susan B. Anthony was the president of the National American Women Suffrage Association and played a crucial role during the women's suffrage movement in the United States. Her efforts led to the Nineteenth Amendment (1920) to the Constitution, giving women the right to vote. She also participated in the abolitionist movement, and the temperance movement.

Anthony gave many speeches around the country to garner support for women's suffrage. 'Woman's Rights to Suffrage' was delivered after her arrest for casting an illegal vote in the presidential election of 1872.

Friends and fellow citizens

I stand before you tonight, under indictment for the alleged crime of having voted at the last Presidential election, without having a lawful right to vote. It shall be my work this evening to prove to you that in thus voting, I not only committed no crime, but, instead, simply exercised my citizen's right, guaranteed to me and all United States citizens by the National Constitution, beyond the power of any State to deny.

Our democratic-republican government is based on the idea of the natural right of every individual member thereof to a voice and a vote in making and executing the laws. We assert the province of government to be to secure the people in the enjoyment of their unalienable rights. We throw to the winds the old dogma that governments can give rights. Before governments were organized, no one denies that each individual possessed the right to protect his own life, liberty and property. And when 100 or 1,000,000 people enter into a free government, they do not barter away their natural rights; they simply pledge themselves to protect each other in the enjoyment of them, through prescribed judicial and legislative tribunals. They agree to abandon the methods of brute force in the adjustment of their differences, and adopt those of civilization.

Nor can you find a word in any of the grand documents left us by the fathers that assumes for government the power to create or to confer rights. The Declaration of Independence, the United States Constitution, the constitutions of the several states and the organic laws of the territories, all alike propose to protect the people in the exercise of their God-given rights. Not one of them pretends to bestow rights.

'All men are created equal, and endowed by their Creator with certain unalienable rights. Among these are life, liberty and the pursuit of happiness. That to secure these, governments are instituted among men, deriving their just powers from the consent of the governed.'

Here is no shadow of government authority over rights, nor exclusion of any from their full and equal enjoyment. Here is pronounced the right of all men, and 'consequently,' as the Quaker preacher said, 'of all women,' to a voice in the government. And here, in this very first paragraph of the declaration, is the assertion of the natural right of all to the ballot; for, how can 'the consent of the governed' be given, if the right to vote be denied. Again:

'That whenever any form of government becomes destructive of these ends, it is the right of the people to alter or abolish it, and to institute a new government, laying its foundations on such principles, and organizing its powers in such forms as to them shall seem most likely to affect their safety and happiness.'

Surely, the right of the whole people to vote is here clearly implied. For however destructive in their happiness this government might become, a disfranchised class could neither alter nor abolish it, nor institute a new one, except by the old brute force method of insurrection and rebellion. One-half of the people of this nation today are utterly powerless to blot from the statute books an unjust law, or to write there a new and a just one. The women, dissatisfied as they are with this form of government, that enforces taxation without representation,—that compels them to obey laws to which they have never given their consent,—that imprisons and hangs them without a trial by a jury of their peers, that robs them, in marriage, of the custody of their own persons, wages and children,—are this half of the people left wholly at the mercy of the other half, in direct violation of the spirit and letter of the declarations of the framers of this government, every one of which was based on the immutable principle of equal rights to all. By those declarations, kings, priests, popes, aristocrats, were all alike dethroned, and placed on a common level politically, with the lowliest born subject or serf. By them, too, me, as such, were deprived of their divine right to rule, and placed on a political level with women. By the practice of those declarations all class and caste distinction will be abolished; and slave, serf, plebeian, wife, woman, all alike, bound from their subject position to the proud platform of equality.

The preamble of the federal constitution says:

'We, the people of the United States, in order to form a more perfect union, establish justice, insure domestic tranquility, provide for the common defense, promote the general welfare and secure the blessings of liberty to ourselves and our posterity, do ordain and established this constitution for the United States of America.'

It was we, the people, not we, the white male citizens, nor yet we, the male citizens; but we, the whole people, who formed this Union. And we formed it, not to give the blessings of liberty, but to secure them; not to the half of ourselves and the half of our posterity, but to the whole people—women as well as men. And it is downright mockery to talk to women of their enjoyment of the blessings of liberty while they are denied the use of the only means of securing them provided by this democratic-republican government—the ballot.

The early journals of Congress show that when the committee reported to that body the original articles of confederation, the very first article which became the subject of discussion was that respecting equality of suffrage. Article 4th said: 'The better to secure and perpetuate mutual friendship and intercourse between the people of the different States of this Union, the free inhabitants of each of the States, (paupers, vagabonds and fugitives from justice excepted,) shall be entitled to all the privileges and immunities of the free citizens of the several States.'

Thus, at the very beginning, did the fathers see the necessity of the universal application of the great principle of equal rights to all—in order to produce the desired result—a harmonious union and a homogeneous people.

Luther Martin, Attorney-General of Maryland, in his report to the Legislature of that State of the convention that framed the United States Constitution, said:

'Those who advocated the equality of suffrage took the matter up on the original principles of government: that the reason why each individual man in forming a State government should have an equal vote, is because each individual, before he enters into government, is equally free and equally independent.'

James Madison said, 'Under every view of the subject, it seems indispensable that the mass of the citizens should not be without a voice in making the laws which they are to obey, and in choosing the magistrate who are to administer them.' Also, 'Let it be remembered, finally, that it has ever been the pride and the boast of America that the rights for which she contended were the rights of human nature.'

And these assertions of the framers of the United States Constitution of the equal and natural rights of all the people to a voice in the government, have been affirmed and reaffirmed by the leading statesmen of the nation, throughout the entire history of our government.

Thaddeus Stevens, of Pennsylvania, said in 1866:

'I have made up my mind that elective franchise is one of the inalienable rights meant to be secured by the declaration of independence.'

B. Gratz Brown, of Missouri, in the three day's discussion in the United States Senate in 1866, on Senator Cowan's motion to strike 'male' from the District of Columbia suffrage bill, said:

'Mr. President, I say here on the floor of the American Senate, I stand for universal suffrage; and as a matter of fundamental principle, do not recognize the right of society to limit on any ground of race or sex. I will go farther and say, that I recognize the right of franchise as being intrinsically a natural right. I do not believe that society is authorized to impose any limitation upon it that do not spring out of the necessities of the social state itself. Sir, I have been shocked, in the course of this debate, to hear Senators declare this right only a conventional and political arrangement, a privilege yielded to you and me and others; not a right in any sense, only a concession! Mr. President, I do not hold my liberties by any such tenure. On the contrary, I believe that whenever you establish that doctrine, whenever you crystallize that idea in the public mind of this country, you ring the death-knell of American liberties.'

Charles Sumner, in his brave protests against the fourteenth and fifteenth amendments, insisted that, so soon as by the thirteenth amendment the slaves became free men, the original powers of the United States Constitution guaranteed to them equal rights—the right to vote and to be voted for. In closing one of his great speeches he said:

'I do not hesitate to say that when the slaves of our country became citizens they took their place in the body politic as a component part of the people, entitled to equal rights, and under the protection of these two guardian principles: First—That all just government stand on the consent of the governed; and second, that taxation without representation is tyranny; and these rights it is the duty of Congress to guarantee as essential to the ideal of a Republic.'

The preamble of the Constitution of the State of New York declares the same purpose. It says: 'We, the people of the State of New York, grateful to Almighty God for our freedom, in order to secure its blessings, do establish this Constitution.'

Here is not the slightest intimation either of receiving freedom from the United States Constitution, or of the State conferring the blessings of liberty upon the people; and the same is true of every one of the thirty-six State Constitutions. Each and all, alike declare rights God-given, and that to secure the people in the enjoyment of their inalienable rights, is their one and only object in ordaining and establishing government. And all of the State Constitutions are equally emphatic in their recognition of the ballot as the means of securing the people in the enjoyment of these rights.

Article 1 of the New York State Constitution says: 'No member of this State shall be disfranchised or deprived of the rights or privileges secured to any citizen thereof, unless by the law of the land, or the judgment of his peers.'

And so carefully guarded is the citizen's right to vote, that the Constitution makes special mention of all who may be excluded. It says:

'Laws may be passed excluding from the right of suffrage all persons who have been or may be convicted of bribery, larceny or any infamous crime.'

In naming the various employments that shall not affect the residence of voters—the 3d section of article 2d says 'that being kept at any alms house, or other asylum, at public expense, nor being confined at any public prison, shall deprive a person of his residence,' and hence his vote. Thus is the right of voting most sacredly hedged about. The only seeming permission in the New York State Constitution for the disfranchisement of women is in section 1st of article 2d, which says: 'Every male citizen of the age of twenty-one years, c., shall be entitled to vote.'

But I submit that in view of the explicit assertions of the equal right of the whole people, both in the preamble and previous article of the constitution, this omission of the adjective 'female' in the second, should not be construed into a denial; but, instead, counted as of no effect. Mark the direct prohibition: 'No member of this State shall be disfranchised, unless by the law of the land, or the judgment of his peers.' 'The law of the land,' is the United States Constitution; and there is no provision in that document that can be fairly construed into a permission to the States to deprive any class of their citizens of their right to vote. Hence New York can get no power from that source to disfranchise one entire half of her members. Nor has 'the judgment of their peers' been pronounced against women exercising their right to vote; no disfranchised person is allowed to be judge or juror—and none but disfranchised persons can be women's peers; nor has the legislature passed laws excluding them on account of idiocy of lunacy; nor yet the courts convicted them of bribery, larceny, or any infamous crime. Clearly, then, there is no constitutional ground for the exclusion of women from the ballot-box in the State of New York, No barriers whatever stand to-day between women and the exercise of their right to vote save those of precedent and prejudice.

The clauses of the United States Constitution, cited by our opponents as giving power to the States to disfranchise any classes of citizens they shall please, are contained in sections 2d and 4th of article 1st. The second says: 'The House of Representatives shall be composed of members chosen every second year by the people of the several States; and the electors in each State shall have the qualifications requisite for electors of the most numerous branch of the State Legislature.'

This cannot be construed into a concession to the States of the power to destroy the right to become an elector, but simply to prescribe what shall be the qualification, such as competency of intellect, maturity of age, length of residence, that shall be deemed necessary to enable them to make an intelligent choice of candidates. If, as our opponents assert, the last clause of this section makes it the duty of the United States to protect citizens in the several States against higher or different qualifications for electors for representatives in Congress, than for members of Assembly, them must the first clause make it equally imperative for the national government to interfere with the States, and forbid them from arbitrarily cutting off the right of one-half of the people to become electors altogether. Section 4th says:

'The time, places and manner of holding elections for Senators and Representatives shall be prescribed in each State by the Legislative thereof; but Congress may at any time, by law, make or alter such regulations, except as to the places by choosing Senators.'

Here is conceded the power only to prescribed times, places and manner of holding the elections; and even with these Congress may interfere, with all excepting the mere place of choosing Senators. Thus you see, there is not the slightest permission in either section for the States to discriminate against the right of any class of citizens to vote. Surely, to regulate cannot be to annihilate! nor to qualify to wholly deprive. And to this principle every true Democrat and Republican said amen, when applied to black men by Senator Sumner in his great speeches for EQUAL RIGHTS TO ALL from 1865 to 1869; and when, in 1871, I asked that Senator to declare the power of the United States Constitution to protect women in their right to vote—as he had done for black men—he handed me a copy of all his speeches during that reconstruction period, and said:

'Miss Anthony, put sex where I have race or color, and you have here the best and strongest argument I can make for woman. There is not a doubt but women have the constitutional right to vote, and I will never vote for a sixteenth amendment to guarantee it to them. I voted for both the fourteenth and fifteenth under protest; would never have done it but for the pressing emergency of that hour; would have insisted that the power of the original Constitution to protect all citizens in the equal enjoyment of their rights should have been vindicated through the courts. But the newly made freedmen had neither the intelligence, wealth nor time to wait that slow process. Women possess all these in an eminent degree, and I insist that they shall appeal to the courts, and through them establish the power of our American Magna Carta, to protect every citizen of the Republic. But, friends, when in accordance with Senator Sumner's counsel, I went to the ballot-box, last November, and exercised my citizen's right to vote, the courts did not wait for me to appeal to them—they appealed to me, and indicted me on the charge of having voted illegally.

Senator Sumner, putting sex where he did color, said:

'Qualifications cannot be in their nature permanent or insurmountable. Sex cannot be a qualification any more than size, race, color, or previous condition of servitude. A permanent or insurmountable qualification is equivalent to a deprivation of the suffrage. In other words, it is the tyranny of taxation without representation, against which our revolutionary mothers, as well as fathers, rebelled.'

For any State to make sex a qualification that must ever result in the disfranchisement of one entire half of the people, is to pass a bill of attainder, or an ex post facto law, and is therefore a violation of the supreme law of the land. By it, the blessings of liberty are forever withheld from women and their female posterity. To them, this government has no just powers derived from the consent of the governed. To them this government is not a democracy. It is not a republic. It is an odious aristocracy; a hateful oligarchy of sex. The most hateful aristocracy ever established on the face of the globe. An oligarchy of wealth, where the rich govern the poor; an oligarchy of learning, where the educated govern the ignorant; or even an oligarchy of race, where the Saxon rules the African, might be endured; but this oligarchy of sex, which makes father, brothers, husband, sons, the oligarchs over the mother and sisters, the wife and daughters of every household; which ordains all men sovereigns, all women subjects, carries dissension, discord and rebellion into every home of the nation. And this most odious aristocracy exists, too, in the face of Section 4, of Article 4, which says: 'The United States shall guarantee to every State in the Union a republican form of government.'

What, I ask you, is the distinctive difference between the inhabitants of a monarchical and those of a republican form of government, save that in the monarchical the people are subjects, helpless, powerless, bound to obey laws made by superiors—while in the republican, the people are citizens, individual sovereigns, all clothed with equal power, to make and unmake both their laws and law makers, and the moment you deprive a person of his right to a voice in the government, you degrade him from the status of a citizen of the republic, to that of a subject, and it matters very little to him whether his monarch be an individual tyrant, as is the Czar of Russia, or a 15,000,000 headed monster, as here in the United States; he is a powerless subject, serf or slave; not a free and independent citizen in any sense.

But is urged, the use of the masculine pronouns he, his and him, in all the constitutions and laws, is proof that only men were meant to be included in their provisions. If you insist on this version of the letter of the law, we shall insist that you be consistent, and accept the other horn of the dilemma, which would compel you to exempt women from taxation for the support of the government, and from penalties for the violation of laws.

A year and a half ago I was at Walla, Walla, Washington Territory. I saw there a theatrical company, called the 'Pixley Sisters,' playing before crowded houses, every night of the whole week of the territorial fair. The eldest of those three fatherless girls was scarce eighteen. Yet every night a United States officer stretched out his long fingers, and clutched six dollars of the proceeds of the exhibition of those orphan girls, who, but a few years before, were half starvelings in the streets of Olympia, the capital of the far-off northwest territory. So the poor widow, who keeps a boarding house, manufacturers shirts, or sells apples and peanuts on the street corners of our cities, is compelled to pay taxes from her scanty pittance. I would that the women of this republic, at once, resolve, never again to submit of taxation, until their right to vote be recognized. Amen.

Miss Sarah E. Wall, of Worcester, Mass., twenty years ago, took this position. For several years, the officers of the law disdained her property, and sold it to meet the necessary amount; still she persisted, and would not yield an iota, though every foot of her lands should be struck off under the hammer. And now, for several years, the assessor has left her name off the tax list, and the collector passed her by without a call.

Mrs. J. S. Weeden, of Viroqua, Wis., for the past six years, has refused to pay her taxes, though the annual assessment is $75.

Mrs. Ellen Van Valkenburg, of Santa Cruz, Cal., who sued the County Clerk for refusing to register her name, declares she will never pay another dollar of tax until allowed to vote; and all over the country, women property holders are waking up to the injustice of taxation without representation, and ere long will refuse, en masse, to submit to the imposition.

There is no she, or her, or hers, in the tax laws.

The statute of New York reads:

'Every person shall be assessed in the town or ward where he resides when the assessment is made, or the lands owned by him.' 'Every collector shall call at least once on the person taxed, or at his usual place of residence, and shall demand payment of the taxes charged on him. If anyone shall refuse to pay the tax imposed on him, the collector shall levy the same by distress and sale of his property'

The same is true of all the criminal laws: 'No person shall be compelled to be a witness against himself.'

The same with the law of May 31st, 1870, the 19th section of which I am charged with having violated; not only are all the pronouns in it masculine, but everybody knows that that particular section was intended expressly to hinder the rebels from voting. It reads 'If any person shall knowingly vote without his having a lawful right,' c. Precisely so with all the papers served on me—the U.S. Marshal's warrant, the bail-bond, the petition for habeas corpus, the bill of indictment—not one of them had a feminine pronoun printed in it; but, to make them applicable to me, the Clerk of the Court made a little carat at the left of 'he' and placed an 's' over it, thus making she out of he. Then the letters 'is' were scratched out, the little carat under and 'er' over, to make her out of his, and I insist if government officials may thus manipulate the pronouns to tax, fine, imprison and hang women, women may take the same liberty with them to secure to themselves their right to a voice in the government.

So long as any classes of men were denied their right to vote, the government made a show of consistency, by exempting them from taxation. When a property qualification of $250 was required of black men in New York, they were not compelled to pay taxes, so long as they were content to report themselves worth less than that sum; but the moment the black man died, and his property fell to his widow or daughter, the black woman's name would be put on the assessor's list, and she be compelled to pay taxes on the same property exempted to her husband. The same is true of ministers in New York. So long as the minister lives, he is exempted from taxation on $1,500 of property, but the moment the breath goes out of his body, his widow's name will go down on the assessor's list, and she will have to pay taxes on the $1,500. So much for the special legislation in favor of women.

In all the penalties and burdens of the government, (except the military,) women are reckoned as citizens, equally with men. Also, in all privileges and immunities, save those of the jury box and ballot box, the two fundamental privileges on which rest all the others. The United States government not only taxes, fines, imprisons and hangs women, but it allows them to pre-empt lands, register ships, and take out passport and naturalization papers. Not only does the law permit single women and widows to the right of naturalization, but Section 2 says: 'A married woman may be naturalized without the concurrence of her husband.' (I wonder the fathers were not afraid of creating discord in the families of foreigners); and again: 'When an alien, having complied with the law, and declared his intention to become a citizen, dies before he is actually naturalized, his widow and children shall be considered citizens, entitled to all rights and privileges as such, on taking the required oath.' If a foreign born woman by becoming a naturalized citizen, is entitled to all the rights and privileges of citizenship, is not a native born woman, by her national citizenship, possessed of equal rights and privileges?

The question of the masculine pronouns, yes and nouns, too, has been settled by the United States Supreme Court, in the Case of Silver versus Ladd, December, 1868, in a decision as to whether a woman was entitled to lands, under the Oregon donation law of 1850. Elizabeth Cruthers, a widow, settled upon a claim, received patents. She died, and her son was heir. He died. Then Messrs. Ladd Nott took possession, under the general pre-emption law, December, 1861. The administrator, E. P. Silver, applied for a writ of ejectment at the land office in Oregon City. Both the Register and Receiver decided that an unmarried woman could not hold land under that law. The Commissioner of the General Land Office, at Washington, and the Secretary of the Interior, also gave adverse opinions. Here patents were issued to Ladd Nott, and duly recorded. Then a suit was brought to set aside Ladd's patent, and it was carried through all the State Courts and the Supreme Court of Oregon, each, in turn, giving adverse decisions. At last, in the United States Supreme Court, Associate Justice Miller reversed the decisions of all the lower tribunals, and ordered the land back to the heirs of Mrs. Cruthers. The Court said:

'In construing a benevolent statute of the government, made for the benefit of its own citizens, inviting and encouraging them to settle on its distant public lands, the words a single man, and unmarried man may, especially if aided by the context and other parts of the statute, be taken in a generic sense. Held, accordingly, that the Fourth Section of the Act of Congress, of September 27th, 1850, granting by way of donation, lands in Oregon Territory, to every white settler or occupant, American half-breed Indians included, embraced within the term single man an unmarried woman.'

And the attorney, who carried this question to its final success, is now the United States senator elect from Oregon, Hon. J. H. Mitchell, in whom the cause of equal rights to women has an added power on the floor of the United States Senate.

Though the words persons, people, inhabitants, electors, citizens, are all used indiscriminately in the national and state constitutions, there was always a conflict of opinion, prior to the war, as to whether they were synonymous terms, as for instance:

'No person shall be a representative who shall not have been seven years a citizen, and who shall not, when elected, be an inhabitant of that state in which he is chosen. No person shall be a senator who shall not have been a citizen of the United States, and an inhabitant of that state in which he is chosen.'

But, whatever there was for a doubt, under the old regime, the adoption of the fourteenth amendment settled that question forever, in its first sentence: 'All persons born or naturalized in the United States and subject to the jurisdiction thereof, are citizens of the United States and of the state wherein they reside.'

And the second settles the equal status of all persons—all citizens:

'No states shall make or enforce any law which shall abridge the privileges or immunities of citizens; nor shall any state deprive any person of life, liberty or property, without due process of law, nor deny to any person within its jurisdiction the equal protection of the laws.'

The only question left to be settled, now, is: Are women persons? And I hardly believe any of our opponents will have the hardihood to say they are not. Being persons, then, women are citizens, and no state has a right to make any new law, or to enforce any old law, that shall abridge their privileges or immunities. Hence, every discrimination against women in the constitutions and laws of the several states, is to-day null and void, precisely as is every one against negroes.

Is the right to vote one of the privileges or immunities of citizens? I think the disfranchised ex-rebels, and the ex-state prisoners will agree with me, that it is not only one of the them, but the one without which all the others are nothing. Seek the first kingdom of the ballot, and all things else shall be given thee, is the political injunction.

Webster, Worcester and Bouvier all define citizen to be a person, in the United States, entitled to vote and hold office.

Prior to the adoption of the thirteenth amendment, by which slavery was forever abolished, and black men transformed from property to persons, the judicial opinions of the country had always been in harmony with these definitions. To be a person was to be a citizen, and to be a citizen was to be a voter.

Associate Justice Washington, in defining the privileges and immunities of the citizen, more than fifty years ago, said: 'they included all such privileges as were fundamental in their nature. And among them is the right to exercise the elective franchise, and to hold office.'

Even the 'Dred Scott' decision, pronounced by the abolitionists and republicans infamous, because it virtually declared 'black men had no rights white men were bound to respect,' gave this true and logical conclusion, that to be one of the people was to be a citizen and a voter.

Chief Judge Daniels said:

'There is not, it is believed, to be found in the theories of writers on government, or in any actual experiment heretofore tried, an exposition of the term citizen, which has not been considered as conferring the actual possession and enjoyment of the perfect right of acquisition and enjoyment of an entire equality of privileges, civil and political.'

Associate Justice Taney said:

'The words people of the United States, and citizens, are synonymous terms, and mean the same thing. They both describe the political body, who, according to our republican institutions, form the sovereignty, and who hold the power and conduct the government, through their representatives. They are what we familiarly call the sovereign people, and every citizen is one of this people, and a constituent member of this sovereignty.'

Thus does Judge Taney's decision, which was such a terrible ban to the black man, while he was a slave, now, that he is a person, no longer property, pronounce him a citizen possessed of an entire equality of privileges, civil and political. And not only the black man, but the black woman, and all women as well.

And it was not until after the abolition of slavery, by which the negroes became free men, hence citizens, that the United States Attorney, General Bates, rendered a contrary opinion. He said:

'The constitution uses the word citizen only to express the political quality, (not equality mark,) of the individual in his relation to the nation; to declare that he is a member of the body politic, and bound to it by the reciprocal obligations of allegiance on the one side, and protection on the other. The phrase, a citizen of the United States, without addition or qualification, means neither more nor less than a member of the nation.'

Then, to be a citizen of this republic, is no more than to be a subject of an empire. You and I, and all true and patriotic citizens must repudiate this base conclusion. We all know that American citizenship, without addition or qualification, means the possession of equal rights, civil and political. We all know that the crowning glory of every citizen of the United States is, that he can either give or withhold his vote from every law and every legislator under the government.

Did 'I am a Roman citizen,' mean nothing more than that I am a 'member' of the body politic of the republic of Rome, bound to it by the reciprocal obligations of allegiance on the one side, and protection on the other? Ridiculously absurd question, you say. When you, young man, shall travel abroad, among the monarchies of the old world, and there proudly boast yourself an 'American citizen,' will you thereby declare yourself neither more nor less than a 'member' of the American nation?

And this opinion of Attorney General Bates, that a black citizen was not a voter, made merely to suit the political exigency of the republican party, in that transition hour between emancipation and enfranchisement, was no less in-famous, in spirit or purpose, than was the decision of Judge Taney, that a black man was not one of the people, rendered in the interest and the behest of the old democratic party, in its darkest hour of subjection to the slave power. Nevertheless, all of the adverse arguments, adverse congressional reports and judicial opinions, thus far, have been based on this purely partisan, time-serving opinion of General Bates, that the normal condition of the citizen of the United States is that of disfranchisement. That only such classes of citizens as have had special legislative guarantee have a legal right to vote.

And if this decision of Attorney General Bates was infamous, as against black men, but yesterday plantation slaves, what shall we pronounce upon Judge Bingham, in the house of Representatives, and Carpenter, in the Senate of the United States, for citing it against the women of the entire nation, vast numbers of whom are the peers of those honorable gentlemen, themselves, in moral!! Intellect, culture, wealth, family—paying taxes on large estates, and contributing equally with them and their sex, in every direction, to the growth, prosperity and well-being of the republic? And what shall be said of the judicial opinions of Judges Carter, Jameson, McKay and Sharswood, all based upon this aristocratic, monarchial idea, of the right of one class to govern another?

I am proud to mention the names of the two United States Judges who have given opinions honorable to our republican idea, and honorable to themselves—Judge Howe, of Wyoming Territory, and Judge Underwood, of Virginia.

The former gave it as his opinion a year ago, when the Legislature seemed likely to revoke the law enfranchising the women of that territory, that, in case they succeeded, the women would still possess the right to vote under the fourteenth amendment.

Judge Underwood, of Virginia, in nothing the recent decision of Judge Carter, of the Supreme Court of the District of Columbia to women the right to vote, under the fourteenth and fifteenth amendment, says:

'If the people of the United States, by amendment of their constitution, could expunge, without any explanatory or assisting legislation, an adjective of five letters from all state and local constitutions, and thereby raise millions of our most ignorant fellow-citizens to all of the rights and privileges of electors, why should not the same people, by the same amendment, expunge an adjective of four letters from the same state and local constitutions, and thereby raise other millions of more educated and better informed citizens to equal rights and privileges, without explanatory or assisting legislation?'

If the fourteenth amendment does not secure to all citizens the right to vote, for what purpose was the grand old charter of the fathers lumbered with its unwieldy proportions? The republican party, and Judges Howard and Bingham, who drafted the document, pretended it was to do something for black men; and if that something was not to secure them in their right to vote and hold office, what could it have been? For, by the thirteenth amendment, black men had become people, and hence were entitled to all the privileges and immunities of the government, precisely as were the women of the country, and foreign men not naturalized. According to Associate Justice Washington, they already had the 'Protection of the government, the enjoyment of life and liberty, with the right to acquire and possess property of every kind, and to pursue and obtain happiness and safety, subject to such restraints as the government may justly prescribe for the general welfare of the whole; the right of a citizen of one state to pass through or to reside in any other state for the purpose of trade, agriculture, professional pursuit, or otherwise; to claim the benefit of the writ of habeas corpus, to institute and maintain actions of any kind in the courts of the state; to take, hold, and dispose of property, either real or personal, and an exemption from higher taxes or impositions than are paid by the other citizens of the state.'

Thus, you see, those newly freed men were in possession of every possible right, privilege and immunity of the government, except that of suffrage, and hence, needed no constitutional amendment for any other purpose. What right, I ask you, has the Irishman the day after he receives his naturalization papers that he did not possess the day before, save the right to vote and hold office? And the Chinamen, now crowding our Pacific coast, are in precisely the same position. What privilege or immunity has California or Oregon the constitutional right to deny them, save that of the ballot? Clearly, then if the fourteenth amendment was not to secure to black men their right to vote, it did nothing for them, since they possessed everything else before. But, if it was meant to be a prohibition of the states, to deny or abridge their right to vote—which I fully believe—then it did the same for all persons, white women included, born or naturalized in the United States; for the amendment does not say all male persons of African descent, but all persons are citizens.

The second section is simply a threat to punish the states, by reducing their representation on the floor of Congress, should they disfranchise any of their male citizens, on account of color, and does not allow of the inference that the states may disfranchise from any, or all other causes, nor in any wise weaken or invalidate the universal guarantee of the first section. What rule of law or logic would allow the conclusion, that the prohibition of a crime to one person, on severe pains and penalties, was a sanction of that crime to any and all other persons save that one?

But, however much the doctors of the law may disagree, as to whether people and citizens, in the original constitution, were once and the same, or whether the privileges and immunities in the fourteenth amendment include the right of suffrage, the question of the citizen's right to vote is settled forever by the fifteenth amendment. 'The citizen's right to vote shall not be denied by the United States, nor any state thereof; on account of race, color, or previous condition of servitude.' How can the state deny or abridge the right of the citizen, if the citizen does not possess it? There is no escape from the conclusion, that to vote is the citizen's right, and the specifications of race, color, or previous condition of servitude can, in no way, impair the force of the emphatic assertion, that the citizen's right to vote shall not be denied or abridged.

The political strategy of the second section of the fourteenth amendment, failing to coerce the rebel states into enfranchising their negroes, and the necessities of the republican party demanding their votes throughout the South, to ensure the re-election of Grant in 1872, that party was compelled to place this positive prohibition of the fifteenth amendment upon the United States and all the states thereof.

If we once establish he false principle, that United States citizenship does not carry with it the right to vote in every state in this Union, there is no end to the petty freaks and cunning devices, that will be resorted to, to exclude one and another class of citizens from the right of suffrage.

It will not always be men combining to disfranchise all women; native born men combining to abridge the rights of all naturalized citizens, as in Rhode Island. It will not always be the rich and educated who may combine to cut off the poor and ignorant; but we may live to see the poor, hardworking, uncultivated day laborers, foreign and native born, learning the power of the ballot and their vast majority of numbers, combine and amend state constitutions so as to disfranchise the Vanderbilts and A. T Stewarts, the Conklings and Fentons. It is poor rule that won't work more ways than one. Establish this precedent, admit the right to deny suffrage to the states, and there is no power to foresee the confusion, discord and disruption that may await us. There is, and can be, but one safe principle of government—equal rights to all. And any and every discrimination against any class, whether on account of color, race, nativity, sex, property, culture, can but embitter and disaffect that class, and thereby endanger the safety of the whole people.

Clearly, then, the national government must not only define the rights of citizens, but it must stretch out its powerful hand and protect them in every state in this Union.

But if you will insist that the fifteenth amendment's emphatic interdiction against robbing United States citizens of their right to vote, 'on account of race, color, or previous condition of servitude,' is a recognition of the right, either of the United States, or any state, to rob citizens of that right, for any or all other reason, I will prove to you that the class of citizens for which I now plead, and to which I belong, may be, and sure, by all the principles of our government, and many of the laws of the states, included under the term 'previous condition of servitude.'

First. —The married women and their legal status. What is servitude? 'The condition of a slave.' What is a slave? 'A person who is robbed of the proceeds of his labour; a person who is subject to the will of another.'

By the law of Georgia, South Carolina, and all the states of the South, the negro had no right to the custody and control of his person. He belonged to his master. If he was disobedient, the master had the right to use correction. If the negro didn't like the correction, and attempted to run away, the master had a right to use coercion to bring him back.

By the law of every state in this Union to-day, North as well as South, the married woman has no right to the custody and control of her person. The wife belongs to her husband; and if the refuses obedience to his will, he may use moderate correction, and if she doesn't like his moderate correction, and attempts to leave his 'bed and board,' the husband may use moderate coercion to bring her back. The little word 'moderate,' you see, is the saving clause for the wife, and would doubtless be overstepped should offended husband administer his correction with the 'cat-o'-nine-tails,' or accomplish his coercion with blood-hounds.

Again, the slave had no right to the earnings of his hands, they belonged to his master; no right to the custody of his children, they belonged to his master; no right to sue or be sued, or testify in the courts. If he committed a crime, it was the master who must sue or be sued.

In many of the states there has been special legislation, giving to married women the right to property inherited, or received by bequest, or earned by the pursuit of any avocation outside of the home; also, giving her the right to sue and be sued in matters pertaining to such separate property; but not a single state of this Union has eve secured the wife in the enjoyment of her right to the joint ownership of the joint earnings of the marriage co-partnership. And since, in the nature of things, the vast majority of married women never earn a dollar, by work outside of their families, nor inherit a dollar from their fathers, it follows that from the day of their marriage to the day of the death of their husbands, not one of them ever has a dollar, except it shall please her husband to let her have it.

In some of the states, also, there have been laws passed giving to the mother a joint right with the father in the guardianship of the children. But twenty years ago, when our woman's rights movement commenced, by the laws of the State of New York, and all the states, the father had the sole custody and control of the children. No matter if he were a brutal, drunken libertine, he had the legal right, without the mother's consent, to apprentice her sons to rum sellers, or her daughters to brothel keepers. He could even will away an unborn child, to some other person than the mother. And in many of the states the law still prevails, and the mothers are still utterly powerless under the common law.

I doubt if there is, to-day, a State in this Union where a married woman can sue or be sued for slander of character, and until quite recently there was not one in which she could sue or be sued for injury of person. However damaging to the wife's reputation any slander may be, she is wholly powerless to institute legal proceedings against her accuser, unless her husband shall join with her; and how often have we hard of the husband conspiring with some outside barbarian to blast the good name of his wife? A married woman cannot testify in courts in cases of joint interest with her husband. A good farmer's wife near Earlville, III., who had all the rights she wanted, went to a dentist of the village and had a full set of false teeth, both upper and under. The dentist pronounced them an admirable fit, and the wife declared they gave her fits to wear them; that she could neither chew nor talk with them in her mouth. The dentist sued the husband; his counsel brought the wife as witness; the judge ruled her off the stand; saying 'a married woman cannot be a witness in matters of joint interest between herself and her husband.' Think of it, ye good wives, the false teeth in your mouths are joint interest with your husbands, about which you are legally incompetent to speak!! If in our frequent and shocking railroad accidents a married woman is injured in her person, in nearly all of the States, it is her husband who must sue the company, and it is to her husband that the damages, if there are any, will be awarded. In Ashfield, Mass., supposed to be the most advanced of any State in the Union in all things, humanitarian as well as intellectual, a married woman was severely injured by a defective sidewalk. Her husband sued the corporation and recovered $13,000 damages. And those $13,000 belong to him bona fide; and whenever that unfortunate wife wishes a dollar of it to supply her needs she must ask her husband for it; and if the man be of a narrow, selfish, nighardly nature, she will have to hear him say, every time, 'What have you done, my dear, with the twenty-five cents I gave you yesterday?' Isn't such a position, ask you, humiliating enough to be called 'servitude?' That husband, as would any other husband, in nearly every State of this Union, sued and obtained damages for the loss of the services of his wife, precisely as the master, under the old slave regime, would have done, had his slave been thus injured, and precisely as he himself would have done had it been his ox, cow or horse instead of his wife.

There is an old saying that 'a rose by any other name would smell as sweet,' and I submit it the deprivation by law of the ownership of one's own person, wages, property, children, the denial of the right as an individual, to sue and be sued, and to testify in the courts, is not a condition of servitude most bitter and absolute, though under the sacred name of marriage?

Does any lawyer doubt my statement of the legal status of married women? I will remind him of the fact that the old common law of England prevails in every State in this Union, except where the Legislature has enacted special laws annulling it. And I am ashamed that not one State has yet blotted from its statue books the old common law of marriage, by which Blackstone, summed up in the fewest words possible, is made to say, 'husband and wife are one, and that one is the husband.'

Thus may all married women, wives and widows, by the laws of the several States, be technically included in the fifteenth amendment's specification of 'condition of servitude,' present or previous. And not only married women, but I will also prove to you that by all the great fundamental principles of our free government, the entire womanhood of the nation is in a 'condition of servitude' as surely as were our revolutionary fathers, when they rebelled against old King George. Women are taxed without representation, governed without their consent, tried, convicted and punished without a jury of their peers. And is all this tyranny any less humiliating and degrading to women under our democratic-republican government to-day than it was to men under their aristocratic, monarchical government one hundred years ago? There is not an utterance of old John Adams, John Hancock or Patrick Henry, but finds a living response in the soul of every intelligent, patriotic woman of the nation. Bring to me a common-sense woman property holder, and

I will show you one whose soul is fired with all the indignation of 1776 every time the tax-gatherer presents himself at her door. You will not find one such but feels her condition of servitude as galling as did James Otis when he said:

'The very act of taxing exercised over those who are not represented appears to me to be depriving them of one of their most essential rights, and if continued, seems to be in effect an entire disfranchisement of every civil right. For, what one civil right is worth a rush after a man's property is subject to be taken from him at pleasure without his consent? If a man is not his own assessor in person, or by deputy, his liberty is gone, or he is wholly at the mercy of others.'

What was the three-penny tax on tea, or the paltry tax on paper and sugar to which our revolutionary fathers were subjected, when compared with the taxation of the women of this Republic? The orphaned Pixley sisters, six dollars a day, and even the women, who are proclaiming the tyranny of our taxation without representation, from city to city throughout the country, are often compelled to pay a tax for the poor privilege of defending our rights. And again, to show that disfranchisement was precisely the slavery of which the fathers complained, allow me to cite to you old Ben. Franklin, who in those olden times was admitted to be good authority, not merely in domestic economy, but in political as well; he said:

'Every man of the commonalty, except infants, insane persons and criminals, is, of common right and the law of God, a freeman and entitled to the free enjoyment of liberty. That liberty or freedom consists in having an actual share in the appointment of those who are to frame the laws, and who are to be the guardians of every man's life, property and peace. For the all of one man is as dear to him as the all of another; and the poor man has an equal right, but more need to have representatives in the Legislature that the rich one. That they who have no voice or vote in the electing of representatives, do not enjoy liberty, but are absolutely enslaved to those who have votes and their representatives; for to be enslaved is to have governors whom other men have set over us, and to be subject to laws made by the representatives of others, without having had representatives of our own to give consent in our behalf.'

Suppose I read it with the feminine gender:

'That women who have no voice nor vote in the electing of representatives, do not enjoy liberty, but are absolutely enslaved to men who have votes and their representatives; for to be enslaved is to have governors whom men have set over us, and to be subject to the laws made by the representatives of men, without having representatives of our own to give consent in our behalf.'

And yet one more authority; that of Thomas Paine, than whom not one of the Revolutionary patriots more ably vindicated the principles upon which our government is founded:

'The right of voting for representatives is the primary right by which other rights are protected. To take away this right is to reduce man to a state of slavery; for slavery consists in being subject to the will of another; and he that has not a vote in the election of representatives is in this case. The proposal, therefore, to disfranchise any class of men is as criminal as the proposal to take away property.'

Is anything further needed to prove woman's condition of servitude sufficiently orthodox to entitle her to the guaranties of the fifteenth amendment?

Is there a man who will not agree with me, that to talk of freedom without the ballot, is mockery—is slavery—to the women of this Republic, precisely as New England's orator Wendell Phillips, at the close of the late war, declared it to be to the newly emancipated black men?

I admit that prior to the rebellion, by common consent, the right to enslave, as well as to disfranchise both native and foreign born citizens, was conceded to the States. But the one grand principle, settled by the war and the reconstruction legislation, is the supremacy of national power to protect the citizens of the United States in their right to freedom and the elective franchise, against any and every interference on the part of the several States. And again and again, have the American people asserted the triumph of this principle, by their overwhelming majorities for Lincoln and Grant.

The one issue of the last two Presidential elections was, whether the fourteenth and fifteenth amendments should be considered the irrevocable will of the people; and the decision was, they shall be—

and that it is only the right, but the duty of the National Government to protect all United States citizens in the full enjoyment and free exercise of all their privileges and immunities against any attempt of any State to deny or abridge.

And in this conclusion Republican and Democrats alike agree.

Senator Frelinghuysen said:

'The heresy of State rights has been completely buried in these amendments, that as amended, the Constitution confers not only national but State citizenship upon all persons born or naturalized within our limits.'

The Call for the national Republican convention said:

'Equal suffrage has been engrafted on the national Constitution; the privileges and immunities of American citizenship have become a part of the organic law.'

The national Republican platform said:

'Complete liberty and exact equality in the enjoyment of all civil, political and public rights, should be established and maintained throughout the Union by efficient and appropriate State and federal legislation.'

If that means anything, it is that Congress should pass a law to require the States to protect women in their equal political rights, and that the States should enact laws making it the duty of inspectors of elections to receive women's votes on precisely the same conditions they do those of men.

Judge Stanley Mathews—a substantial Ohio democrat—in his preliminary speech at the Cincinnati convention, said most emphatically:

'The constitutional amendments have established the political equality of all citizens before the law.'

President Grant, in his message to Congress March 30th, 1870, on the adoption of the fifteenth amendment, said: 'A measure which makes at once four millions of people voters, is indeed a measure of greater importance than any act of the kind from the foundation of the Government to the present time.'

How could four millions negroes be made voter if two millions were not included?

The California State Republican convention said:

'Among the many practical and substantial triumphs of the principles achieved by the Republican party during the past twelve years, it enumerated with pride and pleasure, the prohibiting of any State from abridging the privileges of any citizen of the Republic, the declaring the civil and political equality of every citizen, and the establishing all these principles in the federal constitution by amendments thereto, as the permanent law.'

Benjamin F. Butler, in a recent letter to me, said:

'I do not believe anybody in Congress doubts that the Constitution authorizes the right of women to vote, precisely as if authorizes trial by jury and many other like rights guaranteed to citizens.'

And again, General Butler said:

'It is not laws we want; there are plenty of laws—good enough, too. Administrative ability to enforce law is the great want of the age, in this country especially. Everybody talks of law, law. If everybody would insist on the enforcement of law, the government would stand on a firmer basis, and question would settle themselves.'

An it is upon this just interpretation of the United States Constitution that our National Woman Suffrage Association which celebrates the twenty-fifth anniversary of the woman's rights movement in New York on the 6th of May next, has based all its arguments and action the past five years.

We no longer petition Legislature or Congress to give us the right to vote. We appeal to the women everywhere to exercise their too long neglected 'citizen's right to vote.' We appeal to the inspectors of election everywhere to receive the votes of all United States citizens as it is their duty to do. We appeal to United States commissioners and marshals to arrest the inspectors who reject the names and votes of United States citizens, as it is their duty to do, and leave those alone who, like our eighth ward inspectors, perform their duties faithfully and well.

We ask the juries to fail to return verdicts of 'guilty' against honest, law-abiding, tax-paying United States citizens for offering their votes at our elections. Or against intelligent, worthy young men, inspectors of elections, for receiving and counting such citizens votes.

We ask the judges to render true and unprejudiced opinions of the law, and wherever there is room for a doubt to give its benefit on the side of liberty and equal rights to women, remembering that 'the true rule of interpretation under our national constitution, especially since its amendments, is that anything for human rights is constitutional, everything against human right unconstitutional.'

And it is on this line that we propose to fight our battle for the ballot—all peaceably, but nevertheless persistently through to complete triumph, when all United States citizens shall be recognized as equals before the law.

'I Will Fight No More Forever'

Chief Joseph

Surrender Speech (October 5 1877)

Chief Joseph was the chief of Nez Percé tribe, which was forcibly removed from their ancestral lands in the Wallowa Valley in Oregon by the United States federal government and given a reservation which was much smaller in size in the Idaho Territory. After a series of violent confrontations with the white settlers, the Nez Percé tribe attempted to flee to Canada in order to seek refuge. However, this retreat culminated in what came to be known as the Nez Percé War as members of the Nez Percé tribe were chased by the U.S. Army.

After months of fighting, the Nez Percé were forced to surrender and Chief Joseph gave this poignant speech that highlights the brutality which was inflicted on the Native Americans by the whites.

Tell General Howard I know his heart. What he told me before, I have it in my heart. I am tired of fighting. Our Chiefs are killed; Looking Glass is dead, Ta Hool Hool Shute is dead. The old men are all dead. It is the young men who say yes or no. He who led on the young men is dead. It is cold, and we have no blankets; the little children are freezing to death. My people, some of them, have run away to the hills, and have no blankets, no food. No one knows where they are—perhaps freezing to death. I want to have time to look for my children, and see how many of them I can find. Maybe I shall find them among the dead. Hear me, my Chiefs! I am tired; my heart is sick and sad. From where the sun now stands I will fight no more forever.

The Powder River Council Speech

Sitting Bull

Powder River Council (1877)

Born in the Grand River region of present-day South Dakota, Sitting Bull was a Native American chief under whose leadership the Sioux tribes united in rebellion against the U.S. authorities. The Sioux tribes faced persecution when gold was discovered in the Black Hills of South Dakota in 1874.

Sitting Bull gave this speech at the Powder River Council in 1877, around the time of the Great Sioux War of 1876, also known as the Black Hills War.

Behold, my friends, the spring is come; the earth has gladly received the embraces of the sun, and we shall soon see the results of their love! Every seed is awakened, and all animal life. It is through this mysterious power that we too have our being, and we therefore yield to our neighbors, even to our animal neighbors, the same right as ourselves to inhabit this vast land.

Yet hear me, friends! We have now to deal with another people, small and feeble when our forefathers first met with them, but now great and overbearing. Strangely enough, they have a mind to till the soil, and the love of possessions is a disease in them. These people have made many rules that the rich may break, but the poor may not! They have a religion in which the poor worship, but the rich will not! They even take tithes of the poor and weak to support the rich and those who rule. They claim this mother of ours, the Earth, for their own use, and fence their neighbors away from her, and deface her with their buildings and their refuse. They compel her to produce out of season, and when sterile she is made to take medicine in order to produce again. All this is sacrilege.

'The Solitude of Self'

Elizabeth Cady Stanton

Resignation Speech Before the Committee of the Judiciary of the United States Congress (18 January 1892)

Elizabeth Cady Stanton was an American human rights activist, abolitionist and a prominent leader of the woman's rights movement. Her efforts played an important role in the passing of the 19th Amendment to the Constitution, giving all citizens the right to vote. She served as the first president of the prestigious National Woman Suffrage Association.

'The Solitude of Self' was Stanton's resignation speech, after she had served as President for twenty years. The speech highlights arguments for the equality of women, an issue that preoccupied Stanton for the larger part of her adult life.

The point I wish plainly to bring before you on this occasion is the individuality of each human soul; our Protestant idea, the right of individual conscience and judgment; our republican idea, individual citizenship. In discussing the rights of woman, we are to consider, first, what belongs to her as an individual, in a world of her own, the arbiter of her own destiny, an imaginary Robinson Crusoe, with her woman, Friday, on a solitary island. Her rights under such circumstances are to use all her faculties for her own safety and happiness.

Secondly, if we consider her as a citizen, as a member of a great nation, she must have the same rights as all others members, according to the fundamental principles of our Government.

Thirdly, viewed as a woman, an equal factor in civilization, her rights and duties are still the same—individual happiness and development.

Fourthly, it is only the incidental relations of life, such as mother, wife, sister, daughter, which may involve some special duties and training...

The strongest reason for giving woman all the opportunities for higher education, for the full development of her faculties, her forces of mind and body; for giving her the most enlarged freedom of thought and action; a complete emancipation from all forms of bondage, of custom, dependence, superstition; from all the crippling influences of fear—is the solitude and personal responsibility of her own individual life. The strongest reason why we ask for woman a voice in the government under which she lives; in the religion she is asked to believe; equality in social life, where she is the chief factor; a place in the trades and professions, where she may earn her bread, is because of her birthright to self-sovereignty; because, as an individual, she must rely on herself. No matter how much women prefer to lean, to be protected and supported, nor how much men desire to have them do so, they must make the voyage of life alone, and for safety in an emergency, they must know something of the laws of navigation. To guide our own craft, we must be captain, pilot, engineer; with chart and compass to stand at the wheel; to watch the winds and waves, and know when to take in the sail, and to read the signs in the firmament over all. It matters not whether the solitary voyager is man or woman; nature, having endowed them equally, leaves them to their own skill and judgment in the hour of danger, and, if not equal to the occasion, alike they perish.

To appreciate the importance of fitting every human soul for independent action, think for a moment of the immeasurable solitude of self. We come into the world alone, unlike all who have gone before us, we leave it alone, under circumstances peculiar to ourselves. No mortal ever has been, no mortal ever will be like the soul just launched on the sea of life. There can never again be just such a combination of prenatal influences; never again just such environments as make up the infancy, youth and manhood of this one. Nature never repeats herself, and the possibilities of one human soul will never be found in another. No one has ever found two blades of ribbon grass alike, and no one will ever find two human beings alike. Seeing, then, what must be the infinite diversity in human character, we can in a measure appreciate the loss to a nation when any class of the people is uneducated and unrepresented in the government.

We ask for the complete development of every individual, first, for his own benefit and happiness. In fitting out an army, we give each soldier his own knapsack, arms, powder, his blanket, cup, knife, fork and spoon. We provide alike for all their individual necessities; then each man bears his own burden.

Again, we ask complete individual development for the general good; for the consensus of the competent on the whole round of human interests, on all questions of national life; and here each man must bear his share of the general burden. It is sad to see how soon friendless children are left to bear their own burdens, before they can analyze their feelings; before they can even tell their joys and sorrows, they are thrown on their own resources. The great lesson that nature seems to teach us at all ages in self-dependence, self-protection, self-support…

In youth our most bitter disappointments, our brightest hopes and ambitions, are known only to ourselves. Even our friendship and love we never fully share with another; there is something of every passion, in every situation, we conceal. Even so in our triumphs and our defeats…

We ask no sympathy from others in the anxiety and agony of a broken friendship or shattered love. When death sunders our nearest ties, alone we sit in the shadow of our affliction. Alike amid the greatest triumphs and darkest tragedies of life, we walk alone. On the divine heights of human attainment, eulogized and worshipped as a hero or saint, we stand alone. In ignorance, poverty and vice, as a pauper or criminal, alone we starve or steal; alone we suffer the sneers and rebuffs of our fellows; alone we are hunted and hounded through dark courts and alleys, in by-ways and high-ways; alone we stand in the judgment seat; alone in the prison cell we lament our crimes and misfortunes; alone we expiate them on the gallows. In hours like these we realize the awful solitude of individual life, its pains, its penalties, its responsibilities, hours in which the youngest and most helpless are thrown on their own resources for guidance and consolation. Seeing, then, that life must ever be a march and a battle that each soldier must be equipped for his own protection, it is the height of cruelty to rob the individual of a single natural right.

To throw obstacles in the way of a complete education is like putting out the eyes; to deny the rights of property is like cutting off the hands. To refuse political equality is to rob the ostracized of all self-respect; of credit in the market place; of recompense in the world of work, of a voice in choosing those who make and administer the law, a choice in the jury before whom they are tried, and in the judge who decides their punishment. Think of ... woman's position! Robbed of her natural rights, handicapped by law and custom at every turn, yet compelled to fight her own battles, and in the emergencies of life to fall back on herself for protection...

The young wife and mother, at the head of some establishment, with a kind husband to shield her from the adverse winds of life, with wealth, fortune and position, has a certain harbor of safety, secure against the ordinary ills of life. But to manage a household, have a desirable influence in society, keep her friends and the affections of her husband, train her children and servants well, she must have rare common sense, wisdom, diplomacy, and a knowledge of human nature. To do all this, she needs the cardinal virtues and the strong points of character that the most successful statesman possesses. An uneducated woman trained to dependence, with no resources in herself, must make a failure of any position in life. But society says women do not need a knowledge of the world, the liberal training that experience in public life must give, all the advantages of collegiate education; but when for the lack of all this, the woman's happiness is wrecked, alone she bears her humiliation; and the solitude of the weak and the ignorant is indeed pitiable. In the wild chase for the prizes of life, they are ground to powder.

In age, when the pleasures of youth are passed, children grown up, married and gone, the hurry and bustle of life in a measure over, when the hands are weary of active service, when the old arm chair and the fireside are the chosen resorts, then men and women alike must fall back on their own resources. If they cannot find companionship in books, if they have no interest in the vital questions of the hour, no interest in watching the consummation of reforms with which they might have been identified, they soon pass into their dotage. The more fully the faculties of the mind are developed and kept in use, the longer the period of vigor and active interest in all around us continues. If, from a life-long participation in public affairs, a woman feels responsible for the laws regulating our system of education, the discipline of our jails and prisons, the sanitary condition of our private homes, public buildings and thoroughfares, an interest in commerce, finance, our foreign relations, in any or all these questions, her solitude will at least be respectable, and she will not be driven to gossip or scandal for entertainment.

The chief reason for opening to every soul the doors to the whole round of human duties and pleasures is the individual development thus attained, the resources thus provided under all circumstances to mitigate the solitude that at times must come to everyone...

Inasmuch, then, as woman shares equally the joys and sorrows of time and eternity, is it not the height of presumption in man to propose to represent her at the ballot box and the throne of grace, to do her voting in the state, her praying in the church, and to assume the position of high priest at the family altar?

Nothing strengthens the judgment and quickens the conscience like individual responsibility. Nothing adds such dignity to character as the recognition of one's self-sovereignty; the right to an equal place, everywhere conceded—a place earned by personal merit, not an artificial attainment by inheritance, wealth, family and position. Conceding, then, that the responsibilities of life rest equally on man and woman, that their destiny is the same, they need the same preparation for time and eternity. The talk of sheltering woman from the fierce storms of life is the sheerest mockery, for they beat on her from every point of the compass, just as they do on man, and with more fatal results, for he has been trained to protect himself, to resist, and to conquer. Such are the facts in human experience, the responsibilities of individual sovereignty. Rich and poor, intelligent and ignorant, wise and foolish, virtuous and vicious, man and woman; it is ever the same, each soul must depend wholly on itself.

Whatever the theories may be of woman's dependence on man, in the supreme moments of her life, he cannot bear her burdens. Alone she goes to the gates of death to give life to every man that is born into the world; no one can share her fears, no one can mitigate her pangs; and if her sorrow is greater than she can bear, alone she passes beyond the gates into the vast unknown.

From the mountain-tops of Judea long ago, a heavenly voice bade his disciples, 'Bear ye one another's burdens'; but humanity has not yet risen to that point of self-sacrifice; and if ever so willing, how few the burdens are that one soul can bear for another!...

So it ever must be in the conflicting scenes of life, in the long, weary march, each one walks alone. We may have many friends, love, kindness, sympathy and charity, to smooth our pathway in everyday life, but in the tragedies and triumphs of human experience, each mortal stands alone.

But when all artificial trammels are removed, and women are recognized as individuals, responsible for their own environments, thoroughly educated for all positions in life they may be called to fill; with all the resources in themselves that liberal thought and broad culture can give; guided by their own conscience and judgment, trained to self-protection, by a healthy development of the muscular system, and skill in the use of weapons and defence; and stimulated to self-support by a knowledge of the business world and the pleasure that pecuniary independence must ever give; when women are trained in this way, they will in a measure be fitted for those hours of solitude that come alike to all, whether prepared or otherwise. As in our extremity we must depend on ourselves, the dictates of wisdom point to complete individual development.

In talking of education, how shallow the argument that each class must be educated for the special work it proposes to do, and that all those faculties not needed in this special work must lie dormant and utterly wither for want of use, when, perhaps, these will be the very faculties needed in life's greatest emergencies! Some say, 'Where is the use of drilling girls in the languages, the sciences, in law, medicine, theology. As wives, mothers, housekeepers, cooks, they need a different curriculum from boys who are to fill all positions. The chief cooks in our great hotels and ocean steamers are men.

In our large cities, men run the bakeries; they make our bread, cake and pies. They manage the laundries; they are now considered our best milliners and dressmakers. Because some men fill these departments of usefulness, shall we regulate the curriculum in Harvard and Yale to their present necessities? If not, why this talk in our best colleges of a curriculum for girls who are crowding into the trades and professions, teachers in all our public schools, rapidly filling many lucrative and honorable positions in life?'...

Women are already the equals of men in the whole realm of thought, in art, science, literature and government...The poetry and novels of the century are theirs, and they have touched the keynote of reform, in religion, politics and social life. They fill the editor's and professor's chair, plead at the bar of justice, walk the wards of the hospital, speak from the pulpit and the platform. Such is the type of womanhood that an enlightened public sentiment welcomes today, and such the triumph of the facts of life over the false theories of the past.

Is it, then, consistent to hold the developed woman of this day within the same narrow political limits as the dame with the spinning wheel and knitting needle occupied in the past? No, no! Machinery has taken the labors of woman as well as man on its tireless shoulders; the loom and the spinning wheel are but dreams of the past; the pen, the brush, the easel, the chisel, have taken their places, while the hopes and ambitions of women are essentially changed.

We see reason sufficient in the outer conditions of human beings for individual liberty and development, but when we consider the self-dependence of every human soul, we see the need of courage, judgment and the exercise of every faculty of mind and body, strengthened and developed by use, in woman as well as man.

Whatever may be said of man's protecting power in ordinary conditions, amid all the terrible disasters by land and sea, in the supreme moments of danger, alone woman must ever meet the horrors of the situation. The Angel of Death even makes no royal pathway for her. Man's love and sympathy enter only into the sunshine of our lives. In that solemn solitude of self, that links us with the immeasurable and the eternal, each soul lives alone forever.

A recent writer says: 'I remember once, in crossing the Atlantic, to have gone upon the deck of the ship at midnight, when a dense black cloud enveloped the sky, and the great deep was roaring madly under the lashes of demoniac winds. My feeling was not of danger or fear (which is a base surrender of the immortal soul) but of utter desolation and loneliness; a little speck of life shut in by a tremendous darkness…'

And yet, there is a solitude which each and every one of us has always carried with him, more inaccessible than the ice-cold mountains, more profound than the midnight sea; the solitude of self. Our inner being which we call ourself, no eye nor touch of man or angel has ever pierced. It is more hidden than the caves of the gnome; the sacred adytum of the oracle; the hidden chamber of Eleusinian mystery, for to it only omniscience is permitted to enter.

Such is individual life. Who, I ask you, can take, dare take on himself the rights, the duties, the responsibilities of another human soul?

Address at the Final Session of the Parliament of Religions

Swami Vivekananda

Chicago, Illinois (27 September 1893)

Swami Vivekananda was a Hindu monk, thinker, orator and one of the most celebrated spiritual leaders of India. He played an important role in establishing Hinduism as a revered religion of the world. The young monk inspired many through his message of self-betterment, harmony and brotherhood. In India, 12 January, Swami Vivekananda's birthday, is celebrated as National Youth Day.

Swami Vivekananda represented India and Hinduism at the Parliament of the World's Religions and gave this speech at the final session of the Parliament.

The World's Parliament of Religions has become an accomplished fact, and the merciful Father has helped those who laboured to bring it into existence, and crowned with success their most unselfish labour.

My thanks to those noble souls whose large hearts and love of truth first dreamed this wonderful dream and then realised it. My thanks to the shower of liberal sentiments that has overflowed this platform. My thanks to this enlightened audience for their uniform kindness to me and for their appreciation of every thought that tends to smooth the friction of religions. A few jarring notes were heard from time to time in this harmony. My special thanks to them, for they have, by their striking contrast, made general harmony the sweeter.

Much has been said of the common ground of religious unity. I am not going just now to venture my own theory. But if anyone here hopes that this unity will come by the triumph of any one of the religions and the destruction of the others, to him I say, 'Brother, yours is an impossible hope.' Do I wish that the Christian would become Hindu? God forbid. Do I wish that the Hindu or Buddhist would become Christian? God forbid.

The seed is put in the ground, and earth and air and water are placed around it. Does the seed become the earth, or the air, or the water? No. It becomes a plant. It develops after the law of its own growth, assimilates the air, the earth, and the water, converts them into plant substance, and grows into a plant.

Similar is the case with religion. The Christian is not to become a Hindu or a Buddhist, nor a Hindu or a Buddhist to become a Christian. But each must assimilate the spirit of the others and yet preserve his individuality and grow according to his own law of growth.

If the Parliament of Religions has shown anything to the world, it is this: It has proved to the world that holiness, purity and charity are not the exclusive possessions of any church in the world, and that every system has produced men and women of the most exalted character. In the face of this evidence, if anybody dreams of the exclusive survival of his own religion and the destruction of the others, I pity him from the bottom of my heart, and point out to him that upon the banner of every religion will soon be written in spite of resistance: 'Help and not fight,' 'Assimilation and not Destruction,' 'Harmony and Peace and not Dissension.'

Farewell Address to the Lakota People

Red Cloud

(4 July 1903)

Red Cloud was the chief of the Oglala Lakota people who led them during the successful campaign know as Red Cloud's War (1866-68) against the U.S. government. Considered amongst the most important chiefs of the Lakota people, Red Cloud was a fierce warrior and an important political leader. After the war, he signed a peace treaty with the U.S. government and moved to the Pine Ridge Reservation along with his tribe in the 1870s—a decision he was to regret later.

Red Cloud eventually stepped down as leader in the 1880s and protested peacefully against the U.S. government for better living conditions in the Reservation. On 4 July 1903, he delivered this moving farewell address to the Lakota people.

My sun is set. My day is done. Darkness is stealing over me. Before I lie down to rise no more, I will speak to my people.

Hear me, my friends, for it is not the time for me to tell you a lie. The Great Spirit made us, the Indians, and gave us this land we live in. He gave us the buffalo, the antelope, and the deer for food and clothing. We moved our hunting grounds from the Minnesota to the Platte and from the Mississippi to the great mountains. No one put bounds on us. We were free as the winds, and like the eagle, heard no man's commands.

I was born a Lakota and I shall die a Lakota. Before the white man came to our country, the Lakotas were a free people. They made their own laws and governed themselves as it seemed good to them. The priests and ministers tell us that we lived wickedly when we lived before the white man came among us. Whose fault was this? We lived right as we were taught it was right. Shall we be punished for this? I am not sure that what these people tell me is true.

As a child I was taught the Taku Wakan (Supernatural Powers) were powerful and could do strange things. This was taught me by the wise men and the shamans. They taught me that I could gain their favor by being kind to my people and brave before my enemies; by telling the truth and living straight; by fighting for my people and their hunting grounds.

When the Lakotas believed these things they were happy and they died satisfied. What more than this can that which the white man offers us give?

Taku Shanskan is familiar with my spirit and when I die I will go with him. Then I will be with my forefathers. If this is not in the heaven of the white man I shall be satisfied. Wi is my father. The Wakan Tanka of the white man has overcome him. But I shall remain true to him.

Shadows are long and dark before me. I shall soon lie down to rise no more. While my spirit is with my body the smoke of my breath shall be towards the Sun for he knows all things and knows that I am still true to him.

The Man with the Muck-rake

Theodore Roosevelt

(14 April 1906)

Theodore Roosevelt was the 26th President of the United States who won the Nobel Peace Prize in 1906 for his efforts to end the Russo-Japanese War (1904-1905). He was the youngest President in American history, a fine strategist who knew how to skilfully use the media to influence public opinion.

Roosevelt gave this speech to inaugurate the laying of the cornerstone of the office building of the House of Representatives. Through this speech, he warned the media of biased journalism that led to sensationalism.

Over a century ago Washington laid the corner stone of the Capitol in what was then little more than a tract of wooded wilderness here beside the Potomac. We now find it necessary to provide by great additional buildings for the business of the government.

This growth in the need for the housing of the government is but a proof and example of the way in which the nation has grown and the sphere of action of the national government has grown. We now administer the affairs of a nation in which the extraordinary growth of population has been outstripped by the growth of wealth in complex interests. The material problems that face us today are not such as they were in Washington's time, but the underlying facts of human nature are the same now as they were then. Under altered external form we war with the same tendencies toward evil that were evident in Washington's time, and are helped by the same tendencies for good. It is about some of these that I wish to say a word today.

In Bunyan's 'Pilgrim's Progress' you may recall the description of the Man with the Muck Rake, the man who could look no way but downward, with the muck rake in his hand; who was offered a celestial crown for his muck rake, but who would neither look up nor regard the crown he was offered, but continued to rake to himself the filth of the floor.

In 'Pilgrim's Progress' the Man with the Muck Rake is set forth as the example of him whose vision is fixed on carnal instead of spiritual things. Yet he also typifies the man who in this life consistently refuses to see aught that is lofty, and fixes his eyes with solemn intentness only on that which is vile and debasing.

Now, it is very necessary that we should not flinch from seeing what is vile and debasing. There is filth on the floor, and it must be scraped up with the muck rake; and there are times and places where this service is the most needed of all the services that can be performed. But the man who never does anything else, who never thinks or speaks or writes, save of his feats with the muck rake, speedily becomes, not a help but one of the most potent forces for evil.

There are in the body politic, economic and social, many and grave evils, and there is urgent necessity for the sternest war upon them. There should be relentless exposure of and attack upon every evil man, whether politician or business man, every evil practice, whether in politics, business, or social life. I hail as a benefactor every writer or speaker, every man who, on the platform or in a book, magazine, or newspaper, with merciless severity makes such attack, provided always that he in his turn remembers that the attack is of use only if it is absolutely truthful.

The liar is no whit better than the thief, and if his mendacity takes the form of slander he may be worse than most thieves. It puts a premium upon knavery untruthfully to attack an honest man, or even with hysterical exaggeration to assail a bad man with untruth.

An epidemic of indiscriminate assault upon character does no good, but very great harm. The soul of every scoundrel is gladdened whenever an honest man is assailed, or even when a scoundrel is untruthfully assailed.

Now, it is easy to twist out of shape what I have just said, easy to affect to misunderstand it, and if it is slurred over in repetition not difficult really to misunderstand it. Some persons are sincerely incapable of understanding that to denounce mudslinging does not mean the endorsement of whitewashing; and both the interested individuals who need whitewashing and those others who practice mudslinging like to encourage such confusion of ideas.

One of the chief counts against those who make indiscriminate assault upon men in business or men in public life is that they invite a reaction which is sure to tell powerfully in favor of the unscrupulous scoundrel who really ought to be attacked, who ought to be exposed, who ought, if possible, to be put in the penitentiary. If Aristides is praised overmuch as just, people get tired of hearing it; and over-censure of the unjust finally and from similar reasons results in their favor.

Any excess is almost sure to invite a reaction; and, unfortunately, the reactions instead of taking the form of punishment of those guilty of the excess, is apt to take the form either of punishment of the unoffending or of giving immunity, and even strength, to offenders. The effort to make financial or political profit out of the destruction of character can only result in public calamity. Gross and reckless assaults on character, whether on the stump or in newspaper, magazine, or book, create a morbid and vicious public sentiment, and at the same time act as a profound deterrent to able men of normal sensitiveness and tend to prevent them from entering the public service at any price.

As an instance in point, I may mention that one serious difficulty encountered in getting the right type of men to dig the Panama canal is the certainty that they will be exposed, both without, and, I am sorry to say, sometimes within, Congress, to utterly reckless assaults on their character and capacity.

At the risk of repetition let me say again that my plea is not for immunity to, but for the most unsparing exposure of, the politician who betrays his trust, of the big business man who makes or spends his fortune in illegitimate or corrupt ways. There should be a resolute effort to hunt every such man out of the position he has disgraced. Expose the crime, and hunt down the criminal; but remember that even in the case of crime, if it is attacked in sensational, lurid, and untruthful fashion, the attack may do more damage to the public mind than the crime itself.

It is because I feel that there should be no rest in the endless war against the forces of evil that I ask the war be conducted with sanity as well as with resolution. The men with the muck rakes are often indispensable to the well being of society; but only if they know when to stop raking the muck, and to look upward to the celestial crown above them, to the crown of worthy endeavor. There are beautiful things above and round about them; and if they gradually grow to feel that the whole world is nothing but muck, their power of usefulness is gone.

If the whole picture is painted black there remains no hue whereby to single out the rascals for distinction from their fellows. Such painting finally induces a kind of moral color blindness; and people affected by it come to the conclusion that no man is really black, and no man really white, but they are all gray.

In other words, they neither believe in the truth of the attack, nor in the honesty of the man who is attacked; they grow as suspicious of the accusation as of the offense; it becomes well nigh hopeless to stir them either to wrath against wrongdoing or to enthusiasm for what is right; and such a mental attitude in the public gives hope to every knave, and is the despair of honest men. To assail the great and admitted evils of our political and industrial life with such crude and sweeping generalizations as to include decent men in the general condemnation means the searing of the public conscience. There results a general attitude either of cynical belief in and indifference to public corruption or else of a distrustful inability to discriminate between the good and the bad. Either attitude is fraught with untold damage to the country as a whole.

The fool who has not sense to discriminate between what is good and what is bad is well nigh as dangerous as the man who does discriminate and yet chooses the bad. There is nothing more distressing to every good patriot, to every good American, than the hard, scoffing spirit which treats the allegation of dishonesty in a public man as a cause for laughter. Such laughter is worse than the crackling of thorns under a pot, for it denotes not merely the vacant mind, but the heart in which high emotions have been choked before they could grow to fruition. There is any amount of good in the world, and there never was a time when loftier and more disinterested work for the betterment of mankind was being done than now. The forces that tend for evil are great and terrible, but the forces of truth and love and courage and honesty and generosity and sympathy are also stronger than ever before. It is a foolish and timid, no less than a wicked thing, to blink the fact that the forces of evil are strong, but it is even worse to fail to take into account the strength of the forces that tell for good.

Hysterical sensationalism is the poorest weapon wherewith to fight for lasting righteousness. The men who with stern sobriety and truth assail the many evils of our time, whether in the public press, or in magazines, or in books, are the leaders and allies of all engaged in the work for social and political betterment. But if they give good reason for distrust of what they say, if they chill the ardor of those who demand truth as a primary virtue, they thereby betray the good cause and play into the hands of the very men against whom they are nominally at war.

In his Ecclesiastical Polity that fine old Elizabethan divine, Bishop Hooker, wrote:

He that goeth about to persuade a multitude that they are not so well governed as they ought to be shall never want attentive and favorable hearers, because they know the manifold defects whereunto every kind of regimen is subject, but the secret lets and difficulties, which in public proceedings are innumerable and inevitable, they have not ordinarily the judgment to consider.

This truth should be kept constantly in mind by every free people desiring to preserve the sanity and poise indispensable to the permanent success of self-government. Yet, on the other hand, it is vital not to permit this spirit of sanity and self-command to degenerate into mere mental stagnation. Bad though a state of hysterical excitement is, and evil though the results are which come from the violent oscillations such excitement invariably produces, yet a sodden acquiescence in evil is even worse.

At this moment we are passing through a period of great unrest—social, political, and industrial unrest. It is of the utmost importance for our future that this should prove to be not the unrest of mere rebelliousness against life, of mere dissatisfaction with the inevitable inequality of conditions, but the unrest of a resolute and eager ambition to secure the betterment of the individual and the nation.

So far as this movement of agitation throughout the country takes the form of a fierce discontent with evil, of a determination to punish the authors of evil, whether in industry or politics, the feeling is to be heartily welcomed as a sign of healthy life.

If, on the other hand, it turns into a mere crusade of appetite against appetite, of a contest between the brutal greed of the 'have nots' and the brutal greed of the 'haves,' then it has no significance for good, but only for evil. If it seeks to establish a line of cleavage, not along the line which divides good men from bad, but along that other line, running at right angles thereto, which divides those who are well off from those who are less well off, then it will be fraught with immeasurable harm to the body politic.

We can no more and no less afford to condone evil in the man of capital than evil in the man of no capital. The wealthy man who exults because there is a failure of justice in the effort to bring some trust magnate to account for his misdeeds is as bad as, and no worse than, the so-called labour leader who clamorously strives to excite a foul class feeling on behalf of some other labor leader who is implicated in murder. One attitude is as bad as the other, and no worse; in each case the accused is entitled to exact justice; and in neither case is there need of action by others which can be construed into an expression of sympathy for crime.

It is a prime necessity that if the present unrest is to result in permanent good the emotion shall be translated into action, and that the action shall be marked by honesty, sanity, and self-restraint. There is mighty little good in a mere spasm of reform. The reform that counts is that which comes through steady, continuous growth; violent emotionalism leads to exhaustion.

It is important to this people to grapple with the problems connected with the amassing of enormous fortunes, and the use of those fortunes, both corporate and individual, in business. We should discriminate in the sharpest way between fortunes well won and fortunes ill won; between those gained as an incident to performing great services to the community as a whole and those gained in evil fashion by keeping just within the limits of mere law honesty. Of course, no amount of charity in spending such fortunes in any way compensates for misconduct in making them.

As a matter of personal conviction, and without pretending to discuss the details or formulate the system, I feel that we shall ultimately have to consider the adoption of some such scheme as that of a progressive tax on all fortunes, beyond a certain amount, either given in life or devised or bequeathed upon death to any individual-a tax so framed as to put it out of the power of the owner of one of these enormous fortunes to hand on more than a certain amount to any one individual; the tax of course, to be imposed by the national and not the state government. Such taxation should, of course, be aimed merely at the inheritance or transmission in their entirety of those fortunes swollen beyond all healthy limits. Again, the national government must in some form exercise supervision over corporations engaged in interstate business-and all large corporations engaged in interstate business—whether by license or otherwise, so as to permit us to deal with the far reaching evils of over-capitalization.

This year we are making a beginning in the direction of serious effort to settle some of these economic problems by the railway rate legislation. Such legislation, if so framed, as I am sure it will be, as to secure definite and tangible results, will amount to something of itself; and it will amount to a great deal more in so far as it is taken as a first step in the direction of a policy of superintendence and control over corporate wealth engaged in interstate commerce; this superintendence and control not to be exercised in a spirit of malevolence toward the men who have created the wealth, but with the firm purpose both to do justice to them and to see that they in their turn do justice to the public at large.

The first requisite in the public servants who are to deal in this shape with corporations, whether as legislators or as executives, is honesty. This honesty can be no respecter of persons. There can be no such thing as unilateral honesty. The danger is not really from corrupt corporations; it springs from the corruption itself, whether exercised for or against corporations.

The eighth commandment reads, 'Thou shalt not steal.' It does not read, 'Thou shalt not steal from the rich man.' It does not read, 'Thou shalt not steal from the poor man.' It reads simply and plainly, 'Thou shalt not steal.'

No good whatever will come from that warped and mock morality which denounces the misdeeds of men of wealth and forgets the misdeeds practiced at their expense; which denounces bribery, but blinds itself to blackmail; which foams with rage if a corporation secures favors by improper methods, and merely leers with hideous mirth if the corporation is itself wronged.

The only public servant who can be trusted honestly to protect the rights of the public against the misdeeds of a corporation is that public man who will just as surely protect the corporation itself from wrongful aggression.

If a public man is willing to yield to popular clamor and do wrong to the men of wealth or to rich corporations, it may be set down as certain that if the opportunity comes he will secretly and furtively do wrong to the public in the interest of a corporation.

But in addition to honesty, we need sanity. No honesty will make a public man useful if that man is timid or foolish, if he is a hot-headed zealot or an impracticable visionary. As we strive for reform we find that it is not at all merely the case of a long uphill pull. On the contrary, there is almost as much of breeching work as of collar work. To depend only on traces means that there will soon be a runaway and an upset.

The men of wealth who today are trying to prevent the regulation and control of their business in the interest of the public by the proper government authorities will not succeed, in my judgment, in checking the progress of the movement. But if they did succeed they would find that they had sown the wind and would surely reap the whirlwind, for they would ultimately provoke the violent excesses which accompany a reform coming by convulsion instead of by steady and natural growth.

On the other hand, the wild preachers of unrest and discontent, the wild agitators against the entire existing order, the men who act crookedly, whether because of sinister design or from mere puzzle headedness, the men who preach destruction without proposing any substitute for what they intend to destroy, or who propose a substitute which would be far worse than the existing evils—all these men are the most dangerous opponents of real reform. If they get their way they will lead the people into a deeper pit than any into which they could fall under the present system. If they fail to get their way they will still do incalculable harm by provoking the kind of reaction which in its revolt against the senseless evil of their teaching would enthrone more securely than ever the evils which their misguided followers believe they are attacking.

More important than aught else is the development of the broadest sympathy of man for man. The welfare of the wage worker, the welfare of the tiller of the soil, upon these depend the welfare of the entire country; their good is not to be sought in pulling down others; but their good must be the prime object of all our statesmanship.

Materially we must strive to secure a broader economic opportunity for all men, so that each shall have a better chance to show the stuff of which he is made. Spiritually and ethically we must strive to bring about clean living and right thinking. We appreciate that the things of the body are important; but we appreciate also that the things of the soul are immeasurably more important.

The foundation stone of national life is, and ever must be, the high individual character of the average citizen.

Freedom or Death

Emmeline Pankhurst

Hartford, Connecticut (13 November 1913)

Emmeline Pankhurst was a British suffragist who founded the Women's Social and Political Union (WSPU) in 1903. From 1912 onwards, the WSPU adopted extreme militancy in order to win women's suffrage, and a long struggle ensued which finally culminated in the Representation of the People Act of 1928, giving voting equality to men and women.

In her famous speech 'Freedom or Death', delivered at Hartford, Connecticut, Pankhurst justifies the need for violence in the WSPU's struggle for equality in voting rights, comparing the struggle to a civil war.

Mrs Hepburn, Ladies and Gentlemen

Many people come to Hartford to address meetings as advocates of some reform. Tonight it is not to advocate a reform that I address a meeting in Hartford. I do not come here as an advocate, because whatever position the suffrage movement may occupy in the United States of America, in England it has passed beyond the realm of advocacy and it has entered into the sphere of practical politics. It has become the subject of revolution and civil war, and so tonight I am not here to advocate woman suffrage. American suffragists can do that very well for themselves.

I am here as a soldier who has temporarily left the field of battle in order to explain—it seems strange it should have to be explained—what civil war is like when civil war is waged by women. I am not only here as a soldier temporarily absent from the field at battle; I am here—and that, I think, is the strangest part of my coming—I am here as a person who, according to the law courts of my country, it has been decided, is of no value to the community at all: and I am adjudged because of my life to be a dangerous person, under sentence of penal servitude in a convict prison. So you see there is some special interest in hearing so unusual a person address you. I dare say, in the minds of many of you—you will perhaps forgive me this personal touch—that I do not look either very like a soldier or very like a convict, and yet I am both.

Now, first of all I want to make you understand the inevitableness of revolution and civil war, even on the part of women, when you reach a certain stage in the development of a community's life. It is not at all difficult if revolutionaries come to you from Russia, if they come to you from China, or from any other part of the world, if they are men, to make you understand revolution in five minutes, every man and every woman to understand revolutionary methods when they are adopted by men.

Many of you have expressed sympathy, probably even practical sympathy, with revolutionaries in Russia. I dare say you have followed with considerable interest the story of how the Chinese revolutionary, Sun Yat-sen, conducted the Chinese revolution from England. And yet I find in American newspapers there is a great deal of misunderstanding of the fact that one of the chief minds engaged in conducting the women's revolution is, for purposes of convenience, located in Paris. It is quite easy for you to understand—it would not be necessary for me to enter into explanations at all— the desirability of revolution if I were a man, in any of these countries, even in a part of the British Empire known to you as Ireland. If an Irish revolutionary had addressed this meeting, and many have addressed meetings all over the United States during the last twenty or thirty years, it would not be necessary for that revolutionary to explain the need of revolution beyond saying that the people of his country were denied—and by people, meaning men—were denied the right of self-government. That would explain the whole situation. If I were a man and I said to you, 'I come from a country which professes to have representative institutions and yet denies me, a taxpayer, an inhabitant of the country, representative rights,' you would at once understand that that human being, being a man, was justified in the adoption of revolutionary methods to get representative institutions. But since I am a woman it is necessary in the twentieth century to explain why women have adopted revolutionary methods in order to win the rights of citizenship.

You see, in spite of a good deal that we hear about revolutionary methods not being necessary for American women, because American women are so well off, most of the men of the United States quite calmly acquiesce in the fact that half of the community are deprived absolutely of citizen rights, and we women, in trying to make our case clear, always have to make as part of our argument, and urge upon men in our audience the fact—a very simple fact—that women are human beings. It is quite evident you do not all realize we are human beings or it would not be necessary to argue with you that women may, suffering from intolerable injustice, be driven to adopt revolutionary methods. We have, first of all to convince you we are human beings, and I hope to be able to do that in the course of the evening before I sit down, but before doing that, I want to put a few political arguments before you—not arguments for the suffrage, because I said when I opened, I didn't mean to do that—but arguments for the adoption of militant methods in order to win political rights.

A great many of you have been led to believe, from the somewhat meager accounts you get in the newspapers, that in England there is a strange manifestation taking place, a new form of hysteria being swept across part of the feminist population of those Isles, and this manifestation takes the shape of irresponsible breaking of windows, burning of letters, general inconvenience to respectable, honest business people who want to attend to their business. It is very irrational you say: even if these women had sufficient intelligence to understand what they were doing, and really did want the vote, they have adopted very irrational means for getting the vote. 'How are they going to persuade people that they ought to have the vote by breaking their windows?' you say. Now, if you say that, it shows you do not understand the meaning of our revolution at all, and I want to show you that when damage is done to property it is not done in order to convert people to woman suffrage at all. It is a practical political means, the only means we consider open to voteless persons to bring about a political situation, which can only be solved by giving women the vote.

Suppose the men of Hartford had a grievance, and they laid that grievance before their legislature, and the legislature obstinately refused to listen to them, or to remove their grievance, what would be the proper and the constitutional and the practical way of getting their grievance removed? Well, it is perfectly obvious at the next general election, when the legislature is elected, the men of Hartford in sufficient numbers would turn out that legislature and elect a new one: entirely change the personnel of an obstinate legislature which would not remove their grievance. It is perfectly simple and perfectly easy for voting communities to get their grievances removed if they act in combination and make an example of the legislature by changing the composition of the legislature and sending better people to take the place of those who have failed to do justice.

But let the men of Hartford imagine that they were not in the position of being voters at all, that they were governed without their consent being obtained, that the legislature turned an absolutely deaf ear to their demands, what would the men of Hartford do then? They couldn't vote the legislature out. They would have to choose; they would have to make a choice of two evils: they would either have to submit indefinitely to an unjust state of affairs, or they would have to rise up and adopt some of the antiquated means by which men in the past got their grievances remedied. We know what happened when your forefathers decided that they must have representation for taxation, many, many years ago. When they felt they couldn't wait any longer, when they laid all the arguments before an obstinate British government that they could think of, and when their arguments were absolutely disregarded, when every other means had failed, they began by the tea party at Boston, and they went on until they had won the independence of the United States of America. That is what happened in the old days.

It is perfectly evident to any logical mind that when you have got the vote, by the proper use of the vote in sufficient numbers, by combination, you can get out of any legislature whatever you want, or, if you cannot get it, you can send them about their business and choose other people who will be more attentive to your demands, But, it is clear to the meanest intelligence that if you have not got the vote, you must either submit to laws just or unjust, administration just or unjust, or the time inevitably comes when you will revolt against that injustice and use violent means to put an end to it, That is so logically correct that we hear politicians today talk about the inherent right of revolution and rebellion on the part of human beings suffering from an intolerable injustice, and in England today we are having a situation brought about by men which exactly illustrates the case. We have got in Ireland today a very serious situation. I refer to the fact that for generations Irish agitators, Irish lawbreakers, Irish criminals, who have been sentenced to long terms of imprisonment in English convict prisons, have come over to America and have asked the people of the United States to give them money, to send them help in various forms to fight the Irish rebellion.

The Irish rebellion has at last, during the past few years, come into practical politics, and it has found shape in a measure which has now passed through the House of Commons and through the House of Lords, giving what the Irishmen so long wanted, home rule to Ireland. That is to say, next June, a parliament is going to be set up in Dublin, an Irish parliament, for the management of Irish affairs quite distinct from the government in London. The majority of men in Ireland desired it; presumably the majority of women acquiesced in their desire, but they were not asked whether they wished it or not. It is certain that in the course of the Irish rebellion women have taken a very prominent part; and it is rather a notable point to which I should like to call your attention, that when the imprisonments of Irishmen took place in the course of their political rebellion they were put almost invariably, after a certain amount of struggle, in the first division, and were treated as political offenders; but when women, helping the men, got into the coils of the law, all those women in Ireland who were helping the men to get home rule, were invariably treated as ordinary criminals and got ordinary criminals' treatment. You see, ladies, even in a rebellion, there is an advantage in being a voter, and if you are not a voter you are liable to get very much worse treatment than the voters, even the law-breaking voters, get. Now, the situation today then is, that home rule for Ireland is to take effect early next year, or in the course of next year.

But there is a part of Ireland which does not want home rule. There is a part of Ireland which prefers to be governed from London. That is the north of Ireland, in the County of Ulster. For racial reasons, for religious reasons, for economic reasons, the majority of the people there do not want home rule at all. They call themselves Loyalists, Unionists, and they want to maintain the union with Great Britain in its present form. Directly the home rule bill passed, directly it was perfectly clear that Home Rule was to be granted, these people began to revolt. They had a leader, a man who formed a part of the last Conservative administration, Sir Edward Carson. A distinguished lawyer, a distinguished statesman: he is an Irishman. Sir Edward Carson came to be the leader of the Ulster rebellion. He has advocated civil war: he has not only advocated civil war, he has urged the men of Ulster to drill and prepare to fight if civil war comes to pass. The first stage in this rebellion was the signing of a great declaration on behalf of the Union. It is rather notable that not only men signed that declaration, but women signed it also; the women of Ulster were invited to sign the declaration along with the men. And to those people who say that the province of woman is quite apart from politics, and that women by nature take no interest in politics, I would like to say that more women signed that declaration than did men, considerably more.

Well, the last stage of this struggle, and the struggle is coming to a head, is this; that Sir Edward Carson has been making speeches in which he has gloried in having broken the law; he has challenged the British government to arrest him; arms have been shipped to Ireland; and there is not a club, a young men's club, a workingman's club, or the middle class or the upper class men's club, where they are not drilling and preparing for civil war. The law has already been broken, because there has been considerable riot in the streets of Belfast, and lives even have been lost, and I want to say to you in this meeting how much have you heard of all this in the American newspapers? Have you heard loud condemnation from English newspapers echoed in your own papers? No; the newspapers and you have accepted quite calmly the fact that revolution is preparing in Ireland, and not one of you, whether you are a newspaper editor writing leading articles in your sanctum, or whether you are a business man or a professional man, not one of you has questioned the right of those men in Ulster, although they are voters and have a constitutional means for getting redress for their grievances, the right of those men to resort to revolution if everything else fails.

Well, there is another picture, another contrast I want to draw. We have Sir Edward Carson preaching revolution and justifying bloodshed in defense of what he calls the rights of the manhood of Ulster, the right of having themselves governed in the way they prefer. He has not hesitated to advocate the shedding of blood because he says it is quite worthwhile to shed blood, of your own and other people's, in defense of your citizen rights, in the defense of your having the right to choose the form of government you wish. Sir Edward Carson has not been arrested; Sir Edward Carson has not been charged with conspiracy; Sir Edward Carson has not been sent to jail. He has been making precisely the same kind of speeches that I made up to the month of March last, with this difference: that while he has justified the shedding of human blood in a revolution, I have always said that nothing would bring me to the point of claiming that we should destroy human life in the course of our woman's agitation. That is the only distinction between his speeches and mine, that he has advocated and justified the taking of life where I have always stopped short in my justification, at property, at inanimate objects. I have always said human life is sacred, and in a woman's revolution we respect human life, and we stop short of injury to human life.

Now, to those people who say that women are better treated than men when they break the laws, to those people who say that there is no need for women to take to methods of revolution, I want to draw this contrast; here is Sir Edward Carson, a man who presumably by his education and training, ought to be more respectful of the law than persons who are not either fit to understand the laws or to vote for those who make them. You have Sir Edward Carson, a chartered libertine, going to and fro in England and in Ireland, making these speeches;

whereas you have me, a woman arrested and charged and sentenced to a long term of penal servitude for doing precisely what he has done, although he has not had the justification that I have, because, again I want to call your attention to the point, that Sir Edward Carson and his friends have the vote, and therefore have the legitimate and proper way of getting redress for their grievances, whereas neither I nor any of the women have any constitutional means whatever and no legitimate, recognized methods of getting redress or our grievances except the methods of revolution and violence.

Well now, I want to argue with you as to whether our way is the right one: I want to explain all these things that you have not understood: I want to make you understand exactly what our plan of campaign has been because I have always felt that if you could only make people understand most people's hearts are in the right place and most people's understandings are sound and most people are more or less logical— if you could only make them understand.

Now, I want to come back to the point where I said, if the men of Hartford had a grievance and had no vote to get their redress, if they felt that grievance sufficiently, they would be forced to adopt other methods. That brings me to an explanation of these methods that you have not been able to understand. I am going to talk later on about the grievances, but I want to first of all make you understand that this civil war carried on by women is not the hysterical manifestation which you thought it was, but was carefully and logically thought out, and I think when I have finished you will say, admitted the grievance, admitted the strength of the cause, that we could not do anything else, that there was no other way, that we had either to submit to intolerable injustice and let the woman's movement go back and remain in a worse position than it was before we began, or we had to go on with these methods until victory was secured; and I want also to convince you that these methods are going to win, because when you adopt the methods of revolution there are two justifications which I feel are necessary or to be desired. The first is, that you have good cause for adopting your methods in the beginning, and secondly that you have adopted methods which when pursued with sufficient courage and determination are bound, in the long run, to win.

Now, it would take too long to trace the course of militant methods as adopted by women, because it is about eight years since the word militant was first used to describe what we were doing; it is about eight years since the first militant action was taken by women. It was not militant at all, except that it provoked militancy on the part of those who were opposed to it. When women asked questions in political meetings and failed to get answers, they were not doing anything militant. To ask questions at political meetings is an acknowledged right of all people who attend public meetings; certainly in my country, men have always done it, and I hope they do it in America, because it seems to me that if you allow people to enter your legislatures without asking them any questions as to what they are going to do when they get there you are not exercising your citizen rights and your citizen duties as you ought. At any rate in Great Britain it is a custom, a time-honored one, to ask questions of candidates for parliament and ask questions of members of the government. No man was ever put out of a public meeting for asking a question until Votes for Women came onto the political horizon. The first people who were put out of a political meeting for asking questions, were women; they were brutally ill-used; they found themselves in jail before 24 hours had expired.

But instead of the newspapers, which are largely inspired by the politicians, putting militancy and the reproach of militancy, if reproach there is, on the people who had assaulted the women, they actually said it was the women who were militant and very much to blame. How different the reasoning is that men adopt when they are discussing the cases of men and those of women. Had they been men who asked the questions, and had those men been brutally ill-used, you would have heard a chorus of reprobation on the part of the people toward those who refused to answer those questions. But as they were women who asked the questions, it was not the speakers on the platform who would not answer them, who were to blame, or the ushers at the meeting; it was the poor women who had had their bruises and their knocks and scratches, and who were put into prison for doing precisely nothing but holding a protest meeting in the street after it was all over. However, we were called militant for doing that, and we were quite willing to accept the name, because militancy for us is time-honored; you have the church militant, and in the sense of spiritual militancy we were very militant indeed. We were determined to press this question of the enfranchisement of women to the point where we were no longer to be ignored by the politicians as had been the case for about 50 years, during which time women had patiently used every means open to them to win their political enfranchisement.

We found that all the fine phrases about freedom and liberty were entirely for male consumption, and that they did not in any way apply to women. When it was said taxation without representation is tyranny, when it was 'Taxation of men without representation is tyranny,' everybody quite calmly accepted the fact that women had to pay taxes and even were sent to prison if they failed to pay them—quite right. We found that 'Government of the people, by the people and for the people,' which is also a time-honored Liberal principle, was again only for male consumption; half of the people were entirely ignored; it was the duty of women to pay their taxes and obey the laws and look as pleasant as they could under the circumstances. In fact, every principle of liberty enunciated in any civilized country on earth, with very few exceptions, was intended entirely for men, and when women tried to force the putting into practice of these principles, for women, then they discovered they had come into a very, very unpleasant situation indeed.

Now, I am going to pass rapidly over all the incidents that happened after the two first women went to prison for asking questions of cabinet ministers, and come right up to the time when our militancy became real militancy, when we organised ourselves on an army basis, when we determined, if necessary, to fight for our rights just as our forefathers had fought for their rights. Then people began to say that while they believed they had no criticism of militancy, as militancy, while they thought it was quite justifiable for people to revolt against intolerable injustice, it was absurd and ridiculous for women to attempt it because women could not succeed. After all the most practical criticism of our militancy coming from men has been the argument that it could not succeed. They would say, 'We would be with you if you could succeed but it is absurd for women who are the weaker sex, for women who have not got the control of any large interests, for women who have got very little money, who have peculiar duties as women, which handicaps them extremely—for example, the duty of caring for children—it is absurd for women to think they can ever win their rights by fighting; you had far better give it up and submit because there it is, you have always been subject and you always will be.' Well now, that really became the testing time. Then we women determined to show the world, that women, handicapped as women are, can still fight and can still win, and now I want to show you how this plan of ours was carefully thought out, even our attacks on private property, which has been so much misunderstood. I have managed in London to make audiences of business men who came into the meetings very, very angry with us indeed, some of whom had their telephonic communication cut off for several hours and had not been able to even get telegrams from their stock-brokers in cities far distant, who naturally came to our meetings in a very angry frame of mind, understand the situation: and if it has been possible to make them understand, if some of them even get fairly enthusiastic about our methods, it ought to be possible, Mrs. Hepburn, for me to explain the situation to an audience in Hartford, who, after all, are far enough off to be able to see, unlike men in our own country who are not able to see wood for trees.

I would like to suggest that if later on, while I am explaining these matters to you, there comes into the mind of any man or woman in the audience some better plan for getting what we want out of an obstinate government, I would be thankful and grateful if that person, man or woman, would tell me of some better plan than ours for dealing with the situation.

Here we have a political system where no reforms can get onto the statute book of the old country unless it is initiated by the government of the country, by the cabinet, by the handful of people who really govern the country. It doesn't matter whether you have practically every member of parliament on your side, you cannot get what you want unless the cabinet initiate legislation, a situation by which the private member has become almost of no account at all, the ordinary private member of parliament. He may introduce bills, but he knows himself that he is only registering a pious opinion of a certain number of electors in his constituency; it may be his own; but that pious opinion will never find its way onto the statute book of his country until the government in power, the prime minister and his colleagues, introduces a government measure to carry that reform. Well then, the whole problem of people who want reform is, to bring enough political pressure to bear upon the government to lead them to initiate, to draft a bill, and introduce it in the first instance, into the House of Commons, force it through the House of Commons, press it through the House of Lords, and finally land it safely, having passed through the shoals and rapids of the parliamentary river, safely on the statute book as an Act of Parliament. Well, combinations of voters have tried for generations, even with the power of the vote, to get their reforms registered in legislation, and have failed. You have to get your cause made a first class measure; you have to make the situation in the country so urgent and so pressing that it has become politically dangerous for the government to neglect that question any longer, so politically expedient for them to do it that they realise they cannot present themselves to the country at the next general election unless it has been done.

Well, that was the problem we had to face, and we faced it, a mere handful of women. Well, whether you like our methods or not, we have succeeded in making woman suffrage one of the questions which even cabinet ministers now admit cannot indefinitely be neglected. It must be dealt with within a very short period of time. No other methods than ours would have brought about that result. You may have sentimental articles in magazines by the chancellor of the exchequer who seems to be able to spare time from his ordinary avocations to write magazine articles telling you that militancy is a drag on the movement for woman suffrage. But our answer to that is, methinks our gentlemen doth protest too much, because until militancy became to be known neither Mr. Lloyd George nor any statesman, no, nor any member of parliament, ever thought it was necessary to mention the subject of woman suffrage at all. Now they mention it constantly, to tell us what damage we have done to our cause. They are all urging us to consider the serious position into which we have brought the cause of woman suffrage. Well now, let me come to the situation as we find it. We felt we had to rouse the public to such a point that they would say to the government, you must give women the vote. We had to get the electors, we had to get the business interests, we had to get the professional interests, we had to get the men of leisure all unitedly saying to the government, relieve the strain of this situation and give women the vote; and that is a problem that I think the most astute politician in this meeting would find very difficult. We have done it; we are doing it every day; and I think when you take that fact into consideration you will realize why we have been attacking private property, why we have been attacking the property of men so absorbed in their business that they generally forget to vote in ordinary elections, why we have attacked the pleasures of men whose whole life is spent in a round of pleasure, and who think politics so dull and so beneath their distinguished ossification that they hardly know which party is in power. All these people have had to be moved in order to bring enough pressure to bear upon the government to compel them to deal with the question of woman suffrage. And now that in itself is an explanation. There is a homely English proverb which may help to clear the situation which is this: 'You cannot rouse the Britisher unless you touch his pocket.' That is literally true. Perhaps you now can understand why we women thought we must attack the thing that was of most value in modem life in order to make these people wake up and realise that women wanted the vote, and that things were going to be very uncomfortable until women got the vote, because it is not by making people comfortable you get things in practical life, it is by making them uncomfortable. That is a homely truth that all of us have to learn.

I don't know, Mrs. Hepburn, whether I have used the domestic illustration in Hartford, but it is a very good one: it is quite worth using again. You have two babies very hungry and wanting to be fed. One baby is a patient baby, and waits indefinitely until its mother is ready to feed it. The other baby is an impatient baby and cries lustily, screams and kicks and makes everybody unpleasant until it is fed. Well, we know perfectly well which baby is attended to first. That is the whole history of politics. Putting sentiment aside, people who really want reforms learn that lesson very quickly. It is only the people who are quite content to go on advocating them indefinitely who play the part of the patient baby in politics. You have to make more noise than anybody else, you have to make yourself more obtrusive than anybody else, you have to fill all the papers more than anybody else, in fact you have to be there all the time and see that they do not snow you under, if you are really going to get your reform realised.

That is what we women have been doing, and in the course of our desperate struggle we have had to make a great many people very uncomfortable. Now, one woman was arrested on an occasion when a great many windows were broken in London, as a protest against a piece of trickery on the part of the government, which will be incredible in 50 years, when the history of the movement is read. Women broke some windows as a protest: they broke a good many shopkeepers' windows: they broke the windows of shopkeepers where they spent most of their money when they bought their hats and their clothing. They also broke the windows of many of the clubs, the smart clubs in Piccadilly.

One of the clubs was the Guard Club. Well, the ordinary army man is not much in politics, but he very often, because of his aristocratic and social connections, has considerable influence if he would use it. One woman broke the windows of the Guard Club, and when she broke those windows she stood there quietly until the Guard hall porter came out and seized her and held her until the policemen came to take her to prison. A number of the guards came out to see the kind of woman it was who had broken their windows, and they saw there a quiet little woman. She happened to be an actress, a woman who had come into our militant movement because she knew of the difficulties and dangers and temptations of the actress's life, of how badly paid she is, what her private sorrows are and her difficulties, and so she had come into the militant movement to get votes for actresses as quickly as possible, so that through the vote they could secure better conditions. Some of the guards—I think men who had never known what it was to earn a living, who knew nothing of the difficulties of a man's life, let alone the difficulties of a woman's life—came out, and they said: 'Why did you break our windows? We have done nothing.' She said: 'It is because you have done nothing I have broken your windows.' And perhaps out of that woman's breaking of windows has come this new movement of men of my country, where we find distinguished men who fought through the Boer war are drilling now like Sir Edward Carson in Belfast, drilling men in order to form a bodyguard to protect the militant women. Probably that broken window of the Guard Club did a good deal to rouse men to the defense of women and to the injustice of their situation.

Well, then the shopkeepers who could not understand why we should break the shopkeepers' windows. Why should we alienate the sympathy of the shopkeepers? Well, there is the other side of the question, gentlemen—why should the shopkeepers alienate the sympathy of their customers by refusing to help them to get political power, some power to make the condition of the woman who helps to earn the shopkeepers money by serving in his shop, easier than it is at the present time? Those women broke shopkeepers' windows, and what was the situation? Just at the beginning of the winter season when all the new winter hats and coats were being shown, the shopkeepers had to barricade all their windows with wood and nobody could see the new winter fashions. Well, there again is an impossible situation. The shopkeeper cannot afford to quarrel with his customers, and we have today far more practical sympathy amongst the shopkeepers of London than we ever had when we were quiet, gentle, ladylike suffragists asking nicely for a vote.

Well then, there were the men of pleasure, or the businessmen who were so busy earning money during the week that all they could think of when the week came to an end was recreation, and the great recreation in England today is playing golf. Everywhere on Saturday you see men streaming away into the country for the weekend to play golf. They so monopolize the golf links that they have made a rule that although the ladies may play golf all the week, the golf links are entirely reserved for men on Saturday and Sunday: and you have this spectacle of the exodus of men from London into the country to fill up the week-end with playing golf. They are not, ladies, putting their heads together thinking how best they can govern the country for you, what good laws they can make for you and for the world: they are there, all of them, getting their health, and I do not blame them for it, at the weekend. Well, we attacked the golf links; we wanted to make them think, and if you had been in London and taken a Sunday paper you would have read, especially if you played golf, with consternation, that all the beautiful greens that had taken years to make, had been cut up or destroyed with an acid or made almost impossible to play upon on the Friday night, and in many cases there were going to be important matches on the Saturday afternoon and Sunday.

Just to give you an illustration of the effectiveness of these methods in waking the Britisher up, in conveying to him that women want the vote and are going to get it even if we do not adopt quite the men's methods in order to do so. I was staying at a little house in the country on a golf links, a house that had been loaned to me to use whenever I could get away from my work, and several times in the course of that Sunday morning I got telephone calls from gentlemen who were prominent members of golf clubs in that vicinity. It so happened that the golf links where I was spending the weekend, had not been touched. Those links had been respected because some of the prominent women suffragettes happened to be members of the club, and those women who destroyed the greens—I don't know who they were, but it was no doubt done by women—spared the links where these women, whom they admired and respected, played. Well, then that morning I was rung up over and over again by excited gentlemen who begged that those golf links should be spared, saying: 'I don't know whether your followers know that we are all suffragists, on our committee, we are entirely in favor of woman suffrage.' And I said: 'Well, don't you think you had better tell Mr. Asquith so, because if you are suffragists and do nothing, naturally you will only add to the indignation of the women. If you really want your golf links spared you had better intimate to Mr. Asquith that you think it is high time he put his principles into practice and gave the women the vote.' There was another gentleman who rang up and said: 'The members of our committee, who are all suffragists, are seriously considering turning all the women members out of the club if this sort of thing goes on.' 'Well,' I said, 'don't you think your greater safety is to keep the women in the club as a sort of insurance policy against anything happening to your links?'

But this experience will show you that if you really want to get anything done, it is not so much a matter of whether you alienate sympathy; sympathy is a very unsatisfactory thing if it is not practical sympathy. It does not matter to the practical suffragist whether she alienates sympathy that was never of any use to her. What she wants is to get something practical done, and whether it is done out of sympathy or whether it is done out of fear, or whether it is done because you want to be comfortable again and not be worried in this way, doesn't particularly matter so long as you get it. We had enough of sympathy for 50 years; it never brought us anything, and we would rather have an angry man going to the government and saying, my business is interfered with and I won't submit to its being interfered with any longer because you won't give women the vote, than to have a gentleman come onto our platforms year in and year out and talk about his ardent sympathy with woman suffrage.

Now then, let me come to the more serious matters and to some of the more recent happenings. You know when you have war, many things happen that all of us deplore. We fought a great war not very long ago, in South Africa. Women were expected to face with equanimity the loss of those dearest to them in warfare; they were expected to submit to being impoverished; they were expected to pay the war tax exactly like the men for a war about which the women were never consulted at all. When you think of the object of that war it really makes some of us feel very indignant at the hypocrisy of some of our critics. That war was fought ostensibly to get equal rights for all whites in South Africa. The whole country went wild. We had a disease which was called Mafeka, because when the victory of Mafeking was declared everybody in the country, except a few people who tried to keep their heads steady, went absolutely mad with gratification at the sacrifice of thousands of human beings in the carrying on of that war. That war was fought to get votes for white men in South Africa, a few years sooner than they would have had them under existing conditions, and it was justified on those grounds, to get a voice in the government of South Africa for men who would have had that voice in five or six years if they had waited. That was considered ample justification for one of the most costly and bloody wars of modern times.

Very well, then when you have warfare things happen; people suffer; the noncombatants suffer as well as the combatants. And so it happens in civil war. When your forefathers threw the tea into Boston harbor, a good many women had to go without their tea. It has always seemed to me an extraordinary thing that you did not follow it up by throwing the whiskey overboard; you sacrificed the women; and there is a good deal of warfare for which men take a great deal of glorification which has involved more practical sacrifice on women than it has on any man. It always has been so. The grievances of those who have got power, the influence of those who have got power commands a great deal of attention; but the wrongs and the grievances of those people who have no power at all are apt to be absolutely ignored. That is the history of humanity right from the beginning.

Well, in our civil war people have suffered, but you cannot make omelets without breaking eggs; you cannot have civil war without damage to something. The great thing is to see that no more damage is done than is absolutely necessary, that you do just as much as will arouse enough feeling to bring about peace, to bring about an honorable peace for the combatants, and that is what we have been doing. Within the last few days you have read—I don't know how accurate the news cables are to America. I always take them with a grain of salt—but you have read within the last few days that some more empty houses have been burned, that a cactus house has been destroyed and some valuable plants have suffered in that house, that some pavilion at a pleasure ground has also been burned. Well, it is quite possible that it has happened.

I knew before I came here that for one whole day telegraphic and telephonic communication between Glasgow and London was entirely suspended. We do more in England in our civil war without the sacrifice of a single life than they did in the war of the Balkan States when they had the siege of Adrianople, because during the whole of that siege, in the course of which thousands of people were killed and houses were shelled and destroyed, telegraphic communication was continuous the whole time. If there had been a stock broker in Adrianople who wanted to communicate with a customer in London, he could have done it; there might have been a little delay, but he was able to do it, but we, without the loss of a single life in our war, in this effort to rouse business men to compel the government to give us the vote, because they are the people who can do it in the last resort, we entirely prevented stock brokers in London from telegraphing to stock brokers in Glasgow and vice versa: for one whole day telegraphic and telephonic communication was entirely stopped. I am not going to tell you how it was done. I am not going to tell you how the women got to the mains and cut the wires; but it was done. It was done, and it was proved to the authorities that weak women, suffrage women, as we are supposed to be, had enough ingenuity to create a situation of that kind. Now, I ask you, if women can do that, is there any limit to what we can do except the limit we put upon ourselves?

If you are dealing with an industrial revolution, if you get the men and women of one class to rising up against the men and women of another class, you can locate the difficulty; if there is a great industrial strike, you know exactly where the violence is, and every man knows exactly how the warfare is going to be waged; but in our war against the government you can't locate it. You can take Mrs. Hepburn and myself on this platform, and now, without being told, how could you tell that Mrs. Hepburn is a non-militant and that I am a militant? Absolutely impossible. If any gentleman who is the father of daughters in this meeting went into his home and looked around at his wife and daughters, if he lived in England and was an Englishman, he couldn't tell whether some of his daughters were militants or non-militants. When his daughters went out to post a letter, he couldn't tell if they went harmlessly out to make a tennis engagement at that pillar-box by posting a letter, or whether they went to put some corrosive matter in that would burn all the letters up inside of that box. We wear no mark; we belong to every class, we permeate every class of the community from the highest to the lowest; and so you see in the woman's civil war the dear men of my country are discovering it is absolutely impossible to deal with it: you cannot locate it, and you cannot stop it.

'Put them in prison,' they said, 'that will stop it.' But it didn't stop it. They put women in prison for long terms of imprisonment, for making a nuisance of themselves—that was the expression when they took petitions in their hands to the door of the House of Commons; and they thought that by sending them to prison, giving them a day's imprisonment, would cause them to all settle down again and there would be no further trouble. But it didn't happen so at all: instead of the women giving it up, more women did it, and more and more and more women did it until there were 300 women at a time, who had not broken a single law, only 'made a nuisance of themselves' as the politicians say. Well then they thought they must go a little farther, and so then they began imposing punishments of a very serious kind. The judge who sentenced me last May to three years penal servitude for certain speeches in which I had accepted responsibility for acts of violence done by other women, said that if I could say I was sorry, if I could promise not to do it again, that he would revise the sentence and shorten it, because he admitted that it was a very heavy sentence, especially as the jury recommended me to mercy because of the purity of my motives; and he said he was giving me a determinate sentence, a sentence that would convince me that I would give up my 'evil ways' and would also deter other women from imitating me. But it hadn't that effect at all. So far from it having that effect more and more women have been doing these things and I had incited them to do, and were more determined in doing them: so that the long determinate sentence had no effect in crushing the agitation.

Well then they felt they must do something else, and they began to legislate. I want to tell men in this meeting that the British government, which is not remarkable for having very mild laws to administer, has passed more stringent laws to deal with this agitation than it ever found it necessary during all the history of political agitation in my country. They were able to deal with the revolutionaries of the Chartists' time; they were able to deal with the trades union agitation; they were able to deal with the revolutionaries later on when the Reform Acts of 1867 and 1884 were passed: but the ordinary law has not sufficed to curb insurgent women. They have had to pass special legislation, and now they are on the point of admitting that that special legislation has absolutely failed. They had to dip back into the middle ages to find a means of repressing the women in revolt, and the whole history shows how futile it is for men who have been considered able statesmen to deal with dissatisfied women who are determined to win their citizenship and who will not submit to government until their consent is obtained. That is the whole point of our agitation. The whole argument with the anti-suffragists, or even the critical suffragist man, is this: that you can govern human beings without their consent.

They have said to us government rests upon force, the women haven't force so they must submit. Well, we are showing them that government does not rest upon force at all: it rests upon consent. As long as women consent to be unjustly governed, they can be, but directly women say: 'We withhold our consent, we will not be governed any longer so long as that government is unjust.' Not by the forces of civil war can you govern the very weakest woman. You can kill that woman, but she escapes you then; you cannot govern her. And that is, I think, a most valuable demonstration we have been making to the world. We have been proving in our own person that government does not rest upon force; it rests upon consent; as long as people consent to government, it is perfectly easy to govern, but directly they refuse then no power on earth can govern a human being, however feeble, who withholds his or her consent: and all of the strange happenings that you have read about over here, have been manifestations of a refusal to consent on the part of the women.

When they put us in prison at first, simply for taking petitions, we submitted; we allowed them to dress us in prison clothes; we allowed them to put us in solitary confinement; we allowed them to treat us as ordinary criminals, and put us amongst the most degraded of those criminals; and we were very glad of the experience, because out of that experience we learned of the need for prison reform; we learned of the fearful mistakes that men of all nations have made when it is a question of dealing with human beings; we learned of some of the appalling evils of our so-called civilization that we could not have learned in any other way except by going through the police courts of our country, in the prison vans that take you up to prison and right through that prison experience. It was valuable experience, and we were glad to get it. But there came a time when we said: 'It is unjust to send political agitators to prison in this way for merely asking for justice, and we will not submit any longer.'

And I am always glad to remind American audiences that two of the first women that came to the conclusion that they would not submit to unjust imprisonment any longer were two American girls who are doing some of the most splendid suffrage work in America today up in Washington. I think they are making things extremely lively for the politicians up there, and I don't know whether every American woman knows what those two women, working in conjunction with others, are doing for the enfranchisement of American women at this moment. I am always proud to think that Miss Lucy Burns and Miss Alice Paul served their suffrage apprenticeship in the militant ranks in England, and they were not slow about it either because one of them came, I believe it was, from Heidelberg, travelling all night, to take part in one of those little processions to Parliament with a petition. She was arrested and thrown into prison with about twenty others, and that group of twenty women were the first women who decided they would not submit themselves to the degradation of wearing prison clothes; and they refused, and they were almost the first to adopt the 'hunger strike' as a protest against the criminal treatment. They forced their way out of prison. Well, then it was that women began to withhold their consent.

I have been in audiences where I have seen men smile when they heard the words 'hunger strike', and yet I think there are very few men today who would be prepared to adopt a 'hunger strike' for any cause. It is only people who feel an intolerable sense of oppression who would adopt a means of that kind. I know of no people who did it before us except revolutionaries in Russia—who adopted the hunger strike against intolerable prison conditions. Well, our women decided to terminate those unjust sentences at the earliest possible moment by the terrible means of the hunger strike. It means, you refuse food until you are at death's door, and then the authorities have to choose between letting you die, and letting you go; and then they let the women go.

Now, that went on so long that the government felt they had lost their power, and that they were unable to cope with the situation. Then it was that, to the shame of the British government, they set the example to authorities all over the world of feeding sane, resisting human beings by force. There may be doctors in this meeting: if so, they know it is one thing to treat an insane person, to feed by force an insane person, or a patient who has some form of illness which makes it necessary; but it is quite another thing to feed a sane, resisting human being who resists with every nerve and with every fiber of her body the indignity and the outrage of forcible feeding. Now, that was done in England, and the government thought they had crushed us. But they found that it did not quell the agitation, that more and more women came in and even passed that terrible ordeal, and that they were not able with all their forcible feeding to make women serve out their unjust sentences. They were obliged to let them go.

Then came the legislation to which I have referred, the legislation which is known in England as the 'Cat and Mouse Act'. It got through the British House of Commons because the home secretary assured the House of Commons that he wanted the bill passed in the interests of humanity. He said he was a humane man and he did not like having to resort to forcible feeding; he wanted the House of Commons to give him some way of disposing of them, and this was his way: he said, 'Give me the power to let these women go when they are at death's door, and leave them at liberty under license until they have recovered their health again and then bring them back; leave it to me to fix the time of their licenses: leave it in my hands altogether to deal with this intolerable situation, because the laws must be obeyed and people who are sentenced for breaking the law must be compelled to serve their sentences.' Well, the House of Commons passed the law. They said: 'As soon as the women get a taste of this they will give it up.' In fact, it was passed to repress the agitation, to make the women yield— because that is what it has really come to, Ladies and Gentlemen. It has come to a battle between the women and the government as to who shall yield first, whether they will yield and give us the vote, or whether we will give up our agitation.

Well, they little know what women are. Women are very slow to rouse, but once they are aroused, once they are determined, nothing on earth and nothing in heaven will make women give way; it is impossible. And so this 'Cat and Mouse Act' which is being used against women today has failed: and the home secretary has taken advantage of the fact that parliament is not sitting, to revive and use alongside of it the forcible feeding. At the present time there are women lying at death's door, recovering enough strength to undergo operations, who have had both systems applied to them, and have not given in and won't give in, and who will be prepared, as soon as they get up from their sick beds, to go on as before. There are women who are being carried from their sick beds on stretchers into meetings. They are too weak to speak, but they go amongst their fellow workers just to show that their spirits are unquenched, and that their spirit is alive, and they mean to go on as long as life lasts.

Now, I want to say to you who think women cannot succeed, we have brought the government of England to this position, that it has to face this alternative: either women are to be killed or women are to have the vote. I ask American men in this meeting, what would you say if in your state you were faced with that alternative, that you must either kill them or give them their citizenship—women, many of whom you respect, women whom you know have lived useful lives, women whom you know, even If you do not know them personally, are animated with the highest motives, women who are in pursuit of liberty and the power to do useful public service? Well, there is only one answer to that alternative; there is only one way out of it, unless you are prepared to put back civilization two or three generations: you must give those women the vote. Now that is the outcome of our civil war.

You won your freedom in America when you had the revolution, by bloodshed, by sacrificing human life. You won the civil war by the sacrifice of human life when you decided to emancipate the negro. You have left it to women in your land, the men of all civilized countries have left it to women, to work out their own salvation. That is the way in which we women of England are doing. Human life for us is sacred, but we say if any life is to be sacrificed it shall be ours; we won't do it ourselves, but we will put the enemy in the position where they will have to choose between giving us freedom or giving us death.

Now whether you approve of us or whether you do not, you must see that we have brought the question of women's suffrage into a position where it is of first rate importance, where it can be ignored no longer. Even the most hardened politician will hesitate to take upon himself directly the responsibility of sacrificing the lives of women of undoubted honour, of undoubted earnestness of purpose. That is the political situation as I lay it before you today.

Now then, let me say something about what has brought it about because you must realize that only the very strongest of motives would lead women to do what we have done. Life is sweet to all of us. Every human being loves life and loves to enjoy the good things and the happiness that life gives: and yet we have a state of things in England that has made not two or three women but thousands of women quite prepared to face these terrible situations that I have been trying without any kind of passion or exaggeration to lay before you.

Well, I might spend two or three nights dealing with the industrial situation as it affects women, with the legal position of women, with the social position of women. I want very briefly to say a few words about all. First of all there is the condition of the working woman. One of the things which gives strength to our agitation is that the women who are taking an active part in it are not the poorest women, are not the overworked women; they are the women who are held to be fortunate, the women who have no special personal grievance of their own. Those women have taken up this fight for their own sake, it is true, because they wish to be free, but chiefly for the sake of the women less fortunate than themselves. The industrial workers of Great Britain have an average wage, mind you, not a minimum wage, an average wage, of less than two dollars a week. Think what would happen in any country if the men in industry of that country had to subsist on a wage like that. Thousands upon thousands of these women—because there are over five million wage earners in my country—thousands of these women have dependents; they are women with children dependent upon them, deserted wives with children dependent on them, or wives with sick husbands; they are unmarried mothers, or they are unmarried women who have old parents or younger brothers and sisters, or sick relatives dependent upon them. Their average income, taking the highly skilled woman teacher and averaging her wage with the unskilled home worker, the average income is less than two dollars a week. There you have in itself an explanation of an uprising of a very determined kind to secure better conditions; and when you know that the government is the largest employer of all the employers and sets a horribly bad example to the private employer in the wages that it pays to women, there you have another explanation. Constant economies are being affected in government departments by the substitution of women's labor for men's, and there is always a reduction in wages whenever women are employed. That is the industrial situation. To speak of the sweated home-worker would take too long, but there are women, women even with dependents, only able to earn three or four shillings a week, thousands of them, and having to pay with the increased cost of living, exorbitant rents in our great cities for single rooms, so that you get several families in one room: they cannot afford even to have a room for themselves. So much for the industrial situation.

Then there is the legal situation. The marriage laws of our country are bringing hundreds and hundreds of women into the militant ranks because we cannot get reform, the kind of reform that women want, of our marriage laws. First of all, a girl is held marriageable by English law, at the age of 12 years. When I was on trial they produced a little girl as a witness, a little girl who had found something in the neighborhood of the house of the chancellor of the exchequer, which was destroyed by some women, and this little girl was produced as a witness. It was said that it was a terrible thing to bring a little girl of twelve years of age and put her in the witness box in a court of law. I agreed, but I pointed out to the judge and the jury that one of the reasons why women were in revolt was because that little girl, whose head just appeared over the top of the witness box, was considered old enough by the laws of her country to take upon herself the terrible responsibilities of wifehood and motherhood, and women could not get it altered, no politicians would listen to us, when we asked to have the marriage law altered in that particular.

Then, the position of the wife. It is very frequently said that every woman who wants a vote, wants a vote because she has been disappointed, because she has not been chosen to be a wife. Well, I can assure you that if most women made a study of the laws before they decided to get married, a great many women would seriously consider whether it was worthwhile, whether the price was not too heavy, because, according to English law, a woman may toil all her life for her husband and her family, she may work in her husband's business, she may help him to build up the family income, and if he chooses at the end of a long life to take every penny of the money that woman has helped to earn away from her and her children, he can do it, and she has no redress. She may at the end of a long, hard life find herself and her children absolutely penniless because her husband has chosen to will the money away from her. So that you see when you look at it from the legal point of view, it is not such a very, very great gain to become a wife in my country. There are a great many risks that go along with it.

Then take her as a mother. If the child of two parents has any property inherited from relatives, and that child dies before it is of age to make a will, or without making a will, the only person who inherits the property of that child is the child's father; the mother does not exist as her child's heir at all; and during the father's lifetime she not only cannot inherit from her child but she has no voice whatever in deciding the life of her child. Her husband can give the child away to be educated somewhere else or he can bring whomever he pleases into the house to educate the child. He decides absolutely the conditions in which that child is to live; he decides how it is to be educated; he can even decide what religion it is to profess, and the mother's consent is not obtained to any of these decisions. Women are trying to alter it, have tried for generations, but they cannot because the legislatures have no time to listen to the opinions and the desires of people who have no votes.

Well then, when it comes to the question of how people are to get out of marriage, if they are unhappy, under the laws of divorce, the English law of divorce is the most scandalous divorce law in the civilized world. There may be a few states in America, and I believe in Canada, where the same law obtains, but the English divorce law is in itself such a stigma upon women, such a degradation to women, such an invitation to immorality on the part of the married man, that I think that divorce law in itself would justify a rebellion on the part of the women. You get registered in law unequal standards of morals in marriage, and a married man is encouraged by law to think that he can make as many lapses as he thinks fit in marital fidelity; whereas, if one act of infidelity is proved against her the husband can get rid of her by divorce, can take her children away from her and make her an outcast. Women who have been clamoring for an equal divorce law for generations cannot get any attention. Well now, we have had a royal commission on divorce and we have had a report, but there is no security for women that they are to have justice under a new law so long as men are chosen by men to legislate and those men are likely to register the moral opinions of men, not the moral opinions of women, in legislation.

We have to look facts in the face. Part of the militant movement for woman suffrage has had that effect, that women have learned to look facts in the face; they have got rid of sentimentalities; they are looking at actual facts: and when anti-suffragists talk about chivalry, and when they talk about putting women on pedestals and guarding them from all the difficulties and dangers of life, we look to the facts in life as we see them and we say: 'Women have every reason to distrust that kind of thing, every reason to be dissatisfied; we want to know the truth however bad it is, and we face that truth because it is only through knowing the truth that you ever will get to anything better.' We are determined to have these things faced and cleared up, and it is absolutely ridiculous to say to women that they can safely trust their interests in the hands of men who have already registered in the legislation of their country a standard of morals so unequal for both sexes as we find on the statute books of England today.

When the divorce commission sat, evidence was given by all kinds of people, and women had the experience of reading in the newspapers the evidence of the man who had been chosen by other men to preside over the divorce court, the judge whose duty it was to decide what was legal cruelty and decide whether women were to continue to be bound to their husbands or not. What did he say? I am glad to think that he is not in a position to give effect to his ideas anymore; he now adorns the House of Lords: but he was still judge of the divorce court when he said, that in his opinion the wise wife was the woman who closed her eyes to the moral failings of her husband; and that was the man, women in this meeting, who had for years decided what was legal cruelty and what women were to endure or what they were not to endure in that relationship of husband and wife.

Well, can you wonder that all these things make us more militant? It seems to me that once you look at things from the woman's point of view, once you cease to listen to politicians, once you cease to allow yourself to look at the facts of life through men's spectacles but look at them through your own, every day that passes you are having fresh illustrations of the need there is for women to refuse to wait any longer for their enfranchisement.

Then, the latest manifestation, the latest cause of militancy has been the breaking of the great conspiracy of silence with regard to moral questions and the question of social disease that we have had during the last few years. I want to offer my testimony of gratitude to women like the lady who presides over us today and to the many of the medical men of the United States in making a lead in that direction. Before some of the suffragists had the courage even to study the question, these people spoke out; the medical profession in America has led the way, and through Dr Prince Morrow, and other men whose names we honor, we are at last beginning to know the real facts of the situation. We know this, that whatever women's wishes might be, it is their duty for the sake of the race, itself, to save the race, to insist upon having this question of the moral health of the nation approached from the women's point of view and settled by women in cooperation with men. It is our business to show the close relationship there is between the appalling state of social health and the political degradation of women. The two things go hand in hand. I have been reading a great many articles by very profound thinkers lately, and I see that somehow or other when you get men writing about them, even the best of men, they do evade the real issue, and that is, the status of women.

We women see so clearly the fact that the only way to deal with this thing is to raise the status of women; first the political status, then the industrial and the social status of women. You must make women count as much as men; you must have an equal standard of morals; and the only way to enforce that is through giving women political power so that you can get that equal moral standard registered in the laws of the country. It is the only way. I don't know whether men sufficiently realise it, but we women do realise it: we more and more realise it, and so women have nerved themselves to speak out on this question. First of all, we feel that what is most important is that women should know it. 10 years ago it would have been impossible for any woman or any man to speak openly upon that question on any platform, because women had been taught that they must keep their eyes closed to all these things; women had been taught that they must ignore the fact even that a large section of their sex were living lives of degradation and outlawry. If they knew of it at all, they were told in vague terms that it was in order to make the lives of the rest of the women safe; they were told it was a necessary evil; they were told it was something that the good woman does not understand and must not know anything about. All that is now at an end. Women are refusing, men in this meeting, even if that were true, to have their lives made safe at the expense of their sisters. The women are determined. A good deal of the opposition to woman suffrage is coming from the very worst element in the population, who realize that once you get woman suffrage, a great many places that are tolerated today will have to disappear. It is perhaps a hard saying for many men that there will have to be self-control and an equal standard of morals, but the best men now, the scientists of every country, are supporting the woman's point of view.

It was 30 years ago in England that a splendid woman named Josephine Butler fought to establish an equal moral code for both sexes. She fought all her life; she was stoned; she was hooted; her meetings were broken up; her life was made absolutely dangerous; and yet that woman persisted and she secured the repeal of certain laws relating to prostitution which disgraced the statute books of our country. In those days the doctors were against her; practically everybody was against her. Men were told that it was necessary for their health that we should have an unequal moral code. Now that is all done away with and the foremost medical men and the foremost scientists are agreeing with the women; they are agreeing with the women that it is quite possible, and it is necessary for the sake of the race itself, that this equal moral code shall be established. Well, it is probably difficult; it is perhaps going to be difficult for generations; but it is to come, and it is out of the woman's movement that it is coming, because women today who have had the benefits of education, who have had the benefit of medical training and who have had the benefit of legal training, are informing their sex upon this question, and there is a good deal of opposition coming to it from strange directions; even people who have self-appointed themselves as the custodians of public morals are opposing the facts being told.

One of the strangest things that I have experienced for years is the fact that in New York, quite recently, copies of our paper, The Suffragette, in which were articles written by my daughter, quoting the opinions of medical men all over the world on this question, and relying on those quotations as a statement of fact, were offered for sale, and an attempt, a successful attempt temporarily, was made to prevent that paper being sold because it contained these articles telling the truth: and a book containing the articles in collected form prefaced with an article telling why this book was written, has also had an attack made upon it by that self-constituted guardian of public morals, Mr. Comstock, supported by certain sections of the American press. Well, that book is here tonight: that book is here on sale. That book was written, not for people of my age, not for people who if there are dangers to be faced have either escaped or suffered from them: that book was written for young people. That book was written so that women should know. What is the use of locking the stable after the horse is stolen? Prevention is better than cure. This book was written to convince everybody of the danger, to point out the plain facts of the situation, and to convince thoughtful people that only through the emancipation of women, only through the uplifting of women, can you ever effectively deal with the situation.

We have tried, we women, for generations to undo some of this evil; we have had our rescue societies; we have made all kinds of efforts; we have taken the poor unfortunate children who have been the outcome of this unequal code of morals between men and women, and what has happened? Matters have become sadly worse; we have scratched on the surface instead of cutting out the root of the evil. All that is changed. Today women are working in my country, are sacrificing and suffering to win the political enfranchisement of their sex, so that we may get better laws and better administration of the laws.

I could go on tonight pointing out to you how in my country small crimes against property, small thefts, small injuries to property are punished more severely than are any crimes committed against the physical and the moral integrity of members of my sex. I think I have said enough at least to make you understand that this uprising on the part of the British women has as much justification and as much provocation as any uprising on the part of men in their desire for political liberty in the past. We are not working to get the vote. We are not going to prison to get the vote, merely to say we have the vote. We are going through all this to get the vote so that by means of the vote we can bring about better conditions not only for ourselves but for the community as a whole.

Men have done splendid things in this world; they have made great achievements in engineering; they have done splendid organisation work; but they have failed, they have miserably failed, when it has come to dealing with the lives of human beings. They stand self-confessed failures, because the problems that perplex civilization are absolutely appalling today. Well, that is the function of women in life: it is our business to care for human beings, and we are determined that we must come without delay to the saving of the race. The race must be saved, and it can only be saved through the emancipation of women.

Well, Ladies and Gentlemen, I want to say that I am very thankful to you for listening to me here tonight; I am glad if I have been able even to a small extent to explain to you something of the English situation. I want to say that I am not here to apologize. I do not care very much even whether you really understand, because when you are in a fighting movement, a movement which every fiber of your being has forced you to enter, it is not the approval of other human beings that you want; you are so concentrated on your object that you mean to achieve that object even if the whole world was up in arms against you. So I am not here tonight to apologize or to win very much your approbation. People have said: 'Why does Mrs. Pankhurst come to America? Has she come to America to rouse American women to be militant?' No, I have not come to America to arouse American women to be militant. I believe that American women, as their earnestness increases, as they realise the need for the enfranchisement of their sex, will find out for themselves the best way to secure that object. Each nation must work out its own salvation, and so the American women will find their own way and use their own methods capably.

Other people have said: 'What right has Mrs. Pankhurst to come to America and ask for American dollars?' Well, I think I have the right that all oppressed people have to ask for practical sympathy of others freer than themselves. Your right to send to France and ask for help was never questioned. You did it, and you got that help. Men of all nationalities have come to America, and they have not gone away empty-handed, because American sympathy has been extended to struggling peoples all over the world.

In England, if you could understand it, there is the most pathetic and the most courageous fight going on, because you find the people whom you have been accustomed to look upon as weak and reliant, the people you have always thought leaned upon other people for protection, have stood up and are fighting for themselves. Women have found a new kind of self-respect, a new kind of energy, a new kind of strength: and I think that of all oppressed peoples who might claim your sympathy and support, women who are fighting this fight unknown in the history of humanity before, fighting this fight in the twentieth century for greater powers of self-development, self expression and self-government, might very well attract the sympathy and the practical help of American people.

There hasn't been a victory the women of America have won that we have not rejoiced in. I think as we have read month by month of the new States that have been added to the list of fully enfranchised states, perhaps we who know how hard the fight is, have rejoiced even more than American women themselves.

I have heard cheers ring out in a meeting in London when the news of some new state being added to the list was given, cheers louder and more enthusiastic than I have ever heard for any victory in an American meeting. It is very true that those who are fighting a hard battle, those who are sacrificing greatly in order to win a victory, appreciate victories and are more enthusiastic when victories are won. We have rejoiced wholeheartedly in your victories. We feel that those victories have been easier perhaps because of the hard times that we were having, because out of our militant movement in the storm centre of the suffrage movement have gone waves that have helped to rouse women all over the world. You could only explain the strange phenomena in that way. 10 years ago there was hardly any woman suffrage movement at all. Now even in China and Japan, in India, in Turkey, everywhere women are rising up and asking for these larger opportunities, which modern conditions demand that women should have: and we women think that we have helped. Well, if we have helped at all, if, as has been said from the chair tonight, we have even helped to rouse suffrage enthusiasm in Connecticut, can you blame me very much if I come and tell you of the desperate struggle we are having, of how the government is trying to break us down in every possible way, even by involving us in lawsuits, and trying to frighten our subscribers by threatening to prosecute even people who help us by subscribing money? Can you wonder I come over to America? Have you read about American dollars that have been given the Irish law-breakers?

So here am I. I come in the intervals of prison appearance: I come after having been four times imprisoned under the 'Cat and Mouse Act', probably going back to be rearrested as soon as I set my foot on British soil. I come to ask you to help to win this fight. If we win it, this hardest of all fights, then, to be sure, in the future it is going to be made easier for women all over the world to win their fight when their time comes. So I make no apologies for coming, and I make no apologies, Mrs. Hepburn, for asking this audience if any of them feel inclined to help me to take back some money from America and put it with the money that I know our women are raising by desperate personal sacrifice at home, so that when we begin our next year's campaign, facing a general election, as probably we shall face next year, our anxieties on the money side will not be so heavy as they would have been if I had not found strength and health enough to come and carry out this somewhat arduous tour in the United States of America.

Should Men Vote?

Nellie McClung

Winnipeg, Manitoba (1914)

Nellie Letitia McClung was a Canadian suffragist, reformer, orator and author who played an important role in the Persons Case of 1929. Besides championing the causes of temperance and women's suffrage, McClung was also a prolific writer whose debut novel *Sowing Seeds in Danny* was the bestselling novel in Canada in 1908.

McClung was known for her wit and sense of humour, which she applied brilliantly in 'Should Men Vote'—a mock parliament which ridicules Premier of Manitoba, Rodmond Roblin's sexist views.

Glad to see you—come any time, and ask for anything you like. We like delegations—and I congratulate this delegation on their splendid, gentlemanly manners. If the men in England had come before their Parliament with the frank courtesy you have shown, they might still have been enjoying the privilege of meeting their representatives in this friendly way.

But, gentlemen, you are your own answer to the question; you are the product of an age which has not seen fit to bestow the gift you ask, and who can say that you are not splendid specimens of mankind? No! No! Any system which can produce the virile, splendid type of men we have before us today, is good enough for me, and if it is good enough for me—it is good enough for anybody.

But my dear young friends, I am convinced you do not know what you're asking me to do ; you do not know what you ask. You have not thought of it, of course, with the natural thoughtlessness of your sex. You ask for something which may disrupt the whole course of civilization. Man's place is to provide for his family, a hard enough task in these strenuous days. We hear of women leaving home, and we hear it with deepest sorrow. Do you know why women leave home? There is a reason. Home is not made sufficiently attractive. Would letting politics enter the home help matters? Ah no! Politics would unsettle our men. Unsettled men mean unsettled bills—unsettled bills mean broken homes—broken vows—and then divorce.

Man has a higher destiny than politics! What is home without a bank account? The man who pays the grocer rules the world. Shall I call men away from the useful plow and harrow, to talk loud on street corners about things which do not concern them? Ah, no, I love the farm and the hallowed associations—the dear old farm, with the drowsy tinkle of cowbells at eventide. There I see my father's kindly smile so full of blessing, hardworking, rough-handed man he was, maybe, but able to look the whole world in the face.... You ask me to change all this.

I am the chosen representative of the people, elected to the highest office this fair land has to offer. I must guard well its interests. No upsetting influence must mar our peaceful firesides. Do you never read, gentlemen? Do you not know of the disgraceful happenings in countries cursed by manhood suffrage? Do you not know the fearful odium into which the polls have fallen—is it possible you do not know the origin of that offensive word 'Poll-cat', do you not know that men are creatures of habit—give them an inch—and they will steal the whole sub-division, and although it is quite true, as you say, the polls are only open once in four years—when men once get the habit—who knows where it will end—it is hard enough to keep them at home now! No, history is full of unhappy examples of men in public life; Nero, Herod, King John—you ask me to set these names before your young people. Politics has a blighting, demoralizing influence on men. It dominates them, pursues them even after their earthly career is over. Time and again it has been proven that men came back and voted—even after they were dead.

So you ask me to disturb the sacred calm of our cemeteries? We are doing very well just as we are, very well indeed. Women are the best students of economy. Every woman is a student of political economy. We look very closely at every dollar of public money, to see if we couldn't make a better use of it ourselves, before we spend it. We run our elections as cheaply as they are run anywhere. We always endeavour to get the greatest number of votes for the least possible amount of money. That is political economy.

You think you can instruct a person older than yourself, do you—you, with the brains of a butterfly, the acumen of a bat; the backbone of a jelly-fish. You can tell me something, can you? I was managing governments when you were sitting in your high chair, drumming on a tin plate with a spoon. You dare to tell me how a government should be conducted?

But I must not lose my temper and I never do—never—except when I feel like it—and am pretty sure I can get away with it. I have studied self-control, as you all know—I have had to, in order that I may be a leader. If it were not for this fatal modesty, which on more than one occasion has almost blighted my political career, I would say I believe I have been a leader, a factor in building up this fair province; I would say that I believe I have written my name large across the face of this province.

But gentlemen, I am still of the opinion, even after listening to your cleverly worded speeches, that I will go on just as I have been doing, without the help you so generously offer. My wish for this fair, flower-decked land is that I may long be spared to guide its destiny in world affairs. I know there is no one but me—I tremble when I think of what might happen to these leaderless lambs—but I will go forward confidently, hoping that the good ship may come safely into port, with the same old skipper on the bridge. We are not worrying about the coming election, as you may think. We rest in confidence of the result, and will proudly unfurl, as we have these many years, the same old banner of the grand old party that had gone down many times to disgrace, but thank God, never to defeat.

Graveside Panegyric for Fenian Jeremiah O'Donovan Rossa

Patrick Pearse

Glasnevin Cemetery (1 August 1915)

Patrick Pearse was an Irish nationalist leader, teacher, poet and Commander-in-Chief of the Irish forces in the anti-British Easter Rising of 1916. When the Rising failed, he surrendered to the British. Subsequently, he faced a court martial and was shot dead by a firing squad.

Pearse is considered an important figure in Irish history and helped establish Irish Republicanism. Through 'Graveside Panegyric for Fenian Jeremiah O'Donovan Rossa', Pearse called the Irish people to action.

It has seemed right, before we turn away from this place in which we have laid the mortal remains of O'Donovan Rossa, that one among us should, in the name of all, speak the praise of that valiant man, and endeavour to formulate the thought and the hope that are in us as we stand around his grave. And if there is anything that makes it fitting that I, rather than some other, rather than one of the grey-haired men who were young with him and shared in his labour and in his suffering, should speak here, it is perhaps that I may be taken as speaking on behalf of a new generation that has been re-baptised in the Fenian faith, and that has accepted the responsibility of carrying out the Fenian programme. I propose to you then that, here by the grave of this unrepentant Fenian, we renew our baptismal vows; that, here by the grave of this unconquered and unconquerable man, we ask of God, each one for himself, such unshakable purpose, such high and gallant courage, such unbreakable strength of soul as belonged to O'Donovan Rossa.

Deliberately here we avow ourselves, as he avowed himself in the dock, Irishmen of one allegiance only. We of the Irish Volunteers, and you others who are associated with us in today's task and duty, are bound together and must stand together henceforth in brotherly union for the achievement of the freedom of Ireland. And we know only one definition of freedom: it is Tone's definition, it is Mitchel's definition, it is Rossa's definition. Let no man blaspheme the cause that the dead generations of Ireland served by giving it any other name and definition than their name and their definition.

We stand at Rossa's grave not in sadness but rather in exaltation of spirit that it has been given to us to come thus into so close a communion with that brave and splendid Gael. Splendid and holy causes are served by men who are themselves splendid and holy. O'Donovan Rossa was splendid in the proud manhood of him, splendid in the heroic grace of him, splendid in the Gaelic strength and clarity and truth of him. And all that splendour and pride and strength was compatible with a humility and a simplicity of devotion to Ireland, to all that was olden and beautiful and Gaelic in Ireland, the holiness and simplicity of patriotism of a Michael O'Clery or of an Eoghan O'Growney. The clear true eyes of this man almost alone in his day visioned Ireland as we of today would surely have her: not free merely, but Gaelic as well; not Gaelic merely, but free as well.

In a closer spiritual communion with him now than ever before or perhaps ever again, in a spiritual communion with those of his day, living and dead, who suffered with him in English prisons, in communion of spirit too with our own dear comrades who suffer in English prisons today, and speaking on their behalf as well as our own, we pledge to Ireland our love, and we pledge to English rule in Ireland our hate. This is a place of peace, sacred to the dead, where men should speak with all charity and with all restraint; but I hold it a Christian thing, as O'Donovan Rossa held it, to hate evil, to hate untruth, to hate oppression, and, hating them, to strive to overthrow them. Our foes are strong and wise and wary; but, strong and wise and wary as they are, they cannot undo the miracles of God who ripens in the hearts of young men the seeds sown by the young men of a former generation. And the seeds sown by the young men of '65 and '67 are coming to their miraculous ripening today. Rulers and Defenders of Realms had need to be wary if they would guard against such processes. Life springs from death; and from the graves of patriot men and women spring living nations. The Defenders of this Realm have worked well in secret and in the open. They think that they have pacified Ireland. They think that they have purchased half of us and intimidated the other half. They think that they have foreseen everything, think that they have provided against everything; but the fools, the fools, the fools!—They have left us our Fenian dead, and while Ireland holds these graves, Ireland unfree shall never be at peace.

'Freedom Is My Birthright'

Bal Gangadhar Tilak

1st anniversary of Home Rule League (1917)

Bal Gangadhar Tilak was an Indian nationalist, philosopher, mathematician and scholar who founded the Indian Home Rule League and signed the Lucknow Pact to ensure Hindu-Muslim unity in the nationalist movement. He introduced the method of passive resistance and a boycott of British goods, which was later adopted by Mohandas Karamchand Gandhi.

Tilak delivered his famous 'Freedom Is My Birthright' speech on the first anniversary of the Home Rule League.

I am young in spirit though old in body. I do not wish to lose this privilege of youth. To deny the growing capacity to my thinking power is to admit that I have no right to speak on this resolution. Whatever I am going to speak today is eternally young. The body might grow old, decrepit and it might perish, but the soul is immortal. Similarly, if there might be an apparent lull in our Home Rule activities, the freedom of the spirit behind it is eternal and indestructible, and it will secure liberty for us.

The Soul means Parameshwar and the mind will not get peace till it gets identified with Him. If one body is worn out the soul will take another: so assures the *Gita*. This philosophy is quite old. Freedom is my birthright. So long as it is awake within me, I am not old. No weapon can cut this spirit, no fire can burn it, no water can wet it, no wind can dry it. I say further that no CID can burn it. I declare the same principle to the Superintendent of Police who is sitting before me, to the Collector who had been invited to attend this meeting and to the Government shorthand writer who is busy taking down notes of our speeches.

This principle will not disappear even if it seems to be killed. We ask for Home Rule and we must get it. The Science which ends in Home Rule is the Science of Politics and not the one which ends in slavery. The Science of Politics is the 'Vedas' of the country. You have a soul and I only want to wake it up. I want to tear off the blind that has been let down by ignorant, designing and selfish people. The Science of Politics consists of two parts. The first is Divine and the second is Demonic. The slavery of a Nation comes into the latter part. There cannot be a moral justification for the Demonic part of the Science of Politics. A Nation which might justify this is guilty of sin in the sight of God. Some people have the courage to declare what is harmful to them and some have not that courage. The political and religious teaching consists in giving the knowledge of this principle. Religious and political teachings are not separate, though they appear to be so on account of foreign rule. All philosophies are included in the Science of Politics.

Who does not know the meaning of Home Rule? Who does not want it? Would you like it, if I enter your house and take possession of your cooking department? I must have the right to manage the affairs in my own house. It is only lunatics and children who do not know how to manage their own affairs.

The cardinal creed of the conferences is that a member must be above 21 years of age; do you not, therefore, think that you want your own rights? Not being lunatics or children you understand your own business, your own rights and, therefore, you know Home Rule. We are told we are not fit for Home Rule. A century has passed away and the British Rule has not made us fit for Home Rule; now we will make our own efforts and fit ourselves for it.

To offer irrelevant excuses, to hold out any temptation and to make other offers will be putting a stigma on the English policy. England is trying to protect the small state of Belgium with the help of India; how can it then say that we should not have Home Rule? Those who find fault with us are avaricious people. But there are people who find fault even with the All-Merciful God. We must work hard to save the soul of our Nation without caring for anything. The good of our country consists in guarding this - our birthright. The Congress has passed this Home Rule resolution. The Provincial Conference is only a child of the Congress, which submits to mandates of its father. We will follow Shri Ramachandra in obeying the order of our father the Congress. We are determined to make efforts to get this resolution enforced even if the effort leads us to the desert, compels us to live incognito, makes us suffer any hardship and even if it finally brings us to death. Shri Ramachandra did it. Do not pass this resolution by merely clapping your hands but by taking a solemn vow that you will work for it. We will work for it by every possible constitutional and law-abiding method to get Home Rule.

Through the grace of God, England has changed its mind towards us. We feel our efforts will not be without success. England proudly thought that a tiny nation might be able to protect the Empire by itself. This pride has gone down. England has now begun to feel that it must make changes in the constitution of the Empire. Lloyd George has openly confessed that England cannot go on without the help of India. All notions about a Nation of a 1000 years old have to be changed. The English people have discovered that the wisdom of all their parties is not sufficient. The Indian soldiers have saved the lives of the British soldiers on the French battlefield and have showed their bravery. Those who once considered us as slaves have begun now to call us brothers. God has brought about all these changes. We must push our demands while the notion of this brotherhood is existing in the minds of the English. We must inform them that we, 30 crores of the Indian people, are ready to lay down our lives for the Empire; and that while we are with them none shall dare cast an evil glance at the Empire.

Address to the Jury

Emma Goldman

Anti-Conscription Trial (9 July 1917)

Emma Goldman was a Russian-born American anarchist who championed freedom of expression, use of birth control and freedom of sexual expression, worker's rights and independence of women—issues that continuously made her come into conflict with authorities, and for which she was repeatedly jailed. Considered one of the two most dangerous anarchists in America, she nevertheless persisted and lectured on anarchism across the United States and Europe.

'Address to the Jury' is one of Goldman's most famous and eloquent speeches through which she skilfully defends herself and Alexander Berkman at the trial of 9 July 1917.

Gentlemen of the Jury

As in the case of my co-defendant, Alexander Berkman, this is also the first time in my life I have ever addressed a jury. I once had occasion to speak to three judges. On the day after our arrest it was given out by the U.S. Marshal and the District Attorney's office that the 'big fish' of the No? Conscription activities had been caught, and that there would be no more troublemakers and disturbers to interfere with the highly democratic effort of the Government to conscript its young manhood for the European slaughter. What a pity that the faithful servants of the Government, personified in the U.S. Marshal and the District Attorney, should have used such a weak and flimsy net for their big catch. The moment the anglers pulled their heavily laden net ashore, it broke, and all the labor was so much wasted energy. The methods employed by Marshal McCarthy and his hosts of heroic warriors were sensational enough to satisfy the famous circus men, Barnum & Bailey. A dozen or more heroes dashing up two flights of stairs, prepared to stake their lives for their country, only to discover the two dangerous disturbers and troublemakers, Alexander Berkman and Emma Goldman, in their separate offices, quietly at work at their desks, wielding not a sword, nor a gun or a bomb, but merely their pens! Verily, it required courage to catch such big fish. To be sure, two officers equipped with a warrant would have sufficed to carry out the business of arresting the defendants Alexander Berkman and Emma Goldman. Even the police know that neither of them is in the habit of running away or hiding under the bed. But the farce-comedy had to be properly staged if the Marshal and the District Attorney were to earn immortality. Hence the sensational arrest; hence also, the raid upon the offices of THE BLAST, MOTHER EARTH, and the No-Conscription League. In their zeal to save the country from the troublemakers, the Marshal and his helpers did not even consider it necessary to produce a search warrant. After all, what matters a mere scrap of paper when one is called upon to raid the offices of Anarchists? Of what consequence is the sanctity of property, the right of privacy, to officials in their dealings with Anarchists! In our day of military training for battle, an Anarchist office is an appropriate camping ground. Would the gentlemen who came with Marshal McCarthy have dared to go into the offices of Morgan, or Rockefeller, or any of those men without a search warrant? They never showed us the search warrant, although we asked them for it. Nevertheless, they turned our office into a battlefield, so that when they were through with it, it looked like invaded Belgium, with only the difference that the invaders were not Prussian barbarians but good American patriots bent on making New York safe for democracy. The stage having been appropriately set for the three-act comedy, and the first act successfully played by carrying off the villains in a madly dashing automobile—which broke every traffic regulation and barely escaped crushing everyone in its way—the second act proved even more ludicrous. 50000 dollars bail was demanded, and real estate refused offered by a man whose property is rated at 3000000 dollars, and that after the District Attorney had considered and, in fact, promised to accept the property for one of the defendants, Alexander Berkman, thus breaking every right guaranteed even to the most heinous criminal. Finally the third act, played by the Government in this court during the last week. The pity of it is that the prosecution knows so little of dramatic construction, else it would have equipped itself with better dramatic material to sustain the continuity of the play. As it was, the third act fell flat, utterly, and presents the question, Why such a tempest in a teapot? Gentlemen of the jury, my comrade and co-defendant having carefully and thoroughly gone into the evidence presented by the prosecution, and having demonstrated its entire failure to prove the charge of conspiracy or any overt acts to carry out that conspiracy, I shall not impose upon your patience by going over the same ground, except to emphasize a few points. To charge people with having conspired to do something which they have been engaged in doing most of their lives, namely their campaign against war, militarism and conscription as contrary to the best interests of humanity, is an insult to human intelligence. And how was that charge proven? By the fact that MOTHER EARTH and THE BLAST were printed by the same printer and bound in the same bindery. By the further evidence that the same express man had delivered the two publications! And by the still more illuminating fact that on June 2nd MOTHER EARTH and THE BLAST were given to a reporter at his request, if you please, and gratis. Gentlemen of the jury, you saw the reporter who testified to this overt act. Did any one of you receive the impression that the man was of conscriptable age, and if not, in what possible way is the giving of MOTHER EARTH to a reporter for news purposes proof demonstrating the overt act? It was brought out by our witnesses that the MOTHER EARTH magazine has been published for twelve years; that it was never held up, and that it has always gone through the U.S. mail as second-class mail matter. It was further proven that the magazine appeared each month about the first or second, and that it was sold or given away at the office to whoever wanted a copy. Where, then, is the overt act? Just as the prosecution has utterly failed to prove the charge of conspiracy, so has it also failed to prove the overt act by the flimsy testimony that MOTHER EARTH was given to a reporter. The same holds good regarding THE BLAST. Gentlemen of the jury, the District Attorney must have learned from the reporters the gist of the numerous interviews which they had with us. Why did he not examine them as to whether or not we had counseled young men not to register? That would have been a more direct way of getting at the facts. In the case of the reporter from the New York Times, there can be no doubt that the man would have been only too happy to accommodate the District Attorney with the required information. A man who disregards every principle of decency and ethics of his profession as a newspaper man, by turning material given him as news over to the District Attorney, would have been glad to oblige a friend. Why did Mr. Content neglect such a golden opportunity? Was it not because the reporter of the Times, like all the other reporters, must have told the District Attorney that the two defendants stated, on each and every occasion, they would not tell people not to register? Perhaps the Times reporter refused to go to the extent of perjuring himself. Patrolmen and detectives are not so timid in such matters. Hence Mr. Randolph and Mr. Cadell, to rescue the situation. Imagine employing tenth-rate stenographers to report the very important speeches of dangerous troublemakers! What lack of forethought and efficiency on the part of the District Attorney! But even these two members of the police department failed to prove by their notes that we advised people not to register. But since they had to produce something incriminating against Anarchists, they conveniently resorted to the old standby, always credited to us, 'We believe in violence and we will use violence.' Assuming, gentlemen of the jury, that this sentence was really used at the meeting of May 18th, it would still fail to prove the indictment which charges conspiracy and overt acts to carry out the conspiracy. And that is all we are charged with. Not violence, not Anarchism. I will go further and say, that had the indictment been for the advocacy of violence, you gentlemen of the jury, would still have to render a verdict of 'Not Guilty,' since the mere belief in a thing or even the announcement that you would carry out that belief, cannot possibly constitute a crime. However, I wish to say emphatically that no such expression as 'We believe in violence and we will use violence' was uttered at the meeting of May 18th, or at any other meeting. I could not have employed such a phrase, as there was no occasion for it. If for no other reason, it is because I want my lectures and speeches to be coherent and logical. The sentence credited to me is neither. I have read to you my position toward political violence from a lengthy essay called 'The Psychology of Political Violence.' But to make that position clearer and simpler, I wish to say that I am a social student. It is my mission in life to ascertain the cause of our social evils and of our social difficulties. As a student of social wrongs it is my aim to diagnose a wrong. To simply condemn the man who has committed an act of political violence, in order to save my skin, would be as unpardonable as it would be on the part of the physician, who is called to diagnose a case, to condemn the patient because the patient has tuberculosis, cancer, or some other disease. The honest, earnest, sincere physician does not only prescribe medicine, he tries to find out the cause of the disease. And if the patient is at all capable as to means, the doctor will say to him, 'Get out of this putrid air, get out of the factory, get out of the place where your lungs are being infected.' He will not merely give him medicine. He will tell him the cause of the disease. And that is precisely my position in regard to acts of violence. That is what I have said on every platform. I have attempted to explain the cause and the reason for acts of political violence. It is organized violence on top which creates individual violence at the bottom. It is the accumulated indignation against organized wrong, organized crime, organized injustice which drives the political offender to his act. To condemn him means to be blind to the causes which make him. I can no more do it, nor have I the right to, than the physician who were to condemn the patient for his disease. You and I and all of us who remain indifferent to the crimes of poverty, of war, of human degradation, are equally responsible for the act committed by the political offender. May I therefore be permitted to say, in the words of a great teacher: 'He who is without sin among you, let him cast the first stone.' Does that mean advocating violence? You might as well accuse Jesus of advocating prostitution, because He took the part of the prostitute, Mary Magdalene. Gentlemen of the jury, the meeting of the 18th of May was called primarily for the purpose of voicing the position of the conscientious objector and to point out the evils of conscription. Now, who and what is the conscientious objector? Is he really a shirker, a slacker, or a coward? To call him that is to be guilty of dense ignorance of the forces which impel men and women to stand out against the whole world like a glittering lone star upon a dark horizon. The conscientious objector is impelled by what President Wilson in his speech of Feb. 3, 1917, called 'the righteous passion for justice upon which all war, all structure of family, State and of mankind must rest as the ultimate base of our existence and our liberty.' The righteous passion for justice which can never express itself in human slaughter—that is the force which makes the conscientious objector. Poor indeed is the country which fails to recognize the importance of that new type of humanity as the 'ultimate base of our existence and liberty.' It will find itself barren of that which makes for character and quality in its people. The meeting of May 18th was held before the Draft Bill had actually gone into effect. The President signed it late in the evening of the 18th. Whatever was said at that meeting, even if I had counseled young men not to register, that meeting cannot serve as proof of an overt act. Why, then, has the Prosecuting Attorney dwelt so much, at such length, and with such pains on that meeting, and so little on the other meetings held on the eve of registration and after? Is it not because the District Attorney knew that we had no stenographic notes of that meeting? He knew it because he was approached by Mr. Weinberger and other friends for a copy of the transcript, which request he refused. Evidently, the District Attorney felt safe to use the notes of a patrolman and a detective, knowing that they would swear to anything their superiors wanted. I never like to accuse anyone—I wouldn't go so far as my co-defendant, Mr. Berkman, in saying that the District Attorney doctored the document; I don't know whether he did or not. But I do know that patrolman Randolph and Detective Cadell doctored the notes, for the simple reason that I didn't say those things. But though we could not produce our own stenographic notes, we have been able to prove by men and women of unimpeachable character and high intelligence that the notes of Randolph are utterly false. We have also proven beyond a reasonable doubt, and Mr. Content did not dare question our proof, that at the Hunts' Point Palace, held on the eve of registration, I expressly stated that I cannot and will not tell people not to register. We have further proven that this was my definite stand, which was explained in my statement sent from Springfield and read at the meeting of May 23rd. When we go through the entire testimony given on behalf of the prosecution, I insist that there is not one single point to sustain the indictment for conspiracy or to prove the overt acts we are supposed to have committed. But we were even compelled to bring a man eighty years of age to the witness stand in order to stop, if possible, any intention to drag in the question of German money. It is true, and I appreciate it, that Mr. Content said he had no knowledge of it. But, gentlemen of the jury, somebody from the District Attorney's office or someone from the Marshal's office must have given out the statement that a bank receipt for $2,400 was found in my office and must have told the newspapers the fake story of German money. As if we would ever touch German money, or Russian money, or American money coming from the ruling class, to advance our ideas! But in order to forestall any suspicion, any insinuation, in order to stand clear before you, we were compelled to bring an old man here to inform you that he has been a radical all his life, that he is interested in our ideas, and that he is the man who contributed the money for radical purposes and for the work of Miss Goldman. Gentlemen of the jury, you will be told by the Court, I am sure, that when you render a verdict you must be convinced beyond a reasonable doubt; that you must not assume that we are guilty before we are proven guilty; and that it is your duty to assume that we are innocent. And yet, as a matter of fact, the burden of proof has been laid upon us. We had to bring witnesses. If we had had time we could have brought fifty more witnesses, each corroborating the others. Some of those people have no relation with us. Some are writers, poets, contributors to the most conventional magazines. Is it likely that they would swear to something in our favor if it were not the truth? Therefore I insist, as did my co-defendant Alexander Berkman, that the prosecution has made a very poor showing in proving the conspiracy or any overt act. Gentlemen of the jury, we have been in public life for twenty-seven years. We have been hauled into court, in and out of season—we have never denied our position. Even the police know that Emma Goldman and Alexander Berkman are not shirkers. You have had occasion during this trial to convince yourselves that we do not deny. We have gladly and proudly claimed responsibility, not only for what we ourselves have said and written, but even for things written by others and with which we did not agree. Is it plausible, then, that we would go through the ordeal, trouble and expense of a lengthy trial to escape responsibility in this instance? A thousand times no! But we refuse to be tried on a trumped-up charge, or to be convicted by perjured testimony, merely because we are Anarchists and hated by the class whom we have openly fought for many years. Gentlemen, during our examination of talesmen, when we asked whether you would be prejudiced against us if it were proven that we propagated ideas and opinions contrary to those held by the majority, you were instructed by the Court to say, 'If they are within the law.' But what the Court did not tell you is, that no new faith—not even the most humane and peaceable—has ever been considered 'within the law' by those who were in power. The history of human growth is at the same time the history of every new idea heralding the approach of a brighter dawn, and the brighter dawn has always been considered illegal, outside of the law. Gentlemen of the jury, most of you, I take it, are believers in the teachings of Jesus. Bear in mind that he was put to death by those who considered his views as being against the law. I also take it that you are proud of your Americanism. Remember that those who fought and bled for your liberties were in their time considered as being against the law, as dangerous disturbers and troublemakers. They not only preached violence, but they carried out their ideas by throwing tea into the Boston harbor. They said that 'Resistance to tyranny is obedience to God.' They wrote a dangerous document called the Declaration of Independence. A document which continues to be dangerous to this day, and for the circulation of which a young man was sentenced to ninety days prison in a New York Court, only the other day. They were the Anarchists of their time—they were never within the law. Your Government is allied with the French Republic. Need I call your attention to the historic fact that the great upheaval in France was brought about by extra-legal means? The Dantes, the Robespierres, the Marats, the Herberts, aye even the man who is responsible for the most stirring revolutionary music, the Marseillaise (which unfortunately has deteriorated into a war tune) even Camille Desmoulins, were never within the law. But for those great pioneers and rebels, France would have continued under the yoke of the idle Louis XVI., to whom the sport of shooting jack rabbits was more important than the destiny of the people of France. Ah, gentlemen, on the very day when we were being tried for conspiracy and overt acts, your city officials and representatives welcomed with music and festivities the Russian Commission. Are you aware of the fact that nearly all of the members of that Commission have only recently been released from exile? The ideas they propagated were never within the law. For nearly a hundred years, from 1825 to 1917, the Tree of Liberty in Russia was watered by the blood of her martyrs. No greater heroism, no nobler lives had ever been dedicated to humanity. Not one of them worked within the law. I could continue to enumerate almost endlessly the hosts of men and women in every land and in every period whose ideas and ideals redeemed the world because they were not within the law. Never can a new idea move within the law. It matters not whether that idea pertains to political and social changes or to any other domain of human thought and expression—to science, literature, music; in fact, everything that makes for freedom and joy and beauty must refuse to move within the law. How can it be otherwise? The law is stationary, fixed, mechanical, 'a chariot wheel' which grinds all alike without regard to time, place and condition, without ever taking into account cause and effect, without ever going into the complexity of the human soul. Progress knows nothing of fixity. It cannot be pressed into a definite mould. It cannot bow to the dictum, 'I have ruled,' 'I am the regulating finger of God.' Progress is ever renewing, ever becoming, ever changing—never is it within the law. If that be crime, we are criminals even like Jesus, Socrates, Galileo, Bruno, John Brown and scores of others. We are in good company, among those whom Havelock Ellis, the greatest living psychologist, describes as the political criminals recognized by the whole civilized world, except America, as men and women who out of deep love for humanity, out of a passionate reverence for liberty and an all-absorbing devotion to an ideal are ready to pay for their faith even with their blood. We cannot do otherwise if we are to be true to ourselves—we know that the political criminal is the precursor of human progress—the political criminal of today must needs be the hero, the martyr and the saint of the new age. But, says the Prosecuting Attorney, the press and the unthinking rabble, in high and low station, 'that is a dangerous doctrine and unpatriotic at this time.' No doubt it is. But are we to be held responsible for something which is as unchangeable and unalienable as the very stars hanging in the heavens unto time and all eternity? Gentlemen of the jury, we respect your patriotism. We would not, if we could, have you change its meaning for yourself. But may there not be different kinds of patriotism as there are different kinds of liberty? I for one cannot believe that love of one's country must needs consist in blindness to its social faults, to deafness to its social discords, of inarticulation to its social wrongs. Neither can I believe that the mere accident of birth in a certain country or the mere scrap of a citizen's paper constitutes the love of country. I know many people—I am one of them—who were not born here, nor have they applied for citizenship, and who yet love America with deeper passion and greater intensity than many natives whose patriotism manifests itself by pulling, kicking, and insulting those who do not rise when the national anthem is played. Our patriotism is that of the man who loves a woman with open eyes. He is enchanted by her beauty, yet he sees her faults. So we, too, who know America, love her beauty, her richness, her great possibilities; we love her mountains, her canyons, her forests, her Niagara, and her deserts—above all do we love the people that have produced her wealth, her artists who have created beauty, her great apostles who dream and work for liberty—but with the same passionate emotion we hate her superficiality, her cant, her corruption, her mad, unscrupulous worship at the altar of the Golden Calf. We say that if America has entered the war to make the world safe for democracy, she must first make democracy safe in America. How else is the world to take America seriously, when democracy at home is daily being outraged, free speech suppressed, peaceable assemblies broken up by overbearing and brutal gangsters in uniform; when free press is curtailed and every independent opinion gagged. Verily, poor as we are in democracy, how can we give of it to the world? We further say that a democracy conceived in the military servitude of the masses, in their economic enslavement, and nurtured in their tears and blood, is not democracy at all. It is despotism—the cumulative result of a chain of abuses which, according to that dangerous document, the Declaration of Independence, the people have the right to overthrow. The District Attorney has dragged in our Manifesto, and he has emphasized the passage, 'Resist conscription.' Gentlemen of the jury, please remember that that is not the charge against us. But admitting that the Manifesto contains the expression, 'Resist conscription,' may I ask you, is there only one kind of resistance? Is there only the resistance which means the gun, the bayonet, the bomb or flying machine? Is there not another kind of resistance? May not the people simply fold their hands and declare, 'We will not fight when we do not believe in the necessity of war'? May not the people who believe in the repeal of the Conscription Law, because it is unconstitutional, express their opposition in word and by pen, in meetings and in other ways? What right has the District Attorney to interpret that particular passage to suit himself? Moreover, gentlemen of the jury, I insist that the indictment against us does not refer to conscription. We are charged with a conspiracy against registration. And in no way or manner has the prosecution proven that we are guilty of conspiracy or that we have committed an overt act. Gentlemen of the jury, you are not called upon to accept our views, to approve of them or to justify them. You are not even called upon to decide whether our views are within or against the law. You are called upon to decide whether the prosecution has proven that the defendants Emma Goldman and Alexander Berkman have conspired to urge people not to register. And whether their speeches and writings represent overt acts. Whatever your verdict, gentlemen, it cannot possibly affect the rising tide of discontent in this country against war which, despite all boasts, is a war for conquest and military power. Neither can it affect the ever increasing opposition to conscription which is a military and industrial yoke placed upon the necks of the American people. Least of all will your verdict affect those to whom human life is sacred, and who will not become a party to the world slaughter. Your verdict can only add to the opinion of the world as to whether or not justice and liberty are a living force in this country or a mere shadow of the past. Your verdict may, of course, affect us temporarily, in a physical sense—it can have no effect whatever upon our spirit. For even if we were convicted and found guilty and the penalty were that we be placed against a wall and shot dead, I should nevertheless cry out with the great Luther: 'Here I am and here I stand and I cannot do otherwise.' And gentlemen, in conclusion let me tell you that my co-defendant, Mr. Berkman, was right when he said the eyes of America are upon you. They are upon you not because of sympathy for us or agreement with Anarchism. They are upon you because it must be decided sooner or later whether we are justified in telling people that we will give them democracy in Europe, when we have no democracy here? Shall free speech and free assemblage, shall criticism and opinion—which even the espionage bill did not include—be destroyed? Shall it be a shadow of the past, the great historic American past? Shall it be trampled underfoot by any detective, or policeman, anyone who decides upon it? Or shall free speech and free press and free assemblage continue to be the heritage of the American people? Gentlemen of the jury, whatever your verdict will be, as far as we are concerned, nothing will be changed. I have held ideas all my life. I have publicly held my ideas for 27 years. Nothing on earth would ever make me change my ideas except one thing; and that is, if you will prove to me that our position is wrong, untenable, or lacking in historic fact. But never would I change my ideas because I am found guilty. I may remind you of two great Americans, undoubtedly not unknown to you, gentlemen of the jury; Ralph Waldo Emerson and Henry David Thoreau. When Thoreau was placed in prison for refusing to pay taxes, he was visited by Ralph Waldo Emerson and Emerson said: 'David, what are you doing in jail?' And Thoreau replied: 'Ralph, what are you doing outside, when honest people are in jail for their ideals?' Gentlemen of the jury, I do not wish to influence you. I do not wish to appeal to your passions. I do not wish to influence you by the fact that I am a woman. I have no such desires and no such designs. I take it that you are sincere enough and honest enough and brave enough to render a verdict according to your convictions, beyond the shadow of a reasonable doubt. Please forget that we are Anarchists. Forget that it is claimed that we propagated violence. Forget that something appeared in MOTHER EARTH when I was thousands of miles away, three years ago. Forget all that, and merely consider the evidence. Have we been engaged in a conspiracy? Has that conspiracy been proven? Have we committed overt acts? Have those overt acts been proven? We for the defense say they have not been proven. And therefore your verdict must be not guilty.

But whatever your decision, the struggle must go on. We are but the atoms in the incessant human struggle towards the light that shines in the darkness—the Ideal of economic, political and spiritual liberation of mankind!

Maiden Speech

Nancy Astor

House of Commons, London (24 February 1920)

Nancy Witcher Astor or Viscountess Astor, was a British politician and the first woman to take her seat in the British House of Commons. Her parliamentary work was dedicated to the issues of temperance, women's equality, progressive educational policy and the extension of the Trade Board Acts.

'Maiden Speech' is a debate on alcohol restriction where Astor wittily deflects arguments and gives a strong argument of her own.

I shall not begin by craving the indulgence of the House. I am only too conscious of the indulgence and the courtesy of the House. I know that it was very difficult for some Hon. Members to receive
the first lady M.P. into the House. It was almost as difficult for 1624
some of them as it was for the lady M.P. herself to come in. Hon. Members, however, should not be frightened of what Plymouth sends out into the world. After all, I suppose when Drake and Raleigh wanted to set out on their venturesome careers, some cautious person said, 'Do not do it; it has never been tried before. You stay at home, my sons, cruising around in home waters.' I have no doubt that the same thing occurred when the Pilgrim Fathers set out. I have no doubt that there were cautious Christian brethren who did not understand their going into the wide seas to worship God in their own way. But, on the whole, the world is all the better for those venturesome and courageous west country people, and I would like to say that I am quite certain that the women of the whole world will not forget that it was the fighting men of Devon who

dared to send the first woman to represent women in the Mother of Parliaments. Now, as the west country people are a courageous lot, it is only right that one of their representatives should show some courage, and I am perfectly aware that it does take a bit of courage to address the House on that vexed question, Drink. However, I dare do it. The Hon. Member (Sir J. D. Rees) is more than polite. In fact, I should say that he goes almost a bit too far. However. I will consider his proposal if I can convert him.

The issue raised by the Hon. Member is really quite clear, although I admit that he did not make it as clear as I would have liked. Do we want the welfare of the community, or do we want the prosperity of the Trade? Do we want national efficiency, or do we want national inefficiency? That is what it comes to. So I hope to be able to persuade the House. Are we really trying for a better world, or are we going to slip back to the same old world before 1914? I think that the Hon. Member is not moving with the times. He speaks of vexatious laws and restrictions. I quite agree with him that most laws are vexatious. When we want to go 50 or 60 miles an hour down the Bath Road it is very tiresome, when we come to a village, to have to go 10 miles an hour. Why do we have to do it? It is for the good of the community. We might kill children. He talks about the restrictions. I maintain that they brought a great deal of good to the community. 1625 There were two gains. First, there were the moral gains. I should like to tell you about them. The convictions of drunkenness among women during the War were reduced to one-fifth after these vexatious restrictions were brought in. I take women, because, as the Hon. Member has said, most of the men were away fighting. Does the House realise what that means? The convictions of drunkenness among women were reduced to one-fifth at a time when many women, thousands of them, were earning more than they had ever dreamed of earning in their lives, which generally means, so they say in industrial communities, that there is more spent on drink. Also women were going through not only a physical strain but the most awful mental tortures. Then the deaths from *delirium tremens* were greatly reduced. I do not know whether Hon. Members have seen the tortures of *delirium tremens*, but it is a national gain if you can reduce them. The deaths of children from over-laying were halved. That was after these vexatious restrictions were brought in.

These are some of the gains that you can set out on paper. I could talk for five hours on the moral gains. I will not do it, but I could talk for hours on the moral gains which you cannot put on paper, they are so enormous. I am perfectly certain, if Hon. Members would really stop to think, that they would not cavil at these vexatious restrictions. Already, we have lost some of these gains. The convictions among women have doubled in the last year since the restrictions have been slightly modified, and they are four times as many among men. That is something that I should like the House to think of. Think what these increased convictions mean. Just think, twice as many convictions among women! Does the House realise what that means? How I wish that I was really an orator. I would like to tell you about drink. I have as good a sense of humour as any other Hon. Member, but when I think of the ruin and the desolation and the misery which drink brings into the houses of the working men and women as well as of the well-to-do, I find it a little difficult to be humorous. It was only the other day—I had been down to my constituency—that I was coming back from what they call the poorer parts of the town, and I stopped outside a public 1626
house where I saw a child about five years old waiting for its mother. It did not have to wait long. Presently she reeled out. The child went forward to her, but it soon retreated. Oh the oaths and curses of that poor woman and the shrieks of that child as it fled from her. That is not an easy thing to forget. That is what goes on when you have increased drunkenness among women. I am thinking of the women and children. I am not so tremendously excited about what you call the freedom of the men. The men will get their freedom. I do not want to rob them of anything that is good. I only want to ask them to consider others. There is a story—no, I had better not give it. I do not really want to harrow the feelings of the House! But I do want Hon. Members to think about these things. What really happens? It is a most terrible thing to talk about it. The freedom of the subject! We, the women, know, and the men know, thousands of us in the country who work amongst the slums, and in prisons and hospitals, we know where John Barleycorn, as you are pleased to call him,

leads to. It is not to Paradise. It promises Heaven, and too often it leads to Hell. I will not go on, because it would not be quite fair; but I do beg Hon. Members to think of these things, and when they are talking about freedom, to think of the children.

After all, the thought of every man for himself is a thoroughly materialistic doctrine. There is a doctrine of going out to look for the lost sheep; I feel somehow that that is a better spirit to go on with than to be always clamouring about the freedom of the subject. We talk about our war gains and efficiency. You talk about liquor control. What was it set up for? It was set up for national efficiency. It was not set up for temperance. It did pretty well. The War Office and the Admiralty both commended the Liquor Control Board for having greatly gained that for which it was set up. No one would call the War Office or the Admiralty Pussyfoots. There are several among them, but you can hardly look upon them as prejudiced Pussyfoots. In 1916 the Liquor Control Board unanimously reported that they had enormously increased efficiency by the Regulations which the Hon. Gentleman opposite wants 1627 swept away. The Liquor Board said more, and I would like Hon. Members who are always talking about national efficiency and economy to think of this. I want to see whether you are in earnest about this matter or whether it is camouflage. The Liquor Control Board said that the State could not get the maximum of efficiency so long as the drink trade was in private hands. That is what they said. Why did they say so? It is simple. You cannot reconcile the interests of the State with the interests of the trade. If you could there never would have been any licensing laws; there would never have been any drink question. Why cannot you reconcile the two? I will tell you. Because, Mr. Deputy-Speaker, the interests of the trade is to sell as much of its goods as possible. No one can say that is to the interest of the State. I do not blame the trade, but one must say that its interest is absolutely opposed to the interest of the State. The real lesson for the country, so far as drink is concerned, is that State Purchase gets the largest amount of progress with the least amount of unrest. That is really what is meant by our War lessons.

The Hon. Member spoke of Carlisle. What was the result at Carlisle? The areas all around Carlisle, nearly every one of them, who were originally against the Liquor Control Board's acquisition of the Carlisle area subsequently asked to be taken in. That is really the result of Carlisle. I am glad the Hon. Member mentioned Carlisle. I hope someone who follows will deal with all the facts and figures of Carlisle, because they are something of which to be very proud. There are certain things at Carlisle which we are not able to get anywhere else in England. That is wonderful. I could go on for hours but, as I say, having got the indulgence of the House I will not try it too far.

The Hon. Baronet talks about pacifists and temperance men not being fighting men. I notice that he is a little frightened of revolutions. What makes revolutions? Reactionaries make revolutions. Then the Hon. Gentleman talks about the working man. I suppose when he refers to working men he takes the broad interpretation taken by my Labour friends which interpretation includes anything from a countess to a docker. I know a good deal about the working man. I 1628 would not insult him by telling him, so long as you can prove to him that the conditions of women and children have improved under these restrictions, that he was not willing to have them. I have never found him so. I have spent five years amongst working men in hospitals.

I admit that the country is not ripe for, and does not now want, Prohibition. The Hon. Member is perfectly right there. I am not pressing for Prohibition. I am far too intelligent for that. Frankly, I say that I believe that men will get nearer the Paradise they seek if they try to get it through a greater inspiration than drink. I hope very much from the bottom of my heart that at some time the people of England will come to Prohibition. I myself believe it will come. I say so frankly. I am not frightened of saying it. I am not afraid at all of working men. I have told it to them for five years, and they know perfectly well what I think. I hope the time will come when the working man will go dry. But we are not yet ready. Do not let Hon. Members deceive themselves for one minute. The working man is as good a father as any other man. Show him the figures. Show him what the Liquor Control Board has done for women and children. Tell him the truth. Do not always tell him that his liberty is being taken away, and that the rich man wants to get more work out of him. It is not true, and you know it. I am all for telling the truth, no matter how disagreeable it is. What I find is that if you care enough about people they will listen to the truth. I think the whole world is sick of lies. I believe that you have got to like men or you cannot say 'Boo!' without insulting them. The Hon. Member has said that he and his friends were willing during the War to put up with drink control for the purpose of winning the War. It is not true. Ever since the Liquor Control Board started the Hon. Member and his friends have been kicking against it.

Oh, yes! Oh, yes! It is you, Sir, who are deceiving, it is not I, and if is not the Liquor Control Board. All during the War when the Government and the Admiralty, and the War Office, said that the Liquor Control Board was helping efficiency and helping to win the War, what did you do in the Great War, you and your friends? No, Sir, the Hon. Member and his friends 1629 were always kicking against the Liquor Control Board. [HON. MEMBERS: 'No!'] Oh, yes: look in the OFFICIAL REPORT, and you will see that you were always complaining, and at the time of the nation's dire peril you were always trying to hamper the Liquor Control Board. No, yon have not got a pretty record, you and your friends. I am not saying that there were not some perfectly patriotic brewers. There were, hut I do say that there were some brewers who really were all during the War kicking against restrictions of any kind. That is perfectly true, and the Hon. Member knows it himself. It is really not a pretty story. I thought the Hon. Member was going to complain about the hardships of the trade, but he did not do so. I have, however, heard others do it, and I can tell you that the drink trade, in spite of its hardships, managed to profiteer to the tune of many millions out of the working men. That is what they did in the Great War. Brewery companies which were nearly ruined before the War have now got millions. [HON. MEMBERS: 'No!'] Yes, that is so, and any Hon. Members can look into it and they will see it for themselves. I am not blaming them, but I think if the Hon. Member and his friends are the real friends of the working men they will urge the brewers to disgorge some of their War profits.

What are they doing with their war profits? They are advertising. There are some very offensive posters put up by the brewers, but

I will not deal with them, except to dwell on those which are most likely to mislead the country. There is the poster of a fine English working man pointing to a reformed public house with a beautiful cheerful fire, where it is said that he can get tea, coffee and buns. Do you think the brewing trade are going to press the sale of tea, coffee, and buns? The brewers are spending thousands of pounds to induce Parliament to let them make their public-houses more attractive and more profitable, and this in spite of the record of convictions amongst women being double and amongst men four times what they were. I do not believe that the Government or the House is going to play their game. I do not think the country is really ripe for prohibition, but I am certain it is ripe for drastic drink reforms. [HON. MEMBERS: 'No!'] I know what I am talking about, and you must remember that women have got a vote now and we mean to use it, and use it wisely, not for the benefit of any section of society, but for the benefit of the whole. I want to see what the Government is going to do. As the House knows, I am a great admirer of the Prime Minister, and one of the reasons I have always admired him was the way he faced this vexed question of drink during the War. I know that politicians are a little frightened of the trade, and of this sort of thing, but the Prime Minister was not. He came out and said during the War that the State could not afford to let go its hold on the trade, which had beaten them in the past. I want the Prime Minister to remember those words when he introduces his drink Bill. He also said: that drink was a greater enemy than the German submarine. I want to see that the drink submarine does not torpedo the Prime Minister. I want to see whether the Prime Minister is master in his own house. I do not believe that the Prime Minister is in the strangle hold of the trade and the profiteers. It is not the trade and the profiteers who put the Prime Minister where he is. There are thousands of people who really believe in him over this drink question and they trust him. I do not know whether there are many Hon. Members who feel that way, but I do, and I can tell the House that my name is legion in the country. There is a real awakening throughout the country. [Laughter.] You can laugh, but there really are people in England, and thousands of them, who want to see the country better and they are willing to give up their appetites.

[An HON. MEMBER: 'We all do that!'] If you all do it then you have to face this question of drink. If you want national efficiency you will have to oppose excessive drink for that alone. You know that. When labourers are intoxicated do you really get the maximum out of them?

I do ask Hon. Members not to misread the spirit of the times. Do not go round saying that you want England a country fit for heroes to live in, do not talk about it unless you mean to do it. I do not want to rob the Hon. Member opposite of anything that has given him pleasure. I do not really want to take the joy out of the world, or happiness, or anything that really makes for the betterment of the world; but you know, and I know, that drink really promises everything and gives you nothing. You know it, and the House knows it, and the world is beginning to recognise it. We have no right to think of this question in terms of our appetite, and we have to think of it in something bigger than that. I want you to think of the effect of these restrictions in terms of women and babies. Think of the thousands of children whose fathers even had to put up with more than these vexatious restrictions, who laid down their lives. Think of their fatherless children. Supposing they were your children or my children, would you want them to grow up with the trade flourishing? I do not believe the House would. I do not want you to look on your lady Member as a fanatic or a lunatic. I am simply trying to speak for hundreds of women and children throughout the country who cannot speak for themselves. I want to tell you that I do know the working man, and I know that, if you do not try to fool him, if you tell him the truth about drink, he would be as willing as anybody else to put up with so-called vexatious restrictions.

Pan-Asianism

Sun Yat-sen

Kobe, Japan (28 November 1924)

Sun Yat-sen was the leader of the Chinese Nationalist Party and later the de facto ruler of China. Referred to as the Father of the Nation in the Republic of China, he played an important role in the overthrow of the Qing Dynasty. He is also remembered for his groundbreaking political philosophy—Three Principles of the People—which entails nationalism, democracy and the livelihood of the people.

'Pan-Asianism' by Sun Yat-sen marks the introduction of an important ideology of solidarity of the Asian people.

Gentlemen: I highly appreciate this cordial reception with which you are honoring me today. The topic of the day is 'Pan-Asianism,' but before we touch upon the subject, we must first have a clear conception of Asia's place in the world. Asia, in my opinion, is the cradle of the world's oldest civilization. Several thousand years ago, its peoples had already attained an advanced civilization; even the ancient civilizations of the West, of Greece and Rome, had their origins on Asiatic soil. In Ancient Asia we had a philosophic, religious, logical and industrial civilization. The origins of the various civilizations of the modern world can be traced back to Asia's ancient civilization. It is only during the last few centuries that the countries and races of Asia have gradually degenerated and become weak, while the European countries have gradually developed their resources and become powerful. After the latter had fully developed their strength, they turned their attention to, and penetrated into, East Asia, where they either destroyed or pressed hard upon each and every one of the Asiatic nations, so that thirty years ago there existed, so to speak, no independent country in the whole of Asia. With this, we may say, the low water mark had been reached.

When Asia reached this point, the tide started to turn, and the turn meant the regeneration of Asia. It started thirty years ago when Japan abolished all the Unequal Treaties that she had entered into with the foreign countries. The day when the Unequal Treaties were abolished by Japan was a day of regeneration for all Asiatic peoples. After the abolition of the Unequal Treaties, Japan became the first independent country in Asia. The remaining countries, such as China, India, Persia, Afghanistan, Arabia, and Turkey were not independent, that is to say, they were still dominated, and treated as colonies, by Europe. Thirty years ago, Japan was also a colony of the European countries. But the Japanese were far-sighted. They realized that the only way to power was to struggle with the Europeans and to abolish all Unequal Treaties, which they did, thus turning Japan into an independent country. Since Japan has become an independent country in East Asia, the various nations in this part of the world have been buoyed up with a new hope. They realized that since Japan has been able to achieve her independence through the abolition of the Unequal Treaties, they could do the same. So once again they have mustered courage to conduct their various independent activities with the hope of shaking off the yoke of European restriction and domination and regaining their own rightful position in Asia. This has been the prevailing thought in Asia during the past 30 years, which indeed gives ground for optimism.

Thirty years ago the idea was different. Men thought and believed that European civilization was a progressive one—in science, industry, manufacture, and armament—and that Asia had nothing to compare with it. Consequently, they assumed that Asia could never resist Europe, that European oppression could never be shaken off. Such was the idea prevailing 30 years ago. It was a pessimistic idea. Even after Japan abolished the Unequal Treaties and attained the status of an independent country, Asia, with the exception of a few countries situated near Japan, was little influenced. 10 years later, however, the Russo-Japanese war broke out and Russia was defeated by Japan. For the first time in the history of the last several hundred years, an Asiatic country has defeated a European Power. The effect of this victory immediately spread over the whole Asia, and gave a new hope to all Asiatic peoples. In the year of the outbreak of the Russo-Japanese war I was in Europe. One day news came that Admiral Togo had defeated the Russian navy, annihilating in the Japan Sea the fleet newly dispatched from Europe to Vladivostock. The population of the whole continent was taken aback. Britain was Japan's Ally, yet most of the British people were painfully surprised, for in their eyes Japan's victory over Russia was certainly not a blessing for the White peoples. 'Blood,' after all, 'is thicker than water.' Later on I sailed for Asia. When the steamer passed the Suez Canal a number of natives came to see me. All of them wore smiling faces, and asked me whether I was a Japanese. I replied that I was a Chinese' and inquired what was in their minds, and why they were so happy. They said they had just heard the news that Japan had completely destroyed the Russian fleet recently dispatched from Europe, and were wondering how true the story was. Some of them, living on both banks of the Canal had witnessed Russian hospital ships, with wounded on boards, passing through the Canal from time to time. That was surely a proof of the Russian defeat, they added.

In former days, the colored races in Asia, suffering from the oppression of the Western peoples, thought that emancipation was impossible. We regarded that Russian defeat by Japan as the defeat of the West by the East. We regarded the Japanese victory as our own victory. It was indeed a happy event. Did not therefore this news of Russia's defeat by Japan affect the peoples of the whole of Asia? Was not its effect tremendous? While it may not have seemed so important and consequently have had only a slight effect on the peoples living in East Asia, it had a great effect on the peoples living in West Asia and in the neighborhood of Europe who were in constant touch with Europeans and subject to their oppression daily. The suffering of these Asiatic peoples was naturally greater than that of those living in the further East, and they were therefore more quick to respond to the news of this great victory.

Since the day of Japan's victory over Russia, the peoples of Asia have cherished the hope of shaking off the yoke of European oppression, a hope which has given rise to a series or independence movements—in Egypt, Persia, Turkey, Afghanistan, and finally in India. Therefore, Japan's defeat of Russia gave rise to a great hope for the independence of Asia. From the inception of this hope to the present day only 20 years have elapsed. The Egyptian, Turkish, Persian, Afghan, and Arabian independence movements have already materialized, and even the independence movement in India has, with the passage of time, been gaining ground. Such facts are concrete proofs of the progress of the nationalist idea in Asia. Until this idea reaches its full maturity, no unification or independence movement of the Asiatic peoples as a whole is possible. In East Asia, China and Japan are the two greatest peoples. China and Japan are the driving force of this nationalist movement. What will be the consequences of this driving force still remains to be seen. The present tide of events seems to indicate that not only China and Japan but all the peoples in East Asia will unite together to restore the former status of Asia.

Such a tendency is clearly evident to the eyes of Europe and America. One American scholar has written a book to discuss the rise of the colored peoples, where he maintains that Japan's defeat of Russia amounts to a victory of the Yellow race over the White race, and that such a tendency, if unchecked, will result in the unification of the entire Yellow race, which will be a calamity for the White peoples, and ways and means should therefore be devised to prevent it. Subsequently, he wrote another book in which he described all emancipation movements as Revolts against Civilization. In his view, emancipation movements in Europe should be regarded as revolts against civilization; even more so should such emancipation movements in Asia be regarded. Such views are common among the privileged classes of—people in both Europe and America. A minority, they oppress the majority in their own continent or country. Now they wish to extend their evil practice to Asia, with a view to suppressing the nine hundred million people of Asia, and treating them as their slaves. This American scholar considers the awakening of the Asiatic peoples as a revolt against civilization. Thus, the Westerners consider themselves as the only ones possessed and worthy of true culture and civilization, other peoples with any culture or independent ideas are considered as Barbarians in revolt against Civilization. When comparing Occidental with Oriental civilization they only consider their own civilization logical and humanitarian.

From the aspect of cultural development during the last several hundred years, the material civilization of Europe has reached its height while Oriental civilization has remained stagnant. Outwardly, Europe is superior to Asia. Fundamentally, European civilization during the last several hundred years is one of scientific materialism. Such a civilization, when applied to society, will mean the cult of force, with aeroplanes, bombs, and cannons as its outstanding features. Recently, this cult of force has been repeatedly employed by the Western peoples to oppress Asia, and as a consequence, there is no progress in Asia. To oppress others with the cult of force, in the language of the Ancients, is the rule of Might. Therefore, European civilization is nothing but the rule of Might. The rule of might has always been looked down upon by the Orient. There is another kind of civilization superior to the rule of Might. The fundamental characteristics of this civilization are benevolence, justice and morality: This civilization makes people respect, not fear, it. Such a civilization is, in the language of the Ancients, the rule of Right or the Kingly Way. One may say, therefore, that Oriental civilization is one of the rule of right. Since the development of European materialistic civilization and the cult of Might, the morality of the world has been on the decline. Even in Asia, morality in several countries has degenerated. Of late, a number of European and American scholars have begun to study Oriental civilization and they realize that, while materially the Orient is far behind the Occident, morally the Orient is superior to the Occident.

Which civilization, the rule of Might or the rule of Right, will prove to be beneficial to justice and humanity, to nations and countries? You can give your own answer to this question.

I may cite an example here to illustrate the point. For instance, between 500 and 2000 years ago, there was a period of a thousand years when China was supreme in the world. Her status in the world then was similar to that of Great Britain and America today. What was the situation of the weaker nations toward China then? They respected China as their superior and sent annual tribute to China by their own will, regarding it as an honor to be allowed to do so. They wanted, of their own free will, to be dependencies of China. Those countries which sent tribute to China were not only situated in Asia but in distant Europe as well. But in what way did China maintain her prestige among so many small and weaker nations. Did she send her army or navy, i.e. use Might, to compel them to send their contributions? Not at all. It was not her rule of Might that forced the weaker nations to send tribute to China. It was the influence of her rule of Right. Once they were influenced by the 'Kingly Way' of China they continued to send tribute, not merely once or twice, but the practice was carried on from generation to generation. This influence is felt even at the present moment; there are still traces and evidences of it.

There are two small countries situated to the north of India, namely, Bhutan and Nepal. These countries are small in size, but are inhabited by a brave, strong, and warlike people. During the present British rule of India, Britain often went to Nepal in search of soldiers in order to rule the Indians. A great deal of money by way of subsidies had to be spent before Britain was allowed to dispatch a political observer to Nepal. Even a great Power such as Great Britain had to respect her; Nepal was, in fact, a great Power in Asia. But what is the attitude of Nepal toward Great Britain during the past hundred years? Over hundred years ago India was conquered by Great Britain, and during this period Nepal was able to live peacefully on the border of the British colony. . Although hundred years have passed, Nepal has never sent tribute to Great Britain. Great Britain, on the other hand, has to spend a large 'sum by way of subsidies to Nepal. But what is the attitude of Nepal toward China? The status of China has deteriorated to such an extent that it is now inferior even to that of a British colony Though far away from China Proper and separated from her by Tibet. Nepal considered China as her suzerain State and up to 1911 Nepal sent annual tribute to China via Tibet. In that year, however, when the Nepal commissioners reached Szechuan and found communications interrupted, they returned to their country. The differential attitude of Nepal toward Great Britain and toward China is due to the difference between the Oriental and Occidental civilization. China has degenerated during the last several hundred years, yet Nepal still respects her as a superior State. Great Britain, on the other hand, is a powerful country, but Nepal has been influenced by Chinese civilization, which, in her eyes, is the true civilization, while that of Britain is nothing but the rule of Might.

Now, what is the problem that underlies Pan-Asianism, the Principle of Greater Asia, which we are discussing here to-day?

Briefly, it is a cultural problem, a problem of comparison and conflict between the Oriental and Occidental culture and civilization. Oriental civilization is the rule of Right; Occidental civilization is the rule of Might. The rule of Right respects benevolence and virtue, while the rule of Might only respects force and utilitarianism. The rule of Right always influences people with justice and reason, while the rule of Might always oppresses people with brute force and military measures. People who are influenced by justice and virtue will never forget their superior State, even if that country has become weak. So Nepal even now willingly respects China as a superior State. People who are oppressed by force never submit entirely to the oppressor State. The relations of Great Britain with Egypt and India form a typical example. Although under British rule, Egypt and India have always entertained the thought of independence and separation from Great Britain. If, Great Britain becomes weaker some day, Egypt and India will overthrow British rule and regain their independence within five years. You should now realize which is the superior civilization, the Oriental or the Occidental?

If we want to realize Pan-Asianism in this new world, what should be its foundation if not our ancient civilization and culture? Benevolence and virtue must be the foundations of Pan-Asianism. With this as a sound foundation we must then learn science from Europe for our industrial development and the improvement of our armaments, not, however, with a view to oppressing or destroying other countries and peoples as the Europeans have done, but purely for our self-defense.

Japan is the first nation in Asia to completely master the military civilization of Europe. Japan's military and naval forces are her own creation, independent of European aid or assistance. Therefore,

Japan is the only completely independent country in East Asia. There is another country in Asia who joined with Central Powers during the European War and was partitioned after her final defeat. After the war, however, she was not only able to regain her territory, but to expel all Europeans from that territory. Thus she attained her status of complete independence. This is Turkey. At present Asia has only two independent countries, Japan in the East and Turkey in the West. In other words, Japan and Turkey are the Eastern and Western barricades of Asia. Now Persia, Afghanistan, and Arabia are also following the European example in arming themselves, with the result that the Western peoples dare not look down on them. China at present also possesses considerable armaments, and when her unification is accomplished she too will become a great Power. We advocate Pan-Asianism in order to restore the status of Asia. Only by the unification of all the peoples in Asia on the foundation of benevolence and virtue can they become strong and powerful.

But to rely on benevolence alone to influence the Europeans in Asia to relinquish the privileges they have acquired in China would be an impossible dream. If we want to regain our rights we must resort to force. In the matter of armaments, Japan has already accomplished her aims, while Turkey has recently also completely armed herself. The other Asiatic races, such as the peoples of Persia, Afghanistan, and Arabia are all war-like peoples. China has a population of four hundred millions, and although she needs to modernize her armament and other equipment, and her people are a peace-loving people, yet when the destiny of their country is at stake the Chinese people will also fight with courage and determination. Should all Asiatic peoples thus unite together and present a united front against the Occidentals, they will win the final victory. Compare the populations of Europe and Asia: China has a population of four hundred millions, India three hundred and fifty millions, Japan several scores of millions, totaling, together with other peoples, no less than nine hundred millions. The population in Europe is somewhere around four hundred millions. For the four hundred millions to oppress the nine hundred millions is an intolerable injustice, and in the long run the latter will be defeated. What is more, among the 400 millions some of them have already been influenced by us. Judging from the present tendency of civilization, even in Great Britain and America, there are people who advocate the principles of benevolence and justice. Such an advocacy also exists in some of the barbarian countries. Thus, we realize that the Western civilization of utilitarianism is submitting to the influence of Oriental civilization of benevolence and justice. That is to say the rule of Might gives way to the rule of Right, presaging a bright future for world civilization.

At present there is a new country in Europe which has been looked down upon and expelled from the Family of Nations by the White races of the whole of Europe. Europeans consider it as a poisonous snake or some brutal animal, and dare not approach it. Such a view is also shared by some countries in Asia. This country is Russia. At present, Russia is attempting to separate from the White peoples in Europe. Why? Because she insists on the rule of Right and denounces the rule of Might. She advocates the principle of benevolence and justice and refuses to accept the principles of utilitarianism and force. She maintains Right and opposes the oppression of the majority by the minority. From this point of view, recent Russian civilization is similar to that of our ancient civilization. Therefore, she joins with the Orient and separates from the West. The new principles of Russia were considered as intolerable by Europeans. They are afraid that these principles, when put into effect, would overthrow their rule of Might. Therefore they do not accept the Russian way, which is in accord with the principles of benevolence and justice, but denounce it as contrary to world principles.

What problem does Pan-Asianism attempt to solve? The problem is how to terminate the sufferings of the Asiatic peoples and how to resist the aggression of the powerful European countries. In a word, Pan-Asianism represents the cause of the oppressed Asiatic peoples. Oppressed peoples are found not only in Asia, but in Europe as well. Those countries that practice the rule of Might do not only oppress the weaker people outside their continent, but also those within their own continent. Pan-Asianism is based on the principle of the rule of Right, and justifies the avenging of the wrongs done to others. An American scholar considers all emancipation movements as revolts against civilization. Therefore now we advocate the avenging of the wrong done to those in revolt against the civilization of the rule of Might, with the aim of seeking a civilization of peace and equality and the emancipation of all races. Japan to-day has become acquainted with the Western civilization of the rule of Might, but retains the characteristics of the Oriental civilization of the rule of Right. Now the question remains whether Japan will be the hawk of the Western civilization of the rule of Might, or the tower of strength of the Orient. This is the choice which lies before the people of Japan.

Statement Before the Lahore High Court Bench

Shaheed Bhagat Singh

(13 January 1930)

Bhagat Singh was an Indian revolutionary hero who fought for India's independence. He is referred to as Shaheed Bhagat Singh, 'Shaheed' being an honorary term for a martyr in India. He was involved in a plot to kill the police chief who was responsible for Lala Lajpat Rai's death. However, Singh along with others accidentally killed a junior officer, a crime for which Singh was hanged along with his accomplices.

In his statement at the Lahore High Court, Singh skilfully shifts the focus from the crime to its motivation. He remains a revered figure in Indian history.

My Lords,

We are neither lawyers nor masters of English language, nor holders of degrees. Therefore, please do not expect any oratorial speech from us. We therefore pray that instead of going into the language mistakes of our statement Your Lordships will try to understand the real sense of it.

Leaving other points to our lawyers, I will confine myself to one point only. The point is very important in this case. The point is as to what were our intentions sand to what extent we are guilty. This is a very complicated question and no one will be able to express before you that height to mental elevation which inspired us to think and act in a particular manner. We want that this should be kept in mind while assessing our intentions our offence. According to the famous jurist Solomon, one should not be punished for his criminal offence if his aim is not against law.

We had submitted a written statement in the Sessions Court. That statement explains our aim and, as such, explains our intentions also. But the leaned judge dismissed it with one stroke of pen, saying that 'generally the operation of law is not affected by how or why one committed the offence. In this country the aim of the offence is very rarely mentioned in legal commentaries.'

My Lords, our contention is that under the circumstances the learned judge ought to have judged us either by the result of our action or on the basis of the psychological part of our statement. But he did not take any of these factors into consideration.

The point to be considered is that the two bombs we threw in the Assembly did not harm anybody physically or economically. As such the punishment awarded to us is not only very harsh but revengeful also. Moreover, the motive knowing his psychology. And no one can do justice to anybody without taking his motive into consideration. If we ignore the motive, the biggest general of the words will appear like ordinary murderers; revenue officers will look like thieves and cheats. Even judges will be accused of murder. This way the entire social system and the civilisation will be reduced to murders, thefts and cheating. If we ignore the motive, the government will have no right to expect sacrifice from its people and its officials. Ignore the motive and every religious preacher will be dubbed as a preacher of falsehoods, and every prophet will be charged of misguiding crores of simple and ignorant people.

If we set aside the motive, then Jesus Christ will appear to be a man responsible for creating disturbances, breaking peace and preaching revolt, and will be considered to be a 'dangerous personality' in the language of the law. But we worship him. He commands great respect in our hearts and his image creates vibrations of spiritualism amongst us. Why? Because the inspiration behind his actions was that of a high ideal. The rulers of that age could not recognize that high idealism. They only saw his outward actions. Nineteen centuries have passed since then. Have we not progressed during this period? Shall we repeat that mistake again? It that be so, then we shall have to admit that all the sacrifices of the mankind and all the efforts of the great martyrs were useless and it would appear as if we are still at the same place where we stood twenty centuries back.

From the legal point of view also, the question of motive is of special importance. Take the example of General Dyer. He resorted to firing and killed hundreds of innocent and unarmed people. But the military court did not order him to be shot. It gave him lakhs of rupees as award. Take another example. Shri Kharag Bahadur Singh, a young Gurkha, Killed a Marwari in Calcutta. If the motive be set aside, then Kharag Bahadur Singh ought to have been hanged. But he was awarded a mild sentence of a few years only. He was even released much before the expiry of his sentence. Was there any loophole in the law that he escaped capital punishment? Or, was the charge of murder not proved against him? Like us, he also accepted the full responsibility of his action, but he escaped death. He is free today. I ask Your Lordship, why was he not awarded capital punishment? His action was well calculated and well planned. From the motive end, his action was more serious and fatal than ours. He was awarded a mild punishment because his intentions were good. He was awarded a mild punishment because his intention were good. He saved the society from a dirty leach who had sucked the life-blood of so many pretty young girls. Kharag Singh was given a mild punishment just to uphold the formalities of the law.

This principle (that the law does not take motive into consideration - ed.) is quite absurd. This is against the basic principles of the law which declares that 'the law is for man and not man for the law'. As such, why the same norms are not being applied to us also? It is quite clear that while convicting Kharag Singh his motive was kept in mind, otherwise a murderer can never escape the hangman's noose. Are we being deprived of the ordinary advantage of the law because our offence is against the government, or because our action has a political importance?

My Lords, under these circumstances, please permit us to assert that a government which seeks shelter behind such mean methods has no right to exist. If it is exists, it is for the time being only, and that too with the blood of thousands of people on its head. If the law does not see the motive there can be no justice, nor can there be stable peace.

Mixing of arsenic (poison) in the flour will not be considered to be a crime, provided its purpose is to kill rats. But if the purpose is to kill a man, it becomes a crime of murder. Therefore, such laws which do not stand the test of reason and which are against the principle of justice, should be abolished. Because of such unjust laws, many great intellectuals had to adopt the path of revolt.

The facts regarding our case are very simple. We threw two bombs in the legislative Assembly on April 8, 1929. As a result of the explosion, a few persons received minor scratches. There was pandemonium in the chamber, hundreds of visitors and members of the Assembly ran out. Only my friend B.K. Dutt and myself remained seated in the visitors' gallery and offered ourselves for arrest. We were tried for attempt to murder, and convicted for life. As mentioned above, as a result of the bomb explosion, only four or five persons were slightly injured and one bench got damaged. We offered ourselves for arrest without any resistance. The Sessions Judge admitted that we could have very easily escaped, had we had any intention like that. We accepted our offence and gave a statement explaining our position. We are not afraid of punishment. But we do not want that we should be wrongly understood. The judge remover a few paragraphs from our statement. This we consider to be harmful for our real position.

A proper study of the full text of our statement will make it clear that, according to us, our country is passing through a delicate phase. We saw the coming catastrophe and thought it proper to give a timely warning with a loud voice, and we gave the warning in the manner we thought proper. We may be wrong. Our line of thinking and that of the learned judge may be different, but that does not mean that we be deprived of the permission to express our ideas, and wrong things be propagated in our name.

In our statement we explained in detail what we mean by 'Long Live Revolution' and 'Down With Imperialism'. That formed the crux of our ideas. That portion was removed from our statement. Generally a wrong meaning is attributed to the word revolution. That is not our understanding. Bombs and pistols do not make revolution. That is not our understanding. Bombs and pistols do not make revolution. The sword of revolution is sharpened on the whetting-stone of ideas. This is what we wanted to emphasize. By revolution we mean the end of the miseries of capitalist wars. It was not proper to pronounce judgment without understanding our aims and objects and the process of achieving them. To associate wrong ideas with our names is out and out injustice.

It was very necessary to give the timely warning that the unrest of the people is increasing and that the malady may take a serious turn, if not treated in time and properly. If our warning is not heeded, no human power will be able to stop it. We took this step to give proper direction to the storm. We are serious students of history. We believe that, had the ruling powers acted correctly at the proper time, there would have been no bloody revolutions in France and Russia. Several big power of the world tried to check the storm of ideas and were sunk in the atmosphere of bloodshed. The ruling people cannot change the flow of the current. We wanted to give the first warning. Had we aimed at killing some important personalities, we would have failed in the attainment of our aim.

My Lords, this was the aim and the spirit behind our action, and the result of the action corroborates our statement. There is one more point which needs elucidation, and that is regarding the strength of the bombs. Had we had no idea of the strength of the bombs, there would have been no question of our throwing them in the presence of our respected national leader like Pandit Motilal Nehru, Shri Kelkar, Shri Jayaker and Shri Jinnah. How could we have risked the lives of our leaders? After all we are not mad and, had we been so, we would have certainly been sent to the lunatic asylum, instead of being put in jail. We had full knowledge about the strength of the bombs and that is why we acted with so much confidence. It was very easy to have thrown the bombs on the occupied benches, but it was difficult to have thrown them on unoccupied seats. Had we not of saner mind or had we been mentally unbalanced, the bombs would have fallen on occupied benches and not in empty places. Therefore I would say that we should be rewarded for the courage we showed in carefully selecting the empty places. Under these conditions, My Lords, we think we have not been understood,

My Lords, we think we have not been understood properly. We have not come before you to get our sentences reduced. We have come here to clarify our position. We want that we should not be given any unjust treatment, nor should any unjust opinion be pronounced about us. The question of punishment is of secondary importance before us.

The Pleasure of Books

William Lyon Phelps

(6 April 1933)

William Lyon Phelps was an American scholar, essayist, a literature professor, critic and columnist who played an important role in introducing Americans to Russian novelists. He drew attention to contemporary literature and taught the first American university course in the modern novel.

Phelps was also an engaging orator and he broadcasted this wonderful speech over the radio about the importance of reading.

The habit of reading is one of the greatest resources of mankind; and we enjoy reading books that belong to us much more than if they are borrowed. A borrowed book is like a guest in the house; it must be treated with punctiliousness, with a certain considerate formality. You must see that it sustains no damage; it must not suffer while under your roof. You cannot leave it carelessly, you cannot mark it, you cannot turn down the pages, you cannot use it familiarly. And then, some day, although this is seldom done, you really ought to return it.

But your own books belong to you; you treat them with that affectionate intimacy that annihilates formality. Books are for use, not for show; you should own no book that you are afraid to mark up, or afraid to place on the table, wide open and face down. A good reason for marking favorite passages in books is that this practice enables you to remember more easily the significant sayings, to refer to them quickly, and then in later years, it is like visiting a forest where you once blazed a trail. You have the pleasure of going over the old ground, and recalling both the intellectual scenery and your own earlier self.

Everyone should begin collecting a private library in youth; the instinct of private property, which is fundamental in human beings, can here be cultivated with every advantage and no evils. One should have one's own bookshelves, which should not have doors, glass windows, or keys; they should be free and accessible to the hand as well as to the eye. The best of mural decorations is books; they are more varied in color and appearance than any wallpaper, they are more attractive in design, and they have the prime advantage of being separate personalities, so that if you sit alone in the room in the firelight, you are surrounded with intimate friends. The knowledge that they are there in plain view is both stimulating and refreshing. You do not have to read them all. Most of my indoor life is spent in a room containing six thousand books; and I have a stock answer to the invariable question that comes from strangers. 'Have you read all of these books?' 'Some of them twice.' This reply is both true and unexpected.

There are of course no friends like living, breathing, corporeal men and women; my devotion to reading has never made me a recluse. How could it? Books are of the people, by the people, for the people. Literature is the immortal part of history; it is the best and most enduring part of personality. But book-friends have this advantage over living friends; you can enjoy the most truly aristocratic society in the world whenever you want it. The great dead are beyond our physical reach, and the great living are usually almost as inaccessible; as for our personal friends and acquaintances, we cannot always see them. Perchance they are asleep, or away on a journey. But in a private library, you can at any moment converse with Socrates or Shakespeare or Carlyle or Dumas or Dickens or Shaw or Barrie or Galsworthy. And there is no doubt that in these books you see these men at their best. They wrote for *you*. They 'laid themselves out,' they did their ultimate best to entertain you, to make a favorable impression. You are necessary to them as an audience is to an actor; only instead of seeing them masked, you look into their innermost heart of heart.

The King's Speech

King George VI

London, England (3 September 1939)

George VI, also known as Prince Albert, Duke of York, was the King of the United Kingdom from 1936 to 52. He also served in the Royal Navy, the Royal Naval Air Force and the Royal Air Force during and after the World War I. He became King after the abdication of the throne by his brother Edward VIII. He also became an important symbol of courage for the British people during the World War II.

Overcoming the stammer that afflicted him since childhood through sheer willpower, King George VI gave the 'King's Speech' or the 'First Radio Address', announcing Britain's intention to join the War.

In this grave hour, perhaps the most fateful in our history, I send to every household of my peoples, both at home and overseas, this message, spoken with the same depth of feeling for each one of you as if I were able to cross your threshold and speak to you myself.

For the second time in the lives of most of us we are at war.

Over and over again we have tried to find a peaceful way out of the differences between ourselves and those who are now our enemies. But it has been in vain. We have been forced into a conflict. For we are called, with our allies, to meet the challenge of a principle which, if it were to prevail, would be fatal to any civilised order in the world.

It is the principle which permits a state, in the selfish pursuit of power, to disregard its treaties and its solemn pledges; which sanctions the use of force, or threat of force, against the sovereignty and independence of other states.

Such a principle, stripped of all disguise, is surely the mere primitive doctrine that 'might is right'; and if this principle were established throughout the world, the freedom of our own country and of the whole of the British Commonwealth of Nations would be in danger. But far more than this—the peoples of the world would be kept in the bondage of fear, and all hopes of settled peace and of the security of justice and liberty among nations would be ended.

This is the ultimate issue which confronts us. For the sake of all that we ourselves hold dear, and of the world order and peace, it is unthinkable that we should refuse to meet the challenge.

It is to this high purpose that I now call my people at home and my peoples across the seas, who will make our cause their own. I ask them to stand calm and firm and united in this time of trial. The task will be hard. There may be dark days ahead, and war can no longer be confined to the battlefield. But we can only do the right as we see the right, and reverently commit our cause to God.

If one and all we keep resolutely faithful to it, ready for whatever service or sacrifice it may demand, then, with God's help, we shall prevail.

May He bless and keep us all.

'Luckiest Man on the Face of the Earth'

Lou Gehrig

Farewell to Baseball Address (July 4 1939)

Lou Gehrig, also known as the Iron Horse, was one of the most revered professional baseball players in American history. Gehrig played for the New York Yankees and appeared in 2,130 consecutive games—creating a record at the time. Unfortunately, his successful career was cut short when he developed the nervous disease amyotrophic lateral sclerosis (ALS) in 1939.

On 4 July 1939, Lou Gehrig Appreciation Day was held in his honour and it is on this occasion that he gave his poignant farewell speech.

Fans, for the past two weeks you have been reading about a bad break I got. Yet today I consider myself the luckiest man on the face of the earth. I have been in ballparks for 17 years and have never received anything but kindness and encouragement from you fans.

Look at these grand men. Which of you wouldn't consider it the highlight of his career to associate with them for even one day?

Sure, I'm lucky. Who wouldn't consider it an honor to have known Jacob Ruppert—also the builder of baseball's greatest empire, Ed Barrow—to have spent the next nine years with that wonderful little fellow Miller Huggins—then to have spent the next nine years with that outstanding leader, that smart student of psychology—the best manager in baseball today, Joe McCarthy!

Sure, I'm lucky. When the New York Giants, a team you would give your right arm to beat, and vice versa, sends you a gift, that's something! When everybody down to the groundskeepers and those boys in white coats remember you with trophies, that's something.

When you have a wonderful mother-in-law who takes sides with you in squabbles against her own daughter, that's something. When you have a father and mother who work all their lives so that you can have an education and build your body, it's a blessing! When you have a wife who has been a tower of strength and shown more courage than you dreamed existed, that's the finest I know.

So I close in saying that I might have had a tough break—but I have an awful lot to live for!

Declaration of War on France and England

Benito Mussolini

Palazzo Venezia, Rome (10 June 1940)

Benito Mussolini was an Italian politician and journalist who became the fascist dictator of Italy from 1925 to 45. Mussolini was also the leader of the Italian Fascist Party and the fascists rose to power with Mussolini's regime. During World War II, Mussolini allied with Hitler and extreme fascist activities increased all over Italy.

On 10 June 1940, Mussolini gave this speech, declaring the intention of Italy to side with the Axis powers.

Soldiers, sailors, and aviators! Black shirts of the revolution and of the [Fascist] legions! Men and women of Italy, of the Empire, and of the kingdom of Albania! Pay heed! An hour appointed by destiny has struck in the heavens of our fatherland.

The declaration of war has already been delivered to the ambassadors of Great Britain and France. We go to battle against the plutocratic and reactionary democracies of the west who, at every moment have hindered the advance and have often endangered the very existence of the Italian people. Recent historical events can be summarized in the following phrases: promises, threats, blackmail, and finally to crown the edifice, the ignoble siege by the 52 states of the League of Nations. Our conscience is absolutely tranquil. With you the entire world is witness that Fascist Italy has done all that is humanly possible to avoid the torment which is throwing Europe into turmoil; but all was in vain. It would have sufficed to revise the treaties to bring them up to date with the changing needs of the life of nations and not consider them untouchable for eternity; it would have sufficed not to have begun the stupid policy of guarantees, which has shown itself particularly lethal for those who accepted them; it would have sufficed not to reject the proposal [for peace] that the Fuhrer made on 6 October of last year after having finished the campaign in Poland.

But now all of that belongs to the past. If now today we have decided to face the risks and the sacrifices of a war, it is because the honor, the interests, the future impose and iron necessity, since a great people is truly such if it considers sacred its own duties and noes not evade the supreme trials which determine the course of history.

We take up arms to resolve, after having resolved the problem of our land frontier, the problem of our maritime frontiers; we want to break the territorial chains which suffocate us in our own sea; since a people of 45 million is not truly free if it does not have free access to the ocean.

This gigantic struggle is nothing other than a phase in the logical development of our revolution; it is the struggle of peoples that are poor but rich in workers against the exploiters who hold on ferociously to the monopoly off all the riches and all the gold of the earth; it is the struggle of the fertile and young people against the sterile people moving to the sunset; it is the struggle between two centuries and two ideas. Now that the die are cast and our will has burned our ships at our backs, I solemnly declare that Italy does not intend to drag into the conflict other peoples bordering her on land or on sea. Switzerland, Yugoslavia, Greece, Turkey, Egypt take note of these my words and it depends on them and only on them whether or not they will be rigorously confirmed.

Italiano!

In a memorable meeting, that which took place in Berlin, I said that according to the laws of Fascist morality, when one has a friend, one marches with him to the end. This we have done with Germany, with its people, with its marvelous armed forces. On this eve of an event of century wide scope, we direct our thought to the majesty of the King and Emperor which as always has understood the soul of the fatherland. And we salute with our voices the Fuhrer, the head of great ally Germany. Proletarian and Fascist Italy stands up a third time, strong, proud, and united as never before. The single order of the day is categorical and obligatory for all. It already spreads and fires hearts from the Alps to the Indian Ocean; Victory! And we will win, in order finally to give a long period of peace with justice to Italy, to Europe, and to the world.

People of Italy!

Rush to arms and show your tenacity, your courage, your valor!

Appeal of 18 June 1940

Charles de Gaulle

London (18 June 1940)

Charles de Gaulle was a decorated French soldier and political leader before becoming President of the Fifth Republic in 1959. He worked to improve his country's economic situation and ensured France's autonomy in the face of two superpowers of the world—the United States and the Soviet Union. He was popular amongst the French people and resigned from his post in 1969.

The 'Appeal of June 18' was a famous speech by de Gaulle made during the time he was the leader of the Free French Forces in 1940, and through it he encouraged the French people to resist German occupation.

The leaders who, for many years, were at the head of French armies, have formed a government. This government, alleging our armies to be undone, agreed with the enemy to stop fighting. Of course, we were subdued by the mechanical, ground and air forces of the enemy. Infinitely more than their number, it was the tanks, the airplanes, the tactics of the Germans which made us retreat. It was the tanks, the airplanes, the tactics of the Germans that surprised our leaders to the point to bring them there where they are today.

But has the last word been said? Must hope disappear? Is defeat final? No!

Believe me, I speak to you with full knowledge of the facts and tell you that nothing is lost for France. The same means that overcame us can bring us to a day of victory. For France is not alone! She is not alone! She is not alone! She has a vast Empire behind her. She can align with the British Empire that holds the sea and continues the fight. She can, like England, use without limit the immense industry of United States.

This war is not limited to the unfortunate territory of our country. This war is not finished by the battle of France. This war is a world-wide war. All the faults, all the delays, all the suffering, do not prevent there to be, in the world, all the necessary means to one day crush our enemies. Vanquished today by mechanical force, we will be able to overcome in the future by a superior mechanical force.

The destiny of the world is here. I, General de Gaulle, currently in London, invite the officers and the French soldiers who are located in British territory or who would come there, with their weapons or without their weapons, I invite the engineers and the special workers of armament industries who are located in British territory or who would come there, to put themselves in contact with me.

Whatever happens, the flame of the French resistance not must not be extinguished and will not be extinguished. Tomorrow, as today, I will speak on Radio London.

'Nazis' Aim Is Slavery'

Édouard Daladier

France (29 January 1940)

Édouard Daladier was a Radical-Socialist French politician who served as Prime Minister of France from 1938 to 1940. In order to avoid World War II, he along with British Prime Minister Neville Chamberlain signed the Munich Pact which gave Nazi Germany possession of Sudetenland.

Daladier broadcasted this speech over the radio when Germany invaded Poland, a few months before France was attacked.

At the end of five months of war one thing has become more and more clear. It is that Germany seeks to establish a domination over the world completely different from any known in history.

The domination at which the Nazis aim is not limited to the displacement of the balance of power and the imposition of supremacy of one nation. It seeks the systematic and total destruction of those conquered by Hitler, and it does not treaty with the nations which he has subdued. He destroys them. He takes from them their whole political and economic existence and seeks even to deprive them of their history and their culture. He wishes to consider them only as vital space and a vacant territory over which he has every right.

The human beings who constitute these nations are for him only cattle. He orders their massacre or their migration. He compels them to make room for their conquerors. He does not even take the trouble to impose any war tribute on them. He just takes all their wealth, and, to prevent any revolt, he wipes out their leaders and scientifically seeks the physical and moral degradation of those whose independence he has taken away.

Under this domination, in thousands of towns and villages in Europe there are millions of human beings now living in misery which, some months ago, they could never have imagined. Austria, Bohemia, Slovakia and Poland are only lands of despair. Their whole peoples have been deprived of the means of moral and material happiness. Subdued by treachery or brutal violence, they have no other recourse than to work for their executioners who grant them scarcely enough to assure the most miserable existence.

There is being created a world of masters and slaves in the image of Germany herself. For, while Germany is crushing beneath her tyranny the men of every race and language, she is herself being crushed beneath her own servitude and her domination mania. The German worker and peasant are the slaves of their Nazi masters while the worker and peasant of Bohemia and Poland have become in turn slaves of these slaves. Before this first realization of a mad dream, the whole world might shudder.

Nazi propaganda is entirely founded on the exploitation of the weakness of the human heart. It does not address itself to the strong or the heroic. It tells the rich they are going to lose their money. It tells the worker this is a rich man's war. It tells the intellectual and the artist that all he cherished is being destroyed by war. It tells the lover of good things that soon he would have none of them. It says to the Christian believer: 'How can you accept this massacre?' It tells the adventurer—'a man like you should profit by the misfortunes of your country.'

It is those who speak this way who have destroyed or confiscated all the wealth they could lay their hands on, who have reduced their workers to slavery, who have ruined all intellectual liberty, who have imposed terrible privations on millions of men and women and who have made murder their law. What do contradictions matter to them if they can lower the resistance of those who wish to bar the path of their ambitions to be masters of the world?

For us there is more to do than merely win the war. We shall win it, but we must also win a victory far greater than that of arms. In this world of masters and slaves, which those madmen who rule at Berlin are seeking to forge, we must also save liberty and human dignity.

'Their Finest Hour'

Winston Churchill

House of Commons (18 June 1940)

Sir Winston Churchill was one of the greatest political leaders of the 20th century. An orator and a soldier, he served as Prime Minister of Britain during World War II and led Britain to victory. He was re-elected as Prime Minister in 1951. Churchill was also an accomplished writer and won the Nobel Prize in Literature in 1953.

'Their Finest Hour' is one of the most famous speeches by Churchill.

I spoke the other day of the colossal military disaster which occurred when the French High Command failed to withdraw the northern Armies from Belgium at the moment when they knew that the French front was decisively broken at Sedan and on the Meuse. This delay entailed the loss of fifteen or sixteen French divisions and threw out of action for the critical period the whole of the British Expeditionary Force. Our Army and 120,000 French troops were indeed rescued by the British Navy from Dunkirk but only with the loss of their cannon, vehicles and modern equipment. This loss inevitably took some weeks to repair, and in the first two of those weeks the battle in France has been lost. When we consider the heroic resistance made by the French Army against heavy odds in this battle, the enormous losses inflicted upon the enemy and the evident exhaustion of the enemy, it may well be the thought that these 25 divisions of the best-trained and best-equipped troops might have turned the scale. However, General Weygand had to fight without them. Only three British divisions or their equivalent were able to stand in the line with their French comrades. They have suffered severely, but they have fought well. We sent every man we could to France as fast as we could re-equip and transport their formations.

I am not reciting these facts for the purpose of recrimination. That I judge to be utterly futile and even harmful. We cannot afford it. I recite them in order to explain why it was we did not have, as we could have had, between twelve and fourteen British divisions fighting in the line in this great battle instead of only three. Now I put all this aside. I put it on the shelf, from which the historians, when they have time, will select their documents to tell their stories. We have to think of the future and not of the past. This also applies in a small way to our own affairs at home. There are many who would hold an inquest in the House of Commons on the conduct of the Governments—and of Parliaments, for they are in it, too—during the years which led up to this catastrophe. They seek to indict those who were responsible for the guidance of our affairs. This also would be a foolish and pernicious process. There are too many in it. Let each man search his conscience and search his speeches. I frequently search mine. Of this I am quite sure, that if we open a quarrel between the past and the present, we shall find that we have lost the future. Therefore, I cannot accept the drawing of any distinctions between Members of the present Government. It was formed at a moment of crisis in order to unite all the Parties and all sections of opinion. It has received the almost unanimous support of both Houses of Parliament. Its Members are going to stand together, and, subject to the authority of the House of Commons, we are going to govern the country and fight the war. It is absolutely necessary at a time like this that every Minister who tries each day to do his duty shall be respected; and their subordinates must know that their chiefs are not threatened men, men who are here today and gone tomorrow, but that their directions must be punctually and faithfully obeyed. Without this concentrated power we cannot face what lies before us. I should not think it would be very advantageous for the House to prolong this Debate this afternoon under conditions of public stress. Many facts are not clear that will be clear in a short time. We are to have a secret Session on

Thursday, and I should think that would be a better opportunity for the many earnest expressions of opinion which Members will desire to make and for the House to discuss vital matters without having everything read the next morning by our dangerous foes. The disastrous military events which have happened during the past fortnight have not come to me with any sense of surprise. Indeed, I indicated a fortnight ago as clearly as I could to the House that the worst possibilities were open; and I made it perfectly clear then that whatever happened in France would make no difference to the resolve of Britain and the British Empire to fight on, 'if necessary for years, if necessary alone.' During the last few days we have successfully brought off the great majority of the troops we had on the line of communication in France; and seven-eighths of the troops we have sent to France since the beginning of the war—that is to say, about 350,000 out of 400,000 men—are safely back in this country. Others are still fighting with the French, and fighting with considerable success in their local encounters against the enemy. We have also brought back a great mass of stores, rifles and munitions of all kinds which had been accumulated in France during the last nine months.

We have, therefore, in this Island today a very large and powerful military force. This force comprises all our best-trained and our finest troops, including scores of thousands of those who have already measured their quality against the Germans and found themselves at no disadvantage. We have under arms at the present time in this Island over a million and a quarter men. Behind these we have the Local Defence Volunteers, numbering half a million, only a portion of whom, however, are yet armed with rifles or other firearms. We have incorporated into our Defence Forces every man for whom we have a weapon. We expect very large additions to our weapons in the near future, and in preparation for this we intend forthwith to call up, drill and train further large numbers. Those who are not called up, or else are employed during the vast business of munitions production in all its branches—and their ramifications are innumerable—will serve their country best by remaining at their ordinary work until they receive their summons. We have also over here Dominions armies. The Canadians had actually landed in

France, but have now been safely withdrawn, much disappointed, but in perfect order, with all their artillery and equipment. And these very high-class forces from the Dominions will now take part in the defence of the Mother Country.

Lest the account which I have given of these large forces should raise the question: Why did they not take part in the great battle in France? I must make it clear that, apart from the divisions training and organising at home, only 12 divisions were equipped to fight upon a scale which justified their being sent abroad. And this was fully up to the number which the French had been led to expect would be available in France at the ninth month of the war. The rest of our forces at home have a fighting value for home defence which will, of course, steadily increase every week that passes. Thus, the invasion of Great Britain would at this time require the transportation across the sea of hostile armies on a very large scale, and after they had been so transported they would have to be continually maintained with all the masses of munitions and supplies which are required for continuous battle—as continuous battle it will surely be.

Here is where we come to the Navy—and after all, we have a Navy. Some people seem to forget that we have a Navy. We must remind them. For the last thirty years I have been concerned in discussions about the possibilities of oversea invasion, and I took the responsibility on behalf of the Admiralty, at the beginning of the last war, of allowing all regular troops to be sent out of the country. That was a very serious step to take, because our Territorials had only just been called up and were quite untrained. Therefore, this Island was for several months particularly denuded of fighting troops. The Admiralty had confidence at that time in their ability to prevent a mass invasion even though at that time the Germans had a magnificent battle fleet in the proportion of 10 to 16, even though they were capable of fighting a general engagement every day and any day, whereas now they have only a couple of heavy ships worth speaking of-the Scharnhorst and the Gneisenau. We are also told that the Italian Navy is to come out and gain sea superiority in these waters. If they seriously intend it, I shall only say that we shall be delighted to offer Signor Mussolini a free and safeguarded passage through the Strait of Gibraltar in order that he may play the part to which he aspires. There is a general curiosity in the British Fleet to find out whether the Italians are up to the level they were at in the last war or whether they have fallen off at all.

Therefore, it seems to me that as far as sea-borne invasion on a great scale is concerned, we are far more capable of meeting it today than we were at many periods in the last war and during the early months of this war, before our other troops were trained, and while the B.E.F. had proceeded abroad. Now, the Navy have never pretended to be able to prevent raids by bodies of 5,000 or 10,000 men flung suddenly across and thrown ashore at several points on the coast some dark night or foggy morning. The efficacy of sea power, especially under modern conditions, depends upon the invading force being of large size; It has to be of large size, in view of our military strength, to be of any use. If it is of large size, then the Navy have something they can find and meet and, as it were, bite on. Now, we must remember that even five divisions, however lightly equipped, would require 200 to 250 ships, and with modern air reconnaissance and photography it would not be easy to collect such an armada, marshal it, and conduct it across the sea without any powerful naval forces to escort it; and there would be very great possibilities, to put it mildly, that this armada would be intercepted long before it reached the coast, and all the men drowned in the sea or, at the worst blown to pieces with their equipment while they were trying to land. We also have a great system of minefields, recently strongly reinforced, through which we alone know the channels. If the enemy tries to sweep passages through these minefields, it will be the task of the Navy to destroy the mine-sweepers and any other forces employed to protect them. There should be no difficulty in this, owing to our great superiority at sea.

Those are the regular, well-tested, well-proved arguments on which we have relied during many years in peace and war. But the question is whether there are any new methods by which those solid assurances can be circumvented. Odd as it may seem, some attention has been given to this by the Admiralty, whose prime duty and responsibility is to destroy any large sea-borne expedition before it reaches, or at the moment when it reaches, these shores. It would not be a good thing for me to go into details of this. It might suggest ideas to other people which they have not thought of, and they would not be likely to give us any of their ideas in exchange. All I will say is that untiring vigilance and mind-searching must be devoted to the subject, because the enemy is crafty and cunning and full of novel treacheries and stratagems. The House may be assured that the utmost ingenuity is being displayed and imagination is being evoked from large numbers of competent officers, well-trained in tactics and thoroughly up to date, to measure and counterwork novel possibilities. Untiring vigilance and untiring searching of the mind is being, and must be, devoted to the subject, because, remember, the enemy is crafty and there is no dirty trick he will not do.

Some people will ask why, then, was it that the British Navy was not able to prevent the movement of a large army from Germany into Norway across the Skagerrak? But the conditions in the Channel and in the North Sea are in no way like those which prevail in the Skagerrak. In the Skagerrak, because of the distance, we could give no air support to our surface ships, and consequently, lying as we did close to the enemy's main air power, we were compelled to use only our submarines. We could not enforce the decisive blockade or interruption which is possible from surface vessels. Our submarines took a heavy toll but could not, by themselves, prevent the invasion of Norway. In the Channel and in the North Sea, on the other hand, our superior naval surface forces, aided by our submarines, will operate with close and effective air assistance.

This brings me, naturally, to the great question of invasion from the air, and of the impending struggle between the British and German Air Forces. It seems quite clear that no invasion on a scale beyond the capacity of our land forces to crush speedily is likely to take place from the air until our Air Force has been definitely overpowered. In the meantime, there may be raids by parachute troops and attempted descents of airborne soldiers. We should be able to give those gentry a warm reception both in the air and on the ground, if they reach it in any condition to continue the dispute. But the great question is: Can we break Hitler's air weapon? Now, of course, it is a very great pity that we have not got an Air Force at least equal to that of the most powerful enemy within striking distance of these shores. But we have a very powerful Air Force which has proved itself far superior in quality, both in men and in many types of machine, to what we have met so far in the numerous and fierce air battles which have been fought with the Germans. In France, where we were at a considerable disadvantage and lost many machines on the ground when they were standing round the aerodromes, we were accustomed to inflict in the air losses of as much as two and two-and-a-half to one. In the fighting over Dunkirk, which was a sort of no-man's-land, we undoubtedly beat the German Air Force, and gained the mastery of the local air, inflicting here a loss of three or four to one day after day. Anyone who looks at the photographs which were published a week or so ago of the re-embarkation, showing the masses of troops assembled on the beach and forming an ideal target for hours at a time, must realize that this re-embarkation would not have been possible unless the enemy had resigned all hope of recovering air superiority at that time and at that place.

In the defence of this Island the advantages to the defenders will be much greater than they were in the fighting around Dunkirk. We hope to improve on the rate of three or four to one which was realized at Dunkirk; and in addition all our injured machines and their crews which get down safely—and, surprisingly, a very great many injured machines and men do get down safely in modern air fighting—all of these will fall, in an attack upon these Islands, on friendly soil and live to fight another day; whereas all the injured enemy machines and their complements will be total losses as far as the war is concerned.

During the great battle in France, we gave very powerful and continuous aid to the French Army, both by fighters and bombers; but in spite of every kind of pressure we never would allow the entire metropolitan fighter strength of the Air Force to be consumed. This decision was painful, but it was also right, because the fortunes of the battle in France could not have been decisively affected even if we had thrown in our entire fighter force. That battle was lost by the unfortunate strategical opening, by the extraordinary and unforeseen power of the armored columns, and by the great preponderance of the German Army in numbers. Our fighter Air Force might easily have been exhausted as a mere accident in that great struggle, and then we should have found ourselves at the present time in a very serious plight. But as it is, I am happy to inform the House that our fighter strength is stronger at the present time relatively to the Germans, who have suffered terrible losses, than it has ever been; and consequently we believe ourselves possessed of the capacity to continue the war in the air under better conditions than we have ever experienced before. I look forward confidently to the exploits of our fighter pilots-these splendid men, this brilliant youth-who will have the glory of saving their native land, their island home, and all they love, from the most deadly of all attacks.

There remains, of course, the danger of bombing attacks, which will certainly be made very soon upon us by the bomber forces of the enemy. It is true that the German bomber force is superior in numbers to ours; but we have a very large bomber force also, which we shall use to strike at military targets in Germany without intermission. I do not at all underrate the severity of the ordeal which lies before us; but I believe our countrymen will show themselves capable of standing up to it, like the brave men of Barcelona, and will be able to stand up to it, and carry on in spite of it, at least as well as any other people in the world. Much will depend upon this; every man and every woman will have the chance to show the finest qualities of their race, and render the highest service to their cause. For all of us, at this time, whatever our sphere, our station, our occupation or our duties, it will be a help to remember the famous lines: He nothing common did or mean, Upon that memorable scene.

I have thought it right upon this occasion to give the House and the country some indication of the solid, practical grounds upon which we base our inflexible resolve to continue the war. There are a good many people who say, 'Never mind. Win or lose, sink or swim, better die than submit to tyranny—and such a tyranny.' And I do not dissociate myself from them. But I can assure them that our professional advisers of the three Services unitedly advise that we should carry on the war, and that there are good and reasonable hopes of final victory. We have fully informed and consulted all the self-governing Dominions, these great communities far beyond the oceans who have been built up on our laws and on our civilisation, and who are absolutely free to choose their course, but are absolutely devoted to the ancient Motherland, and who feel themselves inspired by the same emotions which lead me to stake our all upon duty and honour. We have fully consulted them, and I have received from their Prime Ministers, Mr. Mackenzie King of Canada, Mr. Menzies of Australia, Mr. Fraser of New Zealand, and General Smuts of South Africa—that wonderful man, with his immense profound mind, and his eye watching from a distance the whole panorama of European affairs—I have received from all these eminent men, who all have Governments behind them elected on wide franchises, who are all there because they represent the will of their people, messages couched in the most moving terms in which they endorse our decision to fight on, and declare themselves ready to share our fortunes and to persevere to the end. That is what we are going to do.

We may now ask ourselves: In what way has our position worsened since the beginning of the war? It has worsened by the fact that the Germans have conquered a large part of the coast line of Western Europe, and many small countries have been overrun by them. This aggravates the possibilities of air attack and adds to our naval preoccupations. It in no way diminishes, but on the contrary definitely increases, the power of our long-distance blockade. Similarly, the entrance of Italy into the war increases the power of our long-distance blockade. We have stopped the worst leak by that. We do not know whether military resistance will come to an end in France or not, but should it do so, then of course the Germans will be able to concentrate their forces, both military and industrial, upon us. But for the reasons I have given to the House these will not be found so easy to apply. If invasion has become more imminent, as no doubt it has, we, being relieved from the task of maintaining a large army in France, have far larger and more efficient forces to meet it.

If Hitler can bring under his despotic control the industries of the countries he has conquered, this will add greatly to his already vast armament output. On the other hand, this will not happen immediately, and we are now assured of immense, continuous and increasing support in supplies and munitions of all kinds from the United States; and especially of aeroplanes and pilots from the Dominions and across the oceans coming from regions which are beyond the reach of enemy bombers.

I do not see how any of these factors can operate to our detriment on balance before the winter comes; and the winter will impose a strain upon the Nazi regime, with almost all Europe writhing and starving under its cruel heel, which, for all their ruthlessness, will run them very hard. We must not forget that from the moment when we declared war on the 3rd September it was always possible for Germany to turn all her Air Force upon this country, together with any other devices of invasion she might conceive, and that France could have done little or nothing to prevent her doing so. We have, therefore, lived under this danger, in principle and in a slightly modified form, during all these months. In the meanwhile, however, we have enormously improved our methods of defence, and we have learned what we had no right to assume at the beginning, namely, that the individual aircraft and the individual British pilot have a sure and definite superiority. Therefore, in casting up this dread balance sheet and contemplating our dangers with a disillusioned eye, I see great reason for intense vigilance and exertion, but none whatever for panic or despair.

During the first four years of the last war the Allies experienced nothing but disaster and disappointment. That was our constant fear: one blow after another, terrible losses, frightful dangers. Everything miscarried. And yet at the end of those four years the morale of the Allies was higher than that of the Germans, who had moved from one aggressive triumph to another, and who stood everywhere triumphant invaders of the lands into which they had broken. During that war we repeatedly asked ourselves the question: How are we going to win? And no one was able ever to answer it with much precision, until at the end, quite suddenly, quite unexpectedly, our terrible foe collapsed before us, and we were so glutted with victory that in our folly we threw it away.

We do not yet know what will happen in France or whether the French resistance will be prolonged, both in France and in the French Empire overseas. The French Government will be throwing away great opportunities and casting adrift their future if they do not continue the war in accordance with their Treaty obligations, from which we have not felt able to release them. The House will have read the historic declaration in which, at the desire of many Frenchmen—and of our own hearts—we have proclaimed our willingness at the darkest hour in French history to conclude a union of common citizenship in this struggle. However matters may go in France or with the French Government, or other French Governments, we in this Island and in the British Empire will never lose our sense of comradeship with the French people. If we are now called upon to endure what they have been suffering, we shall emulate their courage, and if final victory rewards our toils they shall share the gains, aye, and freedom shall be restored to all. We abate nothing of our just demands; not one jot or tittle do we recede. Czechs, Poles, Norwegians, Dutch, Belgians have joined their causes to our own. All these shall be restored.

What General Weygand called the Battle of France is over. I xpect that the Battle of Britain is about to begin. Upon this battle depends the survival of Christian civilisation. Upon it depends our own British life, and the long continuity of our institutions and our Empire. The whole fury and might of the enemy must very soon be turned on us. Hitler knows that he will have to break us in this Island or lose the war. If we can stand up to him, all Europe may be free and the life of the world may move forward into broad, sunlit uplands. But if we fail, then the whole world, including the United States, including all that we have known and cared for, will sink into the abyss of a new Dark Age made more sinister, and perhaps more protracted, by the lights of perverted science. Let us therefore brace ourselves to our duties, and so bear ourselves that, if the British Empire and its Commonwealth last for a thousand years, men will still say, 'This was their finest hour.'

'A Grave Danger Hangs over Our Country'

Joseph Stalin

(3 July 1941)

Joseph Stalin was the dictator of the Union of Soviet Socialist Republics (USSR) from 1929 to 1953. Under his leadership, the Soviet Union transformed itself from a peasant society to an industrial superpower. However, there was discontent, and several citizens perished under his brutal regime. Stalin aligned with the Allies during World War II.

This speech was broadcasted over radio from Moscow on 3 July 1941 during the German invasion of the Soviet Union during World War II.

Comrades! Citizens! Brothers and sisters! Men of our army and navy! I am addressing you, my friends!

The perfidious military attack on our Fatherland, begun on June 22nd by Hitler Germany, is continuing.

In spite of the heroic resistance of the Red Army, and although the enemy's finest divisions and finest air force units have already been smashed and have met their doom on the field of battle, the enemy continues to push forward, hurling fresh forces into the attack.

Hitler's troops have succeeded in capturing Lithuania, a considerable part of Latvia, the western part of Byelo-Russia, part of Western Ukraine. The fascist air force is extending the range of operations of its bombers, and is bombing Murmansk, Orsha, Mogilev, Smolensk, Kiev, Odessa and Sebastopol.

A grave danger hangs over our country.

How could it have happened that our glorious Red Army surrendered a number of our cities and districts to fascist armies? Is it really true that German fascist troops are invincible, as is ceaselessly trumpeted by the boastful fascist propagandists? Of course not!

History shows that there are no invincible armies and never have been. Napoleon's army was considered invincible but it was beaten successively by Russian, English and German armies. Kaiser Wilhelm's German Army in the period of the first imperialist war was also considered invincible, but it was beaten several times by the Russian and Anglo-French forces and was finally smashed by the Anglo-French forces.

The same must be said of Hitler's German fascist army today. This army had not yet met with serious resistance on the continent of Europe. Only on our territory has it met serious resistance. And if, as a result of this resistance, the finest divisions of Hitler's German fascist army have been defeated by our Red Army, it means that this army too can be smashed and will be smashed as were the armies of Napoleon and Wilhelm.

As to part of our territory having nevertheless been seized by Germany fascist troops, this is chiefly due to the fact that the war of fascist Germany on the USSR began under conditions favorable for the German forces and unfavorable for Soviet forces. The fact of the matter is that the troops of Germany, as a country at war, were already fully mobilized, and the 170 divisions hurled by Germany against the USSR and brought up to the Soviet frontiers, were in a state of complete readiness, only awaiting the signal to move into action, whereas Soviet troops had still to effect mobilization and move up to the frontier.

Of no little importance in this respect is the fact that fascist Germany suddenly and treacherously violated the Non-Aggression Pact she concluded in 1939 with the USSR, disregarding the fact that she would be regarded as the aggressor by the whole world.

Naturally, our peace-loving country, not wishing to take the initiative of breaking the pact, could not resort to perfidy.

It may be asked how could the Soviet Government have consented to conclude a Non-Aggression Pact with such treacherous fiends as Hitler and Ribbentrop? Was this not an error on the part of the Soviet Government? Of course not. Non-Aggression Pacts are pacts of peace between states. It was such a pact that Germany proposed to us in 1939.

Could the Soviet Government have declined such a proposal? I think that not a single peace-loving state could decline a peace treaty with a neighboring state, even though the latter was headed by such fiends and cannibals as Hitler and Ribbentrop. Of course only on one indispensable condition, namely, that this peace treaty does not infringe either directly or indirectly on the territorial integrity, independence and honor of the peace-loving state. As is well known, the Non-Aggression Pact between Germany and the USSR is precisely such a pact.

What did we gain by concluding the Non-Aggression Pact with Germany? We secured our country peace for a year and a half, and the opportunity of preparing its forces to repulse fascist Germany should she risk an attack on our country despite the Pact This was a definite advantage for us and a disadvantage for fascist Germany.

What has fascist Germany gained and what has she lost by treacherously tearing up the pact and attacking the USSR?

She has gained a certain advantageous position for her troops for a short period, but she has lost politically by exposing herself in the eyes of the entire world as a blood-thirsty aggressor.

There can be no doubt that this short-lived military gain for Germany is only an episode, while the tremendous political gain of the USSR is a serious lasting factor that is bound to form the basis for development of decisive military successes of the Red Army in the war with fascist Germany.

That is why our whole valiant Red Army, our whole valiant Navy, all our falcons of the air, all the peoples of our country, all the finest men and women of Europe, America and Asia, finally all the finest men and women of Germany—condemn the treacherous acts of German fascists and sympathize with the Soviet Government, approve the conduct of the Soviet Government, and see that ours is a just cause, that the enemy will be defeated, that we are bound to win.

By virtue of this war which has been forced upon us, our country has come to death-grips with its most malicious and most perfidious enemy—German fascism. Our troops are fighting heroically against an enemy armed to the teeth with tanks and aircraft.

Overcoming innumerable difficulties, the Red Army and Red Navy are self-sacrificingly disputing every inch of Soviet soil. The main forces of the Red Army are coming into action armed with thousands of tanks and airplanes. The men of the Red Army are displaying unexampled valor. Our resistance to the enemy is growing in strength and power.

Side by side with the Red Army, the entire Soviet people are rising in defense of our native land.

What is required to put an end to the danger hovering over our country, and what measures must be taken to smash the enemy?

Above all, it is essential that our people, the Soviet people, should understand the full immensity of the danger that threatens our country and should abandon all complacency, all heedlessness, all those moods of peaceful constructive work which were so natural before the war, but which are fatal today when war has fundamentally changed everything.

The enemy is cruel and implacable. He is out to seize our lands, watered with our sweat, to seize our grain and oil secured by our labor. He is out to restore the rule of landlords, to restore Tsarism, to destroy national culture and the national state existence of the Russians, Ukrainians, Byelo-Russians, Lithuanians, Letts, Esthonians, Uzbeks, Tatars, Moldavians, Georgians, Armenians, Azerbaidzhanians and the other free people of the Soviet Union, to Germanize them, to convert them into the slaves of German princes and barons.

Thus the issue is one of life or death for the Soviet State, for the peoples of the USSR; the issue is whether the peoples of the Soviet Union shall remain free or fall into slavery.

The Soviet people must realize this and abandon all heedlessness, they must mobilize themselves and reorganize all their work on new, wartime bases, when there can be no mercy to the enemy.

Further, there must be no room in our ranks for whimperers and cowards, for panic-mongers and deserters. Our people must know no fear in fight and must selflessly join our patriotic war of liberation, our war against the fascist enslavers.

Lenin, the great founder of our State, used to say that the chief virtue of the Bolshevik must be courage, valor, fearlessness in struggle, readiness to fight, together with the people, against the enemies of our country.

This splendid virtue of the Bolshevik must become the virtue of the millions of the Red Army, of the Red Navy, of all peoples of the Soviet Union.

All our work must be immediately reconstructed on a war footing, everything must be subordinated to the interests of the front and the task of organizing the demolition of the enemy.

The people of the Soviet Union now see that there is no taming of German fascism in its savage fury and hatred of our country which has ensured all working people labor in freedom and prosperity.

The peoples of the Soviet Union must rise against the enemy and defend their rights and their land. The Red Army, Red Navy and all citizens of the Soviet Union must defend every inch of Soviet soil, must fight to the last drop of blood for our towns and villages, must display the daring initiative and intelligence that are inherent in our people.

We must organize all-round assistance for the Red Army, ensure powerful reinforcements for its ranks and the supply of everything it requires, we must organize the rapid transport of troops and military freight and extensive aid to the wounded.

We must strengthen the Red Army's rear, subordinating all our work to this cause. All our industries must be got to work with greater intensity to produce more rifles, machine-guns, artillery, bullets, shells, airplanes; we must organize the guarding of factories, power-stations, telephonic and telegraphic communications and arrange effective air raid precautions in all localities.

We must wage a ruthless fight against all disorganizers of the rear, deserters, panic-mongers, rumor-mongers; we must exterminate spies, diversionists and enemy parachutists, rendering rapid aid in all this to our destroyer battalions.

We must bear in mind that the enemy is crafty, unscrupulous, experienced in deception and the dissemination of false rumors We must reckon with all this and not fall victim to provocation.

All who by their panic-mongering and cowardice hinder the work of defence, no matter who they are, must be immediately hailed before the military tribunal. In case of forced retreat of Red Army units, all rolling stock must be evacuated, the enemy must not be left a single engine, a single railway car, not a single pound of grain or a gallon of fuel.

The collective farmers must drive off all their cattle, and turn over their grain to the safe-keeping of State authorities for transportation to the rear. All valuable property, including non-ferrous metals, grain and fuel which cannot be withdrawn, must without fail be destroyed.

In areas occupied by the enemy, guerrilla units, mounted and on foot, must be formed, diversionist groups must be organized to combat the enemy troops, to foment guerrilla warfare everywhere, to blow up bridges and roads, damage telephone and telegraph lines, set fire to forests, stores, transports.

In the occupied regions conditions must be made unbearable for the enemy and all his accomplices. They must be hounded and annihilated at every step, and all their measures frustrated.

This war with fascist Germany cannot be considered an ordinary war. It is not only a war between two armies, it is also a great war of the entire Soviet people against the German fascist forces.

The aim of this national war in defense of our country against the fascist oppressors is not only elimination of the danger hanging over our country, but also aid to all European peoples groaning under the yoke of German fascism.

In this war of liberation we shall not be alone. In this great war we shall have loyal allies in the peoples of Europe and America, including the German people who are enslaved by the Hitlerite despots.

Our war for the freedom of our country will merge with the struggle of the peoples of Europe and America for their independence, for democratic liberties.

It will be a united front of peoples standing for freedom and against enslavement and threats of enslavement by Hitler's fascist armies.

In this connection the historic utterance of the British Prime Minister Churchill regarding aid to the Soviet Union and the declaration of the United States Government signifying its readiness to render aid to our country, which can only evoke a feeling of gratitude in the hearts of the peoples of the Soviet Union, are fully comprehensible and symptomatic.

Comrades, our forces are numberless. The overweening enemy will soon learn this to his cost. Side by side with the Red Army many thousands of workers, collective farmers, intellectuals are rising to fight the enemy aggressor. The masses of our people will rise up in their millions.

The working people of Moscow and Leningrad have already commenced to form vast popular levies in support of the Red Army. Such popular levies must be raised in every city which is in danger of enemy invasion, all working people must be roused to defend our freedom, our honor, our country—in our patriotic war against German Fascism.

In order to ensure the rapid mobilization of all forces of the peoples of the U.S.S.R. and to repulse the enemy who treacherously attacked our country, a State Committee of Defense has been formed in whose hands the entire power of the State has been vested.

The State Committee of Defense has entered upon its functions and calls upon all people to rally around the Party of Lenin-Stalin and around the Soviet Government, so as to self-denyingly support the Red Army and Navy, demolish the enemy and secure victory.

All our forces for support of our heroic Red Army and our glorious Red Navy! All forces of the people—for the demolition of the enemy! Forward, to our victory!

Infamy Speech

Franklin D. Roosevelt

Joint Session of the US Congress (8 December 1941)

Franklin D. Roosevelt was the 32nd President of the United States and the only president to be elected to the office four times. He led his country through two major crises—the Great Depression and World War II. Undoubtedly, Roosevelt was one of the most successful presidents in American history.

The 'Infamy Speech' was delivered by Roosevelt a day after the Pearl Harbour attack, declaring the United States' intention to retaliate.

'Mr. Vice President, Mr. Speaker, Members of the Senate, and of the House of Representatives:

Yesterday, December 7th, 1941—a date which will live in infamy—the United States of America was suddenly and deliberately attacked by naval and air forces of the Empire of Japan.

The United States was at peace with that nation and, at the solicitation of Japan, was still in conversation with its government and its emperor looking toward the maintenance of peace in the Pacific.

Indeed, one hour after Japanese air squadrons had commenced bombing in the American island of Oahu, the Japanese ambassador to the United States and his colleague delivered to our Secretary of State a formal reply to a recent American message. And while this reply stated that it seemed useless to continue the existing diplomatic negotiations, it contained no threat or hint of war or of armed attack.

It will be recorded that the distance of Hawaii from Japan makes it obvious that the attack was deliberately planned many days or even weeks ago. During the intervening time, the Japanese government has deliberately sought to deceive the United States by false statements and expressions of hope for continued peace. The attack yesterday on the Hawaiian islands has caused severe damage to American naval and military forces. I regret to tell you that very many American lives have been lost. In addition, American ships have been reported torpedoed on the high seas between San Francisco and Honolulu.

Yesterday, the Japanese government also launched an attack against Malaya.

Last night, Japanese forces attacked Hong Kong.

Last night, Japanese forces attacked Guam.

Last night, Japanese forces attacked the Philippine Islands.

Last night, the Japanese attacked Wake Island.

And this morning, the Japanese attacked Midway Island.

Japan has, therefore, undertaken a surprise offensive extending throughout the Pacific area. The facts of yesterday and today speak for themselves. The people of the United States have already formed their opinions and well understand the implications to the very life and safety of our nation.

As Commander in Chief of the Army and Navy, I have directed that all measures be taken for our defense. But always will our whole nation remember the character of the onslaught against us.

No matter how long it may take us to overcome this premeditated invasion, the American people in their righteous might will win through to absolute victory.

I believe that I interpret the will of the Congress and of the people when I assert that we will not only defend ourselves to the uttermost, but will make it very certain that this form of treachery shall never again endanger us.

Hostilities exist. There is no blinking at the fact that our people, our territory, and our interests are in grave danger.

With confidence in our armed forces, with the unbounding determination of our people, we will gain the inevitable triumph—so help us God.

I ask that the Congress declare that since the unprovoked and dastardly attack by Japan on Sunday, December 7th, 1941, a state of war has existed between the United States and the Japanese empire.'

Stalingrad Speech

Adolf Hitler

Address to Senior Members of the Nazi Party, Munich (8 November 1942)

Adolf Hitler was the leader of Germany's Nazi Party and one of the most notorious dictators of the 20th century. He assumed the titles of Chancellor and 'Führer' from 1933 onwards and started World War II with the aim to achieve German world domination. He is marked in history as the reincarnation of evil for his anti-Semitic policies and use of concentration camps.

This speech was delivered by Hitler at the peak of the Battle of Stalingrad on 8 November 1942.

My German fellow-countrymen and women! Party Comrades! It is, I think, something very extraordinary when a man after about 20 years can stand before his old followers, and when in doing so he has not had to make any revisions of his program during these 20 years.

Today's gathering, however, reminds us most of all of the evening which we were able to celebrate in the former hall 10 years ago. It reminds us of this because at that time too we were in the midst of a very hard fight. Our fight to take over power in Germany was just as decisive for our fate as the fight which we are waging today. It was only during the past year that this became known to us in all its meaning, and if victory had not been achieved in 1933, then Germany would have remained what it was then, that is, a powerless nation with an Army of 100,000 men, which would necessarily have (had to submit) to destruction.

And at the same time, a colossus had arisen in the East with only a single thought in mind, to fall upon this weak, lazy, defeatist and internally-torn Europe. And if at that time this challenge had not been successfully taken up, then the power which alone was capable of opposing this danger would not have entered world history.

Today we know that there would probably not be any Europe left. Therefore the battle which we fought then was only apparently an internal struggle for power. In reality, even then it was a struggle for the preservation of Germany and, in the broadest sense of the word, for the preservation of Europe. At that time, we were close to victory. And yet when, 10 years ago, we met in the former hall, no one knew exactly how close it was. Only one thing went without saying as far as we were concerned, namely the conviction that this victory, no matter what happens, must come and will come.

It is with the same conviction that I now stand before you, and it has never left me, either, since the day on which, as an unknown man in this city, I began the struggle, first for the soul of the German people, and then, on beyond this city, forever more and more followers. And in the beginning I did not have much more to give than faith, the faith that if anyone pursues a just aim I with unchanging and undisturbed loyalty and never lets himself be diverted from it, but puts everything into it, then others will be found who are determined to be his followers, and that from this host an ever stronger faith must gradually radiate to the whole people, and that out of this host the worthiest part of the whole people must one day finally find themselves together, and that finally this worthiest part must acquire the power in the state.

And today I stand by this same view. Fate, or Providence, will give the victory to those who most deserve it. We could have had it before, in the year 1918. The German people did not deserve it at that time. They had grown confused and untrue to themselves. And that was the reason that I, an unknown, a nobody, at that time resolved to build up this movement in the midst of utter ruin and complete collapse, the reason why I also had faith that it would have to succeed, because I saw before me, not the defeatist phenomena of a crumbling bourgeois-Marxist world, but the millions of brave men who had done their utmost and who faltered only because the homeland was no longer worthy of them in the critical hour-because it had failed. I then had the conviction that if only the effort to bring back internal order to the German people and to get hold of the soundest kernel in them proved successful, that then another 1918 could never be repeated.

Since I made this resolve, many more than 20 years have gone by. 10 years ago we were about to have a dress rehearsal, after the movement had already encountered the greatest difficulties—in a preceding ten-year period, many had lost their faith, and our opponents already were saying that we were dead. We need only recall that time. It was no wonder, either. A movement which was just getting ready to seize power collapsed completely. Its leaders were either dead or wounded, or in prison or in flight because of their activities.

And yet barely 10 years were enough for this whole movement to rise anew from its ashes, like a phoenix. And when we met here 10 years ago, we had just had another setback. Many—especially our enemies—believed that we had lost our chance because we had not acted at the moment we were offered something which would only have burdened the movement, but not made it at all possible to realize its real aims. At that time, too, I stood before you, my old party comrades, with the same faith as now, absolutely convinced that victory will be his who best deserves it, and that therefore our only task will be to deserve it.

And when now, after 10 years, I again survey this period, I can say that upon no people has Providence ever bestowed more successes than upon us. The miracles we have achieved in the last three years in the face of a whole world of enemies are unique in history, especially the crises we very naturally often had in these years.

I need only remind you of the one great crisis we had to go through in Norway, where, indeed, it was a toss-up, and where we might have asked ourselves, will we be able to hold Narvik? Won't the entire Norwegian undertaking go to pieces? One needed boundless faith in order not to become despondent at that time, and this faith was finally rewarded. Far from the homeland, with barely a single sure line of communication connected with this advanced out-post, a small, heroic German force then was fighting.

Finally they were forced to evacuate Narvik. Our opponents were jubilant. But, thanks to bravery and a fanatical determination not to capitulate under any circumstances, the final result was victory for us and not for our opponents.

If we look back over this entire period, and let everything pass before our eyes, one thing will become obvious to us: We are facing the same opponents, whom we always have had before us nothing has been changed… In the Great War there were the same opponents whom we have had to conquer in this war, and there is only one thing which differentiates the present from that time: First of all, a clearer recognition of the background of the actions of that opponent, of the driving forces, and secondly, the successes which have been gained in the meanwhile, successes which are unique in the history of the world.

For perhaps many a person will ask himself the question, why are we fighting at such great distances? We are fighting at such great distances in order to protect our homeland, in order to keep the war as far removed from it as possible and to spare it what would otherwise be its fate, and which now only certain German cities are experiencing and must experience. It is therefore preferable to keep the front line at a distance of 1,000 and if necessary 2,000 kilometers from the borders of the Reich, than to hold that front somewhere near the border of the Reich and to be forced to hold it there.

Our opponents are the same, and behind these opponents there stands the same eternally driving force, the international Jew. And it is again by no means an accident that these forces were on the inside, and have now met again on the outside. Internally, in the 'coalition' which we know only too well, they included all the enemies of the Reich, beginning with the Frankfurter Zeitung, and the entire stock market speculator-group, all the way to the Rote Fahne (Red Banner) in Berlin, and everything which lay in between.

And outside, we have again today the same coalition as before, from the chief of that international Masonic lodge, the half-Jew Roosevelt, and his Jewish brain trust, to the Jewry of purest water in Marxist-Bolshevik Russia. They are the same enemies as before, the same foes as then. In the World War we had them as external foes, in our struggle as internal foes, and now, as a National-Socialist State, as external foes again.

And again it is no accident that the same State which at that time thought it could bring about the collapse of Germany by a flood of lying propaganda, now again sends a man on the same mission. Then his name was Wilson; now his name is Roosevelt. The Germany of that time, without any education in state and national politics, without any unity, without any enlightenment on the problem of the Jewish question and the working of that power, fell victim to that attack.

The great mistake is that our enemies now imagine it will happen a second time. For if at that time we were perhaps the best organized people in the world, without doubt again we are now the best organized people in the world. And if anyone in the rest of the world imagines he can shatter this people, he does not know the enduring heart of this people today, nor the enduring power, the knowledge which guides this people politically today—the National Socialist Party and its mighty organization.

Neither has he any idea of what this movement has achieved since then, how it has taken hold of our people by its accomplishments, and how it has fulfilled the Socialist ideal—which is free of all international cheating, all the 'lying tirades,' how it has fulfilled these Socialist ideals in a way that no other State has even begun to approach up to now, to say nothing of attain.

I am calm therefore when I face any German who is fighting in the East, or who comes home on leave—and I can tell each one of them, just look at our organization. Compare our home cities, compare the workers' settlements which we are building, compare our social organization with what you have seen on the other side. Compare the fate and the lot of the German farmer with the lot of that Russian farmer. Compare all of that, my dear friend, and then give me your judgment as to who has managed things better, and above all else, who has had more honorable intentions?

Not one man has as yet returned, who could express any other opinion than that if a Socialistic State were in the process of being realized anywhere, it was in Germany only that it was actually taking place. That is still another reason why this other world which so willingly represents capitalistic interests in particular, is attacking us. It is a combine, which even today still pretends to be able to rule the world according to its private capitalistic interests, to manage it, and when necessary, to keep on ruling it.

When, for example, a few days ago, a regular snobbish, perfumed hooligan like this Mr. Eden declared: 'We English have had experience in ruling,' then the only thing one can say is: 'In ruling? In exploitation! In plundering!' What does experience in ruling mean, when in a country which, with 46,000,000 persons itself, is administering 40,000,000 square kilometers over the entire world, there were 2,500,000 unemployed at the beginning of the war.

Where is this art of ruling, to say nothing of the art of leadership? It is only the unscrupulousness for robbery. And when this same man then says: 'We have a fine instinct for idealism and material values.' Yes indeed they have. They have destroyed idealism everywhere, and they have grabbed and taken possession of material worth and always grabbed and taken possession of it, too, by brutal force only. For in 300 years that nation has oppressed and yoked and subjected nation after nation, people after people, race after race.

If they were really such brilliant rulers, then they should now be able to leave after the Indian people have expressed their explicit desire that they do, and then to wait and see whether the Indians call them back again. They have been careful not to leave, although they know how to rule so wonderfully, and in this they are completely of one mind, these plunderers, whether they run around in a Marxist cap or in a capitalistic one.

No, my friends, they don't know how to rule. They can only subjugate peoples and then pauperize them for their own benefit. A handful of people—very rich ones, to be sure—of both Jewish and non-Jewish origin are determining the fate of the world. And we can say with calmness that Germany itself has had an example of the ability of these people to rule. For when in the year 1918 the Reich collapsed, the blinded German people turned then in its blind faith to these people, in the hope that they might be shown a path by them which would lead them back out of their misery, the democratic Germany, not the National-Socialist Germany.

For we would not have come at all, if this democratic Germany had not been plundered and oppressed in that way. They did their best to make a second India out of Germany, and they were even successful to a large extent. They brought it about for us, too, that finally many millions of persons had no sort of livelihood whatever, and many other millions were working part-time. They brought it about for us, too, that finally not ten thousands, but hundreds of thousands of farmers were evicted from their ancestral plots of ground. They brought it about for us, too, that commerce and exchange finally came to a standstill, and that social welfare provisions of any kind were non-existent. They tried out on us their governmental experiments, just as in India or elsewhere, and if this head-tramp—I can't describe him in any other way—Roosevelt comes and declares that they had to rescue Europe by American methods, then the only thing I can say is, that this gentleman could best—or should best—have rescued his own country, and then he would not have had to enter the war at all. It would have been more fitting for him to get rid of his own 13,000,000 unemployed than to throw the world into a war, but he did it, because he could not solve his internal problems and because he was setting out to plunder, just like his British allies, not recognizing merely idealism, but primarily the material values, for Mr. Roosevelt knows as little about idealism as an Englishman.

From out of this art of government of our foes and its horrible results in our democratic Germany, the National Socialist movement gradually developed. For if they had really made Germany happy, we would not have had any reason at all, and I would not have had any ground, for devoting myself to this work day after day, week after week, month after month, and year after year.

You know that too, all my old fellow-combatants. I wasn't loafing then. I didn't speak in a fine club here and there, and I didn't sit down now and then at a fireplace, and deliver a little chat. Then I was making pilgrimages up and down through the German countryside, from North to South and from East to West, and wore myself out, only in order to save my people from this misery, into which these rulers of international capitalism had forced it.

This conspiracy of Jews and capitalists and Bolsheviks of that time, we wanted to do away with. And we finally have got rid of it. And hardly had it been done away with, when this other world immediately began its encirclement.

At that time it was the Germany of the Kaiser. Now it is National Socialist Germany. At that time it was the Kaiser. Now it is I. There is only one difference: the Germany of that time was theoretically an empire, practically it had all gone to pieces internally.

The Kaiser of that time was a man who lacked all force for resistance against these enemies. But in me, now, they have to face an opponent who does not even think of the word 'capitulate.'

That's always been the way, ever since I was a boy-at that time perhaps it was improper behavior but as it is, perhaps it is a virtue after all—my habit of reserving the last word for myself. And all our opponents can be convinced that the Germany of former times laid down its arms at a quarter to twelve. On principle I have never quit before five minutes after 12. My domestic foes found that out 10 years ago. They too did not believe it, and it really was not surprising, because naturally the position of my internal foes was different from the position of my external foes of today, because the internal foes of that time—

God—you know, my Party Comrades, when I began, uh, uh, it was already easy to prophesy that ... my whole work would have to miscarry. On the one side this power of the press, this power of capital, this conspiracy of influential circles, this ... parliamentarians, petty politicians and so forth, and the labor unions, and on the other side the employers' organizations, and then the ... and the parliaments and the Reichstag. How could one single man with a small group of supporters overcome all that? And even in the year 1932, they were still able to believe he would fail regardless, because they could say: 'We are still stronger; we still have more men behind us than the others.'

Today, I must say, the faith that they would stifle by their might is already dead anyway, because in actuality today we are the stronger. When I compute the number of men who are in our camp today, and who are fighting in our camp, working in our camp, it exceeds the number of those who today have taken up positions against us. There is certainly no longer any comparison with the situation of that time. And there is something else besides: this battle is now being waged on a military basis.

And now, my Party Comrades, here we have behind us a great German history. The English say they have never yet lost a war. They have lost many wars; but in every war they have fought to their last ally. That is correct, and that probably distinguishes the English method of waging war from ours. Germany has a great history behind her, and I need only select one hero from this history and compare his fate with our fate-Frederick the Great against whom in his worst time there was actually a coalition of 54,000,000 to about 3,900,000.

And today, when I compare our position with his—our bastions, our fronts advanced everywhere far beyond the borders—then I must say they are completely stupid if they imagine that they can ever crush Germany. And especially if they imagine that they could possibly impress me in any way or could make me afraid. I know perfectly well that the battle is a very hard one, for that is probably just the difference between me and, let us say, a man like Churchill. Churchill said that we—the Reichsmarshal and I—had made whining speeches recently. I don't know if I hit someone right and left and then he says that is absolute defeatism, then one can have a good laugh.

Since 1939 I haven't felt like whining at all. Previously, I was of course very sad, because I had done everything to prevent the war. Recently Sven Hedin published a book in which he gratifyingly now quotes word for word my offer to the Poles which was conveyed at that time through the English. I must say that I really felt a chill when I read through this offer again recently, and I can only thank Providence that it has managed everything otherwise.

Then, too, from what I now know since then, because if at that time this offer had been accepted, then Danzig would be German, to be sure, but for the rest everything would have remained as it was. We would have devoted ourselves to our social tasks, we would have worked, we would have beautified our cities, we would have built dwelling settlements, we would have put our roads in order, we would have established schools, we would have built up a real National Socialist state.

And then, of course, we probably would have expended only very little for the Wehrmacht, and one day this storm would have broken loose from the East, would have passed over Poland, and, before we knew it, would have been a mere 150 kilometers east of Berlin. For that I thank the gentlemen who refused it then. At any rate, three years ago I could not yet guess that either. Three years ago I was sad about it, and therefore when the Polish campaign was at an end, I wanted to offer my hand once more in peace, which would have cost these enemies nothing, either. As you know, it was refused. Then I was forced to conduct another campaign, and still another.

In the year '40 I tried again to offer my hand in peace once more. It was refused again. With that the case was settled for me, because every offer of peace was interpreted by these enemies as weakness, and therefore really turned to the disadvantage of the German Reich. Thus it would have been disloyal to try anything like it again. It was clear to me—now only one thing matters—a state or a world must now fall. Either ours or the other. We shall not fall; consequently the other must fall.

You will recall, my old comrades-in-arms, how often, in exactly the same way, I held out my hand to the internal enemies. How long I wooed them. What pains I took with them. What didn't I do to bring about a sensible understanding! Only after it was useless did I decide to take those measures which are the only ones that can be carried out in this world when reason is stilled. And to this we owe our Brown Shirts, to this we owe our Storm Troops, to this we owe our S. S. Elite Guards; and at last the hour came when we were rid of these enemies, and rid of them how? And this struggle within was perhaps only seemingly easier than the external struggle. In reality the men who led the struggle within were once the fighters externally, too, and they are today the fighters both within and without; because, my Party Comrades, one thing certainly is a reason for us National Socialists to be rather proud.

When bourgeois Germany was fighting, the Germany composed of Marxists and Bourgeois and Center, then, to take but one example, two deputies of the Reichstag were killed in the course of the war out of more than two million dead. The National Socialist Reichstag has thus far already left 39, I believe, on the field of battle, out of a total, however, of hardly 350,000. Yes, that is certainly a different ratio, and when I calculate the ratio of the party comrades

I can say that wherever my Storm Troopers or Party comrades or where the Elite Guards stand at the front, they do their duty in exemplary fashion.

Here too the Reich has changed. And above all, they fight also with a different comprehension: they know the fate that would be in store for us if the other world should be victorious. Because we know this fate and know it well, there is not even the slightest thought there of any compromise. When the gentlemen say from time to time that there is another peace offer from us, they do it only to make up for something to their own people. From us there will be no more peace offers at all. The last one was made in the year 1940.

There is only one thing left, that is to fight. Just as I said at a certain moment to the internal enemies: 'It is not possible to come to an understanding with you peacefully; you want force, so now you'll get it.' And these internal enemies have been taken care of.

Another power, too, which was very strong in Germany has meanwhile been able to learn from experience that the National Socialist prophecies are no mere phrases; it is the main power to which we owe all this misfortune—international Jewry. You will recall the Reichstag session at which I declared: 'If Judaism imagines by any chance that it can bring about an international world war for the extermination of the European races, the result will not be the extermination of the European races, but the extermination of the Jews in Europe.'

They have always derided me as a prophet. Today countless numbers of those who laughed at that time, laugh no longer. Those who are still laughing now, also will perhaps laugh no longer after a while … will spread beyond Europe and over the whole world. International Jewry will be recognized in all its demoniac peril. We National Socialists will see to that. This peril is recognized in Europe, and country after country is adopting our legislation. Thus today we see in this vast struggle only one single possibility; it is that of complete success, and there now remains only the question of whether there are any reasons at all to doubt this success.

If we follow our enemies' propaganda, then I must say that it is to be compared with the quotation: 'Rejoicing to heaven, depressed unto death.' The slightest success anywhere and they literally turn somersaults for joy. They have already destroyed us. Then the page turns and they are again completely cast down, and are again depressed. I need point to only one such example:

If you read the Russian communiqués since June 22, you will read the following every day: 'Fighting of unimportant character' or maybe 'of important character.' 'We have shot down three times as many German planes.' 'The amount of sunken tonnage is already greater than the entire naval tonnage, greater than all types of German tonnage before the war.' They have so many of us missing that they amount to more divisions than we can ever muster. But above all, they are always fighting in the same place. Here and there they then say modestly, after 14 days, 'We have evacuated a city.' But in general they have been fighting since June 22 in the same place, always successfully; we are constantly being beaten back, and in this continued retreat we have slowly come to the Caucasus. I say 'slowly'!

I should say that for my enemies, not for our soldiers. For the speed with which our soldiers have now traversed territory is gigantic. Also what was traversed this year is vast and historically unique. Now I do not always do things just as the others want them done. I consider what the others probably believe, and then do the opposite on principle. So if Mr. Stalin expected that we would attack in the center, I did not want to attack in the center, not only because Mr. Stalin probably believed I would, but because I didn't care about it anymore at all. But I wanted to come to the Volga, to a definite place, to a definite city. It accidentally bears the name of Stalin himself, but do not think that I went after it on that account.

Indeed, it could have an altogether different name. But only because it is an important point, that is, there 30 million tons of traffic can be cut off, including about nine million of oil shipments. There all the wheat pours in from those enormous territories of the Ukraine, of the Kuban territory, then to be transported to the North. There the manganese ore was forwarded. A gigantic terminal was there; I wanted to take it. And do you know, we're modest: that is, we have it; there are only a couple of very small places left there.

Now the others say: Why aren't you fighting there? Because I don't want to make a second Verdun but would rather do it with very small shock units. Time plays no part here. No ships come up the Volga any more—that is the decisive thing.

They have also reproached us, asking why it took us so long at Sevastopol? Because there, too, we did not want to cause an enormous mass murder. Blood is flowing as it is—more than enough. But Sevastopol fell into our hands, and the Crimea fell into our hands. We have reached goal after goal, stubbornly, persistently.

And if the enemy, on his part, makes preparations to attack, don't think I want to forestall him there, but at the same moment we let him attack also. Because then defense still is less expensive. Then just let him attack; he'll bleed to death that way, and thus far we have always taken care of the situation anyhow.

At any rate, the Russians are not at the Pyrenees or before Seville; that, you see, is the same distance as for us to be in Stalingrad today, or on the Terek, let us say; but we are there; that can really not be disputed. That is a fact, after all.

Naturally, when nothing else will do any more, they also say it's a mistake. Then they suddenly turn around and say: 'It is absolutely a mistake for the Germans to have gone to Kirkenes, or to have gone to Narvik, or now perhaps to Stalingrad—what do they expect to do in Stalingrad? For Stalingrad is a capital mistake, a strategic mistake.' We will just wait and see whether that was a strategic mistake.

We see already from present indications whether it was such a great mistake that we took possession of the Ukraine, that we—uh—took possession of the ore region of Krivoi Rog, that we got our hands on the manganese ores, or whether it was really such a great mistake that we got hold of the Kuban region, the greatest granary in the entire world, perhaps, whether it was a mistake that we, and I can safely say this, have now destroyed or got into our own possession four-fifths or five sixths of all their refineries, that we alone either have right in our hands or have completely shut off, a production of nine or 10 million tons of oil, and we have further cut off the transportation of perhaps seven, eight or nine million tons over the Volga.

And everything else which we plan to do there, whether all that was really so mistaken, we will soon see. Now I really don't know, if the English had managed to take the Ruhr valley, or the Rhine too, and then the Danube and the Elbe also, it would be—and then also Upper Silesia, that is just about the same as the Donetz region, and that is the Krivoi Rog ore region, and the Kerch ore region, if they had also after that got a portion of our petroleum sources, and if they had also got the Magdeburg Stock Exchange, whether they would still say to us: 'We made a great mistake to take those things away from the Germans.' That was an extraordinary mistake.

If they impose on their own very narrow-minded, provincial people with that, uh, there may be a certain number of them who will believe it. And yet everyone does not seem to believe it, because you do hear press comments which sometimes become very angry, and say that they should leave off with that stuff now. If they say that in order to impose on us, well, I must say then that they are really confusing present-day Germany with a Germany which may have existed numberless centuries ago. They cannot convince present-day Germany of that, and if they perhaps wish to convince me, then I can only say: 'I have never yet made my strategic plans according to the receipts or ideas of others.'

It was certainly a mistake that we made the break through France that time and went around from above; but still it paid. In any case the English have been marched out of France, even after they had been in France for a rather long period of time. I believe that they had frequently boasted that they had 1,000,000 men there, and we don't want to forget one thing, my Party comrades men and women—they were then very near to our borders. They had 13 divisions there, and besides that more than 130 French divisions, approximately another 24 Belgian divisions, and also 20 Dutch divisions, all right at our borders on our Rhine, and where are they now?

And so if they say today that they are for all I care advancing somewhere or other in the desert, well, they have already made advances several times before, and they moved back again. The decisive thing in this war is who will deal the final blow, and you can be sure of it that we will be the one.

It's the same way with their production. Of course they manufacture everything and above all, they make everything much better than we do. Whenever the Americans come out with something new—for instance, I read a few days ago that they have constructed a new submarine—as I read it, I thought at once: 'Surely, that will again be the best.' And I was right. It said below: 'The best submarine in the world, with by far the most ingenious construction. It is fastest in submerging and the best in every respect.' Compared to them we are real amateurs in the construction of submarines.

My German racial comrades, we are not asleep. Our builders are not asleep either, and let me point out only one thing to you. During the winter of 1939-1940 a certain Mr. Churchill stated: 'The submarine danger is eliminated. Hitler is finished.' He has destroyed two, three, five submarines daily. At that time, he destroyed more than we even had then. He was exhausted. He had destroyed nothing, for then I again committed a very great error. The error was. I had only a very small number of our submarines fighting and held back the greater part of the submarines in order to train the crews for the new submarines being launched.

At that time the number of submarines operating against the enemy was so small that I am today still ashamed even to speak of it. Most of them, more than nine-tenths, remained at that time in our home waters and trained the new crews, for we started mass production at a certain moment. They just can't comprehend anything but American mass production. They always act as if they are the only ones who understand it. We understand it just as well. When they say they build so-and-so many warships per year—well, when they count all their corvettes and all their uh-uh-herring boats and the rest of them and stick a cannon on them, they act as if this ... If we figure in everything, then I guarantee that we are not building fewer ships, only I think we are building more useful ships than they.

In any case, this has again been proved. We have now at any rate sunk more than 24,000,000 tons, that is almost 12,000,000 tons more than in the World War, in all. And the number of U-boats is considerably greater than the number of U-boats in the World War. And we go on building and constructing and do it with all types of weapons, and when the gentlemen over there say they have wonderful new weapons, then they haven't the slightest idea whether we haven't possessed a better one for a long time already.

And here it is my practice only to put out a new weapon when the old one actually is of no use any more. Why disclose new weapons in advance? So far this policy has always proved right. We have always had worse weapons. Of course. We have worse soldiers. That is perfectly clear. We had a far worse organization. Who should be surprised at that? If one compares the organization of such geniuses as, uh, Churchill and Duff Cooper and Chamberlain and all those people, or even Roosevelt, this organizer of...

If one compares these people, then, from the point of view of organization, we, of course, were nothing but blunderers. That is true. But so far we have achieved one success after another. Regarding internal affairs, my dear party members, it has been just the same. We were also continuously worse in internal affairs. We have been incompetent. We have had no qualifications at all, but one day we came into power. That was decisive.

It is understandable that one may not expect a new success perhaps each week in a struggle of world-wide extent such as we are confronted with today. That is an impossibility. Neither is it at all decisive. Decisive is the fact of gradually occupying the positions which must (eventually) crush the enemy, of holding and of fortifying those positions in such a way that they cannot be retaken. You may well believe me: Whatever we once conquer, we actually hold on to so tightly that in this way at least no one else can dislodge us from wherever we gain a foothold. You may rely upon that.

Furthermore, this war has been actually far extended to our allies, the Italians, the Rumanians, the Hungarians, and the Finns and all the other European peoples, such as the Slovaks, the Croats, and the Spaniards, to the volunteers, the Nordic volunteers. A real world power has been achieved, a world power which also has been suffering continuous defeats.

Since the beginning of Japan's entrance, there were nothing but failures; everything the Japanese did was a mistake. But when the mistakes are added up, the result amounts to something brilliant. Just in this process they have acquired about 98 percent of the rubber production of the Americans. In this process they have acquired the greatest tin production in the world. They have acquired an enormous wool production. They have acquired gigantic oil wells.

So if you do nothing but make such mistakes and this is the result, you can be quite content.

And conversely, the others have carried out none but the right operations. Full of genius, brave, heroic, calculating, they have indeed great generals, MacArthur, or Wavell, or one of those very great ones such as the world has never seen before. In between, the generals are already writing books about the other generals. And in spite of this, in spite of all this, the people who had no generals have first of all got a bit further in the war than those blessed with generals. Thus I can speak on the very day that brings us indeed the recollection of the greatest collapse of our movement, a collapse which at that time really seemed to mean also ... the end of the Party. All our enemies (were certain) that National Socialism was dead.

Now on that very day I can only say: For us National Socialists, recollection must now mean an enormous strengthening, a strengthening for the defiance of all dangers, never to waver and never to yield, to meet every emergency with courage and to hold out even when the enemy is ever so menacing.

There one must really adopt Luther's precept: 'And if the world were full of devils, we must and shall succeed.' Precisely today we look into the future with so much confidence, now that we have survived the past winter, a winter which indeed we could not comprehend in all its terrible danger when I spoke to you a year ago. Today I look into the future quite differently.

That time somehow, many even leading and thinking people were oppressed by the recollection of Napoleon's fate in 1812, and the winter of 1812 was exactly 50 percent as cold as the winter we put behind us last year.

This year we are indeed prepared quite differently. Here too, this or that person may lack this or that and miss it, and so on. Then, in any case, we turn to the nation with the request that it might give this, perhaps, or give that or contribute something else besides, but for this winter we are equipped differently. That I can say. Even if it should prove to be exactly as severe as the last one, all that happened to us this last winter will no longer happen to us this time.

And I have already said once: A great philosopher declared that when a blow does not knock a man down it only makes him stronger. There I can only say: The blow which did not knock us down last winter has only made us stronger.

It is immaterial where the front may be, Germany will always ward off the blows and will always advance and attack, and I do not doubt for a moment that our method will be successful in the end.

If today Roosevelt conducts his attack upon North Africa with the remark that he must protect it from Germany and from Italy and so on, we need not waste words regarding these lies by this one scoundrel. He is beyond a doubt the chief gangster of this whole outfit we are confronting. But one may be sure that Mr. Roosevelt will certainly not have the last decisive word in the matter.

We shall prepare all our blows thoroughly, as we always have done, and they always have been struck at the right time. And not one blow which the others intended to strike against us so far has been successful. There was once triumphant shouting, when the first Englishman landed at Boulogne and then advanced. Six months later this triumphant shouting was over. Events turned out differently. They will be different again, today.

You may have full confidence. Your leaders and the Armed Forces will do all that must be done and all that can be done. And I have unyielding confidence that, above all, the German homeland is behind the leadership and the armed forces, and that the entire National Socialist Party particularly, stands behind me as one pledged community. That which distinguishes our period from the last one is the fact that at that time the people did not stand behind the Kaiser while behind me stands one of the most splendid organizations that has ever been built up on this earth, and that organization represents the German people.

Vice versa, however, what distinguishes the present time from then is the fact that at the head of this people there is no one who would ever, in critical times, go to a foreign land, but that at the head of this people is someone who has never known anything but struggle, and who has always known but one principle: 'Strike, strike and strike again.'

Another factor distinguishes the present German people from those of that time. Then there was a leadership that had no roots in the people, because in the last analysis it had been a …

Today we are in the midst of the completion of what grew out of the war of that time, because when I returned from the war I brought the front experience into the homeland with me. From that front experience I built up at home my National Socialist community of the people.

Today the National Socialist community of the people goes to the front, and you will perceive from many things how this Wehrmacht grows more National Socialistic from month to month, how it constantly takes on more and more the imprint of the new Germany, how all privileges, class prejudices and so on are being eliminated more and more, how the German community of the people here becomes more dominant from month to month, and how at the end of this war the German community of the peoples will have proved itself most in this very war, perhaps. This distinguishes the present Germany from the Germany of that time.

And to this we owe, on the one hand, immeasurable heroism at the front, a heroism of millions of iron soldiers, known and unknown, a heroism of tens and tens of thousands of brave officers who today feel themselves more and more in closer community with their men. They have in part already sprung from these men. They have in fact put aside all obstacles.

Just as in the Party, anyone can reach any position, if he is capable, and just as even the poorest child of our nation can aspire to any government position, even the highest one, ever since this Party has been in power, so also it is exactly the same in the armed forces. And as a matter of fact not only theoretically, or merely as an exception which occurs here and there, but in actual practice. Today there are the Oak Leaf wearers, the subordinate officers or the corporals. Knight's Crosses were given to numerous iron men who have distinguished themselves heroically. Countless officers have advanced from the ranks. We are building an army in the midst of the war which is unparalleled in the history of the world.

And back home, on the other hand, a people is working, and here I must also state before the German homeland what I have already stated in the Reichstag: In the year 1917-1918, the munitions factories went on strike. Today we have overtime, and work and more work. Today the German worker in the homeland knows that he is forging the weapons for his comrades out there (on the front).

What is being accomplished here in the country and in the city, by men, and above all also by innumerable women, is tremendous. It is also quite clear, that there is one sphere in which we cannot compete with our opponents.

Just as at one time the Party was the poorest among the parties existing then, and members solely on the strength of idealism, so it is natural today also that the German nation is perhaps the poorest of all the nations in the world as regards its gold reserves.

We have no gold. But what we have, is a capacity for work which is a real value. What we have, is sacred industriousness and a sacred will, and that is in the long run a 1000 times more decisive than gold in such a struggle for life or death.

For of what value are their gold treasure to the Americans now, except for having dentures made, or something of that sort? But of what real benefit is that to them? If they had 10 synthetic rubber factories instead of gold, that would be worth more to them, than the entire gold reserves, which they have accumulated. I have had other things built for me. In any case we didn't go into this war with gold, but with the provisions necessary for the conduct of this struggle, and anyway we Germans do not have a tank which is without rubber treads but the English do have them today.

We will see the war through as to material, and better than ever now. For they have put us in possession of regions providing raw materials which are necessary in order to be able to last through this war under all circumstances. And if anyone says, 'Well, why don't we see more of it?' Well, it's very simple.

Don't get the idea, my internationalist gentlemen, or whatever I might call them—that we just stood there in front of the destroyed railroad bridges or the destroyed railroad tracks or the destroyed water power works or the destroyed ore mines or the destroyed coal mines and, our hands in our pockets, and contemplated them at length. During these years work has been done, and how! And now it is gradually beginning to pay dividends.

And when next year comes, only then will the fruits of this labor really appear, and I can say here with pride that the party has proven itself mightily in this, and innumerable brave party comrades are out there and are organizing with a handful of persons as experienced National Socialist district leaders or local group leaders, and are organizing gigantic regions, and opening up making these regions available for our efficient industrial economy, our nourishment, and in fact, in a broader sense, for the feeding and maintenance of all of Europe.

For this is not a war which Germany is waging for herself alone, but it is a war which is actually being fought for Europe, and only thus is it understandable that such willing—that so many willing volunteers have been found from the North to the South who are in part fighting in our own ranks and in part are arrayed as independent armies or independent detachments with us in this most tremendous front of world history. Therefore, it is our irrevocable determination that the peace which will come sometime, because it has to come, will really be a peace for Europe, and one without the sponsorship of those men with the fine instinct for idealism and material values.

For what instinct Mr. Eden has for idealism we don't know. He has never proved nor shown it anywhere. His behavior doesn't indicate it either. Above all, the culture of his own country is by no means such as could possibly impress us. Of the man across the ocean I shall not speak at all in this connection. So their instinct for idealism is surely smaller than our instinct, for we probably have given more idealism to the world than the society which is in care of Mr. Eden. The same applies to the people who are our allies; some of them look back upon cultures compared to which the culture of the English Island kingdom is really an infinitely young, not to say infantile, culture.

Regarding the material values, however, I believe them; they do have a fine instinct for them. But we have it too. The only difference is that we want to make sure under all circumstances that the material values of Europe will in the future benefit the European peoples also, and not an extra-continental little international finance's clique—that is our unshakable and inexorable resolve. The people of Europe are not fighting afterwards so that a few people of fine instincts should again come along and begin to plunder mankind and make millions of unemployed, just in order to fill their vaults.

We had good reason to depart from the gold standard. We wished to eliminate in that way one of the conditions for this kind of economic conception and economic management. And this is very certain: Europe will come out of this war much healthier economically than before, because a large part of this continent, which was hitherto organized against Europe, has now been placed in the service of the European nations.

If now I am told: 'Ha, ha, so you want to transplant the Dutch,' well, I want to transplant no one, but I believe there will be many people who will be happy to get a bit of earth of their own and to be able to work on it, and not to have to drudge and slave, as is partly the case in this over-settled and overfilled continent. Above all, however, they will be happy if they themselves get the benefit of the reward for this work, if their peoples benefit, if their working men and women benefit, and not a vault which is in the Bank of London, if you wish, or in New York. I believe therefore that at the end of this war there will be collapse of this domination of gold, externally also, and thereby the collapse of this whole society which is to blame for this war.

We all know the mission of the National Socialist Party. I need not repeat it today. We started out to fight this enemy in the interior, we have done everything to find our way through this world by our work. What have we not organized! They have laughed at us, yes, always they have laughed whenever we had new substitute materials (Ersatzstoffe). We have not done this for pleasure. We were compelled to do it. Either millions of men would have not had work and unbelievable values would not have been produced or we would have had to adapt ourselves to new methods. We have done it.

By performing this work we have simultaneously identified ourselves with peace, for by doing so we wanted to maintain peace. Our enemies have rejected it. National Socialism was a fighting phenomenon, for many, many years in the interior, and today it has to be one against the exterior, there against the surroundings against the outside world. And so I expect each party member, above all, to be a representative of this faith in victory and in success, with the utmost fanaticism just as he was during the period of the struggle. Today it is much easier than it was then. Today, I must admire each of my party members of that party, all these many small men, who believed in the unknown nameless soldier of the world war, these men, who followed me at that time, who placed their lives at my disposal, so many of them who gave their lives, not only here, at that time in the old Reich, but also in the Eastern territories and in the Sudeten country, and also elsewhere in other countries.

I must admire them. They followed me at that time, when I was an absolutely unknown man. Today there appears before all of us together, the powerful, great Reich, and above all, what stands before us is the 'to be or not to be' of our entire nation. Every National Socialist who believed in me then, can still be a fanatic for the fight on the outside today, and he must struggle through to the same fanatical consistency that we possessed at that time. We have opponents. There can be no mercy allowed them. On the contrary there is only one possibility: Either we fall or our opponent falls. We are aware of that, and we are men enough to look this knowledge straight in the eye, cool as ice. And that differentiates me from those gentlemen, in London and America; if I require much of the German soldier, I am demanding no more than I myself have always been ready to do also.

If I demand this of the German nation, I am calling for no more work than I myself do also. If I require overtime work of many of them, I don't even know what overtime is in my life. That I don't know at all. For every individual has the good fortune, perhaps, that at a certain time he can leave his work and then he is free. My work is the fate of the Reich. I can't leave it. It pursues me day and night, because I have stepped to the head of the nation.

In these days of gray misery and wretchedness and grief and ruin, any leave at all for me would be ridiculous. After all, what is leave? A leave is always in my eyes one single thing; it is Germany, it is my people, it is its future, it is the future of its children. Therefore I demand from no one else... therefore I demand from no one else more than I demand of myself, or what I am ready to do myself.

I know that my old party comrades now actually constitute the core of this movement, and that in memory of the first blood sacrifices offered by us at that time, they are already leading the nation with their example, and that they are being joined by all the hundreds and hundreds of thousands, the millions, of National Socialist functionaries, of party members, and those who belong to the organizations associated with us are marching with us, all of our men of the Storm Troops, of the S. S. (Schutzstaffel or Elite Guard), are marching with us, the men of our Labor Front are marching with us, the men of the Reich Labor Service; in short, the entire National Socialist German people.

The wonderful thing today is that we are not isolated like people crying in the wilderness, as was once the case with me, but that every word which we address to the nation today, finds a thousand-fold echo.

And if the foe believes that he can soften us by any means whatsoever, he is mistaken. Nor can he influence me to turn aside from an objective. The hour strikes and then I hit back and I do it with interest and compound interest.

You will remember the long period when we had to be legal as party comrades. How often did my old party comrades come to me and say: 'Führer' and they also called me 'Chief' in those days, or they said 'Adolf Hitler, why may we not strike back? Why do we have to take that?' For years I had to force them repeatedly to be legal.

I had to expel party members from the movement with an aching heart, because they believed that they could not obey this command, year after year, until finally the hour came, when I could call upon them.

And that's the way it is today too. Sometimes for months at a time I have to let things go somewhere. But don't you believe that that does not make my heart feel like bursting with anger when I hear about these air-raids. You know that I did not do those things for months. I did not allow a single bomb to be dropped in the city of Paris. Before we attacked Warsaw, I called for surrender five times, I was always refused. I asked that at least the women and children be sent out. Not even the officer bearing the flag of truce was received. Everything was refused, and only then did I decide to do what is permitted by every law of war.

When the English started to drop their bombs, I waited three and a half months and did nothing. At that time there were many who said: 'Why don't we answer them? Why isn't ...? We were already strong enough to do it. I waited, thinking simply that perhaps they would still come to their senses.

It turned out differently. Believe me, it is no different today. I am taking note of it all. They will still learn over there that the German spirit of invention has not rested, and they will get such an answer that it will leave them dizzy.

And I have already had to tell the people several times before that the fact that now and then I don't talk for a long time, does not mean that I have lost my voice, but it means only that I did not consider it expedient to talk. Today it is the same. Why should I talk a lot now? Today in the last analysis it is the front that talks. Everything else is babble. Only on the rarest occasion would I like to take the floor, because what the front says is so forceful, it is such a unique language, that it is binding upon every single German anyway. Whoever reads the army communiqué or the Wehrmacht communiqué and then does not make himself fanatically one with his people, after hearing over and over again this tremendous number of heroic deeds, cannot be helped by talk either.

And as for the outside world—well, I do not speak for the benefit of the outside world at all. I have never yet spoken for the outside world. I speak only for my German people. Whether people abroad listen to me or not is entirely immaterial to me.

If Mr. Roosevelt says he does not hear my speeches, I can only say, I do not talk for Mr. Roosevelt's benefit at all. Once he accosted me by telegraph, and thereupon I gave him my reply, as a polite man would, but otherwise I do not talk to Mr. Roosevelt at all. I now talk through that instrument through which one can only talk today and that instrument talks loud and distinct enough.

Otherwise I talk only on the rarest occasions to the movement and to my own German people, and all that I can say for such a speech is only one thing. Think incessantly, men and women, only of the fact that this war will decide the 'To be or not to be' of our people. And if you understand that, each one of your thoughts and each of your actions will be one single prayer for our Germany.

Quit India Speech

Mahatma Gandhi

Gowalia Tank Maidan (8 August 1942)

Mohandas Karamchand Gandhi, often called Mahatma Gandhi, was an Indian lawyer, politician, social activist and writer, popularly known as the Father of the Nation. The leader of the Indian nationalist movement against British rule, he became renowned worldwide for his non-violent methods of protest.

The 'Quit India Speech' was delivered by Gandhi on the eve of the Quit India movement on 8 August 1942.

Before you discuss the resolution, let me place before you one or two things, I want you to understand two things very clearly and to consider them from the same point of view from which I am placing them before you. I ask you to consider it from my point of view, because if you approve of it, you will be enjoined to carry out all I say. It will be a great responsibility. There are people who ask me whether I am the same man that I was in 1920, or whether there has been any change in me. You are right in asking that question.

Let me, however, hasten to assure that I am the same Gandhi as I was in 1920. I have not changed in any fundamental respect. I attach the same importance to non-violence that I did then. If at all, my emphasis on it has grown stronger. There is no real contradiction between the present resolution and my previous writings and utterances.

Occasions like the present do not occur in everybody's and but rarely in anybody's life. I want you to know and feel that there is nothing but purest Ahimsa in all that I am saying and doing today.

Violence is key. The draft resolution of the Working Committee is based on Ahimsa, the contemplated struggle similarly has its roots in Ahimsa. If, therefore, there is any among you who has lost faith in Ahimsa or is wearied of it, let him not vote for this resolution. Let me explain my position clearly. God has vouchsafed to me a priceless gift in the weapon of Ahimsa. I and my Ahimsa are on our trail today. If in the present crisis, when the earth is being scorched by the flames of Himsa and crying for deliverance, I failed to make use of the God given talent, God will not forgive me and I shall be judged unworthy of the great gift. I must act now. I may not hesitate and merely look on, when Russia and China are threatened.

Ours is not a drive for power, but purely a non-violent fight for India's independence. In a violent struggle, a successful general has been often known to effect a military coup and to set up a dictatorship. But under the Congress scheme of things, essentially non-violent as it is, there can be no room for dictatorship. A non-violent soldier of freedom will covet nothing for himself, he fights only for the freedom of his country. The Congress is unconcerned as to who will rule, when freedom is attained. The power, when it comes, will belong to the people of India, and it will be for them to decide to whom it placed in the entrusted. May be that the reins will be placed in the hands of the Parsis, for instance—as I would love to see happen—or they may be handed to some others whose names are not heard in the Congress today. It will not be for you then to object saying, 'This community is microscopic. That party did not play its due part in the freedom's struggle; why should it have all the power?' Ever since its inception the Congress has kept itself meticulously free of the communal taint. It has thought always in terms of the whole nation and has acted accordingly…I know how imperfect our Ahimsa is and how far away we are still from the ideal, but in Ahimsa there is no final failure or defeat. I have faith, therefore, that if, in spite of our shortcomings, the big thing does happen, it will be because God wanted to help us by crowning with success our silent, unremitting Sadhana for the last 22 years.

I believe that in the history of the world, there has not been a more genuinely democratic struggle for freedom than ours. I read Carlyle's French Revolution while I was in prison, and Pandit

Jawaharlal has told me something about the Russian revolution. But it is my conviction that inasmuch as these struggles were fought with the weapon of violence they failed to realise the democratic ideal. In the democracy which I have envisaged, a democracy established by non-violence, there will be equal freedom for all. Everybody will be his own master. It is to join a struggle for such democracy that I invite you today. Once you realise this you will forget the differences between the Hindus and Muslims, and think of yourselves as Indians only, engaged in the common struggle for independence.

Then, there is the question of your attitude towards the British. I have noticed that there is hatred towards the British among the people. The people say they are disgusted with their behaviour. The people make no distinction between British imperialism and the British people. To them, the two are one. This hatred would even make them welcome the Japanese. It is most dangerous. It means that they will exchange one slavery for another. We must get rid of this feeling. Our quarrel is not with the British people, we fight their imperialism. The proposal for the withdrawal of British power did not come out of anger. It came to enable India to play its due part at the present critical juncture It is not a happy position for a big country like India to be merely helping with money and material obtained willy-nilly from her while the United Nations are conducting the war. We cannot evoke the true spirit of sacrifice and valour, so long as we are not free. I know the British Government will not be able to withhold freedom from us, when we have made enough self-sacrifice. We must, therefore, purge ourselves of hatred. Speaking for myself, I can say that I have never felt any hatred. As a matter of fact, I feel myself to be a greater friend of the British now than ever before. One reason is that they are today in distress. My very friendship, therefore, demands that I should try to save them from their mistakes. As I view the situation, they are on the brink of an abyss. It, therefore, becomes my duty to warn them of their danger even though it may, for the time being, anger them to the point of cutting off the friendly hand that is stretched out to help them. People may laugh, nevertheless that is my claim. At a time when I may have to launch the biggest struggle of my life, I may not harbor hatred against anybody.

'Nation, Rise Up, and Let the Storm Break Loose'

Joseph Goebbels

Berlin (18 February 1943)

Joseph Goebbels was the Minister of Public Enlightenment and Propaganda for the German Third Reich under Hitler's leadership. A skilful propagandist and orator, he ensured a favourable opinion of the Nazis amongst the German people. Following Hitler's suicide, Goebbels and his wife poisoned their six children and committed suicide.

Goebbels was arguably the second-most eloquent Nazi orator after Hitler, drawing large crowds for his orations. This long speech delivered at the end of the Battle of Stalingrad is Goebbels's most famous speech.

Only three weeks ago I stood in this place to read the Führer's proclamation on the 10th anniversary of the seizure of power, and to speak to you and to the German people. The crisis we now face on the Eastern Front was at its height. In the midst of the hard misfortunes the nation faced in the battle on the Volga, we gathered together in a mass meeting on the 30th of January to display our unity, our unanimity and our strong will to overcome the difficulties we faced in the fourth year of the war.

It was a moving experience for me, and probably also for all of you, to be bound by radio with the last heroic fighters in Stalingrad during our powerful meeting here in the Sport Palace. They radioed to us that they had heard the Führer's proclamation, and perhaps for the last time in their lives joined us in raising their hands to sing the national anthems. What an example German soldiers have set in this great age! And what an obligation it puts on us all, particularly the entire German homeland! Stalingrad was and is fate's great alarm call to the German nation! A nation that has the strength to survive and overcome such a disaster, even to draw from it additional strength, is unbeatable. In my speech to you and the German people, I shall remember the heroes of Stalingrad, who put me and all of us under a deep obligation.

I do not know how many millions of people are listening to me over the radio tonight, at home and at the front. I want to speak to all of you from the depths of my heart to the depths of yours. I believe that the entire German people has a passionate interest in what I have to say tonight. I will therefore speak with holy seriousness and openness, as the hour demands. The German people, raised, educated and disciplined by National Socialism, can bear the whole truth. It knows the gravity of the situation, and its leadership can therefore demand the necessary hard measures, yes even the hardest measures. We Germans are armed against weakness and uncertainty. The blows and misfortunes of the war only give us additional strength, firm resolve, and a spiritual and fighting will to overcome all difficulties and obstacles with revolutionary élan.

Now is not the time to ask how it all happened. That can wait until later, when the German people and the whole world will learn the full truth about the misfortune of the past weeks, and its deep and fateful significance. The heroic sacrifices of heroism of our soldiers in Stalingrad has had vast historical significance for the whole Eastern Front. It was not in vain. The future will make clear why.

When I jump over the past to look ahead, I do it intentionally. The time is short! There is no time for fruitless debates. We must act, immediately, thoroughly, and decisively, as has always been the National Socialist way.

The movement has from its beginning acted in that way to master the many crises it faced and overcame. The National Socialist state also acted decisively when faced by a threat. We are not like the ostrich that sticks its head in the sand so as not to see danger. We are brave enough to look danger in the face, to coolly and ruthlessly take its measure, then act decisively with our heads held high. Both as a movement and as a nation, we have always been at our best when we needed fanatic, determined wills to overcome and eliminate danger, or a strength of character sufficient to overcome every obstacle, or bitter determination to reach our goal, or an iron heart capable of withstanding every internal and external battle. So it will be today. My task is to give you an unvarnished picture of the situation, and to draw the hard conclusions that will guide the actions of the German government, but also of the German people.

We face a serious military challenge in the East. The crisis is at the moment a broad one, similar but not identical in many ways to that of the previous winter. Later we will discuss the causes. Now, we must accept things as they are and discover and apply the ways and means to turn things again in our favor. There is no point in disputing the seriousness of the situation. I do not want to give you a false impression of the situation that could lead to false conclusions, perhaps giving the German people a false sense of security that is altogether inappropriate in the present situation.

The storm raging against our venerable continent from the steppes this winter overshadows all previous human and historical experience. The German army and its allies are the only possible defense. In his proclamation on 30 January, the Führer asked in a grave and compelling way what would have become of Germany and Europe if, on 30 January 1933, a bourgeois or democratic government had taken power instead of the National Socialists! What dangers would have followed, faster than we could then have suspected, and what powers of defense would we have had to meet them? 10 years of National Socialism have been enough to make plain to the German people the seriousness of the danger posed by Bolshevism from the East. Now one can understand why we spoke so often of the fight against Bolshevism at our Nuremberg party rallies. We raised our voices in warning to our German people and the world, hoping to awaken Western humanity from the paralysis of will and spirit into which it had fallen. We tried to open their eyes to the horrible danger from Eastern Bolshevism, which had subjected a nation of nearly 200 million people to the terror of the Jews and was preparing an aggressive war against Europe.

When the Führer ordered the army to attack the East on 22 June 1941, we all knew that this would be the decisive battle of this great struggle. We knew the dangers and difficulties. But we also knew that dangers and difficulties always grow over time, they never diminish. It was two minutes before midnight. Waiting any longer could easily have led to the destruction of the Reich and a total Bolshevization of the European continent.

It is understandable that, as a result of broad concealment and misleading actions by the Bolshevist government, we did not properly evaluate the Soviet Union's war potential. Only now do we see its true scale. That is why the battle our soldiers face in the East exceeds in its hardness, dangers and difficulties all human imagining. It demands our full national strength. This is a threat to the Reich and to the European continent that casts all previous dangers into the shadows. If we fail, we will have failed our historic mission. Everything we have built and done in the past pales in the face of this gigantic task that the German army directly and the German people less directly face.

I speak first to the world, and proclaim three theses regarding our fight against the Bolshevist danger in the East.

This first thesis: Were the German army not in a position to break the danger from the East, the Reich would fall to Bolshevism, and all Europe shortly afterwards.

Second: The German army, the German people and their allies alone have the strength to save Europe from this threat.

Third: Danger faces us. We must act quickly and decisively, or it will be too late.

I turn to the first thesis. Bolshevism has always proclaimed its goal openly: to bring revolution not only to Europe, but to the entire world, and plunge it into Bolshevist chaos. This goal has been evident from the beginning of the Bolshevist Soviet Union, and has been the ideological and practical goal of the Kremlin's policies. Clearly, the nearer Stalin and the other Soviet leaders believe they are to realizing their world-destroying objectives, the more they attempt to hide and conceal them. We cannot be fooled. We are not like those timid souls who wait like the hypnotized rabbit until the serpent devours them. We prefer to recognize the danger in good time and take effective action. We see through not only the ideology of Bolshevism, but also its practice, for we had great success with that in our domestic struggles. The Kremlin cannot deceive us. We had 14 years of our struggle for power, and 10 years thereafter, to unmask its intentions and its infamous deceptions.

The goal of Bolshevism is Jewish world revolution. They want to bring chaos to the Reich and Europe, using the resulting hopelessness and desperation to establish their international, Bolshevist-concealed capitalist tyranny.

I do not need to say what that would mean for the German people. A Bolshevization of the Reich would mean the liquidation of our entire intelligentsia and leadership, and the descent of our workers into Bolshevist-Jewish slavery. In Moscow, they find workers for forced labor battalions in the Siberian tundra, as the Führer said in his proclamation on 30 January. The revolt of the steppes is readying itself at the front, and the storm from the East that breaks against our lines daily in increasing strength is nothing other than a repetition of the historical devastation that has so often in the past endangered our part of the world.

That is a direct threat to the existence of every European power. No one should believe that Bolshevism would stop at the borders of the Reich, were it to be victorious. The goal of its aggressive policies and wars is the Bolshevization of every land and people in the world. In the face of such undeniable intentions, we are not impressed by paper declarations from the Kremlin or guarantees from London or Washington. We know that we are dealing in the East with an infernal political devilishness that does not recognize the norms governing relations between people and nations. When for example the English Lord Beaverbrook says that Europe must be given over to the Soviets or when the leading American Jewish journalist Brown cynically adds that a Bolshevization of Europe might solve all of the continent's problems, we know what they have in mind. The European powers are facing the most critical question. The West is in danger. It makes no difference whether or not their governments and intellectuals realize it or not.

The German people, in any event, is unwilling to bow to this danger. Behind the oncoming Soviet divisions we see the Jewish liquidation commandos, and behind them terror, the specter of mass starvation and complete anarchy. International Jewry is the devilish ferment of decomposition that finds cynical satisfaction in plunging the world into the deepest chaos and destroying ancient cultures that it played no role in building.

We also know our historic responsibility. 2000 years of Western civilization are in danger. One cannot overestimate the danger. It is indicative that when one names it as it is, International Jewry throughout the world protests loudly. Things have gone so far in Europe that one cannot call a danger a danger when it is caused by the Jews.

That does not stop us from drawing the necessary conclusions. That is what we did in our earlier domestic battles. The democratic Jewry of the 'Berliner Tageblatt' and the 'Vossischen Zeitung' served communist Jewry by minimizing and downplaying a growing danger, and by lulling our threatened people to sleep and reducing their ability to resist. We could see, if the danger were not overcome, the specter of hunger, misery, and forced labor by millions of Germans. We could see our venerable part of the world collapse, and bury in its ruins the ancient inheritance of the West. That is the danger we face today.

My second thesis: Only the German Reich and its allies are in the position to resist this danger. The European nations, including England, believe that they are strong enough to resist effectively the Bolshevization of Europe, should it come to that. This belief is childish and not even worth refuting. If the strongest military force in the world is not able to break the threat of Bolshevism, who else could do it? The neutral European nations have neither the potential nor the military means nor the spiritual strength to provide even the least resistance to Bolshevism. Bolshevism's robotic divisions would roll over them within a few days. In the capitals of the mid-sized and smaller European states, they console themselves with the idea that one must be spiritually armed against Bolshevism (laughter). That reminds us of the statements by bourgeois parties in 1932, who thought they could fight and win the battle against communism with spiritual weapons. That was too stupid even then to be worth refuting. Eastern Bolshevism is not only a doctrine of terrorism, it is also the practice of terrorism. It strives for its goals with an infernal thoroughness, using every resource at its disposal, regardless of the welfare, prosperity or peace of the peoples it ruthlessly oppresses. What would England and America do if, in the worst case, Europe fell into Bolshevism's arms? Will London perhaps persuade Bolshevism to stop at the English Channel? I have already said that Bolshevism has its foreign legions in the form of communist parties in every democratic nation. None of these states can think it is immune to domestic Bolshevism. In a recent by-election for the House of Commons, the independent, that is communist, candidate got 10,741 of the 22,371 votes cast. This was in a district that had formerly been a conservative stronghold. Within a short time, 10,000 voters, nearly half, had been lost to the communists.

That is proof that the Bolshevist danger exists in England too, and that it will not go away simply because it is ignored. We place no faith in any territorial promises that the Soviet Union may make. Bolshevism set ideological as well as military boundaries, which poses a danger to every nation. The world no longer has the choice between falling back into its old fragmentation or accepting a new order for Europe under Axis leadership. The only choice now is between living under Axis protection or in a Bolshevist Europe.

I am firmly convinced that the lamenting lords and archbishops in London have not the slightest intention of resisting the Bolshevist danger that would result were the Soviet army to enter Europe. Jewry has so deeply infected the Anglo-Saxon states both spiritually and politically that they are no longer have the ability to see the danger. It conceals itself as Bolshevism in the Soviet Union, and plutocratic-capitalism in the Anglo-Saxon states. The Jewish race is an expert at mimicry. They put their host peoples to sleep, paralyzing their defensive abilities. Our insight into the matter led us to the early realization that cooperation between international plutocracy and international Bolshevism was not a contradiction, but rather a sign of deep commonalities. The hand of the pseudo-civilized Jewry of Western Europe shakes the hand of the Jewry of the Eastern ghettos over Germany. Europe is in deadly danger.

I do not flatter myself into believing that my remarks will influence public opinion in the neutral, much less the enemy, states. That is also not my goal or intention. I know that, given our problems on the Eastern Front, the English press tomorrow will furiously attack me with the accusation that I have made the first peace feelers. That is certainly not so. No one in Germany thinks any longer of a cowardly compromise. The entire people thinks only of a hard war. As a spokesman for the leading nation of the continent, however, I claim the right to call a danger a danger if it threatens not threatens not only our own land, but our entire continent. We National Socialists have the duty to sound the alarm against International Jewry's attempt to plunge the European continent into chaos, and to warn that Jewry has in Bolshevism a terroristic military power whose danger cannot be overestimated.

My third thesis is that the danger is immediate. The paralysis of the Western European democracies before their deadliest threat is frightening. International Jewry is doing all it can to encourage such paralysis. During our struggle for power in Germany, Jewish newspapers tried to conceal the danger, until National Socialism awakened the people. It is just the same today in other nations. Jewry once again reveals itself as the incarnation of evil, as the plastic demon of decay and the bearer of an international culture-destroying chaos.

This explains, by the way, our consistent Jewish policies. We see Jewry as a direct threat to every nation. We do not care what other peoples do about the danger. What we do to defend ourselves is our own business, however, and we will not tolerate objections from others. Jewry is a contagious infection. Enemy nations may raise hypocritical protests against our measures against Jewry and cry crocodile tears, but that will not stop us from doing that which is necessary. Germany, in any event, has no intention of bowing before this threat, but rather intends to take the most radical measures, if necessary, in good time.

The military challenges of the Reich in the East are at the center of everything. The war of mechanized robots against Germany and Europe has reached its high point. In resisting the grave and direct threat with its weapons, the German people and its Axis allies are fulfilling in the truest sense of the word a European mission. Our courageous and just battle against this worldwide plague will not be hindered by the worldwide outcry of International Jewry. It can and must end only with victory.

The tragic battle of Stalingrad is a symbol of heroic, manly resistance to the revolt of the steppes. It has not only a military, but also an intellectual and spiritual significance for the German people. Here for the first time our eyes have been opened to the true nature of the war. We want no more false hopes and illusions. We want bravely to look the facts in the face, however hard and dreadful they may be. The history of our party and our state has proven that a danger recognized is a danger defeated. Our coming hard battles in the East will be under the sign of this heroic resistance. It will require previously undreamed of efforts by our soldiers and our weapons. A merciless war is raging in the East. The Führer was right when he said that in the end there will not be winners and losers, but the living and the dead.

The German nation knows that. Its healthy instincts have led it through the daily confusion of intellectual and spiritual difficulties. We know today that the Blitzkrieg in Poland and the campaign in the West have only limited significance to the battle in the East. The German nation is fighting for everything it has. We know that the German people are defending their holiest possessions: their families, women and children, the beautiful and untouched countryside, their cities and villages, their two thousand year old culture, everything indeed that makes life worth living.

Bolshevism of course has not the slightest appreciation for our nation's treasures, and would take no heed of them whatsoever if it came to that. It did not do so even for its own people. The Soviet Union over the last 25 years built up Bolshevism's military potential to an unimaginable degree, and one we falsely evaluated. Terrorist Jewry had 200 million people to serve it in Russia. It cynically used its methods on to create out of the stolid toughness of the Russian people a grave danger for the civilized nations of Europe. A whole nation in the East was driven to battle. Men, women, and even children are employed not only in armaments factories, but in the war itself. 200 million live under the terror of the GPU, partially captives of a devilish viewpoint, partially of absolute stupidity. The masses of tanks we have faced on the Eastern Front are the result of

25 years of social misfortune and misery of the Bolshevist people. We have to respond with similar measures if we do not want to give up the game as lost.

My firm conviction is that we cannot overcome the Bolshevist danger unless we use equivalent, though not identical, methods. The German people face the gravest demand of the war, namely of finding the determination to use all our resources to protect everything we have and everything we will need in the future.

Total war is the demand of the hour. We must put an end to the bourgeois attitude that we have also seen in this war: Wash my back, but don't get me wet! The danger facing us is enormous. The efforts we take to meet it must be just as enormous. The time has come to remove the kid gloves and use our fists. We can no longer make only partial and careless use of the war potential at home and in the significant parts of Europe that we control. We must use our full resources, as quickly and thoroughly as it is organizationally and practically possible. Unnecessary concern is wholly out of place. The future of Europe hangs on our success in the East. We are ready to defend it. The German people are shedding their most valuable national blood in this battle. The rest of Europe should at least work to support us. There are many serious voices in Europe that have already realized this. Others still resist. That cannot influence us. If danger faced them alone, we could view their reluctance as literary nonsense of no significance. But the danger faces us all, and we must all do our share. Those who today do not understand that will thank us tomorrow on bended knees that we courageously and firmly took on the task.

It bothers us not in the least that our enemies abroad claim that our total war measures resemble those of Bolshevism. They claim hypocritically that that means there is no need to fight Bolshevism. The question here is not one of method, but of the goal, namely eliminating the danger. The question is not whether the methods are good or bad, but whether they are successful. The National Socialist government is ready to use every means. We do not care if anyone objects. We are not willing to weaken Germany's war potential by measures that maintain a high, almost peacetime standard of living for a certain class, thereby endangering our war effort. We are voluntarily giving up a significant part of our living standard to increase our war effort as quickly and completely as possible. This is not an end in itself, but rather a means to an end. Our social standard of living will be even higher after the war. We do not need to imitate Bolshevist methods, because we have better people and leaders, which gives us a great advantage. But things have shown that we must do much more than we have done so far to turn the war in the East decisively in our favor.

As countless letters from the homeland and the front have shown, by the way, the entire German people agrees. Everyone knows that if we lose, all will be destroyed. The people and leadership are determined to take the most radical measures. The broad working masses of our people are not unhappy because the government is too ruthless. If anything, they are unhappy because it is too considerate. Ask anyone in Germany, and he will say: The most radical is just radical enough, and the most total is just total enough to gain victory.

The total war effort has become a matter of the entire German people. No one has any excuse for ignoring its demands. A storm of applause greeted my call on 30 January for total war. I can therefore assure you that the leadership's measures are in full agreement with the desires of the German people at home and at the front. The people are willing to bear any burden, even the heaviest, to make any sacrifice, if it leads to the great goal of victory.

This naturally assumes that the burdens are shared equally. We cannot tolerate a situation in which most people carry the burden of the war, while a small, passive portion attempts to escape its burdens and responsibilities. The measures we have taken, and the ones we will yet take, will be characterized by the spirit of National Socialist justice. We pay no heed to class or standing. Rich and poor, high and low must share the burdens equally. Everyone must do his duty in this grave hour, whether by choice or otherwise. We know this has the full support of the people. We would rather do too much rather than too little to achieve victory. No war in history has ever been lost because of too many soldiers or weapons. Many, however, have been lost because the opposite was true.

It is time to get the slackers moving. They must be shaken out of their comfortable ease. We cannot wait until they come to their senses. That might be too late. The alarm must sound throughout the nation. Millions of hands must get to work throughout the country. The measures we have taken, and the ones we will now take, and which I shall discuss later in this speech, are critical for our whole public and private life. The individual may have to make great sacrifices, but they are tiny when compared to the sacrifices he would have to make if his refusal brought down on us the greatest national disaster. It is better to operate at the right time than to wait until the disease has taken root. One may not complain to the doctor or sue him for bodily injury. He cuts not to kill, but to save the patient's life.

Again let me say that the heavier the sacrifices the German people must make, the more urgent it is that they be fairly shared. The people want it that way. No one resists even the heaviest burdens of war. But it angers people when a few always try to escape the burdens. The National Socialist government has both the moral and political duty to oppose such attempts, if necessary with draconian penalties. Leniency here would be completely out of place, leading in time to a confusion in the people's emotions and attitudes that would be a grave danger to our public morale.

We are therefore compelled to adopt a series of measures that are not essential for the war effort in themselves, but seem necessary to maintain moral at home and at the front. The optics of the war, that is, how things outwardly appear, is of decisive importance in this fourth year of war. In view of the superhuman sacrifices that the front makes each day, it has a basic right to expect that no one at home claims the right to ignore the war and its demands. And not only the front demands this, but the overwhelming part of the homeland. The industrious have a right to expect that if they work 10 or 12 or 14 hours a day, a lazy person does not stand next to them who thinks them foolish. The homeland must stay pure and intact in its entirety. Nothing may disturb the picture.

There are therefore a series of measures that take account of the war's optics. We have ordered, for example, the closing of bars and night clubs. I cannot imagine that people who are doing their duty for the war effort still have the energy to stay out late into the night in such places. I can only conclude that they are not taking their responsibilities seriously. We have closed these establishments because they began to offend us, and because they disturb the image of the war. We have nothing against amusements as such. After the war we will happily go by the rule 'Live and let live.' But during a war, the slogan must be 'Fight and let fight!'

We have also closed luxury restaurants that demand far more resources than is reasonable. It may be that an occasional person thinks that, even during war, his stomach is the most important thing. We cannot pay him any heed. At the front everyone from the simple soldier to the general field marshal eats from the field kitchen. I do not believe that it is asking too much to insist that we in the homeland pay heed to at least the basic laws of community thinking. We can become gourmets once again when the war is over. Right now, we have more important things to do than worry about our stomachs.

Countless luxury stores have also been closed. They often offended the buying public. There was generally nothing to buy, unless perhaps one paid here and there with butter or eggs instead of money. What good do shops do that no longer have anything to sell, but only use electricity, heating, and human labor that is lacking everywhere else, particularly in the armaments industry.

It is no excuse to say that keeping some of these shops open gives a lovely impression to foreigners. Foreigners will be impressed only by a German victory! (Stormy applause). Everyone will want to be our friend if we win the war. But if we lose, we will be able to count our friends on the fingers of one hand. We have put an end to such illusions. We want to put these people standing in empty shops to useful work in the war economy. This process is already in motion, and will be completed by 15 March. It is of course a major transformation in our entire economic life. We are following a plan. We do not want to accuse anyone unjustly or open them to complaints and accusations from every side. We are only doing what is necessary. But we are doing it quickly and thoroughly.

We would rather wear worn clothing for a few years than have our people wear rags for a few centuries. What good are fashion salons today? They only use light, heat and workers. They will reappear when the war is over. What good are beauty shops that encourage a cult of beauty and take enormous time and energy? In peace they are wonderful, but a waste of time during war. Our women and girls will be able to greet our victorious returning soldiers without their peacetime finery.

Government offices will work faster and less bureaucratically. It does not leave a good impression when the office closes on the dot after eight hours. The people are not there for the offices, the offices are there for the people. One has to work until the work is done. That is a requirement of the war. If the Führer can do that, so can his paid employees. If there is not enough work to fill the extended hours, 10 or 20 or 30 percent of the workers can be transferred to war production and replace other men for service at the front. That applies to all offices in the homeland. That by itself may make the work in some offices go more quickly and easily. We must learn from the war to operate quickly, not only thoroughly. The soldier at the front does not have weeks to think things over, to pass his thoughts up the line or let them sit in dusty files. He must act immediately or lose his life. In the homeland we do not lose our lives if we work slowly, but we do endanger the life of our people.

Everyone must learn to pay heed to war morale, and pay attention to the just demands of working and fighting people. We are not spoilsports, but neither will we tolerate those who hinder our efforts.

It is, for example, intolerable that certain men and women stay for weeks in spas and trade rumors, taking places away from soldiers on leave or from workers who are entitled to a vacation after a year of hard work. That is intolerable, and we have put an end to it. The war is not a time for amusement. Until it is over, we take our deepest satisfaction in work and battle. Those who do not understand that by themselves must be taught to understand it, and forced if need be. The harshest measures may be needed.

It does not look good, for example, when we devote enormous propaganda to the theme: 'Wheels must roll for victory!' with the result that people avoid unnecessary travel only to see unemployed pleasure-seekers find more room for themselves in the trains.

The railroad serves to transport war goods and travelers on war business. Only those who need a rest from hard work deserve a vacation. The Führer has not had a day of vacation since the war began. Since the first man of the country takes his duty so seriously and responsibly, it must be expected that every citizen will follow his example.

On the other hand, the government is doing all it can to give working people the relaxation they need in these trying times. Theaters, movie houses, and music halls remain in full operation. The radio is working to expand and improve its programming. We have no intention of inflicting a gray winter mood on our people. That which serves the people and keeps up its fighting and working strength is good and essential to the war effort. We want to eliminate the opposite. To balance the measures I have already discussed, I have therefore ordered that cultural and spiritual establishments that serve the people not be decreased, but increased. As long as they aid rather than harm the war effort, they must be supported by the government. That applies to sports as well. Sports are not only for particular circles today, but a matter for the entire people. Military exemptions for athletes are out of place. The purpose of sports is to steel the body, certainly with the goal of using it appropriately in time of the people's greatest need.

The front shares our desires. The entire German people agrees passionately. It is no longer willing to put up with efforts that only waste time and resources. It will not put up with complicated questionnaires on every possible issue. It does not want to worry about a thousand minor matters that may have been important in peace, but are entirely unimportant during war. It also does not need to be constantly reminded of its duty by references to the great sacrifices of our soldiers at Stalingrad. It knows what it has to do. It wants everyone, high and low, rich and poor, to share a spartan life style. The Führer gives us all an example, one that must be followed by everyone. He knows only work and care. We do not want to leave it all to him, but rather we want to take that part of it from him which we are able to bear.

The present day has a remarkable resemblance for every genuine National Socialist to the period of struggle. We have always acted in the same way. We were with the people through thick and thin, and that is why the people followed us. We have always carried our burdens together with the people, and therefore they did not seem heavy to us, but rather light. The people want to be led. Never in history has the people failed a brave and determined leadership a critical hour.

Let me say a few words in this regard about practical measures in our total war effort that we have already taken.

The problem is freeing soldiers for the front, and freeing workers for the armaments industry. These are the primary goals, even at the cost of our standard of social life. This does not mean a permanent decline in our standard of living. It is only a means to reaching an end, that of total war.

As part of this campaign, hundreds of thousands of military exemptions have been canceled. These exemptions were given because we did not have enough skilled labor to fill the positions that would have been left open by revoking them. The reason for our current measures is to mobilize the necessary workers. That is why we have appealed to men not working in the war economy, and to women who were not working at all. They will not and cannot ignore our call. The duty for women to work is broad. That does not however mean that only those included in the law have to work. Anyone is welcome. The more who join the war effort, the more soldiers we can free for the front.

Our enemies maintain that German women are not able to replace men in the war economy. That may be true for certain fields of heavy labor. But I am convinced that the German woman is determined to fill the spot left by the man leaving for the front, and to do so as soon as possible. We do not need to point out Bolshevism's example. For years, millions of the best German women have been working successfully in war production, and they wait impatiently to be joined and assisted by others. All those who join in the work are only giving the proper thanks to those at the front. Hundreds of thousands have already joined, and hundreds of thousands more will join. We hope soon to free up armies of workers who will in turn free up armies of fighting front soldiers.

I would think little of German women if I believed that they do not want to listen to my appeal. They will not seek to follow the letter of the law, or to slip through its loopholes. They few who may try will not succeed. We will not accept a doctor's excuse. Nor will we accept the alibi that one must help one's husband or relative or good friend as a way of avoiding work. We will respond appropriately. The few who may attempt it will only lose the respect of those around them. The people will despise them. No one expects a woman lacking the requisite physical strength to go to work in a tank factory. There are however numerous jobs in war production that do not demand great physical strength, and which a woman can do even if she comes from the better circles. No one is too good to work, and we all have the choice to give up what we have, or to lose everything.

It is also time to ask women with household help if they really need it. One can take care of the house and children oneself, freeing the servant for other tasks, or leave the house and children in care of the servant or the NSV [the party welfare organization], and go to work oneself. Life may not be as pleasant as it is during peace. But we are not at peace, we are at war. We can be comfortable after we have won the war. Now we must sacrifice our comforts to gain victory.

Soldiers' wives surely understand this. They know it is their duty to their husbands to support them by doing work that is important to the war effort. That is true above all in agriculture. The wives of farmers must set a good example. Both men and women must be sure that no one does less during war than they did in peace; more work must instead be done in every area.

One may not, by the way, make the mistake of leaving everything to the government. The government can only set the broad guidelines. To give life to those guidelines is the job of working people, under the inspiring leadership of the party. Fast action is essential.

One must go beyond the legal requirements. 'Volunteer!' is the slogan. As Gauleiter of Berlin, I appeal here above all to my fellow Berliners. They have given enough good examples of noble behavior and bravery during the war such that they will not fail here. Their practical behavior and good cheer even during war have earned them a good name throughout the world. This good name must be maintained and strengthened! If I appeal to my fellow Berliners to do some important work quickly, thoroughly, and without complaint, I know they will all obey. We do not want to complain about the difficulties of the day or grump to one another. Rather we want to behave not only like Berliners, but like Germans, by getting to work, acting, seizing the initiative and doing something, not leaving it to someone else.

What German woman would want to ignore my appeal on behalf of those fighting at the front? Who would want to put personal comfort above national duty? Who in view of the serious threat we face would want to consider his private needs instead of the requirements of the war?

I reject with contempt the enemy's claim that we are imitating Bolshevism. We do not want to imitate Bolshevism, we want to defeat it, with whatever means are necessary. The German woman will best understand what I mean, for she has long known that the war our men are fighting today above all is a war to protect her children. Her holiest possession is guarded by our people's most valuable blood. The German woman must spontaneously proclaim her solidarity with her fighting men. She had better join the ranks of millions of workers in the homeland's army, and do it tomorrow rather than the day after tomorrow. A river of readiness must flow through the German people. I expect that countless women and above all men who are not doing essential war work will report to the authorities. He who gives quickly gives twice as much.

Our general economy is consolidating. That particularly affects the insurance and banking systems, the tax system, newspapers and magazines that are not essential for the war effort, and nonessential party and government activities, and also requires a further simplification of our life style.

I know that many of our people are making great sacrifices. I understand their sacrifices, and the government is trying to keep them to the necessary minimum. But some must remain, and must be borne. When the war is over, we will build up that which we now are eliminating, more generously and more beautifully, and the state will lend its hand.

I energetically reject the charge that our measures will eliminate the middle class or result in a monopoly economy. The middle class will regain its economic and social position after the war.

The current measures are necessary for the war effort. They aim not at a structural transformation of the economy, but merely at winning the war as quickly as possible.

I do not dispute the fact that these measures will cause worry in the coming weeks. They will give us breathing room. We are laying the groundwork for the coming summer, without paying heed to the threats and boasting of the enemy. I am happy to reveal this plan for victory to the German people. They not only accept these measures, they have demanded them, demanded them more strongly than ever before during the war. The people want action! It is time for it! We must use our time to prepare for coming surprises.

I turn now to the entire German people, and particularly to the party, as the leader of the totalization of our domestic war effort. This is not the first major task you have faced. You will bring the usual revolutionary élan to bear on it. You will deal with the laziness and indolence that may occasionally show up. The government has issued general regulations, and will issue further ones in coming weeks. The minor issues not dealt with in these regulations must be taken care of by the people, under the party's leadership. One moral law stands above everything for each of us: to do nothing that harms the war effort, and to do everything that brings victory nearer.

In past years, we have often recalled the example of Frederick the Great in newspapers and on the radio. We did not have the right to do so. For a while during the Third Silesian War, Frederick II had five million Prussians, according to Schlieffen, standing against 90 million enemies. In the second of seven hellish years he suffered a defeat that shook Prussia's foundations. He never had enough soldiers and weapons to fight without risking everything. His strategy was always one of improvisation. But his principle was to attack the enemy whenever it was possible. He suffered defeats, but that was not decisive. What was decisive is that the Great King remained unbroken, that he was unshaken by the changing fortunes of war, that his strong heart overcame every danger. At the end of seven years of war, he was 51 years old, he had no teeth, he suffered from gout, and was tortured by a thousand pains, but he stood above the devastated battlefield as the victor. How does our situation compare with his?! Let us show the same will and decisiveness as he, and when the time comes do as he did, remaining unshakable through all the twists of fate, and like him win the battle even under the most unfavorable circumstances. Let us never doubt our great cause.

I am firmly convinced that the German people have been deeply moved by the blow of fate at Stalingrad. It has looked into the face of hard and pitiless war. It knows now the awful truth, and is resolved to follow the Führer through thick and thin.

The English and American press in recent days has been writing at length about the attitude of the German people during this crisis. The English seem to think that they know the German people much better than we do, its own leadership. They give hypocritical advice on what we should do and not do. They believe that the German people today is the same as the German people of November 1918 that fell victim to their persuasive wiles. I do not need to disprove their assertions. That will come from the fighting and working German people.

To make the truth plain, however, my German comrades, I want to ask you a series of questions. I want you to answer them to the best of your knowledge, according to your conscience. When my audience cheered on 30 January, the English press reported the next day that it was all a propaganda show that did not represent the true opinion of the German people I have invited to today's meeting a cross-section of the German people in the best sense of the word. In front of me are rows of wounded German soldiers from the Eastern Front, missing legs and arms, with wounded bodies, those who have lost their sight, those who have come with nurses, men in the blush of youth who stand with crutches. Among them are 50 who bear the Knight's Cross with Oak Leaves, shining examples of our fighting front. Behind them are armaments workers from Berlin tank factories. Behind them are party officials, soldiers from the fighting army, doctors, scientists, artists, engineers and architects, teachers, officials and employees from offices, proud representatives of every area of our intellectual life that even in the midst of war produce miracles of human genius. Throughout the Sportpalast I see thousands of German women. The youth is here, as are the aged. No class, no occupation, no age remained uninvited. I can rightly say that before me is gathered a representative sample of the German population, both from the homeland and the front. Is that true? Yes or no? You, my hearers, at this moment represent the whole nation. I wish to ask you ten questions that you will answer for the German people throughout the world, but especially for our enemies, who are listening to us on the radio. The English maintain that the German people has lost faith in victory.

I ask you: Do you believe with the Führer and us in the final total victory of the German people?

I ask you: Are you resolved to follow the Führer through thick and thin to victory, and are you willing to accept the heaviest personal burdens?

Second, The English say that the German people are tired of fighting.

I ask you: Are you ready to follow the Führer as the phalanx of the homeland, standing behind the fighting army and to wage war with wild determination through all the turns of fate until victory is ours?

Third: The English maintain that the German people have no desire any longer to accept the government's growing demands for war work.

I ask you: Are you and the German people willing to work, if the Führer orders, 10, 12 and if necessary 14 hours a day and to give everything for victory?

Fourth: The English maintain that the German people is resisting the government's total war measures. It does not want total war, but capitulation! I ask you: Do you want total war? If necessary, do you want a war more total and radical than anything that we can even imagine today?

Fifth: The English maintain that the German people have lost faith in the Führer.

I ask you: Is your confidence in the Führer greater, more faithful and more unshakable than ever before? Are you absolutely and completely ready to follow him wherever he goes and do all that is necessary to bring the war to a victorious end?

Sixth, I ask you: Are you ready from now on to give your full strength to provide the Eastern Front with the men and munitions it needs to give Bolshevism the death blow?

Seventh, I ask you: Do you take a holy oath to the front that the homeland stands firm behind them, and that you will give them everything they need to win the victory?

Eighth, I ask you: Do you, especially you women, want the government to do all it can to encourage German women to put their full strength at work to support the war effort, and to release men for the front whenever possible, thereby helping the men at the front?

Ninth, I ask you: Do you approve, if necessary, the most radical measures against a small group of shirkers and black marketeers who pretend there is peace in the middle of war and use the need of the nation for their own selfish purposes? Do you agree that those who harm the war effort should lose their heads?

Tenth and lastly, I ask you: Do you agree that above all in war, according to the National Socialist Party platform, the same rights and duties should apply to all, that the homeland should bear the heavy burdens of the war together, and that the burdens should be shared equally between high and low and rich and poor?

I have asked; you have given me your answers. You are part of the people, and your answers are those of the German people. You have told our enemies what they needed to hear so that they will have no illusions or false ideas.

Now, just as in the first hours of our rule and through the ten years that followed, we are bound firmly in brotherhood with the German people. The most powerful ally on earth, the people itself, stands behind us and is determined to follow the Führer, come what may. They will accept the heaviest burdens to gain victory. What power on earth can hinder us from reaching our goal. Now we must and will succeed! I stand before you not only as the spokesman of the government, but as the spokesman of the people. My old party friends are here around me, clothed with the high offices of the people and the government. Party comrade Speer sits next to me. The Führer has given him the great task of mobilizing the German armaments industry and supplying the front with all the weapons it needs. Party comrade Dr. Ley sits next to me. The Führer has charged him with the leadership of the German work force, with schooling and training them in untiring work for the war effort. We feel deeply indebted to our party comrade Sauckel, who has been charged by the Führer to bring hundreds of thousands of workers to the Reich to support our national economy, something the enemy cannot do. All the leaders of the party, the army, and government join with us as well.

We are all children of our people, forged together by this most critical hour of our national history. We promise you, we promise the front, we promise the Führer, that we will mold together the homeland into a force on which the Führer and his fighting soldiers can rely on absolutely and blindly. We pledge to do all in our life and work that is necessary for victory. We will fill our hearts with the political passion, with the ever-burning fire that blazed during the great struggles of the party and the state. Never during this war will we fall prey to the false and hypocritical objectivism that has brought the German nation so much misfortune over its history.

When the war began, we turned our eyes to the nation alone. That which serves its struggle for life is good and must be encouraged. What harms its struggle for life is bad and must be eliminated and cut out. With burning hearts and cool heads we will overcome the major problems of this phase of the war. We are on the way to final victory. That victory rests on our faith in the Führer.

This evening I once again remind the whole nation of its duty. The Führer expects us to do that which will throw all we have done in the past into the shadows. We do not want to fail him. As we are proud of him, he should be proud of us.

The great crises and upsets of national life show who the true men and women are. We have no right any longer to speak of the weaker sex, for both sexes are displaying the same determination and spiritual strength. The nation is ready for anything. The Führer has commanded, and we will follow him. In this hour of national reflection and contemplation, we believe firmly and unshakably in victory. We see it before us, we need only reach for it. We must resolve to subordinate everything to it. That is the duty of the hour. Let the slogan be:

Now, people rise up and let the storm break loose!

Address to the U.S. House of Representatives

Soong May-ling

Washington, D.C. (18 February 1943)

Soong May-ling was a renowned Chinese political figure and First Lady of the Republic of China from 1948 to 1975. The New Life Movement of 1934 was launched by her to check the rise of Communism in China. She also played an instrumental role in gaining much-needed American support during the Sino-Chinese War (1937-1945).

Till the late 1960s, her name used to often appear in the U.S. annual list of 10 Most Admired Women in the World. On 18 February 1943, May-ling delivered this address to the U.S. House of Representatives, becoming the first Chinese national and second women to address both houses of the U.S. Congress.

Mr. Speaker, Members of the Congress of the United States:

At any time, it would be a privilege for me to address Congress, more especially this present august body which will have so much to do in shaping the destiny of the world. In speaking to Congress I am literally speaking to the American people. The 77th Congress, as their representatives, fulfilled the obligations and responsibilities of its trust by declaring war on the aggressors.

That part of the duty of the people's representatives was discharged in 1941. The task now confronting you is to help win the war and to create and uphold a lasting peace which will justify the sacrifices and sufferings of the victims of aggression.

Before enlarging on this subject, I should like to tell you a little about my long and vividly interesting trip to your country from my own land, which has bled and borne unflinchingly the burden of war for more than five and a half years. I shall not dwell, however, upon the part China has played in our united effort to free mankind from brutality and violence. I shall try to convey to you, however imperfectly, the impressions gained during the trip.

First of all, I want to assure you that the American people have every right to be proud of their fighting men in so many parts of the world. I am particularly thinking of those of your boys in the far-flung, out-of-the-way stations and areas where life is attended by dreary drabness; this because their duty is not one of spectacular performance and they are not buoyed up by the excitement of battle. They are called upon, day after colorless day, to perform routine duties such as safeguarding defenses and preparing for possible enemy action.

It has been said, and I find it true from personal experience, that it is easier to risk one's life on the battlefield than it is to perform customary humble and humdrum duties which, however, are just as necessary to winning the war.

Some of your troops are stationed in isolated spots, quite out of reach of ordinary communications. Some of your boys have had to fly hundreds of hours over the sea from an improvised airfield in quests, often disappointingly fruitless, of enemy submarines. They, and others, have to stand the monotony of waiting, just waiting. But, as I told them, true patriotism lies in possessing the morale and physical stamina to perform faithfully and conscientiously the daily tasks so that in the sum total the strongest—the weakest link is the strongest. The trivial round, the common task , would furnish all we ought to ask.

Your soldiers have shown conclusively that they are able stoically to endure homesickness, the glaring dryness and scorching heat of the tropics, and keep themselves fit and in excellent fighting trim. They are amongst the unsung heroes of this war, and everything possible to lighten their tedium and buoy up their morale should be done. That sacred duty is yours.

The American Army is better fed than any army in the world. This does not mean, however, that they can live indefinitely on canned food without having the effects tell on them. These admittedly are but minor hardships of war, especially when we pause to consider that in many parts of the world starvation prevails. But peculiarly enough, oftentimes it is not the major problems of existence which irk a man's soul; it is rather the pin pricks, especially those incidental to a life of deadly sameness, with tempers frayed out and nervous systems torn to shreds.

The second impression of my trip is that America is not only the cauldron of democracy but the incubator of democratic principles. At some of the places I visited, I met the crews of your air bases. There, I found first generation Germans, Italians, Frenchmen, Poles, Czechoslovakians, and other nationals. Some of them had accents so thick, that if such a thing were possible, one could not cut them with a butter knife.

But there they were, all Americans, all devoted to the same ideals, all working for the same cause, and united by the same high purpose. No suspicion or rivalry existed between them. This increased my belief and faith that devotion to common principles eliminates differences in race and that identity of ideals is the strongest possible solvent of racial dissimilarities.

I have reached your country, therefore, with no misgivings, but with my belief that the American people are building and carrying out a true pattern of the nation conceived by your forebears, strengthened and confirmed.

You, as representatives of the American people, have before you the glorious opportunity of carrying on the pioneer work of your ancestors, beyond the frontiers of physical and geographical limitations. Their brawn and thews braved undauntedly almost unbelievable hardships to open up a new continent. The modern world lauds them for their vigor and intensity of purpose, and for their accomplishment.

You have today before you the immeasurably greater opportunity to implement these same ideals and to help bring about the liberation of man's spirit in every part of the world. In order to accomplish this purpose, we of the United Nations must now so prosecute the war that victory will be ours decisively and with all good speed.

Sun-Tzu, the well-known Chinese strategist, said: In order to win, 'know thyself' and '[know] thy enemy.' We have also the saying: 'It takes little effort to watch the other fellow carry the load.'

In spite of these teachings from a wise old past, which are shared by every nation, there has been a tendency to belittle the strength of our opponents. When Japan thrust total war on China in 1937, military experts of every nation did not give China even a ghost of a chance. But when Japan failed to bring China cringing to her knees as she vaunted, the world took solace in this phenomenon by declaring that they had overestimated Japan's military might.

Nevertheless, when the greedy flames of war inexorably spread in the Pacific following the perfidious attack on Pearl Harbor, Malaya, and lands in and around the China Sea, and one after another of these places fell, the pendulum swung to the other extreme. Doubts and fears lifted their ugly heads and the world began to think that the Japanese were Nietzschean Supermen—superior in intellect and physical prowess, a belief which the Gobineaus and the Houston Chamberlains and their apt pupils, the Nazi racists, had propounded about the Nordics.

Again, now the prevailing opinion seems to consider the defeat of the Japanese as of relative unimportance and that Hitler is our first concern. This is not borne out by actual facts, nor is it to the interests of the United Nations as a whole to allow Japan to continue, not only as a vital potential threat but as a waiting sword of Damocles, ready—but as a waiting sword of Damocles ready to descend at a moment's notice.

Let us not forget that Japan in her occupied areas today has greater resources at her command than Germany.

Let us not forget that the longer Japan is left in undisputed possessions of these resources, the stronger she must become. Each passing day takes more toll in lives of both Americans and Chinese.

Let us not forget that the Japanese are an intransigent people.

Let us not forget that during the first four and a half years of total aggression China has borne Japan's sadistic fury unaided and alone.

The victories won by the United States Navy at Midway and the Coral Seaare doubtless steps in the right direction, they are merely steps in the right direction—for the magnificent fight that was waged at Guadalcanal during the past six months attests to the fact that the defeat of the forces of evil, though long and arduous, will finally come to pass. For have we not on the side of righteousness and justice staunch allies in Great Britain, Russia, and other brave and indomitable peoples?

Meanwhile, the peril of the Japanese juggernaut remains. Japanese military might must be decimated as a fighting force before its threat to civilization is removed. When the 77th Congress declared war against Japan, Germany, and Italy, Congress, for the moment, had done its work. It now remains for you, the present representatives of the American people, to point the way to win the war, to help construct a world in which all peoples may henceforth live in harmony and peace.

May I not hope that it is the resolve of Congress to devote itself to the creation of the post-war world? To dedicate itself to the preparation for the brighter future that a stricken world so eagerly awaits?

We of this generation who are privileged to help make a better world for ourselves and for posterity should remember that, while we must not be visionary, we must have vision so that peace should not be punitive in spirit and should not be provincial or nationalistic or even continental in concept, but universal in scope and—and humanitarian in action, for modern science has so annihilated distance that what affects one people must of necessity affect all other peoples.

The term 'hands and feet' is often used in China to signify the relationship between brothers. Since international interdependence is now so universally recognized, can we not also say that all nations should become members of one corporate body?

The one hundred and sixty years of traditional friendship between our two great peoples, China and America, which has never been marred by misunderstandings, is unsurpassed in the annals of the world. I can also assure you that China is eager and ready to cooperate with you and other peoples to lay a true and lasting foundation for a sane and progressive world society which would make it impossible for any arrogant or predatory neighbor to plunge future generations into another orgy of blood.

In the past China has not computed the cost to her manpower in her fight against aggression, although she well realized that manpower is [the] real wealth of a nation; and it takes generations to grow it. She—She has been soberly conscious of her responsibilities and has not concerned herself with privileges and gains which she might have obtained through compromise of principles; nor will she demean herself and all she holds dear to the practice of the market place.

We in China, like you, want a better world, not for ourselves alone, but for all mankind, and we must have it. It is not enough, however, to proclaim our ideals or even to be convinced that we have them. In order to preserve, uphold, and maintain them, there are times when we should throw all we cherish into our effort to fulfill these ideals even at the risk of failure.

The teachings drawn from our late leader, Dr. Sun Yat-sen, have given our people the fortitude to carry on. From five and a half years of experience, we in China are convinced that it is the better part of wisdom not to accept failure ignominiously, but to risk it gloriously.

We shall have faith, that, at the writing of peace, America and our other gallant Allies will not be obtunded by the mirage of contingent reasons of expediency.

Man's mettle is tested both in adversity and in success. Twice is this true of the soul of a nation.

Order of the Day

Dwight D. Eisenhower

England (June 6 1944)

Dwight D. Eisenhower was the Supreme Commander of the Allied Forces during World War II, who orchestrated the successful Operation Overlord, which laid the foundations for Allied victory. A decorated army general, he later became the 34th President of the United States, serving two successful terms in the White House.

'Order of the Day' is Eisenhower's famous speech, delivered before Operation Overlord, famously called D-Day.

Soldiers, Sailors, and Airmen of the Allied Expeditionary Force,

You are about to embark upon the Great Crusade, toward which we have striven these many months.

The eyes of the world are upon you. The hopes and prayers of liberty-loving people everywhere march with you.

In company with our brave Allies and brothers-in-arms on other Fronts you will bring about the destruction of the German war machine, the elimination of Nazi tyranny over oppressed peoples of Europe, and security for ourselves in a free world.

Your task will not be an easy one. Your enemy is well trained, well equipped, and battle-hardened. He will fight savagely.

But this is the year 1944. Much has happened since the Nazi triumphs of 1940-41. The United Nations have inflicted upon the Germans great defeats, in open battle, man-to-man. Our air offensive has seriously reduced their strength in the air and their capacity to wage war on the ground. Our Home Fronts have given us an overwhelming superiority in weapons and munitions of war, and placed at our disposal great reserves of trained fighting men. The tide has turned. The free men of the world are marching together to victory.

I have full confidence in your courage, devotion to duty, and skill in battle. We will accept nothing less than full victory.

Good Luck! And let us all beseech the blessing of Almighty God upon this great and noble undertaking.

'Give Me Blood, and I Shall Give You Freedom'

Subhas Chandra Bose

Burma (4 July 1944)

Subhas Chandra Bose was a radical Indian nationalist who wanted to oppose British rule through a violent uprising. At first, a contemporary and ally of Mahatma Gandhi, his militant approach and siding with Axis powers distanced him from Gandhi and other leaders of the Indian National Congress (INC). However, he was given the respected prefix 'Netaji', meaning 'Respected Leader', by Indian soldiers of the Indian National Army and remained popular amongst the young radicals of the INC.

Netaji gave this famous speech to the Indian National Army in Burma (1944).

Friends! 12 months ago a new programme of total mobilisation or maximum sacrifice was placed before Indians in East Asia. Today I shall give you an account of our achievements during the past year and shall place before you are demands for the coming year. But, before I do so, I want you to realise once again what a golden opportunity you have for winning freedom. The British are engaged in a worldwide struggle and in the course of struggle they have suffered defeat after defeat on so many fronts. The enemy having being thus considerably weakened, our fight for liberty has become very much easier than it was five years ago. Such a rare and God-given opportunity comes once in a century for liberating our motherland from the British yoke.

I am so very hopeful and optimistic about the outcome of our struggle, because I do not rely merely on the efforts on three million Indian s in East Asia. There is a gigantic movement going on inside India and millions of our countrymen are prepared for maximum suffering and sacrifice in order to achieve liberty. Unfortunately, ever since the great fight of 1857, our countrymen are disarmed, whereas the enemy is armed to the teeth. Without arms and without a modern army it is impossible for a disarmed people to win freedom in this modern age. Through the grace of Providence and through the help of generous Nippon, it has become possible for Indians in East Asia are united to a man in the endeavour to win freedom and all the religious and other differences that the British tried to engineer inside India, simply do not exist in East Asia. Consequently, we have now an ideal combination of circumstances favoring the success of our struggle—and all that is wanted is that Indians should themselves come forward to pay the price of liberty. According to the programme of 'total mobilisation', I demanded of you men, money, and materials. Regarding men, I am glad to tell you that I have obtained sufficient recruits already. Recruits have come to us from every corner of east Asia-China, Japan, Indo-China, Philippines, Java, Borneo, Celebes, Sumatra, Malaya, Thailand, and Burma…

You must continue the mobilization of men, money and materials with greater vigour and energy, in particular, the problem of supplies and transport has to be solved satisfactorily.

We require more men and women of all categories for administration and reconstruction in liberated areas. We must be prepared for a situation in which the enemy will ruthlessly apply the scorched earth policy, before withdrawing from a particular area and will also force the civilian population to evacuate as was attempted in Burma.

The most important of all is the problem of sending reinforcements in men and in supplies to the fighting fronts. If we do not do so, we cannot hope to maintain our success at the fronts. Nor can we hope to penetrate deeper into India.

Those of you who will continue to work on the Home front should never forget that East Asia—and particularly Burma—form our base for the war of liberation. If this base is not strong, our fighting forces can never be victorious. Remember that this is a 'total war'—and not merely a war between two armies. That is why for a full one year I have been laying so much stress on 'total mobilisation' in the East.

There is another reason why I want you to look after the Home Front properly. During the coming months I and my colleagues on the war committee of the cabinet desire to devote our whole attention to the fighting front—and also to the task of working up the revolution in side India. Consequently, we want to be fully assured that the work at the base will go on smoothly and uninterruptedly even in our absence.

Friends, one year ago, when I made certain demands of you, I told you that if you give me 'total mobilization', I would give you a 'second front'. I have redeemed that pledge. The first phase of our campaign is over. Our victorious troops, fighting side by side with Nipponese troops, have pushed back the enemy and are not fighting bravely on the sacred soil of our dear motherland.

Grid up your loins for the task that now lies ahead. I had asked you for men, money and materials. I have got them in generous measure. Now I demand more of you. Men, money and materials have the motive power that will inspire us to brave deeds and heroic exploits.

It will be a fatal mistake for you to wish to live and see India free simply because victory is now within reach. No one here should have the desire to live to enjoy freedom. A long fight is s till in front of us. We should have but one desire today-the desire to die so that India may live—the desire to face a martyr's death, so that the path to freedom may be paved with the martyr's blood.

Friends! My comrades in the War of Liberation! Today I demand of you one thing, above all. I demand of you blood It is blood alone that can avenge the blood that the enemy has spilt. It is blood alone that can pay the price of freedom. Give me blood and I promise you freedom!

Address at the Fifth Nobel Anniversary Dinner

Albert Einstein

Hotel Astor, New York City (10 December 1945)

Albert Einstein was a German-born physicist considered the most influential physicist of the 20th century. He won the Nobel Prize in Physics in 1921 for his explanation of the photoelectric effect. His theory of general and special relativity had a major impact on the field of Physics.

Einstein was a pacifist who had to flee Nazi Germany due to his Jewish origins. Through this speech, Einstein urged those present to be conscientious in their use of weapons like the atomic bomb, and to take the path of peace and brotherhood.

Ladies and Gentlemen,

The Nobel Anniversary celebration takes on a special significance this year. Well after our deadly struggle of many years, we are at peace again; or what we are supposed to consider as peace. And it bears a still more significant significance for the physicists who, in one way or another, were connected with the construction of the use of the atomic bomb.

For these physicists find themselves in a position not unlike to that of Alfred Nobel himself. Alfred Nobel invented the most powerful explosive ever known up to his time, a means of destruction par excellence. In order to atone for this, in order to relieve his human conscience, he instituted his awards for the promotion of peace and for achievements of peace.

Today, the physicists who participated in forging the most formidable and dangerous weapon of all times are harassed by an equal feeling of responsibility, not to say guilt. We cannot desist from warning, and warning again, we cannot and should not slacken in our efforts to make the nations of the world, and especially their governments, aware of the unspeakable disaster they are certain to provoke unless they change their attitude toward each other and toward the task of shaping the future.

We helped in creating this new weapon in order to prevent the enemies of mankind from achieving it ahead of us, which, given the mentality of the Nazis, would have meant inconceivable destruction and the enslavement of the rest of the world.

We delivered this weapon into the hands of the Americans and the British people as trustees of the whole [of] mankind, as fighters for peace and liberty. But so far, we fail to see any guarantee of peace. We do not see any guarantee of the freedoms that were promised to the nations in the Atlantic Charter. The war is won, but the peace is not.

The great powers, united in fighting, are now divided over the peace settlements.

The world was promised freedom from fear, but in fact fear has increased tremendously since the termination of the war.

The world was promised freedom from want, but large parts of the world are faced with starvation while others are living in abundance.

The nations were promised liberation and justice but we have witnessed, and are witnessing even now, the sad spectacle of liberating armies firing into populations who want their independence and social equality, and supporting in those countries, by force of arms, such parties and personalities as appear to be most suited to serve vested interests.

Territorial questions and arguments of power, obsolete though they are, still prevail over the essential demands of common welfare and justice.

Allow me to be more specific about just one case, which is but a symptom of the general situation: the case of my own people, the Jewish people. As long as Nazi violence was unleashed only, or mainly, against the Jews, the rest of the world looked on passively; and even treaties and agreements were made with the patently criminal government of the Third Reich. Later, when Hitler was on the point of taking over Romania and Hungary, at the time when Maidanek and Oswiecim were in Allied hands, and the methods of the gas chambers were well known all over the world, all attempts to rescue the Romanian and Hungarian Jews came to naught because the doors of Palestine were closed to Jewish immigrants and no country could be found that would admit those forsaken people. They were left to perish like their brothers and sisters in the occupied countries.

We shall never forget the heroic efforts of the small countries, of the Scandinavian, the Dutch, the Swiss nations, and of individuals in the occupied parts of Europe who did all in their power to protect Jewish lives. We do not forget the humane attitude of the Soviet Union who was the only one among the big powers to open her doors to hundreds of thousands of Jews when the Nazi armies were advancing in Poland.

But after all that had happened, and was not prevented from happening—how is it today?

While in Europe territories are being distributed without any qualms about the wishes of the people concerned, the remainders of European Jewry, one-fifth of its prewar population, are again denied access to their haven in Palestine and left to hunger and cold and persisting hostility. There is no country, even today, that would be willing or able to offer them a place where they could live in peace and security. And the fact that many of them are still kept in degrading conditions of concentration camps by the Allies gives sufficient evidence of the shamefulness and hopelessness of the situation.

These people are forbidden to enter Palestine with reference to the principle of democracy, but actually the Western powers, in upholding the ban of the White Paper, are yielding to the threats and the external pressure of five vast and underpopulated Arab

States. It is sheer irony when the British Foreign Minister tells the poor lot of European Jews they should remain in Europe because their genius is needed there, and, on the other hand, advises them not to try to get at the head of the queue lest they might incur new hatred—hatred and persecution. Well, I am afraid they cannot help it; with their six million dead they have been pushed at the head of the queue, of the queue of Nazi victims, most against their will.

The picture of our postwar world is not bright. As far as we, the physicists, are concerned we are no politicians and it has never been our wish to meddle in politics. But we know a few things that the politicians do not know. And we feel the duty to speak up and to remind those responsible that: there is no escape into easy comforts; there is no distance ahead for proceeding little by little and delaying the necessary changes into an indefinite future; there is no time left for petty bargaining.

The situation calls for a courageous effort, for a radical change in our whole attitude in the entire political concept. May the spirit that prompted Alfred Nobel to create this great institution—the spirit of trust and confidence, of generosity and brotherhood among men, prevail in the minds of those upon whose decisions our destiny rests. Otherwise, human civilization will be doomed.

Response to Churchill's Criticism about Neutrality

Eamon de Valera

Ireland (16 May 1945)

Eamon de Valera was an Irish politician who served as taoiseach (Prime Minister of Ireland) for three terms and President from 1959 to 1973, for two terms. A commandant during the Easter Rising, he played an instrumental role in the freedom of Ireland. A strong anti-colonial leader and statesman, de Valera ensured Ireland's rise as a self-sufficient, sovereign state.

In this eloquent and level-headed speech, de Valera demonstrates his leadership skills and gives a balanced response to Churchill's criticism of Ireland's neutrality during World War II.

I have here before me the pencilled notes from which I broadcast to you on 3 September 1939. I had so many other things to do on that day that I could not find time to piece them together into a connected statement. From these notes I see that I said that noting the march of events your Government had decided its policy the previous spring, and had announced its decision to the world.

The aim of our policy, I said, would to keep our people out of the war. I reminded you of what I had said in the Dail that in our circumstances, with our history and our experience after the last war and with a part of our country still unjustly severed from us; no other policy was possible.

Certain newspapers have been very persistent in looking for my answer to Mr. Churchill's recent broadcast . I know the kind of answer I am expected to make. I know the answer that first springs to the lips of every man of Irish blood who heard or read that speech, no matter in what circumstances or in what part of the world he found himself.

I know the reply I would have given a quarter of a century ago. But I have deliberately decided that that is not the reply I shall make tonight. I shall strive not to be guilty of adding any fuel to the flames of hatred and passion which, if continued to be fed, promise to burn up whatever is left by the war of decent human feeling in Europe.

Allowances can be made for Mr. Churchill's statement, however unworthy, in the first flush of his victory. No such excuse could be found for me in this quieter atmosphere. There are, however some things which it is my duty to say, some things which it is essential to say. I shall try to say them as dispassionately as I can.

Mr. Churchill makes it clear that, in certain circumstances, he would have violated our neutrality and that he would justify his action by Britain's necessity. It seems strange to me that Mr. Churchill does not see that this, if accepted, would mean Britain's necessity would become a moral code and that when this necessity became sufficiently great, other people's rights were not to count.

It is quite true that other great Powers believe in this same code—in their own regard—and have behaved in accordance with it. That is precisely why we have the disastrous succession of wars—World War No. 1 and World War No. 2-and shall it be World War No. 3?

Surely Mr. Churchill must see that if his contention be admitted in our regard, a like justification can be framed for similar acts of aggression elsewhere and no small nation adjoining a great Power could ever hope to be permitted to go it own way in peace.

It is indeed fortunate that Britain's necessity did not reach the point when Mr. Churchill would have acted. All credit to him that he successfully resisted the temptation which, I have no doubt, may times assailed him in his difficulties and to which I freely admit many leaders might have easily succumbed. It is indeed; hard for the strong to be just to the weak, but acting justly always has its rewards.

By resisting his temptation in this instance, Mr. Churchill, instead of adding another horrid chapter to the already bloodstained record of the relations between England and this country, has advanced the cause of international morality an important step-one of the most important, indeed, that can be taken on the road to the establishment of any sure basis for peace.

As far as the peoples of these two islands are concerned, it may, perhaps, mark a fresh beginning towards the realisation of that mutual comprehension to which Mr. Churchill has referred for which, I hope, he will not merely pray but work also, as did his predecessor who will yet, I believe, find the honoured place in British history which is due to him, as certainly he will find it in any fair record of the relations between Britain and ourselves.

That Mr. Churchill should be irritated when our neutrality stood in the way of what he thought he vitally needed, I understand, but that he or any thinking person in Britain or elsewhere should fail to see the reason for our neutrality, I find it hard to conceive.

I would like to put a hypothetical question—it is a question I have put to many Englishmen since the last war. Suppose Germany had won the war, had invaded and occupied England, and that after a long lapse of time and many bitter struggles, she was finally brought to acquiesce in admitting England's right to freedom, and let England go, but not the whole of England, all but, let us say, the six southern counties.

These six southern counties, those, let us suppose, commanding the entrance to the narrow seas, Germany had singled out and insisted on holding herself with a view to weakening England as a whole, and maintaining the securing of her own communications through the Straits of Dover.

Let us suppose further, that after all this had happened, Germany was engaged in a great war in which she could show that she was on the side of freedom of a number of small nations, would Mr. Churchill as an Englishman who believed that his own nation had as good a right to freedom as any other, not freedom for a part merely, but freedom for the whole—would he, whilst Germany still maintained the partition of his country and occupied six counties of it, would he lead this partitioned England to join with Germany in a crusade? I do not think Mr. Churchill would.

Would he think the people of partitioned England an object of shame if they stood neutral in such circumstances? I do not think Mr. Churchill would.

Mr. Churchill is proud of Britain's stand alone, after France had fallen and before America entered the War.

Could he not find in his heart the generosity to acknowledge that there is a small nation that stood alone not for one year or two, but for several hundred years against aggression; that endured spoliations, famines, massacres in endless succession; that was clubbed many times into insensibility, but that each time on returning consciousness took up the fight anew; a small nation that could never be got to accept defeat and has never surrendered her soul?

Mr. Churchill is justly proud of his nation's perseverance against heavy odds. But we in this island are still prouder of our people's perseverance for freedom through all the centuries. We, of our time, have played our part in the perseverance, and we have pledged ourselves to the dead generations who have preserved intact for us this glorious heritage, that we, too, will strive to be faithful to the end, and pass on this tradition unblemished.

Many a time in the past there appeared little hope except that hope to which Mr. Churchill referred, that by standing fast a time would come when, to quote his own words: '...the tyrant would make some ghastly mistake which would alter the whole balance of the struggle.'

I sincerely trust, however, that it is not thus our ultimate unity and freedom will be achieved, though as a younger man I confess I prayed even for that, and indeed at times saw not other.

In latter years, I have had a vision of a nobler and better ending, better for both our people and for the future of mankind. For that I have now been long working. I regret that it is not to this nobler purpose that Mr. Churchill is lending his hand rather than, by the abuse of a people who have done him no wrong, trying to find in a crisis like the present excuse for continuing the injustice of the mutilation of our country.

I sincerely hope that Mr. Churchill has not deliberately chosen the latter course but, if he has, however regretfully we may say it, we can only say, be it so.

Meanwhile, even as a partitioned small nation, we shall go on and strive to play our part in the world continuing unswervingly to work for the cause of true freedom and for peace and understanding between all nations.'

'Behold the Land'

W. E. B. Du Bois

Southern Youth Legislature, Columbia, South Carolina
(20 October 1946)

William Edward Burghardt Du Bois was an African-American sociologist, activist, teacher and writer whose *The Souls of Black People* became a classic work of African-American literature. An important activist for African-American rights in the U.S., he made use of sociological studies to solve the several issues faced by the black community.

'Behold the Land' was delivered at the closing session of the Southern Youth Legislature in Columbia, South Carolina. Through this speech, the seasoned activist inspires his audience to continue the fight for racial justice.

The future of American Negroes is in the South. Here 327 years ago, they began to enter what is now the United States of America; here they have made their greatest contribution to American culture; and here they have suffered the damnation of slavery, the frustration of reconstruction and the lynching of emancipation. I trust then that an organization like yours is going to regard the South as the battle-ground of a great crusade. Here is the magnificent climate; here is the fruitful earth under the beauty of the southern sun; and here, if anywhere on earth, is the need of the thinker, the worker and the dreamer. This is the firing line not simply for the emancipation of the American Negro but for the emancipation of the African Negro and the Negroes of the West Indies; for the emancipation of the colored races; and for the emancipation of the white slaves of modern capitalistic monopoly.

Remember here, too, that you do not stand alone. It may seem like a failing fight when the newspapers ignore you; when every effort is made by white people in the South to count you out of citizenship to act as though you did not exist as human beings while all the time they are profiting by your labor; gleaning wealth from your sacrifices and trying to build a nation and a civilization upon your gradation. You must remember that despite all this, you have allies and allies even in the white South. First and greatest of these possible allies are the white working classes about you. The poor whites whom you have been taught to despise and who in turn have learned to fear and hate you. This must not deter you from efforts to make them understand, because in the past in their ignorance and suffering they have been led foolishly to look upon you as the cause of most of their distress. You must remember that this attitude is hereditary from slavery and that it has been deliberately cultivated ever since emancipation.

Slowly but surely the working people of the South, white and black, must come to remember that their emancipation depends upon their mutual cooperation; upon their acquaintanceship with each other; upon their friendship; upon their social intermingling. Unless this happens each is going to be made the football to break the heads and hearts of the other.

White youth is frustrated

White youth in the South is peculiarly frustrated. There is not a single great ideal which they can express or aspire to, that does not bring them into flat contradiction with the Negro problem. The more they try to escape it, the more they land into hypocrisy, lying and double-dealing; the more they become, what they least wish to become, the oppressors and despisers of human beings. Some of them, in larger and larger numbers, are bound to turn toward the truth and recognize you as brothers and sisters, as fellow travelers toward the dawn.

There has always been in the South that intellectual elite who saw Negro problem clearly. They have always lacked and some still lack the courage to stand up for what they know is right.

Nevertheless they can be depended on in the long run to follow their own clear thinking and their own decent choice. Finally even the politicians must eventually recognize the trend in the world, in this country, and the South. James Byrnes, that favorite son of this commonwealth, and Secretary of State of the United States, is today occupying an indefensible and impossible position; and if he survives in the memory of men, he must begin to help establish in his own South Carolina something of that democracy which he has been recently so loudly preaching to Russia. He is the end of a long series of men whose eternal damnation is the fact that they looked truth in the face and did not see it; John C. Calhoun, Wade Hampton, Ben Tillman are men whose names must ever be besmirched by the fact that they fought against freedom and democracy in a land which was founded upon democracy and freedom.

Eventually this class of men must yield to the writing in the stars. That great hypocrite, Jan Smuts, who today is talking of humanity and standing beside Byrnes for a United Nations, is at the same time oppressing the black people of South Africa to an extent which makes their two countries, South Africa and the American South, the most reactionary peoples on earth. Peoples whose exploitation of the poor and helpless reaches the last degree of shame. They must in the long run yield to the forward march of civilization or die.

What does the fight mean

If now you young people, instead of running away from the battle here in Carolina, Georgia, Alabama, Louisiana and Mississippi, instead of seeking freedom and opportunity in Chicago and New York—which do spell opportunity—nevertheless grit your teeth and make up your minds to fight it out right here if it takes every day of your lives and the lives of your children's children; if you do this, you must in meetings like this ask yourselves what does the fight mean? How can be carried on? What are the best tools, arms, and methods? And where does it lead?

I should be the last to insist that the uplift of mankind never calls for force and death. There are times, as both you and I know, when

'Tho' love repine and reason chafe,
There came a voice without reply,

'Tis man's perdition to be safe
When for truth he ought to die.'

At the same time and even more clearly in a day like this, after the millions of mass murders that have been done in the world since 1914, we ought to be the last to believe that force is ever the final word. We cannot escape the clear fact that what is going to win in this world is reason if this ever becomes a reasonable world. The careful reasoning of the human mind backed by the facts of science is the one salvation of man. The world, if it resumes its march toward civilization, cannot ignore reason. This has been the tragedy of the South in the past; it is still its awful and unforgivable sin that it has set its face against reason and against the fact. It tried to build slavery upon freedom; it tried to build tyranny upon democracy; it tried to build mob violence on law and law on lynching and in all that despicable endeavor, the state of South Carolina has led the South for a century. It began not the Civil War—not the War between the States—but the War to Preserve Slavery; it began mob violence and lynching and today it stands in the front rank of those defying the Supreme Court on disfranchisement.

Nevertheless reason can and will prevail; but of course it can only prevail with publicity—pitiless blatant publicity. You have got to make the people of the United States and of the world know what is going on in the South. You have got to use every field of publicity to force the truth into their ears, and before their eyes. You have got to make it impossible for any human being to live in the South and not realize the barbarities that prevail here. You may be condemned for flamboyant methods; for calling a congress like this; for waving your grievances under the noses and in the faces of men. That makes no difference; it is your duty to do it. It is your duty to do more of this sort of thing than you have done in the past. As a result of this you are going to be called upon for sacrifice. It is no easy thing for a young black man or a young black woman to live in the South today and to plan to continue to live here; to marry and raise children; to establish a home. They are in the midst of legal caste and customary insults; they are in continuous danger of mob violence; they are mistreated by the officers of the law and they have no hearing before the courts and the churches and public opinion commensurate with the attention which they ought to receive. But that sacrifice is only the beginning of battle, you must re-build this South.

There are enormous opportunities here for a new nation, a new economy, a new culture in a South really new and not a mere renewal of an old South of slavery, monopoly and race hate. There is a chance for a new cooperative agriculture on renewed land owned by the state with capital furnished by the state, mechanized and coordinated with city life. There is chance for strong, virile trade unions without race discrimination, with high wage, closed shop and decent conditions of work, to beat back and hold in check the swarm of landlords, monopolists and profiteers who are today sucking the blood out of this land. There is chance for cooperative industry, built the cheap power of T.V.A. and its future extensions. There is chance opportunity to organize and mechanize domestic service with decent and high wage and dignified training.

'Behold the land'

There is a vast field for consumers cooperation, building business on public service and not on private profit as the main-spring of Industry. There is chance for a broad, sunny, healthy home life, shorn the fear of mobs and liquor, and rescued from lying, stealing politicians, who build their deviltry on race prejudice.

Here in this South is the gateway to the colored millions of the West Indies, Central and South America. Here is the straight path to Africa, the Indies, China and the South Seas. Here is the path to the greater, freer, truer world. It would be shame and cowardice to surrender this glorious land and its opportunities for civilization and humanity to the thugs and lynchers, the mobs and profiteers, the monopolists and gamblers who today choke its soul and steal its resources. The oil and sulphur; the coal and iron; the cotton and corn; lumber and cattle belong to you the workers, black and white, not to the thieves who hold them and use them to enslave you. They can be rescued and restored to the people if you have the guts to strive for the real right to vote, the right to real education, the right to happiness and health and the total abolition of the father of these scourges of mankind, poverty.

'Behold the beautiful land which the Lord thy God hath given thee. Behold the land, the rich and resourceful land, from which for a hundred years its best elements have been running away, its youth and hope, black and white, scurrying North because they are of each other, and dare not face a future of equal, independent, upstanding human beings, in a real and not a sham democracy.

To rescue this land, in this way, calls for the Great Sacrifice; This is the thing that you are called upon to do because it is the right thing to do. Because you are embarked upon a great and holy crusade, the emancipation of mankind, black and white; the up building of democracy; the breaking down, particularly here in the South, of forces of evil represented by race prejudice in South Carolina; by lynching in Georgia; by disfranchisement in Mississippi; by ignorance in Louisiana and by all these and monopoly of wealth in the whole South.

There could be no more splendid vocation beckoning to the youth of the twentieth century, after the flat failures of white civilization, after the flamboyant establishment of an industrial system which creates poverty and the children of poverty which are ignorance and disease and crime; after the crazy boasting of a white culture that finally ended in wars which ruined civilization in the whole world; in the midst of allied peoples who have yelled about democracy and I never practiced it either in the British Empire or in the American Commonwealth or in South Carolina. Here is the chance for young women and young men of devotion to lift again the banner of humanity and to walk toward a civilization which will be free and intelligent; which will be healthy and unafraid; and build in the world a culture led by black folk and joined by peoples of all colors and all races—without poverty, ignorance and disease!

Once, a great German poet cried: 'Selig der den Er in Sieges Glanze findet.'

'Happy man whom death shall find in Victory's splendor.'

But I know a happier one: he who fights in despair and in defeat still fights. Singing with Arna Bontemps the quiet, determined philosophy of undefeatable men:

'I thought I saw an angel flying low,
I thought I saw the flicker of a wing

Above the mulberry trees; but not again,
Bethesda sleeps. This ancient pool that healed
A host of bearded Jews does not awake.
This pool that once the angels troubled does not move.
No angel stirs it now, no Saviour comes
With healing in His hands to raise the sick
and bid the lame man leap upon the ground.
The golden days are gone. Why do we wait
So long upon the marble steps, blood
Falling from our open wounds? And why
Do our black faces search the empty sky?
Is there something we have forgotten? Some precious thing
We have lost, wandering in strange lands?

There was a day, I remember now,
I beat my breast and cried, 'Wash me God,'
Wash me with a wave of wind upon
The barley; O quiet one, draw near, draw near!
Walk upon the hills with lovely feet
And in the waterfall stand and speak!

‘Tryst with Destiny’

Jawaharlal Nehru

Indian Constituent Assembly (14 Aug 1947)

Jawaharlal Nehru, also known as Pandit Nehru or Chacha Nehru, was an influential political leader and the first Prime Minister of India (1947-1964). His economic, educational and social reforms as well as policies on international relations earned him widespread support of the Indian people. He was one of the nationalists who worked closely with Mahatma Gandhi during India’s freedom struggle.

‘Tryst with Destiny’ was delivered by Nehru to the Indian Constituent Assembly in the Parliament on the eve of independence from British rule.

Long years ago, we made a tryst with destiny, and now the time comes when we shall redeem our pledge, not wholly or in full measure, but very substantially. At the stroke of the midnight hour, when the world sleeps, India will awake to life and freedom. A moment comes, which comes but rarely in history, when we step out from the old to the new, when an age ends, and when the soul of a nation, long suppressed, finds utterance. It is fitting that at this solemn moment we take the pledge of dedication to the service of India and her people and to the still larger cause of humanity.

At the dawn of history India started on her unending quest, and trackless centuries are filled with her striving and the grandeur of her successes and her failures. Through good and ill fortune alike she has never lost sight of that quest or forgotten the ideals which gave her strength. We end today a period of ill fortune and India discovers herself again. The achievement we celebrate today is but a step, an opening of opportunity, to the greater triumphs and achievements that await us. Are we brave enough and wise enough to grasp this opportunity and accept the challenge of the future?

Freedom and power bring responsibility. The responsibility rests upon this Assembly, a sovereign body representing the sovereign people of India. Before the birth of freedom we have endured all the pains of labour and our hearts are heavy with the memory of this sorrow. Some of those pains continue even now. Nevertheless, the past is over and it is the future that beckons to us now.

That future is not one of ease or resting but of incessant striving so that we may fulfil the pledges we have so often taken and the one we shall take today. The service of India means the service of the millions who suffer. It means the ending of poverty and ignorance, and disease and inequality of opportunity. The ambition of the greatest man of our generation has been to wipe every tear from every eye. That may be beyond us, but so long as there are tears and suffering, so long our work will not be over.

And so we have to labour and to work, and work hard, to give reality to our dreams. Those dreams are for India, but they are also for the world, for all the nations and peoples are too closely knit together today for any one of them to imagine that it can live apart Peace has been said to be indivisible; so is freedom, so is prosperity now, and so also is disaster in this One World that can no longer be split into isolated fragments.

To the people of India, whose representatives we are, we make an appeal to join us with faith and confidence in this great adventure. This is no time for petty and destructive criticism, no time for ill-will or blaming others. We have to build the noble mansion of free India where all her children may dwell.

The appointed day has come—the day appointed by destiny—and India stands forth again, after long slumber and struggle, awake, vital, free and independent. The past clings on to us still in some measure and we have to do much before we redeem the pledges we have so often taken. Yet the turning-point is past, and history begins anew for us, the history which we shall live and act and others will write about.

It is a fateful moment for us in India, for all Asia and for the world. A new star rises, the star of freedom in the East, a new hope comes into being, a vision long cherished materializes. May the star never set and that hope never be betrayed!

We rejoice in that freedom, even though clouds surround us, and many of our people are sorrow-stricken and difficult problems encompass us. But freedom brings responsibilities and burdens and we have to face them in the spirit of a free and disciplined people.

On this day our first thoughts go to the architect of this freedom, the Father of our Nation, who, embodying the old spirit of India, held aloft the torch of freedom and lighted up the darkness that surrounded us. We have often been unworthy followers of his and have strayed from his message, but not only we but succeeding generations will remember this message and bear the imprint in their hearts of this great son of India, magnificent in his faith and strength and courage and humility. We shall never allow that torch of freedom to be blown out, however high the wind or stormy the tempest.

Our next thoughts must be of the unknown volunteers and soldiers of freedom who, without praise or reward, have served India even unto death.

We think also of our brothers and sisters who have been cut off from us by political boundaries and who unhappily cannot share at present in the freedom that has come. They are of us and will remain of us whatever may happen, and we shall be sharers in their good [or] ill fortune alike.

The future beckons to us. Whither do we go and what shall be our endeavour? To bring freedom and opportunity to the common man, to the peasants and workers of India; to fight and end poverty and ignorance and disease; to build up a prosperous, democratic and progressive nation, and to create social, economic and political institutions which will ensure justice and fullness of life to every man and woman.

We have hard work ahead. There is no resting for any one of us till we redeem our pledge in full, till we make all the people of India what destiny intended them to be. We are citizens of a great country on the verge of bold advance, and we have to live up to that high standard. All of us, to whatever religion we may belong, are equally the children of India with equal rights, privileges and obligations. We cannot encourage communalism or narrow-mindedness, for no nation can be great whose people are narrow in thought or in action.

To the nations and peoples of the world we send greetings and pledge ourselves to cooperate with them in furthering peace, freedom and democracy.

And to India, our much-loved motherland, the ancient, the eternal and the ever-new, we pay our reverent homage and we bind ourselves afresh to her service.

Jai Hind.

The Struggle for Human Rights

Eleanor Roosevelt

The Sorbonne, Paris (28 September 1948)

First Lady Eleanor Roosevelt was the wife of U.S. President Franklin D. Roosevelt, who was in office from 1933-1945. A human rights activist and writer, she was considered one of the most dynamic first ladies in history. During President Harry S. Truman's term, she was also a United Nations diplomat and served as Chairman of the Commission on Human Rights (1946-1951).

Through this speech, Roosevelt urges nations to grant individual rights and recognise the right of every individual to live with dignity, equality and without racial discrimination.

I have come this evening to talk with you on one of the greatest issues of our time—that is the preservation of human freedom. I have chosen to discuss it here in France, at the Sorbonne, because here in this soil the roots of human freedom have long ago struck deep and here they have been richly nourished. It was here the Declaration of the Rights of Man was proclaimed, and the great slogans of the French Revolution—liberty, equality, fraternity—fired the imagination of men. I have chosen to discuss this issue in Europe because this has been the scene of the greatest historic battles between freedom and tyranny. I have chosen to discuss it in the early days of the General Assembly because the issue of human liberty is decisive for the settlement of outstanding political differences and for the future of the United Nations.

The decisive importance of this issue was fully recognized by the founders of the United Nations at San Francisco. Concern for the preservation and promotion of human rights and fundamental freedoms stands at the heart of the United Nations. Its Charter is distinguished by its preoccupation with the rights and welfare of individual men and women. The United Nations has made it clear that it intends to uphold human rights and to protect the dignity of the human personality. In the preamble to the Charter the keynote is set when it declares: 'We the people of the United Nations determined...to reaffirm faith in fundamental human rights, in the dignity and worth of the human person, in the equal rights of men and women and of nations large and small, and...to promote social progress and better standards of life in larger freedom.' This reflects the basic premise of the Charter that the peace and security of mankind are dependent on mutual respect for the rights and freedoms of all.

One of the purposes of the United Nations is declared in article 1 to be: 'to achieve international cooperation in solving international problems of an economic, social, cultural, or humanitarian character, and in promoting and encouraging respect for human rights and for fundamental freedoms for all without distinction as to race, sex, language, or religion.'

This thought is repeated at several points and notably in articles 55 and 56 the Members pledge themselves to take joint and separate action in cooperation with the United Nations for the promotion of 'universal respect for, and observance of, human rights and fundamental freedoms for all without distinction as to race, sex, language, or religion.'

The Human Rights Commission was given as its first and most important task the preparation of an International Bill of Rights. The General Assembly, which opened its third session here in Paris a few days ago, will have before it the first fruit of the Commission's labors in this task, that is the International Declaration of Human Rights.

The Declaration was finally completed after much work during the last session of the Human Rights Commission in New York in the spring of 1948. The Economic and Social Council has sent it without recommendation to the General Assembly, together with other documents transmitted by the Human Rights Commission.

It was decided in our Commission that a Bill of Rights should contain two parts:

1. A Declaration which could be approved through action of the Member States of the United Nations in the General Assembly. This declaration would have great moral force, and would say to the peoples of the world 'this is what we hope human rights may mean to all people in the years to come.' We have put down here the rights that we consider basic for individual human beings the world over to have. Without them, we feel that the full development of individual personality is impossible.

2. The second part of the bill, which the Human Rights Commission has not yet completed because of the lack of time, is a covenant which would be in the form of a treaty to be presented to the nations of the world. Each nation, as it is prepared to do so, would ratify this covenant and the covenant would then become binding on the nations which adhere to it. Each nation ratifying would then be obligated to change its laws wherever they did not conform to the points contained in the covenant.

This covenant, of course, would have to be a simpler document. It could not state aspirations, which we feel to be permissible in the Declaration. It could only state rights which could be assured by law and it must contain methods of implementation, and no state ratifying the covenant could be allowed to disregard it. The methods of implementation have not yet been agreed upon, nor have they been given adequate consideration by the Commission at any of its meetings. There certainly should be discussion on the entire question of this world Bill of Human Rights and there may be acceptance by this Assembly of the Declaration if they come to agreement on it. The acceptance of the Declaration, I think, should encourage every nation in the coming months to discuss its meaning with its people so that they will be better prepared to accept the covenant with a deeper understanding of the problems involved when that is presented, we hope, a year from now and, we hope, accepted.

The Declaration has come from the Human Rights Commission with unanimous acceptance except for four abstentions—the U.S.S.R., Yugoslavia, Ukraine, and Byelorussia. The reason for this is a fundamental difference in the conception of human rights as they exist in these states and in certain other Member States in the United Nations.

In the discussion before the Assembly, I think it should be made crystal clear what these differences are and tonight I want to spend a little time making them clear to you. It seems to me there is a valid reason for taking the time today to think carefully and clearly on the subject of human rights, because in the acceptance and observance of these rights lies the root, I believe, of our chance of peace in the future, and for the strengthening of the United Nations organization to the point where it can maintain peace in the future.

We must not be confused about what freedom is. Basic human rights are simple and easily understood: freedom of speech and a free press; freedom of religion and worship; freedom of assembly and the right of petition; the right of men to be secure in their homes and free from unreasonable search and seizure and from arbitrary arrest and punishment.

We must not be deluded by the efforts of the forces of reaction to prostitute the great words of our free tradition and thereby to confuse the struggle. Democracy, freedom, human rights have come to have a definite meaning to the people of the world which we must not allow any nation to so change that they are made synonymous with suppression and dictatorship.

There are basic differences that show up even in the use of words between a democratic and a totalitarian country. For instance 'democracy' means one thing to the U.S.S.R. and another the U.S.A. and, I know, in France. I have served since the first meeting of the nuclear commission on the Human Rights Commission, and I think this point stands out clearly.

The U.S.S.R. Representatives assert that they already have achieved many things which we, in what they call the 'bourgeois democracies' cannot achieve because their government controls the accomplishment of these things. Our government seems powerless to them because, in the last analysis, it is controlled by the people. They would not put it that way—they would say that the people in the U.S.S.R. control their government by allowing their government to have certain absolute rights. We, on the other hand, feel that certain rights can never be granted to the government, but must be kept in the hands of the people.

For instance, the U.S.S.R. will assert that their press is free because the state makes it free by providing the machinery, the paper, and even the money for salaries for the people who work on the paper. They state that there is no control over what is printed in the various papers that they subsidize in this manner, such, for instance, as a trade-union paper. But what would happen if a paper were to print ideas which were critical of the basic policies and beliefs of the Communist government.? I am sure some good reason would be found for abolishing the paper.

It is true that they have been many cases where newspapers in the U.S.S.R. have criticized officials and their actions and have been responsible for the removal of those officials, but in doing so they did not criticize anything which was fundamental to Communist beliefs. They simply criticized methods of doing things, so one must differentiate between things which are permissible, such as criticism of any individual or of the manner of doing things, and the criticism of a belief which would be considered vital to the acceptance of Communism.

What are the differences, for instance, between trade-unions in the totalitarian states and in the democracies? In the totalitarian state a trade-union is an instrument used by the government to enforce duties, not to assert rights. Propaganda material which the government desires the workers to have is furnished by the trade-unions to be circulated to their members.

Our trade-unions, on the other hand, are solely the instrument of the workers themselves. They represent the workers in their relations with the government and with management and they are free to develop their own opinions without government help or interference. The concepts of our trade-unions and those in totalitarian countries are drastically different. There is little mutual understanding.

I think the best example one can give of this basic difference of the use of terms is 'the right to work.' The Soviet Union insists that this is a basic right which it alone can guarantee because it alone provides full employment by the government. But the right to work in the Soviet Union means the assignment of workers to do whatever task is given to them by the government without an opportunity for the people to participate in the decision that the government should do this. A society in which everyone works is not necessarily a free society and may indeed be a slave society; on the other hand, a society in which there is widespread economic insecurity can turn freedom into a barren and vapid right for millions of people.

We in the United States have come to realize it means freedom to choose one's job, to work or not to work as one desires. We, in the United States, have come to realize, however, that people have a right to demand that their government will not allow them to starve because as individuals they cannot find work of the kind they are accustomed to doing and this is a decision brought about by public opinion which came as a result of the great depression in which many people were out of work, but we would not consider in the United States that we had gained any freedom if we were compelled to follow a dictatorial assignment to work where and when we were told. The right of choice would seem to us an important, fundamental freedom.

I have great sympathy with the Russian people. They love their country and have always defended it valiantly against invaders. They have been through a period of revolution, as a result of which they were for a time cut off from outside contact. They have not lost their resulting suspicion of other countries and the great difficulty is today that their government encourages this suspicion and seems to believe that force alone will bring them respect.

We, in the democracies, believe in a kind of international respect and action which is reciprocal. We do not think others should treat us differently from the way they wish to be treated. It is interference in other countries that especially stirs up antagonism against the Soviet Government. If it wishes to feel secure in developing its economic and political theories within its territory, then it should grant to others that same security. We believe in the freedom of people to make their own mistakes. We do not interfere with them and they should not interfere with others.

The basic problem confronting the world today, as I said in the beginning, is the preservation of human freedom for the individual and consequently for the society of which he is a part. We are fighting this battle again today as it was fought at the time of the French Revolution and as the time of the American Revolution. The issue of human liberty is as decisive now as it was then. I want to give you my conception of what is meant in my country by freedom of the individual.

Long ago in London during a discussion with Mr. Vyshinsky, he told me there was no such thing as freedom for the individual in the world. All freedom of the individual was conditioned by the rights of other individuals. That of course, I granted. I said: 'We approach the question from a different point of view/ we here in the United Nations are trying to develop ideals which will be broader in outlook, which will consider first the rights of man, which will consider what makes man more free; not governments, but man.'

The totalitarian state typically places the will of the people second to decrees promulgated by a few men at the top. Naturally there must always be consideration of the rights of others; but in a democracy this is not a restriction. Indeed, in our democracies we make our freedoms secure because each of us is expected to respect the rights of others and we are free to make our own laws. Freedom for our peoples is not only a right, but also a tool. Freedom of speech, freedom of the press, freedom of information, freedom of assembly—these are not just abstract ideals to us; they are tools with which we create a way of life, a way of life in which we can enjoy freedom.

Sometimes the processes of democracy are slow, and I have known some of our leaders to say that a benevolent dictatorship would accomplish the ends desired in a much shorter time than it takes to go through the democratic processes of discussion and the slow formation of public opinion. But there is no way of insuring that a dictatorship will remain benevolent or that power once in the hands of a few will be returned to the people without struggle or revolution. This we have learned by experience and we accept the slow processes of democracy because we know that shortcuts compromise principles on which no compromise is possible.

The final expression of the opinion of the people with us is through free and honest elections, with valid choices on basic issues and candidates. The secret ballot is an essential to free elections but you must have a choice before you. I have heard my husband say many times that a people need never lose their freedom if they kept their right to a secret ballot and if they used that secret ballot to the full. Basic decisions of our society are made through the expressed will of the people. That is why when we see these liberties threatened, instead of falling apart, our nation becomes unified and our democracies come together as a unified group in spite of our varied backgrounds and many racial strains.

In the United States we have a capitalistic economy. That is because public opinion favors that type of economy under the conditions in which we live. But we have imposed certain restraints; for instance, we have antitrust laws. These are the legal evidence of the determination of the American people to maintain an economy of free competition and not to allow monopolies to take away the people's freedom.

Our trade-unions grow stronger because the people come to believe that this is the proper way to guarantee the rights of the workers and that the right to organize and to bargain collectively keeps the balance between the actual producer and the investor of money and the manage in industry who watches over the man who works with this hands and who produces the materials which are out tangible wealth.

In the United States we are old enough not to claim perfection. We recognize that we have some problems of discrimination but we find steady progress being made in the solution of these problems. Through normal democratic processes we are coming to understand our needs and how we can attain full equality for all our people. Free discussion on the subject is permitted. Our Supreme Court has recently rendered decisions to clarify a number of our laws to guarantee the rights of all.

The U.S.S.R. claims it has reached a point where all races within her borders are officially considered equal and have equal rights and they insist that they have no discrimination where minorities are concerned.

This is a laudable objective but there are other aspects of the development of freedom for the individual which are essential before the mere absence of discrimination is worth much, and these are lacking in the Soviet Union. Unless they are being denied freedoms which they want and which they see other people have, people do not usually complain of discrimination. It is these other freedoms—the basic freedoms of speech, of the press, of religion and conscience, of assembly, of fair trial and freedom from arbitrary arrest and punishment, which a totalitarian government cannot safely give its people and which give meaning to freedom from discrimination.

It is my belief, and I am sure it is also yours, that the struggle for democracy and freedom is a critical struggle, for their preservation is essential to the great objective of the United Nations to maintain international peace and security. Among free men the end cannot justify the means. We know the patterns of totalitarianism—the single political party, the control of schools, press, radio, the arts, the sciences, and the church to support autocratic authority; these are the age-old patterns against which men have struggled for three thousand years. These are the signs of reaction, retreat, and retrogression. The United Nations must hold fast to the heritage of freedom won by the struggle of its people; it must help us to pass it on to generations to come.

The development of the ideal of freedom and its translation into the everyday life of the people in great areas of the earth is the product of the efforts of many peoples. It is the fruit of a long tradition of vigorous thinking and courageous action. No one race and on one people can claim to have done all the work to achieve greater dignity for human beings and great freedom to develop human personality. In each generation and in each country there must be a continuation of the struggle and new steps forward must be taken since this is preeminently a field in which to stand still is to retreat.

The field of human rights is not one in which compromise on fundamental principles are possible. The work of the Commission on Human Rights is illustrative. The Declaration of Human Rights provides: 'Everyone has the right to leave any country, including his own.' The Soviet Representative said he would agree to this right if a single phrase was added to it—'in accordance with the procedure laid down in the laws of that country.' It is obvious that to accept this would be not only to compromise but to nullify the right stated. This case forcefully illustrates the importance of the proposition that we must ever be alert not to compromise fundamental human rights merely for the sake of reaching unanimity and thus lose them.

As I see it, it is not going to be easy to attain unanimity with respect to our different concepts of government and human rights. The struggle is bound to be difficult and one in which we must be firm but patient. If we adhere faithfully to our principles I think it is possible for us to maintain freedom and to do so peacefully and without recourse to force.

The future must see the broadening of human rights throughout the world. People who have glimpsed freedom will never be content until they have secured it for themselves. In a truest sense, human rights are a fundamental object of law and government in a just society. Human rights exist to the degree that they are respected by people in relations with each other and by governments in relations with their citizens.

The world at large is aware of the tragic consequences for human beings ruled by totalitarian systems. If we examine Hitler's rise to power, we see how the chains are forged which keep the individual a slave and we cans e many similarities in the way things are accomplished in other countries. Politically men must be free to discuss and to arrive at as many facts as possible and there must be at least a two-party system in a country because when there is only one political party, too many things can be subordinated to the interests of that one party and it becomes a tyrant and not an instrument of democratic government.

The propaganda we have witnessed in the recent past, like that we perceive in these days, seeks to impugn, to undermine, and to destroy the liberty and independence of peoples. Such propaganda poses to all peoples the issue whether to doubt their heritage of rights and therefore to compromise the principles by which they live, or try to accept the challenge, redouble their vigilance, and stand steadfast in the struggle to maintain and enlarge human freedoms.

People who continue to be denied the respect to which they are entitled as human beings will not acquiesce forever in such denial.

The Charter of the United Nations is a guiding beacon along the way to the achievement of human rights and fundamental freedoms throughout the world. The immediate test is not only to the extent to which human rights and freedoms have already been achieved, but the direction in which the world is moving. Is there a faithful compliance with the objectives of the Charter if some countries continue to curtail human rights and freedoms instead of to promote the universal respect for an observance of human rights and freedoms for all as called for by the Charter?

The place to discuss the issue of human rights is in the forum of the United Nations. The United Nations has been set up as the common meeting ground for nations, where we can consider together our mutual problems and take advantage of our differences in experience. It is inherent in our firm attachment to democracy and freedom that we stand always ready to use the fundamental democratic procedures of honest discussion and negotiation. It is now as always our hope that despite the wide differences in approach we face in the world today, we can with mutual good faith in the principles of the united Nations Charter, arrive at a common basis of understanding.

We are here to join the meetings of this great international Assembly which meets in your beautiful capital of Paris. Freedom for the individual is an inseparable part of the cherished traditions of France. As one of the Delegates from the United States, I pray Almighty God that we may win another victory here for the rights and freedoms of all men.

Nobel Prize Acceptance Speech

William Faulkner

City Hall, Stockholm (10 December 1950)

William Faulkner, an American author who won the Nobel Prize in Literature in 1949, is considered one of the greatest American novelists of the 20th century. He was notable for using modernist techniques in his works such as stream-of-consciousness and different time frames. Besides these, he was commended for his sophisticated prose and in-depth characterisation. Some of his best works include *The Sound and the Fury* (1929), *As I Lay Dying* (1930) and *Sanctuary* (1931).

In his eloquent acceptance speech, Faulkner reflects on the responsibility of the writer and poet, and the need to shun fear and write of hope.

Ladies and Gentlemen,

I feel that this award was not made to me as a man, but to my work—a life's work in the agony and sweat of the human spirit, not for glory and least of all for profit, but to create out of the materials of the human spirit something which did not exist before. So this award is only mine in trust. It will not be difficult to find a dedication for the money part of it commensurate with the purpose and significance of its origin. But I would like to do the same with the acclaim too, by using this moment as a pinnacle from which I might be listened to by the young men and women already dedicated to the same anguish and travail, among whom is already that one who will someday stand here where I am standing.

Our tragedy today is a general and universal physical fear so long sustained by now that we can even bear it. There are no longer problems of the spirit. There is only the question: When will I be blown up? Because of this, the young man or woman writing today has forgotten the problems of the human heart in conflict with itself which alone can make good writing because only that is worth writing about, worth the agony and the sweat.

He must learn them again. He must teach himself that the basest of all things is to be afraid; and, teaching himself that, forget it forever, leaving no room in his workshop for anything but the old verities and truths of the heart, the old universal truths lacking which any story is ephemeral and doomed—love and honor and pity and pride and compassion and sacrifice. Until he does so, he labors under a curse. He writes not of love but of lust, of defeats in which nobody loses anything of value, of victories without hope and, worst of all, without pity or compassion. His griefs grieve on no universal bones, leaving no scars. He writes not of the heart but of the glands.

Until he relearns these things, he will write as though he stood among and watched the end of man. I decline to accept the end of man. It is easy enough to say that man is immortal simply because he will endure: that when the last dingdong of doom has clanged and faded from the last worthless rock hanging tideless in the last red and dying evening, that even then there will still be one more sound: that of his puny inexhaustible voice, still talking.

I refuse to accept this. I believe that man will not merely endure: he will prevail. He is immortal, not because he alone among creatures has an inexhaustible voice, but because he has a soul, a spirit capable of compassion and sacrifice and endurance. The poet's, the writer's, duty is to write about these things. It is his privilege to help man endure by lifting his heart, by reminding him of the courage and honour and hope and pride and compassion and pity and sacrifice which have been the glory of his past. The poet's voice need not merely be the record of man, it can be one of the props, the pillars to help him endure and prevail.

Secret Speech

Nikita Khrushchev

Moscow, USSR (25 February 1956)

Nikita Khrushchev served as Premier of the Soviet Union (1958-64) during the trying time of the Cold War. He orchestrated the process of 'de-Stalinisation' in the Soviet Union, making the society less repressive. However, he approved the construction of the Berlin Wall and also initiated the Cuban Missile Crisis.

Often called the 'Secret Speech', Khrushchev used it to denounce Stalin and expose his crimes in a special address to the members of the Communist Party.

Comrades! In the Party Central Committee's report at the 20th Congress and in a number of speeches by delegates to the Congress, as also formerly during Plenary CC/CPSU [Central Committee of the Communist Party of the Soviet Union] sessions, quite a lot has been said about the cult of the individual and about its harmful consequences.

After Stalin's death, the Central Committee began to implement a policy of explaining concisely and consistently that it is impermissible and foreign to the spirit of Marxism-Leninism to elevate one person, to transform him into a superman possessing supernatural characteristics, akin to those of a god. Such a man supposedly knows everything, sees everything, thinks for everyone, can do anything, is infallible in his behavior.

Such a belief about a man, and specifically about Stalin, was cultivated among us for many years. The objective of the present report is not a thorough evaluation of Stalin's life and activity.

Concerning Stalin's merits, an entirely sufficient number of books, pamphlets and studies had already been written in his lifetime. The role of Stalin in the preparation and execution of the Socialist Revolution, in the Civil War, and in the fight for the construction of socialism in our country, is universally known. Everyone knows it well.

At present, we are concerned with a question which has immense importance for the Party now and for the future—with how the cult of the person of Stalin has been gradually growing, the cult which became at a certain specific stage the source of a whole series of exceedingly serious and grave perversions of Party principles, of Party democracy, of revolutionary legality.

Because not all as yet realize fully the practical consequences resulting from the cult of the individual, [or] the great harm caused by violation of the principle of collective Party direction and by the accumulation of immense and limitless power in the hands of one person, the Central Committee considers it absolutely necessary to make material pertaining to this matter available to the 20th Congress of the Communist Party of the Soviet Union.

Allow me first of all to remind you how severely the classics of Marxism-Leninism denounced every manifestation of the cult of the individual. In a letter to the German political worker Wilhelm Bloss, [Karl] Marx stated: 'From my antipathy to any cult of the individual, I never made public during the existence of the [1st] International the numerous addresses from various countries which recognized my merits and which annoyed me. I did not even reply to them, except sometimes to rebuke their authors. [Fredrich] Engels and I first joined the secret society of Communists on the condition that everything making for superstitious worship of authority would be deleted from its statute. [Ferdinand] Lassalle subsequently did quite the opposite.'

Sometime later Engels wrote: 'Both Marx and I have always been against any public manifestation with regard to individuals, with the exception of cases when it had an important purpose. We most strongly opposed such manifestations which during our lifetime concerned us personally.'

The great modesty of the genius of the Revolution, Vladimir Ilyich Lenin, is known. Lenin always stressed the role of the people as the creator of history, the directing and organizational roles of the Party as a living and creative organism, and also the role of the Central Committee.

Marxism does not negate the role of the leaders of the working class in directing the revolutionary liberation movement.

While ascribing great importance to the role of the leaders and organizers of the masses, Lenin at the same time mercilessly stigmatized every manifestation of the cult of the individual, inexorably combated [any] foreign-to-Marxism views about a 'hero' and a 'crowd,' and countered all efforts to oppose a 'hero' to the masses and to the people.

Lenin taught that the Party's strength depends on its indissoluble unity with the masses, on the fact that behind the Party follows the people—workers, peasants, and the intelligentsia. Lenin said, 'Only he who believes in the people, [he] who submerges himself in the fountain of the living creativeness of the people, will win and retain power.'

Lenin spoke with pride about the Bolshevik Communist Party as the leader and teacher of the people. He called for the presentation of all the most important questions before the opinion of knowledgeable workers, before the opinion of their Party. He said: 'We believe in it, we see in it the wisdom, the honor, and the conscience of our epoch.'

Lenin resolutely stood against every attempt aimed at belittling or weakening the directing role of the Party in the structure of the Soviet state. He worked out Bolshevik principles of Party direction and norms of Party life, stressing that the guiding principle of Party leadership is its collegiality. Already during the pre-Revolutionary years, Lenin called the Central Committee a collective of leaders and the guardian and interpreter of Party principles. 'During the period between congresses,' Lenin pointed out, 'the Central Committee guards and interprets the principles of the Party.'

Underlining the role of the Central Committee and its authority, Vladimir Ilyich pointed out: 'Our Central Committee constituted itself as a closely centralized and highly authoritative group.'

During Lenin's life the Central Committee was a real expression of collective leadership: of the Party and of the nation. Being a militant Marxist-revolutionist, always unyielding in matters of principle, Lenin never imposed his views upon his co-workers by force. He tried to convince. He patiently explained his opinions to others. Lenin always diligently saw to it that the norms of Party life were realized, that Party statutes were enforced, that Party congresses and Plenary sessions of the Central Committee took place at their proper intervals.

In addition to V. I. Lenin's great accomplishments for the victory of the working class and of the working peasants, for the victory of our Party and for the application of the ideas of scientific Communism to life, his acute mind expressed itself also in this. [Lenin] detected in Stalin in time those negative characteristics which resulted later in grave consequences. Fearing the future fate of the Party and of the Soviet nation, V. I. Lenin made a completely correct characterization of Stalin. He pointed out that it was necessary to consider transferring Stalin from the position of [Party] General Secretary because Stalin was excessively rude, did not have a proper attitude toward his comrades, and was capricious and abused his power.

In December 1922, in a letter to the Party Congress, Vladimir Ilyich wrote: 'After taking over the position of General Secretary, comrade Stalin accumulated immeasurable power in his hands and I am not certain whether he will be always able to use this power with the required care.'

This letter—a political document of tremendous importance, known in the Party's history as Lenin's 'Testament'—was distributed among [you] delegates to [this] 20th Party Congress. You have read it and will undoubtedly read it again more than once. You might reflect on Lenin's plain words, in which expression is given to Vladimir Ilyich's anxiety concerning the Party, the people, the state, and the future direction of Party policy.

Vladimir Ilyich said:

'Stalin is excessively rude, and this defect, which can be freely tolerated in our midst and in contacts among us Communists, becomes a defect which cannot be tolerated in one holding the position of General Secretary. Because of this, I propose that the comrades consider the method by which Stalin would be removed from this position and by which another man would be selected for it, a man who, above all, would differ from Stalin in only one quality, namely, greater tolerance, greater loyalty, greater kindness and more considerate attitude toward the comrades, a less capricious temper, etc.'

This document of Lenin's was made known to the delegates at the 13th Party Congress, who discussed the question of transferring Stalin from the position of General Secretary. The delegates declared themselves in favor of retaining Stalin in this post, hoping that he would heed Vladimir Ilyich's critical remarks and would be able to overcome the defects which caused Lenin serious anxiety.

Comrades! The Party Congress should become acquainted with two new documents, which confirm Stalin's character as already outlined by Vladimir Ilyich Lenin in his 'Testament.' These documents are a letter from Nadezhda Konstantinovna Krupskaya to [Lev] Kamenev, who was at that time head of the Politbiuro, and a personal letter from Vladimir Ilyich Lenin to Stalin.

I will now read these documents:

'LEV BORISOVICH!

'Because of a short letter which I had written in words dictated to me by Vladimir Ilyich by permission of the doctors, Stalin allowed himself yesterday an unusually rude outburst directed at me.

This is not my first day in the Party. During all these 30 years I have never heard one word of rudeness from any comrade. The Party's and Ilyich's business is no less dear to me than to Stalin. I need maximum self-control right now. What one can and what one cannot discuss with Ilyich I know better than any doctor, because I know what makes him nervous and what does not. In any case I know [it] better than Stalin. I am turning to you and to Grigory [Zinoviev] as much closer comrades of V[ladimir] I[lyich]. I beg you to protect me from rude interference with my private life and from vile invectives and threats. I have no doubt what the Control Commission's unanimous decision [in this matter], with which Stalin sees fit to threaten me, will be. However I have neither strength nor time to waste on this foolish quarrel. And I am a human being and my nerves are strained to the utmost.

'N. KRUPSKAYA'

Nadezhda Konstantinovna wrote this letter on December 23, 1922. After two and a half months, in March 1923, Vladimir Ilyich Lenin sent Stalin the following letter:

'TO COMRADE STALIN (COPIES FOR: KAMENEV AND ZINOVIEV):

'Dear comrade Stalin!

'You permitted yourself a rude summons of my wife to the telephone and a rude reprimand of her. Despite the fact that she told you that she agreed to forget what was said, nevertheless Zinoviev and Kamenev heard about it from her. I have no intention to forget so easily that which is being done against me. I need not stress here that I consider as directed against me that which is being done against my wife. I ask you, therefore, that you weigh carefully whether you are agreeable to retracting your words and apologizing, or whether you prefer the severance of relations between us.

'SINCERELY: LENIN, MARCH 5, 1923

Comrades! I will not comment on these documents. They speak eloquently for themselves. Since Stalin could behave in this manner during Lenin's life, could thus behave toward Nadezhda Konstantinovna Krupskaya—whom the Party knows well and values highly as a loyal friend of Lenin and as an active fighter for the cause of the Party since its creation—we can easily imagine how Stalin treated other people. These negative characteristics of his developed steadily and during the last years acquired an absolutely insufferable character.

As later events have proven, Lenin's anxiety was justified. In the first period after Lenin's death, Stalin still paid attention to his advice, but later he began to disregard the serious admonitions of Vladimir Ilyich. When we analyze the practice of Stalin in regard to the direction of the Party and of the country, when we pause to consider everything which Stalin perpetrated, we must be convinced that Lenin's fears were justified. The negative characteristics of Stalin, which, in Lenin's time, were only incipient, transformed themselves during the last years into a grave abuse of power by Stalin, which caused untold harm to our Party.

We have to consider seriously and analyze correctly this matter in order that we may preclude any possibility of a repetition in any form whatever of what took place during the life of Stalin, who absolutely did not tolerate collegiality in leadership and in work, and who practiced brutal violence, not only toward everything which opposed him, but also toward that which seemed, to his capricious and despotic character, contrary to his concepts.

Stalin acted not through persuasion, explanation and patient cooperation with people, but by imposing his concepts and demanding absolute submission to his opinion. Whoever opposed these concepts or tried to prove his [own] viewpoint and the correctness of his [own] position was doomed to removal from the leadership collective and to subsequent moral and physical annihilation. This was especially true during the period following the 17th Party Congress, when many prominent Party leaders and rank-and-file Party workers, honest and dedicated to the cause of Communism, fell victim to Stalin's despotism.

We must affirm that the Party fought a serious fight against the Trotskyites, rightists and bourgeois nationalists, and that it disarmed ideologically all the enemies of Leninism. This ideological fight was carried on successfully, as a result of which the Party became strengthened and tempered. Here Stalin played a positive role.

The Party led a great political-ideological struggle against those in its own ranks who proposed anti-Leninist theses, who represented a political line hostile to the Party and to the cause of socialism. This was a stubborn and a difficult fight but a necessary one, because the political line of both the Trotskyite-Zinovievite bloc and of the Bukharinites led actually toward the restoration of capitalism and toward capitulation to the world bourgeoisie. Let us consider for a moment what would have happened if in 1928-1929 the political line of right deviation had prevailed among us, or orientation toward 'cotton-dress industrialization,' or toward the kulak, etc. We would not now have a powerful heavy industry; we would not have the kolkhozes; we would find ourselves disarmed and weak in a capitalist encirclement.

It was for this reason that the Party led an inexorable ideological fight, explaining to all [its] members and to the non-Party masses the harm and the danger of the anti-Leninist proposals of the Trotskyite opposition and the rightist opportunists. And this great work of explaining the Party line bore fruit. Both the Trotskyites and the rightist opportunists were politically isolated. An overwhelming Party majority supported the Leninist line, and the Party was able to awaken and organize the working masses to apply the Leninist line and to build socialism.

A fact worth noting is that extreme repressive measures were not used against the Trotskyites, the Zinovievites, the Bukharinites, and others during the course of the furious ideological fight against them. The fight [in the 1920s] was on ideological grounds. But some years later, when socialism in our country was fundamentally constructed, when the exploiting classes were generally liquidated, when Soviet social structure had radically changed, when the social basis for political movements and groups hostile to the Party had violently contracted, when the ideological opponents of the Party were long since defeated politically—then repression directed against them began. It was precisely during this period (1935-1937-1938) that the practice of mass repression through the Government apparatus was born, first against the enemies of Leninism—Trotskyites, Zinovievites, Bukharinites, long since politically defeated by the Party—and subsequently also against many honest Communists, against those Party cadres who had borne the heavy load of the Civil War and the first and most difficult years of industrialization and collectivization, who had fought actively against the Trotskyites and the rightists for the Leninist Party line.

Stalin originated the concept 'enemy of the people.' This term automatically made it unnecessary that the ideological errors of a man or men engaged in a controversy be proven. It made possible the use of the cruelest repression, violating all norms of revolutionary legality, against anyone who in any way disagreed with Stalin, against those who were only suspected of hostile intent, against those who had bad reputations. The concept 'enemy of the people' actually eliminated the possibility of any kind of ideological fight or the making of one's views known on this or that issue, even [issues] of a practical nature. On the whole, the only proof of guilt actually used, against all norms of current legal science, was the 'confession' of the accused himself. As subsequent probing has proven, 'confessions' were acquired through physical pressures against the accused. This led to glaring violations of revolutionary legality and to the fact that many entirely innocent individuals— [persons] who in the past had defended the Party line—became victims.

We must assert that, in regard to those persons who in their time had opposed the Party line, there were often no sufficiently serious reasons for their physical annihilation. The formula 'enemy of the people' was specifically introduced for the purpose of physically annihilating such individuals.

It is a fact that many persons who were later annihilated as enemies of the Party and people had worked with Lenin during his life. Some of these persons had made errors during Lenin's life, but, despite this, Lenin benefited by their work; he corrected them and he did everything possible to retain them in the ranks of the Party; he induced them to follow him.

In this connection the delegates to the Party Congress should familiarize themselves with an unpublished note by V. I. Lenin directed to the Central Committee's Politburo in October 1920. Outlining the duties of the [Party] Control Commission, Lenin wrote that the Commission should be transformed into a real 'organ of Party and proletarian conscience.'

'As a special duty of the Control Commission there is recommended a deep, individualized relationship with, and sometimes even a type of therapy for, the representatives of the so-called opposition—those who have experienced a psychological crisis because of failure in their Soviet or Party career. An effort should be made to quiet them, to explain the matter to them in a way used among comrades, to find for them (avoiding the method of issuing orders) a task for which they are psychologically fitted. Advice and rules relating to this matter are to be formulated by the Central Committee's Organizational Bureau, etc.'

Everyone knows how irreconcilable Lenin was with the ideological enemies of Marxism, with those who deviated from the correct Party line. At the same time, however, Lenin, as is evident from the given document, in his practice of directing the Party demanded the most intimate Party contact with people who had shown indecision or temporary non-conformity with the Party line, but whom it was possible to return to the Party path. Lenin advised that such people should be patiently educated without the application of extreme methods.

Lenin's wisdom in dealing with people was evident in his work with cadres.

An entirely different relationship with people characterized Stalin. Lenin's traits—patient work with people, stubborn and painstaking education of them, the ability to induce people to follow him without using compulsion, but rather through the ideological influence on them of the whole collective—were entirely foreign to Stalin. He discarded the Leninist method of convincing and educating, he abandoned the method of ideological struggle for that of administrative violence, mass repressions and terror. He acted on an increasingly larger scale and more stubbornly through punitive organs, at the same time often violating all existing norms of morality and of Soviet laws.

Arbitrary behavior by one person encouraged and permitted arbitrariness in others. Mass arrests and deportations of many thousands of people, execution without trial and without normal investigation created conditions of insecurity, fear and even desperation.

This, of course, did not contribute toward unity of the Party ranks and of all strata of working people, but, on the contrary, brought about annihilation and the expulsion from the Party of workers who were loyal but inconvenient to Stalin.

Our Party fought for the implementation of Lenin's plans for the construction of socialism. This was an ideological fight. Had Leninist principles been observed during the course of this fight, had the Party's devotion to principles been skillfully combined with a keen and solicitous concern for people, had they not been repelled and wasted but rather drawn to our side, we certainly would not have had such a brutal violation of revolutionary legality and many thousands of people would not have fallen victim to the method of terror. Extraordinary methods would then have been resorted to only against those people who had in fact committed criminal acts against the Soviet system.

Let us recall some historical facts.

In the days before the October Revolution, two members of the Central Committee of the Bolshevik Party—Kamenev and Zinoviev—declared themselves against Lenin's plan for an armed uprising. In addition, on October 18 they published in the Menshevik newspaper, *Novaya Zhizn*, a statement declaring that the Bolsheviks were making preparations for an uprising and that they considered it adventuristic. Kamenev and Zinoviev thus disclosed to the enemy the decision of the Central Committee to stage the uprising, and that the uprising had been organized to take place within the very near future.

This was treason against the Party and against the Revolution. In this connection, V. I. Lenin wrote: 'Kamenev and Zinoviev revealed the decision of the Central Committee of their Party on the armed uprising to [Mikhail] Rodzyanko and [Alexander] Kerensky.... He put before the Central Committee the question of Zinoviev's and Kamenev's expulsion from the Party.

However, after the Great Socialist October Revolution, as is known, Zinoviev and Kamenev were given leading positions. Lenin put them in positions in which they carried out most responsible Party tasks and participated actively in the work of the leading Party and Soviet organs. It is known that Zinoviev and Kamenev committed a number of other serious errors during Lenin's life. In his 'Testament' Lenin warned that 'Zinoviev's and Kamenev's October episode was of course not an accident.' But Lenin did not pose the question of their arrest and certainly not their shooting.

Or, let us take the example of the Trotskyites. At present, after a sufficiently long historical period, we can speak about the fight with the Trotskyites with complete calm and can analyze this matter with sufficient objectivity. After all, around Trotsky were people whose origin cannot by any means be traced to bourgeois society. Part of them belonged to the Party intelligentsia and a certain part were recruited from among the workers. We can name many individuals who, in their time, joined the Trotskyites; however, these same individuals took an active part in the workers' movement before the Revolution, during the Socialist October Revolution itself, and also in the consolidation of the victory of this greatest of revolutions. Many of them broke with Trotskyism and returned to Leninist positions. Was it necessary to annihilate such people? We are deeply convinced that, had Lenin lived, such an extreme method would not have been used against any of them.

Such are only a few historical facts. But can it be said that Lenin did not decide to use even the most severe means against enemies of the Revolution when this was actually necessary? No; no one can say this. Vladimir Ilyich demanded uncompromising dealings with the enemies of the Revolution and of the working class and when necessary resorted ruthlessly to such methods. You will recall only V. I. Lenin's fight with the Socialist Revolutionary organizers of the anti-Soviet uprising, with the counterrevolutionary kulaks in 1918 and with others, when Lenin without hesitation used the most extreme methods against the enemies. Lenin used such methods, however, only against actual class enemies and not against those who blunder, who err, and whom it was possible to lead through ideological influence and even retain in the leadership. Lenin used severe methods only in the most necessary cases, when the exploiting classes were still in existence and were vigorously opposing the Revolution, when the struggle for survival was decidedly assuming the sharpest forms, even including a Civil War.

Stalin, on the other hand, used extreme methods and mass repressions at a time when the Revolution was already victorious, when the Soviet state was strengthened, when the exploiting classes were already liquidated and socialist relations were rooted solidly in all phases of national economy, when our Party was politically consolidated and had strengthened itself both numerically and ideologically.

It is clear that here Stalin showed in a whole series of cases his intolerance, his brutality and his abuse of power. Instead of proving his political correctness and mobilizing the masses, he often chose the path of repression and physical annihilation, not only against actual enemies, but also against individuals who had not committed any crimes against the Party and the Soviet Government. Here we see no wisdom but only a demonstration of the brutal force which had once so alarmed V. I. Lenin.

Lately, especially after the unmasking of the Beria gang, the Central Committee looked into a series of matters fabricated by this gang. This revealed a very ugly picture of brutal willfulness connected with the incorrect behavior of Stalin. As facts prove, Stalin, using his unlimited power, allowed himself many abuses, acting in the name of the Central Committee, not asking for the opinion of the Committee members nor even of the members of the Central Committee's Politburo; often he did not inform them about his personal decisions concerning very important Party and government matters.

Considering the question of the cult of an individual, we must first of all show everyone what harm this caused to the interests of our Party.

Vladimir Ilyich Lenin had always stressed the Party's role and significance in the direction of the socialist government of workers and peasants; he saw in this the chief precondition for a successful building of socialism in our country. Pointing to the great responsibility of the Bolshevik Party, as ruling Party of the Soviet state, Lenin called for the most meticulous observance of all norms of Party life; he called for the realization of the principles of collegiality in the direction of the Party and the state.

Collegiality of leadership flows from the very nature of our Party, a Party built on the principles of democratic centralism. 'This means,' said Lenin, 'that all Party matters are accomplished by all Party members—directly or through representatives—who, without any exceptions, are subject to the same rules; in addition, all administrative members, all directing collegia, all holders of Party positions are elective, they must account for their activities and are recallable.'

It is known that Lenin himself offered an example of the most careful observance of these principles. There was no matter so important that Lenin himself decided it without asking for advice and approval of the majority of the Central Committee members or of the members of the Central Committee's Politburo. In the most difficult period for our Party and our country, Lenin considered it necessary regularly to convoke Congresses, Party Conferences and Plenary sessions of the Central Committee at which all the most important questions were discussed and where resolutions, carefully worked out by the collective of leaders, were approved.

We can recall, for an example, the year 1918 when the country was threatened by the attack of the imperialistic interventionists. In this situation the 7th Party Congress was convened in order to discuss a vitally important matter which could not be postponed—the matter of peace. In 1919, while the Civil War was raging, the 8th Party Congress convened which adopted a new Party program, decided such important matters as the relationship with the peasant masses, the organization of the Red Army, the leading role of the Party in the work of the soviets, the correction of the social composition of the Party, and other matters. In 1920 the 9th Party Congress was convened which laid down guiding principles pertaining to the Party's work in the sphere of economic construction. In 1921 the 10th Party Congress accepted Lenin's New Economic Policy and the historic resolution called 'On Party Unity.'

During Lenin's life, Party congresses were convened regularly; always, when a radical turn in the development of the Party and the country took place, Lenin considered it absolutely necessary that the Party discuss at length all the basic matters pertaining to internal and foreign policy and to questions bearing on the development of Party and government.

It is very characteristic that Lenin addressed to the Party Congress as the highest Party organ his last articles, letters and remarks. During the period between congresses, the Central Committee of the Party, acting as the most authoritative leading collective, meticulously observed the principles of the Party and carried out its policy.

So it was during Lenin's life. Were our Party's holy Leninist principles observed after the death of Vladimir Ilyich?

Whereas, during the first few years after Lenin's death, Party Congresses and Central Committee Plenums took place more or less regularly, later, when Stalin began increasingly to abuse his power, these principles were brutally violated. This was especially evident during the last 15 years of his life. Was it a normal situation when over 13 years elapsed between the 18th and 19th Party Congresses, years during which our Party and our country had experienced so many important events? These events demanded categorically that the Party should have passed resolutions pertaining to the country's defense during the [Great] Patriotic War and to peacetime construction after the war.

Even after the end of the war a Congress was not convened for over seven years. Central Committee Plenums were hardly ever called. It should be sufficient to mention that during all the years of the Patriotic War not a single Central Committee Plenum took place. It is true that there was an attempt to call a Central Committee Plenum in October 1941, when Central Committee members from the whole country were called to Moscow. They waited two days for the opening of the Plenum, but in vain. Stalin did not even want to meet and talk to the Central Committee members. This fact shows how demoralized Stalin was in the first months of the war and how haughtily and disdainfully he treated the Central Committee members.

In practice, Stalin ignored the norms of Party life and trampled on the Leninist principle of collective Party leadership.

Stalin's willfulness vis a vis the Party and its Central Committee became fully evident after the 17th Party Congress, which took place in 1934.

Having at its disposal numerous data showing brutal willfulness toward Party cadres, the Central Committee has created a Party commission under the control of the Central Committee's Presidium. It has been charged with investigating what made possible mass repressions against the majority of the Central Committee members and candidates elected at the 17th Congress of the All-Union Communist Party (Bolsheviks).

The commission has become acquainted with a large quantity of materials in the NKVD archives and with other documents. It has established many facts pertaining to the fabrication of cases against Communists, to false accusations, [and] to glaring abuses of socialist legality, which resulted in the death of innocent people. It became apparent that many Party, Soviet and economic activists who in 1937-1938 were branded 'enemies' were actually never enemies, spies, wreckers, etc., but were always honest Communists. They were merely stigmatized [as enemies]. Often, no longer able to bear barbaric tortures, they charged themselves (at the order of the investigative judges/falsifiers) with all kinds of grave and unlikely crimes.

The commission has presented to the Central Committee's Presidium lengthy and documented materials pertaining to mass repressions against the delegates to the 17th Party Congress and against members of the Central Committee elected at that Congress. These materials have been studied by the Presidium..

It was determined that of the 139 members and candidates of the Central Committee who were elected at the 17th Congress, 98 persons, i.e., 70 per cent, were arrested and shot (mostly in 1937-1938). (Indignation in the hall.) What was the composition of the delegates to the 17th Congress? It is known that 80 per cent of the voting participants of the 17th Congress joined the Party during the years of conspiracy before the Revolution and during the Civil War, i.e. meaning before 1921. By social origin the basic mass of the delegates to the Congress were workers (60 per cent of the voting members).

For this reason, it is inconceivable that a Congress so composed could have elected a Central Committee in which a majority [of the members] would prove to be enemies of the Party. The only reasons why 70 per cent of the Central Committee members and candidates elected at the 17th Congress were branded as enemies of the Party and of the people were because honest Communists were slandered, accusations against them were fabricated, and revolutionary legality was gravely undermined.

The same fate met not only Central Committee members but also the majority of the delegates to the 17th Party Congress. Of 1,966 delegates with either voting or advisory rights, 1,108 persons were arrested on charges of anti-revolutionary crimes, i.e., decidedly more than a majority. This very fact shows how absurd, wild and contrary to common sense were the charges of counterrevolutionary crimes made out, as we now see, against a majority of participants at the 17th Party Congress.

We should recall that the 17th Party Congress is known historically as the Congress of Victors. Delegates to the Congress were active participants in the building of our socialist state; many of them suffered and fought for Party interests during the pre-Revolutionary years in the conspiracy and at the civil-war fronts; they fought their enemies valiantly and often nervelessly looked into the face of death.

How, then, can we believe that such people could prove to be 'two-faced' and had joined the camps of the enemies of socialism during the era after the political liquidation of Zinovievites, Trotskyites and rightists and after the great accomplishments of socialist construction? This was the result of the abuse of power by Stalin, who began to use mass terror against Party cadres.

What is the reason that mass repressions against activists increased more and more after the 17th Party Congress? It was because at that time Stalin had so elevated himself above the Party and above the nation that he ceased to consider either the Central Committee or the Party.

Stalin still reckoned with the opinion of the collective before the 17th Congress. After the complete political liquidation of the Trotskyites, Zinovievites and Bukharinites, however, when the Party had achieved unity, Stalin to an ever greater degree stopped considering the members of the Party's Central Committee and even the members of the Politburo. Stalin thought that now he could decide all things alone and that all he needed were statisticians. He treated all others in such a way that they could only listen to him and praise him.

After the criminal murder of Sergey M. Kirov, mass repressions and brutal acts of violation of socialist legality began. On the evening of December 1, 1934 on Stalin's initiative (without the approval of the Politburo–which was given two days later, casually), the Secretary of the Presidium of the Central Executive Committee, [Abel] Yenukidze, signed the following directive:

'1. Investigative agencies are directed to speed up the cases of those accused of the preparation or execution of acts of terror.

'2. Judicial organs are directed not to hold up the execution of death sentences pertaining to crimes of this category in order to consider the possibility of pardon, because the Presidium of the Central Executive Committee of the USSR does not consider as possible the receiving of petitions of this sort.

'3. The organs of the Commissariat of Internal Affairs [NKVD] are directed to execute the death sentences against criminals of the above-mentioned category immediately after the passage of sentences.'

This directive became the basis for mass acts of abuse against socialist legality. During many of the fabricated court cases, the accused were charged with 'the preparation' of terroristic acts; this deprived them of any possibility that their cases might be re-examined, even when they stated before the court that their 'confessions' were secured by force, and when, in a convincing manner, they disproved the accusations against them.

It must be asserted that to this day the circumstances surrounding Kirov's murder hide many things which are inexplicable and mysterious and demand a most careful examination. There are reasons for the suspicion that the killer of Kirov, [Leonid] Nikolayev, was assisted by someone from among the people whose duty it was to protect the person of Kirov.

A month and a half before the killing, Nikolayev was arrested on the grounds of suspicious behavior but he was released and not even searched. It is an unusually suspicious circumstance that when the Chekist assigned to protect Kirov was being brought for an interrogation, on December 2, 1934, he was killed in a car 'accident' in which no other occupants of the car were harmed. After the murder of Kirov, top functionaries of the Leningrad NKVD were given very light sentences, but in 1937 they were shot. We can assume that they were shot in order to cover up the traces of the organizers of Kirov's killing.

Mass repressions grew tremendously from the end of 1936 after a telegram from Stalin and [Andrey] Zhdanov, dated from Sochi on September 25, 1936, was addressed to [Lazar] Kaganovich, [Vyacheslav] Molotov and other members of the Politbiuro. The content of the telegram was as follows:

'We deem it absolutely necessary and urgent that comrade [Nikolay] Yezhov be nominated to the post of People's Commissar for Internal Affairs. [Genrikh] Yagoda definitely has proven himself incapable of unmasking the Trotskyite-Zinovievite bloc. The OGPU is four years behind in this matter. This is noted by all Party workers and by the majority of the representatives of the NKVD.'

Strictly speaking, we should stress that Stalin did not meet with and, therefore, could not know the opinion of Party workers.

This Stalinist formulation that the 'NKVD is four years behind' in applying mass repression and that there is a necessity for 'catching up' with the neglected work directly pushed the NKVD workers on the path of mass arrests and executions.

We should state that this formulation was also forced on the February-March Plenary session of the Central Committee of the All-Union Communist Party (Bolsheviks) in 1937. The Plenary resolution approved it on the basis of Yezhov's report, 'Lessons flowing from the harmful activity, diversion and espionage of the Japanese-German-Trotskyite agents,' stating:

'The Plenum of the Central Committee of the All-Union Communist Party (Bolsheviks) considers that all facts revealed during the investigation into the matter of an anti-Soviet Trotskyite center and of its followers in the provinces show that the People's Commissariat of Internal Affairs has fallen behind at least four years in the attempt to unmask these most inexorable enemies of the people.

The mass repressions at this time were made under the slogan of a fight against the Trotskyites. Did the Trotskyites at this time actually constitute such a danger to our Party and to the Soviet state? We should recall that in 1927, on the eve of the 15th Party Congress, only some 4,000 [Party] votes were cast for the Trotskyite-Zinovievite opposition while there were 724,000 for the Party line. During the 10 years which passed between the 15th Party Congress and the February-March Central Committee Plenum, Trotskyism was completely disarmed. Many former Trotskyites changed their former views and worked in the various sectors building socialism. It is clear that in the situation of socialist victory there was no basis for mass terror in the country.

Stalin's report at the February-March Central Committee Plenum in 1937, 'Deficiencies of Party work and methods for the liquidation of the Trotskyites and of other two-facers,' contained an attempt at theoretical justification of the mass terror policy under the pretext that class war must allegedly sharpen as we march forward toward socialism. Stalin asserted that both history and Lenin taught him this.

Actually Lenin taught that the application of revolutionary violence is necessitated by the resistance of the exploiting classes, and this referred to the era when the exploiting classes existed and were powerful. As soon as the nation's political situation had improved, when in January 1920 the Red Army took Rostov and thus won a most important victory over [General A. I.] Denikin, Lenin instructed [Felix] Dzerzhinsky to stop mass terror and to abolish the death penalty. Lenin justified this important political move of the Soviet state in the following manner in his report at the session of the All-Union Central Executive Committee on February 2, 1920:

'We were forced to use terror because of the terror practiced by the Entente, when strong world powers threw their hordes against us, not avoiding any type of conduct. We would not have lasted two days had we not answered these attempts of officers and White Guardists in a merciless fashion; this meant the use of terror, but this was forced upon us by the terrorist methods of the Entente.

'But as soon as we attained a decisive victory, even before the end of the war, immediately after taking Rostov, we gave up the use of the death penalty and thus proved that we intend to execute our own program in the manner that we promised. We say that the application of violence flows out of the decision to smother the exploiters, the big landowners and the capitalists; as soon as this was accomplished we gave up the use of all extraordinary methods. We have proved this in practice.'

Stalin deviated from these clear and plain precepts of Lenin. Stalin put the Party and the NKVD up to the use of mass terror when the exploiting classes had been liquidated in our country and when there were no serious reasons for the use of extraordinary mass terror.

This terror was actually directed not at the remnants of the defeated exploiting classes but against the honest workers of the Party and of the Soviet state; against them were made lying, slanderous and absurd accusations concerning 'two-facedness,' 'espionage,' 'sabotage,' preparation of fictitious 'plots,' etc.

At the February-March Central Committee Plenum in 1937 many members actually questioned the rightness of the established course regarding mass repressions under the pretext of combating 'two-facedness.'

Comrade [Pavel] Postyshev most ably expressed these doubts. He said:

'I have philosophized that the severe years of fighting have passed. Party members who have lost their backbones have broken down or have joined the camp of the enemy; healthy elements have fought for the Party. These were the years of industrialization and collectivization. I never thought it possible that after this severe era had passed Karpov and people like him would find themselves in the camp of the enemy. Karpov was a worker in the Ukrainian Central Committee whom Postyshev knew well.) And now, according to the testimony, it appears that Karpov was recruited in 1934 by the Trotskyites. I personally do not believe that in 1934 an honest Party member who had trod the long road of unrelenting fight against enemies for the Party and for socialism would now be in the camp of the enemies. I do not believe it...I cannot imagine how it would be possible to travel with the Party during the difficult years and then, in 1934, join the Trotskyites. It is an odd thing...'

Using Stalin's formulation, namely, that the closer we are to socialism the more enemies we will have, and using the resolution of the February-March Central Committee Plenum passed on the basis of Yezhov's report, the provocateurs who had infiltrated the state-security organs together with conscienceless careerists began to protect with the Party name the mass terror against Party cadres, cadres of the Soviet state, and ordinary Soviet citizens. It should suffice to say that the number of arrests based on charges of counterrevolutionary crimes had grown ten times between 1936 and 1937.

It is known that brutal willfulness was practiced against leading Party workers. The [relevant] Party statute, approved at the 17th Party Congress, was based on Leninist principles expressed at the 10th Party Congress. It stated that, in order to apply an extreme method such as exclusion from the Party against a Central

Committee member, against a Central Committee candidate or against a member of the Party Control Commission, 'it is necessary to call a Central Committee Plenum and to invite to the Plenum all Central Committee candidate members and all members of the Party Control Commission'; only if two-thirds of the members of such a general assembly of responsible Party leaders found it necessary, only then could a Central Committee member or candidate be expelled.

The majority of those Central Committee's members and candidates who were elected at the 17th Congress and arrested in 1937-1938 were expelled from the Party illegally through brutal abuse of the Party statute, because the question of their expulsion was never studied at the Central Committee Plenum.

Now, when the cases of some of these so-called 'spies' and 'saboteurs' were examined, it was found that all their cases were fabricated. The confessions of guilt of many of those arrested and charged with enemy activity were gained with the help of cruel and inhuman tortures.

At the same time, Stalin, as we have been informed by members of the Politburo of that time, did not show them the statements of many accused political activists when they retracted their confessions before the military tribunal and asked for an objective examination of their cases. There were many such declarations, and Stalin doubtless knew of them.

The Central Committee considers it absolutely necessary to inform the Congress of many such fabricated 'cases' against the members of the Party's Central Committee elected at the 17th Party Congress.

An example of vile provocation, of odious falsification and of criminal violation of revolutionary legality is the case of the former candidate for the Central Committee Politbiuro, one of the most eminent workers of the Party and of the Soviet Government, comrade [Robert] Eikhe, who had been a Party member since 1905.

Comrade Eikhe was arrested on April 29, 1938 on the basis of slanderous materials, without the sanction of the [State] Prosecutor of the USSR. This was finally received 15 months after the arrest.

The investigation of Eikhe's case was made in a manner which most brutally violated Soviet legality and was accompanied by willfulness and falsification.

Under torture, Eikhe was forced to sign a protocol of his confession prepared in advance by the investigative judges. In it, he and several other eminent Party workers were accused of anti-Soviet activity.

On October 1, 1939 Eikhe sent his declaration to Stalin in which he categorically denied his guilt and asked for an examination of his case. In the declaration he wrote: 'There is no more bitter misery than to sit in the jail of a government for which I have always fought.'

A second declaration of Eikhe has been preserved, which he sent to Stalin on October 27, 1939. In it [Eikhe] cited facts very convincingly and countered the slanderous accusations made against him, arguing that this provocatory accusation was on one hand the work of real Trotskyites whose arrests he had sanctioned as First Secretary of the West Siberian Regional Party Committee and who conspired in order to take revenge on him, and, on the other hand, the result of the base falsification of materials by the investigative judges.

Eikhe wrote in his declaration:

'...On October 25 of this year I was informed that the investigation in my case has been concluded and I was given access to the materials of this investigation. Had I been guilty of only one hundredth of the crimes with which I am charged, I would not have dared to send you this pre-execution declaration. However I have not been guilty of even one of the things with which I am charged and my heart is clean of even the shadow of baseness. I have never in my life told you a word of falsehood, and now, finding both feet in the grave, I am still not lying. My whole case is a typical example of provocation, slander and violation of the elementary basis of revolutionary legality...

'...The confessions which were made part of my file are not only absurd but contain slander toward the Central Committee of the All-Union Communist Party (Bolsheviks) and toward the Council of People's Commissars. [This is] because correct resolutions of the

Central Committee of the All-Union Communist Party (Bolsheviks) and of the Council of People's Commissars which were not made on my initiative and [were promulgated] without my participation are presented as hostile acts of counterrevolutionary organizations made at my suggestion.

'I am now alluding to the most disgraceful part of my life and to my really grave guilt against the Party and against you. This is my confession of counterrevolutionary activity.... The case is as follows: Not being able to suffer the tortures to which I was submitted by [Z.] Ushakov and Nikolayev—especially by the former, who utilized the knowledge that my broken ribs have not properly mended and have caused me great pain—I have been forced to accuse myself and others.

'The majority of my confession has been suggested or dictated by Ushakov. The rest is my reconstruction of NKVD materials from Western Siberia for which I assumed all responsibility. If some part of the story which Ushakov fabricated and which I signed did not properly hang together, I was forced to sign another variation. The same thing was done to [Moisey] Rukhimovich, who was at first designated as a member of the reserve net and whose name later was removed without telling me anything about it. The same also was done with the leader of the reserve net, supposedly created by Bukharin in 1935. At first I wrote my [own] name in, and then I was instructed to insert [Valery] Mezhlauk's. There were other similar incidents.

'...I am asking and begging you that you again examine my case, and this not for the purpose of sparing me but in order to unmask the vile provocation which, like a snake, wound itself around many persons in a great degree due to my meanness and criminal slander. I have never betrayed you or the Party. I know that I perish because of vile and mean work of enemies of the Party and of the people, who have fabricated the provocation against me.'

It would appear that such an important declaration was worth an examination by the Central Committee. This, however, was not done. The declaration was transmitted to Beria while the terrible maltreatment of the Politburo candidate, comrade Eikhe, continued.

On February 2, 1940, Eikhe was brought before the court. Here he did not confess any guilt and said as follows:

'In all the so-called confessions of mine there is not one letter written by me with the exception of my signatures under the protocols, which were forced from me. I have made my confession under pressure from the investigative judge, who from the time of my arrest tormented me. After that I began to write all this nonsense...The most important thing for me is to tell the court, the Party and Stalin that I am not guilty. I have never been guilty of any conspiracy. I will die believing in the truth of Party policy as I have believed in it during my whole life.'

On February 4, Eikhe was shot.

It has been definitely established now that Eikhe's case was fabricated. He has been rehabilitated posthumously.

Comrade [Yan] Rudzutak, a candidate-member of the Politbiuro, a member of the Party since 1905 who spent 10 years in a Tsarist hard-labor camp, completely retracted in court the confession forced from him. The protocol of the session of the Collegium of the Supreme Military Court contains the following statement by Rudzutak:

'...The only plea which [the defendant] places before the court is that the Central Committee of the All-Union Communist Party (Bolsheviks) be informed that there is in the NKVD an as yet not liquidated center which is craftily manufacturing cases, which forces innocent persons to confess. There is no opportunity to prove one's non-participation in crimes to which the confessions of various persons testify. The investigative methods are such that they force people to lie and to slander entirely innocent persons in addition to those who already stand accused. [The defendant] asks the Court that he be allowed to inform the Central Committee of the All-Union Communist Party (Bolsheviks) about all this in writing. He assures the Court that he personally had never any evil designs in regard to the policy of our Party because he has always agreed with Party policy concerning all spheres of economic and cultural activity.'

This declaration of Rudzutak was ignored, despite the fact that Rudzutak was in his time the head of the Central Control

Commission—which had been called into being, in accordance with Lenin's conception, for the purpose of fighting for Party unity. In this manner fell the head of this highly authoritative Party organ, a victim of brutal willfulness. He was not even called before the Politburo because Stalin did not want to talk to him. Sentence was pronounced on him in 20 minutes and he was shot.

After careful examination of the case in 1955, it was established that the accusation against Rudzutak was false and that it was based on slanderous materials. Rudzutak has been rehabilitated posthumously.

The way in which the former NKVD workers manufactured various fictitious 'anti-Soviet centers' and 'blocs' with the help of provocatory methods is seen from the confession of comrade Rozenblum, a Party member since 1906, who was arrested in 1937 by the Leningrad NKVD.

During the examination in 1955 of the Komarov case, Rozenblum revealed the following fact: When Rozenblum was arrested in 1937, he was subjected to terrible torture during which he was ordered to confess false information concerning himself and other persons. He was then brought to the office of [Leonid] Zakovsky, who offered him freedom on condition that he make before the court a false confession fabricated in 1937 by the NKVD concerning 'sabotage, espionage and diversion in a terroristic center in Leningrad.' (Movement in the hall.) With unbelievable cynicism, Zakovsky told about the vile 'mechanism' for the crafty creation of fabricated 'anti-Soviet plots.'

'In order to illustrate it to me,' stated Rozenblum, 'Zakovsky gave me several possible variants of the organization of this center and of its branches. After he detailed the organization to me, Zakovsky told me that the NKVD would prepare the case of this center, remarking that the trial would be public. Before the court were to be brought 4 or 5 members of this center: [Mikhail] Chudov, [Fyodor] Ugarov, [Pyotr] Smorodin, [Boris] Pozern, Chudov's wife [Liudmilla] Shaposhnikova and others together with 2 or 3 members from the branches of this center...

'...The case of the Leningrad center has to be built solidly, and for this reason witnesses are needed. Social origin (of course, in the past) and the Party standing of the witness will play more than a small role. ''You, yourself,' said Zakovsky, 'will not need to invent anything. The NKVD will prepare for you a ready outline for every branch of the center. You will have to study it carefully, and remember well all questions the Court might ask and their answers. This case will be ready in four or five months, perhaps in half a year. During all this time you will be preparing yourself so that you will not compromise the investigation and yourself. Your future will depend on how the trial goes and on its results. If you begin to lie and to testify falsely, blame yourself. If you manage to endure it, you will save your head and we will feed and clothe you at the Government's cost until your death.''

This is the kind of vile thing practiced then.

Even more widely was the falsification of cases practiced in the provinces. The NKVD headquarters of the Sverdlov Province 'discovered' a so-called 'Ural uprising staff'—an organ of the bloc of rightists, Trotskyites, Socialist Revolutionaries, and church leaders—whose chief supposedly was the Secretary of the Sverdlov Provincial Party Committee and member of the Central Committee, All-Union Communist Party (Bolsheviks), [Ivan] Kabakov, who had been a Party member since 1914. Investigative materials of that time show that in almost all regions, provinces and republics there supposedly existed 'rightist Trotskyite, espionage-terror and diversionary-sabotage organizations and centers' and that the heads of such organizations as a rule—for no known reason—were First Secretaries of provincial or republican Communist Party committees or Central Committees.

Many thousands of honest and innocent Communists have died as a result of this monstrous falsification of such 'cases,' as a result of the fact that all kinds of slanderous 'confessions' were accepted, and as a result of the practice of forcing accusations against oneself and others. In the same manner were fabricated the 'cases' against eminent Party and state workers—[Stanislav] Kosior, [Vlas] Chubar, [Pavel] Postyshev, [Alexander] Kosarev, and others.

In those years repressions on a mass scale were applied which were based on nothing tangible and which resulted in heavy cadre losses to the Party.

The vicious practice was condoned of having the NKVD prepare lists of persons whose cases were under the jurisdiction of the Military Collegium and whose sentences were prepared in advance. Yezhov would send these [execution] lists to Stalin personally for his approval of the proposed punishment. In 1937-1938, 383 such lists containing the names of many thousands of Party, Soviet, Komsomol, Army, and economic workers were sent to Stalin. He approved these lists.

A large part of these cases are being reviewed now. A great many are being voided because they were baseless and falsified. Suffice it to say that from 1954 to the present time the Military Collegium of the Supreme Court has rehabilitated 7,679 persons, many of whom have been rehabilitated posthumously.

Mass arrests of Party, Soviet, economic and military workers caused tremendous harm to our country and to the cause of socialist advancement.

Mass repressions had a negative influence on the moral-political condition of the Party, created a situation of uncertainty, contributed to the spreading of unhealthy suspicion, and sowed distrust among Communists. All sorts of slanderers and careerists were active.

Resolutions of the January, 1938 Central Committee Plenum brought some measure of improvement to Party organizations. However, widespread repression also existed in 1938.

Only because our Party has at its disposal such great moral-political strength was it possible for it to survive the difficult events in 1937-1938 and to educate new cadres. There is, however, no doubt that our march forward toward socialism and toward the preparation of the country's defense would have been much more successful were it not for the tremendous loss in the cadres suffered as a result of the baseless and false mass repressions in 1937-1938.

We are accusing Yezhov justly for the degenerate practices of 1937. But we have to answer these questions: Could Yezhov have arrested Kosior, for instance, without Stalin's knowledge? Was there an exchange of opinions or a Politburo decision concerning this?

No, there was not, as there was none regarding other cases of this type. Could Yezhov have decided such important matters as the fate of such eminent Party figures?

No, it would be a display of naiveté to consider this the work of Yezhov alone. It is clear that these matters were decided by Stalin, and that without his orders and his sanction Yezhov could not have done this.

We have examined these cases and have rehabilitated Kosior, Rudzutak, Postyshev, Kosarev and others. For what causes were they arrested and sentenced? Our review of evidence shows that there was no reason for this. They, like many others, were arrested without prosecutorial knowledge.

In such a situation, there is no need for any sanction, for what sort of a sanction could there be when Stalin decided everything? He was the chief prosecutor in these cases. Stalin not only agreed to arrest orders but issued them on his own initiative. We must say this so that the delegates to the Congress can clearly undertake and themselves assess this and draw the proper conclusions.

Facts prove that many abuses were made on Stalin's orders without reckoning with any norms of Party and Soviet legality. Stalin was a very distrustful man, sickly suspicious. We know this from our work with him. He could look at a man and say: 'Why are your eyes so shifty today?' or 'Why are you turning so much today and avoiding to look me directly in the eyes?' The sickly suspicion created in him a general distrust even toward eminent Party workers whom he had known for years. Everywhere and in everything he saw 'enemies,' 'two-facers' and 'spies.' Possessing unlimited power, he indulged in great willfulness and stifled people morally as well as physically. A situation was created where one could not express one's own volition.

When Stalin said that one or another should be arrested, it was necessary to accept on faith that he was an 'enemy of the people.' Meanwhile, Beria's gang, which ran the organs of state security, outdid itself in proving the guilt of the arrested and the truth of materials which it falsified. And what proofs were offered? The confessions of the arrested, and the investigative judges accepted these 'confessions.' And how is it possible that a person confesses to crimes which he has not committed? Only in one way—because of the application of physical methods of pressuring him, tortures, bringing him to a state of unconsciousness, deprivation of his judgment, taking away of his human dignity. In this manner were 'confessions' acquired.

The wave of mass arrests began to recede in 1939. When the leaders of territorial Party organizations began to accuse NKVD workers of using methods of physical pressure on the arrested, Stalin dispatched a coded telegram on January 20, 1939 to the committee secretaries of provinces and regions, to the central committees of republican Communist parties, to the [republican] People's Commissars of Internal Affairs and to the heads of NKVD organizations. This telegram stated:

'The Central Committee of the All-Union Communist Party (Bolsheviks) explains that the application of methods of physical pressure in NKVD practice is permissible from 1937 on in accordance with permission of the Central Committee of the All-Union Communist Party (Bolsheviks)... It is known that all bourgeois intelligence services use methods of physical influence against representatives of the socialist proletariat and that they use them in their most scandalous forms.

'The question arises as to why the socialist intelligence service should be more humanitarian against the mad agents of the bourgeoisie, against the deadly enemies of the working class and of kolkhoz workers. The Central Committee of the All-Union Communist Party (Bolsheviks) considers that physical pressure should still be used obligatorily, as an exception applicable to known and obstinate enemies of the people, as a method both justifiable and appropriate.'

Thus, Stalin had sanctioned in the name of the Central Committee of the All-Union Communist Party (Bolsheviks) the most brutal violation of socialist legality, torture and oppression, which led as we have seen to the slandering and to the self-accusation of innocent people.

Not long ago—only several days before the present Congress—we called to the Central Committee Presidium session and interrogated the investigative judge Rodos, who in his time investigated and interrogated Kosior, Chubar and Kosarev. He is a vile person, with the brain of a bird, and completely degenerate morally. It was this man who was deciding the fate of prominent

Party workers. He also was making judgments concerning the politics in these matters, because, having established their 'crime,' he thereby provided materials from which important political implications could be drawn.

The question arises whether a man with such an intellect could—by himelf—have conducted his investigations in a manner proving the guilt of people such as Kosior and others. No, he could not have done it without proper directives. At the Central Committee Presidium session he told us: 'I was told that Kosior and Chubar were people's enemies and for this reason I, as an investigative judge, had to make them confess that they were enemies.'

He would do this only through long tortures, which he did, receiving detailed instructions from Beria. We must say that at the Central Committee Presidium session he cynically declared: 'I thought that I was executing the orders of the Party.' In this manner, Stalin's orders concerning the use of methods of physical pressure against the arrested were carried out in practice.

These and many other facts show that all norms of correct Party solution of problems were [in]validated and that everything was dependent upon the willfulness of one man.

The power accumulated in the hands of one person, Stalin, led to serious consequences during the Great Patriotic War.

When we look at many of our novels, films and historical-scientific studies, the role of Stalin in the Patriotic War appears to be entirely improbable. Stalin had foreseen everything. The Soviet Army, on the basis of a strategic plan prepared by Stalin long before, used the tactics of so-called 'active defense,' i.e., tactics which, as we know, allowed the Germans to come up to Moscow and Stalingrad. Using such tactics, the Soviet Army, supposedly thanks only to Stalin's genius, turned to the offensive and subdued the enemy. The epic victory gained through the armed might of the land of the Soviets, through our heroic people, is ascribed in this type of novel, film and 'scientific study' as being completely due to the strategic genius of Stalin.

We have to analyze this matter carefully because it has a tremendous significance not only from the historical, but especially from the political, educational and practical points of view. What are the facts of this matter?

Before the war, our press and all our political-educational work was characterized by its bragging tone: When an enemy violates the holy Soviet soil, then for every blow of the enemy we will answer with three, and we will battle the enemy on his soil and we will win without much harm to ourselves. But these positive statements were not based in all areas on concrete facts, which would actually guarantee the immunity of our borders.

During the war and after the war, Stalin advanced the thesis that the tragedy our nation experienced in the first part of the war was the result of an 'unexpected' attack by the Germans against the Soviet Union. But, comrades, this is completely untrue. As soon as Hitler came to power in Germany he assigned to himself the task of liquidating Communism. The fascists were saying this openly. They did not hide their plans.

In order to attain this aggressive end, all sorts of pacts and blocs were created, such as the famous Berlin-Rome-Tokyo Axis. Many facts from the prewar period clearly showed that Hitler was going all out to begin a war against the Soviet state, and that he had concentrated large armies, together with armored units, near the Soviet borders.

Documents which have now been published show that [as early as] April 3, 1941 Churchill, through his ambassador to the USSR, [Sir Stafford] Cripps, personally warned Stalin that the Germans had begun regrouping their armed units with the intent of attacking the Soviet Union.

It is self-evident that Churchill did not do this at all because of his friendly feeling toward the Soviet nation. He had in this his own imperialistic goals—to bring Germany and the USSR into a bloody war and thereby to strengthen the position of the British Empire.

All the same, Churchill affirmed in his writings that he sought to 'warn Stalin and call his attention to the danger which threatened him.' Churchill stressed this repeatedly in his dispatches of April 18 and on the following days. However, Stalin took no heed of these warnings. What is more, Stalin ordered that no credence be given to information of this sort, so as not to provoke the initiation of military operations.

We must assert that information of this sort concerning the threat of German armed invasion of Soviet territory was coming in also from our own military and diplomatic sources. However, because the leadership was conditioned against such information, such data was dispatched with fear and assessed with reservation. Thus, for instance, information sent from Berlin on May 6, 1941 by the Soviet military (sic) attaché, Captain (sic) Vorontsov, stated: 'Soviet citizen Bozer...communicated to the Deputy naval attaché that, according to a statement of a certain German officer from Hitler's headquarters, Germany is preparing to invade the USSR on May 14 through Finland, the Baltic countries and Latvia. At the same time Moscow and Leningrad will be heavily raided and paratroopers landed in border cities...'

In his report of May 22, 1941, the Deputy Military Attaché in Berlin, Khlopov, communicated that '...the attack of the German Army is reportedly scheduled for June 15, but it is possible that it may begin in the first days of June...'

A cable from our London Embassy dated June 18, 1941 stated: 'As of now Cripps is deeply convinced of the inevitability of armed conflict between Germany and the USSR, which will begin not later than the middle of June. According to Cripps, the Germans have presently concentrated 147 divisions (including air force and service units) along the Soviet borders....'

Despite these particularly grave warnings, the necessary steps were not taken to prepare the country properly for defense and to prevent it from being caught unawares.

Did we have time and the capabilities for such preparations? Yes, we had the time and the capability. Our industry was already so developed that it was capable of supplying fully the Soviet Army with everything that it needed. This is proven by the fact that, although during the war we lost almost half of our industry and important industrial and food-production areas as the result of enemy occupation of the Ukraine, Northern Caucasus and other western parts of the country, the Soviet nation was still able to organize the production of military equipment in the eastern parts of the country, to install there equipment taken from the western industrial areas, and to supply our armed forces with everything necessary to destroy the enemy.

Had our industry been mobilized properly and in time to supply the Army with the necessary material, our wartime losses would have been decidedly smaller. However such mobilization had not been started in time. And already in the first days of the war it became evident that our Army was badly armed. We did not have enough artillery, tanks and planes to throw the enemy back.

Soviet science and technology produced excellent models of tanks and artillery pieces before the war. But mass production of all this was not organized. As a matter of fact, we started to modernize our military equipment only on the eve of the war. As a result, when the enemy invaded Soviet territory we did not have sufficient quantities either of old machinery which was no longer used for armament production or of new machinery which we had planned to introduce into armament production.

The situation with anti-aircraft artillery was especially bad. We did not organize the production of anti-tank ammunition. Many fortified regions proved to be indefensible as soon as they were attacked, because their old arms had been withdrawn and new ones were not yet available there.

This pertained, alas, not only to tanks, artillery and planes. At the outbreak of the war we did not even have sufficient numbers of rifles to arm the mobilized manpower. I recall that in those days I telephoned from Kiev to comrade [Georgy] Malenkov and told him, 'People have volunteered for the new Army [units] and are demanding weapons. You must send us arms.'

Malenkov answered me, 'We cannot send you arms. We are sending all our rifles to Leningrad and you have to arm yourselves.'

Such was the armament situation.

In this connection we cannot forget, for instance, the following fact: Shortly before the invasion of the Soviet Union by Hitler's army, [Colonel-General M. P.] Kirponos, who was chief of the Kiev Special Military District (he was later killed at the front), wrote to Stalin that German armies were at the Bug River, were preparing for an attack and in the very near future would probably start their offensive. In this connection, Kirponos proposed that a strong defense be organized, that 300,000 people be evacuated from the border areas and that several strong points be organized there: anti-tank ditches, trenches for the soldiers, etc.

Moscow answered this proposition with the assertions that this would be a provocation, that no preparatory defensive work should be undertaken at the borders, and that the Germans were not to be given any pretext for the initiation of military action against us. Thus our borders were insufficiently prepared to repel the enemy.

When the fascist armies had actually invaded Soviet territory and military operations began, Moscow issued an order that German fire was not to be returned. Why? It was because Stalin, despite the self-evident facts, thought that the war had not yet started, that this was only a provocative action on the part of several undisciplined sections of the German Army, and that our reaction might serve as a reason for the Germans to begin the war.

The following fact is also known: On the eve of the invasion of Soviet territory by Hitler's army, a certain German citizen crossed our border and stated that the German armies had received orders to start [their] offensive against the Soviet Union on the night of June 22 at 3 o'clock. Stalin was informed about this immediately, but even this warning was ignored.

As you see, everything was ignored: warnings of certain Army commanders, declarations of deserters from the enemy army, and even the open hostility of the enemy. Is this an example of the alertness of the chief of the Party and of the state at this particularly significant historical moment?

And what were the results of this carefree attitude, this disregard of clear facts? The result was that already in the first hours and days the enemy had destroyed in our border regions a large part of our Air Force, our artillery and other military equipment. [Stalin] annihilated large numbers of our military cadres and disorganized our military leadership. Consequently we could not prevent the enemy from marching deep into the country.

Very grievous consequences, especially with regard to the beginning of the war, followed Stalin's annihilation of many military commanders and political workers during 1937-1941 because of his suspiciousness and through slanderous accusations. During these years repressions were instituted against certain parts of our military cadres beginning literally at the company- and battalion-commander levels and extending to higher military centers. During this time, the cadre of leaders who had gained military experience in Spain and in the Far East was almost completely liquidated.

The policy of large-scale repression against military cadres led also to undermined military discipline, because for several years officers of all ranks and even soldiers in Party and Komsomol cells were taught to 'unmask' their superiors as hidden enemies.

It is natural that this caused a negative influence on the state of military discipline in the initial stage of the war.

And, as you know, we had before the war excellent military cadres which were unquestionably loyal to the Party and to the Fatherland. Suffice it to say that those of them who managed to survive, despite severe tortures to which they were subjected in the prisons, have from the first war days shown themselves real patriots and heroically fought for the glory of the Fatherland. I have here in mind such [generals] as: [Konstantin] Rokossovsky (who, as you know, had been jailed); [Alexander] Gorbatov; [Kiril] Meretskov (who is a delegate at the present Congress); [K. P.] Podlas (he was an excellent commander who perished at the front); and many, many others. However, many such commanders perished in the camps and the jails and the Army saw them no more.

All this brought about a situation at the beginning of the war that was a great threat to our Fatherland.

It would be wrong to forget that, after [our] severe initial disaster[s] and defeat[s] at the front, Stalin thought that it was the end. In one of his [declarations] in those days he said: 'Lenin left us a great legacy and we've lost it forever.'

After this Stalin for a long time actually did not direct military operations and ceased to do anything whatsoever. He returned to active leadership only when a Politburo delegation visited him and told him that steps needed to be taken immediately so as to improve the situation at the front.

Therefore, the threatening danger which hung over our Fatherland in the initial period of the war was largely due to Stalin's very own faulty methods of directing the nation and the Party.

However, we speak not only about the moment when the war began, which led to our Army's serious disorganization and brought us severe losses. Even after the war began, the nervousness and hysteria which Stalin demonstrated while interfering with actual military operations caused our Army serious damage.

Stalin was very far from understanding the real situation that was developing at the front. This was natural because, during the whole Patriotic War, he never visited any section of the front or any liberated city except for one short ride on the Mozhaisk highway during a stabilized situation at the front. To this incident were dedicated many literary works full of fantasies of all sorts and so many paintings. Simultaneously, Stalin was interfering with operations and issuing orders which did not take into consideration the real situation at a given section of the front and which could not help but result in huge personnel losses.

I will allow myself in this connection to bring out one characteristic fact which illustrates how Stalin directed operations at the fronts. Present at this Congress is Marshal [Ivan] Bagramyan, who was once the head of operations in the Southwestern Front Headquarters and who can corroborate what I will tell you.

When an exceptionally serious situation for our Army developed in the Kharkov region in 1942, we correctly decided to drop an operation whose objective was to encircle [the city]. The real situation at that time would have threatened our Army with fatal consequences if this operation were continued.

We communicated this to Stalin, stating that the situation demanded changes in [our] operational plans so that the enemy would be prevented from liquidating a sizable concentration of our Army.

Contrary to common sense, Stalin rejected our suggestion. He issued the order to continue the encirclement of Kharkov, despite the fact that at this time many [of our own] Army concentrations actually were threatened with encirclement and liquidation.

I telephoned to [Marshal Alexander] Vasilevsky and begged him: 'Alexander Mikhailovich, take a map'—Vasilevsky is present here—'and show comrade Stalin the situation that has developed.' We should note that Stalin planned operations on a globe.

Yes, comrades, he used to take a globe and trace the front line on it. I said to comrade Vasilevsky: 'Show him the situation on a map. In the present situation we cannot continue the operation which was planned. The old decision must be changed for the good of the cause.'

Vasilevsky replied, saying that Stalin had already studied this problem. He said that he, Vasilevsky, would not see Stalin further concerning this matter, because the latter didn't want to hear any arguments on the subject of this operation.

After my talk with Vasilevsky, I telephoned to Stalin at his *dacha*. But Stalin did not answer the phone and Malenkov was at the receiver. I told comrade Malenkov that I was calling from the front and that I wanted to speak personally to Stalin. Stalin informed me through Malenkov that I should speak with Malenkov. I stated for the second time that I wished to inform Stalin personally about the grave situation which had arisen for us at the front. But Stalin did not consider it convenient to pick up the phone and again stated that I should speak to him through Malenkov, although he was only a few steps from the telephone.

After 'listening' in this manner to our plea, Stalin said: 'Let everything remain as it is!'

And what was the result of this? The worst we had expected. The Germans surrounded our Army concentrations and as a result [the Kharkov counterattack] lost hundreds of thousands of our soldiers. This is Stalin's military 'genius.' This is what it cost us.

On one occasion after the war, during a meeting [between] Stalin [and] members of the Politburo, Anastas Ivanovich Mikoyan mentioned that Khrushchev must have been right when he telephoned concerning the Kharkov operation and that it was unfortunate that his suggestion had not been accepted.

You should have seen Stalin's fury! How could it be admitted that he, Stalin, had not been right! He is after all a 'genius,' and a genius cannot help but be right! Everyone can err, but Stalin considered that he never erred, that he was always right. He never acknowledged to anyone that he made any mistake, large or small, despite the fact that he made more than a few in matters of theory and in his practical activity. After the Party Congress we shall probably have to re-evaluate many [of our] wartime military operations and present them in their true light.

The tactics on which Stalin insisted—without knowing the basics of conducting battle operations—cost much blood until we succeeded in stopping the opponent and going over to the offensive.

The military knows that as late as the end of 1941, instead of great operational maneuvers flanking [our] opponent and penetrating behind his back, Stalin was demanding incessant frontal [counter-]attacks and the [re-]capture of one village after another.

Because of this, we paid with great losses—until our generals, upon whose shoulders the whole weight of conducting the war rested, succeeded in altering the situation and shifting to flexible-maneuver operations. [This] immediately brought serious changes at the front [that were] favorable to us.

All the more shameful was the fact that after our great victory over the enemy, which cost us so dearly, Stalin began to downgrade many of the commanders who had contributed so much to it. [This was] because Stalin ruled out any chance that services rendered at the front might be credited to anyone but himself.

Stalin was very much interested in assessments of comrade [Grigory] Zhukov as a military leader. He asked me often for my opinion of Zhukov. I told him then, 'I have known Zhukov for a long time. He is a good general and a good military leader.'

After the war Stalin began to tell all kinds of nonsense about Zhukov. Among it [was] the following: 'You praised Zhukov, but he does not deserve it. They say that before each operation at the front Zhukov used to behave as follows: He used to take a handful of earth, smell it and say, 'We can begin the attack,' or its opposite, 'The planned operation cannot be carried out.'' I stated at the time, 'Comrade Stalin, I do not know who invented this, but it is not true.'

It is possible that Stalin himself invented these things for the purpose of minimizing the role and military talents of Marshal Zhukov.

In this connection, Stalin very energetically popularized himself as a great leader. In various ways he tried to inculcate the notion that the victories gained by the Soviet nation during the Great Patriotic War were all due to the courage, daring, and genius of Stalin and of no one else. Just like [a] Kuzma Kryuchkov, he put one dress on seven people at the same time.

In the same vein, let us take for instance our historical and military films and some [of our] literary creations. They make us feel sick. Their true objective is propagating the theme of praising Stalin as a military genius. Let us recall the film, *The Fall of Berlin*. Here only Stalin acts. He issues orders in a hall in which there are many empty Chairs. Only only one man approaches him to report something to him—it is [Alexander] Poskrebyshev, his loyal shield-bearer.

And where is the military command? Where is the Politburo? Where is the Government? What are they doing, and with what are they engaged? There is nothing about them in the film. Stalin acts for everybody, he does not reckon with anyone. He asks no one for advice. Everything is shown to the people in this false light. Why? To surround Stalin with glory—contrary to the facts and contrary to historical truth.

The question arises: Where is the military, on whose shoulders rested the burden of the war? It is not in the film. With Stalin's inclusion, there was no room left for it.

Not Stalin, but the Party as a whole, the Soviet Government, our heroic Army, its talented leaders and brave soldiers, the whole Soviet nation—these are the ones who assured victory in the Great Patriotic War.

Central Committee members, Ministers, our economic leaders, the leaders of Soviet culture, directors of territorial-party and Soviet organizations, engineers, and technicians—every one of them in his own place of work generously gave of his strength and knowledge toward ensuring victory over the enemy.

Exceptional heroism was shown by our hard core—surrounded by glory are our whole working class, our kolkhoz peasantry, the Soviet intelligentsia, who under the leadership of Party organizations overcame untold hardships and bearing the hardships of war, and devoted all their strength to the cause of the Fatherland's defense.

Our Soviet women accomplished great and brave deeds during the war. They bore on their backs the heavy load of production work in the factories, on the kolkhozes, and in various economic and cultural sectors. Many women participated directly in the

Great Patriotic War at the front. Our brave youth contributed immeasurably, both at the front and at home, to the defense of the Soviet Fatherland and to the annihilation of the enemy.

The services of Soviet soldiers, of our commanders and political workers of all ranks are immortal. After the loss of a considerable part of the Army in the initial war months, they did not lose their heads and were able to reorganize during the course of combat. Over the course of the war they created and toughened a strong, heroic Army. They not only withstood [our] strong and cunning enemy's pressure but smashed him.

The magnificent, heroic deeds of hundreds of millions of people of the East and of the West during the fight against the threat of fascist subjugation which loomed before us will live for centuries, [indeed] for millennia in the memory of thankful humanity.

The main roles and the main credit for the victorious ending of the war belong to our Communist Party, to the armed forces of the Soviet Union, and to the tens of millions of Soviet people uplifted by the Party.

Comrades, let us reach for some other facts. The Soviet Union justly is considered a model multinational state because we have assured in practice the equality and friendship of all [of the] peoples living in our great Fatherland.

All the more monstrous are those acts whose initiator was Stalin and which were rude violations of the basic Leninist principles [behind our] Soviet state's nationalities policies. We refer to the mass deportations of entire nations from their places of origin, together with all Communists and Komsomols without any exception. This deportation was not dictated by any military considerations.

Thus, at the end of 1943, when there already had been a permanent change of fortune at the front in favor of the Soviet Union, a decision concerning the deportation of all the Karachai from the lands on which they lived was taken and executed.

In the same period, at the end of December, 1943, the same lot befell the [Kalmyks] of the Kalmyk Autonomous Republic. In March, 1944, all the Chechens and Ingushi were deported and the Chechen-Ingush Autonomous Republic was liquidated. In April, 1944, all Balkars were deported from the territory of the Kabardino-

Balkar Autonomous Republic to faraway places and their Republic itself was renamed the Autonomous Kabardian Republic.

Ukrainians avoided meeting this fate only because there were too many of them and there was no place to which to deport them. Otherwise, [Stalin] would have deported them also.

No Marxist-Leninist, no man of common sense can grasp how it is possible to make whole nations responsible for inimical activity, including women, children, old people, Communists and Komsomols, to use mass repression against them, and to expose them to misery and suffering for the hostile acts of individual persons or groups of persons.

After the conclusion of the Patriotic War, the Soviet nation proudly stressed the magnificent victories gained through [our] great sacrifices and tremendous efforts. The country experienced a period of political enthusiasm. The Party came out of the war even more united. Its cadres were tempered and hardened by the fire of the war. Under such conditions nobody could have even thought of the possibility of some plot in the Party.

And it was precisely at this time that the so-called 'Leningrad affair' was born. As we have now proven, this case was fabricated. Those who innocently lost their lives included: comrades [Nikolay] Voznesensky, [Aleksey] Kuznetsov, [Mikhail] Rodionov, [Pyotr] Popkov, and others.

As is known, Voznesensky and Kuznetsov were talented and eminent leaders. Once they stood very close to Stalin. It is sufficient to mention that Stalin made Voznesensky First Deputy to the Chairman of the Council of Ministers and Kuznetsov was elected Secretary of the Central Committee. The very fact that Stalin entrusted Kuznetsov with the supervision of the state-security organs shows the trust which he enjoyed.

How did it happen that these persons were branded as enemies of the people and liquidated?

Facts prove that the 'Leningrad affair' is also the result of willfulness which Stalin exercised against Party cadres. Had a normal situation existed in the Party's Central Committee and in the Central Committee Politburo, affairs of this nature would have been examined there in accordance with Party practice, and all pertinent facts assessed; as a result, such an affair as well as others would not have happened.

We must state that, after the war, the situation became even more complicated. Stalin became even more capricious, irritable and brutal. In particular, his suspicion grew. His persecution mania reached unbelievable dimensions. Many workers became enemies before his very eyes. After the war, Stalin separated himself from the collective even more. Everything was decided by him alone without any consideration for anyone or anything.

This unbelievable suspicion was cleverly taken advantage of by the abject provocateur and vile enemy, Beria, who murdered thousands of Communists and loyal Soviet people. The elevation of Voznesensky and Kuznetsov alarmed Beria. As we have now proven, it had been precisely Beria who had 'suggested' to Stalin the fabrication by him and by his confidants of materials in the form of declarations and anonymous letters, and in the form of various rumors and talks.

The Party's Central Committee has examined this so-called 'Leningrad affair'; persons who innocently suffered are now rehabilitated and honor has been restored to the glorious Leningrad Party organization. [V. S.] Abakumov and others who had fabricated this affair were brought before a court; their trial took place in Leningrad and they received what they deserved.

The question arises: Why is it that we see the truth of this affair only now, and why did we not do something earlier, during Stalin's life, in order to prevent the loss of innocent lives? It was because Stalin personally supervised the 'Leningrad affair,' and the majority of the Politburo members did not, at that time, know all of the circumstances in these matters and could not therefore intervene.

When Stalin received certain material from Beria and Abakumov, without examining these slanderous materials he ordered an investigation of the 'affair' of Voznesensky and Kuznetsov. With this, their fate was sealed.

Similarly instructive is the case of the Mingrelian nationalist organization which supposedly existed in Georgia. As is known, resolutions by the Central Committee, Communist Party of the Soviet Union, were made concerning this case in November 1951 and in March 1952. These resolutions were made without prior discussion with the Politburo. Stalin had personally dictated them. They made serious accusations against many loyal Communists. On the basis of falsified documents, it was proven that there existed in Georgia a supposedly nationalistic organization whose objective was the liquidation of the Soviet power in that republic with the help of imperialist powers.

In this connection, a number of responsible Party and Soviet workers were arrested in Georgia. As was later proven, this was a slander directed against the Georgian Party organization.

We know that there have been at times manifestations of local bourgeois nationalism in Georgia as in several other republics. The question arises: Could it be possible that, in the period during which the resolutions referred to above were made, nationalist tendencies grew so much that there was a danger of Georgia's leaving the Soviet Union and joining Turkey?

This is, of course, nonsense. It is impossible to imagine how such assumptions could enter anyone's mind. Everyone knows how Georgia has developed economically and culturally under Soviet rule. Industrial production in the Georgian Republic is 27 times greater than it was before the Revolution. Many new industries have arisen in Georgia which did not exist there before the Revolution: iron smelting, an oil industry, a machine-construction industry, etc. Illiteracy has long since been liquidated, which, in pre-Revolutionary Georgia, included 78 per cent of the population.

Could the Georgians, comparing the situation in their republic with the hard situation of the working masses in Turkey, be aspiring to join Turkey? In 1955, Georgia produced 18 times as much steel per person as Turkey. Georgia produces 9 times as much electrical energy per person as Turkey. According to the available 1950 census, 65 per cent of Turkey's total population is illiterate, and 80 per cent of its women. Georgia has 19 institutions of higher learning which have about 39,000 students; this is 8 times more than in Turkey (for each 1,000 inhabitants). The prosperity of the working people has grown tremendously in Georgia under Soviet rule.

It is clear that, as the economy and culture develop, and as the socialist consciousness of the working masses in Georgia grows, the source from which bourgeois nationalism draws its strength evaporates.

As it developed, there was no nationalistic organization in Georgia. Thousands of innocent people fell victim to willfulness and lawlessness. All of this happened under the 'genius' leadership of Stalin, 'the great son of the Georgian nation,' as Georgians like to refer to him.

The willfulness of Stalin showed itself not only in decisions concerning the internal life of the country but also in the international relations of the Soviet Union.

The July Plenum of the Central Committee studied in detail the reasons for the development of conflict with Yugoslavia. It was a shameful role which Stalin played here. The 'Yugoslav affair' contained no problems which could not have been solved through Party discussions among comrades. There was no significant basis for the development of this 'affair.' It was completely possible to have prevented the rupture of relations with that country. This does not mean, however, that Yugoslav leaders made no mistakes or had no shortcomings. But these mistakes and shortcomings were magnified in a monstrous manner by Stalin, resulting in the break off of relations with a friendly country.

I recall the first days when the conflict between the Soviet Union and Yugoslavia began to be blown up artificially. Once, when I came from Kiev to Moscow, I was invited to visit Stalin, who, pointing to the copy of a letter recently sent to [Yugoslavian President Marshal Joseph] Tito, asked me, 'Have you read this?'

Not waiting for my reply, he answered, 'I will shake my little finger—and there will be no more Tito. He will fall.'

We have paid dearly for this 'shaking of the little finger.' This statement reflected Stalin's mania for greatness, but he acted just that way: 'I will shake my little finger—and there will be no Kosior'; 'I will shake my little finger once more and Postyshev and Chubar will be no more'; 'I will shake my little finger again—and Voznesensky, Kuznetsov and many others will disappear.'

But this did not happen to Tito. No matter how much or how little Stalin shook, not only his little finger but everything else that he could shake, Tito did not fall. Why? The reason was that, in this instance of disagreement with [our] Yugoslav comrades, Tito had behind him a state and a people who had had a serious education in fighting for liberty and independence, a people who gave support to its leaders.

You see what Stalin's mania for greatness led to. He completely lost consciousness of reality. He demonstrated his suspicion and haughtiness not only in relation to individuals in the USSR, but in relation to whole parties and nations.

We have carefully examined the case of Yugoslavia. We have found a proper solution which is approved by the peoples of the Soviet Union and of Yugoslavia as well as by the working masses of all the people's democracies and by all progressive humanity. The liquidation of [our] abnormal relationship with Yugoslavia was done in the interest of the whole camp of socialism, in the interest of strengthening peace in the whole world.

Let us also recall the 'affair of the doctor-plotters.'

Actually there was no 'affair' outside of the declaration of the woman doctor [Lidiya] Timashuk, who was probably influenced or ordered by someone (after all, she was an unofficial collaborator of the organs of state security) to write Stalin a letter in which she declared that doctors were applying supposedly improper methods of medical treatment.

Such a letter was sufficient for Stalin to reach an immediate conclusion that there are doctor-plotters in the Soviet Union. He issued orders to arrest a group of eminent Soviet medical specialists. He personally issued advice on the conduct of the investigation and the method of interrogation of the arrested persons. He said that academician [V. N.] Vinogradov should be put in chains, and that another one [of the alleged plotters] should be beaten. The former Minister of State Security, comrade [Semyen] Ignatiev, is present at this Congress as a delegate. Stalin told him curtly, 'If you do not obtain confessions from the doctors we will shorten you by a head.'

Stalin personally called the investigative judge, gave him instructions, and advised him on which investigative methods should be used. These methods were simple—beat, beat and, beat again.

Shortly after the doctors were arrested, we members of the Politburo received protocols with the doctors' confessions of guilt. After distributing these protocols, Stalin told us, 'You are blind like young kittens. What will happen without me? The country will perish because you do not know how to recognize enemies.'

The case was presented so that no one could verify the facts on which the investigation was based. There was no possibility of trying to verify facts by contacting those who had made the confessions of guilt.

We felt, however, that the case of the arrested doctors was questionable. We knew some of these people personally because they had once treated us. When we examined this 'case' after Stalin's death, we found it to have been fabricated from beginning to end.

This ignominious 'case' was set up by Stalin. He did not, however, have the time in which to bring it to an end (as he conceived that end), and for this reason the doctors are still alive. All of them have been rehabilitated. They are working in the same places they were working before. They are treating top individuals, not excluding members of the Government. They have our full confidence; and they execute their duties honestly, as they did before.

In putting together various dirty and shameful cases, a very base role was played by a rabid enemy of our Party, an agent of a foreign intelligence service—Beria, who had stolen into Stalin's confidence. How could this provocateur have gained such a position in the Party and in the state, so as to become the First Deputy Chair of the Council of Ministers of the Soviet Union and a Politburo member? It has now been established that this villain climbed up the Government ladder over an untold number of corpses.

Were there any signs that Beria was an enemy of the Party? Yes, there were. Already in 1937, at a Central Committee Plenum, former People's Commissar of Health [Grigory] Kaminsky said that Beria worked for the Musavat intelligence service. But the Plenum had barely concluded when Kaminsky was arrested and then shot. Had Stalin examined Kaminsky's statement? No, because Stalin believed in Beria, and that was enough for him. And when Stalin believed in anyone or anything, then no one could say anything that was contrary to his opinion. Anyone daring to express opposition would have met the same fate as Kaminsky.

There were other signs, also. The declaration which comrade [A. V.] Snegov made to the Party's Central Committee is interesting. (Parenthetically speaking, he was also rehabilitated not long ago, after 17 years in prison camps.) In this declaration, Snegov writes:

'In connection with the proposed rehabilitation of the former Central Committee member, [Lavrenty] Kartvelishvili-Lavrentiev, I have entrusted to the hands of the representative of the Committee of State Security a detailed deposition concerning Beria's role in the disposition of the Kartvelishvili case and concerning the criminal motives by which Beria was guided.

'In my opinion, it is indispensable to recall an important fact pertaining to this case and to communicate it to the Central Committee, because I did not consider it as proper to include in the investigation documents.

'On October 30, 1931, at a session of the Organizational Bureau of the Central Committee of the All-Union Communist Party (Bolsheviks), Kartvelishvili, Secretary of the Transcaucasian Regional Committee, made a report. All members of the executive of the Regional Committee were present. Of them I alone am now alive.

'During this session, J. V. Stalin made a motion at the end of his speech concerning the organization of the secretariat of the Transcaucasian Regional Committee composed of the following: First Secretary, Kartvelishvili; Second Secretary, Beria (it was then, for the first time in the Party's history, that Beria's name was mentioned as a candidate for a Party position). Kartvelishvili answered that he knew Beria well and for that reason refused categorically to work together with him. Stalin proposed then that this matter be left open and that it be solved in the process of the work itself. Two days later a decision was arrived at that Beria would receive the Party post and that Kartvelishvili would be deported from the Transcaucasus.

'This fact can be confirmed by comrades Mikoyan and Kaganovich, who were present at that session.'

The long, unfriendly relations between Kartvelishvili and Beria were widely known. They date back to the time when comrade Sergo [Ordzhonikidze] was active in the Transcaucasus. Kartvelishvili was the closest assistant of Sergo. The unfriendly relationship impelled Beria to fabricate a 'case' against Kartvelishvili. It is characteristic that Kartvelishvili was charged with a terroristic act against Beria in this 'case.'

The indictment in the Beria case contains a discussion of his crimes. Some things should, however, be recalled, especially since it is possible that not all delegates to the Congress have read this document. I wish to recall Beria's bestial disposition of the cases of [Mikhail] Kedrov, [V.] Golubev, and Golubev's adopted mother, Baturina—persons who wished to inform the Central Committee concerning Beria's treacherous activity. They were shot without any trial and the sentence was passed ex post facto, after the execution.

Here is what the old Communist, comrade Kedrov, wrote to the Central Committee through comrade [Andrey] Andreyev (comrade Andreyev was then a Central Committee Secretary):

'I am calling to you for help from a gloomy cell of the Lefortovo prison. Let my cry of horror reach your ears; do not remain deaf, take me under your protection; please, help remove the nightmare of interrogations and show that this is all a mistake.

'I suffer innocently. Please believe me. Time will testify to the truth. I am not an agent provocateur of the Tsarist Okhrana. I am not a spy, I am not a member of an anti-Soviet organization of which I am being accused on the basis of denunciations. I am also not guilty of any other crimes against the Party and the Government. I am an old Bolshevik, free of any stain; I have honestly fought for almost 40 years in the ranks of the Party for the good and prosperity of the nation...

'...Today I, a 62-year-old man, am being threatened by the investigative judges with more severe, cruel and degrading methods of physical pressure. They (the judges) are no longer capable of becoming aware of their error and of recognizing that their handling of my case is illegal and impermissible. They try to justify their actions by picturing me as a hardened and raving enemy and are demanding increased repressions. But let the Party know that I am innocent and that there is nothing which can turn a loyal son of the Party into an enemy, even right up to his last dying breath.

'But I have no way out. I cannot divert from myself the hastily approaching new and powerful blows.

'Everything, however, has its limits. My torture has reached the extreme. My health is broken, my strength and my energy are waning, the end is drawing near. To die in a Soviet prison, branded as a vile traitor to the Fatherland—what can be more monstrous for an honest man? And how monstrous all this is! Unsurpassed bitterness and pain grips my heart. No! No! This will not happen; this cannot be, I cry. Neither the Party, nor the Soviet Government, nor the People's Commissar, L. P. Beria, will permit this cruel, irreparable injustice. I am firmly certain that, given a quiet, objective examination, without any foul rantings, without any anger and without the fearful tortures, it would be easy to prove the baselessness of the charges. I believe deeply that truth and justice will triumph. I believe. I believe.'

The old Bolshevik, comrade Kedrov, was found innocent by the Military Collegium. But, despite this, he was shot at Beria's order.

Beria also handled cruelly the family of comrade Ordzhonikidze. Why? Because Ordzhonikidze had tried to prevent Beria from realizing his shameful plans. Beria had cleared from his way all persons who could possibly interfere with him. Ordzhonikidze was always an opponent of Beria, which he told to Stalin. Instead of examining this affair and taking appropriate steps, Stalin allowed the liquidation of Ordzhonikidze's brother and brought Ordzhonikidze himself to such a state that he was forced to shoot himself.

Beria was unmasked by the Party's Central Committee shortly after Stalin's death. As a result of particularly detailed legal proceedings, it was established that Beria had committed monstrous crimes and Beria was shot.

The question arises why Beria, who had liquidated tens of thousands of Party and Soviet workers, was not unmasked during Stalin's life. He was not unmasked earlier because he had utilized very skillfully Stalin's weaknesses; feeding him with suspicions, he assisted Stalin in everything and acted with his support.

Comrades: The cult of the individual acquired such monstrous size chiefly because Stalin himself, using all conceivable methods, supported the glorification of his own person. This is supported by numerous facts. One of the most characteristic examples of Stalin's self-glorification and of his lack of even elementary modesty is the edition of his *Short Biography*, which was published in 1948 (sic).

This book is an expression of the most dissolute flattery, an example of making a man into a godhead, of transforming him into an infallible sage, 'the greatest leader, sublime strategist of all times and nations.' Finally, no other words could be found with which to lift Stalin up to the heavens.

We need not give here examples of the loathsome adulation filling this book. All we need to add is that they all were approved and edited by Stalin personally. Some of them were added in his own handwriting to the draft text of the book.

What did Stalin consider essential to write into this book? Did he want to cool the ardor of the flatterers who were composing his *Short Biography*? No! He marked the very places where he thought that the praise of his services was insufficient. Here are some examples characterizing Stalin's activity, added in Stalin's own hand:

'In this fight against the skeptics and capitulators, the Trotskyites, Zinovievites, Bukharinites and Kamenevites, there was definitely welded together, after Lenin's death, that leading core of the Party... that upheld the great banner of Lenin, rallied the Party behind Lenin's behests, and brought the Soviet people onto the broad paths of industrializing the country and collectivizing the rural economy. The leader of this core and the guiding force of the Party and the state was comrade Stalin.'

Thus writes Stalin himself! Then he adds:

'Although he performed his tasks as leader of the Party and the people with consummate skill, and enjoyed the unreserved support of the entire Soviet people, Stalin never allowed his work to be marred by the slightest hint of vanity, conceit or self-adulation.'

Where and when could a leader so praise himself? Is this worthy of a leader of the Marxist-Leninist type? No. Precisely against this did Marx and Engels take such a strong position. This always was sharply condemned also by Vladimir Ilyich Lenin.

In the draft text of [Stalin's] book appeared the following sentence: 'Stalin is the Lenin of today.' This sentence appeared to

Stalin to be too weak. Thus, in his own handwriting, he changed it to read: 'Stalin is the worthy continuer of Lenin's work, or, as it is said in our Party, Stalin is the Lenin of today.' You see how well it is said, not by the nation but by Stalin himself.

It is possible to offer many such self-praising appraisals written into the draft text of that book in Stalin's hand. He showers himself especially generously with praises regarding his military genius and his talent for strategy. I will cite one more insertion made by Stalin on the theme: 'The advanced Soviet science of war received further development,' he writes, 'at Comrade Stalin's hands. Comrade Stalin elaborated the theory of the permanent operating factors that decide the issue of wars, of active defense and the laws of counteroffensive and offensive, of the cooperation of all services and arms in modern warfare, of the role of big tank masses and air forces in modern war, and of the artillery as the most formidable of the armed services. At various stages of the war, Stalin's genius found correct solutions that took into account all the circumstances of the situation.'

Further, Stalin writes: 'Stalin's military mastership was displayed both in defense and on offense. Comrade Stalin's genius enabled him to divine the enemy's plans and defeat them. The battles in which comrade Stalin directed the Soviet armies are brilliant examples of operational military skill.'

This is how Stalin was praised as a strategist. Who did this? Stalin himself, not in his role as a strategist but in the role of an author-editor, one of the main creators of his [own] self-adulatory biography. Such, comrades, are the facts. Or should be said, rather, the shameful facts.

One additional fact from the same *Short Biography* of Stalin: As is known, the *History of the All-Union Communist Party (Bolsheviks), Short Course* was written by a commission of the Party Central Committee.

This book, parenthetically, was also permeated with the cult of the individual and was written by a designated group of authors. This fact was reflected in the following formulation on the proof copy of the *Short Biography* of Stalin: 'A commission of the Central Committee, All-Union Communist Party (Bolsheviks), under the direction of comrade Stalin and with his most active personal participation, has prepared a *History of the All-Union Communist Party (Bolsheviks), Short Course.*'

But even this phrase did not satisfy Stalin: The following sentence replaced it in the final version of the *Short Biography*: 'In 1938, the book *History of the All-Union Communist Party (Bolsheviks), Short Course* appeared, written by comrade Stalin and approved by a commission of the Central Committee, All-Union Communist Party (Bolsheviks).' Can one add anything more?

As you see, a surprising metamorphosis changed the work created by a group into a book written by Stalin. It is not necessary to state how and why this metamorphosis took place.

A pertinent question comes to our mind: If Stalin is the author of this book, why did he need to praise the person of Stalin so much and to transform the whole post-October historical period of our glorious Communist Party solely into an action of 'the Stalin genius'?

Did this book properly reflect the efforts of the Party in the socialist transformation of the country, in the construction of socialist society, in the industrialization and collectivization of the country, and also other steps taken by the Party which undeviatingly traveled the path outlined by Lenin? This book speaks principally about Stalin, about his speeches, about his reports. Everything without the smallest exception is tied to his name.

And when Stalin himself asserts that he himself wrote the *Short Course,* this calls at least for amazement. Can a Marxist-Leninist thus write about himself, praising his own person to the heavens?

Or let us take the matter of the Stalin Prizes.

Not even the Tsars created prizes which they named after themselves.

Stalin recognized as the best a text of the national anthem of the Soviet Union which contains not a word about the Communist Party; it contains, however, the following unprecedented praise of Stalin: 'Stalin brought us up in loyalty to the people. He inspired us to great toil and deeds.'

In these lines of the anthem, the whole educational, directional and inspirational activity of the great Leninist Party is ascribed to Stalin. This is, of course, a clear deviation from Marxism-Leninism, a clear debasing and belittling of the role of the Party. We should add for your information that the Presidium of the Central Committee has already passed a resolution concerning the composition of a new text of the anthem which will reflect the role of the people and the role of the Party.

And was it without Stalin's knowledge that many of the largest enterprises and towns were named after him? Was it without his knowledge that Stalin monuments were erected in the whole country—these 'memorials to the living'? It is a fact that Stalin himself had signed on July 2, 1951 a resolution of the USSR Council of Ministers concerning the erection on the Volga-Don Canal of an impressive monument to Stalin; on September 4 of the same year he issued an order making 33 tons of copper available for the construction of this impressive monument.

Anyone who has visited the Stalingrad area must have seen the huge statue which is being built there, and that on a site which hardly any people frequent. Huge sums were spent to build it at a time when people of this area had lived since the war in huts. Consider, yourself, was Stalin right when he wrote in his biography that '...he did not allow in himself...even a shadow of conceit, pride, or self-adoration'?

At the same time Stalin gave proofs of his lack of respect for Lenin's memory. It is not a coincidence that, despite the decision taken over 30 years ago to build a Palace of Soviets as a monument to Vladimir Ilyich, this palace was not built, its construction was always postponed and the project allowed to lapse.

We cannot forget to recall the Soviet Government resolution of August 14, 1925 concerning 'the founding of Lenin prizes for educational work.' This resolution was published in the press, but until this day there are no Lenin prizes. This, too, should be corrected.

During Stalin's life—thanks to known methods which I have mentioned, and quoting facts, for instance, from the *Short Biography* of Stalin—all events were explained as if Lenin played only a secondary role, even during the October Socialist Revolution. In many films and in many literary works the figure of Lenin was incorrectly presented and inadmissibly depreciated.

Stalin loved to see the film *The Unforgettable Year of 1919*, in which he was shown on the steps of an armored train and where he was practically vanquishing the foe with his own saber. Let Klimenty Yefremovich [Voroshilov], our dear friend, find the necessary courage and write the truth about Stalin; after all, he knows how Stalin had fought. It will be difficult for comrade Voroshilov to undertake this, but it would be good if he did it. Everyone will approve of it, both the people and the Party. Even his grandsons will thank him.

In speaking about the events of the October Revolution and about the Civil War, the impression was created that Stalin always played the main role, as if everywhere and always Stalin had suggested to Lenin what to do and how to do it. However, this is slander of Lenin.

I will probably not sin against the truth when I say that 99 per cent of the persons present here heard and knew very little about Stalin before the year 1924, while Lenin was known to all. He was known to the whole Party, to the whole nation, from children all the way up to old men.

All this has to be thoroughly revised so that history, literature and the fine arts properly reflect V. I. Lenin's role and the great deeds of our Communist Party and of the Soviet people—a creative people.

Comrades! The cult of the individual caused the employment of faulty principles in Party work and in economic activity. It brought about rude violation of internal Party and Soviet democracy, sterile administration, deviations of all sorts, cover-ups of shortcomings, and varnishings of reality. Our nation bore forth many flatterers and specialists in false optimism and deceit.

We should also not forget that, due to the numerous arrests of Party, Soviet and economic leaders, many workers began to work uncertainly, showed overcautiousness, feared all which was new, feared their own shadows, and began to show less initiative in their work.

Take, for instance, Party and Soviet resolutions. They were prepared in a routine manner, often without considering the concrete situation. This went so far that Party workers, even during the smallest sessions, read [prepared] speeches. All this produced the danger of formalizing the Party and Soviet work and of bureaucratizing the whole apparatus.

Stalin's reluctance to consider life's realities, and the fact that he was not aware of the real state of affairs in the provinces, can be illustrated by his direction of agriculture.

All those who interested themselves even a little in the national situation saw the difficult situation in agriculture, but Stalin never even noted it. Did we tell Stalin about this? Yes, we told him, but he did not support us. Why? Because Stalin never traveled anywhere, did not meet city and kolkhoz workers. He did not know the actual situation in the provinces.

He knew the country and agriculture only from films. And these films dressed up and beautified the existing situation in agriculture. Many films pictured kolkhoz life such that [farmhouse] tables groaned from the weight of turkeys and geese. Evidently, Stalin thought that it was actually so.

Vladimir Ilyich Lenin looked at life differently. He always was close to the people. He used to receive peasant delegates and often spoke at factory gatherings. He used to visit villages and talk with the peasants.

Stalin separated himself from the people and never went anywhere. This lasted ten years. The last time he visited a village was in January, 1928, when he visited Siberia in connection with grain procurements. How then could he have known the situation in the provinces?

Once, [Stalin] was told during a discussion that our situation on the land was a difficult one and that the situation in cattle breeding and meat production was especially bad. [From this] there came a commission charged with the preparation of a resolution called 'Measures toward the further development of animal husbandry in kolkhozes and sovkhozes.' We worked out this project.

Of course, our proposals at that time did not cover all the possibilities. However we did chart ways in which animal husbandry on kolkhozes and sovkhozes could be boosted. We proposed to raise livestock prices so as to create material incentives for kolkhoz, MTS [machine-tractor station] and sovkhoz workers in developing breeding. But our project was not accepted, In February 1953 it was laid aside entirely.

What is more, while reviewing this project Stalin proposed that the taxes paid by kolkhozes and by kolkhoz workers should be raised by 40 billion rubles. According to him, the peasants were well off and a kolkhoz worker would need to sell only one more chicken to pay his tax in full.

Think about what this implied. Forty billion rubles is a sum which [these workers] did not realize for *all* the products which they sold to the State. In 1952, for instance, kolkhozes and kolkhoz workers received 26,280 million rubles for all products delivered and sold to the State.

Did Stalin's position, then, rest on data of any sort whatever? Of course not. In such cases facts and figures did not interest him. If Stalin said anything, it meant it was so – after all, he was a 'genius,' and a genius does not need to count, he only needs to look and can immediately tell how it should be. When he expresses his opinion, everyone has to repeat it and to admire his wisdom.

But how much wisdom was contained in the proposal to raise the agricultural tax by 40 billion rubles? None, absolutely none, because the proposal was not based on an actual assessment of the situation but on the fantastic ideas of a person divorced from reality.

We are currently beginning slowly to work our way out of a difficult agricultural situation. The speeches of the delegates to the Twentieth Congress please us all. We are glad that many delegates have delivered speeches [to the effect] that conditions exist for fulfilling the sixth Five-Year Plan for animal husbandry [early]: not in five years, but within two to three years. We are certain that the commitments of the new Five-Year Plan will be accomplished successfully.

Comrades! If we sharply criticize today the cult of the individual which was so widespread during Stalin's life, and if we speak about the many negative phenomena generated by this cult (which is so alien to the spirit of Marxism-Leninism), some may ask: How could it be? Stalin headed the Party and the country for 30 years and many victories were gained during his lifetime. Can we deny this? In my opinion, the question can be asked in this manner only by those who are blinded and hopelessly hypnotized by the cult of the individual, only by those who do not understand the essence of the revolution and of the Soviet state, only by those who do not understand, in a Leninist manner, the role of the Party and of the nation in the development of the Soviet society.

[Our] Socialist Revolution was attained by the working class and by the poor peasantry with the partial support of middle-class peasants. It was attained by the people under the leadership of the Bolshevik Party. Lenin's great service consisted of the fact that he created a militant Party of the working class, but he was armed with Marxist understanding of the laws of social development and with the science of proletarian victory in the fight with capitalism, and he steeled this Party in the crucible of the revolutionary struggle of the masses of the people.

During this fight the Party consistently defended the interests of the people and became its experienced leader. [The Party] led the working masses to power, to the creation of the first socialist state. You remember well the wise words of Lenin: that the Soviet state is strong because of the awareness of the masses that history is created by the millions and tens of millions of people.

Our historical victories were attained thanks to the Party's organizational work, to the many provincial organizations, and to the self-sacrificing work of our great nation. These victories are the result of the great drive and activity of the nation and of the Party as a whole. They are not at all the fruit of Stalin's leadership, which is how the situation was pictured during the period of the cult of the individual.

If we are to consider this matter as Marxists and as Leninists, then we have to state unequivocally that the leadership practices which came into being during the last years of Stalin's life became a serious obstacle in the path of Soviet social development. Stalin often failed for months to take up some unusually important problems, concerning the life of the Party and of the State, whose solution could not be postponed. During Stalin's leadership our peaceful relations with other nations were often threatened, because one-man decisions could cause, and often did cause, great complications.

In the past [few] years, [after] we managed to free ourselves of the harmful practice of the cult of the individual and took several proper steps in terms of [both] internal and external policies, everyone [has been able to see] how activity has grown before our very eyes, how the creative activity of the broad working masses has developed, and how favorably all this has acted upon economic and cultural development.

Some comrades may ask us: Where were the members of the Politburo? Why did they not assert themselves against the cult of the individual in time? And why is this being done only now? First of all, we have to consider the fact that the members of the Politburo viewed these matters in a different way at different times. Initially, many of them backed Stalin actively because he was one of the strongest Marxists and his logic, his strength and his will greatly influenced [Party] cadres and Party work.

It is known that after Lenin's death, especially during the first years, Stalin actively fought for Leninism against the enemies of Leninist theory and against those who deviated. Beginning with Leninist theory, the Party, with its Central Committee at the head, started on a great scale work on the socialist industrialization of the country, on agricultural collectivization, and on cultural revolution. At that time Stalin gained great popularity, sympathy and support. The Party had to fight those who tried to lead the country away from the correct Leninist path. It had to fight Trotskyites, Zinovievites and rightists, and bourgeois nationalists. This fight was indispensable.

Later, however, Stalin, abusing his power more and more, began to fight eminent Party and Government leaders and to use terroristic methods against honest Soviet people. As we have already shown, Stalin thus handled such eminent Party and State leaders as Kosior, Rudzutak, Eikhe, Postyshev and many others.

Attempts to oppose groundless suspicions and charges resulted in the opponent's falling victim to the repression. This characterized the fall of comrade Postyshev.

In one of his [exchanges] Stalin expressed his dissatisfaction with Postyshev and asked him, 'What are you actually?'

Postyshev answered clearly, 'I am a Bolshevik, comrade Stalin, a Bolshevik.'

At first, this assertion was considered to show [merely] a lack of respect for Stalin. Later it was considered a harmful act. Eventually it resulted in Postyshev's annihilation and castigation as an 'enemy of the people.'

In the situation which then prevailed, I often talked with Nikolay Alexandrovich Bulganin. Once when we two were traveling in a car, he said, 'It has happened sometimes that a man goes to Stalin on his invitation as a friend. And when he sits with Stalin, he does not know where he will be sent next—home or to jail.'

It is clear that such conditions put every member of the Politburo in a very difficult situation. And, when we also consider the fact that in the last years Central Committee Plenary sessions were not convened and that sessions of the Politburo occurred only occasionally, from time to time, then we will understand how difficult it was for any member of the Politburo to take a stand against one or another unjust or improper procedure, against serious errors and shortcomings in leadership practices.

As we have already shown, many decisions were taken either by one person or in a roundabout way, without collective discussion. The sad fate of Politburo member comrade Voznesensky, who fell victim to Stalin's repressions, is known to all. Characteristically, the decision to remove him from the Politburo was never discussed but was reached in a devious fashion. In the same way came the decision regarding Kuznetsov's and Rodionov's removals from their posts.

The importance of the Central Committee's Politburo was reduced and its work was disorganized by the creation within the Politburo of various commissions—the so-called 'quintets,' 'sextets,' 'septets' and 'nonets' Here is, for instance, a Politburo resolution from October 3, 1946:

'Stalin's proposal:

'1. The Politburo Commission for Foreign Affairs ('sextet') is to concern itself in the future, in addition to foreign affairs, also with matters of internal construction and domestic policy.

'2. The Sextet is to add to its roster the Chairman of the State Commission of Economic Planning of the USSR, comrade Voznesensky, and is to be known as a Septet.

'Signed: Secretary of the Central Committee, J. Stalin.'

What [sophistry]!

It is clear that the creation within the Politburo of this type of commissions— 'quintets,' 'sextets,' 'septets' and 'nonets' —was against the principle of collective leadership. The result of this was that some members of the Politburo were in this way kept away from participation in reaching the most important state matters.

One of the oldest members of our Party, Klimenty Yefremovich Voroshilov, found himself in an almost impossible situation. For several years he was actually deprived of the right of participation in Politburo sessions. Stalin forbade him to attend Politburo sessions and to receive documents. When the Politburo was in session and comrade Voroshilov heard about it, he telephoned each time and asked whether he would be allowed to attend. Sometimes Stalin permitted it, but always showed his dissatisfaction.

Because of his extreme suspicion, Stalin toyed also with the absurd and ridiculous suspicion that Voroshilov was an English agent.

It's true—an English agent. A special tap was installed in his home to listen to what was said there.

By unilateral decision, Stalin had also separated one other man from the work of the Politburo—Andrey Andreyevich Andreyev. This was one of the most unbridled acts of willfulness.

Let us consider the first Central Committee Plenum after the 19th Party Congress. Stalin, in his talk at the Plenum, characterized Vyacheslav Mikhailovich Molotov and Anastas Ivanovich Mikoyan and suggested that these old workers of our Party were guilty of some baseless charges. We cannot rule out the possibility that had Stalin remained at the helm for another several months, Comrades Molotov and Mikoyan probably would not have delivered any speeches at this [20th] Congress.

Stalin evidently had plans to finish off the older members of the Politburo. He often stated that Politburo members should be replaced by new ones. His proposal after the 19th Congress to elect 25 persons to the Central Committee Presidium was aimed at the removal of old Politburo members and at bringing in less experienced persons so that these would extol him in all sorts of ways.

We can assume that this was also a design for the future annihilation of the old Politburo members and, in this way, a cover for all shameful acts of Stalin, acts which we are now considering.

Comrades! So as not to repeat errors of the past, the Central Committee has declared itself resolutely against the cult of the individual. We consider that Stalin was extolled to excess. However, in the past Stalin undoubtedly performed great services to the Party, to the working class and to the international workers' movement.

This question is complicated by the fact that all this which we have just discussed was done during Stalin's life under his leadership and with his concurrence; here Stalin was convinced that this was necessary for the defense of the interests of the working classes against the plotting of enemies and against the attack of the imperialist camp.

He saw this from the position of the interest of the working class, of the interest of the laboring people, of the interest of the victory of socialism and communism. We cannot say that these were the deeds of a giddy despot. He considered that this should be done in the interest of the Party, of the working masses, in the name of the defense of the revolution's gains. In this lies the whole tragedy!

Comrades! Lenin had often stressed that modesty is an absolutely integral part of a real Bolshevik. Lenin himself was the living personification of the greatest modesty. We cannot say that we have been following this Leninist example in all respects.

It is enough to point out that many towns, factories and industrial enterprises, kolkhozes and sovkhozes, Soviet institutions and cultural institutions have been referred to by us with a title if I may express it so—of private property of the names of these or those Government or Party leaders who were still active and in good health. Many of us participated in the action of assigning our names to various towns, rayons, enterprises and kolkhozes. We must correct this.

But this should be done calmly and slowly. The Central Committee will discuss this matter and consider it carefully in order to prevent errors and excesses. I can remember how Ukraine learned about Kossior's arrest. Kiev radio used to start its programs thus: 'This is Radio Kosior.' When one day the programs began without mentioning Kosior, everyone was quite certain that something had happened to him and that he probably had been arrested.

Thus, if today we begin to change the signs everywhere and to rename things, people will think that these comrades in whose honor the given enterprises, kolkhozes or cities are named also met some bad fate and that they have also been arrested.

How is the authority and the importance of this or that leader judged? On the basis of how many towns, industrial enterprises and factories, kolkhozes and sovkhozes carry his name. Is it not about time that we eliminate this 'private property' and 'nationalize' the factories, the industrial enterprises, the kolkhozes and the sovkhozes? (Laughter, applause, voices: 'That is right.') This will benefit our cause. After all, the cult of the individual is manifested also in this way.

We should, in all seriousness, consider the question of the cult of the individual. We cannot let this matter get out of the Party, especially not to the press. It is for this reason that we are considering it here at a closed Congress session. We should know the limits; we should not give ammunition to the enemy; we should not wash our dirty linen before their eyes. I think that the delegates to the Congress will understand and assess properly all these proposals.

Comrades! We must abolish the cult of the individual decisively, once and for all; we must draw the proper conclusions concerning both ideological-theoretical and practical work. It is necessary for this purpose:

First, in a Bolshevik manner to condemn and to eradicate the cult of the individual as alien to Marxism-Leninism and not consonant with the principles of Party leadership and the norms of Party life, and to fight inexorably all attempts at bringing back this practice in one form or another.

To return to and actually practice in all our ideological work the most important theses of Marxist-Leninist science about the people as the creator of history and as the creator of all material and spiritual good of humanity, about the decisive role of the Marxist Party in the revolutionary fight for the transformation of society, about the victory of communism.

In this connection we will be forced to do much work in order to examine critically from the Marxist-Leninist viewpoint and to correct the widely spread erroneous views connected with the cult of the individual in the spheres of history, philosophy, economy and of other sciences, as well as in literature and the fine arts. It is especially necessary that in the immediate future we compile a serious textbook of the history of our Party which will be edited in accordance with scientific Marxist objectivism, a textbook of the history of Soviet society, a book pertaining to the events of the Civil War and the Great Patriotic War.

Second, to continue systematically and consistently the work done by the Party's Central Committee during the last years, a work characterized by minute observation in all Party organizations, from the bottom to the top, of the Leninist principles of Party leadership, characterized, above all, by the main principle of collective leadership, characterized by the observance of the norms of Party life described in the statutes of our Party, and, finally, characterized by the wide practice of criticism and self-criticism.

Third, to restore completely the Leninist principles of Soviet socialist democracy, expressed in the Constitution of the Soviet Union, to fight willfulness of individuals abusing their power. The evil caused by acts violating revolutionary socialist legality which have accumulated during a long time as a result of the negative influence of the cult of the individual has to be completely corrected.

Comrades! The 20th Congress of the Communist Party of the Soviet Union has manifested with a new strength the unshakable unity of our Party, its cohesiveness around the Central Committee, its resolute will to accomplish the great task of building communism. And the fact that we present in all their ramifications the basic problems of overcoming the cult of the individual which is alien to Marxism Leninism, as well as the problem of liquidating its burdensome consequences, is evidence of the great moral and political strength of our Party.

We are absolutely certain that our Party, armed with the historical resolutions of the 20th Congress, will lead the Soviet people along the Leninist path to new successes, to new victories.

Long live the victorious banner of our Party—Leninism!

'Wind of Change'

Harold Macmillan

South African Parliament, South Africa (3 February 1960)

Harold Macmillan was Prime Minister of the United Kingdom from 1957 to 1963. He was credited with improving British-American relations during the Suez Canal crisis and his successful foreign policy as well as post-war policies guaranteed full employment to the British people.

The famous 'Wind of Change' speech was made to the Parliament of South Africa in 1960 during a visit to African British colonies, when Macmillan was Prime Minister.

It is, as I have said, a special privilege for me to be here in 1960 when you are celebrating what I might call the golden wedding of the Union. At such a time it is natural and right that you should pause to take stock of your position, to look back at what you have achieved, to look forward to what lies ahead. In the 50 years of their nationhood the people of South Africa have built a strong economy founded upon a healthy agriculture and thriving and resilient industries.

No one could fail to be impressed with the immense material progress which has been achieved. That all this has been accomplished in so short a time is a striking testimony to the skill, energy and initiative of your people. We in Britain are proud of the contribution we have made to this remarkable achievement. Much of it has been financed by British capital.

As I've travelled around the Union I have found everywhere, as I expected, a deep preoccupation with what is happening in the rest of the African continent. I understand and sympathise with your interests in these events and your anxiety about them.

Ever since the breakup of the Roman empire one of the constant facts of political life in Europe has been the emergence of independent nations. They have come into existence over the centuries in different forms, different kinds of government, but all have been inspired by a deep, keen feeling of nationalism, which has grown as the nations have grown.

In the twentieth century, and especially since the end of the war, the processes which gave birth to the nation states of Europe have been repeated all over the world. We have seen the awakening of national consciousness in peoples who have for centuries lived in dependence upon some other power. Fifteen years ago this movement spread through Asia. Many countries there, of different races and civilisations, pressed their claim to an independent national life.

Today the same thing is happening in Africa, and the most striking of all the impressions I have formed since I left London a month ago is of the strength of this African national consciousness. In different places it takes different forms, but it is happening everywhere.

The wind of change is blowing through this continent, and whether we like it or not, this growth of national consciousness is a political fact. We must all accept it as a fact, and our national policies must take account of it.

Well you understand this better than anyone, you are sprung from Europe, the home of nationalism, here in Africa you have yourselves created a free nation. A new nation. Indeed in the history of our times yours will be recorded as the first of the African nationalists. This tide of national consciousness which is now rising in Africa, is a fact, for which both you and we, and the other nations of the western world are ultimately responsible. For its causes are to be found in the achievements of western civilisation, in the pushing forwards of the frontiers of knowledge, the applying of science to the service of human needs, in the expanding of food production, in the speeding and multiplying of the means of communication, and perhaps above all and more than anything else in the spread of education.

As I have said, the growth of national consciousness in Africa is a political fact, and we must accept it as such. That means, I would judge, that we've got to come to terms with it. I sincerely believe that if we cannot do so we may imperil the precarious balance between the East and West on which the peace of the world depends.

The world today is divided into three main groups. First there are what we call the Western Powers. You in South Africa and we in Britain belong to this group, together with our friends and allies in other parts of the Commonwealth. In the United States of America and in Europe we call it the Free World.

Secondly there are the Communists—Russia and her satellites in Europe and China whose population will rise by the end of the next ten years to the staggering total of 800 million. Thirdly, there are those parts of the world whose people are at present uncommitted either to Communism or to our Western ideas.

In this context we think first of Asia and then of Africa. As I see it the great issue in this second half of the twentieth century is whether the uncommitted peoples of Asia and Africa will swing to the East or to the West. Will they be drawn into the Communist camp? Or will the great experiments in self-government that are now being made in Asia and Africa, especially within the Commonwealth, prove so successful, and by their example so compelling, that the balance will come down in favour of freedom and order and justice? The struggle is joined, and it is a struggle for the minds of men. What is now on trial is much more than our military strength or our diplomatic and administrative skill. It is our way of life. The uncommitted nations want to see before they choose.

Address to the United Nations

Haile Selassie

(6 October 1963)

Haile Selassie I was Emperor of Ethiopia from 1930 to1974. He modernised his country and introduced progressive economic, social and political reforms for the betterment of his people. Ethiopia came to the fore in the United Nations and the League of Nations under his leadership, and Addis Ababa became a major centre of the African Union.

In this moving address to the United Nations, Haile Selassie urges African unity and the need to end racial discrimination that hampers development of the African people.

27 years ago, as Emperor of Ethiopia, I mounted the rostrum in Geneva, Switzerland, to address the League of Nations and to appeal for relief from the destruction which had been unleashed against my defenseless nation, by the Fascist invader. I spoke then both to and for the conscience of the world. My words went unheeded, but history testifies to the accuracy of the warning that I gave in 1936.

Today, I stand before the world organisation which has succeeded to the mantle discarded by its discredited predecessor. In this body is enshrined the principle of collective security which I unsuccessfully invoked at Geneva. Here, in this Assembly, reposes the best—perhaps the last—hope for the peaceful survival of mankind.

In 1936, I declared that it was not the Covenant of the League that was at stake, but international morality. Undertakings, I said then, are of little worth if the will to keep them is lacking. The

Charter of the United Nations expresses the noblest aspirations of man: abjuration of force in the settlement of disputes between states; the assurance of human rights and fundamental freedoms for all without distinction as to race, sex, language or religion; the safeguarding of international peace and security.

But these, too, as were the phrases of the Covenant, are only words; their value depends wholly on our will to observe and honor them and give them content and meaning. The preservation of peace and the guaranteeing of man's basic freedoms and rights require courage and eternal vigilance: courage to speak and act— and if necessary, to suffer and die—for truth and justice; eternal vigilance, that the least transgression of international morality shall not go undetected and unremedied. These lessons must be learned anew by each succeeding generation, and that generation is fortunate indeed which learns from other than its own bitter experience. This Organisation and each of its members bear a crushing and awesome responsibility: to absorb the wisdom of history and to apply it to the problems of the present, in order that future generations may be born, and live, and die, in peace.

The record of the United Nations during the few short years of its life affords mankind a solid basis for encouragement and hope for the future. The United Nations has dared to act, when the League dared not in Palestine, in Korea, in Suez, in the Congo. There is not one among us today who does not conjecture upon the reaction of this body when motives and actions are called into question. The opinion of this Organisation today acts as a powerful influence upon the decisions of its members. The spotlight of world opinion, focused by the United Nations upon the transgressions of the renegades of human society, has thus far proved an effective safeguard against unchecked aggression and unrestricted violation of human rights.

The United Nations continues to serve as the forum where nations whose interests clash may lay their cases before world opinion. It still provides the essential escape valve without which the slow build-up of pressures would have long since resulted in catastrophic explosion. Its actions and decisions have speeded the achievement of freedom by many peoples on the continents of

Africa and Asia. Its efforts have contributed to the advancement of the standard of living of peoples in all corners of the world.

For this, all men must give thanks. As I stand here today, how faint, how remote are the memories of 1936. How different in 1963 are the attitudes of men. We then existed in an atmosphere of suffocating pessimism. Today, cautious yet buoyant optimism is the prevailing spirit.

But each one of us here knows that what has been accomplished is not enough. The United Nations judgments have been and continue to be subject to frustration, as individual member-states have ignored its pronouncements and disregarded its recommendations. The Organisation's sinews have been weakened, as member-states have shirked their obligations to it. The authority of the Organisation has been mocked, as individual member-states have proceeded, in violation of its commands, to pursue their own aims and ends. The troubles which continue to plague us virtually all arise among member states of the Organisation, but the Organisation remains impotent to enforce acceptable solutions. As the maker and enforcer of the international law, what the United Nations has achieved still falls regrettably short of our goal of an international community of nations.

This does not mean that the United Nations has failed. I have lived too long to cherish many illusions about the essential high mindedness of men when brought into stark confrontation with the issue of control over their security, and their property interests. Not even now, when so much is at hazard would many nations willingly entrust their destinies to other hands.

Yet, this is the ultimatum presented to us: secure the conditions whereby men will entrust their security to a larger entity, or risk annihilation; persuade men that their salvation rests in the subordination of national and local interests to the interests of humanity, or endanger man's future. These are the objectives, yesterday unobtainable, today essential, which we must labor to achieve.

Until this is accomplished, mankind's future remains hazardous and permanent peace a matter for speculation. There is no single magic formula, no one simple step, no words, whether written into the Organisation's Charter or into a treaty between states, which can automatically guarantee to us what we seek. Peace is a day-to-day problem, the product of a multitude of events and judgements. Peace is not an 'is', it is a 'becoming.' We cannot escape the dreadful possibility of catastrophe by miscalculation.

But we can reach the right decisions on the myriad subordinate problems which each new day poses, and we can thereby make our contribution and perhaps the most that can be reasonably expected of us in 1963 to the preservation of peace. It is here that the United Nations has served us—not perfectly, but well. And in enhancing the possibilities that the Organisation may serve us better, we serve and bring closer our most cherished goals.

I would mention briefly today two particular issues which are of deep concern to all men: disarmament and the establishment of true equality among men. Disarmament has become the urgent imperative of our time. I do not say this because I equate the absence of arms to peace, or because I believe that bringing an end to the nuclear arms race automatically guarantees the peace, or because the elimination of nuclear warheads from the arsenals of the world will bring in its wake that change in attitude requisite to the peaceful settlement of disputes between nations. Disarmament is vital today, quite simply, because of the immense destructive capacity of which men dispose.

Ethiopia supports the atmospheric nuclear test ban treaty as a step towards this goal, even though only a partial step. Nations can still perfect weapons of mass destruction by underground testing. There is no guarantee against the sudden, unannounced resumption of testing in the atmosphere.

The real significance of the treaty is that it admits of a tacit stalemate between the nations which negotiated it, a stalemate which recognizes the blunt, unavoidable fact that none would emerge from the total destruction which would be the lot of all in a nuclear war, a stalemate which affords us and the United Nations a breathing space in which to act.

Here is our opportunity and our challenge. If the nuclear powers are prepared to declare a truce, let us seize the moment to strengthen the institutions and procedures which will serve as the means for the pacific settlement of disputes among men. Conflicts between nations will continue to arise. The real issue is whether they are to be resolved by force, or by resort to peaceful methods and procedures, administered by impartial institutions. This very Organisation itself is the greatest such institution, and it is in a more powerful United Nations that we seek, and it is here that we shall find, the assurance of a peaceful future.

Were a real and effective disarmament achieved and the funds now spent in the arms race devoted to the amelioration of man's state; were we to concentrate only on the peaceful uses of nuclear knowledge, how vastly and in how short a time might we change the conditions of mankind. This should be our goal.

When we talk of the equality of man, we find, also, a challenge and an opportunity; a challenge to breathe new life into the ideals enshrined in the Charter, an opportunity to bring men closer to freedom and true equality and thus, closer to a love of peace.

The goal of the equality of man which we seek is the antithesis of the exploitation of one people by another with which the pages of history and in particular those written of the African and Asian continents, speak at such length. Exploitation, thus viewed, has many faces. But whatever guise it assumes, this evil is to be shunned where it does not exist and crushed where it does. It is the sacred duty of this Organisation to ensure that the dream of equality is finally realized for all men to whom it is still denied, to guarantee that exploitation is not reincarnated in other forms in places whence it has already been banished.

As a free Africa has emerged during the past decade, a fresh attack has been launched against exploitation, wherever it still exists. And in that interaction so common to history, this in turn, has stimulated and encouraged the remaining dependent peoples to renewed efforts to throw off the yoke which has oppressed them and its claim as their birthright the twin ideals of liberty and equality. This very struggle is a struggle to establish peace, and until victory is assured, that brotherhood and understanding which nourish and give life to peace can be but partial and incomplete.

In the United States of America, the administration of President Kennedy is leading a vigorous attack to eradicate the remaining vestige of racial discrimination from this country. We know that this conflict will be won and that right will triumph. In this time of trial, these efforts should be encouraged and assisted, and we should lend our sympathy and support to the American Government today.

Last May, in Addis Ababa, I convened a meeting of Heads of African States and Governments. In three days, the 32 nations represented at that Conference demonstrated to the world that when the will and the determination exist, nations and peoples of diverse backgrounds can and will work together. in unity, to the achievement of common goals and the assurance of that equality and brotherhood which we desire.

On the question of racial discrimination, the Addis Ababa Conference taught, to those who will learn, this further lesson: that until the philosophy which holds one race superior and another inferior is finally and permanently discredited and abandoned; that until there are no longer first class and second class citizens of any nation; that until the color of a man's skin is of no more significance than the color of his eyes; that until the basic human rights are equally guaranteed to all without regard to race; that until that day, the dream of lasting peace and world citizenship and the rule of international morality will remain but a fleeting illusion, to be pursued but never attained.

And until the ignoble and unhappy regimes that hold our brothers in Angola, in Mozambique and in South Africa in subhuman bondage have been toppled and destroyed; until bigotry and prejudice and malicious and inhuman self-interest have been replaced by understanding and tolerance and good-will; until all Africans stand and speak as free beings, equal in the eyes of all men, as they are in the eyes of Heaven; until that day, the African continent will not know peace. We Africans will fight, if necessary, and we know that we shall win, as we are confident in the victory of good over evil.

The United Nations has done much, both directly and indirectly to speed the disappearance of discrimination and oppression from the earth. Without the opportunity to focus world opinion on Africa and Asia which this Organization provides, the goal, for many, might still lie ahead, and the struggle would have taken far longer. For this, we are truly grateful.

But more can be done. The basis of racial discrimination and colonialism has been economic, and it is with economic weapons that these evils have been and can be overcome. In pursuance of resolutions adopted at the Addis Ababa Summit Conference, African States have undertaken certain measures in the economic field which, if adopted by all member states of the United Nations, would soon reduce intransigence to reason. I ask, today, for adherence to these measures by every nation represented here which is truly devoted to the principles enunciated in the Charter.

I do not believe that Portugal and South Africa are prepared to commit economic or physical suicide if honorable and reasonable alternatives exist. I believe that such alternatives can be found. But I also know that unless peaceful solutions are devised, counsels of moderation and temperance will avail for naught; and another blow will have been dealt to this Organisation which will hamper and weaken still further its usefulness in the struggle to ensure the victory of peace and liberty over the forces of strife and oppression. Here, then, is the opportunity presented to us. We must act while we can, while the occasion exists to exert those legitimate pressures available to us, lest time run out and resort be had to less happy means.

Does this Organisation today possess the authority and the will to act? And if it does not, are we prepared to clothe it with the power to create and enforce the rule of law? Or is the Charter a mere collection of words, without content and substance, because the essential spirit is lacking? The time in which to ponder these questions is all too short. The pages of history are full of instances in which the unwanted and the shunned nonetheless occurred because men waited to act until too late. We can brook no such delay.

If we are to survive, this Organisation must survive. To survive, it must be strengthened. Its executive must be vested with great authority. The means for the enforcement of its decisions must be fortified, and, if they do not exist, they must be devised. Procedures must be established to protect the small and the weak when threatened by the strong and the mighty. All nations which fulfill the conditions of membership must be admitted and allowed to sit in this assemblage.

Equality of representation must be assured in each of its organs. The possibilities which exist in the United Nations to provide the medium whereby the hungry may be fed, the naked clothed, the ignorant instructed, must be seized on and exploited for the flower of peace is not sustained by poverty and want.

To achieve this requires courage and confidence. The courage, I believe, we possess. The confidence must be created, and to create confidence we must act courageously.

The great nations of the world would do well to remember that in the modern age even their own fates are not wholly in their hands. Peace demands the united efforts of us all. Who can foresee what spark might ignite the fuse? It is not only the small and the weak who must scrupulously observe their obligations to the United Nations and to each other. Unless the smaller nations are accorded their proper voice in the settlement of the world's problems, unless the equality which Africa and Asia have struggled to attain is reflected in expanded membership in the institutions which make up the United Nations, confidence will come just that much harder. Unless the rights of the least of men are as assiduously protected as those of the greatest, the seeds of confidence will fall on barren soil.

The stake of each one of us is identical—life or death. We all wish to live. We all seek a world in which men are freed of the burdens of ignorance, poverty, hunger and disease. And we shall all be hard-pressed to escape the deadly rain of nuclear fall-out should catastrophe overtake us.

When I spoke at Geneva in 1936, there was no precedent for a head of state addressing the League of Nations. I am neither the first, nor will I be the last head of state to address the United Nations, but only I have addressed both the League and this Organisation in this capacity.

The problems which confront us today are, equally, unprecedented. They have no counterparts in human experience. Men search the pages of history for solutions, for precedents, but there are none.

This, then, is the ultimate challenge. Where are we to look for our survival, for the answers to the questions which have never before been posed?

We must look, first, to Almighty God, Who has raised man above the animals and endowed him with intelligence and reason. We must put our faith in Him, that He will not desert us or permit us to destroy humanity which He created in His image.

And we must look into ourselves, into the depth of our souls. We must become something we have never been and for which our education and experience and environment have ill-prepared us. We must become bigger than we have been: more courageous, greater in spirit, larger in outlook. We must become members of a new race, overcoming petty prejudice, owing our ultimate allegiance not to nations but to our fellow men within the human community.

'Ich bin ein Berliner'

John F. Kennedy

West Berlin (26 June 1963)

John F. Kennedy was the 35th President of the United States who tackled Cold War tensions in Cuba, Vietnam and other places. He gained popularity through his support for the civil rights movement and drive for public service. To this day, he remains one of the most beloved presidents of the United States. He was assassinated on 22 November 1963 in Dallas, Texas, by Lee Harvey Oswald.

Through this speech, considered one of the most famous speeches of the Cold War, Kennedy declares U.S. support for West Germany.

I am proud to come to this city as the guest of your distinguished Mayor, who has symbolized throughout the world the fighting spirit of West Berlin. And I am proud to visit the Federal Republic with your distinguished Chancellor who for so many years has committed Germany to democracy and freedom and progress, and to come here in the company of my fellow American, General Clay, who has been in this city during its great moments of crisis and will come again if ever needed.

Two thousand years ago the proudest boast was *'Civis Romanus Sum.'* Today, in the world of freedom, the proudest boast is *'Ich bin ein Berliner.'*

I appreciate my interpreter translating my German!

There are many people in the world who really don't understand, or say they don't, what is the great issue between the free world and the Communist world. Let them come to Berlin. There are some who say that communism is the wave of the future. Let them come to Berlin. And there are some who say in Europe and elsewhere we can work with the Communists. Let them come to Berlin. And there are even a few who say that it is true that communism is an evil system, but it permits us to make economic progress. *Lass' sie nach Berlin kommen.* Let them come to Berlin.

Freedom has many difficulties and democracy is not perfect, but we have never had to put a wall up to keep our people in, to prevent them from leaving us. I want to say, on behalf of my countrymen, who live many miles away on the other side of the Atlantic, who are far distant from you, that they take the greatest pride that they have been able to share with you, even from a distance, the story of the last 18 years. I know of no town, no city, that has been besieged for 18 years that still lives with the vitality and the force, and the hope and the determination of the city of West Berlin. While the wall is the most obvious and vivid demonstration of the failures of the Communist system, for all the world to see, we take no satisfaction in it, for it is, as your Mayor has said, an offense not only against history but an offense against humanity, separating families, dividing husbands and wives and brothers and sisters, and dividing a people who wish to be joined together.

What is true of this city is true of Germany—real, lasting peace in Europe can never be assured as long as one German out of four is denied the elementary right of free men, and that is to make a free choice. In 18 years of peace and good faith, this generation of Germans has earned the right to be free, including the right to unite their families and their nation in lasting peace, with good will to all people. You live in a defended island of freedom, but your life is part of the main. So let me ask you as I close, to lift your eyes beyond the dangers of today, to the hopes of tomorrow, beyond the freedom merely of this city of Berlin, or your country of Germany, to the advance of freedom everywhere, beyond the wall to the day of peace with justice, beyond yourselves and ourselves to all mankind.

Freedom is indivisible, and when one man is enslaved, all are not free. When all are free, then we can look forward to that day when this city will be joined as one and this country and this great Continent of Europe in a peaceful and hopeful globe. When that day finally comes, as it will, the people of West Berlin can take sober satisfaction in the fact that they were in the front lines for almost two decades.

All free men, wherever they may live, are citizens of Berlin, and, therefore, as a free man, I take pride in the words *'Ich bin ein Berliner.'*

‘I Have a Dream’

Martin Luther King Jr.

The Great March on Washington (28 August 1963)

Martin Luther King Jr. was a social activist who played a major role during the civil rights movement. King challenged racial discrimination and sought equality for African-Americans through peaceful protest. Through his efforts, he helped bring about two important legislations—the Civil Rights Act and the Voting Rights Act. He won the Nobel Peace Prize in 1964. King was assassinated in 1968 by James Earl Ray, a known racist.

‘I Have a Dream’ is one of the most famous speeches in history and was a call for peace and equality for all.

I am happy to join with you today in what will go down in history as the greatest demonstration for freedom in the history of our nation.

Five score years ago, a great American, in whose symbolic shadow we stand today, signed the Emancipation Proclamation. This momentous decree came as a great beacon light of hope to millions of Negro slaves who had been seared in the flames of withering injustice. It came as a joyous daybreak to end the long night of captivity.

But one hundred years later, the Negro still is not free. One hundred years later, the life of the Negro is still sadly crippled by the manacles of segregation and the chains of discrimination. One hundred years later, the Negro lives on a lonely island of poverty in the midst of a vast ocean of material prosperity. One hundred years later, the Negro is still languished in the corners of American society and finds himself in exile in his own land. So we have come here today to dramatize an shameful condition.

In a sense we've come to our nation's Capital to cash a check. When the architects of our republic wrote the magnificent words of the Constitution and the Declaration of Independence, they were signing a promissory note to which every American was to fall heir.

This note was a promise that all men, yes, black men as well as white men, would be guaranteed the unalienable rights of life, liberty, and the pursuit of happiness.

It is obvious today that America has defaulted on this promissory note insofar as her citizens of color are concerned. Instead of honoring this sacred obligation, America has given the Negro people a bad check; a check which has come back marked 'insufficient funds.'

But we refuse to believe that the bank of justice is bankrupt. We refuse to believe that there are insufficient funds in the great vaults of opportunity of this nation. So we have come to cash this check—a check that will give us upon demand the riches of freedom and the security of justice.

We have also come to this hallowed spot to remind America of the fierce urgency of now. This is no time to engage in the luxury of cooling off or to take the tranquilizing drug of gradualism.

Now is the time to make real the promises of democracy. Now is the time to rise from the dark and desolate valley of segregation to the sunlit path of racial justice. Now is the time to lift our nation from the quicksands of racial injustice to the solid rock of brotherhood. Now is the time to make justice a reality for all of God's children.

It would be fatal for the nation to overlook the urgency of the moment. This sweltering summer of the Negro's legitimate discontent will not pass until there is an invigorating autumn of freedom and equality. 1963 is not an end, but a beginning. Those who hope that the Negro needed to blow off steam and will now be content will have a rude awakening if the nation returns to business as usual. There will be neither rest nor tranquility in America until the Negro is granted his citizenship rights. The whirlwinds of revolt will continue to shake the foundations of our nation until the bright day of justice emerges.

But there is something that I must say to my people who stand on the warm threshold which leads into the palace of justice. In the process of gaining our rightful place we must not be guilty of wrongful deeds. Let us not seek to satisfy our thirst for freedom by drinking from the cup of bitterness and hatred. We must forever conduct our struggle on the high plane of dignity and discipline. We must not allow our creative protest to degenerate into physical violence. Again and again we must rise to the majestic heights of meeting physical force with soul force.

The marvelous new militancy which has engulfed the Negro community must not lead us to a distrust of all white people, for many of our white brothers, as evidenced by their presence here today, have come to realize that their destiny is tied up with our destiny. And they have come to realize that their freedom is inextricably bound to our freedom. We cannot walk alone.

And as we walk, we must make the pledge that we shall march ahead. We cannot turn back. There are those who are asking the devotees of civil rights, 'When will you be satisfied?'

We can never be satisfied as long as the Negro is the victim of the unspeakable horrors of police brutality.

We can never be satisfied as long as our bodies, heavy with the fatigue of travel, cannot gain lodging in the motels of the highways and the hotels of the cities.

We cannot be satisfied as long as the Negro's basic mobility is from a smaller ghetto to a larger one.

We can never be satisfied as long as our children are stripped of their selfhood and robbed of their dignity by signs stating 'for whites only.'

We cannot be satisfied as long as a Negro in Mississippi cannot vote and a Negro in New York believes he has nothing for which to vote.

No, no, we are not satisfied, and we will not be satisfied until justice rolls down like waters and righteousness like a mighty stream.

I am not unmindful that some of you have come here out of great trials and tribulations. Some of you have come fresh from narrow jail cells. Some of you have come from areas where your quest for freedom left you battered by the storms of persecution and staggered by the winds of police brutality. You have been the veterans of creative suffering. Continue to work with the faith that unearned suffering is redemptive.

Go back to Mississippi, go back to Alabama, go back to South Carolina, go back to Georgia, go back to Louisiana, go back to the slums and ghettos of our northern cities, knowing that somehow this situation can and will be changed. Let us not wallow in the valley of despair.

I say to you today, my friends, so even though we face the difficulties of today and tomorrow, I still have a dream. It is a dream deeply rooted in the American dream.

I have a dream that one day this nation will rise up and live out the true meaning of its creed: 'We hold these truths to be self-evident; that all men are created equal.'

I have a dream that one day on the red hills of Georgia the sons of former slaves and the sons of former slave owners will be able to sit down together at the table of brotherhood.

I have a dream that one day even the state of Mississippi, a state sweltering with the heat of injustice, sweltering with the heat of oppression, will be transformed into an oasis of freedom and justice.

I have a dream that my four little children will one day live in a nation where they will not be judged by the color of their skin but by the content of their character.

I have a dream today.

I have a dream that one day down in Alabama, with its vicious racists, with its governor having his lips dripping with the words of interposition and nullification, that one day right down in Alabama little black boys and black girls will be able to join hands with little white boys and white girls as sisters and brothers.

I have a dream today.

I have a dream that one day every valley shall be exalted, every hill and mountain shall be made low, the rough places will be made plain, and the crooked places will be made straight, and the glory of the Lord shall be revealed, and all flesh shall see it together.

This is our hope. This is the faith that I will go back to the South with. With this faith we will be able to hew out of the mountain of despair a stone of hope. With this faith we will be able to transform the jangling discords of our nation into a beautiful symphony of brotherhood.

With this faith we will be able to work together, to pray together, to struggle together, to go to jail together, to stand up for freedom together, knowing that we will be free one day.

This will be the day when all of God's children will be able to sing with new meaning, 'My country 'tis of thee, sweet land of liberty, of thee I sing. Land where my fathers died, land of the Pilgrims' pride, from every mountainside, let freedom ring.'

And if America is to be a great nation, this must become true. So let freedom ring from the prodigious hilltops of New Hampshire. Let freedom ring from the mighty mountains of New York. Let freedom ring from the heightening Alleghenies of Pennsylvania.

Let freedom ring from the snow-capped Rockies of Colorado. Let freedom ring from the curvaceous slopes of California. But not only that; let freedom ring from the Stone Mountain of Georgia. Let freedom ring from Lookout Mountain of Tennessee.

Let freedom ring from every hill and molehill of Mississippi. From every mountainside, let freedom ring.

And when this happens, and when we allow freedom ring, when we let it ring from every village and every hamlet, from every state and every city, we will be able to speed up that day when all of God's children, black men and white men, Jews and gentiles, Protestants and Catholics, will be able to join hands and sing in the words of the old Negro spiritual, 'Free at last! Free at last! Thank God Almighty, we are free at last!'

A New Chapter in Silent Spring

Rachel Carson

Garden Club of America, New York City (8 January 1963)

Rachel Carson was a renowned American biologist and writer whose book *The Sea Around Us* (1951) won a National Book Award. Her notable writings on environmental pollution and history of the sea won her international acclaim. Carson remains one of 20th century's most influential writers of nature.

This speech was inspired by Carson's book *Silent Spring* which warns readers about the dangers of chemical pesticides for insects and marine life.

I am particularly glad to have this opportunity to speak to you. Ever since, 10 years ago, you honored me with your Frances Hutchinson medal, I have felt very close to The Garden Club of America. And I should like to pay tribute to you for the quality of your work and for the aims and aspirations of your organization. Through your interest in plant life, your fostering of beauty, your alignment with constructive conservation causes, you promote that onward flow of life that is the essence of our world.

This is a time when forces of a very different nature too often prevail—forces careless of life or deliberately destructive of it and of the essential web of living relationships.

My particular concern, as you know, is with the reckless use of chemicals so unselective in their action that they should more appropriately be called biocides rather than pesticides. Not even their most partisan defenders can claim that their toxic effect is limited to insects or rodents or weeds or whatever the target may be.

The battle for a sane policy for controlling unwanted species will be a long and difficult one. The publication of Silent Spring was neither the beginning nor the end of that struggle. I think, however, that it is moving into a new phase, and I would like to assess with you some of the progress that has been made and take a look at the nature of the struggle that lies before us.

We should be very clear about what our cause is. What do we oppose? What do we stand for? If you read some of my industry-oriented reviewers you will think that I am opposed to any efforts to control insects or other organisms. This, of course, is not my position and I am sure it is not that of The Garden Club of America. We differ from the promoters of biocides chiefly in the means we advocate, rather than the end to be attained.

It is my conviction that if we automatically call in the spray planes or reach for the aerosol bomb when we have an insect problem we are resorting to crude methods of a rather low scientific order. We are being particularly unscientific when we fail to press forward with research that will give us the new kind of weapons we need. Some such weapons now exist—brilliant and imaginative prototypes of what I trust will be the insect control methods of the future. But we need many more, and we need to make better use of those we have. Research men of the Department of Agriculture have told me privately that some of the measures they have developed and tested and turned over to the insect control branch have been quietly put on the shelf.

I criticize the present heavy reliance upon biocides on several grounds: First, on the grounds of their inefficiency. I have here some comparative figures on the toll taken of our crops by insects before and after the DDT era. During the first half of this century, crop loss due to insect attack has been estimated by a leading entomologist at 10 percent a year. It is startling to find, then, that the National Academy of Science last year placed the present crop loss at 25 percent a year. If the percentage of crop loss is increasing at this rate, even as the use of modern insecticides increases, surely something is wrong with the methods used! I would remind you that a non-chemical method gave 100 percent control of the screwworm fly—a degree of success no chemical has ever achieved.

Chemical controls are inefficient also because as now used they promote resistance among insects. The number of insect species resistant to one or more groups of insecticides has risen from about a dozen in pre-DDT days to nearly 150 today. This is a very serious problem, threatening, as it does, greatly impaired control.

Another measure of inefficiency is the fact that chemicals often provoke resurgences of the very insect they seek to control, because they have killed off its natural controls. Or they cause some other organism suddenly to rise to nuisance status: spider mites, once relatively innocuous, have become a worldwide pest since the advent of DDT.

My other reasons for believing we must turn to other methods of controlling insects have been set forth in detail in Silent Spring and I shall not take time to discuss them now. Obviously, it will take time to revolutionize our methods of insect and weed control to the point where dangerous chemicals are minimized. Meanwhile, there is much that can be done to bring about some immediate improvement in the situation through better procedures and controls.

In looking at the pesticide situation today, the most hopeful sign is an awakening of strong public interest and concern. People are beginning to ask questions and to insist upon proper answers instead of meekly acquiescing in whatever spraying programs are proposed. This in itself is a wholesome thing.

There is increasing demand for better legislative control of pesticides. The state of Massachusetts has already set up a Pesticide Board with actual authority. This Board has taken a very necessary step by requiring the licensing of anyone proposing to carry out aerial spraying. Incredible though it may seem, before this was done anyone who had money to hire an airplane could spray where and when he pleased. I am told that the state of Connecticut is now planning an official investigation of spraying practices. And of course on a national scale, the President last summer directed his science advisor to set up a committee of scientists to review the whole matter of the government's activities in this field.

Citizens groups, too, are becoming active. For example, the Pennsylvania Federation of Women's Clubs recently set up a program to protect the public from the menace of poisons in the environment—a program based on education and promotion of legislation. The National Audubon Society has advocated a five-point action program involving both state and federal agencies. The North American Wildlife Conference this year will devote an important part of its program to the problem of pesticides. All these developments will serve to keep public attention focused on the problem.

I was amused recently to read a bit of wishful thinking in one of the trade magazines. Industry 'can take heart,' it said, 'from the fact that the main impact of the book (i.e., Silent Spring) will occur in the late fall and winter—seasons when consumers are not normally active buyers of insecticides…it is fairly safe to hope that by March or April Silent Spring no longer will be an interesting conversational subject.'

If the tone of my mail from readers is any guide, and if the movements that have already been launched gain the expected momentum, this is one prediction that will not come true.

This is not to say that we can afford to be complacent. Although the attitude of the public is showing a refreshing change, there is very little evidence of any reform in spraying practices. Very toxic materials are being applied with solemn official assurances that they will harm neither man nor beast. When wildlife losses are later reported, the same officials deny the evidence or declare the animals must have died from 'something else.'

Exactly this pattern of events is occurring in a number of areas now. For example, a newspaper in East St. Louis, Illinois, describes the death of several hundred rabbits, quail and songbirds in areas treated with pellets of the insecticide, dieldrin. One area involved was, ironically, a 'game preserve.' This was part of a program of Japanese beetle control.

The procedures seem to be the same as those I described in Silent Spring, referring to another Illinois community, Sheldon. At Sheldon the destruction of many birds and small mammals amounted almost to annihilation. Yet an Illinois Agriculture official is now quoted as saying dieldrin has no serious effect on animal life.

A significant case history is shaping up now in Norfolk, Virginia. The chemical is the very toxic dieldrin, the target the white fringed beetle, which attacks some farm crops. This situation has several especially interesting features. One is the evident desire of the state agriculture officials to carry out the program with as little advance discussion as possible. When the Outdoor Edition of the Norfolk Virginian-Pilot 'broke' the story, he reported that officials refused comment on their plans. The Norfolk health officer offered reassuring statements to the public on the grounds that the method of application guaranteed safety: The poison would be injected into the ground by a machine that drills holes in the soil. 'A child would have to eat the roots of the grass to get the poison' he is quoted as saying.

However, alert reporters soon proved these assurances to be without foundation. The actual method of application was to be by seeders, blowers and helicopters: the same type of procedure that in Illinois wiped out robins, brown thrashers and meadowlarks, killed sheep in the pastures, and contaminated the forage so that cows gave milk containing poison.

Yet at a hearing of sorts concerned Norfolk citizens were told merely that the State's Department of Agriculture was committed to the program and that it would therefore be carried out.

The fundamental wrong is the authoritarian control that has been vested in the agricultural agencies. There are, after all, many different interests involved: there are problems of water pollution, of soil pollution, of wildlife protection, of public health. Yet the matter is approached as if the agricultural interest were the supreme, or indeed the only one.

It seems to me clear that all such problems should be resolved by a conference of representatives of all the interests involved.

I wonder whether citizens would not do well to be guided by the strong hint given by the Court of Appeals reviewing the so-called DDT case of the Long Island citizens a few years ago.

This group sought an injunction to protect them from a repetition of the gypsy moth spraying. The lower court refused the injunction and the United States Court of Appeals sustained this ruling on the grounds that the spraying had already taken place and could not be enjoined. However, the court made a very significant comment that seems to have been largely overlooked. Regarding the possibility of a repetition of the Long Island spraying, the judges made this significant general comment: '…out would seem well to point out the advisability for a district court, faced with a claim concerning aerial spraying or any other program which may cause inconvenience and damage as widespread as this 1957 spraying appears to have caused, to inquire closely into the methods and safeguards of any proposed procedures so that incidents of the seemingly unnecessary and unfortunate nature here disclosed, may be reduced to a minimum, assuming, of course, that the government will have shown such a program to be required in the public interest.'

Here the United States Court of Appeals spelled out a procedure whereby citizens may seek relief in the courts from unnecessary, unwise or carelessly executed programs. I hope it will be put to the test in as many situations as possible.

If we are ever to find our way out of the present deplorable situation, we must remain vigilant, we must continue to challenge and to question, we must insist that the burden of proof is on those who would use these chemicals to prove the procedures are safe.

Above all, we must not be deceived by the enormous stream of propaganda that is issuing from the pesticide manufacturers and from industry-related—although ostensibly independent—organizations. There is already a large volume of handouts openly sponsored by the manufacturers. There are other packets of material being issued by some of the state agricultural colleges, as well as by certain organizations whose industry connections are concealed behind a scientific front. This material is going to writers, editors, professional people, and other leaders of opinion.

It is characteristic of this material that it deals in generalities, unsupported by documentation. In its claims for safety to human beings, it ignores the fact that we are engaged in a grim experiment never before attempted. We are subjecting whole populations to exposure to chemicals which animal experiments have proved to be extremely poisonous and in many cases cumulative in their effect. These exposures now begin at or before birth. No one knows what the result will be, because we have no previous experience to guide us.

Let us hope it will not take the equivalent of another thalidomide tragedy to shock us into full awareness of the hazard. Indeed, something almost as shocking has already occurred—a few months ago we were all shocked by newspaper accounts of the tragedy of the Turkish children who have developed a horrid disease through use of an agricultural chemical. To be sure, the use was unintended. The poisoning had been continuing over a period of some seven years, unknown to most of us. What made it newsworthy in 1962 was the fact that a scientist gave a public report on it.

A disease known as toxic porphyria has turned some 5,000 Turkish children into hairy, monkey-faced beings. The skin becomes sensitive to light and is blotched and blistered. Thick hair covers much of the face and arms. The victims have also suffered severe liver damage. Several hundred such cases were noticed in 1955. Five years later, when a South African physician visited Turkey to study the disease, he found 5,000 victims. The cause was traced to seed wheat which had been treated with a chemical fungicide called hexachlorobenzene. The seed, intended for planting, had instead been ground into flour for bread by the hungry people. Recovery of the victims is slow, and indeed worse may be in store for them. Dr. W. C. Hueper, a specialist on environmental cancer, tells me there is a strong likelihood these unfortunate children may ultimately develop liver cancer.

'This could not happen here,' you might easily think.

It would surprise you, then, to know that the use of poisoned seed in our own country is a matter of present concern by the Food and Drug Administration. In recent years there has been a sharp increase in the treatment of seed with chemical fungicides and insecticides of a highly poisonous nature. Two years ago an official of the Food and Drug Administration told me of that agency's fear that treated grain left over at the end of a growing season was finding its way into food channels.

Now, on last October 27, the Food and Drug Administration proposed that all treated food grain seeds be brightly colored so as to be easily distinguishable from untreated seeds or grain intended as food for human beings or livestock. The Food and Drug Administration reported: FDA has encountered many shipments of wheat, corn, oats, rye, barley, sorghum, and alfalfa seed in which stocks of treated seed left over after the planting seasons have been mixed with grains and sent to market for food or feed use. Injury to livestock is known to have occurred.

'Numerous federal court seizure actions have been taken against lots of such mixed grains on charges they were adulterated with a poisonous substance. Criminal cases have been brought against some of the shipping firms and individuals.

'Most buyers and users of grains do not have the facilities or scientific equipment to detect the presence of small amounts of treated seed grains if the treated seed is not colored. The FDA proposal would require that all treated seed be colored in sharp contrast to the natural color of the seed, and that the color be so applied that it could not readily be removed. The buyer could then easily detect a mixture containing treated seed grain, and reject the lot.'

I understood, however, that objection has been made by some segments of the industry and that this very desirable and necessary requirement may be delayed. This is a specific example of the kind of situation requiring public vigilance and public demand for correction of abuses.

The way is not made easy for those who would defend the public interest. In fact, a new obstacle has recently been created, and a new advantage has been given to those who seek to block remedial legislation. I refer to the income tax bill which becomes effective this year. The bill contains a little known provision which permits certain lobbying expenses to be considered a business expense deduction. It means, to cite a specific example, that the chemical industry may now work at bargain rates to thwart future attempts at regulation.

But what of the nonprofit organizations such as the Garden Clubs, the Audubon Societies and all other such tax-exempt groups? Under existing laws they stand to lose their tax-exempt status if they devote any 'substantial' part of their activities to attempts to influence legislation. The word 'substantial' needs to be defined. In practice, even an effort involving less than 5 percent of an organization's activity has been ruled sufficient to cause loss of the tax-exempt status.

What happens, then, when the public interest is pitted against large commercial interests? Those organizations wishing to plead for protection of the public interest do so under the peril of losing the tax-exempt status so necessary to their existence. The industry wishing to pursue its course without legal restraint is now actually subsidized in its efforts.

This is a situation which the Garden Club, and similar organizations, within their legal limitations, might well attempt to remedy.

There are other disturbing factors which I can only suggest. One is the growing interrelations between professional organizations and industry, and between science and industry. For example, the American Medical Association, through its newspaper, has just referred physicians to a pesticide trade association for information to help them answer patients' questions about the effects of pesticides on man. I would like to see physicians referred to authoritative scientific or medical literature—not to a trade organization whose business it is to promote the sale of pesticides.

We see scientific societies acknowledging as 'sustaining associates' a dozen or more giants of a related industry. When the scientific organization speaks, whose voice do we hear—that of science or of the sustaining industry? The public assumes it is hearing the voice of science.

Another cause of concern is the increasing size and number of industry grants to the universities. On first thought, such support of education seems desirable, but on reflection we see that this does not make for unbiased research—it does not promote a truly scientific spirit. To an increasing extent, the man who brings the largest grants to his university becomes an untouchable, with whom even the University president and trustees do not argue.

These are large problems and there is no easy solution. But the problem must be faced.

As you listen to the present controversy about pesticides, I recommend that you ask yourself—Who speaks?—And Why?

'The Ballot or the Bullet'

Malcolm X

Cory Methodist Church, Cleveland (3 April 1964)

Malcolm X was a social activist and eloquent orator who opposed the peaceful protests of the civil rights movement. He championed violent acts to counter white aggression and the ideas of his book The Autobiography of Malcolm X gave rise to the Black Power movement of the late 1960s and 1970s. On 21 February 1965, Malcolm X was assassinated by rival Black Muslims.

In his famous speech 'The Ballot or the Bullet', delivered at the Cory Methodist Church, Cleveland, Ohio, he encourages the black people to exercise their right to vote and to take up arms against white domination if necessary.

Mr. Moderator, Brother Lomax, brothers and sisters, friends and enemies: I just can't believe everyone in here is a friend, and I don't want to leave anybody out. The question tonight, as I understand it, is 'The Negro Revolt, and Where Do We Go From Here?' or 'What Next?' In my little humble way of understanding it, it points toward either the ballot or the bullet.

Before we try and explain what is meant by the ballot or the bullet, I would like to clarify something concerning myself. I'm still a Muslim; my religion is still Islam. That's my personal belief. Just as Adam Clayton Powell is a Christian minister who heads the Abyssinian Baptist Church in New York, but at the same time takes part in the political struggles to try and bring about rights to the black people in this country; and Dr. Martin Luther King is a Christian minister down in Atlanta, Georgia, who heads another organization fighting for the civil rights of black people in this country; and Reverend Galamison, I guess you've heard of him, is another Christian minister in New York who has been deeply involved in the school boycotts to eliminate segregated education; well, I myself am a minister, not a Christian minister, but a Muslim minister; and I believe in action on all fronts by whatever means necessary.

Although I'm still a Muslim, I'm not here tonight to discuss my religion. I'm not here to try and change your religion. I'm not here to argue or discuss anything that we differ about, because it's time for us to submerge our differences and realize that it is best for us to first see that we have the same problem, a common problem, a problem that will make you catch hell whether you're a Baptist, or a Methodist, or a Muslim, or a nationalist. Whether you're educated or illiterate, whether you live on the boulevard or in the alley, you're going to catch hell just like I am. We're all in the same boat and we all are going to catch the same hell from the same man. He just happens to be a white man. All of us have suffered here, in this country, political oppression at the hands of the white man, economic exploitation at the hands of the white man, and social degradation at the hands of the white man.

Now in speaking like this, it doesn't mean that we're anti-white, but it does mean we're anti-exploitation, we're anti-degradation, we're anti-oppression. And if the white man doesn't want us to be anti-him, let him stop oppressing and exploiting and degrading us. Whether we are Christians or Muslims or nationalists or agnostics or atheists, we must first learn to forget our differences. If we have differences, let us differ in the closet; when we come out in front, let us not have anything to argue about until we get finished arguing with the man. If the late President Kennedy could get together with Khrushchev and exchange some wheat, we certainly have more in common with each other than Kennedy and Khrushchev had with each other.

If we don't do something real soon, I think you'll have to agree that we're going to be forced either to use the ballot or the bullet. It's one or the other in 1964. It isn't that time is running out—time has run out!

1964 threatens to be the most explosive year America has ever witnessed. The most explosive year. Why? It's also a political year. It's the year when all of the white politicians will be back in the so-called Negro community jiving you and me for some votes. The year when all of the white political crooks will be right back in your and my community with their false promises, building up our hopes for a letdown, with their trickery and their treachery, with their false promises which they don't intend to keep. As they nourish these dissatisfactions, it can only lead to one thing, an explosion; and now we have the type of black man on the scene in America today—I'm sorry, Brother Lomax—who just doesn't intend to turn the other cheek any longer.

Don't let anybody tell you anything about the odds are against you. If they draft you, they send you to Korea and make you face 800 million Chinese. If you can be brave over there, you can be brave right here. These odds aren't as great as those odds. And if you fight here, you will at least know what you're fighting for.

I'm not a politician, not even a student of politics; in fact, I'm not a student of much of anything. I'm not a Democrat. I'm not a Republican, and I don't even consider myself an American. If you and I were Americans, there'd be no problem. Those Honkies that just got off the boat, they're already Americans; Polacks are already Americans; the Italian refugees are already Americans. Everything that came out of Europe, every blue-eyed thing, is already an American. And as long as you and I have been over here, we aren't Americans yet.

Well, I am one who doesn't believe in deluding myself. I'm not going to sit at your table and watch you eat, with nothing on my plate, and call myself a diner. Sitting at the table doesn't make you a diner, unless you eat some of what's on that plate. Being here in America doesn't make you an American. Being born here in America doesn't make you an American. Why, if birth made you American, you wouldn't need any legislation; you wouldn't need any amendments to the Constitution; you wouldn't be faced with civil-rights filibustering in Washington, D.C., right now. They don't have to pass civil-rights legislation to make a Polack an American.

No, I'm not an American. I'm one of the 22 million black people who are the victims of Americanism. One of the 22 million black people who are the victims of democracy, nothing but disguised hypocrisy. So, I'm not standing here speaking to you as an American, or a patriot, or a flag-saluter, or a flag-waver—no, not I. I'm speaking as a victim of this American system. And I see America through the eyes of the victim. I don't see any American dream; I see an American nightmare.

These 22 million victims are waking up. Their eyes are coming open. They're beginning to see what they used to only look at. They're becoming politically mature. They are realizing that there are new political trends from coast to coast. As they see these new political trends, it's possible for them to see that every time there's an election the races are so close that they have to have a recount. They had to recount in Massachusetts to see who was going to be governor, it was so close. It was the same way in Rhode Island, in Minnesota, and in many other parts of the country. And the same with Kennedy and Nixon when they ran for president. It was so close they had to count all over again. Well, what does this mean? It means that when white people are evenly divided, and black people have a bloc of votes of their own, it is left up to them to determine who's going to sit in the White House and who's going to be in the dog house.

It was the black man's vote that put the present administration in Washington, D.C. Your vote, your dumb vote, your ignorant vote, your wasted vote put in an administration in Washington, D.C., that has seen fit to pass every kind of legislation imaginable, saving you until last, then filibustering on top of that. And your and my leaders have the audacity to run around clapping their hands and talk about how much progress we're making. And what a good president we have. If he wasn't good in Texas, he sure can't be good in Washington, D.C. Because Texas is a lynch state. It is in the same breath as Mississippi, no different; only they lynch you in Texas with a Texas accent and lynch you in Mississippi with a Mississippi accent. And these Negro leaders have the audacity to go and have some coffee in the White House with a Texan, a Southern cracker—that's all he is—and then come out and tell you and me that he's going to be better for us because, since he's from the South, he knows how to deal with the Southerners. What kind of logic is that? Let Eastland be president, he's from the South too. He should be better able to deal with them than Johnson.

In this present administration they have in the House of Representatives 257 Democrats to only 177 Republicans. They control two-thirds of the House vote. Why can't they pass something that will help you and me? In the Senate, there are 67 senators who are of the Democratic Party. Only 33 of them are Republicans. Why, the Democrats have got the government sewed up, and you're the one who sewed it up for them. And what have they given you for it? Four years in office, and just now getting around to some civil-rights legislation. Just now, after everything else is gone, out of the way, they're going to sit down now and play with you all summer long—the same old giant con game that they call filibuster. All those are in cahoots together. Don't you ever think they're not in cahoots together, for the man that is heading the civil-rights filibuster is a man from Georgia named Richard Russell. When Johnson became president, the first man he asked for when he got back to Washington, D.C., was 'Dicky'—that's how tight they are. That's his boy, that's his pal, that's his buddy. But they're playing that old con game. One of them makes believe he's for you, and he's got it fixed where the other one is so tight against you, he never has to keep his promise.

So it's time in 1964 to wake up. And when you see them coming up with that kind of conspiracy, let them know your eyes are open. And let them know you— something else that's wide open too. It's got to be the ballot or the bullet. The ballot or the bullet. If you're afraid to use an expression like that, you should get on out of the country; you should get back in the cotton patch; you should get back in the alley. They get all the Negro vote, and after they get it, the Negro gets nothing in return. All they did when they got to Washington was give a few big Negroes big jobs. Those big Negroes didn't need big jobs, they already had jobs. That's camouflage, that's trickery, that's treachery, window-dressing. I'm not trying to knock out the Democrats for the Republicans. We'll get to them in a minute. But it is true; you put the Democrats first and the Democrats put you last.

Look at it the way it is. What alibis do they use, since they control Congress and the Senate? What alibi do they use when you and I ask, 'Well, when are you going to keep your promise?' They blame the Dixiecrats. What is a Dixiecrat? A Democrat. A Dixiecrat is nothing but a Democrat in disguise. The titular head of the Democrats is also the head of the Dixiecrats, because the Dixiecrats are a part of the Democratic Party. The Democrats have never kicked the Dixiecrats out of the party. The Dixiecrats bolted themselves once, but the Democrats didn't put them out. Imagine, these lowdown Southern segregationists put the Northern Democrats down. But the Northern Democrats have never put the Dixiecrats down. No, look at that thing the way it is. They have got a con game going on, a political con game, and you and I are in the middle. It's time for you and me to wake up and start looking at it like it is, and trying to understand it like it is; and then we can deal with it like it is.

The Dixiecrats in Washington, D.C., control the key committees that run the government. The only reason the Dixiecrats control these committees is because they have seniority. The only reason they have seniority is because they come from states where Negroes can't vote. This is not even a government that's based on democracy. lt. is not a government that is made up of representatives of the people. Half of the people in the South can't even vote. Eastland is not even supposed to be in Washington. Half of the senators and congressmen who occupy these key positions in Washington, D.C., are there illegally, are there unconstitutionally.

I was in Washington, D.C., a week ago Thursday, when they were debating whether or not they should let the bill come onto the floor. And in the back of the room where the Senate meets, there's a huge map of the United States, and on that map it shows the location of Negroes throughout the country. And it shows that the Southern section of the country, the states that are most heavily concentrated with Negroes, are the ones that have senators and congressmen standing up filibustering and doing all other kinds of trickery to keep the Negro from being able to vote. This is pitiful. But it's not pitiful for us any longer; it's actually pitiful for the white man, because soon now, as the Negro awakens a little more and sees the vise that he's in, sees the bag that he's in, sees the real game that he's in, then the Negro's going to develop a new tactic.

These senators and congressmen actually violate the constitutional amendments that guarantee the people of that particular state or county the right to vote. And the Constitution itself has within it the machinery to expel any representative from a state where the voting rights of the people are violated. You don't even need new legislation. Any person in Congress right now, who is there from a state or a district where the voting rights of the people are violated, that particular person should be expelled from Congress. And when you expel him, you've removed one of the obstacles in the path of any real meaningful legislation in this country. In fact, when you expel them, you don't need new legislation, because they will be replaced by black representatives from counties and districts where the black man is in the majority, not in the minority.

If the black man in these Southern states had his full voting rights, the key Dixiecrats in Washington, D. C., which means the key Democrats in Washington, D.C., would lose their seats. The Democratic Party itself would lose its power. It would cease to be powerful as a party. When you see the amount of power that would be lost by the Democratic Party if it were to lose the Dixiecrat wing, or branch, or element, you can see where it's against the interests of the Democrats to give voting rights to Negroes in states where the Democrats have been in complete power and authority ever since the Civil War. You just can't belong to that Party without analyzing it.

I say again, I'm not anti-Democrat, I'm not anti-Republican, I'm not anti-anything. I'm just questioning their sincerity, and some of the strategy that they've been using on our people by promising them promises that they don't intend to keep. When you keep the Democrats in power, you're keeping the Dixiecrats in power. I doubt that my good Brother Lomax will deny that. A vote for a Democrat is a vote for a Dixiecrat. That's why, in 1964, it's time now for you and me to become more politically mature and realize what the ballot is for; what we're supposed to get when we cast a ballot; and that if we don't cast a ballot, it's going to end up in a situation where we're going to have to cast a bullet. It's either a ballot or a bullet.

In the North, they do it a different way. They have a system that's known as gerrymandering, whatever that means. It means when Negroes become too heavily concentrated in a certain area, and begin to gain too much political power, the white man comes along and changes the district lines. You may say, 'Why do you keep saying white man?' Because it's the white man who does it. I haven't ever seen any Negro changing any lines. They don't let him get near the line. It's the white man who does this. And usually, it's the white man who grins at you the most, and pats you on the back, and is supposed to be your friend. He may be friendly, but he's not your friend.

So, what I'm trying to impress upon you, in essence, is this: You and I in America are faced not with a segregationist conspiracy, we're faced with a government conspiracy. Everyone who's filibustering is a senator—that's the government. Everyone who's finagling in Washington, D.C., is a congressman—that's the government. You don't have anybody putting blocks in your path but people who are a part of the government. The same government that you go abroad to fight for and die for is the government that is in a conspiracy to deprive you of your voting rights, deprive you of your economic opportunities, deprive you of decent housing, deprive you of decent education. You don't need to go to the employer alone, it is the government itself, the government of America, that is responsible for the oppression and exploitation and degradation of black people in this country. And you should drop it in their lap. This government has failed the Negro. This so-called democracy has failed the Negro. And all these white liberals have definitely failed the Negro.

So, where do we go from here? First, we need some friends. We need some new allies. The entire civil-rights struggle needs a new interpretation, a broader interpretation. We need to look at this civil-rights thing from another angle—from the inside as well as from the outside. To those of us whose philosophy is black nationalism, the only way you can get involved in the civil-rights struggle is give it a new interpretation. That old interpretation excluded us. It kept us out. So, we're giving a new interpretation to the civil-rights struggle, an interpretation that will enable us to come into it, take part in it. And these handkerchief-heads who have been dillydallying and pussy footing and compromising—we don't intend to let them pussyfoot and dillydally and compromise any longer.

How can you thank a man for giving you what's already yours? How then can you thank him for giving you only part of what's already yours? You haven't even made progress, if what's being given to you, you should have had already. That's not progress. And I love my Brother Lomax, the way he pointed out we're right back where we were in 1954. We're not even as far up as we were in 1954. We're behind where we were in 1954. There's more segregation now than there was in 1954. There's more racial animosity, more racial hatred, more racial violence today in 1964, than there was in 1954. Where is the progress?

And now you're facing a situation where the young Negro's coming up. They don't want to hear that 'turn the-other-cheek' stuff, no. In Jacksonville, those were teenagers, they were throwing Molotov cocktails. Negroes have never done that before. But it shows you there's a new deal coming in. There's new thinking coming in. There's new strategy coming in. It'll be Molotov cocktails this month, hand grenades next month, and something else next month. It'll be ballots, or it'll be bullets. It'll be liberty, or it will be death. The only difference about this kind of death—it'll be reciprocal. You know what is meant by 'reciprocal'? That's one of Brother Lomax's words. I stole it from him. I don't usually deal with those big words because I don't usually deal with big people. I deal with small people. I find you can get a whole lot of small people and whip hell out of a whole lot of big people. They haven't got anything to lose, and they've got everything to gain. And they'll let you know in a minute: 'It takes two to tango; when I go, you go.'

The black nationalists, those whose philosophy is black nationalism, in bringing about this new interpretation of the entire meaning of civil rights, look upon it as meaning, as Brother Lomax has pointed out, equality of opportunity. Well, we're justified in seeking civil rights, if it means equality of opportunity, because all we're doing there is trying to collect for our investment. Our mothers and fathers invested sweat and blood. Three hundred and ten years we worked in this country without a dime in return—I mean without a dime in return. You let the white man walk around here talking about how rich this country is, but you never stop to think how it got rich so quick. It got rich because you made it rich.

You take the people who are in this audience right now. They're poor. We're all poor as individuals. Our weekly salary individually amounts to hardly anything. But if you take the salary of everyone in here collectively, it'll fill up a whole lot of baskets. It's a lot of wealth. If you can collect the wages of just these people right here for a year, you'll be rich—richer than rich. When you look at it like that, think how rich Uncle Sam had to become, not with this handful, but millions of black people. Your and my mother and father, who didn't work an eight-hour shift, but worked from 'can't see' in the morning until 'can't see' at night, and worked for nothing, making the white man rich, making Uncle Sam rich. This is our investment. This is our contribution, our blood.

Not only did we give of our free labor, we gave of our blood. Every time he had a call to arms, we were the first ones in uniform. We died on every battlefield the white man had. We have made a greater sacrifice than anybody who's standing up in America today. We have made a greater contribution and have collected less. Civil rights, for those of us whose philosophy is black nationalism, means: 'Give it to us now. Don't wait for next year. Give it to us yesterday, and that's not fast enough.'

I might stop right here to point out one thing. Whenever you're going after something that belongs to you, anyone who's depriving you of the right to have it is a criminal. Understand that. Whenever you are going after something that is yours, you are within your legal rights to lay claim to it. And anyone who puts forth any effort to deprive you of that which is yours, is breaking the law, is a criminal. And this was pointed out by the Supreme Court decision. It outlawed segregation.

Which means segregation is against the law. Which means a segregationist is breaking the law. A segregationist is a criminal. You can't label him as anything other than that. And when you demonstrate against segregation, the law is on your side. The Supreme Court is on your side.

Now, who is it that opposes you in carrying out the law? The police department itself. With police dogs and clubs. Whenever you demonstrate against segregation, whether it is segregated education, segregated housing, or anything else, the law is on your side, and anyone who stands in the way is not the law any longer. They are breaking the law; they are not representatives of the law. Any time you demonstrate against segregation and a man has the audacity to put a police dog on you, kill that dog, kill him, I'm telling you, kill that dog. I say it, if they put me in jail tomorrow, kill that dog. Then you'll put a stop to it. Now, if these white people in here don't want to see that kind of action, get down and tell the mayor to tell the police department to pull the dogs in. That's all you have to do. If you don't do it, someone else will.

If you don't take this kind of stand, your little children will grow up and look at you and think 'shame.' If you don't take an uncompromising stand, I don't mean go out and get violent; but at the same time you should never be nonviolent unless you run into some nonviolence. I'm nonviolent with those who are nonviolent with me. But when you drop that violence on me, then you've made me go insane, and I'm not responsible for what I do. And that's the way every Negro should get. Any time you know you're within the law, within your legal rights, within your moral rights, in accord with justice, then die for what you believe in. But don't die alone. Let your dying be reciprocal. This is what is meant by equality. What's good for the goose is good for the gander.

When we begin to get in this area, we need new friends, we need new allies. We need to expand the civil-rights struggle to a higher level—to the level of human rights. Whenever you are in a civil-rights struggle, whether you know it or not, you are confining yourself to the jurisdiction of Uncle Sam. No one from the outside world can speak out in your behalf as long as your struggle is a civil-rights struggle. Civil rights comes within the domestic affairs of this country. All of our African brothers and our Asian brothers and our Latin American brothers cannot open their mouths and interfere in the domestic affairs of the United States. And as long as it's civil rights, this comes under the jurisdiction of Uncle Sam.

But the United Nations has what's known as the charter of human rights; it has a committee that deals in human rights. You may wonder why all of the atrocities that have been committed in

Africa and in Hungary and in Asia, and in Latin America are brought before the UN, and the Negro problem is never brought before the UN. This is part of the conspiracy. This old, tricky blue eyed liberal who is supposed to be your and my friend, supposed to be in our corner, supposed to be subsidizing our struggle, and supposed to be acting in the capacity of an adviser, never tells you anything about human rights. They keep you wrapped up in civil rights. And you spend so much time barking up the civil-rights tree, you don't even know there's a human-rights tree on the same floor.

When you expand the civil-rights struggle to the level of human rights, you can then take the case of the black man in this country before the nations in the UN. You can take it before the General Assembly. You can take Uncle Sam before a world court. But the only level you can do it on is the level of human rights. Civil rights keeps you under his restrictions, under his jurisdiction. Civil rights keeps you in his pocket. Civil rights means you're asking Uncle Sam to treat you right. Human rights are something you were born with. Human rights are your God-given rights. Human rights are the rights that are recognized by all nations of this earth. And any time any one violates your human rights, you can take them to the world court.

Uncle Sam's hands are dripping with blood, dripping with the blood of the black man in this country. He's the earth's number-one hypocrite. He has the audacity—yes, he has—imagine him posing as the leader of the free world. The free world! And you over here singing 'We Shall Overcome.' Expand the civil-rights struggle to the level of human rights. Take it into the United Nations, where our African brothers can throw their weight on our side, where our Asian brothers can throw their weight on our side, where our Latin American brothers can throw their weight on our side, and where 800 million Chinamen are sitting there waiting to throw their weight on our side.

Let the world know how bloody his hands are. Let the world know the hypocrisy that's practiced over here. Let it be the ballot or the bullet. Let him know that it must be the ballot or the bullet.

When you take your case to Washington, D.C., you're taking it to the criminal who's responsible; it's like running from the wolf to the fox. They're all in cahoots together. They all work political chicanery and make you look like a chump before the eyes of the world. Here you are walking around in America, getting ready to be drafted and sent abroad, like a tin soldier, and when you get over there, people ask you what are you fighting for, and you have to stick your tongue in your cheek. No, take Uncle Sam to court, take him before the world.

By ballot I only mean freedom. Don't you know—I disagree with Lomax on this issue—that the ballot is more important than the dollar? Can I prove it? Yes. Look in the UN. There are poor nations in the UN; yet those poor nations can get together with their voting power and keep the rich nations from making a move. They have one nation— one vote, everyone has an equal vote. And when those brothers from Asia, and Africa and the darker parts of this earth get together, their voting power is sufficient to hold Sam in check. Or Russia in check. Or some other section of the earth in check. So, the ballot is most important.

Right now, in this country, if you and I, 22 million African-Americans—that's what we are—Africans who are in America. You're nothing but Africans. Nothing but Africans. In fact, you'd get farther calling yourself African instead of Negro. Africans don't catch hell. You're the only one catching hell. They don't have to pass civil-rights bills for Africans. An African can go anywhere he wants right now. All you've got to do is tie your head up. That's right, go anywhere you want. Just stop being a Negro. Change your name to Hoogagagooba. That'll show you how silly the white man is. You're dealing with a silly man. A friend of mine who's very dark put a turban on his head and went into a restaurant in Atlanta before they called themselves desegregated. He went into a white restaurant, he sat down, they served him, and he said, 'What would happen if a Negro came in here? And there he's sitting, black as night, but because he had his head wrapped up the waitress looked back at him and says, 'Why, there wouldn't no nigger dare come in here.'

So, you're dealing with a man whose bias and prejudice are making him lose his mind, his intelligence, every day. He's frightened. He looks around and sees what's taking place on this earth, and he sees that the pendulum of time is swinging in your direction. The dark people are waking up. They're losing their fear of the white man. No place where he's fighting right now is he winning. Everywhere he's fighting, he's fighting someone your and my complexion. And they're beating him. He can't win any more. He's won his last battle. He failed to win the Korean War. He couldn't win it. He had to sign a truce. That's a loss.

Any time Uncle Sam, with all his machinery for warfare, is held to a draw by some rice eaters, he's lost the battle. He had to sign a truce. America's not supposed to sign a truce. She's supposed to be bad. But she's not bad any more. She's bad as long as she can use her hydrogen bomb, but she can't use hers for fear Russia might use hers. Russia can't use hers, for fear that Sam might use his. So, both of them are weapon-less. They can't use the weapon because each's weapon nullifies the other's. So the only place where action can take place is on the ground. And the white man can't win another war fighting on the ground. Those days are over The black man knows it, the brown man knows it, the red man knows it, and the yellow man knows it. So they engage him in guerrilla warfare. That's not his style. You've got to have heart to be a guerrilla warrior, and he hasn't got any heart. I'm telling you now.

I just want to give you a little briefing on guerrilla warfare because, before you know it, before you know it. It takes heart to be a guerrilla warrior because you're on your own. In conventional warfare you have tanks and a whole lot of other people with you to back you up—planes over your head and all that kind of stuff. But a guerrilla is on his own. All you have is a rifle, some sneakers and a bowl of rice, and that's all you need—and a lot of heart. The Japanese on some of those islands in the Pacific, when the American soldiers landed, one Japanese sometimes could hold the whole army off. He'd just wait until the sun went down, and when the sun went down they were all equal. He would take his little blade and slip from bush to bush, and from American to American. The white soldiers couldn't cope with that. Whenever you see a white soldier that fought in the Pacific, he has the shakes, he has a nervous condition, because they scared him to death.

The same thing happened to the French up in French Indochina. People who just a few years previously were rice farmers got together and ran the heavily-mechanized French army out of Indochina. You don't need it—modern warfare today won't work. This is the day of the guerrilla. They did the same thing in Algeria. Algerians, who were nothing but Bedouins, took a rine and sneaked off to the hills, and de Gaulle and all of his highfalutin' war machinery couldn't defeat those guerrillas. Nowhere on this earth does the white man win in a guerrilla warfare. It's not his speed. Just as guerrilla warfare is prevailing in Asia and in parts of Africa and in parts of Latin America, you've got to be mighty naive, or you've got to play the black man cheap, if you don't think some day he's going to wake up and find that it's got to be the ballot or the bullet.

1 would like to say, in closing, a few things concerning the Muslim Mosque, Inc., which we established recently in New York City. It's true we're Muslims and our religion is Islam, but we don't mix our religion with our politics and our economics and our social and civil activities—not any more We keep our religion in our mosque. After our religious services are over, then as Muslims we become involved in political action, economic action and social and civic action. We become involved with anybody, anywhere, any time and in any manner that's designed to eliminate the evils, the political, economic and social evils that are afflicting the people of our community.

The political philosophy of black nationalism means that the black man should control the politics and the politicians in his own community; no more. The black man in the black community has to be re-educated into the science of politics so he will know what politics is supposed to bring him in return. Don't be throwing out any ballots. A ballot is like a bullet. You don't throw your ballots until you see a target, and if that target is not within your reach, keep your ballot in your pocket.

The political philosophy of black nationalism is being taught in the Christian church. It's being taught in the NAACP. It's being taught in CORE meetings. It's being taught in SNCC Student Nonviolent Coordinating Committee meetings. It's being taught in Muslim meetings. It's being taught where nothing but atheists and agnostics come together. It's being taught everywhere. Black people are fed up with the dillydallying, pussyfooting, compromising approach that we've been using toward getting our freedom. We want freedom now, but we're not going to get it saying 'We Shall Overcome.' We've got to fight until we overcome.

The economic philosophy of black nationalism is pure and simple. It only means that we should control the economy of our community. Why should white people be running all the stores in our community? Why should white people be running the banks of our community? Why should the economy of our community be in the hands of the white man? Why? If a black man can't move his store into a white community, you tell me why a white man should move his store into a black community. The philosophy of black nationalism involves a re-education program in the black community in regards to economics. Our people have to be made to see that any time you take your dollar out of your community and spend it in a community where you don't live, the community where you live will get poorer and poorer, and the community where you spend your money will get richer and richer.

Then you wonder why where you live is always a ghetto or a slum area. And where you and I are concerned, not only do we lose it when we spend it out of the community, but the white man has got all our stores in the community tied up; so that though we spend it in the community, at sundown the man who runs the store takes it over across town somewhere. He's got us in a vise. So the economic philosophy of black nationalism means in every church, in every civic organization, in every fraternal order, it's time now for our people to become conscious of the importance of controlling the economy of our community. If we own the stores, if we operate the businesses, if we try and establish some industry in our own community, then we're developing to the position where we are creating employment for our own kind. Once you gain control of the economy of your own community, then you don't have to picket and boycott and beg some cracker downtown for a job in his business.

The social philosophy of black nationalism only means that we have to get together and remove the evils, the vices, alcoholism, drug addiction, and other evils that are destroying the moral fiber of our community. We ourselves have to lift the level of our community, the standard of our community to a higher level, make our own society beautiful so that we will be satisfied in our own social circles and won't be running around here trying to knock our way into a social circle where we're not wanted. So I say, in spreading a gospel such as black nationalism, it is not designed to make the black man re-evaluate the white man—you know him already—but to make the black man re-evaluate himself. Don't change the white man's mind—you can't change his mind, and that whole thing about appealing to the moral conscience of America—America's conscience is bankrupt. She lost all conscience a long time ago. Uncle Sam has no conscience.

They don't know what morals are. They don't try and eliminate an evil because it's evil, or because it's illegal, or because it's immoral; they eliminate it only when it threatens their existence. So you're wasting your time appealing to the moral conscience of a bankrupt man like Uncle Sam. If he had a conscience, he'd straighten this thing out with no more pressure being put upon him. So it is not necessary to change the white man's mind. We have to change our own mind. You can't change his mind about us. We've got to change our own minds about each other. We have to see each other with new eyes. We have to see each other as brothers and sisters. We have to come together with warmth so we can develop unity and harmony that's necessary to get this problem solved ourselves. How can we do this? How can we avoid jealousy? How can we avoid the suspicion and the divisions that exist in the community? I'll tell you how.

I have watched how Billy Graham comes into a city, spreading what he calls the gospel of Christ, which is only white nationalism. That's what he is. Billy Graham is a white nationalist; I'm a black nationalist. But since it's the natural tendency for leaders to be jealous and look upon a powerful figure like Graham with suspicion and envy, how is it possible for him to come into a city and get all the cooperation of the church leaders? Don't think because they're church leaders that they don't have weaknesses that make them envious and jealous—no, everybody's got it. It's not an accident that when they want to choose a cardinal, as Pope I over there in Rome, they get in a closet so you can't hear them cussing and fighting and carrying on.

Billy Graham comes in preaching the gospel of Christ. He evangelizes the gospel. He stirs everybody up, but he never tries to start a church. If he came in trying to start a church, all the churches would be against him. So, he just comes in talking about Christ and tells everybody who gets Christ to go to any church where Christ is; and in this way the church cooperates with him. So we're going to take a page from his book.

Our gospel is black nationalism. We're not trying to threaten the existence of any organization, but we're spreading the gospel of black nationalism. Anywhere there's a church that is also preaching and practicing the gospel of black nationalism, join that church. If the NAACP is preaching and practicing the gospel of black nationalism, join the NAACP. If CORE is spreading and practicing the gospel of black nationalism, join CORE. Join any organization that has a gospel that's for the uplift of the black man. And when you get into it and see them pussyfooting or compromising, pull out of it because that's not black nationalism. We'll find another one.

And in this manner, the organizations will increase in number and in quantity and in quality, and by August, it is then our intention to have a black nationalist convention which will consist of delegates from all over the country who are interested in the political, economic and social philosophy of black nationalism. After these delegates convene, we will hold a seminar; we will hold discussions; we will listen to everyone. We want to hear new ideas and new solutions and new answers. And at that time, if we see fit then to form a black nationalist party, we'll form a black nationalist party. If it's necessary to form a black nationalist army, we'll form a black nationalist army. It'll be the ballot or the bullet. It'll be liberty or it'll be death.

It's time for you and me to stop sitting in this country, letting some cracker senators, Northern crackers and Southern crackers, sit there in Washington, D.C., and come to a conclusion in their mind that you and I are supposed to have civil rights. There's no white man going to tell me anything about my rights. Brothers and sisters, always remember, if it doesn't take senators and congressmen and presidential proclamations to give freedom to the white man, it is not necessary for legislation or proclamation or Supreme Court decisions to give freedom to the black man. You let that white man know, if this is a country of freedom, let it be a country of freedom; and if it's not a country of freedom, change it.

We will work with anybody, anywhere, at any time, who is genuinely interested in tackling the problem head-on, nonviolently as long as the enemy is nonviolent, but violent when the enemy gets violent. We'll work with you on the voter-registration drive, we'll work with you on rent strikes, we'll work with you on school boycotts; I don't believe in any kind of integration; I'm not even worried about it, because I know you're not going to get it anyway; you're not going to get it because you're afraid to die; you've got to be ready to die if you try and force yourself on the white man, because he'll get just as violent as those crackers in Mississippi, right here in Cleveland. But we will still work with you on the school boycotts because we're against a segregated school system. A segregated school system produces children who, when they graduate, graduate with crippled minds. But this does not mean that a school is segregated because it's all black. A segregated school means a school that is controlled by people who have no real interest in it whatsoever.

Let me explain what I mean. A segregated district or community is a community in which people live, but outsiders control the politics and the economy of that community. They never refer to the white section as a segregated community. It's the all-Negro section that's a segregated community. Why? The white man controls his own school, his own bank, his own economy, his own politics, his own everything, his own community; but he also controls yours. When you're under someone else's control, you're segregated. They'll always give you the lowest or the worst that there is to offer, but it doesn't mean you're segregated just because you have your own. You've got to control your own. Just like the white man has control of his, you need to control yours.

You know the best way to get rid of segregation? The white man is more afraid of separation than he is of integration. Segregation means that he puts you away from him, but not far enough for you to be out of his jurisdiction; separation means you're gone. And the white man will integrate faster than he'll let you separate. So we will work with you against the segregated school system because it's criminal, because it is absolutely destructive, in every way imaginable, to the minds of the children who have to be exposed to that type of crippling education.

Last but not least, I must say this concerning the great controversy over rifles and shotguns. The only thing that I've ever said is that in areas where the government has proven itself either unwilling or unable to defend the lives and the property of Negroes, it's time for Negroes to defend themselves. Article number two of the constitutional amendments provides you and me the right to own a rifle or a shotgun. It is constitutionally legal to own a shotgun or a rifle. This doesn't mean you're going to get a rifle and form battalions and go out looking for white folks, although you'd be within your rights—I mean, you'd be justified; but that would be illegal and we don't do anything illegal. If the white man doesn't want the black man buying rifles and shotguns, then let the government do its job.

That's all. And don't let the white man come to you and ask you what you think about what Malcolm says—why, you old Uncle Tom. He would never ask you if he thought you were going to say, 'Amen!' No, he is making a Tom out of you.' So, this doesn't mean forming rifle clubs and going out looking for people, but it is time, in 1964, if you are a man, to let that man know. If he's not going to do his job in running the government and providing you and me with the protection that our taxes are supposed to be for, since he spends all those billions for his defense budget, he certainly can't begrudge you and me spending $12 or $15 for a single-shot, or double-action. I hope you understand. Don't go out shooting people, but any time—brothers and sisters, and especially the men in this audience; some of you wearing Congressional Medals of Honor, with shoulders this wide, chests this big, muscles that big—any time you and I sit around and read where they bomb a church and murder in cold blood, not some grownups, but four little girls while they were praying to the same God the white man taught them to pray to, and you and I see the government go down and can't find who did it.

Why, this man—he can find Eichmann hiding down in Argentina somewhere. Let two or three American soldiers, who are minding somebody else's business way over in South Vietnam, get killed, and he'll send battleships, sticking his nose in their business. He wanted to send troops down to Cuba and make them have what he calls free elections—this old cracker who doesn't have free elections in his own country.

No, if you never see me another time in your life, if I die in the morning, I'll die saying one thing: the ballot or the bullet, the ballot or the bullet.

If a Negro in 1964 has to sit around and wait for some cracker senator to filibuster when it comes to the rights of black people, why, you and I should hang our heads in shame. You talk about a march on Washington in 1963, you haven't seen anything. There's some more going down in '64.

And this time they're not going like they went last year. They're not going singing "We Shall Overcome.' They're not going with white friends. They're not going with placards already painted for them. They're not going with round-trip tickets. They're going with one way tickets. And if they don't want that non-nonviolent army going down there, tell them to bring the filibuster to a halt.

The black nationalists aren't going to wait. Lyndon B. Johnson is the head of the Democratic Party. If he's for civil rights, let him go into the Senate next week and declare himself. Let him go in there right now and declare himself. Let him go in there and denounce the Southern branch of his party. Let him go in there right now and take a moral stand—right now, not later. Tell him, don't wait until election time. If he waits too long, brothers and sisters, he will be responsible for letting a condition develop in this country which will create a climate that will bring seeds up out of the ground with vegetation on the end of them looking like something these people never dreamed of. In 1964, it's the ballot or the bullet.

Thank you

‘I Am Prepared to Die’

Nelson Mandela

The Rivonia Trial (20 April 1964)

Nelson Mandela was a South African activist who became the first black President of South Africa in 1994. He helped abolish apartheid in his country and was well-known as an advocate of human rights globally. Mandela won the Nobel Peace Prize in 1993 along with Frederik Willem de Klerk for their work for the peaceful termination of the apartheid regime, and for laying the foundations for a new democratic South Africa.’

‘I Am Prepared to Die’ is one of the most famous speeches of the 20th century which marked a climactic moment in South African democracy.

I am the First Accused.

I hold a Bachelor`s Degree in Arts and practiced as an attorney in Johannesburg for a number of years in partnership with Oliver Tambo. I am a convicted prisoner serving five years for leaving the country without a permit and for inciting people to go on strike at the end of May 1961.

At the outset, I want to say that the suggestion made by the State in its opening that the struggle in South Africa is under the influence of foreigners or communists is wholly incorrect. I have done whatever I did, both as an individual and as a leader of my people, because of my experience in South Africa and my own proudly felt African background, and not because of what any outsider might have said.

In my youth in the Transkei I listened to the elders of my tribe telling stories of the old days. Amongst the tales they related to me were those of wars fought by our ancestors in defence of the fatherland. The names of Dingane and Bambata, Hintsa and Makana, Squngthi and Dalasile, Moshoeshoe and Sekhukhuni, were praised as the glory of the entire African nation. I hoped then that life might offer me the opportunity to serve my people and make my own humble contribution to their freedom struggle. This is what has motivated me in all that I have done in relation to the charges made against me in this case.

Having said this, I must deal immediately and at some length with the question of violence. Some of the things so far told to the Court are true and some are untrue. I do not, however, deny that I planned sabotage. I did not plan it in a spirit of recklessness, nor because I have any love of violence. I planned it as a result of a calm and sober assessment of the political situation that had arisen after many years of tyranny, exploitation, and oppression of my people by the Whites.

I admit immediately that I was one of the persons who helped to form Umkhonto we Sizwe, and that I played a prominent role in its affairs until I was arrested in August 1962.

In the statement which I am about to make I shall correct certain false impressions which have been created by State witnesses. Amongst other things, I will demonstrate that certain of the acts referred to in the evidence were not and could not have been committed by Umkhonto. I will also deal with the relationship between the African National Congress and Umkhonto, and with the part which I personally have played in the affairs of both organizations. I shall deal also with the part played by the Communist Party. In order to explain these matters properly, I will have to explain what Umkhonto set out to achieve; what methods it prescribed for the achievement of these objects, and why these methods were chosen. I will also have to explain how I became involved in the activities of these organisations.

I deny that Umkhonto was responsible for a number of acts which clearly fell outside the policy of the organisation, and which have been charged in the indictment against us. I do not know what justification there was for these acts, but to demonstrate that they could not have been authorised by Umkhonto, I want to refer briefly to the roots and policy of the organisation.

I have already mentioned that I was one of the persons who helped to form Umkhonto. I, and the others who started the organization, did so for two reasons. Firstly, we believed that as a result of Government policy, violence by the African people had become inevitable, and that unless responsible leadership was given to canalize and control the feelings of our people, there would be outbreaks of terrorism which would produce an intensity of bitterness and hostility between the various races of this country which is not produced even by war. Secondly, we felt that without violence there would be no way open to the African people to succeed in their struggle against the principle of white supremacy. All lawful modes of expressing opposition to this principle had been closed by legislation, and we were placed in a position in which we had either to accept a permanent state of inferiority, or to defy the Government. We chose to defy the law. We first broke the law in a way which avoided any recourse to violence; when this form was legislated against, and then the Government resorted to a show of force to crush opposition to its policies, only then did we decide to answer violence with violence.

But the violence which we chose to adopt was not terrorism. We who formed Umkhonto were all members of the African National Congress, and had behind us the ANC tradition of non-violence and negotiation as a means of solving political disputes. We believe that South Africa belongs to all the people who live in it, and not to one group, be it black or white. We did not want an interracial war, and tried to avoid it to the last minute. If the Court is in doubt about this, it will be seen that the whole history of our organisation bears out what I have said, and what I will subsequently say, when I describe the tactics which Umkhonto decided to adopt. I want, therefore, to say something about the African National Congress.

The African National Congress was formed in 1912 to defend the rights of the African people which had been seriously curtailed by the South Africa Act, and which were then being threatened by the Native Land Act. For 37 years—that is until 1949—it adhered strictly to a constitutional struggle. It put forward demands and resolutions; it sent delegations to the Government in the belief that African grievances could be settled through peaceful discussion and that Africans could advance gradually to full political rights. But White Governments remained unmoved, and the rights of Africans became less instead of becoming greater. In the words of my leader, Chief Lutuli, who became President of the ANC in 1952, and who was later awarded the Nobel Peace Prize:

'Who will deny that thirty years of my life have been spent knocking in vain, patiently, moderately, and modestly at a closed and barred door? What have been the fruits of moderation? The past thirty years have seen the greatest number of laws restricting our rights and progress, until today we have reached a stage where we have almost no rights at all.'

Even after 1949, the ANC remained determined to avoid violence. At this time, however, there was a change from the strictly constitutional means of protest which had been employed in the past. The change was embodied in a decision which was taken to protest against apartheid legislation by peaceful, but unlawful, demonstrations against certain laws. Pursuant to this policy the ANC launched the Defiance Campaign, in which I was placed in charge of volunteers. This campaign was based on the principles of passive resistance. More than 8,500 people defied apartheid laws and went to jail. Yet there was not a single instance of violence in the course of this campaign on the part of any defier. I and 19 colleagues were convicted for the role which we played in organising the campaign, but our sentences were suspended mainly because the Judge found that discipline and non-violence had been stressed throughout. This was the time when the volunteer section of the ANC was established, and when the word `Amadelakufa' was first used: this was the time when the volunteers were asked to take a pledge to uphold certain principles. Evidence dealing with volunteers and their pledges has been introduced into this case, but completely out of context. The volunteers were not, and are not, the soldiers of a black army pledged to fight a civil war against the whites. They were, and are, dedicated workers who are prepared to lead campaigns initiated by the ANC to distribute leaflets, to organise strikes, or do whatever the particular campaign required. They are called volunteers because they volunteer to face the penalties of imprisonment and whipping which are now prescribed by the legislature for such acts.

During the Defiance Campaign, the Public Safety Act and the Criminal Law Amendment Act were passed. These Statutes provided harsher penalties for offences committed by way of protests against laws. Despite this, the protests continued and the ANC adhered to its policy of non-violence. In 1956, 156 leading members of the Congress Alliance, including myself, were arrested on a charge of high treason and charges under the Suppression of Communism Act. The non-violent policy of the ANC was put in issue by the State, but when the Court gave judgement some five years later, it found that the ANC did not have a policy of violence. We were acquitted on all counts, which included a count that the ANC sought to set up a communist state in place of the existing regime. The Government has always sought to label all its opponents as communists. This allegation has been repeated in the present case, but as I will show, the ANC is not, and never has been, a communist organisation.

In 1960 there was the shooting at Sharpeville, which resulted in the proclamation of a state of emergency and the declaration of the ANC as an unlawful organisation. My colleagues and I, after careful consideration, decided that we would not obey this decree. The African people were not part of the Government and did not make the laws by which they were governed. We believed in the words of the Universal Declaration of Human Rights, that `the will of the people shall be the basis of authority of the Government', and for us to accept the banning was equivalent to accepting the silencing of the Africans for all time. The ANC refused to dissolve, but instead went underground. We believed it was our duty to preserve this organisation which had been built up with almost 50 years of unremitting toil. I have no doubt that no self-respecting White political organisation would disband itself if declared illegal by a government in which it had no say.

In 1960 the Government held a referendum which led to the establishment of the Republic. Africans, who constituted approximately 70 per cent of the population of South Africa, were not entitled to vote, and were not even consulted about the proposed constitutional change. All of us were apprehensive of our future under the proposed White Republic, and a resolution was taken to hold an All-In African Conference to call for a National

Convention, and to organise mass demonstrations on the eve of the unwanted Republic, if the Government failed to call the Convention. The conference was attended by Africans of various political persuasions. I was the Secretary of the conference and undertook to be responsible for organising the national stay-at-home which was subsequently called to coincide with the declaration of the Republic. As all strikes by Africans are illegal, the person organising such a strike must avoid arrest. I was chosen to be this person, and consequently I had to leave my home and family and my practice and go into hiding to avoid arrest.

The stay-at-home, in accordance with ANC policy, was to be a peaceful demonstration. Careful instructions were given to organisers and members to avoid any recourse to violence. The Government`s answer was to introduce new and harsher laws, to mobilize its armed forces, and to send Saracens, armed vehicles, and soldiers into the townships in a massive show of force designed to intimidate the people. This was an indication that the Government had decided to rule by force alone, and this decision was a milestone on the road to Umkhonto.

Some of this may appear irrelevant to this trial. In fact, I believe none of it is irrelevant because it will, I hope, enable the Court to appreciate the attitude eventually adopted by the various persons and bodies concerned in the National Liberation Movement. When I went to jail in 1962, the dominant idea was that loss of life should be avoided. I now know that this was still so in 1963.

I must return to June 1961. What were we, the leaders of our people, to do? Were we to give in to the show of force and the implied threat against future action, or were we to fight it and, if so, how?

We had no doubt that we had to continue the fight. Anything else would have been abject surrender. Our problem was not whether to fight, but was how to continue the fight. We of the ANC had always stood for a non-racial democracy, and we shrank from any action which might drive the races further apart than they already were. But the hard facts were that fifty years of non-violence had brought the African people nothing but more and more repressive legislation, and fewer and fewer rights. It may not be easy for this Court to understand, but it is a fact that for a long time the people had been talking of violence—of the day when they would fight the White man and win back their country—and we, the leaders of the ANC, had nevertheless always prevailed upon them to avoid violence and to pursue peaceful methods. When some of us discussed this in May and June of 1961, it could not be denied that our policy to achieve a non-racial State by non-violence had achieved nothing, and that our followers were beginning to lose confidence in this policy and were developing disturbing ideas of terrorism.

It must not be forgotten that by this time violence had, in fact, become a feature of the South African political scene. There had been violence in 1957 when the women of Zeerust were ordered to carry passes; there was violence in 1958 with the enforcement of cattle culling in Sekhukhuniland; there was violence in 1959 when the people of Cato Manor protested against pass raids; there was violence in 1960 when the Government attempted to impose Bantu Authorities in Pondoland. 39 Africans died in these disturbances. In 1961 there had been riots in Warmbaths, and all this time the Transkei had been a seething mass of unrest. Each disturbance pointed clearly to the inevitable growth among Africans of the belief that violence was the only way out—it showed that a Government which uses force to maintain its rule teaches the oppressed to use force to oppose it. Already small groups had arisen in the urban areas and were spontaneously making plans for violent forms of political struggle. There now arose a danger that these groups would adopt terrorism against Africans, as well as Whites, if not properly directed. Particularly disturbing was the type of violence engendered in places such as Zeerust, Sekhukhuniland, and Pondoland amongst Africans. It was increasingly taking the form, not of struggle against the Government—though this is what prompted it—but of civil strife amongst themselves, conducted in such a way that it could not hope to achieve anything other than a loss of life and bitterness.

At the beginning of June 1961, after a long and anxious assessment of the South African situation, I, and some colleagues, came to the conclusion that as violence in this country was inevitable, it would be unrealistic and wrong for African leaders to continue preaching peace and non-violence at a time when the Government met our peaceful demands with force.

This conclusion was not easily arrived at. It was only when all else had failed, when all channels of peaceful protest had been barred to us, that the decision was made to embark on violent forms of political struggle, and to form Umkhonto we Sizwe. We did so not because we desired such a course, but solely because the Government had left us with no other choice. In the Manifesto of Umkhonto published on 16 December 1961, which is Exhibit AD, we said:

'The time comes in the life of any nation when there remain only two choices— submit or fight. That time has now come to South Africa. We shall not submit and we have no choice but to hit back by all means in our power in defense of our people, our future, and our freedom.'

This was our feeling in June of 1961 when we decided to press for a change in the policy of the National Liberation Movement. I can only say that I felt morally obliged to do what I did.

We who had taken this decision started to consult leaders of various organisations, including the ANC. I will not say whom we spoke to, or what they said, but I wish to deal with the role of the African National Congress in this phase of the struggle, and with the policy and objectives of Umkhonto we Sizwe.

As far as the ANC was concerned, it formed a clear view which can be summarized as follows:

a. It was a mass political organisation with a political function to fulfill. Its members had joined on the express policy of non-violence.

b. Because of all this, it could not and would not undertake violence. This must be stressed. One cannot turn such a body into the small, closely knit organisation required for sabotage. Nor would this be politically correct, because it would result in members ceasing to carry out this essential activity: political propaganda and organisation. Nor was it permissible to change the whole nature of the organisation.

c. On the other hand, in view of this situation I have described, the ANC was prepared to depart from its 50-year-old policy of non-violence to this extent that it would no longer disapprove of properly controlled violence. Hence members who undertook such activity would not be subject to disciplinary action by the ANC.

I say `properly controlled violence' because I made it clear that if I formed the organisation I would at all times subject it to the political guidance of the ANC and would not undertake any different form of activity from that contemplated without the consent of the ANC. And I shall now tell the Court how that form of violence came to be determined.

As a result of this decision, Umkhonto was formed in November 1961. When we took this decision, and subsequently formulated our plans, the ANC heritage of non-violence and racial harmony was very much with us. We felt that the country was drifting towards a civil war in which Blacks and Whites would fight each other. We viewed the situation with alarm. Civil war could mean the destruction of what the ANC stood for; with civil war, racial peace would be more difficult than ever to achieve. We already have examples in South African history of the results of war. It has taken more than 50 years for the scars of the South African War to disappear. How much longer would it take to eradicate the scars of inter-racial civil war, which could not be fought without a great loss of life on both sides?

The avoidance of civil war had dominated our thinking for many years, but when we decided to adopt violence as part of our policy, we realised that we might one day have to face the prospect of such a war. This had to be taken into account in formulating our plans. We required a plan which was flexible and which permitted us to act in accordance with the needs of the times; above all, the plan had to be one which recognized civil war as the last resort, and left the decision on this question to the future. We did not want to be committed to civil war, but we wanted to be ready if it became inevitable.

Four forms of violence were possible. There is sabotage, there is guerrilla warfare, there is terrorism, and there is open revolution. We chose to adopt the first method and to exhaust it before taking any other decision.

In the light of our political background the choice was a logical one. Sabotage did not involve loss of life, and it offered the best hope for future race relations. Bitterness would be kept to a minimum and, if the policy bore fruit, democratic government could become a reality. This is what we felt at the time, and this is what we said in our Manifesto (Exhibit AD):

'We of Umkhonto we Sizwe have always sought to achieve liberation without bloodshed and civil clash. We hope, even at this late hour, that our first actions will awaken everyone to a realization of the disastrous situation to which the Nationalist policy is leading. We hope that we will bring the Government and its supporters to their senses before it is too late, so that both the Government and its policies can be changed before matters reach the desperate state of civil war.'

The initial plan was based on a careful analysis of the political and economic situation of our country. We believed that South Africa depended to a large extent on foreign capital and foreign trade. We felt that planned destruction of power plants, and interference with rail and telephone communications, would tend to scare away capital from the country, make it more difficult for goods from the industrial areas to reach the seaports on schedule, and would in the long run be a heavy drain on the economic life of the country, thus compelling the voters of the country to reconsider their position.

Attacks on the economic life lines of the country were to be linked with sabotage on Government buildings and other symbols of apartheid. These attacks would serve as a source of inspiration to our people. In addition, they would provide an outlet for those people who were urging the adoption of violent methods and would enable us to give concrete proof to our followers that we had adopted a stronger line and were fighting back against Government violence.

In addition, if mass action were successfully organised, and mass reprisals taken, we felt that sympathy for our cause would be roused in other countries, and that greater pressure would be brought to bear on the South African Government.

This then was the plan. Umkhonto was to perform sabotage, and strict instructions were given to its members right from the start, that on no account were they to injure or kill people in planning or carrying out operations. These instructions have been referred to in the evidence of 'Mr. X' and 'Mr. Z'.

The affairs of the Umkhonto were controlled and directed by a National High Command, which had powers of co-option and which could, and did, appoint Regional Commands. The High Command was the body which determined tactics and targets and was in charge of training and finance. Under the High Command there were Regional Commands which were responsible for the direction of the local sabotage groups. Within the framework of the policy laid down by the National High Command, the Regional Commands had authority to select the targets to be attacked. They had no authority to go beyond the prescribed framework and thus had no authority to embark upon acts which endangered life, or which did not fit into the overall plan of sabotage. For instance, Umkhonto members were forbidden ever to go armed into operation. Incidentally, the terms High Command and Regional Command were an importation from the Jewish national underground organisation Irgun Zvai Leumi, which operated in Israel between 1944 and 1948.

Umkhonto had its first operation on 16 December 1961, when Government buildings in Johannesburg, Port Elizabeth and Durban were attacked. The selection of targets is proof of the policy to which I have referred. Had we intended to attack life we would have selected targets where people congregated and not empty buildings and power stations. The sabotage which was committed before 16 December 1961 was the work of isolated groups and had no connection whatever with Umkhonto. In fact, some of these and a number of later acts were claimed by other organisations.

The Manifesto of Umkhonto was issued on the day that operations commenced. The response to our actions and Manifesto among the white population was characteristically violent. The Government threatened to take strong action, and called upon its supporters to stand firm and to ignore the demands of the Africans. The Whites failed to respond by suggesting change; they responded to our call by suggesting the laager.

In contrast, the response of the Africans was one of encouragement. Suddenly there was hope again. Things were happening. People in the townships became eager for political news. A great deal of enthusiasm was generated by the initial successes, and people began to speculate on how soon freedom would be obtained.

But we in Umkhonto weighed up the white response with anxiety. The lines were being drawn. The whites and blacks were moving into separate camps, and the prospects of avoiding a civil war were made less. The white newspapers carried reports that sabotage would be punished by death. If this was so, how could we continue to keep Africans away from terrorism?

Already scores of Africans had died as a result of racial friction. In 1920 when the famous leader, Masabala, was held in Port Elizabeth jail, 24 of a group of Africans who had gathered to demand his release were killed by the police and white civilians. In 1921, more than 100 Africans died in the Bulhoek affair. In 1924 over 2000 Africans were killed when the Administrator of South-West Africa led a force against a group which had rebelled against the imposition of dog tax. On 1 May 1950, 18 Africans died as a result of police shootings during the strike. On 21 March 1960, 69 unarmed Africans died at Sharpeville.

How many more Sharpevilles would there be in the history of our country? And how many more Sharpevilles could the country stand without violence and terror becoming the order of the day? And what would happen to our people when that stage was reached? In the long run we felt certain we must succeed, but at what cost to ourselves and the rest of the country?

And if this happened, how could black and white ever live together again in peace and harmony? These were the problems that faced us, and these were our decisions.

Experience convinced us that rebellion would offer the Government limitless opportunities for the indiscriminate slaughter of our people. But it was precisely because the soil of South Africa is already drenched with the blood of innocent Africans that we felt it our duty to make preparations as a long-term undertaking to use force in order to defend ourselves against force. If war were inevitable, we wanted the fight to be conducted on terms most favourable to our people. The fight which held out prospects best for us and the least risk of life to both sides was guerrilla warfare. We decided, therefore, in our preparations for the future, to make provision for the possibility of guerrilla warfare.

All whites undergo compulsory military training, but no such training was given to Africans. It was in our view essential to build up a nucleus of trained men who would be able to provide the leadership which would be required if guerrilla warfare started. We had to prepare for such a situation before it became too late to make proper preparations. It was also necessary to build up a nucleus of men trained in civil administration and other professions, so that Africans would be equipped to participate in the government of this country as soon as they were allowed to do so.

At this stage it was decided that I should attend the Conference of the Pan-African Freedom Movement for Central, East, and Southern Africa, which was to be held early in 1962 in Addis Ababa, and, because of our need for preparation, it was also decided that, after the conference, I would undertake a tour of the African States with a view to obtaining facilities for the training of soldiers, and that I would also solicit scholarships for the higher education of matriculated Africans. Training in both fields would be necessary, even if changes came about by peaceful means. Administrators would be necessary who would be willing and able to administer a non-racial State and so would men be necessary to control the army and police force of such a State.

It was on this note that I left South Africa to proceed to Addis Ababa as a delegate of the ANC. My tour was a success. Wherever I went I met sympathy for our cause and promises of help. All Africa was united against the stand of White South Africa, and even in London I was received with great sympathy by political leaders, such as Mr. Gaitskell and Mr. Grimond. In Africa I was promised support by such men as Julius Nyerere, now President of Tanganyika; Mr. Kawawa, then Prime Minister of Tanganyika; Emperor Haile Selassie of Ethiopia; General Abboud, President of the Sudan; Habib Bourguiba, President of Tunisia; Ben Bella, now President of Algeria; Modibo Keita, President of Mali; Leopold Senghor, President of Senegal; Sekou Toure, President of Guinea; President Tubman of Liberia; and Milton Obote, Prime Minister of Uganda. It was Ben Bella who invited me to visit Oujda, the Headquarters of the Algerian Army of National Liberation, the visit which is described in my diary, one of the Exhibits.

I started to make a study of the art of war and revolution and, whilst abroad, underwent a course in military training. If there was to be guerrilla warfare, I wanted to be able to stand and fight with my people and to share the hazards of war with them. Notes of lectures which I received in Algeria are contained in Exhibit 16, produced in evidence. Summaries of books on guerrilla warfare and military strategy have also been produced. I have already admitted that these documents are in my writing, and I acknowledge that I made these studies to equip myself for the role which I might have to play if the struggle drifted into guerrilla warfare. I approached this question as every African Nationalist should do. I was completely objective. The Court will see that I attempted to examine all types of authority on the subject—from the East and from the West, going back to the classic work of Clausewitz, and covering such a variety as Mao Tse Tung and Che Guevara on the one hand, and the writings on the Anglo-Boer War on the other. Of course, these notes are merely summaries of the books I read and do not contain my personal views.

I also made arrangements for our recruits to undergo military training. But here it was impossible to organise any scheme without the co-operation of the ANC offices in Africa. I consequently obtained the permission of the ANC in South Africa to do this. To this extent then there was a departure from the original decision of the ANC, but it applied outside South Africa only. The first batch of recruits actually arrived in Tanganyika when I was passing through that country on my way back to South Africa.

I returned to South Africa and reported to my colleagues on the results of my trip. On my return I found that there had been little alteration in the political scene save that the threat of a death penalty for sabotage had now become a fact. The attitude of my colleagues in Umkhonto was much the same as it had been before I left. They were feeling their way cautiously and felt that it would be a long time before the possibilities of sabotage were exhausted. In fact, the view was expressed by some that the training of recruits was premature. This is recorded by me in the document which is

Exhibit R.14. After a full discussion, however, it was decided to go ahead with the plans for military training because of the fact that it would take many years to build up a sufficient nucleus of trained soldiers to start a guerrilla campaign, and whatever happened the training would be of value.

I wish to turn now to certain general allegations made in this case by the State. But before doing so, I wish to revert to certain occurrences said by witnesses to have happened in Port Elizabeth and East London. I am referring to the bombing of private houses of pro-Government persons during September, October and November 1962. I do not know what justification there was for these acts, nor what provocation had been given. But if what I have said already is accepted, then it is clear that these acts had nothing to do with the carrying out of the policy of Umkhonto.

One of the chief allegations in the indictment is that the ANC was a party to a general conspiracy to commit sabotage. I have already explained why this is incorrect but how, externally, there was a departure from the original principle laid down by the ANC. There has, of course, been overlapping of functions internally as well, because there is a difference between a resolution adopted in the atmosphere of a committee room and the concrete difficulties that arise in the field of practical activity. At a later stage the position was further affected by banning and house arrests, and by persons leaving the country to take up political work abroad. This led to individuals having to do work in different capacities. But though this may have blurred the distinction between Umkhonto and the ANC, it by no means abolished that distinction. Great care was taken to keep the activities of the two organisations in South Africa distinct. The ANC remained a mass political body of Africans only carrying on the type of political work they had conducted prior to 1961. Umkhonto remained a small organisation recruiting its members from different races and organisations and trying to achieve its own particular object. The fact that members of Umkhonto were recruited from the ANC, and the fact that persons served both organisations, like Solomon Mbanjwa, did not, in our view, change the nature of the ANC or give it a policy of violence. This overlapping of officers, however, was more the exception than the rule. This is why persons such as `Mr. X' and `Mr. Z', who were on the Regional Command of their respective areas, did not participate in any of the ANC committees or activities, and why people such as Mr. Bennett Mashiyana and Mr. Reginald Ndubi did not hear of sabotage at their ANC meetings.

Another of the allegations in the indictment is that Rivonia was the headquarters of Umkhonto. This is not true of the time when I was there. I was told, of course, and knew that certain of the activities of the Communist Party were carried on there. But this is no reason (as I shall presently explain) why I should not use the place.

I came there in the following manner:

1. As already indicated, early in April 1961 I went underground to organise the May general strike. My work entailed travelling throughout the country, living now in African townships, then in country villages and again in cities.

During the second half of the year I started visiting the Parktown home of Arthur Goldreich, where I used to meet my family privately. Although I had no direct political association with him, I had known Arthur Goldreich socially since 1958.

2. In October, Arthur Goldreich informed me that he was moving out of town and offered me a hiding place there. A few days thereafter, he arranged for Michael Harmel to take me to Rivonia. I naturally found Rivonia an ideal place for the man who lived the life of an outlaw. Up to that time I had been compelled to live indoors during the daytime and could only venture out under cover of darkness. But at Liliesleaf [farm, Rivonia] I could live differently and work far more efficiently.

3. For obvious reasons, I had to disguise myself and I assumed the fictitious name of David. In December, Arthur Goldreich and his family moved in. I stayed there until I went abroad on 11 January 1962. As already indicated, I returned in July 1962 and was arrested in Natal on 5 August.

4. Up to the time of my arrest, Liliesleaf farm was the headquarters of neither the African National Congress nor Umkhonto. With the exception of myself, none of the officials or members of these bodies lived there, no meetings of the governing

bodies were ever held there, and no activities connected with them were either organised or directed from there. On numerous occasions during my stay at Liliesleaf farm I met both the Executive Committee of the ANC, as well as the NHC, but such meetings were held elsewhere and not on the farm.

5. Whilst staying at Liliesleaf farm, I frequently visited Arthur Goldreich in the main house and he also paid me visits in my room. We had numerous political discussions covering a variety of subjects. We discussed ideological and practical questions, the Congress Alliance, Umkhonto and its activities generally, and his experiences as a soldier in the Palmach, the military wing of the Haganah. Haganah was the political authority of the Jewish National Movement in Palestine.

6. Because of what I had got to know of Goldreich, I recommended on my return to South Africa that he should be recruited to Umkhonto. I do not know of my personal knowledge whether this was done.

Another of the allegations made by the State is that the aims and objects of the ANC and the Communist Party are the same. I wish to deal with this and with my own political position, because I must assume that the State may try to argue from certain Exhibits that I tried to introduce Marxism into the ANC. The allegation as to the ANC is false. This is an old allegation which was disproved at the Treason Trial and which has again reared its head. But since the allegation has been made again, I shall deal with it as well as with the relationship between the ANC and the Communist Party and Umkhonto and that party.

The ideological creed of the ANC is, and always has been, the creed of African Nationalism. It is not the concept of African Nationalism expressed in the cry, 'Drive the White man into the sea'. The African Nationalism for which the ANC stands is the concept of freedom and fulfillment for the African people in their own land. The most important political document ever adopted by the ANC is the 'Freedom Charter'. It is by no means a blueprint for a socialist state. It calls for redistribution, but not nationalisation, of land; it provides for nationalisation of mines, banks, and monopoly industry, because big monopolies are owned by one race only, and without such nationalization racial domination would be perpetuated despite the spread of political power. It would be a hollow gesture to repeal the Gold Law prohibitions against Africans when all gold mines are owned by European companies. In this respect the ANC's policy corresponds with the old policy of the present Nationalist Party which, for many years, had as part of its programme the nationalization of the gold mines which, at that time, were controlled by foreign capital. Under the Freedom Charter, nationalization would take place in an economy based on private enterprise. The realisation of the Freedom Charter would open up fresh fields for a prosperous African population of all classes, including the middle class. The ANC has never at any period of its history advocated a revolutionary change in the economic structure of the country, nor has it, to the best of my recollection, ever condemned capitalist society.

As far as the Communist Party is concerned, and if I understand its policy correctly, it stands for the establishment of a State based on the principles of Marxism. Although it is prepared to work for the Freedom Charter, as a short term solution to the problems created by white supremacy, it regards the Freedom Charter as the beginning, and not the end, of its programme.

The ANC, unlike the Communist Party, admitted Africans only as members. Its chief goal was, and is, for the African people to win unity and full political rights. The Communist Party's main aim, on the other hand, was to remove the capitalists and to replace them with a working-class government. The Communist Party sought to emphasise class distinctions whilst the ANC seeks to harmonise them. This is a vital distinction.

It is true that there has often been close co-operation between the ANC and the Communist Party. But co-operation is merely proof of a common goal—in this case the removal of white supremacy—and is not proof of a complete community of interests.

The history of the world is full of similar examples. Perhaps the most striking illustration is to be found in the co-operation between Great Britain, the United States of America, and the Soviet Union in the fight against Hitler. Nobody but Hitler would have dared to suggest that such co-operation turned Churchill or Roosevelt into communists or communist tools, or that Britain and America were working to bring about a communist world.

Another instance of such co-operation is to be found precisely in Umkhonto. Shortly after Umkhonto was constituted, I was informed by some of its members that the Communist Party would support Umkhonto, and this then occurred. At a later stage the support was made openly.

I believe that communists have always played an active role in the fight by colonial countries for their freedom, because the short-term objects of communism would always correspond with the long-term objects of freedom movements. Thus communists have played an important role in the freedom struggles fought in countries such as Malaya, Algeria, and Indonesia, yet none of these States today are communist countries. Similarly in the underground resistance movements which sprung up in Europe during the last World War, communists played an important role. Even General Chiang Kai-Shek, today one of the bitterest enemies of communism, fought together with the communists against the ruling class in the struggle which led to his assumption of power in China in the 1930s.

This pattern of co-operation between communists and non-communists has been repeated in the National Liberation Movement of South Africa. Prior to the banning of the Communist Party, joint campaigns involving the Communist Party and the Congress movements were accepted practice. African communists could, and did, become members of the ANC, and some served on the National, Provincial, and local committees. Amongst those who served on the National Executive are Albert Nzula, a former Secretary of the Communist Party, Moses Kotane, another former Secretary, and J. B. Marks, a former member of the Central Committee.

I joined the ANC in 1944, and in my younger days I held the view that the policy of admitting communists to the ANC, and the close co-operation which existed at times on specific issues between the ANC and the Communist Party, would lead to a watering down of the concept of African Nationalism. At that stage I was a member of the African National Congress Youth League, and was one of a group which moved for the expulsion of communists from the ANC. This proposal was heavily defeated. Amongst those who voted against the proposal were some of the most conservative sections of African political opinion. They defended the policy on the ground that from its inception the ANC was formed and built up, not as a political party with one school of political thought, but as a Parliament of the African people, accommodating people of various political convictions, all united by the common goal of national liberation. I was eventually won over to this point of view and I have upheld it ever since.

It is perhaps difficult for white South Africans, with an ingrained prejudice against communism, to understand why experienced African politicians so readily accept communists as their friends. But to us the reason is obvious. Theoretical differences amongst those fighting against oppression is a luxury we cannot afford at this stage. What is more, for many decades communists were the only political group in South Africa who were prepared to treat Africans as human beings and their equals; who were prepared to eat with us; talk with us, live with us, and work with us. They were the only political group which was prepared to work with the Africans for the attainment of political rights and a stake in society. Because of this, there are many Africans who, today, tend to equate freedom with communism. They are supported in this belief by a legislature which brands all exponents of democratic government and African freedom as communists and bans many of them (who are not communists) under the Suppression of Communism Act. Although I have never been a member of the Communist Party, I myself have been named under that pernicious Act because of the role I played in the Defiance Campaign. I have also been banned and imprisoned under that Act.

It is not only in internal politics that we count communists as amongst those who support our cause. In the international field, communist countries have always come to our aid. In the United Nations and other Councils of the world the communist bloc has supported the Afro-Asian struggle against colonialism and often seems to be more sympathetic to our plight than some of the Western powers. Although there is a universal condemnation of apartheid, the communist bloc speaks out against it with a louder voice than most of the white world. In these circumstances, it would take a brash young politician, such as I was in 1949, to proclaim that the Communists are our enemies.

I turn now to my own position. I have denied that I am a communist, and I think that in the circumstances I am obliged to state exactly what my political beliefs are.

I have always regarded myself, in the first place, as an African patriot. After all, I was born in Umtata, 46 years ago. My guardian was my cousin, who was the acting paramount chief of Tembuland, and I am related both to the present paramount chief of Tembuland, Sabata Dalindyebo, and to Kaizer Matanzima, the Chief Minister of the Transkei.

Today I am attracted by the idea of a classless society, an attraction which springs in part from Marxist reading and, in part, from my admiration of the structure and organisation of early African societies in this country. The land, then the main means of production, belonged to the tribe. There were no rich or poor and there was no exploitation.

It is true, as I have already stated, that I have been influenced by Marxist thought. But this is also true of many of the leaders of the new independent States. Such widely different persons as Gandhi, Nehru, Nkrumah, and Nasser all acknowledge this fact. We all accept the need for some form of socialism to enable our people to catch up with the advanced countries of this world and to overcome their legacy of extreme poverty. But this does not mean we are Marxists.

Indeed, for my own part, I believe that it is open to debate whether the Communist Party has any specific role to play at this particular stage of our political struggle. The basic task at the present moment is the removal of race discrimination and the attainment of democratic rights on the basis of the Freedom Charter. In so far as that Party furthers this task, I welcome its assistance. I realise that it is one of the means by which people of all races can be drawn into our struggle.

From my reading of Marxist literature and from conversations with Marxists, I have gained the impression that communists regard the parliamentary system of the West as undemocratic and reactionary. But, on the contrary, I am an admirer of such a system.

The Magna Carta, the Petition of Rights, and the Bill of Rights are documents which are held in veneration by democrats throughout the world.

I have great respect for British political institutions, and for the country's system of justice. I regard the British Parliament as the most democratic institution in the world, and the independence and impartiality of its judiciary never fail to arouse my admiration.

The American Congress, that country's doctrine of separation of powers, as well as the independence of its judiciary, arouses in me similar sentiments.

I have been influenced in my thinking by both West and East. All this has led me to feel that in my search for a political formula, I should be absolutely impartial and objective. I should tie myself to no particular system of society other than of socialism. I must leave myself free to borrow the best from the West and from the East ...

There are certain Exhibits which suggest that we received financial support from abroad, and I wish to deal with this question.

Our political struggle has always been financed from internal sources—from funds raised by our own people and by our own supporters. Whenever we had a special campaign or an important political case—for example, the Treason Trial—we received financial assistance from sympathetic individuals and organisations in the Western countries. We had never felt it necessary to go beyond these sources.

But when in 1961 the Umkhonto was formed, and a new phase of struggle introduced, we realized that these events would make a heavy call on our slender resources, and that the scale of our activities would be hampered by the lack of funds. One of my instructions, as I went abroad in January 1962, was to raise funds from the African states.

I must add that, whilst abroad, I had discussions with leaders of political movements in Africa and discovered that almost every single one of them, in areas which had still not attained independence, had received all forms of assistance from the socialist countries, as well as from the West, including that of financial support. I also discovered that some well-known African states, all of them non-communists, and even anti-communists, had received similar assistance.

On my return to the Republic, I made a strong recommendation to the ANC that we should not confine ourselves to Africa and the Western countries, but that we should also send a mission to the socialist countries to raise the funds which we so urgently needed.

I have been told that after I was convicted such a mission was sent, but I am not prepared to name any countries to which it went, nor am I at liberty to disclose the names of the organisations and countries which gave us support or promised to do so.

As I understand the State case, and in particular the evidence of `Mr. X', the suggestion is that Umkhonto was the inspiration of the Communist Party which sought by playing upon imaginary grievances to enrol the African people into an army which ostensibly was to fight for African freedom, but in reality was fighting for a communist state. Nothing could be further from the truth. In fact the suggestion is preposterous. Umkhonto was formed by Africans to further their struggle for freedom in their own land. Communists and others supported the movement, and we only wish that more sections of the community would join us.

Our fight is against real, and not imaginary, hardships or, to use the language of the State Prosecutor, 'so-called hardships'. Basically, we fight against two features which are the hallmarks of African life in South Africa and which are entrenched by legislation which we seek to have repealed. These features are poverty and lack of human dignity, and we do not need communists or so-called `agitators' to teach us about these things.

South Africa is the richest country in Africa, and could be one of the richest countries in the world. But it is a land of extremes and remarkable contrasts. The whites enjoy what may well be the highest standard of living in the world, whilst Africans live in poverty and misery. Forty per cent of the Africans live in hopelessly overcrowded and, in some cases, drought-stricken Reserves, where soil erosion and the overworking of the soil makes it impossible for them to live properly off the land. 30 per cent are labourers, labour tenants, and squatters on white farms and work and live under conditions similar to those of the serfs of the Middle Ages. The other 30 per cent live in towns where they have developed economic and social habits which bring them closer in many respects to white standards. Yet most Africans, even in this group, are impoverished by low incomes and high cost of living.

The highest-paid and the most prosperous section of urban African life is in Johannesburg. Yet their actual position is desperate. The latest figures were given on 25 March 1964 by Mr. Carr, Manager of the Johannesburg Non-European Affairs Department. The poverty datum line for the average African family in Johannesburg (according to Mr. Carr's department) is R 42.84 per month. He showed that the average monthly wage is R 32.24 and that 46 per cent of all African families in Johannesburg do not earn enough to keep them going.

Poverty goes hand-in-hand with malnutrition and disease. The incidence of malnutrition and deficiency diseases is very high amongst Africans. Tuberculosis, pellagra, kwashiorkor, gastro-enteritis, and scurvy bring death and destruction of health. The incidence of infant mortality is one of the highest in the world. According to the Medical Officer of Health for Pretoria, tuberculosis kills 40 people a day (almost all Africans), and in 1961 there were 58,491 new cases reported. These diseases not only destroy the vital organs of the body, but they result in retarded mental conditions and lack of initiative, and reduce powers of concentration. The secondary results of such conditions affect the whole community and the standard of work performed by African labourers.

The complaint of Africans, however, is not only that they are poor and the whites are rich, but that the laws which are made by the whites are designed to preserve this situation. There are two ways to break out of poverty. The first is by formal education, and the second is by the worker acquiring a greater skill at his work and thus higher wages. As far as Africans are concerned, both these avenues of advancement are deliberately curtailed by legislation.

The present Government has always sought to hamper Africans in their search for education. One of their early acts, after coming into power, was to stop subsidies for African school feeding. Many African children who attended schools depended on this supplement to their diet. This was a cruel act.

There is compulsory education for all white children at virtually no cost to their parents, be they rich or poor. Similar facilities are not provided for the African children, though there are some who receive such assistance. African children, however, generally have to pay more for their schooling than whites. According to figures quoted by the South African Institute of Race Relations in its 1963 journal, approximately 40 per cent of African children in the age group between seven to 14 do not attend school. For those who do attend school, the standards are vastly different from those afforded to white children. In 1960-61 the per capita Government spending on African students at State-aided schools was estimated at R 12.46. In the same years, the per capita spending on white children in the Cape Province (which are the only figures available to me) was R 144.57. Although there are no figures available to me, it can be stated, without doubt, that the white children on whom R 144.57 per head was being spent all came from wealthier homes than African children on whom R 12.46 per head was being spent.

The quality of education is also different. According to the Bantu Educational Journal, only 5,660 African children in the whole of South Africa passed their Junior Certificate in 1962, and in that year only 362 passed Matric. This is presumably consistent with the policy of Bantu education about which the present Prime Minister said, during the debate on the Bantu Education Bill in 1953:

'When I have control of Native education I will reform it so that Natives will be taught from childhood to realise that equality with Europeans is not for them ... People who believe in equality are not desirable teachers for Natives. When my Department controls Native education it will know for what class of higher education a Native is fitted, and whether he will have a chance in life to use his knowledge.'

The other main obstacle to the economic advancement of the African is the industrial colour-bar under which all the better jobs of industry are reserved for Whites only. Moreover, Africans who do obtain employment in the unskilled and semi-skilled occupations which are open to them are not allowed to form trade unions which have recognition under the Industrial Conciliation Act. This means that strikes of African workers are illegal, and that they are denied the right of collective bargaining which is permitted to the better-paid White workers. The discrimination in the policy of successive South African Governments towards African workers is demonstrated by the so-called 'civilised labour policy' under which sheltered, unskilled Government jobs are found for those white workers who cannot make the grade in industry, at wages which far exceed the earnings of the average African employee in industry.

The Government often answers its critics by saying that Africans in South Africa are economically better off than the inhabitants of the other countries in Africa. I do not know whether this statement is true and doubt whether any comparison can be made without having regard to the cost-of-living index in such countries. But even if it is true, as far as the African people are concerned it is irrelevant. Our complaint is not that we are poor by comparison with people in other countries, but that we are poor by comparison with the white people in our own country, and that we are prevented by legislation from altering this imbalance.

The lack of human dignity experienced by Africans is the direct result of the policy of white supremacy. White supremacy implies black inferiority. Legislation designed to preserve white supremacy entrenches this notion. Menial tasks in South Africa are invariably performed by Africans. When anything has to be carried or cleaned the white man will look around for an African to do it for him, whether the African is employed by him or not. Because of this sort of attitude, whites tend to regard Africans as a separate breed. They do not look upon them as people with families of their own; they do not realize that they have emotions—that they fall in love like white people do; that they want to be with their wives and children like white people want to be with theirs; that they want to earn enough money to support their families properly, to feed and clothe them and send them to school. And what `house-boy' or `garden-boy' or labourer can ever hope to do this?

Pass laws, which to the Africans are among the most hated bits of legislation in South Africa, render any African liable to police surveillance at any time. I doubt whether there is a single African male in South Africa who has not at some stage had a brush with the police over his pass. Hundreds and thousands of Africans are thrown into jail each year under pass laws. Even worse than this is the fact that pass laws keep husband and wife apart and lead to the breakdown of family life.

Poverty and the breakdown of family life have secondary effects. Children wander about the streets of the townships because they have no schools to go to, or no money to enable them to go to school, or no parents at home to see that they go to school, because both parents (if there be two) have to work to keep the family alive. This leads to a breakdown in moral standards, to an alarming rise in illegitimacy, and to growing violence which erupts not only politically, but everywhere. Life in the townships is dangerous. There is not a day that goes by without somebody being stabbed or assaulted. And violence is carried out of the townships in the white living areas. People are afraid to walk alone in the streets after dark. Housebreakings and robberies are increasing, despite the fact that the death sentence can now be imposed for such offences. Death sentences cannot cure the festering sore.

Africans want to be paid a living wage. Africans want to perform work which they are capable of doing, and not work which the Government declares them to be capable. Africans want to be allowed to live where they obtain work, and not be endorsed out of an area because they were not born there. Africans want to be allowed to own land in places where they work, and not to be obliged to live in rented houses which they can never call their own. Africans want to be part of the general population, and not confined to living in their own ghettoes. African men want to have their wives and children to live with them where they work, and not be forced into an unnatural existence in men's hostels. African women want to be with their menfolk and not be left permanently widowed in the Reserves. Africans want to be allowed out after 11 o'clock at night and not to be confined to their rooms like little children. Africans want to be allowed to travel in their own country and to seek work where they want to and not where the Labour Bureau tells them to. Africans want a just share in the whole of South Africa; they want security and a stake in society.

Above all, we want equal political rights, because without them our disabilities will be permanent. I know this sounds revolutionary to the whites in this country, because the majority of voters will be Africans. This makes the white man fear democracy.

But this fear cannot be allowed to stand in the way of the only solution which will guarantee racial harmony and freedom for all. It is not true that the enfranchisement of all will result in racial domination. Political division, based on colour, is entirely artificial and, when it disappears, so will the domination of one colour group by another. The ANC has spent half a century fighting against racialism. When it triumphs it will not change that policy.

This then is what the ANC is fighting. Their struggle is a truly national one. It is a struggle of the African people, inspired by their own suffering and their own experience. It is a struggle for the right to live.

During my lifetime I have dedicated myself to this struggle of the African people. I have fought against white domination, and I have fought against black domination. I have cherished the ideal of a democratic and free society in which all persons live together in harmony and with equal opportunities. It is an ideal which I hope to live for and to achieve. But if needs be, it is an ideal for which I am prepared to die.

Judge Carswell and the Sex Plus Doctrine

Betty Friedan

U.S. Senate, Washington, DC (29 January 1970)

Betty Friedan was an American feminist, author, activist, co-founder and the first President of National Organisation for Women (NOW). She was a pioneer of the women's rights movement, and her groundbreaking novel *The Feminine Mystique* (1963) paved the way for the idea of women finding fulfillment outside traditional gender roles.

Through this speech, Friedan was instrumental in the U.S. Senate's rejection of Judge Carswell's nomination; the same judge had opposed the 1964 Civil Rights Act.

I am here to testify before this committee to oppose Judge Carswell's appointment to Supreme Court Justice on the basis of his proven insensitivity to the problems of the 53 percent of United States citizens who are women, and specifically on the basis of his explicit discrimination in a circuit court decision in 1969 against working mothers.

I speak in my capacity as national president of the National Organization for Women, which has led the exploding new movement in this country for 'full equality for women in truly equal partnership with men,' and which was organized in 1966 to take action to break through discrimination against women in employment, education, government and in all fields of American life.

On October 13, 1969, in the Fifth Circuit Court of Appeals, Judge Carswell was party to a most unusual judiciary action which would permit employers, in defiance of the law of the land as embodied in Title VII of the 1964 Civil Rights Act, to refuse to hire women who have children.

The case involved Mrs. Ida Phillips, who was refused employment by Martin Marietta Corporation as an aircraft assembler because she had pre-school aged children, although the company said it would hire a man with pre-school aged children. This case was considered a clear-cut violation of the law which forbids job discrimination on the grounds of sex as well as race. The E.E.O.C., empowered to administer Title VII, filed an amicus brief on behalf of Mrs. Phillips; an earlier opinion of the Fifth Circuit filed in May upholding the company was considered such a clear violation of the Civil Rights Act by Chief Judge John Brown that he vacated the opinion and asked to convene the full court to consider the case.

Judge Carswell voted to deny a rehearing of the case, an action which in effect would have permitted employers to fire the 4.1 million working mothers in the U.S. today who have children under six. They comprise 38.9 percent of the nearly 10.6 million mothers in the labor force today.

In his dissent to this ruling in which Judge Carswell claimed no sex discrimination was involved, Chief Judge Brown said: 'The case is simple. A woman with pre-school aged children may not be employed, a man with pre-school children may. The distinguishing factor seems to be motherhood versus fatherhood. The question then arises: Is this sex related? To the simple query, the answer is just as simple: Nobody—and this includes judges, Solomonic or life-tenured—has yet seen a male mother. A mother, to over-simplify the simplest biology, must then be a woman.

'It is the fact of the person being a mother, i.e., a woman—not the age of the children, which denies employment opportunity to a woman which is open to men.'

It is important for this committee to understand the dangerous insensitivity of Judge Carswell to sex discrimination, when the desire and indeed the necessity of women to take a fully equal place in American society has already emerged as one of the most explosive issues in the 1970's, entailing many new problems which will ultimately have to be decided by the Supreme Court.

According to government figures, over 25 percent of mothers who have children under six are in the labor force today. Over 85 percent of them work for economic reasons. Over half a million are widowed, divorced or separated. Their incomes are vitally important to their children. Perhaps even more important, as a portent of the future, is the fact that there has been an astronomical increase in the last three decades in the number of working mothers. Between 1950 and the most recent compilation of government statistics, the number of working mothers in the United States nearly doubled. For every mother of children who worked in 1940, ten mothers are working today, an increase from slightly over 1.5 million to nearly 11 million.

In his pernicious action, Judge Carswell not only flaunted the Civil Rights Act, designed to end the job discrimination which denied women, along with other minority groups, equal opportunity in employment, but specifically defied the policy of this administration to encourage women in poverty, who have children, to work by expanding day-care centers, rather than having them depend on the current medieval welfare system which perpetuates the cycle of poverty from generation to generation. Mothers and children today comprise 80 percent of the welfare load in major cities.

Judge Carswell justified discrimination against such women by a peculiar doctrine of 'sex plus,' which claimed that discrimination which did not apply to all women but only to women who did not meet special standards—standards not applied to men—was not sex discrimination.

In his dissent, Chief Judge Brown said, 'the sex plus rule in this case sows the seed for future discrimination against black workers through making them meet extra standards not imposed on whites.' The 'sex plus' doctrine would also penalize the very women who most need jobs.

Chief Judge Brown said, 'Even if the 'sex plus' rule is not expanded, in its application to mothers of pre-school children, it will deal a serious blow to the objectives of Title VII. If the law against sex discrimination means anything, it must protect employment opportunities for those groups of women who most need jobs because of economic necessity. Working mothers of pre-schoolers are such a group. Studies show that, as compared to women with older children or no children, these mothers of pre-school children were much more likely to have gone to work because of pressing need...because of financial necessity and because their husbands are unable to work. Frequently, these women are a key or only source of income for their families. 68 percent of working women do not have husbands present in the household, and two-thirds of these women are raising children in poverty. Moreover, a barrier to jobs for mothers of pre-schoolers tends to harm non-white mothers more than white mothers.'

I am not a lawyer, but the wording of Title VII of the Civil Rights Act so clearly conveys its intention to provide equal job opportunity to all oppressed groups, including women—who today in America earn on the average less than half the earnings of men—that only outright sex discrimination or sexism, as we new feminists call it, can explain Judge Carswell's ruling.

Human rights are indivisible, and I, and those for whom I speak, would oppose equally the appointment to the Supreme Court of a racist judge who had been totally blind to the humanity of black men and women since 1948, as the appointment of a sexist judge totally blind to the humanity of women in 1969.

To countenance outright sexism, not only in words, but by judicial flaunting of the law in an appointee to the Supreme Court in 1970, when American women—not in the hundreds or thousands but in the millions—are finally beginning to assert their human rights, is unconscionable.

I trust that you gentlemen of the committee do not share Judge Carswell's inability to see women as human beings, too. I will, however, put these questions to you.

How would you feel if in the event you were not reelected, you applied for a job at some company or law firm or university, and were told you weren't eligible because you had a child?

How would you feel if your sons were told explicitly or implicitly that they could not get or keep certain jobs if they had children?

Then how do you feel about appointing to the Supreme Court a man who has said your daughters may not hold a job if they have children?

The economic misery and psychological conflicts entailed for untold numbers of American women, and their children and husbands, by Judge Carswell's denial of the protection of a law that was enacted for their benefit suggest only a faint hint of the harm that would be done in appointing such a sexually backward judge to the Supreme Court. For during the next decade I can assure you that the emerging revolution of the no-longer-quite-so-silent majority will pose many pressing new problems to our society, problems which will inevitably come before the courts and which indeed will probably preoccupy the Supreme Court of the 1970's as did questions arising from the civil rights movement in the 1960's.

It is already apparent from decisions made by judges in other circuit courts that Judge Carswell is unusually blind in the matter of sex prejudice and that his blindness will make it impossible for him to judge fairly the cases of sex prejudice that will surely come up.

Recently, courts have begun to outlaw forms of discrimination against women long accepted in society. The Fifth Circuit Court of Appeals (convened as a three-judge court without Judge Carswell), on March 4, 1969, in Weeks v. Southern Bell Telephone ruled that weight-lifting limitations barring women, but not men, from jobs, were illegal under Title VII. The Seventh Circuit Court of Appeals, on September 26, 1969, in Bowe v. Colgate Palmolive Co. ruled that, if retained, a weight-lifting test must apply to ALL employees, male and female, and that each individual must be permitted to 'bid on and fill any job which his or her seniority entitled him or her.' Separate seniority lists for men and women were forbidden.

Here are a few existing instances of discrimination against women, that are or will be before the courts:

1. In New York City, male, but not female, teachers are paid for their time spent on jury duty.
2. In Syracuse, New York, male, but not female, teachers are paid for athletic coaching.
3. In Syracuse, an employer wants to challenge the rule that forbids her to hire female employees at night in violation of New York State restrictive laws.

4. In Pennsylvania, a woman has requested help in obtaining a tax deduction for household help necessary for her to work.
5. In Arizona, a female law professor is fighting a rule that forbids her to be hired by the same university that employs her husband in another department.
6. In California, a wife is challenging a community property law which makes it obligatory for a husband to control their joint property.
7. And all over the country the E.E.O.C. regulation, which made it illegal to have separate want ads for males and females, have not been followed by most newspapers.

The Honorable Shirley Chisholm, a national board member of NOW, has summed it all up in her statement that she has been more discriminated against as a woman than as a black.

It would show enormous contempt for every woman of this country and contempt for every black American, as well as contempt for the Supreme Court itself, if you confirm Judge Carswell's appointment.

'What Educated Women Can Do'

Indira Gandhi

Golden Jubilee Celebrations of the Indraprastha College for Women
(23 November 1974)

Indira Gandhi was a former Prime Minister of India who served for three terms, making her the second-longest serving Indian prime minister after her father Jawaharlal Nehru. She enjoyed widespread support due to her agricultural reforms that led to the Green Revolution and for the success of the war with Pakistan, resulting in the creation of Bangladesh.

Following Operation Blue Star, Indira Gandhi was assassinated in 1984 by her two trusted Sikh bodyguards.

In this speech delivered at the Indraprastha College for Women, New Delhi, Gandhi talks about the importance of women's education.

An ancient Sanskrit saying says, 'Woman is the home and the home is the basis of society.' It is as we build our homes that we can build our country. If the home is inadequate— either inadequate in material goods and necessities or inadequate in the sort of friendly, loving atmosphere that every child needs to grow and develop—then that country cannot have harmony and no country which does not have harmony can grow in any direction at all.

That is why women's education is almost more important than the education of boys and men. We—and by 'we' I do not mean only we in India but all the world— have neglected women education. It is fairly recent. Of course, not to you but when I was a child, the story of early days of women's education in England, for instance, was very current. Everybody remembered what had happened in the early days.

I remember what used to happen here. I still remember the days when living in old Delhi even as a small child of seven or eight. I had to go out in a doli if I left the house. We just did not walk. Girls did not walk in the streets. First, you had your sari with which you covered your head, then you had another shawl or something with which you covered your hand and all the body, then you had a white shawl, with which everything was covered again although your face was open fortunately. Then you were in the doli, which again was covered by another cloth. And this was in a family or community which did not observe purdah of any kind at all. In fact, all our social functions always were mixed functions but this was the atmosphere of the city and of the country.

Now, we have got education and there is a debate all over the country whether this education is adequate to the needs of society or the needs of our young people. I am one of those who always believe that education needs a thorough overhauling. But at the same time, I think that everything in our education is not bad, that even the present education has produced very fine men and women, specially scientists and experts in different fields, who are in great demand all over the world and even in the most affluent countries. Many of our young people leave us and go abroad because they get higher salaries, they get better conditions of work.

But it is not all a one-sided business because there are many who are persuaded and cajoled to go even when they are reluctant. We know of first class students, especially in medicine or nuclear energy for instance, they are approached long before they have passed out and offered all kinds of inducements to go out. Now, that shows that people do consider that they have a standard of knowledge and capability which will be useful anywhere in the world.

So, that is why I say that there is something worthwhile. It also shows that our own ancient philosophy has taught us that nothing in life is entirely bad or entirely good. Everything is somewhat of a mixture and it depends on us and our capability how we can extract the good, how we can make use of what is around us. There are people who through observation can learn from anything that is around them. There are others who can be surrounded by the most fascinating people, the most wonderful books, and other things and who yet remain quite closed in and they are unable to take anything from this wealth around them.

Our country is a very rich country. It is rich in culture, it is rich in many old traditions—old and even modern tradition. Of course, it has a lot of bad things too and some of the bad things are in the society—superstition, which has grown over the years and which sometimes clouds over the shining brightness of ancient thought and values, eternal values. Then, of course, there is the physical poverty of large numbers of our people. That is something which is ugly and that hampers the growth of millions of young boys and girls. Now, all these bad things we have to fight against and that is what we are doing since Independence.

But, we must not allow this dark side of the picture which, by the way, exists in every country in the world. Even the most rich country in the world has its dark side, but usually other people hide their dark sides and they try to project the shining side or the side of achievement. Here in India, we seem to want to project the worst side of society. Before anybody does anything, he has to have, of course, knowledge and capability, but along with it he has to have a certain amount of pride in what he or she is doing. He has to have self-confidence in his own ability. If your teacher tells, 'You cannot do this,' even if you are a very bright student I think every time you will find, it will be more and more difficult for you to do it. But if your teacher encourages saying, 'Go along you have done very good work, now try a little harder,' then you will try a little harder and you will be able to do it. And it is the same with societies and with countries.

This country, India, has had remarkable achievements to its credit, of course in ancient times, but even in modern times, I think there are a few modern stories, success stories, which are as fascinating as the success story of our country. It is true that we have not banished poverty, we have not banished many of our social ills, but if you compare us to what we were just about 27 years ago,

I think that you will not find a single other country that has been able to achieve so much under the most difficult circumstances.

Today, we are passing through specially dark days. But these are not dark days for India alone. Except for the countries which call themselves socialist and about which we do not really know very much, every other country has the same sort of economic problems, which we have. Only a few countries, which have very small populations, have no unemployment. Otherwise, the rich countries also today have unemployment. They have shortages of essential articles. They have shortages even of food.

I do not know how many of you know that the countries of Western Europe and Japan import 41 per cent of their food needs, whereas India imports just under two per cent. Yet, somehow we ourselves project an image that India is out with the begging bowl. And naturally when we ourselves say it, other people will say it much louder and much stronger. It is true, of course, that our two per cent is pretty big because we are a very big country and we have a far bigger population than almost any country in the world with the exception of China. We have to see and you, the educated women, because it is great privilege for you to have higher education, you have to try and see our problems in the perspective of what has happened here in this country and what is happening all over the world.

There is today great admiration for certain things that have happened in other countries where the society is quite differently formed, where no dissent is allowed. The same people who admire that system or the achievements of that system are the ones who say there is dictatorship here even though, I think, nobody has yet been able to point out to me which country has more freedom of expression or action. So, something is said and a lot of people without thinking keep on repeating it with additions until an entirely distorted picture of the country and of our people is presented.

As I said, we do have many shortcomings, whether it is the government, whether it is the society. Some are due to our traditions because, as I said, not all tradition is good. And one of the biggest responsibilities of the educated women today is how to synthesise what has been valuable and timeless in our ancient traditions with what is good and valuable in modern thought. All that is modern is not good just as all that is old is neither all good nor all bad. We have to decide, not once and for all but almost every week, every month what is coming out that is good and useful to our country and what of the old we can keep and enshrine in our society. To be modern, most people think that it is something of a manner of dress or a manner of speaking or certain habits and customs, but that is not really being modern. It is a very superficial part of modernity.

For instance, when I cut my hair, it was because of the sort of life that I was leading. We were all in the movement. You simply could not have long hair and go in the villages and wash it every day. So, when you lead a life, a particular kind of life, your clothes, your everything has to fit into that life if you are to be efficient. If you have to go in the villages and you have to bother whether your clothes are going to be dirty, then you cannot be a good worker. You have to forget everything of that kind. That is why, gradually, clothes and so on have changed in some countries because of the changes in the life-style. Does it suit our life-style or what we want to do or not? If it does, maybe we have to adopt some of these things not merely because it is done in another country and perhaps for another purpose. But what clothes we wear is really quite unimportant. What is important is how we are thinking.

Sometimes, I am very sad that even people who do science are quite unscientific in their thinking and in their other actions— not what they are doing in the laboratories but how they live at home or their attitudes towards other people. Now, for India to become what we want it to become with a modern, rational society and firmly based on what is good in our ancient tradition and in our soil, for this we have to have a thinking public, thinking young women who are not content to accept what comes from any part of the world but are willing to listen to it, to analyse it and to decide whether it is to be accepted or whether it is to be thrown out and this is the sort of education which we want, which enables our young people to adjust to this changing world and to be able to contribute to it.

Some people think that only by taking up very high jobs, you are doing something important or you are doing national service. But we all know that the most complex machinery will be ineffective if one small screw is not working as it should and that screw is just as important as any big part. It is the same in national life. There is no job that is too small; there is no person who is too small. Everybody has something to do. And if he or she does it well, then the country will run well.

In our superstition, we have thought that some work is dirty work. For instance, sweeping has been regarded as dirty. Only some people can do it; others should not do it. Now we find that manure is the most valuable thing that the world has today and many of the world's economies are shaking because there is not enough fertilizer—and not just the chemical fertilizer but the ordinary manure, night-soil and all that sort of thing, things which were considered dirty.

Now it shows how beautifully balanced the world was with everything fitted in with something else. Everything, whether dirty or small, had a purpose. We, with our science and technology, have tried to—not purposely, but somehow, we have created an imbalance and that is what is troubling, on a big scale, the economies of the world and also people and individuals. They are feeling alienated from their societies, not only in India but almost in every country in the world, except in places where the whole purpose of education and government has to be to make the people conform to just one idea. We are told that people there are very happy in whatever they are doing. If they are told to clean the streets, well, if he is a professor he has to clean the streets, if he is a scientist he has to do it, and we were told that they are happy doing it. Well, if they are happy, it is alright.

But I do not think in India we can have that kind of society where people are forced to do things because we think that they can be forced maybe for 25 years, maybe for 50 years, but sometime or the other there will be an explosion. In our society, we allow lots of smaller explosions because we think that that will guard the basic stability and progress of society and prevent it from having the kind of chaotic explosion which can retard our progress and harmony in the country.

So, I hope that all of you who have this great advantage of education will not only do whatever work you are doing keeping the national interests in view, but you will make your own contribution to creating peace and harmony, to bringing beauty in the lives of our people and our country. I think this is the special responsibility of the women of India. We want to do a great deal for our country, but we have never regarded India as isolated from the rest of the world. What we want to do is to make a better world. So, we have to see India's problems in the perspective of the larger world problems.

It has given me great pleasure to be with you here. I give my warm congratulations to those who are doing well and my very good wishes to all the others that they will also do much better. This college has had a high reputation but we must always see that we do better than those who were there before us. So, good luck and good wishes to you.

The Hope Speech

Harvey Milk

San Francisco City Hall, San Francisco (25 June 1978)

Harvey Milk was a pioneer social and political activist for the gay community in San Francisco, winning a seat on the city's Board of Supervisors. He was one of the most notable openly gay elected officials of his time. Charismatic, witty and eloquent, he was adoringly called the 'Mayor of Castro Street'. He was posthumously awarded the Presidential Medal of Freedom by Barack Obama in 2009 for his efforts to end discrimination based on sexual orientation. In his honour, 22 May is celebrated as Harvey Milk Day in California.

Harvey Milk delivered 'The Hope Speech' during a mass rally in San Francisco to celebrate California Gay Freedom Day on 25 June 1978.

My name is Harvey Milk and I'm here to recruit you. I've been saying this one for years. It's a political joke. I can't help it—I've got to tell it. I've never been able to talk to this many political people before, so if I tell you nothing else you may be able to go home laughing a bit. This ocean liner was going across the ocean and it sank. And there was one little piece of wood floating and three people swam to it and they realized only one person could hold on to it. So they had a little debate about which was the person. It so happened that the three people were the Pope, the President, and Mayor Daley. The Pope said he was titular head of one of the greatest religions of the world and he was spiritual adviser to many, many millions and he went on and pontificated and they thought it was a good argument. Then the President said he was leader of the largest and most powerful nation of the world. What takes place in this country affects the whole world and they thought that was a good argument. And Mayor Daley said he was mayor of the backbone of the United States and what took place in Chicago affected the world, and what took place in the archdiocese of Chicago affected Catholicism. And they thought that was a good argument. So they did it the democratic way and voted. And Daley won, seven to two. About six months ago, Anita Bryant in her speaking to God said that the drought in California was because of the gay people. On November 9, the day after I got elected, it started to rain. On the day I got sworn in, we walked to City Hall and it was kinda nice, and as soon as I said the word 'I do,' it started to rain again. It's been raining since then and the people of San Francisco figure the only way to stop it is to do a recall petition. That's the local joke. So much for that. Why are we here? Why are gay people here? And what's happening? What's happening to me is the antithesis of what you read about in the papers and what you hear about on the radio. You hear about and read about this movement to the right. That we must band together and fight back this movement to the right. And I'm here to go ahead and say that what you hear and read is what they want you to think because it's not happening. The major media in this country has talked about the movement to the right so the legislators think that there is indeed a movement to the right and that the Congress and the legislators and the city councils will start to move to the right the way the major media want them. So they keep on talking about this move to the right. So let's look at 1977 and see if there was indeed a move to the right. In 1977, gay people had their rights taken away from them in Miami. But you must remember that in the week before Miami and the week after that, the word homosexual or gay appeared in every single newspaper in this nation in articles both pro and con. In every radio station, in every TV station and every household. For the first time in the history of the world, everybody was talking about it, good or bad. Unless you have dialogue, unless you open the walls of dialogue, you can never reach to change people's opinion. In those two weeks, more good and bad, but more about the word homosexual and gay was written than probably in the history of mankind. Once you have dialogue starting, you know you can break down prejudice. In 1977 we saw a dialogue start. In 1977, we saw a gay person elected in San Francisco. In 1977 we saw the state of Mississippi decriminalize marijuana. In 1977, we saw the convention of conventions in Houston. And I want to know where the movement to the right is happening. What that is a record of what happened last year. What we must do is make sure that 1978 continues the movement that is really happening that the media don't want you to know about. That is the movement to the left. It's up to CDC to put the pressures on Sacramento—but to break down the walls and the barriers so the movement to the left continues and progress continues in the nation. We have before us coming up several issues we must speak out on. Probably the most important issue outside the Briggs—which we will come to—but we do know what will take place this June. We know there's an issue on the ballot called Jarvis-Gann. We hear the taxpayers talk about it on both sides. But what you don't hear is that it's probably the most racist issue on the ballot in a long time. In the city and county of San Francisco, if it passes and we indeed have to lay off people, who will they be? The last in, and the first in, and who are the last in but the minorities? Jarvis-Gann is a racist issue. We must address that issue. We must not talk away from it. We must not allow them to talk about the money it's going to save, because look at who's going to save the money and who's going to get hurt. We also have another issue that we've started in some of the north counties and I hope in some of the south counties it continues. In San Francisco elections we're asking—at least we hope to ask—that the U.S. government put pressure on the closing of the South African consulate. That must happen. There is a major difference between an embassy in Washington which is a diplomatic bureau, and a consulate in major cities. A consulate is there for one reason only—to promote business, economic gains, tourism, investment. And every time you have business going to South Africa, you're promoting a regime that's offensive. In the city of San Francisco, if everyone of 51 percent of that city were to go to South Africa, they would be treated as second-class citizens. That is an offense to the people of San Francisco and I hope all my colleagues up there will take every step we can to close down that consulate and hope that people in other parts of the state follow us in that lead. The battles must be started some place and CDC is the greatest place to start the battles. I know we are pressed for time so I'm going to cover just one more little point. That is to understand why it is important that gay people run for office and that gay people get elected. I know there are many people in this room who are running for central committee who are gay. I encourage you. There's a major reason why. If my non-gay friends and supporters in this room understand it, they'll probably understand why I've run so often before I finally made it. Y'see right now, there's a controversy going on in this convention about the gay governor. Is he speaking out enough? Is he strong enough for gay rights? And there is controversy and for us to say it is not would be foolish. Some people are satisfied and some people are not. You see there is a major difference—and it remains a vital difference—between a friend and a gay person, a friend in office and a gay person in office. Gay people have been slandered nationwide. We've been tarred and we've been brushed with the picture of pornography. In Dade County, we were accused of child molestation. It's not enough anymore just to have friends represent us. No matter how good that friend may be. The black community made up its mind to that a long time ago. That the myths against blacks can only be dispelled by electing black leaders, so the black community could be judged by the leaders and not by the myths or black criminals. The Spanish community must not be judged by Latin criminals or myths. The Asian community must not be judged by Asian criminals or myths. The Italian community must not be judged by the mafia, myths. And the time has come when the gay community must not be judged by our criminals and myths. Like every other group, we must be judged by our leaders and by those who are themselves gay, those who are visible. For invisible, we remain in limbo—a myth, a person with no parents, no brothers, no sisters, no friends who are straight, no important positions in employment. A tenth of the nation supposedly composed of stereotypes and would-be seducers of children—and no offense meant to the stereotypes. But today, the black community is not judged by its friends, but by its black legislators and leaders. And we must give people the chance to judge us by our leaders and legislators. A gay person in office can set a tone, con command respect not only from the larger community, but from the young people in our own community who need both examples and hope. The first gay people we elect must be strong. They must not be content to sit in the back of the bus. They must not be content to accept pablum. They must be above wheeling and dealing. They must be—for the good of all of us—independent, unbought. The anger and the frustrations that some of us feel is because we are misunderstood, and friends can't feel the anger and frustration. They can sense it in us, but they can't feel it. Because a friend has never gone through what is known as coming out. I will never forget what it was like coming out and having nobody to look up toward. I remember the lack of hope—and our friends can't fulfill it. I can't forget the looks on faces of people who've lost hope. Be they gay, be they seniors, be they blacks looking for an almost-impossible job, be they Latins trying to explain their problems and aspirations in a tongue that's foreign to them. I personally will never forget that people are more important than buildings. I use the word 'I' because I'm proud. I stand here tonight in front of my gay sisters, brothers and friends because I'm proud of you. I think it's time that we have many legislators who are gay and proud of that fact and do not have to remain in the closet. I think that a gay person, up-front, will not walk away from a responsibility and be afraid of being tossed out of office. After Dade County, I walked among the angry and the frustrated night after night and I looked at their faces. And in San Francisco, three days before Gay Pride Day, a person was killed just because he was gay. And that night, I walked among the sad and the frustrated at City Hall in San Francisco and later that night as they lit candles on Castro Street and stood in silence, reaching out for some symbolic thing that would give them hope. These were strong people, whose faces I knew from the shop, the streets, meetings and people who I never saw before but I knew. They were strong, but even they needed hope.

And the young gay people in the Altoona, Pennsylvanias, and the Richmond, Minnesotas, who are coming out and hear Anita Bryant on television and her story. The only thing they have to look forward to is hope. And you have to give them hope. Hope for a better world, hope for a better tomorrow, hope for a better place to come to if the pressures at home are too great. Hope that all will be all right. Without hope, not only gays, but the blacks, the seniors, the handicapped, the us'es, the us'es will give up. And if you help elect to the central committee and other offices, more gay people, that gives a green light to all who feel disenfranchised, a green light to move forward. It means hope to a nation that has given up, because if a gay person makes it, the doors are open to everyone. So if there is a message I have to give, it is that I've found one overriding thing about my personal election, it's the fact that if a gay person can be elected, it's a green light. And you and you and you, you have to give people hope. Thank you very much.

Nobel Prize Acceptance Speech

Mother Teresa

Oslo, Norway (11 December 1979)

Saint Teresa was a Roman Catholic nun who founded the Missionaries of Charity in Kolkata in 1950. Today it has a presence in numerous countries with over four thousand sisters serving under its name. The institution looked after the poorest of the poor, ailing and destitute people suffering from tuberculosis, HIV/AIDS and leprosy. The missionaries dedicated to her work observed a vow of poverty, chastity, obedience and helping those in need. Saint Teresa won the Nobel Peace Prize, amongst other accolades, for her pioneering work.

In her moving acceptance speech, Teresa spreads her message of universal peace, love and devotion to God.

Let us all together thank God for this beautiful occasion where we can all together proclaim the joy of spreading peace, the joy of loving one another and the joy acknowledging that the poorest of the poor are our brothers and sisters.

As we have gathered here to thank God for this gift of peace, I have given you all the prayer for peace that St Francis of Assisi prayed many years ago, and I wonder he must have felt the need what we feel today to pray for. I think you have all got that paper? We'll say it together.

Lord, make me a channel of your peace, that where there is hatred, I may bring love; that where there is wrong, I may bring the spirit of forgiveness; that where there is discord, I may bring harmony; that where there is error, I may bring truth; that where there is doubt, I may bring faith; that where there is despair, I may bring hope; that where there are shadows, I may bring light; that where there is sadness, I may bring joy.

Lord, grant that I may seek rather to comfort than to be comforted; to understand, than to be understood; to love, than to be loved. For it is by forgetting self, that one finds. It is by forgiving that one is forgiven. It is by dying, that one awakens to eternal life. Amen.

God loved the world so much that he gave his son and he gave him to a virgin, the blessed virgin Mary, and she, the moment he came in her life, went in haste to give him to others. And what did she do then? She did the work of the handmaid, just so. Just spread that joy of loving to service. And Jesus Christ loved you and loved me and he gave his life for us, and as if that was not enough for him, he kept on saying: Love as I have loved you, as I love you now, and how do we have to love, to love in the giving. For he gave his life for us. And he keeps on giving, and he keeps on giving right here everywhere in our own lives and in the lives of others.

It was not enough for him to die for us, he wanted that we loved one another, that we see him in each other, that's why he said: Blessed are the clean of heart, for they shall see God.

And to make sure that we understand what he means, he said that at the hour of death we are going to be judged on what we have been to the poor, to the hungry, naked, the homeless, and he makes himself that hungry one, that naked one, that homeless one, not only hungry for bread, but hungry for love, not only naked for a piece of cloth, but naked of that human dignity, not only homeless for a room to live, but homeless for that being forgotten, been unloved, uncared, being nobody to nobody, having forgotten what is human love, what is human touch, what is to be loved by somebody, and he says: Whatever you did to the least of these my brethren, you did it to me.

It is so beautiful for us to become holy to this love, for holiness is not a luxury of the few, it is a simple duty for each one of us, and through this love we can become holy. To this love for one another and today when I have received this reward, I personally am most unworthy, and I having avowed poverty to be able to understand the poor, I choose the poverty of our people. But I am grateful and I am very happy to receive it in the name of the hungry, of the naked, of the homeless, of the crippled, of the blind, of the leprous, of all those people who feel unwanted, unloved, uncared, thrown away of the society, people who have become a burden to the society, and are ashamed by everybody.

In their name I accept the award. And I am sure this award is going to bring an understanding love between the rich and the poor. And this is what Jesus has insisted so much, that is why Jesus came to earth, to proclaim the good news to the poor. And through this award and through all of us gathered here together, we are wanting to proclaim the good news to the poor that God loves them, that we love them, that they are somebody to us, that they too have been created by the same loving hand of God, to love and to be loved. Our poor people are great people, are very lovable people, they don't need our pity and sympathy, they need our understanding love. They need our respect; they need that we treat them with dignity. And I think this is the greatest poverty that we experience, that we have in front of them who may be dying for a piece of bread, but they die to such dignity. I never forget when I brought a man from the street. He was covered with maggots; his face was the only place that was clean. And yet that man, when we brought him to our home for the dying, he said just one sentence: I have lived like an animal in the street, but I am going to die like an angel, love and care, and he died beautifully. He went home to God, for dead is nothing but going home to God. And he having enjoyed that love, that being wanted, that being loved, that being somebody to somebody at the last moment, brought that joy in his life.

And I feel one thing I want to share with you all, the greatest destroyer of peace today is the cry of the innocent unborn child. For if a mother can murder her own child in her womb, what is left for you and for me to kill each other? Even in the scripture it is written: Even if mother could forget her child—I will not forget you—I have carved you in the palm of my hand. Even if mother could forget, but today millions of unborn children are being killed. And we say nothing. In the newspapers you read numbers of this one and that one being killed, this being destroyed, but nobody speaks of the millions of little ones who have been conceived to the same life as you and I, to the life of God, and we say nothing, we allow it. To me the nations who have legalized abortion, they are the poorest nations. They are afraid of the little one, they are afraid of the unborn child, and the child must die because they don't want to feed one more child, to educate one more child, the child must die.

And here I ask you, in the name of these little ones, for it was that unborn child that recognized the presence of Jesus when Mary came to visit Elizabeth, her cousin. As we read in the gospel, the moment Mary came into the house, the little one in the womb of his mother, lift with joy, recognized the Prince of Peace. And so today, let us here make a strong resolution, we are going to save every little child, every unborn child, give them a chance to be born. And what we are doing, we are fighting abortion by adoption, and the good God has blessed the work so beautifully that we have saved thousands of children, and thousands of children have found a home where they are loved, they are wanted, they are cared. We have brought so much joy in the homes that there was not a child, and so today, I ask His Majesties here before you all who come from different countries, let us all pray that we have the courage to stand by the unborn child, and give the child an opportunity to love and to be loved, and I think with God's grace we will be able to bring peace in the world. We have an opportunity here in Norway, you are with God's blessing, you are well to do. But I am sure in the families and many of our homes, maybe we are not hungry for a piece of bread, but maybe there is somebody there in the family who is unwanted, unloved, uncared, forgotten, there isn't love. Love begins at home. And love to be true has to hurt. I never forget a little child who taught me a very beautiful lesson. They heard in Calcutta, the children, that Mother Teresa had no sugar for her children, and this little one, Hindu boy four years old, he went home and he told his parents: I will not eat sugar for three days, I will give my sugar to Mother Teresa. How much a little child can give. After three days they brought into our house, and there was this little one who could scarcely pronounce my name, he loved with great love, he loved until it hurt. And this is what I bring before you, to love one another until it hurts, but don't forget that there are many children, many children, many men and women who haven't got what you have. And remember to love them until it hurts. Sometime ago, this to you will sound very strange, but I brought a God child from the street, and I could see in the face of the child that the child was hungry. God knows how many days that not eaten. So I give her a piece of bread. And then the little one started eating the bread crumb by crumb. And I said to the child, eat the bread, eat the bread. And she looked at me and said: I am afraid to eat the bread because I'm afraid when it is finished I will be hungry again. This is a reality, and yet there is a greatness of the poor. One evening a gentleman came to our house and said, there is a Hindu family and the eight children have not eaten for a long time. Do something for them. And I took rice and I went immediately, and there was this mother, those little one's faces, shining eyes from sheer hunger. She took the rice from my hand, she divided into two and she went out. When she came back, I asked her, where did you go? What did you do? And one answer she gave me: They are hungry also. She knew that the next door neighbor, a Muslim family, was hungry.

What surprised me most, not that she gave the rice, but what surprised me most, that in her suffering, in her hunger, she knew that somebody else was hungry, and she had the courage to share, share the love. And this is what I mean, I want you to love the poor, and never turn your back to the poor, for in turning your back to the poor, you are turning it to Christ. For he had made himself the hungry one, the naked one, the homeless one, so that you and I have an opportunity to love him, because where is God? How can we love God? It is not enough to say to my God I love you, but my God, I love you here. I can enjoy this, but I give up. I could eat that sugar, but I give that sugar. If I stay here the whole day and the whole night, you would be surprised of the beautiful things that people do, to share the joy of giving. And so, my prayer for you is that truth will bring prayer in our homes, and from the foot of prayer will be that we believe that in the poor it is Christ. And we will really believe, we will begin to love. And we will love naturally, we will try to do something. First in our own home, next door neighbor in the country we live, in the whole world. And let us all join in that one prayer, God give us courage to protect the unborn child, for the child is the greatest gift of God to a family, to a nation and to the whole world. God bless you!

Nobel Prize Acceptance Speech

Adolfo Pérez Esquivel

Oslo, Norway (10 December 1980)

Adolfo Pérez Esquivel is an Argentine sculptor, architect, professor and human rights activist whose efforts for non-violent reform throughout Latin America earned him a Nobel Peace Prize in 1980. In the 1970s, Esquivel was imprisoned and tortured for 14 months for expressing his dissent against the Argentine Military Junta. He continues to be an outspoken advocate of human rights, and travels extensively to campaign for the same.

The following is his Nobel Prize acceptance speech, delivered on 10 December in Oslo, Norway.

Your Majesty, Mr. President of the Nobel Committee, Committee Members, Ladies and Gentlemen,

With humility I stand before you to receive the high distinction that the Nobel Committee and the Parliament grant to those who have committed their lives on behalf of peace and to the pursuit of justice and solidarity among nations.

I would like to receive this award in the name of the people of Latin America and especially in the name of the poorest and smallest of my brothers and sisters, who are the most beloved children of God. I receive it in the name of my indigenous brothers and sisters, the peasants, workers, and young people, in the name of the thousands of members of religious orders and of men and women of goodwill, who renounce privileges to share the life and way of the poor, and who struggle to build a new society.

For a man like myself, *a small voice for those who have no voice*, who struggles so that the *cry of the people* may be heard in all its power, for one without any special identity except as a *veritable Latin American man* and as a Christian, —this is, without any doubt, the highest honour that I can receive: to be considered *a servant of peace*.

I come from a continent that lives between anguish and hope, where my own history is being written. I am convinced that the gospel power of nonviolence presents a choice that opens up for us a challenge of new and radical perspectives. It is an option which gives priority to the essential Christian value: *the dignity of the human being*; the sacred, transcendent and irrevocable dignity that belongs to the human being by reason of being a child of God and a brother or sister in Christ, and therefore, our own brother and sister.

In these long years of struggle for our organisation, the Service for Peace and Justice in Latin America, we have shared the path together with the poorest and most necessitous.

We have not much to say but much to share in order to achieve by nonviolent struggle the abolition of injustice and the attainment of a more just and humane society for all.

It is walking together with our brothers and sisters, those who are persecuted, who hunger and thirst for justice, who suffer oppression, who live in anguish by the prospect of war, who suffer aggressive violence or see regularly postponed the attainment of their elemental rights.

It is for all these that I am here today.

Would that my voice could have the strength of voice of the humble, a voice that denounces injustice and proclaims hope in God and humanity. This is the hope of all human beings who long to live in harmony in common with all persons as brothers and sisters and as children of God.

Latin America is a continent young and vital, which was described by Pope Paul VI as the 'Continent of Hope'.

To understand this is to value this reality and be called to share in its destiny. It means to achieve a profound identity with the people who are the protagonists in this historic process. It means being ready to redeem pain and suffering with love in the way that Jesus taught.

When we see the world our people inhabit, we see it as an affront to God in which millions of our children, youths, adults, and the elderly live under the mark of under-development.

The institutionalised violence, misery and oppression generate a dual reality, fruit of the political and economic systems that create injustice, sanctifying a social order that benefits only a few: the rich becomes ever richer at the expense of the poor who becomes ever poorer.

Confronting that reality—like the Catholic bishops at Puebla, like the Christians committed to the struggle for human rights, like all persons of goodwill—I want to share the anguish on the suffering face of the Latin American man or woman in whom we see the suffering face of Christ, our Lord, questioning us.

As I speak to you, I see before my eyes the vivid images of my brothers and sisters:

—faces of the workers and peasants living at sub-human levels, whose rights to organise are severely limited;

—faces of children who suffer from malnutrition;

—of young people who see their hopes frustrated;

—of the marginal urban poor;

—of our indigenous people;

—of the mothers searching for their missing sons and daughters;

—of the disappeared, many of them mere children;

—of thousands of exiles;

—of the people who clamour for liberty and justice of all.

In spite of so much suffering and pain, I live in hope because I feel that Latin America is a continent on the rise. Its liberation may be delayed but never denied.

We live in hope because, like St. Paul, we believe that love never dies. Human beings in the historical process have created enclaves of love with their active practice of solidarity throughout the world, with the goal of the full liberation of humanity.

For me it is essential to have the inner peace and serenity of prayer in order to listen to the silence of God, which speaks to us in our personal life and the history of our times, of the power of love.

Because of this faith in Christ and humankind, we must apply our humble efforts to build a more just and humane world. I want to affirm emphatically: such a world is possible.

To create this new society we must reach out our hands, fraternally, without hatred and rancour, for reconciliation and peace, with unfaltering determination in the defense of truth and justice.

We know we cannot plant seeds with closed fists. To sow we must open our hands.

I want to thank all of you and the Nobel Committee for this high distinction given the humble people of Latin America. I am deeply moved and even more committed to redouble my efforts in the struggle for peace and justice.

We know that peace is only possible when it is the fruit of justice. True peace is a profound transformation by means of the force of nonviolence that is the power of love.

I would like to tell you that, thanks to the support and understanding of my wife and children even in the hardest and most difficult moments of this struggle, I could continue this work together with my brothers and sisters of Latin America. With my family's love, silence and solidarity they have always helped to give me strength and courage to serve my brothers and sisters.

Invoking the strength of Christ, our Lord, I would like to share with you, with my people, and with the world what He has taught us in the Sermon on the Mount:

Blessed are the poor in spirit;
—theirs is the kingdom of heaven.
Blessed are the gentle;
they shall inherit the earth.
Blessed are they who mourn;
—they shall be comforted.
Blessed are those who hunger and thirst for righteousness;
—they shall be satisfied.
Blessed are the merciful;

—they shall obtain mercy.
Blessed are the pure in heart;
—they shall see God.
Blessed are the peacemakers;
—they shall be called children of God.
Blessed are those who are persecuted for righteousness' sake;
—theirs is the kingdom of heaven.

Blessed are you when people abuse you and persecute you and speak all kinds of falsehoods against you for my sake.

Rejoice and be glad, for great will be your reward in heaven. In the same way they persecuted the prophets before you.

(Matthew 5, 1-12)

Receive my deep gratitude and my wish for peace and well-being.

Nobel Lecture

Desmond Tutu

Oslo, Norway (11 December 1984)

Desmond Tutu, Archbishop Emeritus of Cape Town, won among many several other accolades, the Nobel Peace Prize in 1984 for his efforts to end apartheid in South Africa,. An Anglican cleric, he became the first black South African to become Dean of St. Mary's Cathedral in Johannesburg in 1975. In 1995, Archbishop Tutu was also appointed Head of Truth and Reconciliation Commission, which sought to redress the human rights abuses during the apartheid era.

In his Nobel acceptance speech, Desmond Tutu denounces the system of apartheid and calls for peace in South Africa and beyond.

Ladies and Gentlemen,

Before I left South Africa, a land I love passionately, we had an emergency meeting of the Executive Committee of the South African Council of Churches with the leaders of our member churches. We called the meeting because of the deepening crisis in our land, which has claimed nearly 200 lives this year alone. We visited some of the trouble-spots on the Witwatersrand. I went with others to the East Rand. We visited the home of an old lady. She told us that she looked after her grandson and the children of neighbors while their parents were at work. One day the police chased some pupils who had been boycotting classes, but they disappeared between the township houses. The police drove down the old lady's street. She was sitting at the back of the house in her kitchen, whilst her charges were playing in the front of the house in the yard. Her daughter rushed into the house, calling out to her to come quickly. The old lady dashed out of the kitchen into the living room. Her grandson had fallen just inside the door, dead. He had been shot in the back by the police. He was 6 years old. A few weeks later, a white mother, trying to register her black servant for work, drove through a black township. Black rioters stoned her car and killed her baby of a few months old, the first white casualty of the current unrest in South Africa. Such deaths are two too many. These are part of the high cost of apartheid.

Every day in a squatter camp near Cape Town, called K.T.C., the authorities have been demolishing flimsy plastic shelters which black mothers have erected because they were taking their marriage vows seriously. They have been reduced to sitting on soaking mattresses, with their household effects strewn round their feet, and whimpering babies on their laps, in the cold Cape winter rain. Everyday the authorities have carried out these callous demolitions. What heinous crime have these women committed, to be hounded like criminals in this manner? All they have wanted is to be with their husbands, the fathers of their children. Everywhere else in the world they would be highly commended, but in South Africa, a land which claims to be Christian, and which boasts a public holiday called Family Day, these gallant women are treated so inhumanely, and yet all they want is to have a decent and stable family life. Unfortunately, in the land of their birth, it is a criminal offence for them to live happily with their husbands and the fathers of their children. Black family life is thus being undermined, not accidentally, but by deliberate Government policy. It is part of the price human beings, God's children, are called to pay for apartheid. An unacceptable price.

I come from a beautiful land, richly endowed by God with wonderful natural resources, wide expanses, rolling mountains, singing birds, bright shining stars out of blue skies, with radiant sunshine, golden sunshine. There is enough of the good things that come from God's bounty, there is enough for everyone, but apartheid has confirmed some in their selfishness, causing them to grasp greedily a disproportionate share, the lion's share, because of their power. They have taken 87 of the land, though being only about 20 of our population. The rest have had to make do with the remaining 13. Apartheid has decreed the politics of exclusion. 73 of the population is excluded from any meaningful participation in the political decision-making processes of the land of their birth. The new constitution, making provision of three chambers, for whites, coloreds, and Indians, mentions blacks only once, and thereafter ignores them completely. Thus this new constitution, lauded in parts of the West as a step in the right direction, entrenches racism and ethnicity. The constitutional committees are composed in the ratio of 4 whites to 2 coloreds and 1 Indian. 0 black. 2 + 1 can never equal, let alone be more than, 4. Hence this constitution perpetuates by law and entrenches white minority rule. Blacks are expected to exercise their political ambitions in unviable, poverty-stricken, arid, bantustan homelands, ghettoes of misery, inexhaustible reservoirs of cheap black labor, bantustans into which South Africa is being balkanized. Blacks are systematically being stripped of their South African citizenship and being turned into aliens in the land of their birth. This is apartheid's final solution, just as Nazism had its final solution for the Jews in Hitler's Aryan madness. The South African Government is smart. Aliens can claim but very few rights, least of all political rights.

In pursuance of apartheid's ideological racist dream, over 3.000.000 of God's children have been uprooted from their homes, which have been demolished, whilst they have then been dumped in the bantustan homeland resettlement camps. I say dumped advisedly: only things or rubbish is dumped, not human beings. Apartheid has, however, ensured that God's children, just because they are black, should be treated as if they were things, and not as of infinite value as being created in the image of God. These dumping grounds are far from where work and food can be procured easily. Children starve, suffer from the often irreversible consequences of malnutrition – this happens to them not accidentally, but by deliberate Government policy. They starve in a land that could be the bread basket of Africa, a land that normally is a net exporter of food.

The father leaves his family in the bantustan homeland, there eking out a miserable existence, whilst he, if he is lucky, goes to the so-called white man's town as a migrant, to live an unnatural life in a single sex hostel for 11 months of the year, being prey there to prostitution, drunkenness, and worse. This migratory labor policy is declared Government policy, and has been condemned, even by the white Dutch Reformed Church,1 not noted for being quick to criticize the Government, as a cancer in our society. This cancer, eating away at the vitals of black family life, is deliberate Government policy. It is part of the cost of apartheid, exorbitant in terms of human suffering.

Apartheid has spawned discriminatory education, such as Bantu Education, education for serfdom, ensuring that the Government spends only about one tenth on one black child per annum for education what it spends on a white child. It is education that is decidedly separate and unequal. It is to be wantonly wasteful of human resources, because so many of God's children are prevented, by deliberate Government policy, from attaining to their fullest potential. South Africa is paying a heavy price already for this iniquitous policy because there is a desperate shortage of skilled manpower, a direct result of the short-sighted schemes of the racist regime. It is a moral universe that we inhabit, and good and right equity matter in the universe of the God we worship. And so, in this matter, the South African Government and its supporters are being properly hoisted with their own petard.

Apartheid is upheld by a phalanx of iniquitous laws, such as the Population Registration Act, which decrees that all South Africans must be classified ethnically, and duly registered according to these race categories. Many times, in the same family one child has been classified white whilst another, with a slightly darker hue, has been classified colored, with all the horrible consequences for the latter of being shut out from membership of a greatly privileged caste. There have, as a result, been several child suicides. This is too high a price to pay for racial purity, for it is doubtful whether any end, however desirable, can justify such a means. There are laws, such as the Prohibition of Mixed Marriages Act, which regard marriages between a white and a person of another race as illegal. Race becomes an impediment to a valid marriage. Two persons who have fallen in love are prevented by race from consummating their love in the marriage bond. Something beautiful is made to be sordid and ugly. The Immorality Act decrees that fornication and adultery are illegal if they happen between a white and one of another race. The police are reduced to the level of peeping Toms to catch couples red-handed. Many whites have committed suicide rather than face the disastrous consequences that follow in the train of even just being charged under this law. The cost is too great and intolerable.

Such an evil system, totally indefensible by normally acceptable methods, relies on a whole phalanx of draconian laws such as the security legislation which is almost peculiar to South Africa. There are the laws which permit the indefinite detention of persons whom the Minister of Law and Order has decided are a threat to the security of the State. They are detained at his pleasure, in solitary confinement, without access to their family, their own doctor, or a lawyer. That is severe punishment when the evidence apparently available to the Minister has not been tested in an open court – perhaps it could stand up to such rigorous scrutiny, perhaps not; we are never to know. It is a far too convenient device for a repressive regime, and the minister would have to be extra special not to succumb to the temptation to circumvent the awkward process of testing his evidence in an open court, and thus he lets his power under the law to be open to the abuse where he is both judge and prosecutor. Many, too many, have died mysteriously in detention. All this is too costly in terms of human lives. The minister is able, too, to place people under banning orders without being subjected to the annoyance of the checks and balances of due process. A banned person for 3 or 5 years becomes a non-person, who cannot be quoted during the period of her banning order. She cannot attend a gathering, which means more than one other person. Two persons together talking to a banned person are a gathering! She cannot attend the wedding or funeral of even her own child without special permission. She must be at home from 6:00 pm of one day to 6:00 am of the next and on all public holidays, and from 6.00 pm on Fridays until 6:00 am on Mondays for 3 years. She cannot go on holiday outside the magisterial area to which she has been confined. She cannot go to the cinema, nor to a picnic. That is severe punishment, inflicted without the evidence allegedly justifying it being made available to the banned person, nor having it scrutinized in a court of law. It is a serious erosion and violation of basic human rights, of which blacks have precious few in the land of their birth. They do not enjoy the rights of freedom of movement and association. They do not enjoy freedom of security of tenure, the right to participate in the making of decisions that affect their lives. In short, this land, richly endowed in so many ways, is sadly lacking in justice.

Once a Zambian and a South African, it is said, were talking. The Zambian then boasted about their Minister of Naval Affairs. The South African asked, 'But you have no navy, no access to the sea. How then can you have a Minister of Naval Affairs?' The Zambian retorted, 'Well, in South Africa you have a Minister of Justice, don't you?'

It is against this system that our people have sought to protest peacefully since 1912 at least, with the founding of the African National Congress. They have used the conventional methods of peaceful protest – petitions, demonstrations, deputations, and even a passive resistance campaign. A tribute to our people's commitment to peaceful change is the fact that the only South Africans to win the Nobel Peace Prize are both black. Our people are peace-loving to a fault. The response of the authorities has been an escalating intransigence and violence, the violence of police dogs, tear gas, detention without trial, exile, and even death. Our people protested peacefully against the Pass Laws in 1960, and 69 of them were killed on March 21, 1960, at Sharpeville, many shot in the back running away. Our children protested against inferior education, singing songs and displaying placards and marching peacefully. Many in 1976, on June 16th and subsequent times, were killed or imprisoned. Over 500 people died in that uprising. Many children went into exile. The whereabouts of many are unknown to their parents. At present, to protest that self-same discriminatory education, and the exclusion of blacks from the new constitutional dispensation, the sham local black government, rising unemployment, increased rents and General Sales Tax, our people have boycotted and demonstrated. They have staged a successful two-day stay away. Over 150 people have been killed. It is far too high a price to pay. There has been little revulsion or outrage at this wanton destruction of human life in the West. In parenthesis, can somebody please explain to me something that has puzzled me. When a priest goes missing and is subsequently found dead, the media in the West carry his story in very extensive coverage.2 I am glad that the death of one person can cause so much concern. But in the self-same week when this priest is found dead, the South African Police kill 24 blacks who had been participating in the protest, and 6.000 blacks are sacked for being similarly involved, and you are lucky to get that much coverage. Are we being told something I do not want to believe, that we blacks are expendable and that blood is thicker than water, that when it comes to the crunch, you cannot trust whites, that they will club together against us? I don't want to believe that is the message being conveyed to us.

Be that as it may, we see before us a land bereft of much justice, and therefore without peace and security. Unrest is endemic, and will remain an unchanging feature of the South African scene until apartheid, the root cause of it all, is finally dismantled. At this time, the Army is being quartered on the civilian population. There is a civil war being waged. South Africans are on either side. When the African National Congress and the Pan-Africanist Congress3 were banned in 1960, they declared that they had no option but to carry out the armed struggle. We in the South African Council of Church have said we are opposed to all forms of violence – that of a repressive and unjust system, and that of those who seek to overthrow that system. However, we have added that we understand those who say they have had to adopt what is a last resort for them. Violence is not being introduced into the South African situation *de novo* from outside by those who are called terrorists or freedom fighters, depending on whether you are oppressed or an oppressor. The South African situation is violent already, and the primary violence is that of apartheid, the violence of forced population removals, of inferior education, of detention without trial, of the migratory labor system, etc.

There is war on the border of our country. South African faces fellow South African. South African soldiers are fighting against Namibians who oppose the illegal occupation of their country by

South Africa, which has sought to extend its repressive system of apartheid, unjust and exploitative.

There is no peace in Southern Africa. There is no peace because there is no justice. There can be no real peace and security until there be first justice enjoyed by all the inhabitants of that beautiful land. The Bible knows nothing about peace without justice, for that would be crying 'Peace, peace, where there is no peace'. God's Shalom, peace, involves inevitably righteousness, justice, wholeness, fullness of life, participation in decision-making, goodness, laughter, joy, compassion, sharing and reconciliation.

I have spoken extensively about South Africa, first because it is the land I know best, but because it is also a microcosm of the world and an example of what is to be found in other lands in differing degree – when there is injustice, invariably peace becomes a casualty. In El Salvador, in Nicaragua, and elsewhere in Latin America, there have been repressive regimes which have aroused opposition in those countries. Fellow citizens are pitted against one another, sometimes attracting the unhelpful attention and interest of outside powers, who want to extend their spheres of influence. We see this in the Middle East, in Korea, in the Philippines, in Kampuchea, in Vietnam, in Ulster, in Afghanistan, in Mozambique, in Angola, in Zimbabwe, behind the Iron Curtain.

Because there is global insecurity, nations are engaged in a mad arms race, spending billions of dollars wastefully on instruments of destruction, when millions are starving. And yet, just a fraction of what is expended so obscenely on defense budgets would make the difference in enabling God's children to fill their stomachs, be educated, and given the chance to lead fulfilled and happy lives. We have the capacity to feed ourselves several times over, but we are daily haunted by the spectacle of the gaunt dregs of humanity shuffling along in endless queues, with bowls to collect what the charity of the world has provided, too little too late. When will we learn, when will the people of the world get up and say, Enough is enough. God created us for fellowship. God created us so that we should form the human family, existing together because we were made for one another. We are not made for an exclusive self-sufficiency but for interdependence, and we break the law of our being at our peril. When will we learn that an escalated arms race merely escalates global insecurity? We are now much closer to a nuclear holocaust than when our technology and our spending were less.

Unless we work assiduously so that all of God's children, our brothers and sisters, members of our one human family, all will enjoy basic human rights, the right to a fulfilled life, the right of movement, of work, the freedom to be fully human, with a humanity measured by nothing less than the humanity of Jesus Christ Himself, then we are on the road inexorably to self-destruction, we are not far from global suicide; and yet it could be so different.

When will we learn that human beings are of infinite value because they have been created in the image of God, and that it is a blasphemy to treat them as if they were less than this and to do so ultimately recoils on those who do this? In dehumanizing others, they are themselves dehumanized. Perhaps oppression dehumanizes the oppressor as much as, if not more than, the oppressed. They need each other to become truly free, to become human. We can be human only in fellowship, in community, in koinonia, in peace.

Let us work to be peacemakers, those given a wonderful share in Our Lord's ministry of reconciliation. If we want peace, so we have been told, let us work for justice. Let us beat our swords into ploughshares.

God calls us to be fellow workers with Him, so that we can extend His Kingdom of Shalom, of justice, of goodness, of compassion, of caring, of sharing, of laughter, joy and reconciliation, so that the kingdoms of this world will become the Kingdom of our God and of His Christ, and He shall reign forever and ever. Amen. Then there will be a fulfillment of the wonderful vision in the *Revelation of St. John the Divine* (Rev. 6:9ff):

9. After this I beheld, and lo, a great multitude, which no man could number, of all nations and kindreds and people and tongues, stood before the throne and before the Lamb, clothed with white robes, and palms in their hands,

10. And cried with a loud voice saying, 'Salvation to our God, who sitteth upon the throne, and unto the Lamb.'

11. And all the angels stood round about the throne, and about the elders and the four beasts, and fell before the throne on their faces, and worshipped God

12. saying, 'Amen; Blessing and glory and wisdom and thanksgiving and honor and power and might, be unto our God forever and ever. Amen.'

On the 40th Anniversary of D-Day

Ronald Regan

Pointe du Hoc, France (6 June 1984)

Ronald Reagan, a former actor and Governor of California, served as the 40th President of the United States, for two terms. He is credited with bringing the Cold War to an end, negotiating a nuclear arms reduction agreement with the Soviet Union and convincing Soviet leader Mikhail Gorbachev to bring down the Berlin Wall.

President Reagan gave this speech to the war veterans of World War II and several world leaders on the 40th anniversary of D-Day, the dangerous mission that established Allied victory.

We're here to mark that day in history when the Allied armies joined in battle to reclaim this continent to liberty. For four long years, much of Europe had been under a terrible shadow. Free nations had fallen, Jews cried out in the camps, millions cried out for liberation. Europe was enslaved and the world prayed for its rescue. Here, in Normandy, the rescue began. Here, the Allies stood and fought against tyranny, in a giant undertaking unparalleled in human history.

We stand on a lonely, windswept point on the northern shore of France. The air is soft, but 40 years ago at this moment, the air was dense with smoke and the cries of men, and the air was filled with the crack of rifle fire and the roar of cannon. At dawn, on the morning of the 6th of June, 1944, 225 Rangers jumped off the British landing craft and ran to the bottom of these cliffs.

Their mission was one of the most difficult and daring of the invasion: to climb these sheer and desolate cliffs and take out the enemy guns. The Allies had been told that some of the mightiest of these guns were here, and they would be trained on the beaches to stop the Allied advance.

The Rangers looked up and saw the enemy soldiers at the edge of the cliffs, shooting down at them with machine guns and throwing grenades. And the American Rangers began to climb. They shot rope ladders over the face of these cliffs and began to pull themselves up. When one Ranger fell, another would take his place. When one rope was cut, a Ranger would grab another and begin his climb again. They climbed, shot back, and held their footing. Soon, one by one, the Rangers pulled themselves over the top, and in seizing the firm land at the top of these cliffs, they began to seize back the continent of Europe. 225 came here. After two days of fighting, only 90 could still bear arms.

And behind me is a memorial that symbolizes the Ranger daggers that were thrust into the top of these cliffs. And before me are the men who put them there. These are the boys of Pointe du Hoc. These are the men who took the cliffs. These are the champions who helped free a continent. And these are the heroes who helped end a war. Gentlemen, I look at you and I think of the words of Stephen Spender's poem. You are men who in your 'lives fought for life and left the vivid air signed with your honor.'

I think I know what you may be thinking right now—thinking 'we were just part of a bigger effort; everyone was brave that day.' Well everyone was. Do you remember the story of Bill Millin of the 51st Highlanders? 40 years ago today, British troops were pinned down near a bridge, waiting desperately for help. Suddenly, they heard the sound of bagpipes, and some thought they were dreaming. Well, they weren't. They looked up and saw Bill Millin with his bagpipes, leading the reinforcements and ignoring the smack of the bullets into the ground around him.

Lord Lovat was with him—Lord Lovat of Scotland, who calmly announced when he got to the bridge, 'Sorry, I'm a few minutes late,' as if he'd been delayed by a traffic jam, when in truth he'd just come from the bloody fighting on Sword Beach, which he and his men had just taken.

There was the impossible valor of the Poles, who threw themselves between the enemy and the rest of Europe as the invasion took hold; and the unsurpassed courage of the Canadians who had already seen the horrors of war on this coast. They knew what awaited them there, but they would not be deterred. And once they hit Juno Beach, they never looked back.

All of these men were part of a roll call of honor with names that spoke of a pride as bright as the colors they bore; The Royal Winnipeg Rifles, Poland's 24th Lancers, the Royal Scots' Fusiliers, the Screaming Eagles, the Yeomen of England's armored divisions, the forces of Free France, the Coast Guard's 'Matchbox Fleet,' and you, the American Rangers.

Forty summers have passed since the battle that you fought here. You were young the day you took these cliffs; some of you were hardly more than boys, with the deepest joys of life before you. Yet you risked everything here. Why? Why did you do it? What impelled you to put aside the instinct for self-preservation and risk your lives to take these cliffs? What inspired all the men of the armies that met here? We look at you, and somehow we know the answer. It was faith and belief. It was loyalty and love.

The men of Normandy had faith that what they were doing was right, faith that they fought for all humanity, faith that a just God would grant them mercy on this beachhead, or on the next. It was the deep knowledge—and pray God we have not lost it—that there is a profound moral difference between the use of force for liberation and the use of force for conquest. You were here to liberate, not to conquer, and so you and those others did not doubt your cause. And you were right not to doubt.

You all knew that some things are worth dying for. One's country is worth dying for, and democracy is worth dying for, because it's the most deeply honorable form of government ever devised by man. All of you loved liberty. All of you were willing to fight tyranny, and you knew the people of your countries were behind you.

The Americans who fought here that morning knew word of the invasion was spreading through the darkness back home. They fought—or felt in their hearts, though they couldn't know in fact, that in Georgia they were filling the churches at 4:00 am. In Kansas they were kneeling on their porches and praying. And in Philadelphia they were ringing the Liberty Bell.

Something else helped the men of D-day; their rock-hard belief that Providence would have a great hand in the events that would unfold here; that God was an ally in this great cause. And so, the night before the invasion, when Colonel Wolverton asked his parachute troops to kneel with him in prayer, he told them: 'Do not bow your heads, but look up so you can see God and ask His blessing in what we're about to do.' Also, that night, General Matthew Ridgway on his cot, listening in the darkness for the promise God made to Joshua: 'I will not fail thee nor forsake thee.'

These are the things that impelled them; these are the things that shaped the unity of the Allies.

When the war was over, there were lives to be rebuilt and governments to be returned to the people. There were nations to be reborn. Above all, there was a new peace to be assured. These were huge and daunting tasks. But the Allies summoned strength from the faith, belief, loyalty, and love of those who fell here. They rebuilt a new Europe together. There was first a great reconciliation among those who had been enemies, all of whom had suffered so greatly. The United States did its part, creating the Marshall Plan to help rebuild our allies and our former enemies. The Marshall Plan led to the Atlantic alliance—a great alliance that serves to this day as our shield for freedom, for prosperity, and for peace.

In spite of our great efforts and successes, not all that followed the end of the war was happy or planned. Some liberated countries were lost. The great sadness of this loss echoes down to our own time in the streets of Warsaw, Prague, and East Berlin. The Soviet troops that came to the center of this continent did not leave when peace came. They're still there, uninvited, unwanted, unyielding, almost 40 years after the war. Because of this, allied forces still stand on this continent. Today, as 40 years ago, our armies are here for only one purpose: to protect and defend democracy. The only territories we hold are memorials like this one and graveyards where our heroes rest.

We in America have learned bitter lessons from two world wars. It is better to be here ready to protect the peace, than to take blind shelter across the sea, rushing to respond only after freedom is lost. We've learned that isolationism never was and never will be an acceptable response to tyrannical governments with an expansionist intent. But we try always to be prepared for peace, prepared to deter aggression, prepared to negotiate the reduction of arms, and yes, prepared to reach out again in the spirit of reconciliation. In truth, there is no reconciliation we would welcome more than a reconciliation with the Soviet Union, so, together, we can lessen the risks of war, now and forever.

It's fitting to remember here the great losses also suffered by the Russian people during World War II. 20 million perished, a terrible price that testifies to all the world the necessity of ending war. I tell you from my heart that we in the United States do not want war. We want to wipe from the face of the earth the terrible weapons that man now has in his hands. And I tell you, we are ready to seize that beachhead. We look for some sign from the Soviet Union that they are willing to move forward, that they share our desire and love for peace, and that they will give up the ways of conquest. There must be a changing there that will allow us to turn our hope into action.

We will pray forever that someday that changing will come. But for now, particularly today, it is good and fitting to renew our commitment to each other, to our freedom, and to the alliance that protects it.

We're bound today by what bound us 40 years ago, the same loyalties, traditions, and beliefs. We're bound by reality. The strength of America's allies is vital to the United States, and the American security guarantee is essential to the continued freedom of Europe's democracies. We were with you then; we're with you now. Your hopes are our hopes, and your destiny is our destiny.

Here, in this place where the West held together, let us make a vow to our dead. Let us show them by our actions that we understand what they died for. Let our actions say to them the words for which Matthew Ridgway listened: 'I will not fail thee nor forsake thee.'

Strengthened by their courage and heartened by their value [valor] and borne by their memory, let us continue to stand for the ideals for which they lived and died.

Thank you very much, and God bless you all.

Nobel Peace Prize Acceptance Speech

His Holiness the 14th Dalai Lama of Tibet

Oslo, Norway (10 December 1989)

His Holiness the 14th Dalai Lama, Tenzin Gyatso, is a Buddhist monk and the spiritual leader of Tibet. At the tender age of 2, he was recognised as the reincarnation of the 13th Dalai Lama. After the failed Tibetan national uprising of 1959, he was forced to escape to India, and ever since, has been leading the Tibetan government-in-exile from Dharamshala, India. His Holiness was awarded the Nobel Peace Prize in 1989 for his non-violent struggle for the liberation of Tibet and for his concern for global environmental problems.

In his Nobel Prize acceptance speech, His Holiness once again reiterated his message for universal peace.

Your Majesty, Members of the Nobel Committee, Brothers and Sisters.

I am very happy to be here with you today to receive the Nobel Prize for Peace. I feel honoured, humbled and deeply moved that you should give this important prize to a simple monk from Tibet I am no one special. But I believe the prize is a recognition of the true value of altruism, love, compassion and non-violence which I try to practice, in accordance with the teachings of the Buddha and the great sages of India and Tibet

I accept the prize with profound gratitude on behalf of the oppressed everywhere and for all those who struggle for freedom and work for world peace. I accept it as a tribute to the man who founded the modern tradition of non-violent action for change Mahatma Gandhi whose life taught and inspired me. And, of course, I accept it on behalf of the six million Tibetan people, my brave countrymen and women inside Tibet, who have suffered and continue to suffer so much. They confront a calculated and systematic strategy aimed at the destruction of their national and cultural identities. The prize reaffirms our conviction that with truth, courage and determination as our weapons, Tibet will be liberated.

No matter what part of the world we come from, we are all basically the same human beings. We all seek happiness and try to avoid suffering. We have the same basic human needs and is concerns. All of us human beings want freedom and the right to determine our own destiny as individuals and as peoples. That is human nature. The great changes that are taking place everywhere in the world, from Eastern Europe to Africa are a clear indication of this.

In China the popular movement for democracy was crushed by brutal force in June this year. But I do not believe the demonstrations were in vain, because the spirit of freedom was rekindled among the Chinese people and China cannot escape the impact of this spirit of freedom sweeping many parts of the world. The brave students and their supporters showed the Chinese leadership and the world the human face of that great nation.

Last week a number of Tibetans were once again sentenced to prison terms of up to nineteen years at a mass show trial, possibly intended to frighten the population before today's event. Their only 'crime' was the expression of the widespread desire of Tibetans for the restoration of their beloved country's independence.

The suffering of our people during the past forty years of occupation is well documented. Ours has been a long struggle. We know our cause is just Because violence can only breed more violence and suffering, our struggle must remain non-violent and free of hatred. We are trying to end the suffering of our people, not to inflict suffering upon others

It is with this in mind that I proposed negotiations between Tibet and China on numerous occasions. In 1987, I made specific proposals in a Five-Point plan for the restoration of peace and human rights in Tibet. This included the conversion of the entire Tibetan plateau into a Zone of Ahimsa, a sanctuary of peace and non-violence where human beings and nature can live in peace and harmony.

Last year, I elaborated on that plan in Strasbourg, at the European Parliament I believe the ideas I expressed on those occasions are both realistic and reasonable although they have been criticised by some of my people as being too conciliatory. Unfortunately, China's leaders have not responded positively to the suggestions we have made, which included important concessions. If this continues we will be compelled to reconsider our position.

Any relationship between Tibet and China will have to be based on the principle of equality, respect, trust and mutual benefit. It will also have to be based on the principle which the wise rulers of Tibet and of China laid down in a treaty as early as 823 AD, carved on the pillar which still stands today in front of the Jokhang, Tibet's holiest shrine, in Lhasa, that 'Tibetans will live happily in the great land of Tibet, and the Chinese will live happily in the great land of China.'

As a Buddhist monk, my concern extends to all members of the human family and, indeed, to all sentient beings who suffer. I believe all suffering is caused by ignorance. People inflict pain on others in the selfish pursuit of their happiness or satisfaction. Yet true happiness comes from a sense of brotherhood and sisterhood. We need to cultivate a universal responsibility for one another and the planet we share. Although I have found my own Buddhist religion helpful in generating love and compassion, even for those we consider our enemies, I am convinced that everyone can develop a good heart and a sense of universal responsibility with or without religion.

With the ever growing impact of science on our lives, religion and spirituality have a greater role to play reminding us of our humanity. There is no contradiction between the two. Each gives us valuable insights into the other. Both science and the teachings of the Buddha tell us of the fundamental unity of all things. This understanding is crucial if we are to take positive and decisive action on the pressing global concern with the environment.

I believe all religions pursue the same goals, that of cultivating human goodness and bringing happiness to all human beings. Though the means might appear different the ends are the same.

As we enter the final decade of this century I am optimistic that the ancient values that have sustained mankind are today reaffirming themselves to prepare us for a kinder, happier 21st century.

I pray for all of us, oppressor and friend, that together we succeed in building a better world through human understanding and love, and that in doing so we may reduce the pain and suffering of all sentient beings. Thank you.

'Freedom from Fear'

Aung San Suu Kyi

(1990)

Daw Aung San Suu Kyi is a politician, author and the first State Counsellor of Myanmar, who won the Nobel Peace Prize in 1991. Through the late 1990s and 2000s, she has been under house arrest several times for her protest of the military government. Aung San Suu Kyi also co-founded the National League for Democracy in 1988 and serves as its President.

'Freedom from Fear' is one of Aung San Suu Kyi's most famous speeches, delivered at a mass rally in 1990, as she began her campaign for the restoration of democratic institutions in Myanmar.

It is not power that corrupts but fear. Fear of losing power corrupts those who wield it and fear of the scourge of power corrupts those who are subject to it. Most Burmese are familiar with the four a-gati, the four kinds of corruption. Chanda-gati, corruption induced by desire, is deviation from the right path in pursuit of bribes or for the sake of those one loves. Dosa-gati is taking the wrong path to spite those against whom one bears ill will, and moga-gati is aberration due to ignorance. But perhaps the worst of the four is bhaya-gati, for not only does bhaya, fear, stifle and slowly destroy all sense of right and wrong, it so often lies at the root of the other three kinds of corruption. Just as chanda-gati, when not the result of sheer avarice, can be caused by fear of want or fear of losing the goodwill of those one loves, so fear of being surpassed, humiliated or injured in some way can provide the impetus for ill will. And it would be difficult to dispel ignorance unless there is freedom to pursue the truth unfettered by fear. With so close a relationship between fear and corruption it is little wonder that in any society where fear is rife corruption in all forms becomes deeply entrenched.

Public dissatisfaction with economic hardships has been seen as the chief cause of the movement for democracy in Burma, sparked off by the student demonstrations 1988. It is true that years of incoherent policies, inept official measures, burgeoning inflation and falling real income had turned the country into an economic shambles. But it was more than the difficulties of eking out a barely acceptable standard of living that had eroded the patience of a traditionally good-natured, quiescent people—it was also the humiliation of a way of life disfigured by corruption and fear.

The students were protesting not just against the death of their comrades but against the denial of their right to life by a totalitarian regime which deprived the present of meaningfulness and held out no hope for the future. And because the students' protests articulated the frustrations of the people at large, the demonstrations quickly grew into a nationwide movement. Some of its keenest supporters were businessmen who had developed the skills and the contacts necessary not only to survive but to prosper within the system. But their affluence offered them no genuine sense of security or fulfillment, and they could not but see that if they and their fellow citizens, regardless of economic status, were to achieve a worthwhile existence, an accountable administration was at least a necessary if not a sufficient condition. The people of Burma had wearied of a precarious state of passive apprehension where they were 'as water in the cupped hands' of the powers that be.

Emerald cool we may be. As water in cupped hands. But oh that we might be. As splinters of glass. In cupped hands.

Glass splinters, the smallest with its sharp, glinting power to defend itself against hands that try to crush, could be seen as a vivid symbol of the spark of courage that is an essential attribute of those who would free themselves from the grip of oppression. Bogyoke Aung San regarded himself as a revolutionary and searched tirelessly for answers to the problems that beset Burma during her times of trial. He exhorted the people to develop courage: 'Don't just depend on the courage and intrepidity of others. Each and every one of you must make sacrifices to become a hero possessed of courage and intrepidity. Then only shall we all be able to enjoy true freedom.'

The effort necessary to remain uncorrupted in an environment where fear is an integral part of everyday existence is not immediately apparent to those fortunate enough to live in states governed by the rule of law. Just laws do not merely prevent corruption by meting out impartial punishment to offenders. They also help to create a society in which people can fulfill the basic requirements necessary for the preservation of human dignity without recourse to corrupt practices. Where there are no such laws, the burden of upholding the principles of justice and common decency falls on the ordinary people. It is the cumulative effect on their sustained effort and steady endurance which will change a nation where reason and conscience are warped by fear into one where legal rules exist to promote man's desire for harmony and justice while restraining the less desirable destructive traits in his nature.

In an age when immense technological advances have created lethal weapons which could be, and are, used by the powerful and the unprincipled to dominate the weak and the helpless, there is a compelling need for a closer relationship between politics and ethics at both the national and international levels. The Universal Declaration of Human Rights of the United Nations proclaims that 'every individual and every organ of society' should strive to promote the basic rights and freedoms to which all human beings regardless of race, nationality or religion are entitled. But as long as there are governments whose authority is founded on coercion rather than on the mandate of the people, and interest groups which place short-term profits above long-term peace and prosperity, concerted international action to protect and promote human rights will remain at best a partially realised struggle. There will continue to be arenas of struggle where victims of oppression have to draw on their own inner resources to defend their inalienable rights as members of the human family.

The quintessential revolution is that of the spirit, born of an intellectual conviction of the need for change in those mental attitudes and values which shape the course of a nation's development. A revolution which aims merely at changing official policies and institutions with a view to an improvement in material conditions has little chance of genuine success. Without a revolution of the spirit, the forces which produced the iniquities of the old order would continue to be operative, posing a constant threat to the process of reform and regeneration. It is not enough merely to call for freedom, democracy and human rights. There has to be a united determination to persevere in the struggle, to make sacrifices in the name of enduring truths, to resist the corrupting influences of desire, ill will, ignorance and fear.

Saints, it has been said, are the sinners who go on trying. So free men are the oppressed who go on trying and who in the process make themselves fit to bear the responsibilities and to uphold the disciplines which will maintain a free society. Among the basic freedoms to which men aspire that their lives might be full and uncramped, freedom from fear stands out as both a means and an end. A people who would build a nation in which strong, democratic institutions are firmly established as a guarantee against state-induced power must first learn to liberate their own minds from apathy and fear.

Always one to practice what he preached, Aung San himself constantly demonstrated courage—not just the physical sort but the kind that enabled him to speak the truth, to stand by his word, to accept criticism, to admit his faults, to correct his mistakes, to respect the opposition, to parley with the enemy and to let people be the judge of his worthiness as a leader. It is for such moral courage that he will always be loved and respected in Burma—not merely as a warrior hero but as the inspiration and conscience of the nation. The words used by Jawaharlal Nehru to describe Mahatma Gandhi could well be applied to Aung San:

'The essence of his teaching was fearlessness and truth, and action allied to these, always keeping the welfare of the masses in view.'

Gandhi, that great apostle of non-violence, and Aung San, the founder of a national army, were very different personalities, but as there is an inevitable sameness about the challenges of authoritarian rule anywhere at any time, so there is a similarity in the intrinsic qualities of those who rise up to meet the challenge. Nehru, who considered the instillation of courage in the people of India one of Gandhi's greatest achievements, was a political modernist, but as he assessed the needs for a twentieth-century movement for independence, he found himself looking back to the philosophy of ancient India: 'The greatest gift for an individual or a nation was abhaya, fearlessness, not merely bodily courage but absence of fear from the mind.'

Fearlessness may be a gift but perhaps more precious is the courage acquired through endeavour, courage that comes from cultivating the habit of refusing to let fear dictate one's actions, courage that could be described as 'grace under pressure'—grace which is renewed repeatedly in the face of harsh, unremitting pressure.

Within a system which denies the existence of basic human rights, fear tends to be the order of the day. Fear of imprisonment, fear of torture, fear of death, fear of losing friends, family, property or means of livelihood, fear of poverty, fear of isolation, fear of failure. A most insidious form of fear is that which masquerades as common sense or even wisdom, condemning as foolish, reckless, insignificant or futile the small, daily acts of courage which help to preserve man's self-respect and inherent human dignity. It is not easy for a people conditioned by fear under the iron rule of the principle that might is right to free themselves from the enervating miasma of fear. Yet even under the most crushing state machinery courage rises up again and again, for fear is not the natural state of civilised man.

The wellspring of courage and endurance in the face of unbridled power is generally a firm belief in the sanctity of ethical principles combined with a historical sense that despite all setbacks the condition of man is set on an ultimate course for both spiritual and material advancement. It is his capacity for self-improvement and self-redemption which most distinguishes man from the mere brute. At the root of human responsibility is the concept of perfection, the urge to achieve it, the intelligence to find a path towards it, and the will to follow that path if not to the end at least the distance needed to rise above individual limitations and environmental impediments. It is man's vision of a world fit for rational, civilised humanity which leads him to dare and to suffer to build societies free from want and fear. Concepts such as truth, justice and compassion cannot be dismissed as trite when these are often the only bulwarks which stand against ruthless power.

Nobel Prize Acceptance Speech (read by Mr Andrej Kovaljov)

Mikhail Gorbachev

Oslo, Norway (10 December 1990)

Mikhail Gorbachev was General Secretary of the Communist Party of the Soviet Union and the last leader of the Soviet Union. He is credited with bringing an end to the Cold War, democratising politics in his country, bringing down the Berlin Wall, leading to the downfall of Communism and the break-up of the Soviet Union. He was awarded the Nobel Peace Prize in 1990.

In his acceptance speech, Gorbachev spreads the message of hope, mutual trust and peace in the world.

Your Majesty, Esteemed Chairman of the Norwegian Nobel Committee, Ladies and Gentlemen,

I have been requested by the President of the USSR, Mikhail Gorbachev, to present his address to the Norwegian Nobel Committee and to all those present today at this award ceremony:

To the Chairman of the Norwegian Nobel Committee, Mrs. Gidske Anderson: Esteemed Mrs. Anderson,

I am deeply and personally moved by the decision of the Nobel Committee to award me the 1990 Nobel Peace Prize.

The prestige and authority of the Nobel Peace Prize are universally recognized. The prize has been awarded ever since the beginning of this century. The disasters and tragedies of this period, which have not managed to subdue man's optimism and unflagging belief in human reason, have given the Peace Prize the unique aura associated with it today.

Immanuel Kant prophesied that mankind would one day be faced with a dilemma: either to be joined in a true union of nations or to perish in a war of annihilation ending in the extinction of the human race. Now, as we move from the second to the third millennium, the clock has struck the moment of truth.

In this respect, the year 1990 represents a turning point. It marks the end of the unnatural division of Europe. Germany has been reunited. We have begun resolutely to tear down the material foundations of a military, political and ideological confrontation. But there are some very grave threats that have not been eliminated: the potential for conflict and the primitive instincts which allow it, aggressive intentions, and totalitarian traditions.

I would like to assure you that the leadership of the USSR is doing and will continue to do everything in its power to ensure that future developments in Europe and the world as a whole are based on openness, mutual trust, international law and universal values.

The recent meeting in Paris of heads of state and government from the European nations, the United States and Canada, embodying all the best elements in international movements such as the Helsinki Process, has established the framework for a Europe based on the rule of law, stability, good relations between neighboring countries and humane attitudes. It is my hope that such a Europe will be understood and accepted by nations and governments in other parts of the world as an example of universal security and genuine cooperation.

I do not regard the 1990 Nobel Peace Prize as an award to me personally, but as a recognition of what we call perestroika and innovative political thinking, which is of vital significance for human destinies all over the world.

The Nobel Peace Prize for 1990 confirms that perestroika and innovative political thinking no longer belong only to us, the people of the Soviet Union. They are the property of the whole of mankind and are an inseparable part of its destiny and of a safe, peaceful future. We are deeply grateful to Norway and other members of the international community who have shown such understanding and who, through their conduct in international issues and in their relations with the Soviet Union, have shown their solidarity as we proceed with our perestroika and their sympathy as we struggle to resolve our problems. If we all took this as our point of departure, mankind would have no cause to regret the loss of a unique opportunity for reason and the logic of peace to prevail over that of war and alienation.

Once more, I would like to express my appreciation for this very great honor. I intend to do everything in my power to live up to the expectations and hopes of my countrymen and all those who support the Nobel Committee's choice.

With my sincere wishes for peace and prosperity,

Mikhail Gorbachev President of the USSR

This was the address by the winner of the Nobel Peace Prize for 1990, which I, as his personal representative, have had the honor of making on his behalf.

Thank you for your attention.

Speech at the Rio Earth Summit

Severn Suzuki

Rio de Janeiro, Brazil (1992)

Severn Cullis-Suzuki is a Canadian author, speaker and environmental activist who gave a speech at the Earth Summit in Rio de Janeiro as a 12-year-old in 1992, that stunned all present, and who was applauded by all the delegates. For her efforts, she was honoured in the United Nations Environment Programme's Global 500 Roll of Honour. She also hosted Suzuki's Nature Quest, a children's television series that aired on Discovery Kids in 2002.

Here is the speech she delivered at the Earth Summit in Rio de Janeiro, urging people to conserve the environment for the future generations.

Hello, I'm Severn Suzuki, speaking for ECO-the Environmental Children's Organization. We are a group of 12 and 13-year olds trying to make a difference: Vanessa Suttie, Morgan Geisler, Michelle Quigg and me. We raised all the money to come here five thousand miles to tell you adults you must change your ways. Coming up here today, I have no hidden agendas. I am fighting for my future. Losing my future is not like losing an election or a few points on the stock market. I am here to speak for all generations to come. I am here to speak on behalf of the starving children around the world whose cries go unheard. I am here to speak for the countless animals dying across this planet because they have nowhere left to go. I am afraid to go out in the sun now because of the holes in the ozone. I am afraid to breathe the air because I don't know what chemicals are in it. I used to go fishing in Vancouver, my home, with my Dad until just a few years ago we found the fish full of cancers. And now we hear of animals and plants going extinct every day—vanishing forever. In my life, I have dreamt of seeing the great herds of wild animals, jungles and rain forests full of birds and butterflies, but now I wonder if they will even exist for my children to see. Did you have to worry about these things when you were my age? All this is happening before our eyes and yet we act as if we have all the time we want and all the solutions. I'm only a child and I don't have all the solutions, but I want you to realize, neither do you… You don't know how to bring the salmon back up a dead stream. You don't know how to bring back an animal now extinct. And you can't bring back the forests that once grew where there is now desert. If you don't know how fix it, please stop breaking it!

At school even in kindergarten, you teach us how to behave in the world. You teach us: not to fight with others, to work things out, to respect elders, to clean up our mess, not to hurt other creatures, to share—not be greedy. Then why do you go out and do the things you tell us not to do? Do not forget why you are attending these conferences, who you're doing this for—we are your own children. You are deciding what kind of world we are growing up in. Parents should be able to comfort their children by saying 'everything's going to be all right', 'it's not the end of the world', and 'we're doing the best we can'. But I don't think you can say that to us anymore. Are we even on your list of priorities?

My Dad always says, 'You are what you do, not what you say.' Well, what you do makes me cry at night. You grown-ups say you love us, but I challenge you. Please make your actions reflect your words. Thank you.

ESPY Awards Speech

Jim Valvano

Madison Square Garden, New York City (4 March 1993)

James Thomas Anthony Valvano, also known as Jimmy V, was an American college basketball player and one of the most successful coaches of his time. He was also a broadcaster for ESPN and ABC sports, and the prestigious ESPY Awards were renamed Jimmy V Awards in his honour and in support of cancer patients.

An optimist at heart, Valvano in his moving acceptance speech, urges his audience to never give up and have hope, love and persistence. He died of cancer less than two months after delivering this speech.

Thank you, Thank you very much. I can't tell you what an honor it is, to even be mentioned in the same breath with Arthur Ashe. This is something I certainly will treasure forever. But, as it was said on the tape…I'm going to speak longer than anybody else has spoken tonight. That's the way it goes. Time is very precious to me. I don't know how much I have left and I have some things that I would like to say. Hopefully, at the end, I will have said something that will be important to other people too. When people say to me how do you get through life or each day, it's the same thing. To me, there are three things we all should do every day. We should do this every day of our lives. Number one is laugh. You should laugh every day. Number two is think. You should spend some time in thought. Number three is, you should have your emotions moved to tears, could be happiness or joy. But think about it. If you laugh, you think, and you cry, that's a full day. That's a heck of a day. You do that seven days a week, you're going to have something special. I always have to think about what's important in life to me are these three things. Where you started, where you are and where you're going to be. When I think of where I started, I have to remember the first speech I ever gave. I was coaching at Rutgers University, that was my first job, and I was the freshman coach. That's when freshmen played on freshman teams, and I was so fired up about my first job...The very first time I stood in the locker room to give a pep talk. That's a special place, the locker room, for a coach to give a talk. So my idol as a coach was Vince Lombardi...Lombardi talked about the first time he spoke before his Green Bay Packers team in the locker room, and they were perennial losers. He wanted it to be emotional, so it would be brief. So here's what he did. Normally you get in the locker room, I don't know, twenty-five minutes, a half hour before the team takes the field, you do your little x and o's, and then you give the great Knute Rockne talk. You get your squad ready...Lombardi, what he said was he didn't go in, he waited. His team wondering, where is he? Where is this great coach? He's not there. Ten minutes he's still not there. Three minutes before they could take the field Lombardi comes in, bangs the door open, and He walked in and he walked back and forth, like this, just walked, staring at the players. He said, 'All eyes on me.' and he said 'Gentlemen, we will be successful this year, if you can focus on three things, and three things only. Your family, your religion and the Green Bay Packers.' They knocked the walls down and the rest was history. I said, that's beautiful. I'm going to do that. Your family, your religion and Rutgers basketball...I'm practicing outside of the locker room...Not yet, not yet, family, religion, Rutgers Basketball. All eyes on me. I got it, I got it. Then finally, three minutes...I go to knock the doors open just like Lombardi. Boom! They don't open. I almost broke my arm. Now I was down, the players were looking. Help the coach out, help him out. Now I did like Lombardi, I walked back and forth, and I was going like that with my arm getting the feeling back in it. Finally I said, 'Gentlemen, all eyes on me.' These kids wanted to play, they're nineteen. 'Let's go,' I said. 'Gentlemen, we'll be successful this year if you can focus on three things, and three things only. Your family, your religion and the Green Bay

Packers,' I told them.. I remember that. I remember where I came from. It's so important to know where you are. I know where I am right now. How do you go from where you are to where you want to be? I think you have to have an enthusiasm for life. You have to have a dream, a goal. You have to be willing to work for it. I just got one last thing, I urge all of you, all of you, to enjoy your life, the precious moments you have. To spend each day with some laughter and some thought, to get your emotions going. To be enthusiastic every day and as Ralph Waldo Emerson said, 'Nothing great could be accomplished without enthusiasm,' to keep your dreams alive in spite of problems whatever you have. The ability to be able to work hard for your dreams to come true, to become a reality. Now I look at where I am now and I know what I want to do... We need money for research. It may not save my life. It may save my children's lives. It may save someone you love—we are starting the Jimmy V Foundation for Cancer Research. And its motto is 'Don't give up, don't ever give up.'...I'm going to work as hard as I can for cancer research and hopefully, maybe, we'll have some cures and some breakthroughs. I'd like to think, I'm going to fight my brains out to be back here again next year for the Arthur Ashe recipient. I want to give it next year! I know, I gotta go, I gotta go, and I got one last thing and I said it before, and I want to say it again. Cancer can take away all my physical abilities. It cannot touch my mind, it cannot touch my heart and it cannot touch my soul. And those three things are going to carry on forever. I thank you and God bless you all.

On the Pulse of Morning

Maya Angelou

Presidential Inauguration (1993)

Maya Angelou was an American novelist, poet, actor, dancer and human rights activist best-known for her memoir *I Know Why the Caged Bird Sings* (1969) which became the first bestselling work of non-fiction by an African-American woman. Angelou was an outspoken activist for black people and women, and received the Presidential Medal of Freedom in 2011.

She recited her poem 'On the Pulse of Morning' at the first inauguration of Bill Clinton, becoming the first poet since Robert Frost to make an inaugural recitation.

A Rock, A River, A Tree
Hosts to species long since departed,
Marked the mastodon.

The dinosaur, who left dry tokens
Of their sojourn here
On our planet floor,
Any broad alarm of their hastening doom
Is lost in the gloom of dust and ages.

But today, the Rock cries out to us, clearly, forcefully,
Come, you may stand upon my
Back and face your distant destiny,
But seek no haven in my shadow.
I will give you no hiding place down here.

You, created only a little lower than
The angels, have crouched too long in
The bruising darkness,
Have lain too long
Face down in ignorance.

Your mouths spilling words
Armed for slaughter.

The Rock cries out to us today, you may stand upon me,
But do not hide your face.

Across the wall of the world,
A River sings a beautiful song,
It says come rest here by my side.

Each of you a bordered country,
Delicate and strangely made proud,
Yet thrusting perpetually under siege.

Your armed struggles for profit
Have left collars of waste upon
My shore, currents of debris upon my breast.

Yet, today I call you to my riverside,
If you will study war no more. Come,

Clad in peace and I will sing the songs
The Creator gave to me when I and the
Tree and the rock were one.

Before cynicism was a bloody sear across your
Brow and when you yet knew you still
Knew nothing.

The River sang and sings on.

There is a true yearning to respond to
The singing River and the wise Rock.

So say the Asian, the Hispanic, the Jew
The African, the Native American, the Sioux,
The Catholic, the Muslim, the French, the Greek
The Irish, the Rabbi, the Priest, the Sheikh,
The Gay, the Straight, the Preacher,
The privileged, the homeless, the Teacher.
They all hear
The speaking of the Tree.

They hear the first and last of every Tree
Speak to humankind today. Come to me, here beside
the River.

Plant yourself beside the River.

Each of you, descendant of some passed
On traveller, has been paid for.

You, who gave me my first name, you
Pawnee, Apache, Seneca, you
Cherokee Nation, who rested with me, then
Forced on bloody feet, left me to the employment of
Other seekers—desperate for gain,
Starving for gold.

You, the Turk, the Arab, the Swede, the German, the Eskimo, the
Scot...
You the Ashanti, the Yoruba, the Kru, bought
Sold, stolen, arriving on a nightmare
Praying for a dream.

Here, root yourselves beside me.

I am that Tree planted by the River,
Which will not be moved.

I, the Rock, I the River, I the Tree
I am yours—your Passages have been paid.

Lift up your faces, you have a piercing need
For this bright morning dawning for you.

History, despite its wrenching pain,
Cannot be unlived, but if faced
With courage, need not be lived again.

Lift up your eyes upon
This day breaking for you.

Give birth again
To the dream.

Women, children, men,
Take it into the palms of your hands.

Mold it into the shape of your most
Private need. Sculpt it into
The image of your most public self.
Lift up your hearts
Each new hour holds new chances
For new beginnings.

Do not be wedded forever
To fear, yoked eternally
To brutishness.

The horizon leans forward,
Offering you space to place new steps of change.
Here, on the pulse of this fine day
You may have the courage

To look up and out and upon me, the
Rock, the River, the Tree, your country.

No less to Midas than the mendicant.

No less to you now than the mastodon then.

Here on the pulse of this new day
You may have the grace to look up and out
And into your sister's eyes, and into
Your brother's face, your country
And say simply
Very simply
With hope
Good morning.

'Women's Rights Are Human Rights'

Hillary Clinton

U.N. 4th World Conference on Women Plenary Session
(5 September 1995)

Hillary Clinton is one of the most accomplished (former) first ladies in American history. A trained lawyer, she had a thriving career both in the public and private sectors. Clinton was also an important political advisor to her husband, Bill Clinton, who became the 42nd President of the United States. She also served as the U.S. Secretary of State from 2009 to 2013, making human rights and women's rights the central focus of her tenure.

Clinton gave this notable speech at the United Nation's 4th World Conference on Women Plenary Session, stressing the importance of women's rights and making famous the phrase 'Women's rights are human rights.'

Thank you very much, Gertrude Mongella, for your dedicated work that has brought us to this point, distinguished delegates, and guests:

I would like to thank the Secretary General for inviting me to be part of this important United Nations Fourth World Conference on Women. This is truly a celebration, a celebration of the contributions women make in every aspect of life: in the home, on the job, in the community, as mothers, wives, sisters, daughters, learners, workers, citizens, and leaders.

It is also a coming together, much the way women come together every day in every country. We come together in fields and factories, in village markets and supermarkets, in living rooms and board rooms. Whether it is while playing with our children in the park, or washing clothes in a river, or taking a break at the office water cooler, we come together and talk about our aspirations and concern. And time and again, our talk turns to our children and our families. However different we may appear, there is far more that unites us than divides us. We share a common future, and we are here to find common ground so that we may help bring new dignity and respect to women and girls all over the world, and in so doing bring new strength and stability to families as well.

By gathering in Beijing, we are focusing world attention on issues that matter most in our lives—the lives of women and their families: access to education, health care, jobs and credit, the chance to enjoy basic legal and human rights and to participate fully in the political life of our countries.

There are some who question the reason for this conference. Let them listen to the voices of women in their homes, neighborhoods, and workplaces. There are some who wonder whether the lives of women and girls matter to economic and political progress around the globe. Let them look at the women gathered here and at Huairou—the homemakers and nurses, the teachers and lawyers, the policymakers and women who run their own businesses. It is conferences like this that compel governments and peoples everywhere to listen, look, and face the world's most pressing problems. Wasn't it after all—after the women's conference in Nairobi ten years ago that the world focused for the first time on the crisis of domestic violence?

Earlier today, I participated in a World Health Organization forum. In that forum, we talked about ways that government officials, NGOs, and individual citizens are working to address the health problems of women and girls. Tomorrow, I will attend a gathering of the United Nations Development Fund for Women. There, the discussion will focus on local—and highly successful—programs that give hard-working women access to credit so they can improve their own lives and the lives of their families.

What we are learning around the world is that if women are healthy and educated, their families will flourish. If women are free from violence, their families will flourish. If women have a chance to work and earn as full and equal partners in society, their families will flourish. And when families flourish, communities and nations do as well. That is why every woman, every man, every child, every family, and every nation on this planet does have a stake in the discussion that takes place here.

Over the past 25 years, I have worked persistently on issues relating to women, children, and families. Over the past two and a half years, I've had the opportunity to learn more about the challenges facing women in my own country and around the world.

I have met new mothers in Indonesia, who come together regularly in their village to discuss nutrition, family planning, and baby care. I have met working parents in Denmark who talk about the comfort they feel in knowing that their children can be cared for in safe, and nurturing after-school centers. I have met women in South Africa who helped lead the struggle to end apartheid and are now helping to build a new democracy. I have met with the leading women of my own hemisphere who are working every day to promote literacy and better health care for children in their countries. I have met women in India and Bangladesh who are taking out small loans to buy milk cows, or rickshaws, or thread in order to create a livelihood for themselves and their families. I have met the doctors and nurses in Belarus and Ukraine who are trying to keep children alive in the aftermath of Chernobyl.

The great challenge of this conference is to give voice to women everywhere whose experiences go unnoticed, whose words go unheard. Women comprise more than half the world's population, 70% of the world's poor, and two-thirds of those who are not taught to read and write. We are the primary caretakers for most of the world's children and elderly. Yet much of the work we do is not valued—not by economists, not by historians, not by popular culture, not by government leaders.

At this very moment, as we sit here, women around the world are giving birth, raising children, cooking meals, washing clothes, cleaning houses, planting crops, working on assembly lines, running companies, and running countries. Women also are dying from diseases that should have been prevented or treated. They are watching their children succumb to malnutrition caused by poverty and economic deprivation. They are being denied the right to go to school by their own fathers and brothers. They are being forced into prostitution, and they are being barred from the bank lending offices and banned from the ballot box.

Those of us who have the opportunity to be here have the responsibility to speak for those who could not. As an American, I want to speak for those women in my own country, women who are raising children on the minimum wage, women who can't afford health care or child care, women whose lives are threatened by violence, including violence in their own homes.

I want to speak up for mothers who are fighting for good schools, safe neighborhoods, clean air, and clean airwaves; for older women, some of them widows, who find that, after raising their families, their skills and life experiences are not valued in the marketplace; for women who are working all night as nurses, hotel clerks, or fast food chefs so that they can be at home during the day with their children; and for women everywhere who simply don't have time to do everything they are called upon to do each and every day.

Speaking to you today, I speak for them, just as each of us speaks for women around the world who are denied the chance to go to school, or see a doctor, or own property, or have a say about the direction of their lives, simply because they are women. The truth is that most women around the world work both inside and outside the home, usually by necessity.

We need to understand there is no one formula for how women should lead our lives. That is why we must respect the choices that each woman makes for herself and her family. Every woman deserves the chance to realize her own God-given potential. But we must recognize that women will never gain full dignity until their human rights are respected and protected.

Our goals for this conference, to strengthen families and societies by empowering women to take greater control over their own destinies, cannot be fully achieved unless all governments here and around the world—accept their responsibility to protect and promote internationally recognized human rights. The—The international community has long acknowledged and recently reaffirmed at Vienna that both women and men are entitled to a range of protections and personal freedoms, from the right of personal security to the right to determine freely the number and spacing of the children they bear. No one—No one should be forced to remain silent for fear of religious or political persecution, arrest, abuse, or torture.

Tragically, women are most often the ones whose human rights are violated. Even now, in the late 20th century, the rape of women continues to be used as an instrument of armed conflict. Women and children make up a large majority of the world's refugees. And when women are excluded from the political process, they become even more vulnerable to abuse. I believe that now, on the eve of a new millennium, it is time to break the silence. It is time for us to say here in Beijing, and for the world to hear, that it is no longer acceptable to discuss women's rights as separate from human rights.

These abuses have continued because, for too long, the history of women has been a history of silence. Even today, there are those who are trying to silence our words. But the voices of this conference and of the women at Huairou must be heard loudly and clearly:

It is a violation of human rights when babies are denied food, or drowned, or suffocated, or their spines broken, simply because they are born girls.

It is a violation of human rights when women and girls are sold into the slavery of prostitution for human greed—and the kinds of reasons that are used to justify this practice should no longer be tolerated.

It is a violation of human rights when women are doused with gasoline, set on fire, and burned to death because their marriage dowries are deemed too small.

It is a violation of human rights when individual women are raped in their own communities and when thousands of women are subjected to rape as a tactic or prize of war.

It is a violation of human rights when a leading cause of death worldwide among women ages 14 to 44 is the violence they are subjected to in their own homes by their own relatives.

It is a violation of human rights when young girls are brutalized by the painful and degrading practice of genital mutilation.

It is a violation of human rights when women are denied the right to plan their own families, and that includes being forced to have abortions or being sterilized against their will.

If there is one message that echoes forth from this conference, let it be that human rights are women's rights and women's rights are human rights once and for all. Let us not forget that among those rights are the right to speak freely—and the right to be heard.

Women must enjoy the rights to participate fully in the social and political lives of their countries, if we want freedom and democracy to thrive and endure. It is indefensible that many women in nongovernmental organizations who wished to participate in this conference have not been able to attend—or have been prohibited from fully taking part.

Let me be clear. Freedom means the right of people to assemble, organize, and debate openly. It means respecting the views of those who may disagree with the views of their governments. It means not taking citizens away from their loved ones and jailing them, mistreating them, or denying them their freedom or dignity because of the peaceful expression of their ideas and opinions.

In my country, we recently celebrated the 75th anniversary of Women's Suffrage. It took 150 years after the signing of our Declaration of Independence for women to win the right to vote. It took 72 years of organized struggle, before that happened, on the part of many courageous women and men. It was one of America's most divisive philosophical wars. But it was a bloodless war. Suffrage was achieved without a shot being fired.

But we have also been reminded, in V-J Day observances last weekend, of the good that comes when men and women join together to combat the forces of tyranny and to build a better world. We have seen peace prevail in most places for a half century. We have avoided another world war. But we have not solved older, deeply-rooted problems that continue to diminish the potential of half the world's population.

Now it is the time to act on behalf of women everywhere. If we take bold steps to better the lives of women, we will be taking bold steps to better the lives of children and families too. Families rely on mothers and wives for emotional support and care. Families rely on women for labor in the home. And increasingly, everywhere, families rely on women for income needed to raise healthy children and care for other relatives.

As long as discrimination and inequities remain so commonplace everywhere in the world, as long as girls and women are valued less, fed less, fed last, overworked, underpaid, not schooled, subjected to violence in and outside their homes—the potential of the human family to create a peaceful, prosperous world will not be realized.

Let—Let this conference be our—and the world's—call to action. Let us heed that call so we can create a world in which every woman is treated with respect and dignity, every boy and girl is loved and cared for equally, and every family has the hope of a strong and stable future. That is the work before you. That is the work before all of us who have a vision of the world we want to see—for our children and our grandchildren.

The time is now. We must move beyond rhetoric. We must move beyond recognition of problems to working together, to have the comment efforts to build that common ground we hope to see.

God's blessing on you, your work, and all who will benefit from it. Godspeed and thank you very much.

'Your Education Is a Dress Rehearsal for a Life That Is Yours to Lead'

Nora Ephron

Commencement Address to Wellesley Class of 1996

Nora Ephron was an American author, essayist, playwright, screenwriter and film director who won the BAFTA Award for Best Original Screenplay for *When Harry Met Sally* (1989) besides several other accolades and Academy Award nominations for her other works. She was popular for her romantic comedies featuring witty and strong female protagonists.

In her inspiring commencement address to the college from which she graduated, Nora Ephron wittily inspires the students to break the glass ceiling and achieve their goals.

President Walsh, trustees, faculty, friends, noble parents...and dear class of 1996, I am so proud of you. Thank you for asking me to speak to you today. I had a wonderful time trying to imagine who had been ahead of me on the list and had said no; I was positive you'd have to have gone to Martha Stewart first. And I meant to call her to see what she would have said, but I forgot. She would probably be up here telling you how to turn your lovely black robes into tents. I will try to be at least as helpful, if not quite as specific as that.

I'm very conscious of how easy it is to let people down on a day like this, because I remember my own graduation from Wellesley very, very well, I am sorry to say. The speaker was Santha Rama Rau who was a woman writer, and I was going to be a woman writer. And in fact, I had spent four years at Wellesley going to lectures by women writers hoping that I would be the beneficiary of some terrific secret—which I never was. And now here I was at graduation, under these very trees, absolutely terrified. Something was over. Something safe and protected. And something else was about to begin. I was heading off to New York and I was sure that I would live there forever and never meet anyone and end up dying one of those New York deaths where no one even notices you're missing until the smell drifts into the hallway weeks later. And I sat here thinking, 'OK, Santha, this is my last chance for a really terrific secret, lay it on me,' and she spoke about the need to place friendship over love of country, which I must tell you had never crossed my mind one way or the other.

I want to tell you a little bit about my class, the class of 1962. When we came to Wellesley in the fall of 1958, there was an article in the *Harvard Crimson* about the women›s colleges, one of those stupid mean little articles full of stereotypes, like girls at Bryn Mawr wear black. We were girls then, by the way, Wellesley girls. How long ago was it? It was so long ago that while I was here, Wellesley actually threw six young women out for lesbianism. It was so long ago that we had curfews. It was so long ago that if you had a boy in your room, you had to leave the door open six inches, and if you closed the door you had to put a sock on the doorknob. In my class of, I don›t know, maybe 375 young women, there were six Asians and 5 Blacks. There was a strict quota on the number of Jews. Tuition was $2,000 a year and in my junior year it was raised to $2,250 and my parents practically had a heart attack.

How long ago? If you needed an abortion, you drove to a gas station in Union, New Jersey, with $500 in cash in an envelope and you were taken, blindfolded, to a motel room and operated on without an anesthetic. On the lighter side, and as you no doubt read in the *New York Times* magazine, and were flabbergasted to learn, there were the posture pictures. We not only took off most of our clothes to have our posture pictures taken, we took them off without ever even thinking, this is weird, why are we doing this? —not only that, we had also had speech therapy—I was told I had a New Jersey accent I really ought to do something about, which was a shock to me since I was from Beverly Hills, California, and had never set foot in the state of New Jersey...not only that, we were required to take a course called Fundamentals, Fundies, where we actually were taught how to get in and out of the back seat of the car. Some of us were named things like Winkie. We all parted our hair in the middle. How long ago was it? It was so long ago that among the things that I honestly cannot conceive of life without, that had not yet been invented: panty hose, lattes, Advil, pasta (there was no pasta then, there was only spaghetti and macaroni)—I sit here writing this speech on a computer next to a touch tone phone with an answering machine and a Rolodex, there are several CDs on my desk, a bottle of Snapple, there are felt-tip pens and an electric pencil sharpener...well, you get the point, it was a long time ago.

Anyway, as I was saying, the *Crimson* had this snippy article which said that Wellesley was a school for tunicata—tunicata apparently being small fish who spend the first part of their lives frantically swimming around the ocean floor exploring their environment, and the second part of their lives just lying there breeding. It was mean and snippy, but it had the horrible ring of truth, it was one of those do-not-ask-for-whom-the-bell-tolls things, and it burned itself into our brains. Years later, at my 25th reunion, one of my classmates mentioned it, and everyone remembered what tunicata were, word for word.

My class went to college in the era when you got a master's degrees in teaching because it was 'something to fall back on' in the worst case scenario, the worst case scenario being that no one married you and you actually had to go to work. As this same classmate said at our reunion, 'Our education was a dress rehearsal for a life we never led.' Isn't that the saddest line? We weren't meant to have futures, we were meant to marry them. We weren't' meant to have politics, or careers that mattered, or opinions, or lives; we were meant to marry them. If you wanted to be an architect, you married an architect. *Non Ministrare sed Ministrari*—you know the old joke, not to be ministers but to be ministers' wives.

I've written about my years at Wellesley, and I don't want to repeat myself any more than is necessary. But I do want to retell one anecdote from the piece I did about my 10th Wellesley reunion. I'll tell it a little differently for those of you who read it. Which was that, during my junior year, when I was engaged for a very short period of time, I thought I might transfer to Barnard my senior year. I went to see my class dean and she said to me, 'Let me give you some advice. You've worked so hard at Wellesley, when you marry, take a year off. Devote yourself to your husband and your marriage.' Of course it was stunning piece of advice to give me because I'd always intended to work after college. My mother was a career woman, and all of us, her four daughters, grew up understanding that the question, 'What do you want to be when you grow up?' was as valid for girls as for boys. Take a year off being a wife. I always wondered what I was supposed to do in that year. Iron? I repeated the story for years, as proof that Wellesley wanted its graduates to be merely housewives. But I turned out to be wrong, because years later I met another Wellesley graduate who had been as hell-bent on domesticity as I had been on a career. And she had gone to the same dean with the same problem, and the dean had said to her, 'Don't have children right away. Take a year to work.' And so I saw that what Wellesley wanted was for us to avoid the extremes. To be instead, that thing in the middle. A lady. We were to take the fabulous education we had received here and use it to preside at dinner table or at a committee meeting, and when two people disagreed we would be intelligent enough to step in and point out the remarkable similarities between their two opposing positions. We were to spend our lives making nice.

Many of my classmates did exactly what they were supposed to when they graduated from Wellesley, and some of them, by the way, lived happily ever after. But many of them didn't. All sorts of things happened that no one expected. They needed money so they had to work. They got divorced so they had to work. They were bored witless so they had to work. The women's movement came along and made harsh value judgments about their lives—judgments that caught them by surprise, because they were doing what they were supposed to be doing, weren't they? The rules had changed, they were caught in some kind of strange time warp. They had never intended to be the heroines of their own lives, they'd intended to be—what?—First Ladies, I guess, first ladies in the lives of big men. They ended up feeling like victims. They ended up, and this is really sad, thinking that their years in college were the best years of their lives.

Why am I telling you this? It was a long time ago, right? Things have changed, haven't they? Yes, they have. But I mention it because I want to remind you of the undertow, of the specific gravity. American society has a remarkable ability to resist change, or to take whatever change has taken place and attempt to make it go away. Things are different for you than they were for us. Just the fact that you chose to come to a single-sex college makes you smarter than we were—we came because it's what you did in those days—and the college you are graduating from is a very different place. All sorts of things caused Wellesley to change, but it did change, and today it's a place that understands its obligations to women in today's world. The women's movement has made a huge difference, too, particularly for young women like you. There are women doctors and women lawyers. There are anchorwomen, although most of them are blonde. But at the same time, the pay differential between men and women has barely changed. In my business, the movie business, there are many more women directors, but it's just as hard to make a movie about women as it ever was, and look at the parts the Oscar-nominated actresses played this year: hooker, hooker, hooker, hooker, and nun. It's 1996, and you are graduating from Wellesley in the Year of the Wonderbra. The Wonderbra is not a step forward for women. Nothing that hurts that much is a step forward for women.

What I'm saying is, don't delude yourself that the powerful cultural values that wrecked the lives of so many of my classmates have vanished from the earth. Don't let the *New York Times* article about the brilliant success of Wellesley graduates in the business world fool you—there›s still a glass ceiling. Don›t let the number of women in the work force trick you—there are still lots of magazines devoted almost exclusively to making perfect casseroles and turning various things into tents.

Don't underestimate how much antagonism there is toward women and how many people wish we could turn the clock back. One of the things people always say to you if you get upset is, don't take it personally, but listen hard to what's going on and, please, I beg you, take it personally. Understand: Every attack on Hillary Clinton for not knowing her place is an attack on you. Underneath almost all those attacks are the words: Get back, get back to where you once belonged. When Elizabeth Dole pretends that she isn't serious about her career, that is an attack on you. The acquittal of O.J. Simpson is an attack on you. Any move to limit abortion rights is an attack on you—whether or not you believe in abortion. The fact that Clarence Thomas is sitting on the Supreme Court today is an attack on you.

Above all, be the heroine of your life, not the victim. Because you don't have the alibi my class had—this is one of the great achievements and mixed blessings you inherit: Unlike us, you can't say nobody told you there were other options. Your education is a dress rehearsal for a life that is yours to lead. Twenty-five years from now, you won't have as easy a time making excuses as my class did. You won't be able to blame the deans, or the culture, or anyone else: you will have no one to blame but yourselves. Whoa.

So what are you going to do? This is the season when a clutch of successful women—who have it all —give speeches to women like you and say, to be perfectly honest, you can't have it all. Maybe young women don't wonder whether they can have it all any longer, but in case any of you are wondering, of course you can have it all. What are you going to do? Everything, is my guess. It will be a little messy, but embrace the mess. It will be complicated, but rejoice in the complications. It will not be anything like what you think it will be like, but surprises are good for you. And don't be frightened: you can always change your mind. I know: I've had four careers and three husbands. And this is something else I want to tell you, one of the hundreds of things I didn't know when I was sitting here so many years ago: you are not going to be you, fixed and immutable you, forever. We have a game we play when we're waiting for tables in restaurants, where you have to write the five things that describe yourself on a piece of paper. When I was your age, I would have put: ambitious, Wellesley graduate, daughter, Democrat, single. Ten years later not one of those five things turned up on my list. I was: journalist, feminist, New Yorker, divorced, funny. Today not one of those five things turns up in my list: writer, director, mother, sister, happy. Whatever those five things are for you today, they won't make the list in ten years—not that you still won't be some of those things, but they won't be the five most important things about you. Which is one of the most delicious things available to women, and more particularly to women than to men. I think. It's slightly easier for us to shift, to change our minds, to take another path. Yogi Berra, the former New York Yankee who made a specialty of saying things that were famously maladroit, quoted himself at a recent commencement speech he gave. 'When you see a fork in the road,' he said, 'take it.' Yes, it's supposed to be a joke, but as someone said in a movie I made, don't laugh this is my life, this is the life many women lead: Two paths diverge in a wood, and we get to take them both. It's another of the nicest things about being women; we can do that. Did I say it was hard? Yes, but let me say it again so that none of you can ever say the words, nobody said it was so hard. But it's also incredibly interesting. You are so lucky to have that life as an option.

Whatever you choose, however many roads you travel, I hope that you choose not to be a lady. I hope you will find some way to break the rules and make a little trouble out there. And I also hope that you will choose to make some of that trouble on behalf of women. Thank you. Good luck. The first act of your life is over. Welcome to the best years of your lives.

Eulogy of Diana Spencer, Princess of Wales

Charles Spencer, 9th Earl Spencer

Westminster Abbey, London (6 September 1997)

Charles Edward Maurice Spencer, 9th Earl Spencer is a British nobleman, peer, author, broadcaster and journalist who is the younger brother of the late Diana, Princess of Wales, and maternal uncle of Prince William, Duke of Cambridge and Prince Harry, Duke of Sussex.

In his moving eulogy for his sister, Princess Diana, Earl Spencer shocked and rebuked both the royal family and the media, and took this opportunity to highlight his sister's goodness, charity and spirited nature.

I stand before you today the representative of a family in grief, in a country in mourning before a world in shock.

We are all united not only in our desire to pay our respects to Diana, but rather in our need to do so.

For such was her extraordinary appeal that the tens of millions of people taking part in this service all over the world via television and radio who never actually met her, feel that they, too, lost someone close to them in the early hours of Sunday morning. It is a more remarkable tribute to Diana than I can ever hope to offer her today.

Diana was the very essence of compassion, of duty, of style, of beauty. All over the world she was a symbol of selfless humanity, a standard-bearer for the rights of the truly downtrodden, a truly British girl who transcended nationality, someone with a natural nobility who was classless, who proved in the last year that she needed no royal title to continue to generate her particular brand of magic.

Today is our chance to say 'thank you' for the way you brightened our lives, even though God granted you but half a life. We will all feel cheated that you were taken from us so young and yet we must learn to be grateful that you came along at all.

Only now you are gone do we truly appreciate what we are now without and we want you to know that life without you is very, very difficult.

We have all despaired at our loss over the past week and only the strength of the message you gave us through your years of giving has afforded us the strength to move forward.

There is a temptation to rush to canonize your memory. There is no need to do so. You stand tall enough as a human being of unique qualities not to need to be seen as a saint. Indeed to sanctify your memory would be to miss out on the very core of your being, your wonderfully mischievous sense of humor with the laugh that bent you double, your joy for life transmitted wherever you took your smile, and the sparkle in those unforgettable eyes, your boundless energy which you could barely contain.

But your greatest gift was your intuition, and it was a gift you used wisely. This is what underpinned all your wonderful attributes. And if we look to analyze what it was about you that had such a wide appeal, we find it in your instinctive feel for what was really important in all our lives.

Without your God-given sensitivity, we would be immersed in greater ignorance at the anguish of AIDS and HIV sufferers, the plight of the homeless, the isolation of lepers, the random destruction of land mines. Diana explained to me once that it was her innermost feelings of suffering that made it possible for her to connect with her constituency of the rejected.

And here we come to another truth about her. For all the status, the glamour, the applause, Diana remained throughout a very insecure person at heart, almost childlike in her desire to do good for others so she could release herself from deep feelings of unworthiness of which her eating disorders were merely a symptom.

The world sensed this part of her character and cherished her for her vulnerability, whilst admiring her for her honesty. The last time I saw Diana was on July the first, her birthday, in London, when typically she was not taking time to celebrate her special day with friends but was guest of honor at a charity fund-raising evening.

She sparkled of course, but I would rather cherish the days I spent with her in March when she came to visit me and my children in our home in South Africa. I am proud of the fact that apart from when she was on public display meeting President Mandela, we managed to contrive to stop the ever-present paparazzi from getting a single picture of her.

That meant a lot to her.

These are days I will always treasure. It was as if we'd been transported back to our childhood, when we spent such an enormous amount of time together, the two youngest in the family. Fundamentally she hadn't changed at all from the big sister who mothered me as a baby, fought with me at school and endured those long train journeys between our parents' homes with me at weekends. It is a tribute to her level-headedness and strength that despite the most bizarre life imaginable after her childhood, she remained intact, true to herself.

There is no doubt that she was looking for a new direction in her life at this time. She talked endlessly of getting away from England, mainly because of the treatment she received at the hands of the newspapers.

I don't think she ever understood why her genuinely good intentions were sneered at by the media, why there appeared to be a permanent quest on their behalf to bring her down. It is baffling. My own, and only, explanation is that genuine goodness is threatening to those at the opposite end of the moral spectrum.

It is a point to remember that of all the ironies about Diana, perhaps the greatest is this; that a girl given the name of the ancient goddess of hunting was, in the end, the most hunted person of the modern age.

She would want us today to pledge ourselves to protecting her beloved boys William and Harry from a similar fate. And I do this here, Diana, on your behalf. We will not allow them to suffer the anguish that used regularly to drive you to tearful despair.

Beyond that, on behalf of your mother and sisters, I pledge that we, your blood family, will do all we can to continue the imaginative and loving way in which you were steering these two exceptional young men, so that their souls are not simply immersed by duty and tradition but can sing openly as you planned.

We fully respect the heritage into which they have both been born, and will always respect and encourage them in their royal role. But we, like you, recognize the need for them to experience as many different aspects of life as possible, to arm them spiritually and emotionally for the years ahead. I know you would have expected nothing less from us.

William and Harry, we all care desperately for you today. We are all chewed up with sadness at the loss of a woman who wasn't even our mother. How great your suffering is we cannot even imagine.

I would like to end by thanking God for the small mercies he has shown us at this dreadful time; for taking Diana at her most beautiful and radiant and when she had so much joy in her private life.

Above all, we give thanks for the life of a woman I am so proud to be able to call my sister: the unique the complex, the extraordinary and irreplaceable Diana, whose beauty, both internal and external, will never be extinguished from our minds.

'Rise Up and Walk!'

Wangari Maathai

The Third Annual Nelson Mandela Lecture,
Johannesburg, South Africa (19 July 2004)

Wangari Maathai was a Kenyan author, professor, politician and environmental activist who became the first black African woman to win the Nobel Peace Prize (2004). The Green Belt Movement founded by her empowers Kenyan women to conserve the environment, fight deforestation, gain self-sustenance and improve their livelihoods.

In her empowering speech, Wangari Maathai encourages the several African leaders in attendance to work for the betterment of their people and become environmentally conscious and self-sufficient.

Your Excellencies, Presidents Nelson Mandela and Bill Clinton,
Your Grace the Archbishop Desmond Tutu,
Her Excellency Graca Machel
Ministers, Excellencies,
Distinguished guests,
Ladies and Gentlemen,

Allow me to thank the Nelson Mandela Foundation for inviting me to share these unforgettable days with South Africa. It is both a privilege and an honour to be in your midst and to give this year's Nelson Mandela Lecture.

This is a very special time when we are celebrating Madiba's birthday. Madiba, you are a source of great joy and pride for all of us in

Africa and indeed in the whole world. Thank you for your dedication and commitment for the cause of freedom and human dignity.

We thank God for the gift that is Nelson Mandela. We salute you Madiba, we love you and we shall remain forever grateful to you. It is a privilege to be here to say, Happy Birthday, and may you have many more.

I am very aware of the extraordinary speakers of previous Mandela lectures. Both President Bill Clinton and the Archbishop Desmond Tutu have set very high standards for these lectures. I am deeply honored to share this platform with them.

In the last few weeks the world and G8 leaders have focused on Africa. In Gleneagles, Scotland, G8 leaders were joined by African statesmen, among them Presidents Thabo Mbeki of South Africa, Olesegun Obasanjo of Nigeria, Benjamin Mkapa of Tanzania and Prime Minister Meles Zenawi of Ethiopia.

Leading up to the G8 meeting, another global campaign was picking up: Live8. Inspired by Geldof, Bono and other concerned artists around the world, the concerts were organised in support of Africa, attracting millions of ordinary citizens in industrialised countries. They went to enjoy the music but they also went to be informed and educated about Africa. They used that forum to express their support for Africa. The G8 leaders listened and watched as their citizens gathered to support the call to make dehumanising poverty unacceptable.

But even as I appreciated and was encouraged by the efforts at Gleneagles and around the world I had some concerns. This is because I knew that the G8 leaders had their own concerns and constraints. I also knew that they had some doubts about leadership and governance in Africa. They were therefore unlikely to, for example, cancel all the unpayable debts. Yet they knew that in some countries like Kenya, essential services are denied citizens so that debt obligations can be met. In other countries, the average income used to determine eligibility for debt cancellation is misleading. This is because of inequitable distribution of resources, which has created large disparities between the few very rich and many citizens who are very poor. When such countries are denied debt relief, it is the many poor people who are punished.

The G8 leaders had their reasons for their doubts. It was reported that some of these reasons included the fact that some African governments do not respect the rule of law and human rights, that some leaders are corrupt and often siphon the same money into personal accounts, that some governments spend funds inefficiently and excessively. It is important to realise, however, that those who may be guilty do not suffer; it is the poor who suffer.

Despite the challenges, there has been much progress in Africa. There are already good indications of good governance in many countries. In many others, civil society continues to grow with moral support from governments and the African Union. For example, the African Union is currently overseeing the formation of a civil society organ (ECOSOCC), to advise it on issues related to the African people and to ensure that they participate in the affairs of the Union. I have the honor of presiding over this process and I consider it an important window of opportunity.

Further, many countries in the region are resolving their conflicts and are working for peace and stability. For sure, much remains to be done. But we must appreciate and encourage those who are making bold decisions.

Nevertheless, as I stated earlier, it is the ordinary citizens who suffer when debts are not cancelled, when financial assistance is not forthcoming or when trade barriers are raised.

It is on their behalf that the African leaders traveled to Gleneagles to meet G8 leaders. It is on their behalf that the Live8 concerts were held. It is for them that the Jubilee 2000 campaign was carried out by global citizens. Yet many ordinary citizens in Africa had no idea that such discussions and concerts were taking place on their behalf.

I wonder how many consultations and concerts will be held before a sustainable solution is found not only by the G8 leaders but also by the African leadership and people. What will it take for a solution to be found?

I ask these questions because the poor people the world is concerned about come from Africa, which is one of the richest continents on the planet. It is endowed with a large number of men and women; it has a lot of sunshine, oil, precious stones, forests, water, wildlife, soil, land and agricultural products. So, why are her people so poor?

The problem is that many Africans lack knowledge, skills and tools to create wealth from their resources. They are unable to add value to their raw materials so that they can take processed goods into the local and international markets and negotiate better prices and better trade rules. Without that capacity, opportunities will continue to slip by or others will continue to take advantage of them without the benefits reaching the people in whose name these negotiations take place.

What can be done to prepare Africa so that she benefits from the concessions and opportunities that surely lie ahead?

During the last thirty years of working with the Green Belt Movement I saw the need to give our people values. The man whose birthday we celebrate today exemplifies these values. For example, the value of service for the common good. How shall we motivate our men and women in the region, willing to sacrifice and volunteer so that others may have it better? The values of commitment, persistence and patience, to stay with it until the goal is realised.

The love for the land and desire to protect it from desertification and other destructive processes. Perhaps it is due to lack of information and ignorance, or perhaps it is due to poverty, but we need people who love Africa so much that they want to protect her from destructive processes. Some that are threatening the entire continent include desertification due to deforestation, encroachment into forests for subsistence farming, overgrazing and loss of biodiversity and soil. Of particular importance for Africa and the world is the protection of the Congo Basin Forest Ecosystem.

These two values are important for African leaders, who should govern and serve for the benefit of the people, rather than themselves. Working at the grassroots level and with the poor people, it was depressing to see those in power fail to provide necessary services and protect the land. Instead they facilitated the exploitation of the people and their resources. Because I have experienced irresponsible governance in the course of my work for the environment, it is difficult to dismiss the reservations and concerns expressed by the G8 leaders

Another value we must espouse is the love and concern for the youth. One of the most devastating experiences at the grassroots level today is to see the youth wasting away because they are unemployed, even after they have completed secondary and tertiary education. Governments should prioritise the youth and their health. This should involve investments in technical education, HIV and AIDS prevention, treatment and care/support programs.

One of the constraints, even for the government, is that we have not invested enough in education and especially in technical education. Technical education would give citizens knowledge, skills and experience, which would make them competent, confident and competitive. Such personnel would create opportunities for entrepreneurship and wealth creation. Such investments in Asia have contributed significantly to the economic growth and alleviation of poverty in the region.

Without skills, people will always find themselves locked out of productive, rewarding economic activities that would give them a better share of their national wealth. They find themselves unemployed or underemployed and they are certainly underpaid. They may wish to secure a well-paid job, but if they do not have the skills and the tools, nobody will hire them. Consequently they will not be able to meet their needs for housing, healthcare, nutrition, and other family and personal needs. They get trapped in a vicious cycle of poverty and sometimes crime.

Besides these values Africa needs to prepare herself by deliberately working for peace and security. I believe much of the poverty in Africa has been fuelled by conflicts. In the course of my work I learnt that whether it is at the national or regional level, most conflicts between communities are over resources: who will access, control and utilise them; who will be included or excluded.

Often, those in power invent excuses to justify the exclusion and other injustices against those perceived to be weak and vulnerable. But when resources are scarce, so degraded that they can no longer sustain livelihoods, or when they are not equitably distributed, conflicts will invariably ensue.

Equitable distribution of resources cannot be effected unless there is democratic space, which respects the rule of law and human rights. Such democratic space gives citizens an enabling environment to be creative and productive. What is clear is that there is a close linkage between sustainable management of resources and equitable distribution of the same on the one hand and democratic governance and peace on the other. These are the pillars of any stable and secure state. Such a state has the enabling environment for development. People who are denied the three pillars eventually become angry and frustrated, and undermine peace and security in their neighborhoods and beyond.

For that reason, we need to manage our resources sustainably, accountably and responsibly. We need to share those resources equitably. Otherwise, we shall continue to invest in wars and conflicts, fighting crime and domestic instability, rather than promoting development and thereby eliminating poverty.

Over the past thirty years of work in Kenya I discovered something that is still not very clear to me. It is perhaps the most unrecognised problem in Africa today, especially at the grassroots level. It is the level of disempowerment of our people. Wherever it comes from, it manifests itself in the form of fear, lack of confidence, low self-esteem, apathy and lack of enthusiasm to take charge of one's life and destiny. To the disempowered, it seems much easier and acceptable to leave their lives completely in the hands of third parties, especially governments.

At the Green Belt Movement, to assist community members understand the need to take charge of their destiny and overcome apathy, we initiated education seminars to identify problems, their sources and solutions. This became a process of self-discovery and self-empowerment. It would take a long time but eventually participants believed in themselves and became more independent and self-reliant. They embraced some of these values mentioned above and developed a deep desire to better themselves and their immediate environments. Eventually they were even willing to work for the common resources like forests and public parks.

For Africa to benefit from the opportunities which come her way, she must empower her people. Education will help, peace and security are important, and sustainable management of resources is essential. But the people must be allowed to gain confidence, dignity and a sense of self-worth. Ultimately, they must also be empowered with knowledge, skills and tools to take action. This is why debt relief is very important. It allows governments additional resources to invest in initiatives that empower.

The phenomenon of disempowerment is very common and perhaps that is why it is not addressed. But I believe that it is one of the main reasons why so many people are unable to take advantage of the many opportunities available in Africa today. Such disempowerment and the triumph over it remind me of a story in the Bible that I love. (It is in Acts 3:1–10.) It's the story where Peter and John went to the temple for prayer. As they approached, they came across a beggar, who was crippled since birth. The beggar must have had all the characteristics of a disempowered person: poor, self-effacing, dejected, low self-esteem, no self-pride and no sense of well-being. He did not even dare to look up to the people from whom he was begging. He was too ashamed of his status. The Bible says that he bowed his head, hid his face and stretched his hand for alms.

Peter and John, upon seeing him in that dehumanised and humiliated state, said to him 'Look up'! That must have been a bit startling, because people did not usually talk to him. Peter went on, 'Silver and gold we do not have, but what we have we give to you.' And, taking him by the right hand Peter helped the lame man stand up saying, 'In the name of Jesus Christ of Nazareth, Rise up and walk!'

And much to his surprise, he felt his limbs get strong and he rose up and walked forward with confidence and pride. The Bible says he went with Peter and John into the temple 'jumping and praising God.' He was an empowered man: no longer a beggar, no longer dehumanised. Now he could go and take care of himself with dignity, self-respect and confidence.

There must have been many worshippers who had given him a few coins many times but never thought of doing anything different. But Peter and John reacted differently and decided to empower him, to give him wholeness. They encouraged him to believe in himself and walk with them into the temple.

Friends and leaders of Africa should be like Peter and John. They should strive to empower Africa and not only give her alms.

African governments should be responsible and accountable to their people, lifting them from ignorance, diseases and poverty, which cripple them.

In closing, we must remember that Peter and John called on the beggar to rise up and walk. It was not Peter and John who had to do the rising and the walking. It was the beggar. On his part, the beggar made a choice to respond to the call. He could have preferred to stay put and continue to beg the rich worshippers. But he decided to respond to an opportunity which presented itself, he was ready for it and his life was changed for the better.

With African leaders like those here today, President Nelson Mandela, Archbishop Desmond Tutu and many friends like President Bill Clinton we have the 'Peters' and 'Johns' we need. They call on all of us to 'Rise up and walk.' Walk away from ignorance, inertia, apathy and fatalism. Walk towards the temple of economic and political freedom. An Africa free of dehumanising poverty.

There are simple actions we can take. Start by planting ten trees we each need to absorb the carbon dioxide we exhale. Practice the 3R campaign (reduce, re-use, repair and re-use, which is mottainai in Japanese), get involved in local initiatives and volunteer your time for services in your community. Governments should prioritise technical schools and give people knowledge and skills for self-employment.

Madiba, I know this is the dream you have for Africa. An Africa free of poverty. An Africa with economic and political freedom. An empowered Africa.

So my fellow Africans. Let's heed the call of Madiba: 'Rise Up and Walk!' Thank you.

'This Is Water'

David Foster Wallace

Commencement Speech at Kenyon College (2005)

David Foster Wallace was an American author and professor best-known for his novel *Infinite Jest* (1996), which was ranked amongst the 100 best English-language novels published between 1923-2005 by *Time magazine*. He was an influential writer and wrote witty journalistic pieces, short stories and novels as well as other works of non-fiction.

Wallace's famous commencement speech at Kenyon College in 2005 is full of wisdom, through which he urges the students to live a meaningful life. The speech was later converted into a book titled *This Is Water: Some Thoughts, Delivered on a Significant Occasion, about Living a Compassionate Life.*

'Greetings parents and congratulations to Kenyon's graduating class of 2005. There are these two young fish swimming along and they happen to meet an older fish swimming the other way, who nods at them and says 'Morning, boys. How's the water?' And the two young fish swim on for a bit, and then eventually one of them looks over at the other and goes 'What the hell is water?'

This is a standard requirement of US commencement speeches, the deployment of didactic little parable-ish stories. The story thing turns out to be one of the better, less bullshitty conventions of the genre, but if you're worried that I plan to present myself here as the wise, older fish explaining what water is to you younger fish, please don't be. I am not the wise old fish. The point of the fish story is merely that the most obvious, important realities are often the ones that are hardest to see and talk about. Stated as an English sentence, of course, this is just a banal platitude, but the fact is that in the day to day trenches of adult existence, banal platitudes can have a life or death importance, or so I wish to suggest to you on this dry and lovely morning.

Of course the main requirement of speeches like this is that I'm supposed to talk about your liberal arts education's meaning, to try to explain why the degree you are about to receive has actual human value instead of just a material payoff. So let's talk about the single most pervasive cliché in the commencement speech genre, which is that a liberal arts education is not so much about filling you up with knowledge as it is about 'teaching you how to think.' If you're like me as a student, you've never liked hearing this, and you tend to feel a bit insulted by the claim that you needed anybody to teach you how to think, since the fact that you even got admitted to a college this good seems like proof that you already know how to think. But I'm going to posit to you that the liberal arts cliché turns out not to be insulting at all, because the really significant education in thinking that we're supposed to get in a place like this isn't really about the capacity to think, but rather about the choice of what to think about. If your total freedom of choice regarding what to think about seems too obvious to waste time discussing, I'd ask you to think about fish and water, and to bracket for just a few minutes your scepticism about the value of the totally obvious.

Here's another didactic little story. There are these two guys sitting together in a bar in the remote Alaskan wilderness. One of the guys is religious, the other is an atheist, and the two are arguing about the existence of God with that special intensity that comes after about the fourth beer. And the atheist says: 'Look, it's not like I don't have actual reasons for not believing in God. It's not like I haven't ever experimented with the whole God and prayer thing. Just last month I got caught away from the camp in that terrible blizzard, and I was totally lost and I couldn't see a thing, and it was 50 below, and so I tried it: I fell to my knees in the snow and cried out 'Oh, God, if there is a God, I'm lost in this blizzard, and I'm gonna die if you don't help me." And now, in the bar, the religious guy looks at the atheist all puzzled. 'Well then you must believe now,' he says, 'After all, here you are, alive.' The atheist just rolls his eyes. 'No, man, all that was a couple Eskimos happened to come wandering by and showed me the way back to camp.'

It's easy to run this story through kind of a standard liberal arts analysis: the exact same experience can mean two totally different things to two different people, given those people's two different belief templates and two different ways of constructing meaning from experience. Because we prize tolerance and diversity of belief, nowhere in our liberal arts analysis do we want to claim that one guy's interpretation is true and the other guy's is false or bad. Which is fine, except we also never end up talking about just where these individual templates and beliefs come from. Meaning, where they come from INSIDE the two guys. As if a person's most basic orientation toward the world, and the meaning of his experience were somehow just hard-wired, like height or shoe-size; or automatically absorbed from the culture, like language. As if how we construct meaning were not actually a matter of personal, intentional choice. Plus, there's the whole matter of arrogance. The nonreligious guy is so totally certain in his dismissal of the possibility that the passing Eskimos had anything to do with his prayer for help. True, there are plenty of religious people who seem arrogant and certain of their own interpretations, too. They're probably even more repulsive than atheists, at least to most of us. But religious dogmatists' problem is exactly the same as the story's unbeliever: blind certainty, a close-mindedness that amounts to an imprisonment so total that the prisoner doesn't even know he's locked up.

The point here is that I think this is one part of what teaching me how to think is really supposed to mean. To be just a little less arrogant. To have just a little critical awareness about myself and my certainties. Because a huge percentage of the stuff that I tend to be automatically certain of is, it turns out, totally wrong and deluded. I have learned this the hard way, as I predict you graduates will, too.

Here is just one example of the total wrongness of something I tend to be automatically sure of: everything in my own immediate experience supports my deep belief that I am the absolute centre of the universe; the realest, most vivid and important person in existence. We rarely think about this sort of natural, basic self-centredness because it's so socially repulsive. But it's pretty much the same for all of us. It is our default setting, hard-wired into our boards at birth. Think about it: there is no experience you have had that you are not the absolute centre of. The world as you experience it is there in front of YOU or behind YOU, to the left or right of YOU, on YOUR TV or YOUR monitor. And so on. Other people's thoughts and feelings have to be communicated to you somehow, but your own are so immediate, urgent, real.

Please don't worry that I'm getting ready to lecture you about compassion or other-directedness or all the so-called virtues. This is not a matter of virtue. It's a matter of my choosing to do the work of somehow altering or getting free of my natural, hard-wired default setting which is to be deeply and literally self-centered and to see and interpret everything through this lens of self. People who can adjust their natural default setting this way are often described as being 'well-adjusted', which I suggest to you is not an accidental term.

Given the triumphant academic setting here, an obvious question is how much of this work of adjusting our default setting involves actual knowledge or intellect. This question gets very tricky. Probably the most dangerous thing about an academic education—least in my own case—is that it enables my tendency to over-intellectualise stuff, to get lost in abstract argument inside my head, instead of simply paying attention to what is going on right in front of me, paying attention to what is going on inside me.

As I'm sure you guys know by now, it is extremely difficult to stay alert and attentive, instead of getting hypnotised by the constant monologue inside your own head (may be happening right now). Twenty years after my own graduation, I have come gradually to understand that the liberal arts cliché about teaching you how to think is actually shorthand for a much deeper, more serious idea: learning how to think really means learning how to exercise some control over how and what you think. It means being conscious and aware enough to choose what you pay attention to and to choose how you construct meaning from experience. Because if you cannot exercise this kind of choice in adult life, you will be totally hosed.

Think of the old cliché about 'the mind being an excellent servant but a terrible master.'

This, like many clichés, so lame and unexciting on the surface, actually expresses a great and terrible truth. It is not the least bit coincidental that adults who commit suicide with firearms almost always shoot themselves in: the head. They shoot the terrible master. And the truth is that most of these suicides are actually dead long before they pull the trigger.

And I submit that this is what the real, no bullshit value of your liberal arts education is supposed to be about: how to keep from going through your comfortable, prosperous, respectable adult life dead, unconscious, a slave to your head and to your natural default setting of being uniquely, completely, imperially alone day in and day out. That may sound like hyperbole, or abstract nonsense. Let's get concrete. The plain fact is that you graduating seniors do not yet have any clue what 'day in day out' really means. There happen to be whole, large parts of adult American life that nobody talks about in commencement speeches. One such part involves boredom, routine and petty frustration. The parents and older folks here will know all too well what I'm talking about.

By way of example, let's say it's an average adult day, and you get up in the morning, go to your challenging, white-collar, college-graduate job, and you work hard for eight or 10 hours, and at the end of the day you're tired and somewhat stressed and all you want is to go home and have a good supper and maybe unwind for an hour, and then hit the sack early because, of course, you have to get up the next day and do it all again. But then you remember there's no food at home. You haven't had time to shop this week because of your challenging job, and so now after work you have to get in your car and drive to the supermarket. It's the end of the work day and the traffic is apt to be: very bad. So getting to the store takes way longer than it should, and when you finally get there, the supermarket is very crowded, because of course it's the time of day when all the other people with jobs also try to squeeze in some grocery shopping. And the store is hideously lit and infused with soul-killing muzak or corporate pop and it's pretty much the last place you want to be but you can't just get in and quickly out; you have to wander all over the huge, over-lit store's confusing aisles to find the stuff you want and you have to manoeuvre your junky cart through all these other tired, hurried people with carts (et cetera, et cetera, cutting stuff out because this is a long ceremony) and eventually you get all your supper supplies, except now it turns out there aren't enough check-out lanes open even though it's the end-of-the-day rush. So the checkout line is incredibly long, which is stupid and infuriating. But you can't take your frustration out on the frantic lady working the register, who is overworked at a job whose daily tedium and meaninglessness surpasses the imagination of any of us here at a prestigious college.

But anyway, you finally get to the checkout line's front, and you pay for your food, and you get told to 'Have a nice day' in a voice that is the absolute voice of death. Then you have to take your creepy, flimsy, plastic bags of groceries in your cart with the one crazy wheel that pulls maddeningly to the left, all the way out through the crowded, bumpy, littery parking lot, and then you have to drive all the way home through slow, heavy, SUV-intensive, rush-hour traffic, et cetera et cetera.

Everyone here has done this, of course. But it hasn't yet been part of you graduates' actual life routine, day after week after month after year.

But it will be. And many more dreary, annoying, seemingly meaningless routines besides. But that is not the point. The point is that petty, frustrating crap like this is exactly where the work of choosing is gonna come in. Because the traffic jams and crowded aisles and long checkout lines give me time to think, and if I don't make a conscious decision about how to think and what to pay attention to, I'm gonna be pissed and miserable every time I have to shop. Because my natural default setting is the certainty that situations like this are really all about me. About MY hungriness and MY fatigue and MY desire to just get home, and it's going to seem for all the world like everybody else is just in my way. And who are all these people in my way? And look at how repulsive most of them are, and how stupid and cow-like and dead-eyed and nonhuman they seem in the checkout line, or at how annoying and rude it is that people are talking loudly on cell phones in the middle of the line. And look at how deeply and personally unfair this is.

Or, of course, if I'm in a more socially conscious liberal arts form of my default setting, I can spend time in the end-of-the-day traffic being disgusted about all the huge, stupid, lane-blocking SUV's and Hummers and V-12 pickup trucks, burning their wasteful, selfish, 40-gallon tanks of gas, and I can dwell on the fact that the patriotic or religious bumper-stickers always seem to be on the biggest, most disgustingly selfish vehicles, driven by the ugliest—this is an example of how NOT to think, though—most disgustingly selfish vehicles, driven by the ugliest, most inconsiderate and aggressive drivers. And I can think about how our children's children will despise us for wasting all the future's fuel, and probably screwing up the climate, and how spoiled and stupid and selfish and disgusting we all are, and how modern consumer society just sucks, and so forth and so on.

You get the idea.

If I choose to think this way in a store and on the freeway, fine. Lots of us do. Except thinking this way tends to be so easy and automatic that it doesn't have to be a choice. It is my natural default setting. It's the automatic way that I experience the boring, frustrating, crowded parts of adult life when I'm operating on the automatic, unconscious belief that I am the centre of the world, and that my immediate needs and feelings are what should determine the world's priorities.

The thing is that, of course, there are totally different ways to think about these kinds of situations. In this traffic, all these vehicles stopped and idling in my way, it's not impossible that some of these people in SUV's have been in horrible auto accidents in the past, and now find driving so terrifying that their therapist has all but ordered them to get a huge, heavy SUV so they can feel safe enough to drive. Or that the Hummer that just cut me off is maybe being driven by a father whose little child is hurt or sick in the seat next to him, and he's trying to get this kid to the hospital, and he's in a bigger, more legitimate hurry than I am: it is actually I who am in HIS way.

Or I can choose to force myself to consider the likelihood that everyone else in the supermarket's checkout line is just as bored and frustrated as I am, and that some of these people probably have harder, more tedious and painful lives than I do.

Again, please don't think that I'm giving you moral advice, or that I'm saying you are supposed to think this way, or that anyone expects you to just automatically do it. Because it's hard. It takes will and effort, and if you are like me, some days you won't be able to do it, or you just flat out won't want to.

But most days, if you're aware enough to give yourself a choice, you can choose to look differently at this fat, dead-eyed, over-made-up lady who just screamed at her kid in the checkout line. Maybe she's not usually like this. Maybe she's been up three straight nights holding the hand of a husband who is dying of bone cancer. Or maybe this very lady is the low-wage clerk at the motor vehicle department, who just yesterday helped your spouse resolve a horrific, infuriating, red-tape problem through some small act of bureaucratic kindness. Of course, none of this is likely, but it's also not impossible. It just depends what you want to consider. If you're automatically sure that you know what reality is, and you are operating on your default setting, then you, like me, probably won't consider possibilities that aren't annoying and miserable. But if you really learn how to pay attention, then you will know there are other options. It will actually be within your power to experience a crowded, hot, slow, consumer-hell type situation as not only meaningful, but sacred, on fire with the same force that made the stars: love, fellowship, the mystical oneness of all things deep down.

Not that that mystical stuff is necessarily true. The only thing that's capital-T True is that you get to decide how you're gonna try to see it.

This, I submit, is the freedom of a real education, of learning how to be well-adjusted. You get to consciously decide what has meaning and what doesn't. You get to decide what to worship.

Because here's something else that's weird but true: in the day-to-day trenches of adult life, there is actually no such thing as atheism. There is no such thing as not worshipping. Everybody worships. The only choice we get is what to worship. And the compelling reason for maybe choosing some sort of god or spiritual-type thing to worship–be it JC or Allah, be it YHWH or the Wiccan Mother

Goddess, or the Four Noble Truths, or some inviolable set of ethical principles—is that pretty much anything else you worship will eat you alive. If you worship money and things, if they are where you tap real meaning in life, then you will never have enough, never feel you have enough. It's the truth. Worship your body and beauty and sexual allure and you will always feel ugly. And when time and age start showing, you will die a million deaths before they finally grieve you. On one level, we all know this stuff already. It's been codified as myths, proverbs, clichés, epigrams, parables; the skeleton of every great story. The whole trick is keeping the truth up front in daily consciousness.

Worship power, you will end up feeling weak and afraid, and you will need ever more power over others to numb you to your own fear. Worship your intellect, being seen as smart, you will end up feeling stupid, a fraud, always on the verge of being found out. But the insidious thing about these forms of worship is not that they're evil or sinful, it's that they're unconscious. They are default settings.

They're the kind of worship you just gradually slip into, day after day, getting more and more selective about what you see and how you measure value without ever being fully aware that that's what you're doing.

And the so-called real world will not discourage you from operating on your default settings, because the so-called real world of men and money and power hums merrily along in a pool of fear and anger and frustration and craving and worship of self. Our own present culture has harnessed these forces in ways that have yielded extraordinary wealth and comfort and personal freedom. The freedom all to be lords of our tiny skull-sized kingdoms, alone at the centre of all creation. This kind of freedom has much to recommend it. But of course there are all different kinds of freedom, and the kind that is most precious you will not hear much talk about much in the great outside world of wanting and achieving... The really important kind of freedom involves attention and awareness and discipline, and being able truly to care about other people and to sacrifice for them over and over in myriad petty, unsexy ways every day.

That is real freedom. That is being educated, and understanding how to think. The alternative is unconsciousness, the default setting, the rat race, the constant gnawing sense of having had, and lost, some infinite thing.

I know that this stuff probably doesn't sound fun and breezy or grandly inspirational the way a commencement speech is supposed to sound. What it is, as far as I can see, is the capital-T Truth, with a whole lot of rhetorical niceties stripped away. You are, of course, free to think of it whatever you wish. But please don't just dismiss it as just some finger-wagging Dr Laura sermon. None of this stuff is really about morality or religion or dogma or big fancy questions of life after death.

The capital-T Truth is about life BEFORE death.

It is about the real value of a real education, which has almost nothing to do with knowledge, and everything to do with simple awareness; awareness of what is so real and essential, so hidden in plain sight all around us, all the time, that we have to keep reminding ourselves over and over:

'This is water.'

'This is water.'

It is unimaginably hard to do this, to stay conscious and alive in the adult world day in and day out. Which means yet another grand cliché turns out to be true: your education really IS the job of a lifetime. And it commences: now.

I wish you way more than luck.

'You've Got to Find What You Love'

Steve Jobs

Stanford University Commencement Speech (12 June 2005)

Steve Jobs was an American business executive, computer programmer and entrepreneur who was a co-founder of Apple Inc., Founder of NeXT and chairman and shareholder of Pixar. He is widely recognised as the pioneer of the microcomputer revolution along with his Apple co-founder Steve Wozniak.

In his powerful commencement address at Stanford University, Jobs urged the students to find meaning in their lives and strive hard to achieve their goals.

I am honored to be with you today at your commencement from one of the finest universities in the world. I never graduated from college. Truth be told, this is the closest I've ever gotten to a college graduation. Today I want to tell you three stories from my life. That's it. No big deal. Just three stories.

The first story is about connecting the dots.

I dropped out of Reed College after the first 6 months, but then stayed around as a drop-in for another 18 months or so before I really quit. So why did I drop out?

It started before I was born. My biological mother was a young, unwed college graduate student, and she decided to put me up for adoption. She felt very strongly that I should be adopted by college graduates, so everything was all set for me to be adopted at birth by a lawyer and his wife. Except that when I popped out they decided at the last minute that they really wanted a girl. So my parents, who were on a waiting list, got a call in the middle of the night asking: 'We have an unexpected baby boy; do you want him?' They said: 'Of course.' My biological mother later found out that my mother had never graduated from college and that my father had never graduated from high school. She refused to sign the final adoption papers. She only relented a few months later when my parents promised that I would someday go to college.

And 17 years later I did go to college. But I naively chose a college that was almost as expensive as Stanford, and all of my working-class parents' savings were being spent on my college tuition. After six months, I couldn't see the value in it. I had no idea what I wanted to do with my life and no idea how college was going to help me figure it out. And here I was spending all of the money my parents had saved their entire life. So I decided to drop out and trust that it would all work out OK. It was pretty scary at the time, but looking back it was one of the best decisions I ever made. The minute I dropped out I could stop taking the required classes that didn't interest me, and begin dropping in on the ones that looked interesting.

It wasn't all romantic. I didn't have a dorm room, so I slept on the floor in friends' rooms, I returned coke bottles for the 5¢ deposits to buy food with, and I would walk the 7 miles across town every Sunday night to get one good meal a week at the Hare Krishna temple. I loved it. And much of what I stumbled into by following my curiosity and intuition turned out to be priceless later on. Let me give you one example:

Reed College at that time offered perhaps the best calligraphy instruction in the country. Throughout the campus every poster, every label on every drawer, was beautifully hand calligraphed. Because I had dropped out and didn't have to take the normal classes, I decided to take a calligraphy class to learn how to do this. I learned about serif and sans serif typefaces, about varying the amount of space between different letter combinations, about what makes great typography great. It was beautiful, historical, artistically subtle in a way that science can't capture, and I found it fascinating.

None of this had even a hope of any practical application in my life. But 10 years later, when we were designing the first Macintosh computer, it all came back to me. And we designed it all into the Mac. It was the first computer with beautiful typography. If I had never dropped in on that single course in college, the Mac would have never had multiple typefaces or proportionally spaced fonts. And since Windows just copied the Mac, it's likely that no personal computer would have them. If I had never dropped out, I would have never dropped in on this calligraphy class, and personal computers might not have the wonderful typography that they do. Of course it was impossible to connect the dots looking forward when I was in college. But it was very, very clear looking backwards 10 years later.

Again, you can't connect the dots looking forward; you can only connect them looking backwards. So you have to trust that the dots will somehow connect in your future. You have to trust in something—your gut, destiny, life, karma, whatever. This approach has never let me down, and it has made all the difference in my life.

My second story is about love and loss.

I was lucky—I found what I loved to do early in life. Woz and I started Apple in my parents' garage when I was 20. We worked hard, and in 10 years Apple had grown from just the two of us in a garage into a $2 billion company with over 4000 employees. We had just released our finest creation—the Macintosh—a year earlier, and I had just turned 30. And then I got fired. How can you get fired from a company you started? Well, as Apple grew we hired someone who I thought was very talented to run the company with me, and for the first year or so things went well. But then our visions of the future began to diverge and eventually we had a falling out. When we did, our Board of Directors sided with him. So at 30 I was out. And very publicly out. What had been the focus of my entire adult life was gone, and it was devastating.

I really didn't know what to do for a few months. I felt that I had let the previous generation of entrepreneurs down—that I had dropped the baton as it was being passed to me. I met with David Packard and Bob Noyce and tried to apologize for screwing up so badly. I was a very public failure, and I even thought about running away from the valley. But something slowly began to dawn on me—AZI still loved what I did. The turn of events at Apple had not changed that one bit. I had been rejected, but I was still in love. And so I decided to start over.

I didn't see it then, but it turned out that getting fired from Apple was the best thing that could have ever happened to me. The heaviness of being successful was replaced by the lightness of being a beginner again, less sure about everything. It freed me to enter one of the most creative periods of my life.

During the next five years, I started a company named NeXT, another company named Pixar, and fell in love with an amazing woman who would become my wife. Pixar went on to create the world's first computer animated feature film, *Toy Story*, and is now the most successful animation studio in the world. In a remarkable turn of events, Apple bought NeXT, I returned to Apple, and the technology we developed at NeXT is at the heart of Apple's current renaissance. And Laurene and I have a wonderful family together.

I'm pretty sure none of this would have happened if I hadn't been fired from Apple. It was awful tasting medicine, but I guess the patient needed it. Sometimes life hits you in the head with a brick. Don't lose faith. I'm convinced that the only thing that kept me going was that I loved what I did. You've got to find what you love. And that is as true for your work as it is for your lovers. Your work is going to fill a large part of your life, and the only way to be truly satisfied is to do what you believe is great work. And the only way to do great work is to love what you do. If you haven't found it yet, keep looking. Don't settle. As with all matters of the heart, you'll know when you find it. And, like any great relationship, it just gets better and better as the years roll on. So keep looking until you find it. Don't settle.

My third story is about death

When I was 17, I read a quote that went something like: 'If you live each day as if it was your last, someday you'll most certainly be right.' It made an impression on me, and since then, for the past 33 years, I have looked in the mirror every morning and asked myself: 'If today were the last day of my life, would I want to do what I am about to do today?' And whenever the answer has been 'No' for too many days in a row, I know I need to change something.

Remembering that I'll be dead soon is the most important tool I've ever encountered to help me make the big choices in life. Because almost everything—all external expectations, all pride, all fear of embarrassment or failure—these things just fall away in the face of death, leaving only what is truly important. Remembering that you are going to die is the best way I know to avoid the trap of thinking you have something to lose. You are already naked. There is no reason not to follow your heart.

About a year ago I was diagnosed with cancer. I had a scan at 7:30 in the morning, and it clearly showed a tumor on my pancreas. I didn't even know what a pancreas was. The doctors told me this was almost certainly a type of cancer that is incurable, and that I should expect to live no longer than three to six months. My doctor advised me to go home and get my affairs in order, which is doctor's code for prepare to die. It means to try to tell your kids everything you thought you'd have the next 10 years to tell them in just a few months. It means to make sure everything is buttoned up so that it will be as easy as possible for your family. It means to say your goodbyes.

I lived with that diagnosis all day. Later that evening I had a biopsy, where they stuck an endoscope down my throat, through my stomach and into my intestines, put a needle into my pancreas and got a few cells from the tumor. I was sedated, but my wife, who was there, told me that when they viewed the cells under a microscope the doctors started crying because it turned out to be a very rare form of pancreatic cancer that is curable with surgery. I had the surgery and I'm fine now.

This was the closest I've been to facing death, and I hope it's the closest I get for a few more decades. Having lived through it, I can now say this to you with a bit more certainty than when death was a useful but purely intellectual concept:

No one wants to die. Even people who want to go to heaven don't want to die to get there. And yet death is the destination we all share. No one has ever escaped it. And that is as it should be, because Death is very likely the single best invention of Life. It is

Life's change agent. It clears out the old to make way for the new. Right now the new is you, but someday not too long from now, you will gradually become the old and be cleared away. Sorry to be so dramatic, but it is quite true.

Your time is limited, so don't waste it living someone else's life. Don't be trapped by dogma—which is living with the results of other people's thinking. Don't let the noise of others' opinions drown out your own inner voice. And most important, have the courage to follow your heart and intuition. They somehow already know what you truly want to become. Everything else is secondary.

When I was young, there was an amazing publication called *The Whole Earth Catalog*, which was one of the bibles of my generation. It was created by a fellow named Stewart Brand not far from here in Menlo Park, and he brought it to life with his poetic touch. This was in the late 1960's, before personal computers and desktop publishing, so it was all made with typewriters, scissors, and polaroid cameras. It was sort of like Google in paperback form, 35 years before Google came along: it was idealistic, and overflowing with neat tools and great notions.

Stewart and his team put out several issues of *The Whole Earth Catalog*, and then when it had run its course, they put out a final issue. It was the mid-1970s, and I was your age. On the back cover of their final issue was a photograph of an early morning country road, the kind you might find yourself hitchhiking on if you were so adventurous. Beneath it were the words: 'Stay Hungry. Stay Foolish.' It was their farewell message as they signed off. Stay Hungry. Stay Foolish. And I have always wished that for myself. And now, as you graduate to begin anew, I wish that for you.

Stay Hungry. Stay Foolish.

Thank you all very much.

Speech on World Peace

Dr. A.P.J. Abdul Kalam

European Union (25 April 2007)

Dr. A.P.J. Abdul Kalam was an Indian scientist, author and politician who served as the 11th President of India from 2002 to 2007. A leading scientist, he played an important role in India's missile and nuclear weapons programmes, which earned him the nickname 'Missile Man' of India. For his efforts in the fields of science and technology, Kalam was awarded two of the country's highest honours, the Padma Vibhushan (1990) and the Bharat Ratna (1997).

This is one of the most famous speeches by Kalam, in which he stresses on the importance of world peace and harmony and spreads the message of unity in diversity, which is central to the Indian spirit.

Friends, my greetings to all of you. I would particularly like to greet Mr Hans-Gert Pöttering, Mr Harald Rømer, Mr Klaus Welle and Mr Ciril Stokelj.

Good afternoon, Ladies and Gentlemen.

I am delighted to be with the honourable Members of the European Parliament on the occasion of the Golden Jubilee year of the European Union. I was wondering what thoughts I could share with you. As you are aware, as a democratic nation India has experience in providing leadership to over one billion people with multi-language, multicultural and multi-religious systems. I wish to share this experience with you, friends.

European civilisation has a unique place in human history. Its people were valiantly engaged in the adventure of exploring the Planet Earth, resulting in the discovery of many ideas and systems.

Europe has seen the birth of pioneers in science, leading to the development of technologies. Europe was the theatre of conflicts among the nations lasting hundreds of years, including the two World Wars. Now, with this backdrop and these dynamics, you have established the European Union with a vision of peace and prosperity for the entire region. The European Union has become an example for connectivity among nations, probably with no possibility of war, leading to lasting regional peace.

Before I started out on my journey to Europe, I was thinking: why are Europe and India unique and natural partners? Do we share a common history and heritage and, possibly in the future, a common destiny? This was the question. I was astonished by what I found: the depth and vitality of our inter-connectedness, through language, culture, ancient beliefs, ideologies and the movement of people, have stood the test of time. This has matured into a very strong bond through sustained trade and intellectually satisfying collaboration in many areas of science and technology. For example, on 23 April 2007, the Italian scientific satellite Agile was launched by the Indian Polar Satellite Launch Vehicle rocket system into a very precise orbit. Scientists from India and Europe are very excited. Let us congratulate them.

India is a country that has learnt over the years to evolve and maintain a unique unity amid diversity. Similarly, the European Union's greatest contribution has been to demonstrate to the world that it is possible to build a strong union of nations without compromising national identities. It has become an inspirational model and an example to emulate for every region in the world. The European Union and India support a social form of economic development and we encourage a model of growth with equity. Both are conscious of the need for growth to respect the environment and to make it sustainable for future generations. With India's and the European Union's centuries of valuable experience, we can develop a doctrine of global cooperation based on the foundation of regional collaboration and core competencies of our nations.

The European Union and India radiate a message to the world that regional cooperation and interregional collaboration will lead to a win-win situation for all, so that we can have a politically and socio-economically emergent civilisation. Our contribution will be successful if, before the 21st century is over, we are able to make all regions transform into happy unions leading to the emergence of a world of unions. In this context, I am reminded of the dream of an Indian poet who said 3000 years ago in the Tamil classic: ,which means, 'I am a world citizen. Every citizen is my own kith and kin'. He said that 3000 years ago.

Against this backdrop, I have brought from India a message to launch three important Indo-European tasks that could contribute to global peace and prosperity. I propose these missions on the basis of India's experience and the European Union's dynamics.

The first task is the evolution of an enlightened society, in which citizens have a system of values, leading to a prosperous and peaceful world.

The second idea is creating energy independence. Normally people talk about energy security. I am talking about energy independence: a three-dimensional approach to energy choice that aims to achieve a clean world.

The third aim is a World Knowledge Platform to bring together the core skills of the European Union and India in certain areas in order to provide solutions to critical issues like water, healthcare and capacity-building.

When nations join together to build a cohesive society, it is necessary to ensure that the benefits of development encompass all sections of society. Worldwide poverty, illiteracy, unemployment and deprivation are driving forward the forces of anger and violence. These forces are linked to some earlier real or perceived historical enmities, tyrannies, injustice, inequalities, ethnic issues and religious fundamentalism that are flowing into an outburst of extremism worldwide. Both India and the European Union have witnessed and are witnessing the unsavoury acts of certain misguided sections of society. Together we must address the root causes of such phenomena in order to find lasting ways to promote peace. How do we do that?

We need a carrier of eternal goodness and wholesomeness in human conduct, which is called 'righteousness'. As we say in India:

'Where there is righteousness in the heart
There is beauty in the character.
When there is beauty in the character,
There is harmony in the home.
When there is harmony in the home,
There is order in the nation.
When there is order in the nation,
There is peace in the world.'

Honourable Members, this is true for the whole world. When we need peace in the world, we need order in the nation. We need harmony in the home. Whether in Europe, India or in any part of the world the origin is righteousness in the heart. How do we instil righteousness in the heart of every citizen of the world? This is my area of specialisation and I would like to talk to you about it.

First, I wish to discuss the evolution of an enlightened society. With this spirit of righteousness in the heart, I would like to present to this important gathering a methodology for developing a happy, prosperous and peaceful society in our world, which I call 'Evolution of Enlightened society'. I have shared these thoughts with many intellectuals in national and international circles. We need to create an enlightened society with three components: 1) education with a value system; 2) religion transforming into spirituality; and 3) economic development for societal transformation.

Beginning with the first component, we have seen that the seeds of peace in the world have their origin in the righteousness in the heart of every individual. Such righteous citizens lead to the emergence of an enlightened society. Education with a value system has to be designed so that the righteousness in the heart is developed in young minds. That should be the mission of education. The prime learning environment is five to seventeen years of age. That reminds me of what an ancient Greek teacher said a few thousand years ago: 'Give me a child for seven years; afterwards, let God or the devil take the child. They cannot change my child'.

This shows the power of great teachers and what they can inculcate in young minds. Parents and teachers must instill moral leadership in children. It requires the ability to have insight into the uniqueness and universality of human consciousness. True education is the acquisition of enlightened feelings and enlightened powers to understand daily events and to understand the permanent truth linking man to his environment, human and planetary.

I remember the lectures given when I was a student a long time ago – nearly 57 years ago – at the Jesuit institution of St Joseph's College in Tiruchirappalli in southern India by the college's highest authority, the Reverend Father Rector Kalathil. Every Monday, the Reverend Father would take an hour-long class. He used to talk about good human beings present and past and about what makes a good human being. In this class, he used to give lectures on people such as Buddha, Confucius, St Augustine, Caliph Omar, Mahatma Gandhi, Einstein, and Abraham Lincoln and to tell moral stories related to our civilisational heritage. In the moral science class, Father Kalathil used to highlight the best aspect of how these great people had evolved as good human beings through parental care, teaching and the companionship of great books. Even though these lessons were given to me in 1950 during my college days, they inspire me even today.

It is essential that in schools and colleges in every nation, important teachers at the institution give hour-long weekly lectures on civilisational heritage and the derived value system. This may be called a Moral Science class and will teach young minds to love their country and other human beings and to elevate them to higher planes. I have suggested this methodology to education experts in my country. The European Union may like to consider developing a system that would enable a student to learn these fundamental lessons for the benefit of all.

Let me turn to the issue of transforming religion into spiritual force. Many in the world believe it is a difficult task, but I disagree. I would like to share an experience that convinced me that it is possible for religion to be transformed into a spiritual force.

How do we do that? As you all know, religion has two components: theology and spirituality. Even though theology is unique to every religion, the spiritual component spreads the value to be absorbed by human beings in order to promote a good life and the welfare of society in the pursuit of material life. I witnessed the coming together of religion and science in a major task.

In the early 1960s, the founder of the Indian Space Research Programme, Professor Vikram Sarabhai, and his team had located the most technically suitable place for space research after considering many alternatives. The town of Thumba in Kerala in southern India was selected for space research as it was near the magnetic equator. This made it ideally suited to ionospheric and electrojet research in the upper atmosphere. I was fortunate to work with Professor Vikram Sarabhai for about eight years.

The major challenge for Vikram Sarabhai was to locate the site in a specific area. As was usual, Professor Sarabhai approached the Kerala Government administrators first. After seeing the land and the sea coast, he was told that thousands of fishermen lived there and that the place had an ancient church, the St Mary Magdalene Church, a Bishop's House and a school. It would be very difficult, therefore, to allocate this land and the administration was willing to provide land in an alternative area. Similarly, the political authorities also believed that it would be a difficult situation owing to the existence of important institutions and concern for people who were to be relocated. However, the Professor was very determined.

It was suggested that he should approach the only person who could advise and help. That was the Bishop, Father Peter Bernard Pereira. Professor Sarabhai, approached the Bishop one Saturday evening. I still remember their meeting, which proved to be historic. Many of us witnessed the event. Father Pereira exclaimed, 'Oh Vikram, you are asking for my children's home, the fishermen's home, my home, the Bishop's House, and God's home, the church. How is it possible?'. Both had a special quality: they could smile even in difficult situations. Father Pereira asked Professor Sarabhai to come to church on Sunday morning at 9 a.m. and he turned up on Sunday with his team. Prayers were taking place with a reading from the Bible by Father Pereira. After the prayer was over, the Bishop invited Professor Sarabhai to come to the dais. The Reverend Father introduced him to the congregation. 'Dear children', said the Bishop, 'here is a scientist, Professor Vikram Sarabhai. What does science do? All of us, including this church, experience the light from electricity. I am able to talk to you through the microphone because of technology. Doctors treat patients thanks to medical science. Science through technology enhances the comfort and quality of human life. What do I do as a preacher? I pray for you people, for your wellbeing and for your peace. In short, Vikram and I are doing the same: both science and spirituality seek the Almighty's blessings for human prosperity in body and mind. Professor Sarabhai says that he will build within a year alternative facilities near the coast. Now, dear children, can we give our homes, my home and God's home for a great scientific mission?'

He asked the question. There total silence, as there is now. Then the entire congregation got up and said 'Amen', which made the whole church reverberate.

That was the church where we had our design centre and where we started rocket assembly, and the Bishop's house was where the scientists worked. Later, the Thumba Equatorial Rocket Launching Station led to the establishment of the Vikram Sarabhai Space Centre and the space activities led to the emergence of multiple space centres throughout the country. This church has become an important centre of learning, where thousands of people learn about the dynamic history of India's space programme and the great minds of a scientist and a spiritual leader. Of course, the people of Thumba received well-equipped facilities, a place of worship and an educational centre elsewhere as promised.

When I think of this event, I can see how enlightened spiritual and scientific leaders can come together to give reverence to human life. Of course, the birth of TERLS and the VSSC gave the country the ability to launch vehicles, spacecraft and space applications that have accelerated social and economic development in India to unprecedented levels.

Professor Vikram Sarabhai and Father Peter Bernard Pereira are no longer with us, but those who are responsible for creation and making flowers blossom will themselves be a different kind of flower, as described in the *Bhagwat Gita*. It says, 'See the flower, how generously it distributes perfume, honey. It gives to all, gives freely of its love. When its work is done, it falls away quietly. Try to be like the flower, unassuming despite all its qualities'. What a beautiful message to humanity on the purpose of life, reflecting the spiritual component. Can we bridge the spiritual component of the religions to bring peace to nations and to the world?

I was asked to talk about cultural dialogue and would like to recall an incident that commonly occurs in many parts of my country. I witnessed this event as a young boy of 10. In our house, periodically, I used to see three unique people meet: Pakshi Lakshmana Shastrigal, who was the head priest of the famous Rameshwaram Temple, a Vedic scholar, Reverend Father Bodal, who built the first church on Rameshwaram Island, and my father who was an imam in the mosque. All three used to sit and discuss the island's problems and find solutions. In addition, they built several religious connectivities with compassion. These connectivities quietly spread to others on the island like the fragrance from the flowers. This sight always comes to my mind whenever I discuss with people the dialogue of religions. India has had this advantage of integration of minds for thousands of years. Throughout the world, the need to have a frank dialogue among cultures, religions and civilisations has been felt now more than ever.

These two instances give me confidence that religions can be bridged through spiritual components. Whenever I meet the young and experienced in my country, I narrate these two experiences. Many in my country and the world over may have such experiences. We have to spread such 'glad tidings' to every part of the world.

Now let us discuss the third important component of enlightened society, which is to achieve economic development for societal transformation. Let me take India as an example; it may be true to many parts of the world, including the European Union.

The Indian Economy is in an ascent phase. There is considerable growth in the manufacturing and service sectors. We have a mission of spreading this economic growth throughout the country, including the rural sector. Nearly 220 million people out of a billion people must have their quality of life raised in both rural and urban areas. Even though GDP growth indicates our economic growth, people's participation is essential to achieving the required targets. It is essential to ensure that citizens are empowered with good quality of life encompassing nutritious food, good habitat, clean environment, affordable healthcare, quality education and productive employment, integrated with our value system drawn from civilisational heritage leading to the comprehensive development of the nation that will bring smiles to one billion people. These are indicators for the growth of the National Prosperity Index. To achieve that growth rate, we have identified five areas where India has a core competence for integrated action: 1) agriculture and food processing; 2) education and healthcare; 3) information and communication technology; 4) infrastructure development, including PURA (Providing Urban Amenities in Rural Areas); and 5) self-reliance in critical technologies. We propose to realise the vision of transforming India into a developed nation before 2020 by energising and igniting the minds of the 540 million youth of the nation below 25 years of age.

So far we have discussed the three-dimensional approach of providing value-based education, religion transforming India's spiritual force and economic development for societal transformation leading to the evolution of an enlightened society. This integrated three-dimensional methodology for the evolution of enlightened society will pave the way for peaceful, prosperous, happy nations and, thereby, for a world free from extremisms and further seeds of extremism. On my website www.presidentofindia.nic.in, I have stated how an empowered world body is essential to evolve the nations of enlightened citizens. I will be very happy to exchange thoughts, ideas and action related to this mission with the honourable Members after they have seen my website.

Let me now discuss the second mission, 'Leading to Energy Independence'. When we analyse the critical problems facing the planet today, two important issues come to our minds. Firstly, the continuous depletion of fossil-material-derived oil, gas and coal reserves, as predicted by the World Energy Forum, of which you are all aware. The second is the continuous degradation of the environment, primarily due to extensive use of fossil materials to generate energy. The solution to these problems can be found through energy independence, which I have presented to my country. It may be applicable to many nations. What form of energy independence do I propose in India?

India has 17% of the world's population, but only about 0.8% of the world's known oil and natural gas resources. Based on the progress visualised for the nation during the next two decades, its power-generating capacity has to increase to 400 000 MW by the year 2030 from the present capacity of 130 000 MW. This takes into consideration the energy economies planned and the design and production of energy-efficient equipment and systems.

I have proposed various systems. Solar cell efficiency, common to the European Union and India, has to increase from the present level of 20% to 55% through intensified research on carbon-nanotube-based solar cells. Regarding thorium reactors, thorium is a non-fissile material. It has to be converted into a fissile material using fast breeder technology. In the biofuels area, the challenge is biofuel plantation for higher yield, esterification technologies for higher output and changes to automobile power plants. These three research areas need intensive cooperation between the European Union and India. I would suggest setting up an India-EU renewable energy development programme for advanced R[amp]D in all forms of renewable energy, leading to the availability of commercial-class large-scale power plants within the next decade.

I should like to conclude with the 'World Knowledge Platform'. With India's experience of two successful international cooperative ventures from concept to realisation and marketing, I would suggest developing the 'World Knowledge Platform' to bring together the core competences of the nations of the EU and India in science and technology, leading to the development of unique systems for global applications. The 'World Knowledge Platform' will enable joint design, development, cost-effective production and marketing of the knowledge products, systems and services in various domains based on the core competence of partner nations in the international market. The 'World Knowledge Platform' is a meeting place for science, technology, industry, management and marketing.

You may ask about the missions of the 'World Knowledge Platform'. The convergence of biotechnology, nanotechnology and IT is expected to touch every area of concern to humanity. The 'World Knowledge Platform' will take up missions in some of the areas discussed further, which are of the utmost importance to all of us and to making our world a safe, sustainable, peaceful and prosperous place to live.

The first is water: desalination of sea water using solar energy, channelisation, networking of rivers and cost-effective safe drinking water.

The second is healthcare: diagnosis, drug delivery system, development and production of vaccines for HIV, TB, malaria and cardiac diseases.

The third is agriculture and food processing: increased production of food grain in an environment of reduced land, reduced water and reduced manpower; preservation of food; food processing; cost effective storage and distribution.

The fourth is knowledge products: hardware, software and networking and storage products, including hand-held micro and nano electronic devices.

The fifth is transportation systems: fossil-fuel-free transportation systems using renewable energies, safety systems, hardware and embedded software integration.

The sixth is habitat: an energy-efficient, water-efficient, pollution-free habitat.

The seventh is disaster prediction and management: earthquake forecasting, assessing in advance the quantum of rain for particular cloud conditions.

Finally, capacity-building: quality human resource development for all the above areas, including the development of personnel with world-class skills.

The European Union represents a wealth of scientific potential with a rich culture for research. India has emerged as a leading country, with its demonstrated scientific and technological potential in many societal missions, and is now on the ascent. The combined strength of the nations can be utilised for the advantage of both India and the EU by joining together as partners in creating the 'World Knowledge Platform'.

In conclusion, as we have seen, there is a visible common thread to our dreams and problems. When I am with you, I have a feeling that there are beautiful solutions from beautiful minds. Beautiful minds generate creativity. This is the common heritage of both India and the European Union.

I have presented three missions: 'the evolution of an enlightened society', 'leading to energy independence' and 'creating the 'World Knowledge Platform'. These Indo-EU missions will reinforce further our strategic partnership and become the foundation for making changes to the life of 1.5 billion people, ultimately leading to the confluence of civilisations.

To meet the challenges of these missions, we can draw inspiration from the saying of Maharishi Patanjali from about 2 500 years ago. He said: 'When you are inspired by some great purpose, some extraordinary project, all your thoughts break their bounds. Your mind transcends limitations, your consciousness expands in every direction, and you find yourself in a new, great and wonderful world. Dormant forces, faculties and talents come alive, and you discover yourself to be a greater person by far than you ever dreamt yourself to be.'

I have great admiration for the European Union. In this context I have composed a poem which I should like to share with you.

The title of the poem is 'The message from Mother India to the European Union'.

'Beautiful environment leads to beautiful minds.
Beautiful environment leads to beautiful minds.
Beautiful minds generate freshness and creativity,
Created the explorers of land and sea,
Created the European Union,
Created the explorers of land and sea,
Create minds that innovate,
Create great scientific minds everywhere. Why?
Go back to the many discoveries.
Discover the continent.
Do you realise you have discovered a continent?
Discover the continent and unknown lands.
Venture into unexplored parts.
Create new highways.
In the minds of the best,
In the minds of the best was to us also born,

Generated seeds of the battle and hatred,
Hundreds of years of war and blood.
Millions of my wonderful children lost in the land and sea.
Tears flooded many nations,
Many engulfed in an ocean of sadness.
Then came the vision of the European Union.
Took the vote never to turn human knowledge against ourselves or others.
United in their thinking, action emanated to make Europe prosperous,
And peace bound the European Union.
Those glad tidings captivated the people of the planet of my galaxy.
Those glad tidings captivated the people of the planet of my galaxy.
Oh, European Union let your mission spread everywhere like the air we breathe.

That is my poem.

Finally, friends, let me convey the greetings of the one billion people of my country to all the honourable Members of the European Parliament and, through you, to all the citizens of European Union countries.

May God bless you all.

On Failure and Success

Viswanathan Anand

Chennai (2007)

Viswanathan Anand is an Indian chess grandmaster and a former World Chess Champion. He held the number one position in chess for 21 months, making it the 6th longest record in history. For his excellence in chess, Anand became the first recipient of the Rajiv Gandhi Khel Ratna Award in 1991-92, India's highest sporting honour. In 2007, he became the first sportsperson to receive the Padma Vibhushan, India's second-highest civilian award.

The chess prodigy spoke extemporaneously on the importance of success and failure in his hometown of Chennai in 2007, an important year in Anand's career.

I started playing chess at the age of six. I used to observe my elder siblings play chess and asked my mom if I could learn the game too. I never really thought I would make it big. I just enjoyed playing chess.

My sister decided I should join a chess club. Three days after joining the club I realised I could play my first tournament. I don't know if it was such a bright idea but when you are six optimism is never a problem.

I promptly lost my first three games in the tournament; the fourth I won by default. My opponent failed to turn up. I counted the seconds, anxiously praying that my rival wouldn't turn up at the last minute and spoil the fun. This was my first victory in chess. From then on, I played in many weekend events and state-level tournaments.

There was no specific goal or big picture. It was just a natural progression from one level to the other.

The Holy Grail of Indian chess till 1987 was when and who would become India's first Grandmaster. I chased the GM title for two full years. Every time I would come close enough, but would miss it by the narrowest margin.

At the end of 1986 I took a small break from chess and decided to do something unusual. I prepared for my exams. I was so happy to study for my Class 12 exams. My fellow students found it difficult to grasp that preparing for exams could be pleasurable. Right after my 12th standard exam I won the world junior and subsequently the Grandmaster title.

Sometimes when you have a goal in front of you it is easy to focus. Cyclists have peletons who give them that focus as to what they should achieve in short bursts. After becoming a Grandmaster I realised I no longer had a goal. It didn't matter whether I scored 5 or 6 points in a tournament. Soon, my results started to decline.

As long as you know what your destination is, you know how fast you want to get there. But once you have reached your destination you start looking back rather looking at new peaks.

When I played the Linares tournament in 1991, I beat Anatoly Karpov. I was offered a bonus if I defeated Karpov. I thought if I do beat him I would pay the organiser my bonus. When I first defeated Karpov I realised I could play the Soviet Grandmasters and even defeat them.

Slowly guys started trash-talking me. People used to describe me as a talent, so this was a new experience. Later I realised that when they flatter you it means they show pity. And when they actually say something negative, it means they respect you.

I slowly started understanding that the occasional win over Karpov or Garry Kasparov wasn't enough. One had to play the whole event well and be consistent.

In the beginning beating anyone among the top five Grandmasters in an event would more or less make me content. After going through four or five events with just an upset over a top seed, I thought of actually trying to be a top player. I had to make a podium finish and even aim for first place.

This happened in Regio Emilia when I beat both Karpov and Kasparov and won the event. I think I used all these lessons came together in 2000 when I became the World Champion.

Soon after winning the most exalted title a sportsperson can aspire to, came the vacuum.

What was the next big thing?

I did have some good results, but crisis struck in the Dortmund tournament in 2001. I started with two losses and tried hard not to lose. Then I lost a further game. Thinking I had hit rock bottom I decided to play very passively. I was duly punished with a fourth defeat. This was my worst performance ever.

So what went wrong in Dortmund?

I had done some good preparation. I was very disciplined and kept up my routine. But the spark was missing. I was so scared of avoiding failure and taking risks that I was staring the abyss in the face.

It is extremely difficult to change a winning formula, but one has to experiment even when you succeed.

Defeat gives you the courage to experiment. Success can never motivate you the same way.

After Dortmund I decided I had to do something different. I decided to work on new areas. I went through several months of indifferent results.

After a few months I played a rapid Grand Prix in Dubai. I was eliminated in the second round. This was quite a rude shock as rapid chess was always my forte.

The tournament had a strange rule that meant that even if you were eliminated you played on for the final standings. So I thought I could have seven days of suffering and silent torture or have one week of fun and play chess. I decided to take the second route. I played different openings, stopped worrying about results.

All of a sudden, I was Anand the six-year-old boy. The same boy who played chess at lightning speed. Who could calculate fast and who thoroughly enjoyed the game.

After Dubai I played in Prague. This was the strongest rapid chess event in the world and all the players participated. For the first time I was not even counted among the favourites. That too in a rapid chess event.

This was something of a wakeup call. I reached the event waiting to play chess. I was not worried about being eliminated or losing. I wanted to try new things, enjoy myself and learn from the event. I won the event without the slightest problem.

Everything came together in Prague.

So what went right?

There were various points that I had started to work on.

Enjoy the challenge

I decided to enjoy the challenge. Not being the favourite meant I had to make my critics notice me again.

I had to play like Viswanathan Anand, and not try to play like someone else.

You don't have to search for big challenges or goals. Doing what you do a little better is a challenge in itself.

Spark off creativity

I stopped working permanently with my coach. I started travelling to events alone to spark off creativity. I needed to get that spark and it had to come from within me. I decided to stop doing things by routine, but do things that added value to my chess.

Change something!

I gave up a couple of big events in 2002 (Wijk and Monaco). I wanted to just change something.

Work with new people

I began to work with young players with new styles and knowledge of cutting edge developments. These guys grow up with the latest techniques.

In the 1980s chess information used to arrive three months late. In the 1990s the information used to be posted in the form of diskettes. Nowadays, we download games and data in real time. So these were all inflection points.

Your chess and thought process has to change accordingly. Working with new people gives you a fresh perspective.

The most important lesson I learnt was that one had to experiment even when the going is good.

When you are in good form you have to keep constantly analysing yourself. When you are very resistant to change or are content with the way things are it is a sure sign that something is going wrong.

The temptation is always there to get into cruise control mode. You have to be willing to take the occasional hits so that you succeed over a longer period.

I also realised that passion is something that you need to keep, however small the event. Process and perfection are all good qualities, but passion has to be the guiding force.

Each challenge and game should be a challenge and a learning experience.

Self criticism is also essential.

It is difficult to be objective about success or failure, but they are the two pillars on which you hinge your performance.

It is a lesson I try to learn every day. No amount of tutoring can teach you how to deal with success or failure. It is your passion within that will make the difference.

Election Victory Speech

Barack Obama

Grant Park, Chicago (4 November 2008)

Barack Obama was the 44th President of the United States of America and the first African-American to hold that post, serving two consecutive terms in office. Before joining politics, he trained to become a lawyer at the Harvard Law School and in 1990, he became the first African-American editor of the *Harvard Law Review*. He practised as a civil rights lawyer before securing a seat in the U.S. Senate in 2004.

Obama's victory speech from the 2008 presidential election is one of his most famous speeches, from which the famous phrase: 'Yes, we can' is derived.

If there is anyone out there who still doubts that America is a place where all things are possible; who still wonders if the dream of our founders is alive in our time; who still questions the power of our democracy, tonight is your answer.

It's the answer told by lines that stretched around schools and churches in numbers this nation has never seen; by people who waited three hours and four hours, many for the very first time in their lives, because they believed that this time must be different; that their voice could be that difference.

It's the answer spoken by young and old, rich and poor, Democrat and Republican, black, white, Latino, Asian, Native American, gay, straight, disabled and not disabled—Americans who sent a message to the world that we have never been a collection of Red States and Blue States: we are, and always will be, the United States of America.

It's the answer that led those who have been told for so long by so many to be cynical, and fearful, and doubtful of what we can achieve to put their hands on the arc of history and bend it once more toward the hope of a better day.

It's been a long time coming, but tonight, because of what we did on this day, in this election, at this defining moment, change has come to America.

I just received a very gracious call from Senator McCain. He fought long and hard in this campaign, and he's fought even longer and harder for the country he loves. He has endured sacrifices for America that most of us cannot begin to imagine, and we are better off for the service rendered by this brave and selfless leader. I congratulate him and Governor Palin for all they have achieved, and I look forward to working with them to renew this nation's promise in the months ahead.

I want to thank my partner in this journey, a man who campaigned from his heart and spoke for the men and women he grew up with on the streets of Scranton and rode with on that train home to Delaware, the Vice President-elect of the United States, Joe Biden.

I would not be standing here tonight without the unyielding support of my best friend for the last sixteen years, the rock of our family and the love of my life, our nation's next First Lady, Michelle Obama. Sasha and Malia, I love you both so much, and you have earned the new puppy that's coming with us to the White House. And while she's no longer with us, I know my grandmother is watching, along with the family that made me who I am. I miss them tonight, and know that my debt to them is beyond measure.

To my campaign manager David Plouffe, my chief strategist David Axelrod, and the best campaign team ever assembled in the history of politics—you made this happen, and I am forever grateful for what you've sacrificed to get it done.

But above all, I will never forget who this victory truly belongs to—it belongs to you.

I was never the likeliest candidate for this office. We didn't start with much money or many endorsements. Our campaign was not hatched in the halls of Washington—it began in the backyards of Des Moines and the living rooms of Concord and the front porches of Charleston.

It was built by working men and women who dug into what little savings they had to give five dollars and 10 dollars and 20 dollars to this cause. It grew strength from the young people who rejected the myth of their generation's apathy; who left their homes and their families for jobs that offered little pay and less sleep; from the not-so-young people who braved the bitter cold and scorching heat to knock on the doors of perfect strangers; from the millions of Americans who volunteered, and organized, and proved that more than two centuries later, a government of the people, by the people and for the people has not perished from this Earth. This is your victory.

I know you didn't do this just to win an election and I know you didn't do it for me. You did it because you understand the enormity of the task that lies ahead. For even as we celebrate tonight, we know the challenges that tomorrow will bring are the greatest of our lifetime—two wars, a planet in peril, the worst financial crisis in a century. Even as we stand here tonight, we know there are brave Americans waking up in the deserts of Iraq and the mountains of Afghanistan to risk their lives for us. There are mothers and fathers who will lie awake after their children fall asleep and wonder how they'll make the mortgage, or pay their doctor's bills, or save enough for college. There is new energy to harness and new jobs to be created; new schools to build and threats to meet and alliances to repair.

The road ahead will be long. Our climb will be steep. We may not get there in one year or even one term, but America—I have never been more hopeful than I am tonight that we will get there. I promise you—we as a people will get there.

There will be setbacks and false starts. There are many who won't agree with every decision or policy I make as President, and we know that government can't solve every problem. But I will always be honest with you about the challenges we face. I will listen to you, especially when we disagree. And above all, I will ask you join in the work of remaking this nation the only way it's been done in America for 200 and 21 years—block by block, brick by brick, calloused hand by calloused hand.

What began 21 months ago in the depths of winter must not end on this autumn night. This victory alone is not the change we seek—it is only the chance for us to make that change. And that cannot happen if we go back to the way things were. It cannot happen without you.

So let us summon a new spirit of patriotism; of service and responsibility where each of us resolves to pitch in and work harder and look after not only ourselves, but each other. Let us remember that if this financial crisis taught us anything, it's that we cannot have a thriving Wall Street while Main Street suffers—in this country, we rise or fall as one nation; as one people.

Let us resist the temptation to fall back on the same partisanship and pettiness and immaturity that has poisoned our politics for so long. Let us remember that it was a man from this state who first carried the banner of the Republican Party to the White House—a party founded on the values of self-reliance, individual liberty, and national unity. Those are values we all share, and while the Democratic Party has won a great victory tonight, we do so with a measure of humility and determination to heal the divides that have held back our progress. As Lincoln said to a nation far more divided than ours, 'We are not enemies, but friends…though passion may have strained it must not break our bonds of affection.' And to those Americans whose support I have yet to earn—I may not have won your vote, but I hear your voices, I need your help, and I will be your President too.

And to all those watching tonight from beyond our shores, from parliaments and palaces to those who are huddled around radios in the forgotten corners of our world— our stories are singular, but our destiny is shared, and a new dawn of American leadership is at hand. To those who would tear this world down—we will defeat you. To those who seek peace and security—we support you. And to all those who have wondered if America's beacon still burns as bright—tonight we proved once more that the true strength of our nation comes not from our the might of our arms or the scale of our wealth, but from the enduring power of our ideals: democracy, liberty, opportunity, and unyielding hope.

For that is the true genius of America—that America can change. Our union can be perfected. And what we have already achieved gives us hope for what we can and must achieve tomorrow.

This election had many firsts and many stories that will be told for generations. But one that's on my mind tonight is about a woman who cast her ballot in Atlanta. She's a lot like the millions of others who stood in line to make their voice heard in this election except for one thing—Ann Nixon Cooper is 106 years old.

She was born just a generation past slavery; a time when there were no cars on the road or planes in the sky; when someone like her couldn't vote for two reasons—because she was a woman and because of the color of her skin.

And tonight, I think about all that she's seen throughout her century in America—the heartache and the hope; the struggle and the progress; the times we were told that we can't, and the people who pressed on with that American creed: Yes we can.

At a time when women's voices were silenced and their hopes dismissed, she lived to see them stand up and speak out and reach for the ballot. Yes we can.

When there was despair in the dust bowl and depression across the land, she saw a nation conquer fear itself with a New Deal, new jobs and a new sense of common purpose. Yes we can.

When the bombs fell on our harbor and tyranny threatened the world, she was there to witness a generation rise to greatness and a democracy was saved. Yes we can.

She was there for the buses in Montgomery, the hoses in Birmingham, a bridge in Selma, and a preacher from Atlanta who told a people that 'We Shall Overcome.' Yes we can.

A man touched down on the moon, a wall came down in Berlin, a world was connected by our own science and imagination. And this year, in this election, she touched her finger to a screen, and cast her vote, because after 106 years in America, through the best of times and the darkest of hours, she knows how America can change. Yes we can.

America, we have come so far. We have seen so much. But there is so much more to do. So tonight, let us ask ourselves—if our children should live to see the next century; if my daughters should be so lucky to live as long as Ann Nixon Cooper, what change will they see? What progress will we have made?

This is our chance to answer that call. This is our moment. This is our time—to put our people back to work and open doors of opportunity for our kids; to restore prosperity and promote the cause of peace; to reclaim the American Dream and reaffirm that fundamental truth—that out of many, we are one; that while we breathe, we hope, and where we are met with cynicism, and doubt, and those who tell us that we can't, we will respond with that timeless creed that sums up the spirit of a people:

Yes We Can. Thank you, God bless you, and may God Bless the United States of America.

‘The Fringe Benefits of Failure, and the Importance of Imagination’

J.K. Rowling

Commencement Speech at Harvard (2008)

J.K. Rowling is a British author, philanthropist, screenwriter, film and television producer best-known as the creator of the international blockbuster book and film franchise, the Harry Potter series. The Harry Potter novels have become the bestselling book series of all time and have been translated to over 50 languages. Rowling became the world's first billionaire author before giving away much of her earnings to charity. She is considered one of the most influential women of Britain.

In her famous commencement speech delivered at Harvard, Rowling encourages students to dream, embrace failure and stay resilient in the face of adversity.

President Faust, members of the Harvard Corporation and the Board of Overseers, members of the faculty, proud parents, and, above all, graduates.

The first thing I would like to say is ‘thank you’. Not only has Harvard given me an extraordinary honour, but the weeks of fear and nausea I have endured at the thought of giving this commencement address have made me lose weight. A win-win situation! Now all I have to do is take deep breaths, squint at the red banners and convince myself that I am at the world's largest Gryffindor reunion.

Delivering a commencement address is a great responsibility; or so I thought until I cast my mind back to my own graduation. The commencement speaker that day was the distinguished British philosopher Baroness Mary Warnock. Reflecting on her speech has helped me enormously in writing this one, because it turns out that I can't remember a single word she said. This liberating discovery enables me to proceed without any fear that I might inadvertently influence you to abandon promising careers in business, the law or politics for the giddy delights of becoming a gay wizard.

You see? If all you remember in years to come is the 'gay wizard' joke, I've come out ahead of Baroness Mary Warnock. Achievable goals: the first step to self improvement.

Actually, I have wracked my mind and heart for what I ought to say to you today. I have asked myself what I wish I had known at my own graduation, and what important lessons I have learned in the 21 years that have expired between that day and this.

I have come up with two answers. On this wonderful day when we are gathered together to celebrate your academic success, I have decided to talk to you about the benefits of failure. And as you stand on the threshold of what is sometimes called 'real life', I want to extol the crucial importance of imagination.

These may seem quixotic or paradoxical choices, but please bear with me.

Looking back at the 21-year-old that I was at graduation, is a slightly uncomfortable experience for the 42-year-old that she has become. Half my lifetime ago, I was striking an uneasy balance between the ambition I had for myself, and what those closest to me expected of me.

I was convinced that the only thing I wanted to do, ever, was to write novels. However, my parents, both of whom came from impoverished backgrounds and neither of whom had been to college, took the view that my overactive imagination was an amusing personal quirk that would never pay a mortgage, or secure a pension. I know that the irony strikes with the force of a cartoon anvil, now.

So they hoped that I would take a vocational degree; I wanted to study English Literature. A compromise was reached that in retrospect satisfied nobody, and I went up to study Modern Languages. Hardly had my parents' car rounded the corner at the end of the road than I ditched German and scuttled off down the Classics corridor.

I cannot remember telling my parents that I was studying Classics; they might well have found out for the first time on graduation day. Of all the subjects on this planet, I think they would have been hard put to name one less useful than Greek mythology when it came to securing the keys to an executive bathroom.

I would like to make it clear, in parenthesis, that I do not blame my parents for their point of view. There is an expiry date on blaming your parents for steering you in the wrong direction; the moment you are old enough to take the wheel, responsibility lies with you. What is more, I cannot criticise my parents for hoping that I would never experience poverty. They had been poor themselves, and I have since been poor, and I quite agree with them that it is not an ennobling experience. Poverty entails fear, and stress, and sometimes depression; it means a thousand petty humiliations and hardships. Climbing out of poverty by your own efforts, that is indeed something on which to pride yourself, but poverty itself is romanticised only by fools.

What I feared most for myself at your age was not poverty, but failure.

At your age, in spite of a distinct lack of motivation at university, where I had spent far too long in the coffee bar writing stories, and far too little time at lectures, I had a knack for passing examinations, and that, for years, had been the measure of success in my life and that of my peers.

I am not dull enough to suppose that because you are young, gifted and well-educated, you have never known hardship or heartbreak. Talent and intelligence never yet inoculated anyone against the caprice of the Fates, and I do not for a moment suppose that everyone here has enjoyed an existence of unruffled privilege and contentment.

However, the fact that you are graduating from Harvard suggests that you are not very well-acquainted with failure. You might be driven by a fear of failure quite as much as a desire for success.

Indeed, your conception of failure might not be too far from the average person's idea of success, so high have you already flown.

Ultimately, we all have to decide for ourselves what constitutes failure, but the world is quite eager to give you a set of criteria if you let it. So I think it fair to say that by any conventional measure, a mere seven years after my graduation day, I had failed on an epic scale. An exceptionally short-lived marriage had imploded, and I was jobless, a lone parent, and as poor as it is possible to be in modern Britain, without being homeless. The fears that my parents had had for me, and that I had had for myself, had both come to pass, and by every usual standard, I was the biggest failure I knew.

Now, I am not going to stand here and tell you that failure is fun. That period of my life was a dark one, and I had no idea that there was going to be what the press has since represented as a kind of fairy tale resolution. I had no idea then how far the tunnel extended, and for a long time, any light at the end of it was a hope rather than a reality.

So why do I talk about the benefits of failure? Simply because failure meant a stripping away of the inessential. I stopped pretending to myself that I was anything other than what I was, and began to direct all my energy into finishing the only work that mattered to me. Had I really succeeded at anything else, I might never have found the determination to succeed in the one arena I believed I truly belonged. I was set free, because my greatest fear had been realised, and I was still alive, and I still had a daughter whom I adored, and I had an old typewriter and a big idea. And so rock bottom became the solid foundation on which I rebuilt my life.

You might never fail on the scale I did, but some failure in life is inevitable. It is impossible to live without failing at something, unless you live so cautiously that you might as well not have lived at all—in which case, you fail by default.

Failure gave me an inner security that I had never attained by passing examinations. Failure taught me things about myself that I could have learned no other way. I discovered that I had a strong will, and more discipline than I had suspected; I also found out that I had friends whose value was truly above the price of rubies.

The knowledge that you have emerged wiser and stronger from setbacks means that you are, ever after, secure in your ability to survive. You will never truly know yourself, or the strength of your relationships, until both have been tested by adversity. Such knowledge is a true gift, for all that it is painfully won, and it has been worth more than any qualification I ever earned.

So given a Time Turner, I would tell my 21-year-old self that personal happiness lies in knowing that life is not a check-list of acquisition or achievement. Your qualifications, your CV, are not your life, though you will meet many people of my age and older who confuse the two. Life is difficult, and complicated, and beyond anyone's total control, and the humility to know that will enable you to survive its vicissitudes.

Now you might think that I chose my second theme, the importance of imagination, because of the part it played in rebuilding my life, but that is not wholly so. Though I personally will defend the value of bedtime stories to my last gasp, I have learned to value imagination in a much broader sense. Imagination is not only the uniquely human capacity to envision that which is not, and therefore the fount of all invention and innovation. In its arguably most transformative and revelatory capacity, it is the power that enables us to empathise with humans whose experiences we have never shared.

One of the greatest formative experiences of my life preceded Harry Potter, though it informed much of what I subsequently wrote in those books. This revelation came in the form of one of my earliest day jobs. Though I was sloping off to write stories during my lunch hours, I paid the rent in my early 20s by working at the African research department at Amnesty International's headquarters in London.

There in my little office I read hastily scribbled letters smuggled out of totalitarian regimes by men and women who were risking imprisonment to inform the outside world of what was happening to them. I saw photographs of those who had disappeared without trace, sent to Amnesty by their desperate families and friends. I read the testimony of torture victims and saw pictures of their injuries. I opened handwritten, eyewitness accounts of summary trials and executions, of kidnappings and rapes.

Many of my co-workers were ex-political prisoners, people who had been displaced from their homes, or fled into exile, because they had the temerity to speak against their governments. Visitors to our offices included those who had come to give information, or to try and find out what had happened to those they had left behind.

I shall never forget the African torture victim, a young man no older than I was at the time, who had become mentally ill after all he had endured in his homeland. He trembled uncontrollably as he spoke into a video camera about the brutality inflicted upon him. He was a foot taller than I was, and seemed as fragile as a child. I was given the job of escorting him back to the Underground Station afterwards, and this man whose life had been shattered by cruelty took my hand with exquisite courtesy, and wished me future happiness.

And as long as I live I shall remember walking along an empty corridor and suddenly hearing, from behind a closed door, a scream of pain and horror such as I have never heard since. The door opened, and the researcher poked out her head and told me to run and make a hot drink for the young man sitting with her. She had just had to give him the news that in retaliation for his own outspokenness against his country's regime, his mother had been seized and executed.

Every day of my working week in my early 20s I was reminded how incredibly fortunate I was, to live in a country with a democratically elected government, where legal representation and a public trial were the rights of everyone.

Every day, I saw more evidence about the evils humankind will inflict on their fellow humans, to gain or maintain power. I began to have nightmares, literal nightmares, about some of the things I saw, heard, and read.

And yet I also learned more about human goodness at Amnesty International than I had ever known before.

Amnesty mobilises thousands of people who have never been tortured or imprisoned for their beliefs to act on behalf of those who have. The power of human empathy, leading to collective action, saves lives, and frees prisoners. Ordinary people, whose personal well-being and security are assured, join together in huge numbers to save people they do not know, and will never meet. My small participation in that process was one of the most humbling and inspiring experiences of my life.

Unlike any other creature on this planet, humans can learn and understand, without having experienced. They can think themselves into other people's places.

Of course, this is a power, like my brand of fictional magic, that is morally neutral. One might use such an ability to manipulate, or control, just as much as to understand or sympathise.

And many prefer not to exercise their imaginations at all. They choose to remain comfortably within the bounds of their own experience, never troubling to wonder how it would feel to have been born other than they are. They can refuse to hear screams or to peer inside cages; they can close their minds and hearts to any suffering that does not touch them personally; they can refuse to know.

I might be tempted to envy people who can live that way, except that I do not think they have any fewer nightmares than I do. Choosing to live in narrow spaces leads to a form of mental agoraphobia, and that brings its own terrors. I think the willfully unimaginative see more monsters. They are often more afraid.

What is more, those who choose not to empathise enable real monsters. For without ever committing an act of outright evil ourselves, we collude with it, through our own apathy.

One of the many things I learned at the end of that Classics corridor down which I ventured at the age of 18, in search of something I could not then define, was this, written by the Greek author Plutarch: What we achieve inwardly will change outer reality.

That is an astonishing statement and yet proven a thousand times every day of our lives. It expresses, in part, our inescapable connection with the outside world, the fact that we touch other people's lives simply by existing.

But how much more are you, Harvard graduates of 2008, likely to touch other people's lives? Your intelligence, your capacity for hard work, the education you have earned and received, give you unique status, and unique responsibilities. Even your nationality sets you apart. The great majority of you belong to the world's only remaining superpower. The way you vote, the way you live, the way you protest, the pressure you bring to bear on your government, has an impact way beyond your borders. That is your privilege, and your burden.

If you choose to use your status and influence to raise your voice on behalf of those who have no voice; if you choose to identify not only with the powerful, but with the powerless; if you retain the ability to imagine yourself into the lives of those who do not have your advantages, then it will not only be your proud families who celebrate your existence, but thousands and millions of people whose reality you have helped change. We do not need magic to change the world, we carry all the power we need inside ourselves already: we have the power to imagine better.

I am nearly finished. I have one last hope for you, which is something that I already had at 21. The friends with whom I sat on graduation day have been my friends for life. They are my children's godparents, the people to whom I've been able to turn in times of trouble, people who have been kind enough not to sue me when I took their names for Death Eaters. At our graduation we were bound by enormous affection, by our shared experience of a time that could never come again, and, of course, by the knowledge that we held certain photographic evidence that would be exceptionally valuable if any of us ran for Prime Minister.

So today, I wish you nothing better than similar friendships. And tomorrow, I hope that even if you remember not a single word of mine, you remember those of Seneca, another of those old Romans I met when I fled down the Classics corridor, in retreat from career ladders, in search of ancient wisdom: As is a tale, so is life: not how long it is, but how good it is, is what matters. I wish you all very good lives.

Thank you very much.

Tulane University Commencement Speech

Ellen DeGeneres

(16 May 2009)

Ellen DeGeneres is an American comedian, LGBT rights activist, television host, author, actress and producer who is one of the most famous contemporary comedians. She has been hosting a successful daytime television show called 'The Ellen DeGeneres Show' since 2003. Her show has won several Daytime Emmy Awards as well as People's Choice Awards, breaking the previous record held by 'The Oprah Winfrey Show'. In 2016, she was awarded the Presidential Medal of Freedom for advocating equality and fairness for all.

In her witty and humorous commencement speech, DeGeneres motivates students to be true to themselves, work hard and chase their dreams.

Thank you, President Cowan, Mrs. President Cowen; distinguished guests, undistinguished guests, you know who you are, honored faculty and creepy Spanish teacher. And thank you to all the graduating class of 2009, I realize most of you are hungover and have splitting headaches and haven't slept since Fat Tuesday, but you can't graduate 'til I finish, so listen up.

When I was asked to make the commencement speech, I immediately said yes. Then I went to look up what commencement meant which would have been easy if I had a dictionary, but most of the books in our house are Portia's, and they're all written in

Australian. So I had to break the word down myself, to find out the meaning.

Commencement: common, and cement, common cement. You commonly see cement on sidewalks. Sidewalks have cracks, and if you step on a crack, you break your mother's back. So there's that. But I'm honored that you've asked me here to speak at your common cement.

I thought that you had to be a famous alumnus, alumni, aluminum, alumis; you had to graduate from this school. And I didn't go to college here, and I don't know if President Cowan knows, I didn't go to any college at all, any college. And I'm not saying you wasted your time, or money, but look at me, I'm a huge celebrity.

Although I did graduate from the school of hard knocks, our mascot was the knockers. I spent a lot of time here growing up. My mom worked at Newcomb and I would go there every time I needed to steal something out of her purse. But why am I here today? Clearly not to steal, you're too far away and I'd never get away with it. I'm here because of you. Because I can't think of a more tenacious, more courageous graduating class. I mean, look at you all, wearing your robes. Usually when you're wearing a robe at 10 in the morning, it means you've given up. I'm here because I love New Orleans. I was born and raised here, I spent my formative years here, and like you, while I was living here I only did laundry six times. When I finished school, I was completely lost and by school, I mean middle school, but I went ahead and finished high school anyway. And I really, I had no ambition; I didn't know what I wanted to do. I did everything from: I shucked oysters, I was a hostess, I was a bartender, I was a waitress, I painted houses, I sold vacuum cleaners; I had no idea and I thought I'd just finally settle in some job and I would make enough money to pay my rent, maybe have basic cable, maybe not, I didn't really have a plan, my point is that, by the time I was your age, I really thought I knew who I was but I had no idea. Like for example, when I was your age, I was dating men. So what I'm saying is, when you're older, most of you will be gay. Anyone writing this stuff down? Parents?

Anyway, I had no idea what I wanted to do with my life and the way I ended up on this path was from a very tragic event. I was maybe nineteen, and my girlfriend at the time was killed in a car accident. And I passed the accident, and I didn't know it was her and I kept going and I found out shortly after that, it was her. And I was living in a basement apartment; I had no money; I had no heat, no air, I had a mattress on the floor and the apartment was infested with fleas. And I was soul-searching, I was like, why is she suddenly gone, and there are fleas here? I don't understand, there must be a purpose and wouldn't it be so convenient if we could pick up the phone and call God and ask these questions. And I started writing and what poured out of me was an imaginary conversation with God, which was one-sided and I finished writing it and I looked at it and I said to myself, and I hadn't even been doing stand-up, ever, there was no club in town. I said, 'I'm going do this on the Tonight Show with Johnny Carson' at the time he was the king 'and I'm going be the first woman in the history of the show to be called over to sit down.' And several years later, I was the first woman in the history of the show, and only woman in the history of the show to sit down, because of that phone conversation with God that I wrote. And I started this path of stand-up and it was successful and it was great but it was hard because I was trying to please everybody and I had this secret that I was keeping, that I was gay. And I thought if people found out they wouldn't like me, they wouldn't laugh at me. Then my career turned into, I got my own sitcom, and that was very successful, another level of success. And I thought, what if they find out I'm gay, then they'll never watch, and this was a long time ago, this was when we just had white presidents but anyway, this was back many years ago and I finally decided that I was living with so much shame, and so much fear, that I just couldn't live that way anymore and I decided to come out and make it creative. And my character would come out at the same time, and it wasn't to make a political statement, it wasn't to do anything other than to free myself up from this heaviness that I was carrying around, and I just wanted to be honest. And I thought, 'What's the worst that could happen? I can lose my career'. I did. I lost my career. The show was cancelled after six years without even telling me; I read it in the paper. The phone didn't ring for three years. I had no offers. Nobody wanted to touch me at all. Yet, I was getting letters from kids that almost committed suicide, but didn't because of what I did. And I realized that I had a purpose. And it wasn't just about me and it wasn't about celebrity, but I felt like I was being punished and it was a bad time, I was angry, I was sad, and then I was offered a talk show. And the people that offered me the talk show tried to sell it. And most stations didn't want to pick it up. Most people didn't want to buy it because they thought nobody would watch me. Really when I look back on it, I wouldn't change a thing. I mean, it was so important for me to lose everything because I found out what the most important thing is, is to be true to yourself. Ultimately, that's what's gotten me to this place. I don't live in fear, I'm free; I have no secrets and I know I'll always be ok, because no matter what, I know who I am. So In conclusion, when I was younger I thought success was something different. I thought when I grow up, I want to be famous. I want to be a star. I want to be in movies. When I grow up I want to see the world, drive nice cars, I want to have groupies. To quote the Pussycat Dolls. How many people thought it was 'boobies', by the way? It's not, it's 'groupies'.

But my idea of success is different today. And as you grow, you'll realize the definition of success changes. For many of you, today, success is being able to hold down 20 shots of tequila. For me, the most important thing in your life is to live your life with integrity and not to give into peer pressure to try to be something that you're not, to live your life as an honest and compassionate person, to contribute in some way. So to conclude my conclusion, follow your passion, stay true to yourself. Never follow anyone else's path, unless you're in the woods and you're lost and you see a path and by all means you should follow that. Don't give advice, it will come back and bite you in the ass. Don't take anyone's advice. So my advice to you is to be true to yourself and everything will be fine.

And I know that a lot of you are concerned about your future, but there's no need to worry. The economy is booming, the job market is wide open, the planet is just fine. It's going be great. You've already survived a hurricane. What else can happen to you? And as I mentioned before, some of the most devastating things that happen to you will teach you the most. And now you know the right questions to ask in your first job interview. Like, 'Is it above sea level?' So to conclude my conclusion that I've previously concluded, in the common cement speech, I guess what I'm trying to say is life is like one big Mardi Gras. But instead of showing your boobs, show people your brain, and if they like what they see, you'll have more beads than you know what to do with and you'll be drunk, most of the time. So the Katrina class of 2009, I say congratulations and if you don't remember a thing I said today, remember this, you're going to be ok, dum de dumdumdum, just dance.

'Your Elusive Creative Genius'

Elizabeth Gilbert

TED Talk (9 February 2009)

Elizabeth Gilbert is a famous American author, journalist and orator best-known for her memoir *Eat, Pray, Love* (2006) that was adapted into a blockbuster movie starring Julia Roberts in 2010. Her other major works include *Pilgrims* (1997) and *The Last American Man* (2002).

'Your Elusive Creative Genius' is a famous TED talk by Elizabeth Gilbert in which she elaborates on the need to distance the artist from their work and create barriers that help to work despite fear and anxiety about criticism.

I am a writer. Writing books is my profession but it's more than that, of course. It is also my great lifelong love and fascination. And I don't expect that that's ever going to change. But, that said, something kind of peculiar has happened recently in my life and in my career, which has caused me to have to recalibrate my whole relationship with this work. And the peculiar thing is that I recently wrote this book, this memoir called 'Eat, Pray, Love' which, decidedly unlike any of my previous books, went out in the world for some reason, and became this big, mega-sensation, international bestseller thing. The result of which is that everywhere I go now, people treat me like I'm doomed. Seriously—doomed, doomed! Like, they come up to me now, all worried, and they say, 'Aren't you afraid you're never going to be able to top that? Aren't you afraid you're going to keep writing for your whole life and you're never again going to create a book that anybody in the world cares about at all, ever again?'

So that's reassuring, you know. But it would be worse, except for that I happen to remember that over 20 years ago, when I was a teenager, when I first started telling people that I wanted to be a writer, I was met with this same sort of fear-based reaction. And people would say, 'Aren't you afraid you're never going to have any success? Aren't you afraid the humiliation of rejection will kill you? Aren't you afraid that you're going to work your whole life at this craft and nothing's ever going to come of it and you're going to die on a scrap heap of broken dreams with your mouth filled with bitter ash of failure?'

Like that, you know.

The answer—the short answer to all those questions is, 'Yes.' Yes, I'm afraid of all those things. And I always have been. And I'm afraid of many, many more things besides that people can't even guess at, like seaweed and other things that are scary. But, when it comes to writing, the thing that I've been sort of thinking about lately, and wondering about lately, is why? You know, is it rational? Is it logical that anybody should be expected to be afraid of the work that they feel they were put on this Earth to do. And what is it specifically about creative ventures that seems to make us really nervous about each other's mental health in a way that other careers kind of don't do, you know? Like my dad, for example, was a chemical engineer and I don't recall once in his 40 years of chemical engineering anybody asking him if he was afraid to be a chemical engineer, you know? 'That chemical-engineering block, John, how's it going?' It just didn't come up like that, you know? But to be fair, chemical engineers as a group haven't really earned a reputation over the centuries for being alcoholic manic-depressives.

We writers, we kind of do have that reputation, and not just writers, but creative people across all genres, it seems, have this reputation for being enormously mentally unstable. And all you have to do is look at the very grim death count in the 20th century alone, of really magnificent creative minds who died young and often at their own hands, you know? And even the ones who didn't literally commit suicide seem to be really undone by their gifts, you know. Norman Mailer, just before he died, last interview, he said, 'Every one of my books has killed me a little more.' An extraordinary statement to make about your life's work. But we don't even blink when we hear somebody say this, because we've heard that kind of stuff for so long and somehow we've completely internalized and accepted collectively this notion that creativity and suffering are somehow inherently linked and that artistry, in the end, will always ultimately lead to anguish.

And the question that I want to ask everybody here today is are you guys all cool with that idea? Are you comfortable with that? Because you look at it even from an inch away and, you know—I'm not at all comfortable with that assumption. I think it's odious. And I also think it's dangerous, and I don't want to see it perpetuated into the next century. I think it's better if we encourage our great creative minds to live.

And I definitely know that, in my case—in my situation—it would be very dangerous for me to start sort of leaking down that dark path of assumption, particularly given the circumstance that I'm in right now in my career. Which is—you know, like check it out, I'm pretty young, I'm only about 40 years old. I still have maybe another four decades of work left in me. And it's exceedingly likely that anything I write from this point forward is going to be judged by the world as the work that came after the freakish success of my last book, right? I should just put it bluntly, because we're all sort of friends here now—it's exceedingly likely that my greatest success is behind me. So Jesus, what a thought! That's the kind of thought that could lead a person to start drinking gin at nine o'clock in the morning, and I don't want to go there.

I would prefer to keep doing this work that I love.

And so, the question becomes, how? And so, it seems to me, upon a lot of reflection, that the way that I have to work now, in order to continue writing, is that I have to create some sort of protective psychological construct, right? I have to sort of find some way to have a safe distance between me, as I am writing, and my very natural anxiety about what the reaction to that writing is going to be, from now on. And, as I've been looking, over the last year, for models for how to do that, I've been sort of looking across time, and I've been trying to find other societies to see if they might have had better and saner ideas than we have about how to help creative people sort of manage the inherent emotional risks of creativity.

And that search has led me to ancient Greece and ancient Rome. So stay with me, because it does circle around and back. But, ancient Greece and ancient Rome—people did not happen to believe that creativity came from human beings back then, OK? People believed that creativity was this divine attendant spirit that came to human beings from some distant and unknowable source, for distant and unknowable reasons. The Greeks famously called these divine attendant spirits of creativity 'daemons.' Socrates, famously, believed that he had a daemon who spoke wisdom to him from afar.

The Romans had the same idea, but they called that sort of disembodied creative spirit a genius. Which is great, because the Romans did not actually think that a genius was a particularly clever individual. They believed that a genius was this, sort of magical divine entity, who was believed to literally live in the walls of an artist's studio, kind of like Dobby the house elf, and who would come out and sort of invisibly assist the artist with their work and would shape the outcome of that work.

So brilliant—there it is, right there, that distance that I'm talking about—that psychological construct to protect you from the results of your work. And everyone knew that this is how it functioned, right? So the ancient artist was protected from certain things, like, for example, too much narcissism, right? If your work was brilliant, you couldn't take all the credit for it, everybody knew that you had this disembodied genius who had helped you. If your work bombed, not entirely your fault, you know? Everyone knew your genius was kind of lame.

And this is how people thought about creativity in the West for a really long time. And then the Renaissance came and everything changed, and we had this big idea, and the big idea was, let's put the individual human being at the center of the universe above all gods and mysteries, and there's no more room for mystical creatures who take dictation from the divine. And it's the beginning of rational humanism, and people started to believe that creativity came completely from the self of the individual. And for the first time in history, you start to hear people referring to this or that artist as being a genius, rather than having a genius.

And I got to tell you, I think that was a huge error. You know, I think that allowing somebody, one mere person to believe that he or she is like, the vessel, you know, like the font and the essence and the source of all divine, creative, unknowable, eternal mystery is just a smidge too much responsibility to put on one fragile, human psyche. It's like asking somebody to swallow the sun. It just completely warps and distorts egos, and it creates all these unmanageable expectations about performance. And I think the pressure of that has been killing off our artists for the last 500 years.

And, if this is true, and I think it is true, the question becomes, what now? Can we do this differently? Maybe go back to some more ancient understanding about the relationship between humans and the creative mystery. Maybe not. Maybe we can't just erase 500 years of rational humanistic thought in one 18 minute speech. And there's probably people in this audience who would raise really legitimate scientific suspicions about the notion of, basically, fairies who follow people around rubbing fairy juice on their projects and stuff. I'm not, probably, going to bring you all along with me on this.

But the question that I kind of want to pose is—you know, why not? Why not think about it this way? Because it makes as much sense as anything else I have ever heard in terms of explaining the utter maddening capriciousness of the creative process. A process which, as anybody who has ever tried to make something—which is to say basically everyone here—knows does not always behave rationally. And, in fact, can sometimes feel downright paranormal.

I had this encounter recently where I met the extraordinary American poet Ruth Stone, who's now in her 90s, but she's been a poet her entire life and she told me that when she was growing up in rural Virginia, she would be out working in the fields, and she said she would feel and hear a poem coming at her from over the landscape. And she said it was like a thunderous train of air. And it would come barreling down at her over the landscape. And she felt it coming, because it would shake the earth under her feet. She knew that she had only one thing to do at that point, and that was to, in her words, 'run like hell.' And she would run like hell to the house and she would be getting chased by this poem, and the whole deal was that she had to get to a piece of paper and a pencil fast enough so that when it thundered through her, she could collect it and grab it on the page. And other times she wouldn't be fast enough, so she'd be running and running, and she wouldn't get to the house and the poem would barrel through her and she would miss it and she said it would continue on across the landscape, looking, as she put it 'for another poet.' And then there were these times— this is the piece I never forgot—she said that there were moments where she would almost miss it, right? So, she's running to the house and she's looking for the paper and the poem passes through her, and she grabs a pencil just as it's going through her, and then she said, it was like she would reach out with her other hand and she would catch it. She would catch the poem by its tail, and she would pull it backwards into her body as she was transcribing on the page. And in these instances, the poem would come up on the page perfect and intact but backwards, from the last word to the first.

So when I heard that I was like—that's uncanny, that's exactly what my creative process is like.

That's not at all what my creative process is—I'm not the pipeline! I'm a mule, and the way that I have to work is I have to get up at the same time every day, and sweat and labor and barrel through it really awkwardly. But even I, in my mulishness, even I have brushed up against that thing, at times. And I would imagine that a lot of you have too. You know, even I have had work or ideas come through me from a source that I honestly cannot identify. And what is that thing? And how are we to relate to it in a way that will not make us lose our minds, but, in fact, might actually keep us sane?

And for me, the best contemporary example that I have of how to do that is the musician Tom Waits, who I got to interview several years ago on a magazine assignment. And we were talking about this, and you know, Tom, for most of his life, he was pretty much the embodiment of the tormented contemporary modern artist, trying to control and manage and dominate these sort of uncontrollable creative impulses that were totally internalized.

But then he got older, he got calmer, and one day he was driving down the freeway in Los Angeles, and this is when it all changed for him. And he's speeding along, and all of a sudden he hears this little fragment of melody, that comes into his head as inspiration often comes, elusive and tantalizing, and he wants it, it's gorgeous, and he longs for it, but he has no way to get it. He doesn't have a piece of paper, or a pencil, or a tape recorder.

So he starts to feel all of that old anxiety start to rise in him like, 'I'm going to lose this thing, and I'll be haunted by this song forever. I'm not good enough, and I can't do it.' And instead of panicking, he just stopped. He just stopped that whole mental process and he did something completely novel. He just looked up at the sky, and he said, 'Excuse me, can you not see that I'm driving?'

'Do I look like I can write down a song right now? If you really want to exist, come back at a more opportune moment when I can take care of you. Otherwise, go bother somebody else today. Go bother Leonard Cohen.'

And his whole work process changed after that. Not the work, the work was still oftentimes as dark as ever. But the process, and the heavy anxiety around it was released when he took the genie, the genius out of him where it was causing nothing but trouble, and released it back where it came from, and realized that this didn't have to be this internalized, tormented thing. It could be this peculiar, wondrous, bizarre collaboration, kind of conversation between Tom and the strange, external thing that was not quite Tom.

When I heard that story, it started to shift a little bit the way that I worked too, and this idea already saved me once. It saved me when I was in the middle of writing *Eat, Pray, Love,* and I fell into one of those sort of pits of despair that we all fall into when we're working on something and it's not coming and you start to think this is going to be a disaster, the worst book ever written. Not just bad, but the worst book ever written. And I started to think I should just dump this project. But then I remembered Tom talking to the open air and I tried it. So I just lifted my face up from the manuscript and I directed my comments to an empty corner of the room. And I said aloud, 'Listen you, thing, you and I both know that if this book isn't brilliant that is not entirely my fault, right? Because you can see that I am putting everything I have into this, I don't have any more than this. If you want it to be better, you've got to show up and do your part of the deal. But if you don't do that, you know what, the hell with it. I'm going to keep writing anyway because that's my job. And I would please like the record to reflect today that I showed up for my part of the job.'

Because—because in the end it's like this, OK—centuries ago in the deserts of North Africa, people used to gather for these moonlight dances of sacred dance and music that would go on for hours and hours, until dawn. They were always magnificent, because the dancers were professionals and they were terrific, right? But every once in a while, very rarely, something would happen, and one of these performers would actually become transcendent. And I know you know what I'm talking about, because I know you've all seen, at some point in your life, a performance like this. It was like time would stop, and the dancer would sort of step through some kind of portal and he wasn't doing anything different than he had ever done, 1,000 nights before, but everything would align. And all of a sudden, he would no longer appear to be merely human. He would be lit from within, and lit from below and all lit up on fire with divinity.

And when this happened, back then, people knew it for what it was, you know, they called it by its name. They would put their hands together and they would start to chant, 'Allah, Allah, Allah, God, God, God.' That's God, you know. Curious historical footnote: when the Moors invaded southern Spain, they took this custom with them and the pronunciation changed over the centuries from 'Allah, Allah, Allah,' to 'Olé, olé, olé,' which you still hear in bullfights and in flamenco dance. In Spain, when a performer has done something impossible and magic,'Allah, olé, olé, Allah, magnificent, bravo,' incomprehensible, there it is—a glimpse of God. Which is great, because we need that.

But, the tricky bit comes the next morning, for the dancer himself, when he wakes up and discovers that it's Tuesday at 11 a.m., and he's no longer a glimpse of God. He's just an aging mortal with really bad knees, and maybe he's never going to ascend to that height again. And maybe nobody will ever chant God's name again as he spins, and what is he then to do with the rest of his life? This is hard. This is one of the most painful reconciliations to make in a creative life. But maybe it doesn't have to be quite so full of anguish if you never happened to believe, in the first place, that the most extraordinary aspects of your being came from you. But maybe if you just believed that they were on loan to you from some unimaginable source for some exquisite portion of your life to be passed along when you're finished, with somebody else. And, you know, if we think about it this way, it starts to change everything.

This is how I've started to think, and this is certainly how I've been thinking in the last few months as I've been working on the book that will soon be published, as the dangerously, frighteningly over-anticipated follow up to my freakish success.

And what I have to sort of keep telling myself when I get really psyched out about that is don't be afraid. Don't be daunted. Just do your job. Continue to show up for your piece of it, whatever that might be. If your job is to dance, do your dance. If the divine, cockeyed genius assigned to your case decides to let some sort of wonderment be glimpsed, for just one moment through your efforts, then 'Olé!' And if not, do your dance anyhow. And 'Olé!' to you, nonetheless. I believe this and I feel that we must teach it. 'Olé!' to you, nonetheless, just for having the sheer human love and stubbornness to keep showing up.

Thank you.

'What Matters More Than Your Talents'

Jeff Bezos

Baccalaureate Remarks to Graduates from Princeton University (2010)

Jeff Bezos is an American entrepreneur, investor and philanthropist who is the founder and CEO of Amazon.com and the owner of The Washington Post. Bezos ranks amongst the richest people in the world. According to Forbes, Bezos became 'the richest man in modern history' after his wealth increased to a record $150 billion in July 2018.

Bezos gave this inspiring speech at Princeton University, he motivated the students to dream big, work hard, take risks and ensure they choose a future that would be meaningful to them.

As a kid, I spent my summers with my grandparents on their ranch in Texas. I helped fix windmills, vaccinate cattle, and do other chores. We also watched soap operas every afternoon, especially 'Days of our Lives.' My grandparents belonged to a Caravan Club, a group of Airstream trailer owners who travel together around the U.S. and Canada. And every few summers, we'd join the caravan. We'd hitch up the Airstream trailer to my grandfather's car, and off we'd go, in a line with 300 other Airstream adventurers. I loved and worshipped my grandparents and I really looked forward to these trips. On one particular trip, I was about 10 years old. I was rolling around in the big bench seat in the back of the car. My grandfather was driving. And my grandmother had the passenger seat. She smoked throughout these trips, and I hated the smell.

At that age, I'd take any excuse to make estimates and do minor arithmetic. I'd calculate our gas mileage—figure out useless statistics on things like grocery spending. I'd been hearing an ad campaign about smoking. I can't remember the details, but basically the ad said, every puff of a cigarette takes some number of minutes off of your life: I think it might have been two minutes per puff. At any rate, I decided to do the math for my grandmother. I estimated the number of cigarettes per days, estimated the number of puffs per cigarette and so on. When I was satisfied that I'd come up with a reasonable number, I poked my head into the front of the car, tapped my grandmother on the shoulder, and proudly proclaimed, 'At two minutes per puff, you've taken nine years off your life!'

I have a vivid memory of what happened, and it was not what I expected. I expected to be applauded for my cleverness and arithmetic skills. 'Jeff, you're so smart. You had to have made some tricky estimates, figure out the number of minutes in a year and do some division.' That's not what happened. Instead, my grandmother burst into tears. I sat in the backseat and did not know what to do. While my grandmother sat crying, my grandfather, who had been driving in silence, pulled over onto the shoulder of the highway. He got out of the car and came around and opened my door and waited for me to follow. Was I in trouble? My grandfather was a highly intelligent, quiet man. He had never said a harsh word to me, and maybe this was to be the first time? Or maybe he would ask that I get back in the car and apologize to my grandmother. I had no experience in this realm with my grandparents and no way to gauge what the consequences might be. We stopped beside the trailer. My grandfather looked at me, and after a bit of silence, he gently and calmly said, 'Jeff, one day you'll understand that it's harder to be kind than clever.'

What I want to talk to you about today is the difference between gifts and choices. Cleverness is a gift, kindness is a choice. Gifts are easy—they're given after all. Choices can be hard. You can seduce yourself with your gifts if you're not careful, and if you do, it'll probably be to the detriment of your choices.

This is a group with many gifts. I'm sure one of your gifts is the gift of a smart and capable brain. I'm confident that's the case because admission is competitive and if there weren't some signs that you're clever, the dean of admission wouldn't have let you in.

Your smarts will come in handy because you will travel in a land of marvels. We humans—plodding as we are—will astonish ourselves. We'll invent ways to generate clean energy and a lot of it. Atom by atom, we'll assemble tiny machines that will enter cell walls and make repairs. This month comes the extraordinary but also inevitable news that we've synthesized life. In the coming years, we'll not only synthesize it, but we'll engineer it to specifications. I believe you'll even see us understand the human brain. Jules Verne, Mark Twain, Galileo, Newton—all the curious from the ages would have wanted to be alive most of all right now. As a civilization, we will have so many gifts, just as you as individuals have so many individual gifts as you sit before me.

How will you use these gifts? And will you take pride in your gifts or pride in your choices?

I got the idea to start Amazon 16 years ago. I came across the fact that Web usage was growing at 2,300 percent per year. I'd never seen or heard of anything that grew that fast, and the idea of building an online bookstore with millions of titles—something that simply couldn't exist in the physical world—was very exciting to me. I had just turned 30 years old, and I'd been married for a year. I told my wife MacKenzie that I wanted to quit my job and go do this crazy thing that probably wouldn't work since most startups don't, and I wasn't sure what would happen after that. MacKenzie (also a Princeton grad and sitting here in the second row) told me I should go for it. As a young boy, I'd been a garage inventor. I'd invented an automatic gate closer out of cement-filled tires, a solar cooker that didn't work very well out of an umbrella and tinfoil, baking-pan alarms to entrap my siblings. I'd always wanted to be an inventor, and she wanted me to follow my passion.

I was working at a financial firm in New York City with a bunch of very smart people, and I had a brilliant boss that I much admired. I went to my boss and told him I wanted to start a company selling books on the Internet. He took me on a long walk in Central Park, listened carefully to me, and finally said, 'That sounds like a really good idea, but it would be an even better idea for someone who didn't already have a good job.' That logic made some sense to me, and he convinced me to think about it for 48 hours before making a final decision. Seen in that light, it really was a difficult choice, but ultimately, I decided I had to give it a shot. I didn't think I'd regret trying and failing. And I suspected I would always be haunted by a decision to not try at all. After much consideration, I took the less safe path to follow my passion, and I'm proud of that choice.

Tomorrow, in a very real sense, your life—the life you author from scratch on your own—begins.

How will you use your gifts? What choices will you make?

Will inertia be your guide, or will you follow your passions?

Will you follow dogma, or will you be original?

Will you choose a life of ease, or a life of service and adventure?

Will you wilt under criticism, or will you follow your convictions?

Will you bluff it out when you're wrong, or will you apologize?

Will you guard your heart against rejection, or will you act when you fall in love?

Will you play it safe, or will you be a little bit swashbuckling?

When it's tough, will you give up, or will you be relentless?

Will you be a cynic, or will you be a builder?

Will you be clever at the expense of others, or will you be kind?

I will hazard a prediction. When you are 80 years old, and in a quiet moment of reflection narrating for only yourself the most personal version of your life story, the telling that will be most compact and meaningful will be the series of choices you have made. In the end, we are our choices. Build yourself a great story. Thank you and good luck!

Main Address at St. Bridge's Church

Marie Colvin

London (10 November 2010)

Marie Colvin was an American war correspondent who worked as the foreign affairs correspondent for *The Sunday Times*. Fearless and headstrong, Colvin worked in the most dangerous areas of the world to tell stories which might otherwise not have seen the light of day. She lost her left eye in Colombo while reporting on the Sri Lankan Civil War. Colvin died on 22 February 2012, while covering the Siege of Homs in Syria.

In this moving address, Colvin remembers the sacrifices and efforts of the journalists who worked and continue to work in dangerous circumstances to tell stories of those oppressed.

Your Royal Highness, Ladies and Gentlemen, I am honoured and humbled to be speaking to you at this service tonight to remember the journalists and their support staff who gave their lives to report from the war zones of the 21st Century. I have been a war correspondent for most of my professional life. It has always been a hard calling. But the need for front line, objective reporting has never been more compelling.

Covering a war means going to places torn by chaos, destruction, and death, and trying to bear witness. It means trying to find the truth in a sandstorm of propaganda when armies, tribes or terrorists clash. And yes, it means taking risks, not just for yourself but often for the people who work closely with you.

Despite all the videos you see from the Ministry of Defence or the Pentagon, and all the sanitised language describing smart bombs and pinpoint strikes, the scene on the ground has remained remarkably the same for hundreds of years. Craters. Burned houses. Mutilated bodies. Women weeping for children and husbands. Men for their wives, mothers children.

Our mission is to report these horrors of war with accuracy and without prejudice. We always have to ask ourselves whether the level of risk is worth the story. What is bravery, and what is bravado?

Journalists covering combat shoulder great responsibilities and face difficult choices. Sometimes they pay the ultimate price. Tonight we honour the 49 journalists and support staff who were killed bringing the news to our shores. We also remember journalists around the world who have been wounded, maimed or kidnapped and held hostage for months. It has never been more dangerous to be a war correspondent, because the journalist in the combat zone has become a prime target.

I lost my eye in an ambush in the Sri Lankan civil war. I had gone to the northern Tamil area from which journalists were banned and found an unreported humanitarian disaster. As I was smuggled back across the internal border, a soldier launched a grenade at me and the shrapnel sliced into my face and chest. He knew what he was doing.

Just last week, I had a coffee in Afghanistan with a photographer friend, Joao Silva. We talked about the terror one feels and must contain when patrolling on an embed with the armed forces through fields and villages in Afghanistan ... putting one foot in front of the other, steeling yourself each step for the blast. The expectation of that blast is the stuff of nightmares. Two days after our meeting Joao stepped on a mine and lost both legs at the knee.

Many of you here must have asked yourselves, or be asking yourselves now, is it worth the cost in lives, heartbreak, loss? Can we really make a difference?

I faced that question when I was injured. In fact one paper ran a headline saying, has Marie Colvin gone too far this time? My answer then, and now, was that it is worth it.

Today in this church are friends, colleagues and families who know exactly what I am talking about, and bear the cost of those experiences, as do their families and loved ones.

Today we must also remember how important it is that news organisations continue to invest in sending us out at great cost, both financial and emotional, to cover stories.

We go to remote war zones to report what is happening. The public have a right to know what our government, and our armed forces, are doing in our name. Our mission is to speak the truth to power. We send home that first rough draft of history. We can and do make a difference in exposing the horrors of war and especially the atrocities that befall civilians.

The history of our profession is one to be proud of. The first war correspondent in the modern era was William Howard Russell of The Times, who was sent to cover the Crimean conflict when a British-led coalition fought an invading Russian army.

Billy Russell, as the troops called him, created a firestorm of public indignation back home by revealing inadequate equipment, scandalous treatment of the wounded, especially when they were repatriated—does this sound familiar?—and an incompetent high command that led to the folly of the Charge of the Light Brigade. It was a breakthrough in war reporting. Until then, wars were reported by junior officers who sent back dispatches to newspapers. Billy Russell went to war with an open mind, a telescope, a notebook and a bottle of brandy. I first went to war with a typewriter, and learned to tap out a telex tape. It could take days to get from the front to a telephone or telex machine.

War reporting has changed greatly in just the last few years. Now we go to war with a satellite phone, laptop, video camera and a flak jacket. I point my satellite phone to South Southwest in Afghanistan, press a button and I have filed.

In an age of 24/7 rolling news, blogs and twitters, we are on constant call wherever we are. But war reporting is still essentially the same—someone has to go there and see what is happening. You can't get that information without going to places where people are being shot at, and others are shooting at you. The real difficulty is having enough faith in humanity to believe that enough people be they government, military or the man on the street, will care when your file reaches the printed page, the website or the TV screen.

We do have that faith because we believe we do make a difference.

And we could not make that difference—or begin to do our job—without the fixers, drivers, and translators, who face the same risks and die in appalling numbers. Today we honour them as much as the front line journalists who have died in pursuit of the truth. They have kept the faith as we who remain must continue to do.'

'Fall Forward'

Denzel Washington

Penn Commencement Address (2011)

Denzel Washington is an Oscar-winning American actor, filmmaker, director and philanthropist known for starring in movies such as *Malcolm X, The Hurricane* and *Training Day*. In 2016, Washington was awarded the prestigious Cecil B. DeMille Lifetime Achievement Award at the 73rd Golden Globe Awards.

Washington gave his inspiring commencement speech at the University of Pennsylvania, through which he asks the students to 'fall forward'—take risks and not be afraid to explore their talents.

President Gutmann; Provost Price; Board Chair Cohen; fellow honorees; and today's graduates:

I'm honored and grateful for the invitation today.

It's always great to be on the Penn campus. I've been to a lot of basketball games at the Palestra because my son played on the team. Coach didn't give him enough playing time, but we'll talk about that later. No, I'm very pleased with the progress Coach Allen has made and I wish them success in the future.

I'd always get a warm welcome here—except on the few occasions when I'd wear my Yankees cap.

It's like taking your life in your hands. People would say: 'We love you Denzel. But you walking around with that hat on…we don't care who you are.'

So you'll be happy to see that I'm not wearing my Yankees cap today.

But I am wearing my Yankees socks, my Yankees t-shirt, and my Yankees underwear.

Still, I'll be honest with you: I'm a little nervous. Speaking at a graduation of this magnitude is a little overwhelming.

This is out of my comfort zone.

Dress me up in army fatigues. Throw me on top of a moving train. Ask me to play Malcolm X, Rubin Hurricane Carter, Alonzo from *Training Day*: I can do all that.

But a commencement speech? It's a very serious affair. Different ballgame. There's literally thousands and thousands of people here.

And for those who say—you're a movie star, millions of people watch you speak all the time…

Yes, that's technically true. But I'm not actually there in the theater—watching *them* watching *me*.

I'm not there when they cough…or fidget…or pull out their iPhone and text their boyfriend…or scratch their behinds.

From up here: I can see *every single one of you*. And that makes me uncomfortable.

So *please*, don't pull out your iPhone and text your boyfriend until after I'm done.

But if you need to scratch your behinds, go right ahead. I'll understand.

Thinking about the speech, I figured the best way to keep your attention would be to talk about some really, juicy Hollywood stuff.

I thought I could start with me and Russell Crowe getting into some arguments on the set of *American Gangster*…

…but no. You're a group of high-minded intellectuals. You're not interested in that.

Or how about that 'private' moment I had with Angelina Jolie half naked in her dressing room backstage at the Oscars?… Who wants to hear about that?

I don't think so. This is an Ivy League school. Angelina Jolie in her dressing room…?

No, this is *Penn*. That stuff wouldn't go over well here. Maybe at Drexel—but not here. I'm in trouble now.

I was back to square one—and feeling the pressure.

So now you're probably thinking—if it was gonna be this difficult, why'd I even accept today's invitation in the first place?

Well, you know my son goes here. That's a good reason. And I always like to check to see how my money's being spent.

And I'm sure there's some parents out there who can relate to what I'm talking about!

And there were other good reasons for me to show up.

Sure, I got an Academy Award...but I never had something called 'Magic Meatballs' after waiting in line for half an hour at a food truck.

True, I've talked face-to-face with President Obama... but I never met a guy named 'Kweeder' who sings bad cover songs at Smokes on a Tuesday night.

Yes, I've played a detective battling demons...but I've never been to a school in my life where the squirrel population has gone bananas, breaking into the dorm rooms and taking over campus. I think I've even seen some carrying books on the way to class!

So I had to be here. I had to come...even though I was afraid I might make a fool of myself.

In fact...if you really want to know the truth:

I had to come...*exactly because* I might make a fool of myself.

What am I talking about?

Well, here it is:

I've found that nothing in life is worthwhile unless you take risks.

Nothing.

Nelson Mandela said:

'There is no passion to be found playing small—in settling for a life that's less than the one you're capable of living.'

I'm sure in your experiences—in school... in applying to college...in picking your major...in deciding what you want to do with life—people have told you to make sure you have something to 'fall back on.'

But I've never understood that concept, having something to fall back on.

If I'm going to fall, I don't want to fall back on anything, except my faith. I want to fall...*forward*.

At least I figure that way I'll see what I'm about to hit.

Fall forward.

Here's what I mean:

Reggie Jackson struck out 2600 times in his career—the most in the history of baseball.

But you don't hear about the strikeouts. People remember the home runs.

Fall forward.

Thomas Edison conducted 1,000 failed experiments. Did you know that?

I didn't either—because #1,001 was the light bulb.

Fall forward.

Every failed experiment is one step closer to success.

You've got to take risks. And I'm sure you've probably heard that before.

But I want to talk about why it's so important.

I've got three reasons—and then you can pick up your iPhones.

First…you *will* fail at some point in your life. Accept it. You will lose. You will embarrass yourself. You will suck at something. There is no doubt about it.

That's probably not a traditional message for a graduation ceremony. But, hey, I'm telling you—embrace it.

Because it's inevitable.

And I should know: In the acting business, you fail all the time.

Early in my career, I auditioned for a part in a Broadway musical. A perfect role for me, I thought—except for the fact that I can't sing.

So I'm in the wings, about to go on stage but the guy in front of me is singing like Pavarotti and I am just shrinking getting smaller and smaller...

So I come out with my little sheet music and it was 'Just My Imagination' by the Temptations, that's what I came up with.

So I hand it to the accompanist, and she looks at it and looks at me and looks at the director, so I start to sing and they're not saying anything. I think I must be getting better, so I start getting into it.

But after the first verse, the director cuts me off: 'Thank you. Thank you very much, you'll be hearing from me.'

The next part of the audition is the acting part. I figure, I can't sing, but I know I can act.

But the guy I was paired with to do the scene couldn't be more over-dramatic and over-the top.

Suffice to say, I didn't get the part.

But here's the thing: I didn't quit. I didn't fall back.

I walked out of there to prepare for the next audition, and the next audition, and the next one. I prayed and I prayed, but I continued to fail, and I failed, and I failed.

But it didn't matter. Because you know what? You hang around a barbershop long enough—sooner or later you will get a haircut.

You will catch a break.

Last year I did a play called *Fences* on Broadway and I won a Tony Award. And I didn't have to sing for it, by the way.

And here's the kicker—it was at the Court Theater, the same theater where I failed that first audition 30 years prior.

The point is, every graduate here today has the training and the talent to succeed.

But do you have guts to fail?

Here's my second point about failure:

If you don't fail...you're not even trying.

My wife told me this expression: 'To get something you never had, you have to do something you never did.'

Les Brown, a motivational speaker, made an analogy about this.

Imagine you're on your deathbed—and standing around your bed are the ghosts representing your unfilled potential.

The ghosts of the ideas you never acted on. The ghosts of the talents you didn't use.

And they're standing around your bed. Angry. Disappointed. Upset.

'We came to you because you could have brought us to life,' they say. 'And now we go to the grave together.'

So I ask you today: How many ghosts are going to be around your bed when your time comes?

You invested a lot in your education. And people invested in *you*.

And let me tell you, the world needs your talents.

Man, does it ever.

I just got back from four months of filming in South Africa—beautiful country, but there are places with terrible poverty that need help.

And Africa is just the tip of the iceberg.

The Middle East needs your help. Japan needs your help. Alabama and Tennessee need your help. Louisiana needs your help. Philadelphia needs your help.

The world needs a lot—and we need it from you, the young people.

So get out there. Give it everything you've got—whether it's your time, your talent, your prayers, or your treasure.

Because remember this: You'll never see a U-haul behind a hearse.

You can't take it with you. The Ancient Egyptians tried it—and all they got was robbed!

So what are you going to do with what you have? And I'm not talking *how much* you have.

Some of you are business majors. Some of you are theologians, nurses, sociologists. Some of you have money. Some of you have patience. Some have kindness. Some have love. Some of you have the gift of long-suffering.

Whatever it is... what are you going to do with what you have?

Now here's my last point about failure:

Sometimes it's the best way to figure out where you're going.

Your life will never be a straight path.

I began at Fordham University as a pre-med student. That lasted until I took a course called 'Cardiac Morphogenesis.'

I couldn't pronounce it...and I couldn't pass it.

Then I decided to go pre-law. Then journalism.

With no academic focus, my grades took off in their own direction: down.

My GPA was 1.8 one semester, and the university very politely suggested it might be better to take some time off.

I was 20 years old, at my lowest point.

And then one day—and I remember the exact day: March 27th, 1975—I was helping out in the beauty shop my mother owned in Mount Vernon.

An older woman who belonged to my mother's church, one of the elders of the town, was in there getting her hair done and kept giving me these strange looks.

She finally took the drier off her head and said something to me I'll never forget:

'Young boy,' she said. 'I have a spiritual prophecy: you are going to travel the world and speak to millions of people.'

Like a wise-ass, I'm thinking to myself: 'Does she got anything in that crystal ball about me getting back to college in the fall?'

But maybe she was on to something. Because later that summer, while working as a counselor at a YMCA camp in Connecticut, we put on a talent show for the campers.

After the show, another counselor came up to me and asked: 'Have you ever thought of acting? You should. You're good at that.'

When I got back to Fordham that fall I changed my major once again—*for the last time.*

And in the years that followed—just as that woman getting her hair done predicted—I *have* traveled the world and I *have* spoken to millions of people through my movies.

Millions who—up 'till today—I couldn't see while I was talking to them.

But I *do* see you today. And I'm encouraged by what I see. I'm strengthened by what I see. I love what I see.

Let me conclude with one final point. Many years ago I did this movie called *Philadelphia*. We actually filmed some scenes right here on campus.

Philadelphia came out in 1993, when most of you were probably still crawling around in diapers. Some of the professors, too.

But it's a good movie. Rent it on Netflix. I get 23 cents every time you do. Tell your friends, too!

It's about a man, played by Tom Hanks, who's fired from his law firm because he has AIDS.

He wants to sue the firm, but no one's willing to represent him until a homophobic, ambulance-chasing lawyer—played by yours truly—takes on the case.

In a way, if you watch the movie, you'll see everything I'm talking about today.

You'll see what I mean about taking risks or being willing to fail.

Because taking a risk is not just about going for a job.

It's also about knowing what you know and what you don't know. It's about being open to people and ideas.

Over the course of the film, the character I play begins to take risks. He slowly overcomes his fears, and ultimately his heart becomes flooded with love.

And I can't think of a better message as we send you off today.

To not only take risks, but to be open to life.

To accept new views and to be open to new opinions.

To be willing to speak at commencement at one of the country's best universities… even though you're scared stiff.

While it may be frightening, it will also be rewarding.

Because the chances you take…the people you meet…the people you love...the faith that you have—*that's* what's going to define your life.

So… members of the class of 2011: This is your mission:

When you leave the friendly confines of West Philly: Never be discouraged. Never hold back. Give everything you've got.

And when you fall throughout life—and maybe even tonight after a few too many glasses of champagne—*fall forward*.

Congratulations, I love you, God bless you, I respect you.

'We Should All Be Feminists'

Chimamanda Ngozi Adichie

TEDx Euston, London (2012)

Chimamanda Ngozi Adichie is a Nigerian author and orator who divides her time between Nigeria and the United States. A successful author, her work has been translated to over 30 languages and she has won the National Book Critics Circle Award for her novel *Americanah* (2013).

'We Should All Be Feminists' by Adichie was an inspiring TED talk which was later published as a book in 2014.

My brother Chuks and my best friend Ike are part of the organizing team, and so when they ask me to come, I couldn't say no. But I'm so happy to be here. What a fantastic team of people who care about Africa. I feel so humble and so happy to be here.

And I'm also told that the most beautiful, most amazing little girl in the world is in the audience. Her name is Kamzia Adichie and I want her to stand up… she's my niece!

So, I would like to start by telling you about one of my greatest friends, Okuloma.

Okuloma lived on my street and looked after me like a big brother. If I liked a boy, I would ask Okuloma's opinion. Okuloma died in the notorious Sosoliso Plane Crash in Nigeria in December of 2005. Almost exactly seven years ago.

Okuloma was a person I could argue with, laugh with, and truly talk to. He was also the first person to call me a feminist. I was about fourteen, we were at his house, arguing. Both of us bristling with half bit knowledge from books that we had read. I don't remember what this particular argument was about, but I remember that as I argued and argued, Okuloma looked at me and said, 'You know, you're a feminist.' It was not a compliment. I could tell from his tone, the same tone that you would use to say something like 'You're a supporter of terrorism.'

I did not know exactly what this word 'feminist' meant, and I did not want Okuloma to know that I did not know, so I brushed it aside and I continued to argue. And the first thing I planned to do when I got home was to look up the word 'feminist' in the dictionary.

Now fast forward to some years later, I wrote a novel about a man who among other things beats his wife and whose story doesn't end very well. While I was promoting the novel in Nigeria, a journalist, a nice well-meaning man, told me he wanted to advise me. And for the Nigerians here, I'm sure we're all familiar with how quick our people are to give unsolicited advice. He told me that people were saying that my novel was feminist and his advice to me—and he was shaking his head sadly as he spoke—was that I should never call myself a feminist because feminists are women who are unhappy because they cannot find husbands. So I decided to call myself 'a happy feminist.'

Then an academic, a Nigerian woman told me that feminism was not our culture and that feminism wasn't African, and that I was calling myself a feminist because I had been corrupted by 'Western books.' Which amused me, because a lot of my early readings were decidedly unfeminist. I think I must have read every single Mills & Boon romance published before I was sixteen. And each time I tried to read those books called 'the feminist classics' I'd get bored and I really struggled to finish them.

But anyway, since feminism was un-African, I decided that I would now call myself 'a happy African feminist.' At some point I was a happy African feminist who does not hate men and who likes lip gloss and who wears high heels for herself but not for men. Of course a lot of these was tongue-in-cheek, but that word feminist is so heavy with baggage, negative baggage. You hate men, you hate bras, you hate African culture, that sort of thing.

Now here's a story from my childhood. When I was in primary school, my teacher said at the beginning of term that she would give the class a test and whoever got the highest score would be the class monitor. Now, class monitor was a big deal. If you were a class monitor, you got to write down the names of noise makers, which was having enough power of its own. But my teacher would also give you a cane to hold in your hand while you walk around and patrol the class for noise makers.

Now of course you're not actually allowed to use the cane. But it was an exciting prospect for the nine-year-old me. I very much wanted to be the class monitor. And I got the highest score on the test.

Then, to my surprise, my teacher said that the monitor had to be a boy. She'd forgotten to make that clear earlier because she assumed it was…obvious. A boy had the second highest score on the test and he would be monitor.

Now what was even more interesting about this is that the boy was a sweet, gentle soul who had no interest in patrolling the class with the cane, while I was full of ambition to do so. But I was female, and he was male and so he became the class monitor.

And I've never forgotten that incident. I often make the mistake of thinking that something that is obvious to me is just as obvious to everyone else. Now, take my dear friend Louis for example. Louis is a brilliant, progressive man, and we would have conversations and he would tell me, 'I don't know what you mean by things being different or harder for women. Maybe in the past, but not now.'

And I didn't understand how Louis could not see what seems so self-evident. Then one evening, in Lagos, Louis and I went out with friends. And for people here who are not familiar with Lagos, there's that wonderful Lagos' fixture, the sprinkling of energetic man who hung around outside establishments and very dramatically 'help' you park your car. I was impressed with the particular theatrics of the man who found us a parking spot that evening, and so as we were leaving, I decided to leave him a tip.

I opened my bag, put my hand inside my bag, brought out my money that I had earned from doing my work, and I gave it to the man.

And he, this man who was very grateful, and very happy, took the money from me, looked across at Louis, and said 'Thank you, sir!'

Louis looked at me, surprised, and asked 'Why is he thanking me? I didn't give him the money.'

Then I saw realization dawned on Louis' face. The man believed that whatever money I had had ultimately come from Louis. Because Louis is a man.

The men and women are different. We have different hormones, we have different sexual organs, we have different biological abilities, women can have babies, men can't. At least not yet. Men have testosterone and are in general physically stronger than women. There's slightly more women than men in the world, about 52% of the world's population is female. But most of the positions of power and prestige are occupied by men.

The late Kenyan Nobel Peace Laureate, Wangari Maathai, put it simply and well when she said: 'The higher you go, the fewer women there are.'

In the recent US elections we kept hearing of the Lilly Ledbetter law, and if we go beyond the nicely alliterative name of that law, it was really about a man and a woman doing the same job being equally qualified and the man being paid more because he's a man. So in the literal way, men rule the world, and this made sense a thousand years ago because human beings lived then in a world in which physical strength was the most important attribute for survival. The physically stronger person was more likely to lead, and men, in general, are physically stronger. Of course there are many exceptions.

But today we live in a vastly different world. The person more likely to lead is not the physically stronger person, it is the more creative person, the more intelligent person, the more innovative person, and there are no hormones for those attributes. A man is as likely as a woman to be intelligent, to be creative, to be innovative. We have evolved; but it seems to me that our ideas of gender have not evolved.

Some weeks ago I walked into a lobby of one of the best Nigerian hotels. I thought about naming the hotel, but I thought I probably shouldn't, and a guard at the entrance stopped me and ask me annoying questions, because their automatic assumption is that a Nigerian female walking into a hotel alone is a sex worker.

And by the way, why do these hotels focus on the ostensible supply rather than the demand for sex workers?

In Lagos I cannot go alone into many 'reputable' bars and clubs. They just don't let you in if you're a woman alone, you have to be accompanied by a man. Each time I walk into a Nigerian restaurant with a man, the waiter greets the man and ignores me. The waiters are products…at this some women felt like 'Yes! I thought that!' The waiters are products of a society that has taught them that men are more important than women. And I know that waiters don't intend any harm. But it's one thing to know intellectually and quite another to feel it emotionally. Each time they ignore me, I feel invisible. I feel upset. I want to tell them I'm just as human as the man, that I'm just as worthy of acknowledgement. These are little things, but sometimes it's the little things that sting the most.

And not long ago I wrote an article about what it means to be young and female in Lagos, and the printers told me 'It was so angry.' Of course it was angry!

I am angry. Gender as it functions today is a grave injustice. We should all be angry. Anger has a long history of bringing about positive change; but in addition to being angry, I'm also hopeful. Because I believe deeply in the ability of human beings to make and remake themselves for the better.

Gender matters everywhere in the world, but I want to focus on Nigeria and on Africa in general, because it is where I know, and because it is where my heart is. And I would like today to ask that we begin to dream about and plan for a different world, a fairer world; a world of happier men and happier women who are truer to themselves. And this is how to start: we must raise our daughters differently. We must also raise our sons differently.

We do a great disservice to boys on how we raise them; we stifle the humanity of boys. We define masculinity in a very narrow way, masculinity becomes this hard, small cage and we put boys inside the cage. We teach boys to be afraid of fear. We teach boys to be afraid of weakness, of vulnerability. We teach them to mask their true selves, because they have to be, in Nigerian speak, 'hard man!'

In secondary school, a boy and a girl, both of them teenagers, both of them with the same amount of pocket money, would go out and then the boy would be expected always to pay, to prove his masculinity. And yet we wonder why boys are more likely to steal money from their parents.

What if both boys and girls were raised not to link masculinity with money? What if the attitude was not 'the boy has to pay' but rather 'whoever has more should pay'? Now of course because of that historical advantage, it is mostly men who will have more today, but if we start raising children differently, then in fifty years, in a hundred years, boys will no longer have the pressure of having to prove this masculinity.

But by far the worst thing we do to males, by making them feel that they have to be hard, is that we leave them with very fragile egos. The more 'hard-man' the man feels compelled to be, the weaker his ego is.

And then we do a much greater disservice to girls because we raise them to cater to the fragile egos of men. We teach girls to shrink themselves, to make themselves smaller, we say to girls, 'You can have ambition, but not too much.' 'You should aim to be successful, but not too successful, otherwise you would threaten the man.' If you are the breadwinner in your relationship with a man, you have to pretend that you're not, especially in public, otherwise you will emasculate him.

But what if we question the premise itself, why should a woman's success be a threat to a man? What if we decide to simply dispose of that word, and I don't think there's an English word I dislike more than 'emasculation.' A Nigerian acquaintance once asked me if I was worried that men would be intimidated by me. I was not worried at all. In fact it had not occurred to me to be worried because a man who would be intimidated by me is exactly the kind of man I would have no interest in. But still I was really struck by this. Because I'm female, I'm expected to aspire to marriage; I'm expected to make my life choices always keeping in mind that marriage is the most important.

A marriage can be a good thing; it can be a source of joy and love and mutual support. But why do we teach girls to aspire to marriage and we don't teach boys the same? I know a woman who decided to sell her house because she didn't want to intimidate a man who might marry her. I know an unmarried woman in Nigeria who, when she goes to conferences, wears a wedding ring because according to her, she wants the other participants in the conference to 'give her respect.'

I know young women who are under so much pressure from family, from friends, even from work to get married and they're pushed to make terrible choices. A woman at a certain age who is unmarried, our society teaches her to see it as a deep, personal failure. And a man at a certain age who is unmarried we just think he hasn't come around to making his pick. It's easy for us to say, 'Oh but women can just say no to all of this'. But the reality is more difficult and more complex. We're all social beings. We internalize ideas from our socialization. Even the language we use in talking about marriage and relationships illustrates this. The language of marriage is often the language of ownership rather than the language of partnership.

We use the word 'respect' to mean something that a woman shows a man but often not something a man shows a woman. Both men and women in Nigeria will say—and this is an expression I'm very amused by—'I did it for peace in my marriage.' Now when men say it, it is usually about something that they should not be doing anyway. Sometimes they say it to their friends, it's something to say to their friends in a kind of fondly exasperated way, you know, something that ultimately proves how masculine they are, how needed, how loved— 'Oh my wife said I can't go to club every night, so for peace in my marriage, I do it only on weekends.'

Now when a woman says, 'I did it for peace in my marriage,' she's usually talking about having giving up a job, a dream, a career. We teach females that in relationships, compromise is what women do. We raise girls to see each other as competitors not for job or for accomplishments, which I think could be a good thing, but for attention of men. We teach girls that they cannot be sexual beings in the way that boys are. If we have sons, we don't mind knowing about our sons' girlfriends. But our daughters' boyfriends? God forbid.

But of course when the time is right, we expect those girls to bring back the perfect man to be their husbands. We police girls, we praise girls for virginity, but we don't praise boys for virginity, and it's always made me wonder how exactly this is supposed to work out because...I mean, the loss of virginity is usually a process that involves...

Recently a young woman was gang raped in a University in Nigeria, I think some of us know about that. And the response of many young Nigerians, both male and female, was something along the lines of this: 'Yes, rape is wrong. But what is a girl doing in a room with four boys?'

Now if we can forget the horrible inhumanity of that response, these Nigerians have been raised to think of women as inherently guilty, and have been raised to expect so little of men that the idea of men as savage beings without any control is somehow acceptable. We teach girls shame. 'Close your legs', 'Cover yourself'. We make them feel as though by being born female they're already guilty of something. And so, girls grow up to be women who cannot see they have desire. They grow up to be women who silence themselves. They grow up to be women who cannot see what they truly think, and they grow up—and this is the worst thing we did to girls—they grow up to be women who have turned pretense into an art form.

I know a woman who hates domestic work, she just hates it, but she pretends that she likes it, because she's been taught that to be 'good wife material' she has to be—to use that Nigerian word—very 'homely.' And then she got married, and after a while her husband's family began to complain that she had changed. Actually she had not changed, she just got tired of pretending.

The problem with gender is that it prescribes how we should be rather than recognizing how we are. Now imagine how much happier we would be, how much freer to be our true individual selves, if we didn't have the weight of gender expectations. Boys and girls are undeniably different biologically, but socialization exaggerates the differences and then it becomes a self-fulfilling process.

Now take cooking for example. Today women in general are more likely to do the house work than men, the cooking and cleaning. But why is that? Is it because women are born with a cooking gene? Or because over years they have been socialized to see cooking as their rule? Actually I was going to say that maybe women are born with a cooking gene, until I remember that the majority of the famous cooks in the world, whom we give the fancy title of 'chefs,' are men.

I used to look up to my grandmother who was a brilliant, brilliant woman, and wonder how she would have been if she had the same opportunity as men when she was growing up. Now today, there are many more opportunities for women than there were during my grandmother's time because of changes in policy, changes in law, all of which are very important. But what matters even more is our attitude, our mindset, what we believe and what we value about gender.

What if in raising children we focus on ability instead of gender? What if in raising children we focus on interest instead of gender? I know a family who have a son and a daughter, both of whom are brilliant at school, who are wonderful, lovely children. When the boy is hungry, the parents say to the girl 'Go and cook Indomie noodles for your brother.' Now the daughter doesn't particularly like to cook Indomie noodles, but she's a girl, and so she has to.

Now, what if the parents, from the beginning, taught both the boy and the girl to cook Indomie? Cooking, by the way, is a very useful skill for boys to have. I've never thought it made sense to leave such a crucial thing, the ability to nourish oneself, in the hands of others.

I know a woman who has the same degree and the same job as her husband, when they get back from work she does most of the house work, which I think is true for many marriages. But what struck me about them was that whenever her husband changed the baby's diaper, she said 'thank you' to him.

Now what if she saw this as perfectly normal and natural that he should, in fact, care for his child? I'm trying to unlearn many of the lessons of gender that I internalized when I was growing up. But I sometimes still feel very vulnerable in the face of gender expectations. The first time I taught a writing class in graduate school I was worried. I wasn't worried about the material I would teach because I was well-prepared and I was going to teach what I enjoy teaching. Instead, I was worried about what to wear. I wanted to be taken seriously. I knew that because I was female I will automatically have to prove my worth. And I was worried if I looked too feminine

I would not be taken seriously. I really wanted to wear my shiny lip gloss and my girly skirt, but I decided not to.

Instead, I wore a very serious, very manly, and very ugly suit. Because the sad truth is that when it comes to appearance we start off with man as the standard, as the norm. If a man is getting ready for a business meeting he doesn't worry about looking too masculine and therefore not being taken for granted. If a woman has to get ready for business meeting, she has to worry about looking too feminine, and what it says and whether or not she will be taken seriously.

I wish I had not worn that ugly suit that day. I've actually banished it from my closet, by the way. Had I then the confidence that I have now to be myself my students would have benefited even more from my teaching, because I would have been more comfortable, and more fully and more truly myself. I have chosen to no longer be apologetic for my femaleness and for my femininity. And I want to be respected in all of my femaleness because I deserve to be.

Gender is not an easy conversation to have. For both men and women, to bring up gender, sometimes encounters almost immediate resistance. I can imagine some people here are actually thinking 'Women, true to selves? ' Some of the men here might be thinking 'Okay, all of this is interesting, but I don't think like that.' And that is part of the problem. That many men do not actively think about gender or notice gender, is part of the problem of gender. That many men, say, like my friend Louis, that everything is fine now. And that many men do nothing to change it. If you are a man and you walk into a restaurant with a woman and the waiter greets only you, does it occur to you to ask the waiter 'Why haven't you greeted her?'

Because gender can be...Actually we may repose part of a longer version of this talk. So, because gender can be a very uncomfortable conversation to have, there are very easy ways to close it, to close the conversation. So some people will bring up evolutionary biology and apes, how, you know, female apes bow down to male apes and that sort of thing.

But the point is we're not apes. Apes also live on trees and have earth worms for breakfast but we don't. Some people will say, 'Well, poor men also have a hard time.' And this is true. But that is not what this... But this is not what this conversation is about. Gender and class are different forms of oppression. I actually learned quite a bit about systems of oppression and how they can be blind to one another by talking to black men.

I was once talking to a black man about gender and he said to me, 'Why do you have to say 'my experience as a woman'? why can't it be 'your experience as a human being'?' Now this was the same man who would often talk about his experience as a black man.

Gender matters. Men and women experience the world differently. Gender colors the way we experience the world. But we can change that.

Some people will say, 'Oh but women have the real power, bottom power.' And for non-Nigerians, bottom power is an expression which—I suppose means something like a woman who uses her sexuality to get favors from men. But bottom power is not power at all. Bottom power means that a woman simply has a good root to tap into, from time to time, somebody else's power. And then of course we have to wonder what happens when that somebody else is in a bad mood, or sick, or impotent.

Some people will say that a woman being subordinate to a man is our culture. But culture is constantly changing. I have beautiful twin nieces who are fifteen and live in Lagos, if they had been born a hundred years ago they would have been taken away and killed. Because it was our culture, it was our culture to kill twins.

So what is the point of culture? I mean there's the decorative, the dancing...but also, culture really is about preservation and continuity of a people. In my family, I am the child who is most interested in the story of who we are, in our tradition, in the knowledge about ancestral lands. My brothers are not as interested as I am. But I cannot participate, I cannot go to their meetings, I cannot have a say. Because I'm female.

Culture does not make people, people make culture. So if it's in fact true that the full humanity of women is not our culture, then we must make it our culture. I think very often of my dear friend Okuloma, may he and all the others that passed away in that Sosoliso Crash continue to rest in peace. He will always be remembered by those of us who loved him. And he was right that day many years ago when he called me a feminist. I am a feminist. And when I looked up the word in the dictionary that day, this is what it said: Feminist, a person who believes in the social, political and economic equality of the sexes.

My great grandmother, from the stories I've heard, was a feminist. She ran away from the house of the man she did not want to marry, and ended up marrying the man of her choice. She refused, she protested, she spoke up whenever she felt she's being deprived of access, of land, that sort of thing. My great grandmother did not know that word 'feminist,' but it doesn't mean that she wasn't one. More of us should reclaim that word.

My own definition of feminist is: a feminist is a man or a woman who says—a feminist is a man or a woman who says 'Yes, there's a problem with gender as it is today, and we must fix it. We must do better.'

The best feminist I know is my brother Kenny. He's also a kind, good-looking, lovely man, and he's very masculine.

Thank you.

Misogyny Speech

Julia Gillard

Parliament (9 October 2012)

Julia Gillard is a former politician who served as the 27th Prime Minister of Australia, becoming the first woman to hold the post. To date, she is the only woman to hold the positions of Prime Minister, Deputy Prime Minister and leader of a major party in Australia. In 2014, Gillard's political memoir *My Story* became the highest selling politics-related book in Australia.

'Misogyny Speech' by Gillard was delivered at the Australian Parliament in which she calls out the Opposition leader Tony Abbott for his sexist behaviour. This speech was praised by feminists all round the world.

Thank you very much Deputy Speaker and I rise to oppose the motion moved by the Leader of the Opposition. And in so doing I say to the Leader of the Opposition I will not be lectured about sexism and misogyny by this man. I will not. And the Government will not be lectured about sexism and misogyny by this man. Not now, not ever.

The Leader of the Opposition says that people who hold sexist views and who are misogynists are not appropriate for high office. Well I hope the Leader of the Opposition has got a piece of paper and he is writing out his resignation. Because if he wants to know what misogyny looks like in modern Australia, he doesn't need a motion in the House of Representatives, he needs a mirror. That's what he needs.

Let's go through the Opposition Leader's repulsive double standards, repulsive double standards when it comes to misogyny and sexism. We are now supposed to take seriously that the Leader of the Opposition is offended by Mr Slipper's text messages, when this is the Leader of the Opposition who has said, and this was when he was a minister under the last government—not when he was a student, not when he was in high school—when he was a minister under the last government.

He has said, and I quote, in a discussion about women being under-represented in institutions of power in Australia, the interviewer was a man called Stavros. The Leader of the Opposition says 'If it's true, Stavros, that men have more power generally speaking than women, is that a bad thing?'

And then a discussion ensues, and another person says 'I want my daughter to have as much opportunity as my son.' To which the Leader of the Opposition says 'Yeah, I completely agree, but what if men are by physiology or temperament, more adapted to exercise authority or to issue command?'

Then ensues another discussion about women's role in modern society, and the other person participating in the discussion says 'I think it's very hard to deny that there is an underrepresentation of women,' to which the Leader of the Opposition says, 'But now, there's an assumption that this is a bad thing.'

This is the man from whom we're supposed to take lectures about sexism. And then of course it goes on. I was very offended personally when the Leader of the Opposition, as Minister of Health, said, and I quote, 'Abortion is the easy way out.' I was very personally offended by those comments. You said that in March 2004, I suggest you check the records.

I was also very offended on behalf of the women of Australia when in the course of this carbon pricing campaign, the Leader of the Opposition said 'What the housewives of Australia need to understand as they do the ironing…' Thank you for that painting of women's roles in modern Australia.

And then of course, I was offended too by the sexism, by the misogyny of the Leader of the Opposition catcalling across this table at me as I sit here as Prime Minister, 'If the Prime Minister wants to, politically speaking, make an honest woman of herself…' something that would never have been said to any man sitting in this chair. I was offended when the Leader of the Opposition went outside in the front of Parliament and stood next to a sign that said 'Ditch the witch.'

I was offended when the Leader of the Opposition stood next to a sign that described me as a man's bitch. I was offended by those things. Misogyny, sexism, every day from this Leader of the Opposition. Every day in every way, across the time the Leader of the Opposition has sat in that chair and I've sat in this chair, that is all we have heard from him.

And now, the Leader of the Opposition wants to be taken seriously, apparently he's woken up after this track record and all of these statements, and he's woken up and he's gone 'Oh dear, there's this thing called sexism, oh my lords, there's this thing called misogyny. Now who's one of them? Oh, the Speaker must be because that suits my political purpose.'

Doesn't turn a hair about any of his past statements, doesn't walk into this Parliament and apologise to the women of Australia. Doesn't walk into this Parliament and apologise to me for the things that have come out of his mouth. But now seeks to use this as a battering ram against someone else.

Well this kind of hypocrisy must not be tolerated, which is why this motion from the Leader of the Opposition should not be taken seriously.

And then second, the Leader of the Opposition is always wonderful about walking into this Parliament and giving me and others a lecture about what they should take responsibility for.

Always wonderful about that—everything that I should take responsibility for, now apparently including the text messages of the Member for Fisher. Always keen to say how others should assume responsibility, particularly me.

Well can anybody remind me if the Leader of the Opposition has taken any responsibility for the conduct of the Sydney Young Liberals and the attendance at this event of members of his front-bench?

Has he taken any responsibility for the conduct of members of his political party and members of his front-bench who apparently when the most vile things were being said about my family, raised no voice of objection? Nobody walked out of the room; no-one walked up to Mr Jones and said that this was not acceptable.

Instead of course, it was all viewed as good fun until it was run in a Sunday newspaper and then the Leader of the Opposition and others started ducking for cover.

Big on lectures of responsibility, very light on accepting responsibility himself for the vile conduct of members of his political party.

Third, Deputy Speaker, why the Leader of the Opposition should not be taken seriously on this motion.

The Leader of the Opposition and the Deputy Leader of the Opposition have come into this place and have talked about the Member for Fisher. Well, let me remind the Opposition and the Leader of the opposition party about their track record and association with the Member for Fisher.

I remind them that the National Party preselected the Member for Fisher for the 1984 election, that the National Party preselected the Member for Fisher for the 1987 election, that the Liberals preselected Mr Slipper for the 1993 election, then the 1996 election, then the 1998 election, then for the 2001 election, then for the 2004 election, then for the 2007 election and then for the 2010 election.

And across these elections, Mr Slipper enjoyed the personal support of the Leader of the Opposition. I remind the Leader of the Opposition that on 28 September 2010, following the last election campaign, when Mr Slipper was elected as Deputy Speaker, the Leader of the Opposition at that stage said this, and I quote.

He referred to the Member for Maranoa, who was also elected to a position at the same time, and then went on as follows: 'And the Member for Fisher will serve as a fine complement to the Member for Scullin in the chair. I believe that the Parliament will be well-served by the team which will occupy the chair in this chamber. I congratulate the Member for Fisher, who has been a friend of mine for a very long time, who has served this Parliament in many capacities with distinction.'

The words of the Leader of the Opposition on record, about his personal friendship with Mr [Slipper], and on record about his view about Mr Slipper's qualities and attributes to be the Speaker.

No walking away from those words, they were the statement of the Leader of the Opposition then. I remind the Leader of the Opposition, who now comes in here and speaks about apparently his inability to work with or talk to Mr Slipper. I remind the Leader of the Opposition he attended Mr Slipper's wedding.

Did he walk up to Mr Slipper in the middle of the service and say he was disgusted to be there? Was that the attitude he took? No, he attended that wedding as a friend.

The Leader of the Opposition keen to lecture others about what they ought to know or did know about Mr Slipper. Well with respect, I'd say to the Leader of the Opposition after a long personal association including attending Mr Slipper's wedding, it would be interesting to know whether the Leader of the Opposition was surprised by these text messages.

He's certainly in a position to speak more intimately about Mr Slipper than I am, and many other people in this Parliament, given this long personal association.

Then of course the Leader of the Opposition comes into this place and says, and I quote, 'Every day the Prime Minister stands in this Parliament to defend this Speaker will be another day of shame for this Parliament, another day of shame for a government which should already have died of shame.'

Well can I indicate to the Leader of the Opposition the Government is not dying of shame, my father did not die of shame, what the Leader of the Opposition should be ashamed of is his performance in this Parliament and the sexism he brings with it. Now about the text messages that are on the public record or reported in the—that's a direct quote from the Leader of the Opposition so I suggest those groaning have a word with him.

On the conduct of Mr Slipper, and on the text messages that are in the public domain, I have seen the press reports of those text messages. I am offended by their content. I am offended by their content because I am always offended by sexism. I am offended by their content because I am always offended by statements that are anti-women.

I am offended by those things in the same way that I have been offended by things that the Leader of the Opposition has said, and no doubt will continue to say in the future. Because if this today was an exhibition of his new feminine side, well I don't think we've got much to look forward to in terms of changed conduct.

I am offended by those text messages. But I also believe, in terms of this Parliament making a decision about the speakership, that this Parliament should recognise that there is a court case in progress. That the judge has reserved his decision, that having waited for a number of months for the legal matters surrounding Mr Slipper to come to a conclusion, that this Parliament should see that conclusion.

I believe that is the appropriate path forward, and that people will then have an opportunity to make up their minds with the fullest information available to them.

But whenever people make up their minds about those questions, what I won't stand for, what I will never stand for is the Leader of the Opposition coming into this place and peddling a double standard. Peddling a standard for Mr Slipper he would not set for himself. Peddling a standard for Mr Slipper he has not set for other members of his front-bench.

Peddling a standard for Mr Slipper that has not been acquitted by the people who have been sent out to say the vilest and most revolting things like his former Shadow Parliamentary Secretary Senator Bernardi.

I will not ever see the Leader of the Opposition seek to impose his double standard on this Parliament. Sexism should always be unacceptable. We should conduct ourselves as it should always be unacceptable. The Leader of the Opposition says do something; well he could do something himself if he wants to deal with sexism in this Parliament.

He could change his behaviour, he could apologise for all his past statements, he could apologise for standing next to signs describing me as a witch and a bitch, terminology that is now objected to by the front bench of the Opposition.

He could change a standard himself if he sought to do so. But we will see none of that from the Leader of the Opposition because on these questions he is incapable of change. Capable of double standards, but incapable of change. His double standards should not rule this Parliament.

Good sense, common sense, proper process is what should rule this Parliament. That's what I believe is the path forward for this Parliament, not the kind of double standards and political game-playing imposed by the Leader of the Opposition now looking at his watch because apparently a woman's spoken too long.

I've had him yell at me to shut up in the past, but I will take the remaining seconds of my speaking time to say to the Leader of the Opposition I think the best course for him is to reflect on the standards he's exhibited in public life, on the responsibility he should take for his public statements; on his close personal connection with Peter Slipper, on the hypocrisy he has displayed in this House today.

And on that basis, because of the Leader of the Opposition's motivations, this Parliament today should reject this motion and the Leader of the Opposition should think seriously about the role of women in public life and in Australian society because we are entitled to a better standard than this.

Speech at the GoSports Foundation Athletes' Conclave

Abhinav Bindra

Bengaluru (17 July 2013)

Abhinav Bindra is an Indian businessman and former Indian shooter who was a World and Olympic champion in the 10m Air Rifle event. After his 2008 Beijing Olympic Games win, Bindra became the first Indian to win an individual gold medal at the Olympic Games. Following his retirement, Bindra received the prestigious Blue Cross, which is the International Shooting Sport Federation's highest shooting honour.

Bindra gave this inspiring speech at the GoSport Foundation Athletes' Conclave, of which he is a member of the advisory board.

Good morning Ladies and Gentlemen,

Think of a boy. The youngest in the family, adored and indulged by his parents and older sister. A mama's boy. I used to be that boy. Picture me when I was 9 years old. A normal boy who liked goofing off with friends; didn't like reading, hated physical activity. I think I worked hardest at bunking PE classes at school.

See me as I was then. Fat. Wearing glasses, because I was short-sighted. Everything was perfect. Except that my dad kept pushing me, saying, 'Try sport.' I tried cricket and football, but I hated the exertion, and my heart wasn't in it.

Like most boys, I loved the idea of guns—the power, the 'bang-bang' noise. One Sunday, as my dad was cleaning his three guns,

I thought: 'Maybe I should try shooting as a sport. At least I won't have to run around.'

That's how it began. So how does a boy who is neither talented nor athletic win the Olympic gold?

Friends, there are a thousand ways to be successful, and I am nobody to tell you the way that is right for you. No one can do that. Each one of us has to find our own path, the way that works best for us.

At the same time, I welcome the opportunity to share with you some of my experiences, and hope that they will help you find your individual path in your journey to success. Because you know, that no matter how many people support you and help you, when you perform, you are alone

Some of what I'm sharing are things I wish someone had said to me when I was your age—hungry, desperate, eager to win; my whole life staked on each competition.

So how does a boy who is neither talented nor athletic become both World and Olympic champion? The answer is a four-letter word; in fact, it is two four-letter words: HARD WORK.

I was tenacious. I hung on despite disappointments.

I was stubborn as a mule. I refused to give up.

I believed in myself. And when my belief in myself faltered, I had the sense to listen to my team—my family and coaches—who believed in me for me.

I was fortunate to be coached by Lt. Col. Dhillon, a taskmaster of the old school. Every day, he seemed to be waiting for me to come late for practice, or take short-cuts, or give up, or go home early, disheartened by my performance that day. Every day, he seemed to wait for me to begin complaining, like the spoilt boy he believed I was.

I was determined never to give him the satisfaction of having his expectations fulfilled. Every day he waited in vain. Till he suddenly shifted his expectations of me, and began enrolling me in shooting competitions.

Meanwhile, I was undergoing a transformation of another sort. What began as bloody-mindedness—I would never give the Colonel the satisfaction that I gave up or gave in—ended in seduction. I was seduced by the call of the bulls eye. One tiny dot that called to me over and over again, saying, 'Come and get me.' And I followed the call gladly, willingly.

Of course I paid the price for following my passion. My friends faded away. It was such an alien sport—shooting. Nobody knew anything about it. Had it been cricket, I'd have kept my friends—maybe our friendship might even have been strengthened. But with shooting, there was no chance. A gun and a target don't allow talk—not even encouraging talk.

You must understand that those days, children lived very different lives. You went to school, came home, played outside with your friends, and got back home. There were no malls at which you could hang out, so I just kept on going to school and shooting every afternoon. My mother managed my schedule with military precision, and life was full.

I was still 13 when I saw the wonderful Jaspal Rana at the 1996 Olympics in Atlanta. My sister swears I told her then that I would win an Olympic gold for India.

For the first time in my life, I had dedicated myself, committed myself to something, and as I spent more and more time shooting, I found myself fascinated by the sport.

In the beginning, obviously, I wanted to maximize my score. I had one, single focus—hit as many shots as I can into the very centre of the bulls eye. But as I got better, I found that just a great score alone did not make me feel good.

You know—you are athletes—some days seem to be charmed. You're not making any special effort, but you're breaking records in training. Your action is so smooth that you might well be gliding on air. Everything goes right. But there's a 'BUT' in your head and your heart.

You know that this is just a lucky chance—you can neither predict nor control when it will happen again. In fact, it may never happen again. So what good is a 'lucky' performance? Not much good.

I wish someone had told me that more than getting the perfect score, what would give me satisfaction, what would give me a sense of achievement as an athlete, was when I knew that this score came from my effort—from something I had done—rather than because I was having a lucky day.

It shocked me—shooting 600/600 and feeling lousy. I thought to myself: If even winning is not enough, then what is it I'm trying to do here?

And I groped my way forward, to find another goal to focus on. Now what I wanted was: to win and feel good about winning.

Friends, this is a point in your path you may already have reached. I want to assure you that dissatisfaction with perfect scores is normal. Because you know that in reality, you will be competing against a whole bunch of very talented, skilled practitioners of your sport. And you need more than luck to get you the gold you want.

And so there is this strange feeling: I may feel better about shooting 594/600 than 597/600. Because 594 was my effort, and 597 was a lucky chance.

In those days, there was no organization or system that exposed athletes to the facilities, training, and equipment of sport in the international arena. You, dear friends, are in a fortunate position in comparison. Organisations such as the GoSports Foundation are committed to your welfare, working actively to ensure young athletes with world-class potential receive all the support, knowledge and encouragement necessary to empower them to achieve their dreams.

I attended shooting camps in Germany where I shot against the best marksmen, and saw no shame in losing to them. Instead, I learned. It helped that I was a boy, and awe-struck at shooting alongside such illustrious people.

But this itself became a problem. If you look up to someone, you can never seriously compete against them. Think about it. If you find yourself in a swimming competition against Michael Phelps, would you really be able to put your heart and soul into beating him? Even if you did try, in your heart of hearts, do you really believe you could beat him?

I wish someone had told me that it's not always about how good you are and how hard you work and how much practice you put in. You need to be mentally tough. Even if you have to shoot against the person you most admire, you have to be able to put that admiration aside. Otherwise, you might as well not compete. Because you have already lost this competition in your mind.

My Swiss-German coaches Gaby Buehlmann and Heinz Reinkemeier saw my 'niceness' as a major hurdle in my ability to win matches. Now I don't think I'm so much nicer than the average person. I am a regular, gentle, polite person. But regular, gentle and polite does not win matches. I needed 'killer instinct', 'me vs. you all' type of mental toughness. Today many people misunderstand it for arrogance or aloofness. But it was a shield I developed against people because I had to develop it if I wanted to have a serious shot at winning my dreams.

I wish someone had told me that I would be misunderstood by so many people as I worked to attain a quest that would make us all proud. It hurt—it hurt then and it hurts now. Only now, it doesn't hurt as much, because you get used to things; you don't let them affect you as much.

I have always been a diligent student. No detail is too small to interest me. I want to know everything about everything that has to do with shooting. Even today, when I do know a few things, I keep looking for new things to learn to get better—always better. I may never be perfect. That's okay. But I can always be better than I was yesterday.

My next challenge was clear – how could I get better? Yes, it's the same old thing—hard work. But instead of just aiming my rifle at the bulls eye and reading my score, I began to look at other things: improving my technique, customizing my equipment, learning more about myself, and so on.

Was my body comfortable when I sank into my stance to shoot? When I became tired, it was harder to shoot well. Alright, so I have to find ways to delay the tiredness. Maybe I should train my muscles to be stronger, so they won't get tired so quickly. And so, ironically, I began working hard at working out, because I wanted my body to cope better with muscle strain and fatigue, because I wanted to get better results; because I wanted to win.

Are there pellets which can improve my shooting accuracy? Research, find out, experiment. Go deeper.

When I see that I'm close to a perfect score, my heart starts hammering in excitement, anticipating that perfect result. Do I spoil the last shot because I'm too excited? Yes, I do. Okay, I have to find a way to be less excited.

I'd like to emphasize that I did all this at various times in my life to break out of stuck situations, but always, whether I was stuck or not, whether I was winning or losing, what I followed rigorously—almost religiously—was my training.

I never compromised. One day, I was doing crunches in reps of 10. My trainer said, 'Good job. 10 done.' There's nobody there to check, the trainer has counted 10, but I know it's 8, so I said, 'No. It was 8, not 10.' And then I do two more to make it 10.

When people ask me what helped me win gold, this is what I say to them. 'I slogged my guts out—I did it without compromise, when there was no one to see, no one to be impressed. I did it when I did not feel like it. And the reason I did it is: my desire to win was, and is, much greater, than my desire to make excuses or find reasons not to win.

I wish someone had told me that no matter how hard you work, how dedicatedly, how much you push yourself, you will not always win. And you have to learn to pick up the broken pieces of yourself after you lose, knit yourself back together again, and start the process all over again.

It is impossible that you will win everything all the time. Even in his prime, the supreme athlete Roger Federer, did lose some matches. So you need to think about and prepare yourself for failure as well. Because it will come, as surely as night follows day.

I was 17 when a wild card entry, called a hardship quota in shooting, allowed me to participate at the Sydney Olympics in 2000. I think that is when I understood the range and depth and height of what the Olympic Games mean to a sportsperson. Once in 4 years, you get the chance to shoot the best you can for 2 hours. That's it. If you haven't done it then, you begin all over again, preparing for the 2 hours you want to get after 4 years, in the next Olympics. My ambition solidified. This time around, I was an inexperienced shooter. Next time, I would be ready.

I wish someone had told me that winning at sport was about so much more than sport. For instance, I needed to be able to deal with my luggage getting lost—when I needed my equipment to train for a competition.

Once I had to wait at the airport for hours, because someone forgot to reserve a hotel room, and I was literally stranded in another country with nowhere to go until the organisers booked me a hotel room. I had to be able to get over this so that it would not affect my mood, my state of mind as I went into the competition. I needed to focus.

I wish someone had told me that I wouldn't always get home food, and might have to make do with food that was unappetizing and much lower in nutrition than I was used to—on the eve of international events. I learned all this the hard way. By going hungry, not eating enough, getting upset tummies. You know that a feeling of nervousness is called getting butterflies in your tummy. Well, I for one, have had butterflies, goats, elephants and the odd dinosaur or two in my tummy. But I have had to ignore all these creatures and prepare to shoot my best. Sometimes on a glass of milk.

But your desire to win, to achieve your goal has to be big enough, strong enough to overcome any such hurdles you face. And frankly, the win that you struggle for is the win that you are proud of. If the win comes too easily, you are always left with a feeling of doubt: was it really me? Am I really good enough? And the taste of victory turns to ashes in your mouth.

2004, Athens. The Olympic Games. I have done everything I can to prepare myself. Many people believe I have a good chance of winning the gold. I don't win the gold. I don't win any medals. In fact, I come seventh.

I wish someone had told me that winning at sport was about so much more than sport. Days later, I find out that the tile beneath my shooting position, Position No. 3, was wobbly, and that everyone who shot from that position performed considerably worse than they were expected to.

Do the reasons really matter when your mind and spirit have been shattered? Months later, when I became capable of thinking again, my only thought was to give up shooting. I put away my equipment and immersed myself in viewing, collecting and painting art.

I did not lose focus. I gave it up. What was the point of focusing if any arbitrary event could throw off years and years of focus and work? I lost faith in myself, in shooting as the right way of life for myself.

My coaches, my family and friends—they all walked the tightrope between giving me the time and space to heal, jollying me along, and giving me stern 'put-the-past-behind-you-and-pick-up-the-gun' talks.

More than a year later, my spirit began to stir feebly. The 2006 World Championships were a pain in the back. Literally. My muscles and core were not sufficiently developed to support the long periods of time I spent in my stance. Shooters stand with their hips thrown out, and their vertebrae go through severe punishment. I invested myself in a deeper study of the body, doing weights, Pilates, strengthening my core and increasing my cardio-vascular fitness. I had also got back to my old holy grail, technique.

I had learnt that success was a fickle mistress. I decided to pursue excellence. Focus on excellence. Soldier on.

2006—the world championships in Zagreb—I won a gold. This win created some good feelings and somewhat restored my faith in my abilities. But I did not lose sight of my goal—the Olympic gold.

Continuing to focus on excellence, on every detail from my shoes to my clothes to the angles at which I stood, held my gun, and so on, I trained my body. You need to repeat something at least 10,000 times to make it a habit, I believe. And if you've practiced maybe 100,000 times or 1 million or 10 million times, your muscles develop a memory of your movement. This is the beginning of command, of mastery—over your sport and your body.

As the Beijing Olympics of 2008 approached, I knew I had to plan my strategy very carefully. The enemy was within me. My enemy was my mind. I needed to develop the mental strength to take pressure of the competition in my stride; not to let it affect my performance. But I had prepared for this. I had practiced keeping a calm clear mind and reducing the voice in my head worrying about how I was doing, and what my score was, and how others were shooting, and a hundred other things. I had trained myself to mute this voice.

Okay. Game time.

I won. And the world erupted. Months later, after a whirlwind of congratulations and celebrations, I was left feeling like an open bottle of Coke. Flat, no fizz, stale.

I wish someone had told me that in some ways, winning was harder than losing. Because when you lose, you still have your goal—you simply need to take a break to process your emotions, refocus yourself and work towards achieving your goal.

But when you win, you lose your goal. Where now, will you find the motivation to work when you've already achieved your dream? 10 crunches? 5 is enough. No. Wait a minute, why do any crunches at all? Why train?

A peculiar lack of energy, of drive, took hold of me. I found myself drifting.

I wish someone had told me that after I had won, I would need to find goals beyond winning. Those were dark days too, because I was petrified. If I didn't want to shoot, what would I do with the rest of my life? Shooting is all I knew!

Obviously, I had to keep participating in competitions, but I didn't win anything.

We Indians are a warm-hearted people. We are a whole-hearted people. We either love or hate. There is nothing between the two extremes. Everyone loved me after I won in Beijing. But oh, how they hated me when I did not continue my winning spree.

I wish someone had told me how each doubt cast at my ability to win would be like a fresh dart thrown at my already-wounded self. Even though I thought I had developed a thick hide, and did not care much about what people thought or said, I cared passionately, and I suffered.

My coaches were prepared for my post-victory depression. Raging controversies added insult to injury—the medal was won, what more did they want? —I withdrew into myself to find the sustenance to keep me going. The Vipassana course I did, for instance, showed me clearly that I still felt passionately about shooting.

In subsequent world championships, I did not bring home any medals. I was working hard on my technique and myself, but I had not yet dug deep enough inside, not yet found a reason I wanted badly enough to win.

Till I found it: to be the only person to win the Olympic gold in air-rifle shooting twice in a row.

And then: London. 'Will he repeat his feat?' The thought was deafening in its volume, even when it was not voiced. I am prepared—fully, in every way. I have foreseen and prepared for every kind of eventuality. I know this, and it strengthens my resolve to win.

Of course it didn't happen. Life is always throwing you new curve balls. By this time, shooting has been firmly established as a spectator sport, and the noise from the spectators is—literally—deafening. And I'm supposed to shut them out and shoot to win… I didn't.

I wish someone had told me that not every loss feels earth-shattering.

How differently I handled the aftermath of this not-win! I was calm—disappointed, but calm. No end-of-the-world scenarios were playing out in my mind. When one journalist asked me if I planned to retire, I replied, 'I might look old, but actually, I'm pretty young.' He withdrew, bemused.

I'm back home in Chandigarh, training, shooting. I'm traveling to shoot in other events all over the world. I've found a quiet confidence, an excited hum within me as I prepare for Rio in 2016. I am focusing again.

Somewhere, in a corner of my mind, I sometimes think: at least I've got this focus thing right. First, I need something to focus on. Secondly, what I focus on will keep shifting, depending on what happens in my life, and in my head. I have never been more committed to my sport, and as I explore it more deeply, I also get to know myself better—what motivates me, what excites me, what keeps me going, what I am indifferent to.

I wanted to quit shooting after Beijing, not imagining what more I could aspire to. But I dug deep and found the courage to put myself on the line. So I put myself on the line and I failed—but failure only brings out my defiant streak, pushes me to be even better, to see what else I can find inside myself.

The London Olympics were a failure as far as the result was concerned, but I count it as one of the victories in my journey of growing as a sportsperson. I am learning more, getting better, readying myself for Rio in 2016.

Today, I know there will be roadblocks, but the only way is around them. And I am determined to find a way, a solution to overcome them. I have dug my feet in the ground and decided that victory is mine. When the next win will come, I don't know. But victory is more than winning.

Victory is my relentless pursuit of excellence, victory is my commitment to my sport, victory is never giving up, never losing sight of my goal. Victory is knowing that I will do whatever it takes to get better.

I would like to close by telling you about my heroes. I don't know their names. They are the ones who work quietly, tirelessly, training whether or not they have facilities, equipment, or support. They may win medals—district-level, zonal, national, international—or they may not win anything. They show up every day when they aren't feeling well, when they're disheartened, when it's bad weather—they triumph over every circumstance to show up and train. Alone and driven by the spark that lights a fire in them, and propels them 'Faster, Higher, Stronger'.

And in that they are already victorious. Their medals will come. If not at this event, then next time.

Till next time, my friends, our next time—yours and mine…

Thank you for listening.

Speech at *Economic Times* Award Function

Azim Premji

(7 December 2013)

Azim Premji is an Indian businessman and philanthropist who served as the chairman of Wipro Limited and made it a leading company in the software industry. He is one of the wealthiest people in the world. In 2001, he established the Azim Premji Foundation which aims to improve elementary education in rural regions of India.

In his speech at the *Economic Times* Award Function, Premji implored those present to engage in charity, help the poor and follow the path of philanthropy.

Good evening. It's a pleasure to be here with all of you.

I want to thank the *Economic Times* for bestowing this honor on me.

While I receive this honor, the simple fact is that it is actually an honor for the thousands of my colleagues and partners, who have helped build Wipro in to what it is, over the past few decades.

Thank you.

It was suggested by the *Economic Times* that I share some thoughts on Philanthropy on this occasion. So let me do so.

Let's think about tonight. We will all go home or go to our hotels and sleep. No matter where we are, within a couple of kilometers of where we are sleeping safely and soundly, there will be a young girl, who is our daughters' age or our granddaughter's age, trying to sleep in the cold night of December on the roads.

She has been abused in the past, and she will be abused in the future. She is probably desperately hungry. In her circumstances, going to school or having anything else that every child must have is not even a remote possibility.

When she wakes up tomorrow morning, it's just the start of another day of trying to survive, to again sleep shivering on the cold pavement somewhere.

This girl is not alone. There are probably 3 million children, who are homeless and will sleep on the streets in India tonight and every night. She is also not alone in sleeping hungry. More than 200 million of our people will probably sleep hungry, like her.

In very simple terms: can we be indifferent to this?

To my mind that is the basic question that we need to ask ourselves, do we feel connected to our country, to the people around us? Should not every Indian have the very basic, very bare necessities of a life of dignity? This is certainly not hoping for too much, it's just basic safety, adequate food, a roof to sleep, basic education and the healthcare.

Most of us would we feel this way. I think we just need to act.

I have mentioned only a few kinds of issues. But as all of us know, our country is facing challenges of similar kind on every front. Be it education, healthcare, nutrition, sanitation or of deep inequality and discrimination.

Each one is as complex as the other, and each one as necessary for a life of basic dignity.

We can perhaps justifiably say that many of these issues need to be addressed by the government. Certainly the government needs to do more and better. But that doesn't in any way lessen the responsibility that we have. I and you, who have the privilege of being successful, have a greater responsibility.

To me Philanthropy is the connection that we can have if we are not indifferent to all these issues that face us. It is the mechanism for us to contribute to making some positive change. And I think greater our success, the greater the responsibility for us.

I must also say that, the desire to engage must come from within. No one can be told to be philanthropic. At its core Philanthropy is about the connection that you feel with the people around you or the world around you. Many, who feel this connection and have taken action, have experienced that there is enough reason for hope in our country, and that one can genuinely contribute.

The Foundation that we have set up has been working with various state governments to improve equity and quality of government schools for the past 12 years. I have learnt that trying to improve education is a very long process, but I think that basic education is the basic route to building a better society, so we remain totally committed to it. Let me narrate one of many things that give us hope in this journey.

We work in some of the most disadvantaged districts of the country. We have 50-70 of our own people in each of these districts. They are all deeply committed to the cause of education, and are capable of educating teachers.

In all these places we run voluntary learning forums for government school teachers, amongst many other initiatives. What this means is that teachers come to these learning sessions on their own. They spend their own money for transportation; they come from up to 30 km away in difficult conditions. They also spend their own money on food. They do this on a holiday, usually a Sunday.

Can we imagine this happening in the best of the companies? How many employees of such companies will spend their holidays and their own money, so that they can do their jobs better? How completely contrary is this experience of ours, to the notion of the disinterested government employee? These are all government employees, but they are deeply committed and they genuinely care.

Our experience has been that between 12-18% teachers in a district become a part of such forums over a period of time. And if you ask them why they do it, they all have the same answer, which is that they want to learn so that they can teach better. We are not talking about small numbers. In a typical district with 5000 teachers, this implies that 600-800 teachers are engaged in such forums.

I find this a great reason for hope. When so many people from within the government school system have this kind of commitment, I am sure education will improve, given time and sustained effort.

As I said before we have been at it for 12 years. I have only regret about my Philanthropy, which is that, I wish I had started earlier.

There is so much to do, and this kind of work takes so much time that the earlier we try to contribute, the better it is.

With these 12 years' of our experience, let me share three other things that I have learnt about Philanthropy. Those of you, who are very active in Philanthropy, would perhaps resonate with these lessons that I have learnt.

First, involving your family early on in Philanthropy is very important. Their understanding, endorsement and involvement may eventually be the most determining factor. There is another positive aspect to this early involvement. Some of the smartest people that I know have been those who chose to become home makers. They can perhaps play a significant role in starting off their families philanthropic efforts.

Second, the key to scaling up Philanthropy and doing good work is getting good people in the team. This is exactly the same, as in our businesses. The work in Philanthropy is perhaps more complex than business, because social issues are more complex. So it needs really good people. I think that the most serious start to anyone's philanthropic work would be to pick one of their top people from within the business, a person who has the intent, empathy, ability, and trust and move him or her to the Philanthropy side.

Third, philanthropic work needs patience, tenacity and empathy. It is different from business. We all know that intellectually, but it's very challenging when one gets in to it. One has to change ones' mindset significantly, if one has to make a difference. I have learnt this only slowly in the past 12 years.

Thank you for hearing me out. I absolutely believe that we are trustees of our wealth for this society, and we must use it as such. We must do Philanthropy because it is the Right thing to do.

I also believe that every one of us has the basic empathy with the people around us; we just need to let it find expression. I am certain that none of us wants to let the young girl I talked about earlier, to go hungry, to get abused, or to sleep in the cold night of December on the road, when our daughters and granddaughters are sleeping safe and sound—as they should.

Thank you.

‘Our Books and Our Pens Are the Most Powerful Weapons’

Malala Yousafzai

Youth Takeover of the United Nations (12 July 2013)

Malala Yousafzai is a Pakistani children’s and women’s rights activist who defied the Taliban and asserted the right of the girl child to be educated. Despite being shot in the head for her efforts, she nevertheless persevered and became the youngest person to receive the Nobel Peace Prize at the age of 17 in 2014.

At the Youth Takeover of the United Nations, Yousafzai made her first public speech since being shot by the Taliban, and spoke once again on the importance of education for the girl child.

In the name of God, the Most Beneficent, the Most Merciful.

Honorable UN Secretary General Mr Ban Ki-moon, respected president of the General Assembly Vuk Jeremic, honorable UN envoy for global education Mr Gordon Brown, respected elders and my dear brothers and sisters: *Assalamu alaikum.*

Today is it an honor for me to be speaking again after a long time. Being here with such honorable people is a great moment in my life and it is an honor for me that today I am wearing a shawl of the late Benazir Bhutto. I don’t know where to begin my speech. I don’t know what people would be expecting me to say, but first of all thank you to God for whom we all are equal and thank you to every person who has prayed for my fast recovery and new life. I cannot believe how much love people have shown me. I have received thousands of good wish cards and gifts from all over the world. Thank you to all of them. Thank you to the children whose innocent words encouraged me. Thank you to my elders whose prayers strengthened me. I would like to thank my nurses, doctors and the staff of the hospitals in Pakistan and the UK and the UAE government who have helped me to get better and recover my strength.

I fully support UN Secretary General Ban Ki-moon in his Global Education First Initiative and the work of UN Special Envoy for Global Education Gordon Brown and the respectful president of the UN General Assembly Vuk Jeremic. I thank them for the leadership they continue to give. They continue to inspire all of us to action. Dear brothers and sisters, do remember one thing: Malala Day is not my day. Today is the day of every woman, every boy and every girl who have raised their voice for their rights.

There are hundreds of human rights activists and social workers who are not only speaking for their rights, but who are struggling to achieve their goal of peace, education and equality. Thousands of people have been killed by the terrorists and millions have been injured. I am just one of them. So here I stand. So here I stand, one girl, among many. I speak not for myself, but so those without a voice can be heard. Those who have fought for their rights. Their right to live in peace. Their right to be treated with dignity. Their right to equality of opportunity. Their right to be educated.

Dear friends, on 9 October 2012, the Taliban shot me on the left side of my forehead. They shot my friends, too. They thought that the bullets would silence us, but they failed. And out of that silence came thousands of voices. The terrorists thought they would change my aims and stop my ambitions. But nothing changed in my life except this: weakness, fear and hopelessness died. Strength, power and courage was born.

I am the same Malala. My ambitions are the same. My hopes are the same. And my dreams are the same. Dear sisters and brothers, I am not against anyone. Neither am I here to speak in terms of personal revenge against the Taliban or any other terrorist group. I am here to speak for the right of education for every child. I want education for the sons and daughters of the Taliban and all the terrorists and extremists. I do not even hate the Talib who shot me.

Even if there was a gun in my hand and he was standing in front of me, I would not shoot him. This is the compassion I have learned from Mohammed, the prophet of mercy, Jesus Christ and Lord Buddha. This the legacy of change I have inherited from Martin Luther King, Nelson Mandela and Mohammed Ali Jinnah.

This is the philosophy of nonviolence that I have learned from Gandhi, Bacha Khan and Mother Teresa. And this is the forgiveness that I have learned from my father and from my mother. This is what my soul is telling me: be peaceful and love everyone.

Dear sisters and brothers, we realize the importance of light when we see darkness. We realise the importance of our voice when we are silenced. In the same way, when we were in Swat, the north of Pakistan, we realised the importance of pens and books when we saw the guns. The wise saying, 'The pen is mightier than the sword.' It is true. The extremists are afraid of books and pens. The power of education frightens them. They are afraid of women. The power of the voice of women frightens them. This is why they killed 14 innocent students in the recent attack in Quetta. And that is why they kill female teachers. That is why they are blasting schools every day because they were and they are afraid of change and equality that we will bring to our society. And I remember that there was a boy in our school who was asked by a journalist why are the Taliban against education? He answered very simply by pointing to his book, he said, 'a Talib doesn't know what is written inside this book.'

They think that God is a tiny, little conservative being who would point guns at people's heads just for going to school. These terrorists are misusing the name of Islam for their own personal benefit. Pakistan is a peace loving, democratic country. Pashtuns want education for their daughters and sons. Islam is a religion of peace, humanity and brotherhood. It is the duty and responsibility to get education for each child, that is what it says. Peace is a necessity for education. In many parts of the world, especially Pakistan and Afghanistan, terrorism, war and conflicts stop children from going to schools. We are really tired of these wars. Women and children are suffering in many ways in many parts of the world.

In India, innocent and poor children are victims of child labor. Many schools have been destroyed in Nigeria. People in Afghanistan have been affected by extremism. Young girls have to do domestic child labor and are forced to get married at an early age. Poverty, ignorance, injustice, racism and the deprivation of basic rights are the main problems, faced by both men and women.

Today I am focusing on women's rights and girls' education because they are suffering the most. There was a time when women activists asked men to stand up for their rights. But this time we will do it by ourselves. I am not telling men to step away from speaking for women's rights, but I am focusing on women to be independent and fight for themselves. So dear sisters and brothers, now it's time to speak up. So today, we call upon the world leaders to change their strategic policies in favor of peace and prosperity. We call upon the world leaders that all of these deals must protect women and children's rights. A deal that goes against the rights of women is unacceptable.

We call upon all governments to ensure free, compulsory education all over the world for every child. We call upon all the governments to fight against terrorism and violence. To protect children from brutality and harm. We call upon the developed nations to support the expansion of education opportunities for girls in the developing world. We call upon all communities to be tolerant, to reject prejudice based on caste, creed, sect, color, religion or agenda to ensure freedom and equality for women so they can flourish. We cannot all succeed when half of us are held back. We call upon our sisters around the world to be brave, to embrace the strength within themselves and realise their full potential.

Dear brothers and sisters, we want schools and education for every child's bright future. We will continue our journey to our destination of peace and education. No one can stop us. We will speak up for our rights and we will bring change to our voice. We believe in the power and the strength of our words. Our words can change the whole world because we were all together, united for the cause of education. And if we want to achieve our goal, then let us empower ourselves with the weapon of knowledge and let us shield ourselves with unity and togetherness.

Dear brothers and sisters, we must not forget that millions of people are suffering from poverty and injustice and ignorance. We must not forget that millions of children are out of their schools. We must not forget that our sisters and brothers are waiting for a bright, peaceful future.

So let us wage, so let us wage a glorious struggle against illiteracy, poverty and terrorism, let us pick up our books and our pens, they are the most powerful weapons. One child, one teacher, one book and one pen can change the world. Education is the only solution. Education first. Thank you.

Farewell Speech

Sachin Tendulkar

Wankhede Stadium, Mumbai (16 November 2013)

Sachin Tendulkar is a retired Indian cricketer and former captain of the Indian national team, who is considered one of the greatest batsmen in history. He became India's youngest Test cricketer at the age of 16. Throughout his outstanding career, he has been awarded several prestigious accolades such as the Arjuna Award, Rajiv Gandhi Khel Ratna Award, Padma Shri, Padma Vibhushan and the Bharat Ratna, India's highest civilian award.

Tendulkar gave this moving farewell speech on 16 November 2013, on the day of his 200th Test match, announcing his retirement from cricket.

All my friends. Settle down let me talk, I will get more and more emotional. My life, between 22 yards for 24 years, it is hard to believe that that wonderful journey has come to an end, but I would like to take this opportunity to thank people who have played an important role in my life. Also, for the first time in my life I am carrying this list, to remember all the names in case I forget someone. I hope you understand. It's getting a little bit difficult to talk but I will manage.

The most important person in my life, and I have missed him a lot since 1999 when he passed away, my father. Without his guidance, I don't think I would have been standing here in front of you. He gave me freedom at the age of 11, and told me that [I should] chase my dreams, but make sure you do not find shortcuts. The path might be difficult but don't give up, and I have simply followed his instructions. Above all, he told me to be a nice human being, which I will continue to do and try my best. Every time I have done something special [and] showed my bat, it was [for] my father.

My mother, I don't know how she dealt with such a naughty child like me. I was not easy to manage. She must be extremely patient. For a mother, the most important thing is that her child remains safe and healthy and fit. That was what she was most bothered and worried about. She took care of me for the last 24 years that I have played for India, but even before that she started praying for me the day I started playing cricket. She just prayed and prayed and I think her prayers and blessings have given me the strength to go out and perform, so a big thank you to my mother for all the sacrifices.

In my school days, for four years, I stayed with my uncle and aunt because my school was quite far from my home, and they treated me like their son. My aunt, after having had a hard day's play, I would be half asleep and she would be feeding me food so I could go again and play tomorrow. I can't forget these moments. I am like their son and I am glad it has continued to be the same way.

My eldest brother, Nitin, and his family, have always encouraged me. My eldest brother doesn't like to talk much, but the one thing he always told me is that whatever you do, I know you will always give it 100%, and that I have full faith and confidence in you. His encouragement meant a lot to me. My sister, Savita, and her family, was no different. The first cricket bat of my life was presented to me by my sister. It was a Kashmir willow bat. But that is where the journey began. She is one of those many who still continue to fast when I bat, so thank you very much.

Ajit, my brother, now what do I talk about him? I don't know. We have lived this dream together. He was the one who sacrificed his career for my cricket. He spotted the spark in me. And it all started from the age of 11 when he took me to Archrekar sir, my coach, and from there on my life changed. You will find this hard to believe but even last night he called to discuss my dismissal, knowing that there was a remote chance of batting again, but just the habit we have developed, the rapport we have developed, since my birth, has continued and it will continue. Maybe when I'm not playing cricket we will still be discussing technique.

Various things we agreed upon, my technique, and so many technical things which I didn't agree with him, we have had arguments and disagreements, but when I look back at all these things in my life, I would have been a lesser cricketer.

The most beautiful thing happened to me in 1990 when I met my wife, Anjali. Those were special years and it has continued and will always continue that way. I know Anjali, being a doctor; there was a wonderful career in front of her. When we decided to have a family, Anjali took the initiative to step back and say that 'you continue with your cricket and I will take the responsibility of the family'.

Without that, I don't think I would have been able to play cricket freely and without stress. Thanks for bearing with all my fuss and all my frustrations, and all sorts of rubbish that I have spoken. Thanks for bearing with me and always staying by my side through all the ups and downs. You are the best partnership I've had in my life. Then, the two precious diamonds of my life, Sara and Arjun. They have already grown up. My daughter is 16, my son is 14. Time has flown by. I wanted to spend so much time with them on special occasions like their birthdays, their annual days, their sports day, going on holidays, whatever. I have missed out on all those things. Thanks for your understanding. Both of you have been so, so special to me you cannot imagine. I promise you [that] for 14 and 16 years I have not spent enough time with both of you, but the next 16 years or even beyond that, everything is for you.

My in-laws, Anand Mehta and Annabel, both have been so, so supportive [and] loving and caring. I have discussed on various things in life, generally with them, and have taken their advice. You know, it's so important to have a strong family who is always with you and who are guiding you. Before you start clapping, the most important thing they did was allowing me to marry Anjali, so thank you very much.

In the last 24 years that I have played for India I have made new friends, and before that I have had friends from my childhood. They have all had a terrific contribution. As and when I have called them to come and bowl to me at the nets, they have left their work aside to come and help me. Be it joining me on holidays and having discussions with me on cricket, or how I was a little stressed and wanting to find a solution so I can perform better. All those moments my friends were with me. Even for when I was injured, I would wake up in the morning because I couldn't sleep and thought that my career was over because of injuries, that is when my friends have woken up at 3 o'clock in the morning to drive with me and make me believe that my career was not over. Life would be incomplete without all those friends. Thanks for being there for me.

My cricket career started when I was 11. The turning point of my career was when my brother (Ajit) took me to Achrekar Sir. I was extremely delighted to see him up in the stands. Normally he sits in front of the television and he watches all the games that I play. When I was 11/12, those were the days when I used to hop back on his scooter and play a couple of practice matches a day. The first half the innings I would be batting at Shivaji Park, the second half, at some other match in Azad Maidan. He would take me all over Mumbai to make sure I got match practice.

On a lighter note, in the last 29 years, sir has never ever said 'well played' to me because he thought I would get complacent and I would stop working hard. Maybe he can push his luck and wish me now, well done on my career, because there are no more matches, sir, in my life. I will be witnessing cricket, and cricket will always stay in my heart, but you have had an immense contribution in my life, so thank you very much.

My cricket for Mumbai started right here on this ground, the Mumbai Cricket Association (MCA), which is so dear to me. I remember landing from New Zealand at four o'clock in the morning, and turning up for a game here at eight o'clock just because I wanted to be a part of Mumbai cricket, and not that somebody forced me. That was for the love of Mumbai cricket, and thank you very much. The president is here so thank you very much, along with your team, for taking care of me and looking after my cricket.

The dream was obviously to play for India, and that is where my association with BCCI started. BCCI was fantastic, right from my debut they believed in my ability and selecting me into the squad at the age of 16 was a big step, so thanks to all the selectors for having faith in me and the BCCI for giving me the freedom to express myself out in the middle. Things would have been different if you had not been behind me, and I really appreciate your support. Especially when I was injured, you were right with me and making sure that all the treatments were taken care of, and that I got fit and fine and playing [right] back for India.

The journey has been special, the last 24 years, I have played with many senior cricketers, and even before that there were many senior cricketers with whom I watched on television. They inspired me to play cricket, and to play in the right way. Thanks to all those senior cricketers, and unfortunately I have not been able to play with them, but I have high regards for all their achievements and all their contributions.

We see it on the mega-screen, Rahul, Laxman, Sourav, and Anil, who is not here, and my team-mates right here in front me. You are like my family away from home. I have had some wonderful times with you. It is going to be difficult to not be part of the dressing room, sharing those special moments. All the coaches for their guidance, it has been special for me. I know when MS Dhoni presented me the 200th Test match cap on Day One morning. I had a brief message for the team. I would like to repeat that. I just feel that all of us are so, so fortunate and proud to be part of the Indian cricket team and serving the nation.

Knowing all of you guys, I know you will continue to serve the nation in the right spirit and right values. I believe we have been the lucky ones to be chosen by the Almighty to serve this sport. Each generation gets this opportunity to take care of this sport and serve it to the best of our ability. I have full faith in you to continue to serve the nation in the right spirit and to the best of your ability, to bring all the laurels to the country. All the very best.

I would be failing in my duties if I did not thank all the doctors, the physios, the trainers, who have put this difficult body together to go back on the field and be able to play. The amount of injuries that I have had in my career, I don't know how you have managed to keep me fit, but without your special efforts, it would never have happened. The doctors have met me at weird hours. I mean I have called them from Mumbai to Chennai, Mumbai to Delhi, I mean wherever. They have just taken the next flight and left their work and families to be with me, which has allowed me to play. So a big thank you to all three of you for keeping me in good shape.

My dear friend, late Mark Mascarenhas, my first manager. We unfortunately lost him in a car accident in 2001, but he was such a well-wisher of cricket, my cricket, and especially Indian cricket. He was so passionate. He understood what it takes to represent a nation and gave me all the space to go out and express myself, and never pressurised me to do this ad or promotion or whatever the sponsors demanded. He took care of that and today I miss him, so thank you Mark for all your contribution.

My current management team, WSG, for repeating what Mark has done, because when I signed the contract I exactly told them what I want from them, and what it requires to represent me. They have done that and respected that.

Someone who has worked closely with me for 14 years is my manager, Vinod Nayudu. He is more like my family and all the sacrifices, spending time away from his family for my work, has been special, so big thank you to his family as well for giving up so much time for my work with Vinod.

In my school days, when I performed well, the media backed me a lot. They continue to do that till this morning. Thank you so much to the media for supporting and appreciating my performances. It surely had a positive effect on me. Thank you so much to all the photographers as well for those wonderfully captured moments that will stay with me for the rest of my life, so a big thank you to all the photographers.

I know my speech is getting a bit too long, but this is the last thing I want to say. I want to thank all the people here who have flown in from various parts of the world, and have supported me endlessly, whether I scored a 0 or a 100-plus. Your support was so dear to me and meant a lot to me. Whatever you have done for me.

I know I have met so many guys who have fasted for me, prayed for me, done so much for me. Without that life wouldn't have been like this for me. I want to thank you from the bottom of my heart, and also say that time has flown by rather quickly, but the memories you have left with me will always be with me forever and ever, especially 'Sachin, Sachin' which will reverberate in my ears till I stop breathing. Thank you very much. If I have missed out on saying something, I hope you understand. Goodbye.

‘Gender Equality Is Your Issue Too’

Emma Watson

United Nations Headquarters, New York (20 September 2014)

Emma Watson is an English actor, model and activist best-known for playing Hermione Granger in the Harry Potter series. Her other major roles include *Beauty and the Beast, The Perks of Being a Wallflower* and *Regression*. In 2014, she was honoured by the BAFTA, winning the British Artist of the Year. She was also appointed the UN Women Goodwill ambassador in the same year and she helped launch the HeForShe campaign.

Through her speech, Watson stresses on the importance of men too supporting the cause of gender equality.

Today we are launching a campaign called ‘HeForShe.’

I am reaching out to you because I need your help. We want to end gender inequality—and to do that we need everyone to be involved.

This is the first campaign of its kind at the UN: we want to try and galvanise as many men and boys as possible to be advocates for gender equality. And we don’t just want to talk about it, but make sure it is tangible.

I was appointed six months ago and the more I have spoken about feminism the more I have realised that fighting for women’s rights has too often become synonymous with man-hating. If there is one thing I know for certain, it is that this has to stop.

For the record, feminism by definition is: 'The belief that men and women should have equal rights and opportunities. It is the theory of the political, economic and social equality of the sexes.'

I started questioning gender-based assumptions when at eight I was confused at being called 'bossy,' because I wanted to direct the plays we would put on for our parents—When at 14 I started being sexualized by certain elements of the press.

When at 15 my girlfriends started dropping out of their sports teams because they didn't want to appear 'muscly.'

When at 18 my male friends were unable to express their feelings.

I decided I was a feminist and this seemed uncomplicated to me. But my recent research has shown me that feminism has become an unpopular word.

Apparently I am among the ranks of women whose expressions are seen as too strong, too aggressive, isolating, anti-men and, unattractive.

Why is the word such an uncomfortable one?

I am from Britain and think it is right that as a woman I am paid the same as my male counterparts. I think it is right that I should be able to make decisions about my own body. I think it is right that women be involved on my behalf in the policies and decision-making of my country. I think it is right that socially I am afforded the same respect as men. But sadly I can say that there is no one country in the world where all women can expect to receive these rights.

No country in the world can yet say they have achieved gender equality.

These rights I consider to be human rights but I am one of the lucky ones. My life is a sheer privilege because my parents didn't love me less because I was born a daughter. My school did not limit me because I was a girl. My mentors didn't assume I would go less far because I might give birth to a child one day. These influencers were the gender equality ambassadors that made me who I am today. They may not know it, but they are the inadvertent feminists who are changing the world today. And we need more of those.

And if you still hate the word—it is not the word that is important but the idea and the ambition behind it. Because not all women have been afforded the same rights that I have. In fact, statistically, very few have been.

In 1995, Hilary Clinton made a famous speech in Beijing about women's rights. Sadly many of the things she wanted to change are still a reality today.

But what stood out for me the most was that only 30 per cent of her audience were male. How can we affect change in the world when only half of it is invited or feel welcome to participate in the conversation?

Men—I would like to take this opportunity to extend your formal invitation. Gender equality is your issue too.

Because to date, I've seen my father's role as a parent being valued less by society despite my needing his presence as a child as much as my mother's.

I've seen young men suffering from mental illness unable to ask for help for fear it would make them look less 'macho'—in fact in the UK suicide is the biggest killer of men between 20-49 years of age; eclipsing road accidents, cancer and coronary heart disease. I've seen men made fragile and insecure by a distorted sense of what constitutes male success. Men don't have the benefits of equality either.

We don't often talk about men being imprisoned by gender stereotypes but I can see that that they are and that when they are free, things will change for women as a natural consequence.

If men don't have to be aggressive in order to be accepted women won't feel compelled to be submissive. If men don't have to control, women won't have to be controlled.

Both men and women should feel free to be sensitive. Both men and women should feel free to be strong... It is time that we all perceive gender on a spectrum not as two opposing sets of ideals.

If we stop defining each other by what we are not and start defining ourselves by what we are—we can all be freer and this is what HeForShe is about. It's about freedom.

I want men to take up this mantle. So their daughters, sisters and mothers can be free from prejudice but also so that their sons have permission to be vulnerable and human too—reclaim those parts of themselves they abandoned and in doing so be a more true and complete version of themselves.

You might be thinking who is this Harry Potter girl? And what is she doing up on stage at the UN. It's a good question and trust me, I have been asking myself the same thing. I don't know if I am qualified to be here. All I know is that I care about this problem. And I want to make it better.

And having seen what I've seen—and given the chance—I feel it is my duty to say something. English Statesman Edmund Burke said: 'All that is needed for the forces of evil to triumph is for enough good men and women to do nothing.'

In my nervousness for this speech and in my moments of doubt I've told myself firmly—if not me, who, if not now, when. If you have similar doubts when opportunities are presented to you I hope those words might be helpful.

Because the reality is that if we do nothing it will take 75 years, or for me to be nearly a hundred before women can expect to be paid the same as men for the same work. 15.5 million girls will be married in the next 16 years as children. And at current rates it won't be until 2086 before all rural African girls will be able to receive a secondary education.

If you believe in equality, you might be one of those inadvertent feminists I spoke of earlier.

And for this I applaud you.

We are struggling for a uniting word but the good news is we have a uniting movement. It is called HeForShe. I am inviting you to step forward, to be seen to speak up, to be the 'he' for 'she'. And to ask yourself if not me, who? If not now, when?

Thank you.

Commencement Speech

Jim Carrey
Maharishi University of Management
(24 May 2014)

Jim Carrey is a Canadian-American comedian, actor, screenwriter and painter known for his roles in blockbuster movies such as *Ace Ventura: Pet Detective, Dumb and Dumber* and *The Mask.* Carrey won two Golden Globe Awards for Best Actor for his films *The Truman Show* and *Man on the Moon.*

In 2014, Carrey gave this witty and humorous commencement speech at the Maharishi University of Management and received an honorary doctorate for his achievements as a comedian, artist, author and philanthropist.

Thank you Bevan, thank you all!

I brought one of my paintings to show you today. Hope you guys are gonna be able see it okay. It's not one of my bigger pieces. You might wanna move down front—to get a good look at it.

Faculty, Parents, Friends, Dignitaries…Graduating Class of 2014, and all the dead baseball players coming out of the corn to be with us today. After the harvest there's no place to hide—the fields are empty—there is no cover there!

I am here to plant a seed that will inspire you to move forward in life with enthusiastic hearts and a clear sense of wholeness. The question is, will that seed have a chance to take root, or will I be sued by Monsanto and forced to use their seed, which may not be totally 'Ayurvedic.'

Excuse me if I seem a little low energy tonight—today—whatever this is. I slept with my head to the North last night. Oh man! Oh man! You know how that is, right kids? Woke up right in the middle of Pitta and couldn't get back to sleep till Vata rolled around, but I didn't freak out. I used that time to eat a large meal and connect with someone special on Tinder.

Life doesn't happen to you, it happens for you. How do I know this? I don't, but I'm making sound, and that's the important thing. That's what I'm here to do. Sometimes, I think that's one of the only things that are important. Just letting each other know we're here, reminding each other that we are part of a larger self. I used to think Jim Carrey is all that I was…

Just a flickering light

A dancing shadow

The great nothing masquerading as something you can name

Dwelling in forts and castles made of witches—wishes! Sorry, a Freudian slip there

Seeking shelter in caves and foxholes, dug out hastily

An archer searching for his target in the mirror

Wounded only by my own arrows

Begging to be enslaved

Pleading for my chains

Blinded by longing and tripping over paradise—can I get an 'Amen'?!

You didn't think I could be serious did ya? I don't think you understand who you're dealing with! I have no limits! I cannot be contained because I'm the container. You can't contain the container, man! You can't contain the container!

I used to believe that who I was ended at the edge of my skin, that I had been given this little vehicle called a body from which to experience creation, and though I couldn't have asked for a sportier model, it was after all a loaner and would have to be returned. Then, I learned that everything outside the vehicle was a part of me, too, and now I drive a convertible. Top down wind in my hair!

I am elated and truly, truly, truly excited to be present and fully connected to you at this important moment in your journey. I hope you're ready to open the roof and take it all in?! (Audience doesn't react) Okay, four more years then!

I want to thank the Trustees, Administrators and Faculty of MUM for creating an institution worthy of Maharishi's ideals of education. A place that teaches the knowledge and experience necessary to be productive in life, as well as enabling the students, through Transcendental Meditation and ancient Vedic knowledge to slack off twice a day for an hour and a half!!—Don't think you're fooling me!!!—But, I guess it has some benefits. It does allow you to separate who you truly are and what's real, from the stories that run through your head.

You have given them the ability to walk behind the mind's elaborate set decoration, and to see that there is a huge difference between a dog that is going to eat you in your mind and an actual dog that's going to eat you. That may sound like no big deal, but many never learn that distinction and spend a great deal of their lives living in fight or flight response.

I'd like to acknowledge all you wonderful parents—way to go for the fantastic job you've done—for your tireless dedication, your love, your support, and most of all, for the attention you've paid to your children. I have a saying, 'Beware the unloved,' because they will eventually hurt themselves...or me!

But when I look at this group here today, I feel really safe! I do! I'm just going to say it—my room is not locked! My room is not locked! No doubt some of you will turn out to be crooks! But white-collar stuff—Wall St. you know, that type of thing—crimes committed by people with self-esteem! Stuff a parent can still be proud of in a weird way.

And to the graduating class of 2017—minus 3! You didn't let me finish!—Congratulations! Yes, give yourselves a round of applause, please. You are the vanguard of knowledge and consciousness; a new wave in a vast ocean of possibilities. On the other side of that door, there is a world starving for new leadership, new ideas.

I've been out there for 30 years! She's a wild cat! (laughter) Oh, she'll rub up against your leg and purr until you pick her up and start pettin' her, and out of nowhere she'll swat you in the face. Sure it's rough sometimes but that's OK, 'cause they've got soft serve ice cream with sprinkles! I guess that's what I'm really here to say; sometimes it's okay to eat your feelings!

Fear is going to be a player in your life, but you get to decide how much. You can spend your whole life imagining ghosts, worrying about your pathway to the future, but all there will ever be is what's happening here, and the decisions we make in this moment, which are based in either love or fear.

So many of us choose our path out of fear disguised as practicality. What we really want seems impossibly out of reach and ridiculous to expect, so we never dare to ask the universe for it. I'm saying, I'm the proof that you can ask the universe for it—please! And if it doesn't happen for you right away, it's only because the universe is so busy fulfilling my order. It's party size!

My father could have been a great comedian, but he didn't believe that was possible for him, and so he made a conservative choice. Instead, he got a safe job as an accountant, and when I was 12 years old, he was let go from that safe job and our family had to do whatever we could to survive.

I learned many great lessons from my father, not the least of which was that you can fail at what you don't want, so you might as well take a chance on doing what you love.

That's not the only thing he taught me though: I watched the affect my father's love and humor had on the world around me, and I thought, 'That's something to do, that's something worth my time.'

It wasn't long before I started acting up. People would come over to my house and they would be greeted by a seven year old throwing himself down a large flight of stairs. They would say, 'What happened?' And I would say, 'I don't know—let's check the replay.' And I would go back to the top of the stairs and come back down in slow motion. (Jim reenacts coming down the stairs in slow-mo) It was a very strange household.

My father used to brag that I wasn't a ham—I was the whole pig. And he treated my talent as if it was his second chance. When I was about 28, after a decade as a professional comedian, I realized one night in LA that the purpose of my life had always been to free people from concern, like my dad. When I realized this, I dubbed my new devotion, 'The Church of Freedom From Concern'— 'The Church of FFC'—and I dedicated myself to that ministry.

What's yours? How will you serve the world? What do they need that your talent can provide? That's all you have to figure out. As someone who has done what you are about to go do, I can tell you from experience, the effect you have on others is the most valuable currency there is.

Everything you gain in life will rot and fall apart, and all that will be left of you is what was in your heart. My choosing to free people from concern got me to the top of a mountain. Look where I am—look what I get to do! Everywhere I go—and I'm going to get emotional because when I tap into this, it really is extraordinary to me—I did something that makes people present their best selves to me wherever I go. I am at the top of the mountain and the only one I hadn't freed was myself and that's when my search for identity deepened.

I wondered who I'd be without my fame. Who would I be if I said things that people didn't want to hear, or if I defied their expectations of me? What if I showed up to the party without my Mardi Gras mask and I refused to flash my breasts for a handful of beads? I'll give you a moment to wipe that image out of your mind.

But you guys are way ahead of the game. You already know who you are and that peace, that peace that we're after, lies somewhere beyond personality, beyond the perception of others, beyond invention and disguise, even beyond effort itself. You can join the game, fight the wars, play with form all you want, but to find real peace, you have to let the armor fall. Your need for acceptance can make you invisible in this world. Don't let anything stand in the way of the light that shines through this form. Risk being seen in all of your glory. (A sheet drops and reveals Jim's painting.)

(Re: the painting) It's not big enough! This painting is big for a reason. This painting is called 'High Visibility.' It's about picking up the light and daring to be seen. Here's the tricky part. Everyone is attracted to the light. The party host up in the corner (refers to painting) who thinks unconsciousness is bliss and is always offering a drink from the bottles that empty you; Misery, below her, who despises the light—can't stand when you're doing well—and wishes you nothing but the worst; The Queen of Diamonds who needs a King to build her house of cards; And the Hollow One, who clings to your leg and begs, 'Please don't leave me behind for I have abandoned myself.'

Even those who are closest to you and most in love with you; the people you love most in the world can find clarity confronting at times. This painting took me thousands of hours to complete and—thank you—yes, thousands of hours that I'll never get back, I'll never get them back—I worked on this for so long, for weeks and weeks, like a mad man alone on a scaffolding—and when I was finished one of my friends said, 'This would be a cool black light painting.'

So I started over. (All the lights go off in the Dome and the painting is showered with black light.) Whooooo! Welcome to Burning Man! Some pretty crazy characters right? Better up there than in here. Painting is one of the ways I free myself from concern, a way to stop the world through total mental, spiritual and physical involvement.

But even with that, comes a feeling of divine dissatisfaction. Because ultimately, we're not the avatars we create. We're not the pictures on the film stock. We are the light that shines through it. All else is just smoke and mirrors. Distracting, but not truly compelling.

I've often said that I wished people could realize all their dreams of wealth and fame so they could see that it's not where you'll find your sense of completion. Like many of you, I was concerned about going out in the world and doing something bigger than myself, until someone smarter than myself made me realize that there is nothing bigger than myself!

My soul is not contained within the limits of my body. My body is contained within the limitlessness of my soul—one unified field of nothing dancing for no particular reason, except maybe to comfort and entertain itself. As that shift happens in you, you won't be feeling the world you'll be felt by it—you will be embraced by it. Now, I'm always at the beginning. I have a reset button called presence and I ride that button constantly.

Once that button is functional in your life, there's no story the mind could create that will be as compelling. The imagination is always manufacturing scenarios—both good and bad—and the ego tries to keep you trapped in the multiplex of the mind. Our eyes are not only viewers, but also projectors that are running a second story over the picture we see in front of us all the time. Fear is writing that script and the working title is, 'I'll never be enough.'

You look at a person like me and say, 'How could we ever hope to reach those kinds of heights, Jim? How can I make a painting that's too big for any reasonable home? How do you fly so high without a special breathing apparatus?' This is the voice of your ego. If you listen to it, there will always be someone who seems to be doing better than you. No matter what you gain, ego will not let you rest. It will tell you that you cannot stop until you've left an indelible mark on the earth, until you've achieved immortality. How tricky is the ego that it would tempt us with the promise of something we already possess.

So I just want you to relax—that's my job—relax and dream up a good life! I had a substitute teacher from Ireland in the second grade that told my class during Morning Prayer that when she wants something, anything at all, she prays for it, and promises something in return and she always gets it. I'm sitting at the back of the classroom, thinking that my family can't afford a bike, so I went home and I prayed for one, and promised I would recite the rosary every night in exchange. Broke it—broke that promise.

Two weeks later, I got home from school to find a brand new mustang bike with a banana seat and easy rider handlebars—from fool to cool! My family informed me that I had won the bike in a raffle that a friend of mine had entered my name in, without my knowledge. That type of thing has been happening ever since, and as far as I can tell, it's just about letting the universe know what you want and working toward it while letting go of how it might come to pass.

Your job is not to figure out how it's going to happen for you, but to open the door in your head and when the doors open in real life, just walk through it. Don't worry if you miss your cue. There will always be another door opening. They keep opening.

And when I say, 'life doesn't happen to you, it happens for you.' I really don't know if that's true. I'm just making a conscious choice to perceive challenges as something beneficial so that I can deal with them in the most productive way. You'll come up with your own style, that's part of the fun!

Oh, and why not take a chance on faith as well? Take a chance on faith—not religion, but faith. Not hope, but faith. I don't believe in hope. Hope is a beggar. Hope walks through the fire. Faith leaps over it.

You are ready and able to do beautiful things in this world and after you walk through those doors today, you will only ever have two choices: love or fear. Choose love, and don't ever let fear turn you against your playful heart.

Thank you. Jai Guru Dev. I'm so honored. Thank you.

Speech at the United Nations Climate Summit

Leonardo DiCaprio

(23 September 2014)

Leonardo DiCaprio is an Oscar-winning American actor, producer, philanthropist and environmental activist known for blockbuster films such as *Titanic, The Great Gatsby* and *The Wolf of Wall Street*. DiCaprio is also widely known for his environmental activism and in 1998, he established the Leonardo DiCaprio Foundation, a non-profit organisation that promotes environmental awareness.

DiCaprio delivered this speech at the United Nations Climate Summit in 2014, encouraging world leaders to weigh the problems of the environment more carefully and take swift action.

Thank you, Mr. Secretary-General, Your Excellencies, Ladies and Gentleman, and distinguished guests. I'm honored to be here today, I stand before you not as an expert but as a concerned citizen, one of the 400,000 people who marched in the streets of New York on Sunday, and the billions of others around the world who want to solve our climate crisis.

As an actor I pretend for a living. I play fictitious characters often solving fictitious problems.

I believe mankind has looked at climate change in that same way: as if it were a fiction, as if pretending that climate change wasn't real would somehow make it go away.

But I think we know better than that. Every week , we're seeing new and undeniable climate events, evidence that accelerated climate change is here right now. Droughts are intensifying, our oceans are acidifying, with methane plumes rising up from the ocean floor. We are seeing extreme weather events, and the West Antarctic and Greenland ice sheets melting at unprecedented rates, decades ahead of scientific projections.

None of this is rhetoric, and none of it is hysteria. It is fact. The scientific community knows it, industry knows it, governments know it, even the United States military knows it. The Chief of the U.S. Navy's Pacific Command, Admiral Samuel Locklear, recently said that climate change is our single greatest security threat.

My Friends, this body—perhaps more than any other gathering in human history—now faces this difficult, but achievable task. You can make history…or be vilified by it.

To be clear, this is not about telling people to change their light bulbs or buy a hybrid car. This disaster has grown BEYOND the choices that individuals make. This is now about our industries, and governments around the world taking decisive, large-scale action.

Now must be our moment for action.

We need to put a price tag on carbon emissions, and eliminate government subsidies for oil, coal and gas companies. We need to end the free ride that industrial polluters have been given in the name of a free-market economy, they do not deserve our tax dollars, they deserve our scrutiny. For the economy itself will die if our ecosystems collapse.

The good news is that renewable energy is not only achievable but good economic policy.

This is not a partisan debate; it is a human one. Clean air and a livable climate are inalienable human rights. And solving this crisis is not a question of politics, it is a question of our own survival.

This is the most urgent of times, and the most urgent of messages.

Honored delegates, leaders of the world, I pretend for a living. But you do not.

The people made their voices heard on Sunday around the world and the momentum will not stop. But now it is YOUR turn, the time to answer humankind's greatest challenge is now.

We beg of you to face it with courage. And honesty. Thank you.

Speech on 68th Independence Day

Narendra Damodardas Modi

Red Fort, New Delhi (15 August 2014)

Narendra Damodardas Modi is the current Prime Minster of India and former Chief Minister of Gujarat. His term as Chief Minister was one that garnered mixed reviews due to the communal riots of 2002. However, his continued political successes established his position within the Bharatiya Janata Party and he became an influential political leader, finally becoming the Prime Minister of India in 2014. His promise of economic reforms has provided him a large following and his charismatic persona is expected to bring him back in power in the general elections in 2019.

This is one of the most famous speeches by Modi, delivered soon after he assumed office.

My dear countrymen,

Today, all Indians in the country and also abroad are celebrating the festival of independence. On this day of sacred festival of independence, the prime servant of India extends greetings to all dear countrymen

I am present amidst you not as the Prime Minister, but as the Prime Servant. The freedom struggle was fought for so many years, so many generations laid down their lives, innumerable people sacrificed their lives and youth, spent their entire lives behind bars. Today, I pay my respect, greetings and homage to all those who laid their lives for the country's independence.

I also pay my respects to the crores of citizens of this country on the pious occasion of India`s independence, and recall all those martyrs who had laid down their lives in India`s struggle for freedom. The day of independence is a festival when we take a solemn pledge of working for the welfare of mother India, and also for the welfare of the poor, oppressed, Dalits, the exploited & the backward people of our country.

My dear countrymen, a national festival is an occasion to refine and rebuild the national character. This National festival inspires us to resolve ourselves to lead a life where our character gets refined further, to dedicate ourselves to the nation and our every activity is linked to the interest of the nation and only then this festival of freedom can be a festival of inspiration to take India to newer heights. My dear countrymen, this nation has neither been built by political leaders nor by rulers nor by governments. This nation has been built by our farmers, our workers, our mothers and sisters, our youth. The country has reached here today because of generation to generation rigours undertaken by our sages, our saints, our maestros, our teachers, our scientists and social workers. These great people and these great generations, who had worked for the country throughout their lives, deserve our deepest respect. This is the beauty of India's Constitution, this is its capability which has made it possible that today a boy from small town, a poor family has got the opportunity to pay homage to the tricolour of India at the ramparts of Lal Quila (Red Fort). This is the strength of India's democracy. This is an invaluable legacy which we have inherited from our architects of the constitution. I pay my respects to those architects of the constitution of India today. Brothers and sisters, today if we have reached here after independence, it is because of the contribution of all the Prime Ministers, all the governments and even the governments of all the States. I want to express my feelings of respect and gratitude to all those previous governments and ex-Prime Ministers who have endeavoured to take our present day India to such heights and who have added to the country's glory.

This country has been built on such foundation of ancient cultural heritage, where we were told of only one mantra during Vedic period, which is indicative of our work culture, which we have learnt, we have memorised—*'Sangachchhdhvam Samvadadhvam sam wo manansi jaanataam.'* We walk together, we move together, we think together, we resolve together and together we take this country forward. Having imbibed this basic mantra, 125 crores of countrymen have taken the nation forward. Yesterday only the first Parliamentary Session of the new Government had concluded. Today, I can proudly say that the Session of Parliament reflects our thinking and it is a reflection of our intentions. We are not for moving forward on the basis of majority, we are not interested to move forward by virtue of majority. We want to move ahead on the basis of strong consensus. *'Sangachhadhwam'* and, therefore, the nation has witnessed the entire Session of Parliament. Having taken all the Parties and Opposition along while working shoulder to shoulder, we achieved an unprecedented success and the credit for this does not go to the Prime Minister alone, the credit does not go to the people sitting in the Government, the credit for this goes to the Opposition also, the credit goes to all the leaders of Opposition too and also all the Members from Opposition. From the ramparts of Red Fort, quite proudly I salute all the Members of Parliament, I also salute all the Political Parties and by virtue of their strong support, we could take some important decisions intended to take the nation forward and yesterday the Session of Parliament had concluded.

Brothers and sisters, I am an outsider for Delhi, I am not a native of Delhi. I have no idea about the administration and working of this place. I have been quite isolated from the elite class of this place but during the last two months while being an outsider, I had an insider view and I was astonished. It is not a political platform, rather it is a platform of a national policy and, therefore, my views should not be evaluated from a political perspective. I have already said, I salute all the ex-Prime Ministers and earlier governments who have brought the country thus far. But I am going to say something else and it may not be seen from political point of view. When I came to Delhi and noticed an insider view, I felt what it was and I was surprised to see it. It seemed as if dozens of separate governments are running at the same time in one main government. It appeared that everyone has its own fiefdom. I could observe disunity and conflict among them. One department is taking on the other department and taking on to the extent that two departments of the same government are fighting against each other by approaching Supreme Court. This disunity, this conflict among people of the same country! How come we can take the country forward? And that is why I have started making efforts for razing those walls; I have started making efforts at making the Government, not an assembled entity, but an organic unity, an organic entity, a harmonious whole— with one aim, one mind, one direction, one energy. Let's resolve to steer the country to one destination. We have it in us to move in that direction. A few days back...Nowadays newspapers are full of news that Modiji's Government has come, officers are reaching office on time, offices open in time, and people get there in time. I observed that India's National newspapers, TV media were carrying these news items prominently. As the Head of the Government I could have derived pleasure in the fact that everything started going on time, cleanliness got the attention, but I was not taking pleasure, I was feeling pained. That thing, I want to tell today in public. And why, because if government officers arrive office in time, does that make a news? And if that makes news, it shows how low we have fallen. It becomes a proof of that, and that's how, brothers and sisters, the governments have run? Today in the face of global competition, when we have to realise the dreams of millions of Indians, the country cannot run on the lines of 'it happens', 'it goes'. In order to fulfill the aspirations of masses, we have to sharpen the tool called the Government machinery, we have to make it keen, more dynamic, and it is in this direction that we are working.

My countrymen, it`s not long since I have come from outside Delhi, but I give you an assurance that the people in the Government are very capable—from the peon to the Cabinet Secretary, everybody is capable, everybody has a power, they have experience. I want to awaken that power, I want to unite that power and want to accelerate the pace of the welfare of nation through that power and I shall definitely do it. I want to assure the countrymen that we will achieve that, we will definitely do that. I could not say this on 16th May, but today after my experience of two-two and half months, keeping the tricolor as witness, I am saying on 15th of August that it is possible, it will be achieved.

Brothers and sisters, time has come to give a serious thought to the fact that whether we have a duty to create India of the dreams of those great people who gave us freedom, whether we have a national character? Brothers and sisters, can someone please tell me as to whether he or she has ever introspected in the evening after a full day's work as to whether his or her acts have helped the poor of the country or not, whether his or her actions have resulted in safeguarding the interest of the country or not, whether the actions have been directed in country's welfare or not? Whether it should not be the motto of one and a quarter billion countrymen that every step in life should be in the country's interests? Unfortunately, we have an environment today wherein if you approach anyone with some work, he begins by saying 'What does it mean for me?' He begins by saying 'What does it involve for me?' And when he come to know that it does not entail any benefit for him, immediately he says 'Why should I bother?' We have to rise above the feelings of 'what does it mean for me' and 'why should I bother'. Everything is not for self interest only. There are certain things which are meant for the country and we have to refine this national character. We have to rise above the feelings of 'Why should I bother' and 'What does it mean for me' and instead we have to think that 'I am for nation`s interest and in this field, I am going to lead.' We have to inculcate this sentiment.

Brothers and sisters, when we hear about the incidents of rape, we hang our heads in shame. People come out with different arguments, someone indulges in psycho analysis, but brothers and sisters, today from this platform, I want to ask those parents, I want to ask every parent that you have a daughter of 10 or 12 years age, you are always on the alert, every now and then you keep on asking where are you going, when would you come back, inform immediately after you reach. Parents ask their daughters hundreds of questions, but have any parents ever dared to ask their son as to where he is going, why he is going out, who his friends are. After all, a rapist is also somebody's son. He also has parents. As parents, have we ever asked our son as to what he is doing and where he is going.

If every parent decides to impose as many restrictions on the sons as have been imposed on our daughters, try to do this with your sons, try to ask such questions of them.

My dear brothers and sisters, the law will take its own course, strict action will be taken, but as a member of the society, as parents, we also have some responsibilities. If somebody tells me that those who have taken guns on their shoulders and kill innocent people are Maoists, are terrorists, but they are also somebody's children. I would like to ask of such parents if they had ever asked their children as to why they were taking a wrong path. Every parent must take this responsibility, he must know that his misguided son is bent on killing innocent people. He is not able to serve himself nor his family nor the country. I want to say to those youngsters who have chosen the path of violence that whatever they are and wherever they are, it is all because of mother India only that they have got it. Whoever you are it is all because of your parents. I want to ask you to think how green, how beautiful and how beneficial this earth can become if you shoulder the plough instead of the gun which spills blood on this land. How long shall we have bloodshed on this land, how long shall we take the lives of the innocent people and what have we got after all this? The path of violence has not yielded anything to us.

Brothers and sisters, I had gone to Nepal recently. There I said something publicly to draw the attention of the whole world. There was a time when the Emperor Ashoka who had chosen the path of wars, got converted to the path of Buddha at the sight of violence. There was a time in Nepal when their youngsters had opted for the path of violence but today I witness that the same youngsters are waiting for their constitution. The same people associated with them are framing the constitution. And I further said that if Nepal could present the best example of moving from the weapons to the books then it could provide inspiration to the youngsters in the world to abandon the path of violence.

Brothers and sisters, If Nepal, land of Buddha, can give message to the world then why can't India too do the same? So it`s the call of the hour that we renounce the path of violence and take the path of brotherhood.

Brothers and sisters, for one reason or the other, we have had communal tensions for ages. This led to the division of the country. Even after Independence, we have had to face the poison of casteism and communalism. How long these evils will continue? Whom does it benefit? We have had enough of fights, many have been killed. Friends, look behind and you will find that nobody has benefited from it. Except casting a slur on Mother India, we have done nothing. Therefore, I appeal to all those people that whether it is the poison of casteism, communalism, regionalism, discrimination on social and economic basis, all these are obstacles in our way forward. Let's resolve for once in our hearts, let`s put a moratorium on all such activities for ten years, we shall march ahead to a society which will be free from all such tensions. And you will see that how much strength we get from peace, unity, goodwill and brotherhood. Let`s experiment it for once.

My dear countrymen, believe in my words, I do assure you. Shun all the sins committed so far, give up that way, follow the way of goodwill and brotherhood, and let's resolve to take the country forward. I believe we can do that.

With advancement of science, brothers and sisters, we have a rising feeling of modernity in our mind, but what do we do? Have we ever thought what the sex ratio in the country is like? 940 girls are born against per thousand boys. Who is causing this imbalance in the society? Certainly not God. I request the doctors not to kill the girl growing in the womb of a mother just to line their own pockets. I advise mothers and sisters not to sacrifice daughters in the hope of son. Sometimes mother-father feel tempted to have son in the hope of supporting them in old age. I am a person who has worked in public life. I have come across families with five sons, each having bungalows, access to fleet of cars, but parents are forced to live in old-age homes, Vriddhashrams. I have seen such families. I have also seen families with only daughter as progeny, that daughter sacrifices her dreams, doesn't get married, and spends entire life in taking care of old parents. This disparity points to female foeticide and the polluted and tainted mind the 21st century has. We will have to liberate from it, and that is message to us of this Freedom festival.

Recently Commonwealth Games were organised. Indian sportspersons brought glory to the country. Nearly 64 of our sportspersons won. Our sportspersons brought 64 medals. But of them 29 are girls. Let's feel proud and clap for them. Girls also contribute to India's fame and glory. Let's recognise it. Let's take them along, shoulder to shoulder. This way we can get over the evils that have crept in social life. Therefore, brothers and sisters, we have to proceed in that direction as a social and national character. Brothers and Sisters, Development is the only way forward for the country. Good governance is the only way. There are only these two tracks to take the country forward—good governance and development, we can move forward only by taking them with us. We wish to move forward with the intent of taking them with us. When I talk of good governance, you tell me, when I ask a person in private job, he tells that he does the job; when you ask the same from a person in government job, he says that I do the service. Both earn, but for one it is job while for the other it is service. I ask a question from all brothers and sisters in government service, whether the word 'Service' has not lost its strength, its identity? Persons in government service are not doing 'job', they are doing 'service'. We have to revive this feeling, we have to take this feeling forward as a national character, we have to move forward in this direction.

Brothers and Sisters, whether the citizens of the country should take steps for the welfare of the nation or not? You imagine, if this 125 crores of countrymen move one step forward, then the country moves 125 crore steps forward. The meaning of democracy is not just limited to electing a government, but its meaning is that 125 crore of citizens work together joining shoulder with the government to fulfill hopes and aspirations of the country, this is the meaning of democracy. We have to create partnership with the people. We have to proceed under Public-Private Partnership. We have to proceed along with the participation of the people. But, please tell me why our farmers commit suicide? A farmer takes loan from the moneylender, but fails to repay his loans. He takes loan for the wedding of his daughter, but fails to repay. He will have to suffer hardships during his whole life. He chooses to commit suicide. Who will save the poor families of such farmers?

Brothers and sisters, I have come here with a pledge to launch a scheme on this festival of Freedom. It will be called 'Pradhanmantri Jan-Dhan Yojana'. I wish to connect the poorest citizens of the country with the facility of bank accounts through this yojana. There are millions of families who have mobile phones but no bank accounts. We have to change this scenario. Economic resources of the country should be utilized for the well-being of the poor. The change will commence from this point. This yojana will open the window. Therefore, an account holder under `Pradhanmantri Jan-Dhan Yojana' will be given a debit card. An insurance of One Lakh Rupees will be guaranteed with that debit card for each poor family, so that such families are covered with the insurance of One Lakh Rupees in case of any crisis in their lives.

My brothers and sisters, it is a country of young people. The 65 percent population of the country happens to be under the age of 35 years. Our country has the largest number of youths in the world. Have we ever thought of deriving an advantage out of it? Today, the world needs a skilled workforce. Today, India also needs a skilled workforce. At times, we look for a good driver but he is not available, we look for a plumber, but he is not available. If we need a good cook, he is not available. We have young people, they are unemployed but the kind of young people we seek for are not available. If we have to promote the development of our country then our mission has to be 'skill development' and 'skilled India'. Millions and Millions of Indian youth should go for acquisition of skills and there should be a network across the country for this and not the archaic systems. They should acquire the skills which could contribute towards making India a modern country. Whenever they go to any country in the world, their skills must be appreciated and we want to go for a two pronged development. I also want to create a pool of young people who are able to create jobs and the ones who are not capable of creating jobs and do not have the opportunities, they must be in a position to face their counterparts in any corner of the world while keeping their heads high by virtue of their hard work and their dexterity of hands and win the hearts of people around the world through their skills. We want to go for the capacity building of such young people. My brothers and sisters, having taken a resolve to enhance the skill development at a highly rapid pace, I want to accomplish this.

Brothers and sisters, the world has undergone a change. My dear countrymen, the world has changed. Now India cannot decide its future by remaining isolated and sitting alone in a corner. The economics of the world have changed and, therefore, we will have to act accordingly. Government have taken many decisions recently, made some announcements in the budget and I call upon the world and call upon the Indians spread world over that if we have to provide more and more employment to the youth, we will have to promote manufacturing sector. If we have to develop a balance between imports and exports, we will have to strengthen manufacturing sector. If we have to put in use the education, the capability of the youth, we will have to go for manufacturing sector and for this Hindustan also will have to lend its full strength, but we also invite world powers. Therefore I want to appeal all the people world over, from the ramparts of the Red Fort, 'Come, make in India', 'Come, manufacture in India'. Sell in any country of the world but manufacture here. We have got skill, talent, discipline, and determination to do something. We want to give the world an favourable opportunity that come here, 'Come, Make in India' and we will say to the world, from electrical to electronics, 'Come, Make in India', from automobiles to agro value addition 'Come, Make in India', paper or plastic, 'Come, Make in India', satellite or submarine 'Come, Make in India'. Our country is powerful. Come, I am giving you an invitation.

Brothers and sisters, I want to call upon the youth of the country, particularly the small people engaged in the industrial sector. I want to call upon the youth working in the field of technical education in the country. As I say to the world 'Come, Make in India', I say to the youth of the country—it should be our dream that this message reaches every corner of the world, 'Made in India'. This should be our dream. Whether, to serve the country, is it necessary for the youth of the country to be hanged like Bhagat Singh? Brothers and sisters, Lal Bahadur Shastri had given the slogan 'Jai Jawan, Jai Kisan'. A soldier sacrifices himself at the border and protects Mother India. Similarly, a farmer serves

Mother India by filling the godowns with grains. This is also nation`s service. Filling the granary is the biggest nation`s service that a farmer provides. That is why Lal Bahadur Shashtri had given the slogan of 'Jai Jawan, Jai Kisan'.

Brothers and Sisters, I would like to pose a question to my youngsters as to why despite them, we are forced to import even the smallest of things? My country's youth can resolve it, they should conduct research, try to find out as to what type of items are imported by India and then each one should resolve that, through may be micro or small industries only, he would manufacture at least one such item so that we need not import the same in future. We should even advance to a situation wherein we are able to export such items. If each one of our millions of youngsters resolves to manufacture at least one such item, India can become a net exporter of goods. I, therefore, urge upon the youth, in particular our small entrepreneurs that they would never compromise, at least on two counts. First, zero defect and, second again zero effect. We should manufacture goods in such a way that they carry zero defect, that our exported goods are never returned to us. We should manufacture goods with zero effect that they should not have a negative impact on the environment. If we march ahead with the dream of zero defect in the manufacturing sector then, my brothers and sisters, I am confident that we would be able to achieve our goals.

Brothers and sisters, the youth of India has completely transformed the identity of India in the world. Earlier, in what manner did the world know our country? Till only 25-30 years back, if not more, there were many people in the world who thought that India was a country of snake charmers, it was a country which practiced in black magic. The real identity of India had not reached the world, but my dear brothers and sisters, our youngsters, 20-22-23 years old youngsters have mesmerized the whole world with their skills in computers. Our young I.T. professionals have given a new path of making a new identity of India. If our country has this strength, can we think something about the country? Our dream is, therefore, of 'Digital India'. When I talk of 'Digital India', I don`t speak of the elite, it is for the poor people. You can imagine what a quality education the children in villages will get, if all the villages of India are connected with Broadband Connectivity and if we are able to give long distance education to the schools in every remote corner of the villages. If we create a network of telemedicine in the places where there is a shortage of doctors, we can have a clear guideline of the way in which health facilities have to be provided to the poor people living in those areas. The citizens of India have mobile phones in their hands, they have mobile connectivity, but can we walk in the direction of mobile governance? We have to move in a direction where every poor person is able to operate his bank account from his mobile, is able to demand various things from the government, can submit applications, can conduct all his business, while on the move, through mobile governance and if this has to be done, we have to move towards `digital India' and if we have to move towards 'digital India' then we have a dream. Today we are importing electronic goods on a large scale. Friends, you will be surprised that we are bringing in these televisions, mobile phones, i-pads and all these electronic goods. It is a necessity to import petroleum products, oil, diesel and petrol. Second to this is the import of our electronic goods. If we move ahead with the dream of 'digital India' to manufacture electronic goods and become self reliant at least there, how big can be the benefit for the treasury! Therefore, e-governance is what we need to take this idea of 'digital India' forward. E-governance is easy governance, effective governance and also economic governance. E-governance paves the way for good governance. There was a time when we used to say that the railways provided connectivity to the country. That was it. I say that today it is IT that has the potential to connect each and every citizen of the country and that is why we want to realise the mantra of unity with the help of `digital India'.

Brothers and sisters, if we move ahead with all this then I believe that a `digital India' will have the potential to stand with the world on equal footing. Our youth have that capability, it is an opportunity for them.

Brothers and sisters, we want to promote tourism. Tourism provides employment to the poorest of the poor. Gram seller earns something, auto-rickshaw driver earns something, *pakoda* seller earns something and tea seller also earns something. When there is talk of tea seller, I feel a sense of belongingness. Tourism provide employment to the poorest of the poor. But there is a big obstacle in promoting tourism and in our national character and that is—the filthiness all around us. Whether after independence, after so many years of independence, when we stand at the threshold of one and half decade of 21st century, we still want to live in filthiness? The first work I started here after formation of Government is of cleanliness. People wondered whether it is a work of a Prime Minister? People may feel that it is a trivial work for a Prime Minister but for me this a big work. Cleanliness is very big work. Whether our country cannot be clean? If one hundred and twenty five crore countrymen decide that they will never spread filthiness, which power in the world has ability to spread filthiness in our cities and villages? Can`t we resolve this much?

Brothers and sisters it will be 150th birth anniversary of Mahatma Gandhi in 2019. How do we celebrate 150th birth anniversary of Mahatma Gandhi? Mahatma Gandhi, who gave us freedom, who brought so much honour to such a big country in the world, what do we give to Mahatma Gandhi? Brothers and Sisters, Mahatma Gandhi had cleanliness and sanitation closest to his heart. Whether we resolve not to leave a speck of dirt in our village, city, street, area, school, temple, hospital, and what have you, by 2019 when we celebrate 150th anniversary of Mahatma Gandhi? This happens not just with the Government, but with public participation. That`s why we have to do it together.

Brother and Sisters, we are living in 21st century. Has it ever pained us that our mothers and sisters have to defecate in open? Whether dignity of women is not our collective responsibility? The poor womenfolk of the village wait for the night; until darkness descends, they can't go out to defecate. What bodily torture they must be feeling, how many diseases that act might engender. Can't we just make arrangements for toilets for the dignity of our mothers and sisters? Brothers and Sisters, somebody might feel that a big festival like 15th August is an occasion to talk big. Brothers and Sisters, talking big has its importance, making announcements too has importance, but sometimes announcements raise hopes and when the hopes are not fulfilled, the society sinks into a state of despondency. That`s why are in favour of telling those things, which we can fulfill just within our sight. Brothers and sisters, you must be getting shocked to hear the Prime Minister speaking of cleanliness and the need to build toilets from the ramparts of the Red Fort.

Brothers and sisters, I do not know how my speech is going to be criticised and how will people take it. But this is my heartfelt conviction. I come from a poor family, I have seen poverty. The poor need respect and it begins with cleanliness. I, therefore, have to launch a 'Clean India' campaign from 2nd October this year and carry it forward in 4 years. I want to make a beginning today itself and that is—all schools in the country should have toilets with separate toilets for girls. Only then our daughters will not be compelled to leave schools midway. Our parliamentarians utilising MPLAD fund are there. I appeal to them to spend it for constructing toilets in schools for a year. The government should utilise its budget on providing toilets. I call upon the corporate sector also to give priority to the provision of toilets in schools with your expenditure under Corporate Social Responsibility. This target should be finished within one year with the help of state governments and on the next 15th August, we should be in a firm position to announce that there is no school in India without separate toilets for boys and girls.

Brothers and sisters, if we proceed with the dreams, we are in a position to realise them. Today, I wish to tell one more specific thing. It has its own importance to discuss the matters and express the views of nation's interest. However, our Members of Parliament do not get opportunity though they are willing to do something. They can express themselves, write to the government, agitate, give memoranda. Still they do not get opportunity to do something on their own. Today I have come to you with a new idea. We are running so many schemes in the name of the Prime Minister in our country, there are numerous schemes in the name of various leaders. However, today I am going to announce a scheme on behalf of the Member of Parliament–'Sansad Aadarsh Gram Yojana'. We shall fix some parameters. I urge upon the Members of Parliament to select any one of the villages having population of three to five thousand in your constituency. The parameters will be according to the time, space and situation of that locality. It will include the conditions of health, cleanliness, atmosphere, greenery, cordiality etc. On the basis of those parameters, each of our MPs should make one village of his or her constituency a Model Village by 2016. Can`t we do at least this? Shouldn't we do this? If we have to build a nation, we should start from the village. Make a Model Village. The reason of fixing this target for 2016 is that it is a new scheme. It takes time to formulate a scheme and then to implement it. After 2016, select two more villages for this purpose, before we go for the General Elections in 2019. And after 2019, each Member of Parliament, during his/her tenure of 5 years must establish at-least five model villages in his/her area. I also call upon the Members of Parliament from urban areas to adopt one village of their choice. I also urge upon the Members of Parliament from Rajya Sabha to adopt one of the villages. If we provide one model village in each district of India then the surrounding villages shall be automatically inspired to follow that model. Let us establish a model village, let us establish a village well equipped with all systems and facilities. The birth anniversary of Jai Prakash Narayan Ji happens to be on 11th October. On 11th October, the occasion of birth anniversary of Jai Prakash Narayan Ji, I will present a complete blueprint of 'Sãnsad Adharsh Grãm Yojana' (Members of Parliament Model Village Scheme) before all Members of Parliament and State Governments, and I urge upon State Governments also that as per the feasibility in their respective states, all the Members of Legislative Assembly resolve to establish a model village. You can imagine all the Members of Legislative Assembly and all the Members of Parliament in the country establishing a model village. All of a sudden, there would be a model village in each block of India which could inspire us to transform the amenities in rural areas and could give us a new direction and, therefore, we want to move ahead under this 'Sãnsad Adarsh Grãm Yojana'.

My dear brothers and sisters, ever since our government has taken charge, there has been a discussion in the newspapers, on TV channels as to what would happen to Planning Commission. I believe that when Planning Commission was constituted, it was done on the basis of the circumstances and the needs of those times. In recent years, Planning Commission has contributed to the growth of the country in its own way. I respect that, I am proud of that, but the prevalent situation in the country is different, global scenario has also changed, governments are no longer the centre of economic activities, the scope of such activities has broadened. State governments have been at the center of development and I consider this a good indication. If we have to take India forward, it can happen only by taking the states forward. India's federal structure is more important today than in the last 60 years. To strengthen our federal structure, to make our federal structure vibrant, to take our federal structure as a heritage of development, a team of Chief Minister and Prime Minister should be there, a joint team of the Centre and the states should move forward, then to do this job, we will have to think about giving the Planning Commission a look. So, I am saying from the rampart of the Red Fort that it is a very old system and it will have to be rejuvenated, it will have to be changed a lot. Sometimes it costs more to repair the old house, but, it gives us no satisfaction. Thereafter, we have a feeling that it would be better to construct a new house altogether and therefore within a short period, we will replace the planning commission with a new institution having a new design and structure, a new body, a new soul, a new thinking, a new direction, a new faith towards forging a new direction to lead the country based on creative thinking, public-private partnership, optimum utilisation of resources, utilisation of youth power of the nation, to promote the aspirations of state governments seeking development, to empower the state governments and to empower the federal structure. Very shortly, we are about to move in a direction when this institute would be functioning in place of Planning Commission.

Brothers and sisters, today, on 15th August, we also have the birth anniversary of Maharishi Aurobindo. Maharishi Aurobindo, being a rebel, moved on to achieve the status of a Yoga Guru. With regard to the destiny of India, he remarked, 'I have a faith that the divine power and spiritual heritage of India will play an important role towards the welfare of the world.' Such sentiments were echoed by Maharishi Arvind. I strongly believe in the words of legends. I have great faith in the statements made by ascetics, sages & saints and that's why today at the ramparts of Lal Quila I am reminded of the words of Swami Viveknanda. He had said— 'I can see before my eyes Mother India awakening once again. My Mother India would be seated as the World Guru. Every Indian would render service towards welfare of humanity. This legacy of India would be useful for the welfare of the world'. These words were spoken by Swami Viveknanda ji in his own style. Friends, the words of Viveknanda ji can never be untrue. The words of Viveknanda ji, his dream of seeing India ensconced as World Guru, his vision, it is incumbent upon us to realise that dream. This capable country, blessed with natural bounty, this country of youth can do much for the world in the coming days.

Brothers and sisters, our foreign policy is a much talked about issue. I clearly believe that India's foreign policy can be multi-dimensional. But there is an important issue to which I want to draw your attention that the way we fought for freedom, we fought together, we were not separate at that time. We were together. Which was the government with us? What were the weapons available to us? There was a Gandhi, a Sardar and lakhs of freedom fighters and such a huge empire. Didn't we win in the struggle of freedom against that empire? Did we not defeat the foreign powers? Did we not force them to leave India? We were the ones, they were our ancestors only who showed this might. If the people of India could remove such a big empire without the power of the government, without weapons and even without resources, then friends, it is the need of the hour to eradicate poverty, can we not overcome poverty? Can we not defeat poverty? My 125 crore dear countrymen, let us resolve to eradicate poverty, to win against it. Let us move with the dream of poverty eradication from India. Our neighbouring countries are also faced with the same problem. Why not get together with all the SAARC nations to plan out the fight against poverty? Let's fight together and defeat poverty. Let us see at-least for once as to how wonderful is the feeling of being alive instead of killing and getting killed. This is the land where incidents from Siddharth's life happened. One bird was shot with an arrow by one brother and the other took out that arrow to save it. They went to mother— whose bird, whose swan? Whether killer's or saviour's, they asked of mother. The mother replied, saviour's. The saviour has more power than the killer and that makes him Buddha in future. And that`s why I seek cooperation from neighbouring countries for fighting against poverty in concert and cooperate with them, so that together with SAARC countries we can create our importance and emerge as a power in the world. It is imperative that we work together with a dream to win a fight against poverty, shoulder to shoulder. I went to Bhutan, Nepal, all the dignitaries from SAARC countries took part in oath-taking ceremony; this marked a good beginning. This will definitely yield good results, it is my belief and this thinking of India, in the country and the world, that we want to do well to the countrymen and be useful for the welfare of the world, India wants such a hand to be extended. We are trying to move forward with these dreams to achieve them.

Brothers and Sisters, today on 15th August we will resolve to do something for the country. Let`s be useful for the country, we will move ahead with a resolve to take the country forward, and I assure you, Brothers and Sisters, as well as my colleagues in the Government, that if you work for 12 hours, I will do so for 13 hours. If you work for 14 hours, I will do for 15 hours. Why? Because I`m amidst you not as a Prime Minister, but as the first servant. I have formed the Government not as a ruler, but as a servant. Brothers and sisters, I assure that this country has a destiny. It is destined to work for the welfare of the world, it was said by Vivekanand ji. India is born, this Hindustan is born in order to achieve this destiny. 125 crore countrymen have to move forward wholeheartedly for the welfare of the nation.

Once again I feel proud of the devotion, the sacrifices of the security forces of the country, para-military forces of the country, all the security forces of the country to protect Mother India. I say to the countrymen, 'Eternal vigilance is the price of liberty'. The army is vigilant, we should also be vigilant and the country scales new heights, we have to move forward with this resolution. Speak loudly with me with full force—

Bharat Mata ki Jai, Bharat Mata ki Jai, Bharat Mata ki Jai.

Jai Hind, Jai Hind, Jai Hind.

Vande Mataram, Vande Mataram, Vande Mataram!

'I Haven't Broken Through Any Glass Ceilings'

Shonda Rhimes

The Hollywood Reporter Sherry Lansing Award Acceptance Speech (10 December 2014)

Shonda Rhimes is an award-winning American television producer, screenwriter and author best-known for her successful shows 'Grey's Anatomy', 'How to Get Away with Murder' and 'Scandal'. In 2007, *TIME magazine* ranked her amongst '100 People Who Help Shape the'. Rhimes also published a memoir in 2015, *Year of Yes: How to Dance It Out, Stand in the Sun, and Be Your Own Person.*

In her moving acceptance speech, Rhimes modestly stated that she hasn't 'broken through any glass ceiling' but that it is the many hardworking women before her who made this day possible.

When my publicist called to tell me that I was receiving this honor, I screwed up my face and I said, 'Are you sure? Me?' And he said, 'Yes.'

And I said, 'Why?' And then I said, 'No really, WHY?'

And I made him call and ask for some written reason why I was getting this award. Because I really and truly was worried that there might have been some kind of mistake.

I want to pause for a beat here to say that I don't say these things to be self deprecating and humble. I am not a self-deprecating, humble person. I think I'm pretty fantastic. But I also think that The Hollywood Reporter Sherry Lansing Award is extraordinary—as is Sherry Lansing herself. So…no, really, WHY?

They sent a written reason why I was getting this award. It said many nice things but the main thing that it was said was that I was getting the award in recognition of my breaking through the industry's glass ceiling as a woman and an African-American.

Well. I call my publicist back. Because I just don't know about this. I mean, I'm concerned now.

I come from a very large, very competitive family. Extremely competitive. And by competitive, I mean, my mother says we're not allowed to play Scrabble anymore when we get together because of the injuries and the tears. One of the rules in my family is you don't ever get a trophy for participation, you don't get a trophy for just being you. So getting an award today BECAUSE I'm a woman and an African-American feels...I was born with an awesome vagina and really gorgeous brown skin. I didn't do anything to make either of those things happen.

To get all Beyonce about it, people: *'I woke up like this.'*

Seriously. I know this isn't an award because I'm a woman or BECAUSE I'm African American. I know that it's really about breaking the glass ceiling that exists in the face of being a woman and being black in this very male, very white town.

But I haven't broken through any glass ceilings.

Do they know I haven't broken through any glass ceilings? I ask my publicist. He assures me that I have. I assure him that I have not. I have not broken through any glass ceilings. If I had broken through any glass ceilings, I would know. If I had broken through a glass ceiling, I would have felt some cuts, I would have some bruises. There'd be shards of glass in my hair. I'd be bleeding, I'd have wounds.

If I'd broken the glass ceiling, that would mean I would have made it through to the other side. Where the air is rare. I would feel the wind on my face. The view from here—way up here where the glass ceiling is broken—would be incredible. Right? So how come I don't remember the moment? When me with my woman-ness and my brown skin went running full speed, gravity be damned, into that thick layer of glass and smashed right through it? How come I don't remember that happening?

Here's why: It's 2014.

This moment right here, me standing up here all brown with my boobs and my Thursday night of network television full of women of color, competitive women, strong women, women who own their bodies and whose lives revolve around their work instead of their men, women who are big dogs, that could only be happening right now.

Think about it.

Look around this room. It's filled with women of all colors in Hollywood who are executives and heads of studios and VPs and show creators and directors. There are a lot of women in Hollywood in this room who have the game-changing ability to say yes or no to something.

15 years ago, that would not have been as true. There'd have been maybe a few women in Hollywood who could say yes or no. And a lot of D girls and assistants who were gritting their teeth and working really hard. And for someone like me, if I was very very VERY lucky, there'd have been maybe one small show. One small shot. And that shot would not have involved a leading actress of color, any three dimensional LGBT characters, any women characters with high powered jobs AND families, and no more than two characters of color in any scene at one time—because that only happened in sitcoms.

30 years ago, I'd think maybe there'd be a thousand secretaries fending off their handsy bosses back at the office and about two women in Hollywood in this room. And if I were here, I would serving those two women breakfast.

50 years ago, if women wanted to gather in a room, well it had better be about babies or charity work. And the brown women were in one room over there and the white women were in a room over here.

From then to now...we've all made such an incredible leap.

Think of all of them.

50 years ago trying to get out of separate rooms, 30 years ago trying to not serve breakfast or be groped by their bosses, 15 years ago trying to make clear that they could run a department as well as that guy over there.

All the women, white or black or brown who woke up like this, who came before me in this town.

Think of them. Heads up, eyes on the target. Running. Full speed. Gravity be damned. Towards that thick layer of glass that is the ceiling. Running, full speed and crashing. Crashing into that ceiling and falling back. Crashing into it and falling back. Into it and falling back. Woman after woman. Each one running and each one crashing. And everyone falling.

How many women had to hit that glass before the first crack appeared? How many cuts did they get, how many bruises? How hard did they have to hit the ceiling? How many women had to hit that glass to ripple it, to send out a thousand hairline fractures? How many women had to hit that glass before the pressure of their effort caused it to evolve from a thick pane of glass into just a thin sheet of splintered ice?

So that when it was my turn to run, it didn't even look like a ceiling anymore. I mean, the wind was already whistling through—I could always feel it on my face. And there were all these holes giving me a perfect view to other side. I didn't even notice the gravity, I think it had worn itself away. So I didn't have to fight as hard, I had time to study the cracks. I had time to decide where the air felt the rarest, where the wind was the coolest, where the view was the most soaring. I picked my spot in the glass and called it my target. And I ran. And when I hit finally that ceiling, it just exploded into dust.

Like *that*.

My sisters who went before me had already handled it.

No cuts. No bruises. No bleeding.

Making it through the glass ceiling to the other side was simply a matter of running on a path created by every other woman's footprints.

I just hit at exactly the right time in exactly the right spot.

So I'm breaking my family's rule today. This is a trophy for participation. And I am beyond honored and proud to receive it. Because this? Was a group effort.

Thank you to all the women in this room. Thank you to all the women who never made it to this room. And thank you to all the women who will hopefully fill a room 100 times this size when we are all gone.

You are all an inspiration.

Caring for the Earth—Reasons for Hope

Dr. Jane Goodall

12th Khazanah Global Lecture, Kuala Lumpur, Malaysia
(31 October 2016)

Dr. Jane Goodall is an English ethologist and animal rights activist who is well-known for her long-term research on the chimpanzees of the Gombe Stream National Park in Tanzania. She has published several works on her study of the behaviour of chimpanzees as well as founded the Jane Goodall Institute. In 2002, she was appointed UN Messenger of Peace.

In this speech, Goodall recounts her journey as well as stresses on the importance of conservation.

Well, thank you for a wonderful introduction and thank everybody who is here tonight. I'm going to greet you in my traditional way, and I'm willing to bet that the voice of the wild chimpanzee has never been heard in this room before. And if you're with me in the hills of Gombe, and you climbed up in the morning, you would almost certainly hear the chimpanzees greeting the day.

(Jane Goodall imitates a chimpanzee call) This is me, this is Jane.

Well, you've just heard all this stuff about my life, and what I've done in my 82 years. And sometimes, I really wonder how it's all happened. How is it that when I go to a country like Malaysia, all of you people have come to listen to me? And I've worked out that there are actually two Janes. There's one Jane that has become somehow the sort of conservation icon, and I think it probably started with the National Geographic Society. But there's also the other Jane, and that's me. I'm just me, just an ordinary human being who started off as a very shy little girl with a dream.

I want to thank one person in particular and but for her, I think possibly I would not be standing here tonight. We can't choose our parents, and I was lucky. I was born with an extraordinary mother, I was also born loving animals. When I was one and a half—I don't remember this, of course—but she tells me she came into my room to say goodnight to me, and she found I had taken a whole handful of earthworms to bed with me. Well, most mothers would be kind of cross because there was a lot of earth in the bed as well but she just said quietly 'Jane, they need to go back into the garden or they'll die.' And we carried them back.

And then, when I was four and a half, and I don't know how many of you can think of a four and a half year old—I'm sure quite a lot of you—and loving animals but living in London, there weren't so many animals. And so, what I remember so well was going for a holiday into the country and staying on a farm. And in those days, farms were farms where animals roamed about in the fields, there was none of this intensive farming. And meeting cows and pigs and horses face to face, was really exciting. And they gave me a job to help collect the hen's eggs. And the hens were pecking around in the farmyard but they mostly went into these little hen-houses where they also slept at night, to lay their eggs. And the eggs were in little boxes around the edge, and I would go and lift up the lid and if there was an egg, put it in my basket. But apparently, I began asking everybody, 'but where's the hole on the hen? Where does the egg come out? I couldn't see a hole big enough for an egg.'

And obviously, nobody told me to my satisfaction. And what I do remember so clearly is seeing a hen, she was a brown hen, and she was going into one of these hen houses, I think there were about six or eight of them, and thinking she's going to lay an egg, and crawling after her. Well, that was a big mistake. And with squawks of I suppose fear, she flew out. And you know, I—four and a half years old—but I thought well, no hen would lay an egg here. This is a frightening place. And I went into an empty hen house and hid in the straw at the back and I waited and I waited and I waited. And the family had no idea where I was. And as it was beginning to get dark, they were searching and in fact, they even called the police. And yet, when my mother met me, instead of 'how dare you go off without telling us? Don't you dare do it again' which would have killed all the excitement, she saw my shining eyes and sat down to hear the wonderful story of how a hen lays an egg.

And I can still close my eyes and see it as though if it was happening yesterday. And the reason I tell that story is isn't that the making of a little scientist, the curiosity, asking questions, not getting the right answer, deciding to find out for myself, making a mistake, not giving up, and learning patience. It was all there, in that little four and a half year old girl. And with a different kind of mother, that little scientific curiosity might have been crushed.

And that's why I say I might not be standing here tonight. She decided that if she got books about animals, I would learn to read more quickly, and of course, she was right. The war in 3 Europe had started by this time, and I don't think they were even making new books, so my books came from the library. Anyway, we had very little money. And so one day, I was given from the library this book about Dr Dolittle, someone who could actually talk to the animals, and he was taught by his parrot Polynesia. And if you don't know the Dr Dolittle stories, they are wonderful. And I wanted a parrot to teach me animal language, and so I was eight years old, and I pretended to all my friends that I could understand the dogs and the cats and the squirrels and the birds. They believed me, I would translate what they were saying.

And then when I was 10, as I say, we had very little money and the books mostly came from libraries. But there were some wonderful secondhand bookshops, and this one particular one was run by a funny little old man. And really, the books were just piled up higgledy piggledy, he didn't know where anything was. And I used to spend hours in there and I found this little book, I just had saved up enough of my few pennies pocket money to buy it. And I took it home and I climbed my favourite tree in the garden. I read that book from cover to cover. I still have it today, and that was called Tarzan of the Apes.

And of course, I fell passionately in love with Tarzan. Little girls of 10 are very romantic. And what did Tarzan do? He married the wrong Jane. Well, of course, I was very jealous. But equally, I knew that there wasn't a Tarzan. That's when my dream began. I will grow up, go to Africa, live with animals and write books about them. That was my dream. And everybody at school laughed at me: 'how will you get to Africa, it's very far away.' We talked about it as the Dark Continent, we didn't have any money. And girls didn't do that sort of thing. 'Jane, dream about something you can achieve, forget this nonsense about Africa.' But not my mother. And what she said to me, or at least words to this effect, is the message that I take around the world today and share with children everywhere.

Basically, she said 'Jane, if you really want this thing, you're going to have to work really hard. You're going to have to take advantage of opportunity and never give up.' And I think one of the most rewarding things about my life today is the number of children whom I meet or who write to me and say, 'you taught me that because you did it, I can do it too.' I can't think of anything more rewarding than that.

So as you heard, there was no money for university. You couldn't get a scholarship unless you were good in a foreign language. And we had just enough money for this secretarial course. And when I got the letter from my school friend ... you couldn't save money in London where I was working at that time, so I worked, I think it was about five months in a hotel, an old fashioned hotel where people came for a week's holiday, and after the war, they didn't have much money. So, I was serving breakfast, lunch and dinner. And always, when I'm at an event like this, I'm always thinking of the waiters and waitresses, and what a hard job they actually have. But at any rate, thank you waiters and waitresses if you are listening in here.

So eventually, I had saved up enough money, by boat which is how one went in those days. It should have been a journey taking about slightly less than two weeks, from Britain through the Suez Canal and down to Mombasa. But there was this stupid little war between England and Egypt, and the Suez Canal was closed. And so, the boat went all the way around Cape Town, took over three weeks. And can you imagine what it was like? I was 23 years old, and I got onto the boat and it was grey and dull in England, and the water was grey. And then, as we went further south, so the water got bluer and the air got warmer. And I can never forget the first flying fish, and the dolphins that were gamboling around the boat as we got down to Cape Town.

Arriving in Mombasa, going by train, all the animals were there then, we went past them in the train, being met by my friend. And the very first morning I woke up, she came running to my room and said 'Jane, come and look.' And there, just outside the house were the paw prints of a large male leopard. Now, I had really arrived in Africa.

And how wonderful to hear about Dr Lewis Leakey, and somebody said 'Jane, if you're interested in animals, you should meet Lewis.' And he was curator of the National History Museum at that time. And I made an appointment to see him, just to talk about animals. And he took me all around, he asked me many, many questions about the different animals that were in the museum. And because I had read so many books about Africa and animals, because I had spent hours when I was in London in the Natural History Museum, I could answer most of his questions. And so, that's why he gave me a job as his secretary, assistant, took me on one of his digs to Olduvai Gorge in the days when all the animals were there. Meeting rhinoceros long before they became endangered, meeting a young male lion who followed me and this other young girl, at least the length of this large room, which was a bit scary but very exciting.

And I think it was that evening, around the campfire, that Lewis decided I was the person he'd been looking for. He said for years to go and learn about chimpanzees in the wild, nobody knew anything, nobody had studied them in the wild. And he was searching for the fossilised remains of our earliest ancestors. And you can tell an awful lot from the fossils about those creatures from the wear on the teeth, the sort of diet they had, and from the structure of the bones, the sort of gait, the way they walked. And from the remnants of tools on the living floors, you could tell the level of their sophistication. But behaviour doesn't fossilise.

And Lewis argued that if we could, if I could find behaviour that was similar or even the same in chimpanzees, our closest living relatives today, similar behaviour in them and us, maybe that behaviour was present in the common ancestor about seven million years ago. And therefore, he could better imagine early humans, kissing, embracing, holding hands, patting one another on the back, perhaps waging war. All of those things which I was to find out, similar in chimpanzee and human society. But none of that was known when I first got to Gombe National Park.

It took him a year to find money. I mean, who was going to give money for this, young girl with no degree, new out of Africa. So I had go back and wait in England while he searched and searched for money. And eventually it was a wealthy American businessman who provided money just for half a year. He said, 'well, we'll see how she does.'

And then at that time, you know, the British Empire was crumbling but it was still in its last throes. And what is Tanzania today was Tanganyika, and it was under British protectorate rule and the authorities were not prepared to take responsibility for this young girl. It was ridiculous. But in the end, because Lewis never gave up, they said, 'oh well, all right, but she can't come alone. She has to come with a companion.' And who volunteered? That same amazing mother. She packed up for four whole months, and left her life in England, and shared an old ex-Army tent, none of your neat little zips that you have today so that you can shut out the mosquitoes. If you wanted air, you rolled up the side flaps and in came the air, yes, but also snakes and spiders and goodness knows what.

And it was fine for me, I was up in the hills every single morning, searching for chimpanzees. But she was left on her own in the camp and there were buffaloes around at that time. But she set up a little clinic for the local fishermen. And although she wasn't a doctor or a nurse, her brother was a surgeon, her sister was a physiotherapist, and we'd come armed with simple things like aspirin and bandages and so forth. And because she spent hours with the different people who came with their ailments, she made some amazing cures, and people began coming from further and further away. And I learnt later that she was known as a white witch doctor. The good kind.

So, she established, for me, from the very beginning, a really good relationship with the local people, and these were fishermen coming down over the hills to the shore of Lake Tanganyika. And then when the moon was full and the fish didn't rise to their lights, they went back to their village and sold the fish. So she did another really important thing for me because in those early days, the chimpanzees would take one look and run away. They are very conservative, they have never seen a white ape before. And they would take one look and vanish in the vegetation.

And I was in my dream world but you know, I knew if I didn't see something exciting before the money ran out, that would have been the end and I would have let Lewis Leakey down. So, it was wonderful when I got back in the evening, there she was, and she was boosting my morale. 'Jane, you are learning more than you think. You found this peak that you said, and from it, you can see the chimpanzees moving around, sometimes alone, sometimes in small groups, sometimes obviously a family—a mother and her younger children.'

She said, 'you'd seen them all meet up and greet one another when there's a delicious fruit come into season. And you're learning a lot more than you think. You see how they make nests at night, bending over the branches,' just like your orangutans do here. So, she did help to boost my morale. And it was really sad that she left before the breakthrough observation which was when I saw a chimpanzee through the vegetation, with my binoculars, I saw a black hand reach out and break off a grass stem and push it carefully into a termite mound, leave it for a moment, pull it slowly out and pick off the termites with his lips. And I saw him break off a leafy twig, and before he could use that as a tool, he had to strip the leaves. He was making a tool.

That wouldn't be exciting today, we know today that various animals can use and make tools. Birds, crows have been known to make tools. But in those days, it was really exciting because it was thought in our arrogant way, that we humans were the only individuals, only creatures to use and make tools. We were actually defined as man the tool maker. So that when I sent Lewis Leakey this information, waited of course until I had seen it a few more times with a few more chimps to be sure, he said well, we shall have to redefine man, redefine tool or accept chimpanzee as human.

So, it was that that brought in the National Geographic Society. And not only did they provide money so that I could relax, knowing that the study could go on after the six months was over, but they also sent a photographer and a cameraman Hugo van Lawick who became my first husband and the father of my only child, my son.

And so, as the chimpanzees came to accept me, thanks really to this one individual David Greybeard who I had seen using and making tools, who's the first one to demonstrate that sometimes chimpanzees hunt and eat meat, not very often but sometimes. And because he began to accept me and not run away, if he was with a group that were all ready to flee as usual, and David just sat there calmly, the others would look from him to me and back, and I suppose they thought well, she can't be so dangerous after all.

And so, in a way, he introduced me to his friends in the forest, and there was his close companion Goliath. And then there was the very low-ranking Mike, and there was the old female Flo, and Melissa and Passion and all the rest of the characters that I got to know so well. And as the months turn into years, I began to realise that there are good and bad mothers in chimp society just as in human society. And the good mothers are those who are protective but not over protective. They allow their child some freedom, they are affectionate, they are playful but most importantly, they are supportive. In other words, my mother behaved like a good chimpanzee mother.

And it was very clear as I learnt more and more that the offspring of the good mothers did better, they became more self-assured. The males rose higher in the dominance hierarchy, the females were better mothers. And learning more and more about the ways they resemble us in their communication, gestures, kissing and embracing, and holding hands and patting on the back, and swaggering and shaking the fist.

And yes, I learnt that they, like us, have a dark side. They can be violent and brutal but like us, they can show compassion, altruism, true altruism as when a mother dies, leaves a small infant. If that child is older than three years and no longer dependent on the mother's milk, then the child will have a chance of surviving, if it's cared for and that's usually by an older brother or sister. But if there's no older brother or sister, then an unrelated individual may care for that infant, and the infant may actually survive.

So it was when I had been in field two years, didn't know all of this by then but I was beginning to learn quite a bit about the chimpanzees and I certainly knew their various personalities. And I got a letter from Lewis Leakey telling me that he wouldn't always be around to help me get money, I would have to stand on my own two feet and I would need a degree. And there was no time to mess about, as he put it, with a BA. I would have to go straight for a PhD, and he had me a place, Cambridge University.

Well, you can imagine I was a little bit nervous. I had never been to college. I imagined that the other students resented me, 'who does she think she is? You know, coming in just because she studied exotic things like chimpanzees, she thinks she doesn't have to do all the work for a BA.' It wasn't like that at all but they didn't know. But then when the professors told me that I had done everything wrong, that was a blow. I shouldn't have given them names, they should have had numbers, that was scientific. And I shouldn't be talking about them having personalities, minds capable of thinking and absolutely not emotions. I was guilty of the worst scientific sin of anthropomorphism. Well, fortunately, when I was a child, I had a wonderful teacher. And that teacher had taught me that of course, animals have personality, of course they can think, and of course they have emotions like happiness and sadness and fear and despair. And that teacher? That was my dog, Rusty.

Yes, let's give dogs a hand.

If you share your life in a meaningful way with a dog, a cat, a horse, a cow, a bird, I don't care what it is, you know the professors were wrong. And fortunately my sternest critic, initially, was my supervisor Dr Robert Hinde, but then he came to Gombe and he said in two weeks there, he learned more about animal behaviour than in all his previous life. And he helped me to write my observations in such a way that I wouldn't be completely torn apart by my scientific colleagues. And I got the PhD, and I went back to Gombe and I built up a research station so that other students could come and help to learn more and more about the chimpanzees. It was my dream life. I had a child by then, he was there with me, he was being home schooled. And I had time for analysing the data which I had loved doing, time for writing some popular books, and I had time every day to be out in the forest with the chimpanzees who were just out in nature.

So why did I leave? I left because in 1986, we brought together the various people who by then was studying chimpanzees in eight different parts of Africa. And it seemed important to try to share the knowledge that we jointly had. Because we now know that chimpanzees have simple cultures, the young ones learned by observing and imitating, and one definition of human culture is behaviour passed from one generation to the next through observational learning. And so bringing these different people together, looking at slides at how the chimps behaved differently in different parts of Africa, it was really exciting but we had a session on conservation.

And that was a shock, everywhere, all of these eight different places, chimpanzee numbers were dropping, forests were disappearing. There was the beginning of the bush meat trade, the commercial hunting of wild animals for food, chimpanzees were being caught in wire snares and losing a hand or a foot or dying. The mothers were being shot to steal their babies as pets, to sell in the local markets or to sell overseas through dealers to be exhibited in zoos in far off lands, to be used in the entertainment business in circuses and so forth. And at that time, in medical research.

We had another session on conditions in some captive situations, and that was an even worse shock, seeing the cruelty with which the chimpanzees are trained to perform in a circus. And this was undercover, of course, nobody was going to admit the cruelty but there were people who found, there were whistle-blowers.

And then, came worst of all, secretly filmed footage in a medical research lab. Our closest living relatives, they were there because their bodies are so like ours, we share over 98 per cent of DNA, composition of DNA with chimpanzees. The immune system, the composition of the blood, the anatomy of the brain, all of these things are so like us. And so, the scientists were very happy to use these bodies because chimpanzees can be infected with diseases which other animals, less like us, cannot be infected with. Yes, so here we are, we have the perfect model. We learn about ways to cure disease, vaccines and so forth with these chimpanzees. And they were not prepared to admit the equally striking psychological similarities between us and them. And so here were these close relatives of ours, in five foot by five foot, bleak cages with bars all around. I actually have stood in one of those cages with maybe if they were lucky, with limited time on the ground. Maybe for 30 or 40 years, they can live for 60 years. I couldn't sleep for weeks after that, these images went round and round in my mind.

So, I went to that conference in 1986, 30 years ago, I went as a scientist with a magical life and I left as an activist. I didn't make any conscious decision, I just left knowing that I had to try and do something for these amazing beings who had taught me so much. They taught all of us so much. It was chimpanzees because they are so like us in so many ways that finally began opening the mind of science to understand that we are a part of, and not separated, from the rest of the animal kingdom. And honestly, in 1961 when I went to Cambridge, it was thought that the difference between us and all the other animals, was one of kind. Now we know that it's one of degree but back then, it was one of kind. And it was a sharp line which should never be crossed.

And as I say, because chimps are so like us in so many ways, gradually, science opened its mind, and you know that today, for you young students, any of you who want to go into animal behaviour, this is the most exciting time because we are now understanding that all kinds of animals that we never thought were particularly intelligent before, or at least science didn't, now we find that they are capable of amazing intelligent behaviour.

The crow, I mentioned before. And the octopus. It's unbelievable what octopus can do, and if you haven't seen this, then I beg you afterwards google octopus and coconut shell. And you will be amazed to see what happens as an octopus under the water, a wild octopus, with two tentacles on each side, walking on the other four, goes across the ocean bed with half coconut shells on each side of him. And when he gets to an area where there are no rocks, and he's of course soft-bodied, he lays one half on the coconut shell on the ground, he gets himself wriggling, wriggling, making himself smaller and smaller and smaller, until he's more or less inside the bottom half, and then he reaches out and puts the top half over him. This is magic, and it hasn't only happened once, does it with clam shells as well, different octopus.

So here we are, it's wide open. The animal kingdom has never been so wide open to exploration. And this is just one reason why, in Malaysia, you're so lucky with the amazing animals that are out there, and I saw a film and some photographs this morning of some of these extraordinary animals that you have here in Malaysia.

But at any rate, as I say, I left that conference as an activist and since then, 30 years, I haven't been more than three weeks in any one place consecutively. And I began travelling around in Africa, I thought I must learn more about what's happening to the chimpanzees and their forests. And so, I learnt a lot but at the same time, I was learning more and more about the problems faced by so many African people, those living in and around the rainforest, suffering from tremendous poverty and hunger, and a lack of educational and health facilities, struggling to survive. And this all came to a head in 1991, when I flew over Gombe National Park which had been part of a belt of forest stretching along the western part Tanzania and Uganda, and curling around to the west coast of Africa. But I flew over in '91, I looked down on a tiny island of forest, surrounded by completely bare hills. More people living there than the land could support, overused farm land, no longer fertile. People desperate to try and grow more food to feed their families, and so cutting down the last of the trees. Steep, steep country so as the tree cover disappears, there was terrible erosion and the soil washed down into the little streams which were getting silted up. And I realised, it hit me so forcibly, we can't even try to save these chimpanzees while people are living in this terrible situation.

And so, that's when the Jane Goodall Institute began our programme that we call Take Care, or TACARE, and it's—I won't get into it now—but it's basically a very holistic programme because everything is inter-connected. And it was growing more food, and obviously without chemicals. But they also wanted better education and health facilities, and we did this by working with the Tanzanian government. We had very little money, a small grant from the European Union.

And then introducing projects to restore the flow of the streams, protecting the watershed, beginning to allow the steep hills to reforest from the seeds in the soil, and introducing the micro credit programmes, and I was so happy to see Muhammad Yunus made one of these lectures, he's one of my true heroes. He took me with him to Bangladesh, he introduced me to the women whose lives have been changed when they took out a tiny grant. And what I've noticed as we have developed this, we have nine of these little micro credit lending areas just around Gombe, is that if you just don't hand out money but you loan the money, and you loan it for some environmentally sustainable project, like one woman wanted to start a pineapple farm, another one wanted a few chickens to sell the eggs, and then they pay back. When they pay back, they can, if they wish, take out a larger loan but because they have done it themselves, they have been able to pay back, they are proud, I did it. And so, they are empowered and carrying on with this same theme, we provide as many scholarships as we can to keep girls in school after puberty. And it's been shown all around the world that as women's education improves, as women are empowered, so family size tends to drop. And that is desperately important in the world today. And we provide family planning information which is delivered by women in the villages, not by us. In fact, all of this programme has been done by local people, we've kept right in the background.

So successful has this Take Care / TACARE programme been that we've been able to introduce it around chimpanzee habitat in seven other African countries, and it has been successful in all of them. So helping to save the environment and the chimpanzees by helping the people. And the people are now truly our partners in conservation. We work around Gombe in 55 villages now and all of these villages provide one or two, depending on the size of the village, one or two volunteers to monitor the forests that are now coming back. The trees are growing where we once saw the bare slopes, some of them are 30 foot high already. And they go out, and now, they've got smart phones and i-tablets and things like this, and they use GPS, and they can go and monitor where there is an illegally cut tree, or where there is an animal trap or a cartridge. But they can also monitor a chimpanzee nest or a sighting of a leopard and so on. And all of this information goes out to a platform in the cloud, Global Forest Watch. And it's adding to what people are trying to do around the world to protect our precious rainforests. So, as I was traveling around developing this programme, and also trying to raise funds for these programmes, I was learning more and more about what was happening to our planet.

Let me go back for a moment to the chimpanzees. I talked a lot about the similarities between them and us, but clearly, there are major differences as well. You won't have chimpanzees dressed up in jackets and ties, and pretty dresses for a dinner, listening to a lecture. And chimpanzees are way smarter than we used to think, they can learn more than 400 of the signs of the American Sign Language (ASL) and use them in meaningful ways. Some of them love to paint, some of them will spontaneously sign to you what they think they have painted. It may not look like it to you but one painting I have is labelled Banana Flower. That's what the chimpanzee said it was. They can also do very, very clever things on computers, remembering the order of numbers much faster than I can.

But chimpanzees can't make rockets going up to the moon or to Mars, and I think personally, the biggest difference between us and them, us and any other animal, is this explosive development of the human intellect. And I believe a main contributory factor of this development is that we, at some point, developed this way of communicating with words so that we can learn from the distant past. We can make teach children about things that aren't present, we can make plans for the distant future. I mean, I could plan to come back here in three years.

And most important of all, we can have discussions. We had a discussion this morning, a round-table and when we bring different people together, as this morning, there were corporates, there were NGOs, there were scientists, conservationists, and discuss problems, then this sometimes leads to solutions. So, isn't it peculiar that this most intellectual creature that has ever walked on planet Earth, surely we are, nevertheless we are destroying our only home. That's not very intelligent, is it?

So, what's happened? It seems to me that there's been some kind of disconnect between this really clever brain and the human heart, love and compassion. And I have this conviction that we can only attain our true human potential, we can only begin to heal the harm we have inflicted on this beautiful planet when head and heart work in harmony. And when we realise that there is more to life than the bottom-line.

And I think that one of the things that has gone wrong is that while we all need money to live, there are too many people today who live for money. And I always like to say it's fine to live for money, if you live for money to make the world a better place like donating money to the Jane Goodall Institute, for example. At any rate, as I'm going around learning more about the pollution, the destruction of the rainforest, the creation of greenhouse gases, the CO2 that is released when you cut down and burn a forest, the gradual pollution of the ocean, the heating up of the ocean as the ice is melting thanks to global warming, these greenhouse gases that form an envelope around the planet and trap the heat of the sun. Then, I've been in Greenland, I've seen the ice melting at a time of year when no melting should take place. I've met people who've had to leave island homes because the melting of the ice has raised the level of the ocean, and there's been an increase in storms and hurricanes and so forth. And so, at high tide or during storms, their homes had been flooded and they had to leave their islands. And it's only getting worse.

Not really surprising that as I'm traveling around the world, I'm meeting a lot of young people, high school students and university students particularly, but also young people out in their first jobs. Well, and everybody really, meeting people of all kinds in all these different countries, who seem not to have much hope for the future. And it's not really surprising when you think about what's going on. I began talking to these young people, particularly, because if our young people lose hope, well then there is no hope, right, because there is no hope at all. So, I began talking to them, and basically, they all said more or less the same thing. 'Well, we feel like this because you've compromised our future and there's nothing we can do about it.'

Have we compromised the future of our young people? Have we compromised the future of our children and grandchildren? We have. We know we have. I know the planet's changed since I was a young child, and it's not changed for the better. And I'm so tired of hearing this phrase 'we haven't inherited this planet from our parents, we borrowed it from our children'. We haven't borrowed anything, we've stolen, and we are still stealing. And it's time we get together with the young people and to try to heal the harm that we have inflicted before it's too late. Because I don't believe it when people say it's too late. I think we have a window of time to turn things around.

So, that's when I began the programme for young people, Roots and Shoots. It began in Tanzania with 12 high school students. They came and told me all the things that were bothering them like the destruction of the coral reef, the street children. They were worried, some of them, about the treatment of animals in the markets, and stray dogs. They were worried about all kinds of things like that. And they wanted me to fix all those problems. And I said I love Tanzania but I'm not Tanzanian. And I really can't fix these problems but maybe together, we can talk about them. So, they got friends from their schools, they came from nine different schools, and we had a big meeting, and from that meeting, this youth programme was born. The main message: every single one of us, every single one of us makes impact on this planet every single day. We cannot live through a day without making some kind of impact.

And we have a choice. Certainly everybody in this room has a choice. Some people don't have that much choice in their lives but we do. And if we start thinking about the consequences of the choices we make each day, the little things: what we buy, what we eat, what we wear, where did they come from, how was it made, did it result, the making of it, in cruelty to animals, was it child slave labour in a faraway place, did it harm the environment, that kind of thing, then we start making wiser choices. We can also ask ourselves do we really need it, is it necessary, do we have to buy this thing? And so, I feel that the biggest problem that people face today, is yes, we are getting wiser and wiser about what's happening to the planet but it's daunting.

If you think about everything, it's daunting. And I'm one person, what can I do? There's no point in doing anything because I'm helpless and hopeless. And so, people do nothing and they shut it all away, and they don't even think about it. They don't want to think about it because that would be depressing. So, it's this apathy that has to be overcome and I found particularly with young people that when they start realising that yes, me alone, I can't do anything but when there's hundreds or thousands or millions or maybe eventually billions of people all making the right choices, all trying to leave a slightly lighter ecological footprint, then we begin moving to the kind of world that we can be happier to leave to our descendants.

So, that's how Roots and Shoots was born. That was its main message that every individual matters and has a role to play, and makes a difference. And why is it called Roots and Shoots? Well, you have beautiful trees in this country. I was just in a little park outside somewhere near here, and there were these strangling figs. They are such gorgeous things, we took photographs. And this strangling fig, when it starts, it's from a very tiny little seed, and from that tiny little seed, little roots appear and little tiny shoots. And you can pick it up, and how teeny and weak and fragile it seems but it's, you know what I call it, it's a magic. It's a life force in that seed so powerful that those little roots to reach the water can work though rocks and eventually push them aside. And that little shoot, to reach the sun, can work its way through cracks in a brick wall or a pavement, and eventually, break it down.

So, Roots and Shoots is hope that hundreds and thousands of young people around the world can break through and make a difference. And we are now in almost 100 countries. We started in Malaysia last year but there's already over 50 groups in 50 different schools, thanks to the volunteers in Roots and Shoots, and TP Lim who is the chairman. I wouldn't be here but for him. Stand up, TP, and where are the Roots and Shoots volunteers? You stand up too, I don't know where you are, I can't see but they're there. (Claps)

So, to give you a tiny taste of what Roots and Shoots is doing around the world. Every group chooses three kinds of projects to make the world better. One to help people, one to help animals, one to help the environment. And the kind that they choose will depend on how old they are because we now have members from kindergarten all the way to university. It will depend if they are rich or poor, it'll depend on the country that they are in or the part of the country that they are in because the problems will be different and the solutions will be different. But basically, it's about talking about the problems, deciding what you can do and rolling up your sleeves and getting out. It's about taking action.

And this little tiny four minutes of a film will give you just a little idea of what's going on around the world.

(Video clip plays)

Well, maybe you can understand why my greatest reason for hope is the young people, and as I'm travelling around the world, everywhere I'm greeted with these shining eyes and young people of all ages wanting to tell Dr Jane what they have been doing, what they plan to do to make world a better place. And it's growing so fast, this programme, and I think it's because young people feel so empowered when they see the difference they make. When they see a place that was bare, and a forest beginning to grow back, when they remove invasive species, when they plant mangroves, when they raise money to help the victims of tsunamis or earthquakes. There are so many, many projects that these young people think of and take action and make change. It isn't that young people can change the world, they are changing the world and that's my greatest reason for hope.

But I have four other reasons for hope, and we wanted to talk about hope this evening.

My next reason is this human brain.

And yes, we have done some pretty bad things with our brain, we still are doing some pretty bad things with this amazing intellect of ours, but think of all the good things that are being done. Think of all the technology that's been created that will enable us to live in greater harmony with this planet, the clean green energy. And if governments would just subsidise that, instead of always subsidising fossil fuel, then it would start to really bloom and we'd move much faster towards the kind of world we all want.

And the human brain is working in individuals too. We are learning that we can make a difference, we are learning to make different life choices which makes us feel better. Luckily when we do something, especially if it's a bit hard, it makes you feel better and that's really lucky. So, the human brain is my next reason for hope.

The resilience of nature.

Around Gombe, there were these bare hills. If you fly over it today, there are no more bare hills. The trees are growing back, that magic in the seeds in the soil is working, we haven't even had to plant the trees there. And in Malaysia, there were two animal species that were on the brink of extinction and that's the leatherback turtle and the green turtle, and they are now making a comeback.

And your forests in Sabah are being protected, I was hearing about that this morning, large areas of forests being protected, plans made to protect it even more and people determined to fight, to go on, so that the orangutans will have a home. And all the other extraordinary creatures in those forests will survive for your great-great grandchildren. And this is happening all over the world, and so the resilience of nature is one of my great reasons for hope. And I've seen it happening, I've seen it happening in so many countries.

And then, social media.

That is fairly new, I hadn't thought about it before but I was in New York two years ago, and there was a climate march. And it was arranged by, I don't know who arranged it but Al Gore was there and Ban Ki-moon. And the organisers hoped for about 80,000 people, in fact 400,000 people, the police had to stop more coming. So, what was happening? Everybody was on their little gadgets, you know facebooking and tweeting and twittering, and all the different things that get done these days. And there were also people on cell phones, I could hear them, I could hear what they were saying. And they were saying come and join us, it's great weather, there's all these famous people here. One of them said, I just saw Leonardo DiCaprio, one of them said I saw Angelina Jolie and one of them truly said I saw Jane Goodall. Yes!

That was happening in major cities around the world. It was said to be the biggest gathering of human beings around a single issue in the history of the Earth. So where in the old days, we would write letters and drop them through letter boxes, or we would make long telephone calls and gather as many people as we could for a demonstration or something, now, we can just spread it out around the world and get all these different people coming together. It's very powerful.

And finally, my last reason for hope is the indomitable human spirit.

And this is something very special. There are people who, you know they suffered the slings and arrows of outrageous fortune as Shakespeare said, they have been knocked down, they have perhaps lost all their savings, people have fled the country where they grew up because of war and violence, and arrive as refugees with nothing and yet, because of this indomitable spirit, somehow they find a way forward and make a living for themselves.

And there are icons like Nelson Mandela, like Martin Luther King, I'm sure you have your own in this part of the world. And then, there are those people who overcome tremendous physical disabilities and lead lives that are shining inspiration to everybody around them. And that's why I carry Mr H, you probably saw him in the piece of film. And Mr H is now 24 years old. He was given to me for my birthday 24 years ago by a man called Gary Horn which is why he is Mr H, who thought he was giving me a stuffed chimpanzee. Well, Gary Horn was blind, I made him hold the tail. And Gary Horn, having been blinded at 21 in the US Marines, for some odd reason, decided that he wanted to become a magician.

So everybody said, 'But Gary, you can't be a good magician if you can't see.' He said, 'well, I can try.' And he's such a good magician that the children don't realise he's blind. And at the end, he'll tell them and say 'things may go wrong in your life because we never know. But if they do, don't give up, there's always some way forward.' And he does sky diving. I mean I think it's crackers to jump out of a plane anyway but to jump out into a pitch black world is the height of insanity. But anyway, he does it. And he has just produced a book called the Blind Artist. He paints, he's learnt to paint, he has done an amazing portrait of Mr H just by holding him and feeling him, and putting it on paper. And in the book, he explains how he does it, how he does all these extraordinary pictures that he has produced. So I'm sure every single of you has had experience of this indomitable human spirit.

There are hundreds of stories, and so, those are my reasons for hope.

The young people all around the world, not just Roots and Shoots, so many other youth organisations. There is a new sense of urgency in young people. They seem to be growing up faster, they seem to have more sense of responsibility. And once they are educated and empowered to take action, there's no limit to the effort that they put in to making this a better world. And then, this amazing human brain that can enable us to live in a very different way, if we will only push that side of it. And then, the resilience of nature, the power of social media, and that, of course, is due to the amazing brain. And then, the indomitable human spirit.

So, I want to thank all of you for coming tonight. And it is wonderful to look around and see so many faces in this lovely setting. So, I hope that this message of hope will inspire you to just think a little bit more about the way you live because that's what's going to make the difference. And that's what's going to enable you to go to sleep with a happier mind every night. And that's my greatest hope for the future. Thank You.

New Hampshire Speech

Michelle Obama

Manchester, New Hampshire (2016)

Michelle Obama is a former First Lady, lawyer, author, orator and activist who was a major aide during former President Barack Obama's election campaign. She continues to serve as a role model for Americans, advocating for healthy living, education and the eradication of poverty. Besides a successful career as a lawyer and her humanitarian ventures, Michelle Obama is also considered a fashion icon by many notable designers.

During her 'New Hampshire Speech', Michelle Obama denounced Donald Trump's sexist behaviour and showed support for Hillary Clinton.

My goodness! You guys are fired up!

Well, let me just say hello everyone. I am so thrilled to be here with you all today in New Hampshire. This is like home to me, and this day—thank you for a beautiful fall day. You just ordered this day up for me, didn't you? It's great to be here.

Let me start by thanking your fabulous governor, your next US senator, Maggie Hassan. I want to thank her for that lovely introduction. I also want to recognize your Congresswoman Annie McKlane Kuster, who's a dear, dear friend. Your soon-to-be congresswoman once again, Carol Shea Porter—all of whom have been just terrific friends to us. And your executive council and candidate for governor, Colin Van Ostern.

And, of course, thanks to all of you for taking the time to be here today.

(Audience member: We love you!)

Thanks so much. That's very sweet of you. I love you guys too. I can't believe it's just a few weeks before election day, as we come together to support the next president and vice-president of the United States, Hillary Clinton *and Tim Kaine! And New Hampshire is going to be important, as always.*

So I'm going to get a little serious here, because I think we can all agree that this has been a rough week in an already rough election. This week has been particularly interesting for me personally because it has been a week of profound contrast.

See, on Tuesday, at the White House, we celebrated the International Day of the Girl and Let Girls Learn, and it was a wonderful celebration. It was the last event that I'm going to be doing as first lady for Let Girls Learn. And I had the pleasure of spending hours talking to some of the most amazing young women you will ever meet, young girls here in the US and all around the world. And we talked about their hopes and their dreams. We talked about their aspirations. See, because many of these girls have faced unthinkable obstacles just to attend school, jeopardizing their personal safety, their freedom, risking the rejection of their families and communities.

So I thought it would be important to remind these young women how valuable and precious they are. I wanted them to understand that the measure of any society is how it treats its women and girls. And I told them that they deserve to be treated with dignity and respect, and I told them that they should disregard anyone who demeans or devalues them, and that they should make their voices heard in the world. And I walked away feeling so inspired, just like I'm inspired by all the young people here—and I was so uplifted by these girls. That was Tuesday.

And now, here I am, out on the campaign trail in an election where we have consistently been hearing hurtful, hateful language about women—language that has been painful for so many of us, not just as women, but as parents trying to protect our children and raise them to be caring, respectful adults, and as citizens who think that our nation's leaders should meet basic standards of human decency.

The fact is that in this election, we have a candidate for president of the United States who, over the course of his lifetime and the course of this campaign, has said things about women that are so shocking, so demeaning that I simply will not repeat anything here today. And last week, we saw this candidate actually bragging about sexually assaulting women. And I can't believe that I'm saying that a candidate for president of the United States has bragged about sexually assaulting women.

And I have to tell you that I can't stop thinking about this. It has shaken me to my core in a way that I couldn't have predicted. So while I'd love nothing more than to pretend like this isn't happening, and to come out here and do my normal campaign speech, it would be dishonest and disingenuous of me to just move on to the next thing like this was all just a bad dream.

This is not something that we can ignore. It's not something we can just sweep under the rug as just another disturbing footnote in a sad election season. Because this was not just a 'lewd conversation'. This wasn't just locker-room banter. This was a powerful individual speaking freely and openly about sexually predatory behavior, and actually bragging about kissing and groping women, using language so obscene that many of us were worried about our children hearing it when we turn on the TV.

And to make matters worse, it now seems very clear that this isn't an isolated incident. It's one of countless examples of how he has treated women his whole life. And I have to tell you that I listen to all of this and I feel it so personally, and I'm sure that many of you do too, particularly the women. The shameful comments about our bodies. The disrespect of our ambitions and intellect. The belief that you can do anything you want to a woman.

It is cruel. It's frightening. And the truth is, it hurts. It hurts. It's like that sick, sinking feeling you get when you're walking down the street minding your own business and some guy yells out vulgar words about your body. Or when you see that guy at work that stands just a little too close, stares a little too long, and makes you feel uncomfortable in your own skin.

It's that feeling of terror and violation that too many women have felt when someone has grabbed them, or forced himself on them and they've said no but he didn't listen—something that we know happens on college campuses and countless other places every single day. It reminds us of stories we heard from our mothers and grandmothers about how, back in their day, the boss could say and do whatever he pleased to the women in the office, and even though they worked so hard, jumped over every hurdle to prove themselves, it was never enough.

We thought all of that was ancient history, didn't we? And so many have worked for so many years to end this kind of violence and abuse and disrespect, but here we are in 2016 and we're hearing these exact same things every day on the campaign trail. We are drowning in it. And all of us are doing what women have always done: we're trying to keep our heads above water, just trying to get through it, trying to pretend like this doesn't really bother us maybe because we think that admitting how much it hurts makes us as women look weak.

Maybe we're afraid to be that vulnerable. Maybe we've grown accustomed to swallowing these emotions and staying quiet, because we've seen that people often won't take our word over his. Or maybe we don't want to believe that there are still people out there who think so little of us as women. Too many are treating this as just another day's headline, as if our outrage is overblown or unwarranted, as if this is normal, just politics as usual.

But, New Hampshire, be clear: this is not normal. This is not politics as usual. This is disgraceful. It is intolerable. And it doesn't matter what party you belong to— Democrat, Republican, independent—no woman deserves to be treated this way. None of us deserves this kind of abuse.

And I know it's a campaign, but this isn't about politics. It's about basic human decency. It's about right and wrong. And we simply cannot endure this, or expose our children to this any—not for another minute, and let alone for four years. Now is the time for all of us to stand up and say enough is enough. This has got to stop right now.

Because consider this: if all of this is painful to us as grown women, what do you think this is doing to our children? What message are our little girls hearing about who they should look like, how they should act? What lessons are they learning about their value as professionals, as human beings, about their dreams and aspirations? And how is this affecting men and boys in this country? Because I can tell you that the men in my life do not talk about women like this. And I know that my family is not unusual. And to dismiss this as everyday locker-room talk is an insult to decent men everywhere.

The men that you and I know don't treat women this way. They are loving fathers who are sickened by the thought of their daughters being exposed to this kind of vicious language about women. They are husbands and brothers and sons who don't tolerate women being treated and demeaned and disrespected. And like us, these men are worried about the impact this election is having on our boys who are looking for role models of what it means to be a man.

In fact, someone recently told me a story about their six-year-old son who one day was watching the news—they were watching the news together. And the little boy, out of the blue, said, 'I think Hillary Clinton will be president.' And his mom said, 'Well, why do you say that?' And this little six-year-old said, 'Because the other guy called someone a piggy and,' he said, 'You cannot be president if you call someone a piggy.'

So even a six-year-old knows better. A six-year-old knows that this is not how adults behave. This is not how decent human beings behave. And this is certainly not how someone who wants to be president of the United States behaves.

Because let's be very clear: strong men—men who are truly role models—don't need to put down women to make themselves feel powerful. People who are truly strong lift others up. People who are truly powerful bring others together. And that is what we need in our next president. We need someone who is a uniting force in this country. We need someone who will heal the wounds that divide us, someone who truly cares about us and our children, someone with strength and compassion to lead this country forward.

And let me tell you, I'm here today because I believe with all of my heart that Hillary Clinton will be that president.

See, we know that Hillary is the right person for the job because we've seen her character and commitment not just in this campaign, but over the course of her entire life. The fact is that Hillary embodies so many of the values that we try so hard to teach our young people. We tell our young people 'work hard in school, get a good education'. We encourage them to use that education to help others—which is exactly what Hillary did with her college and law degrees, advocating for kids with disabilities, fighting for children's healthcare as first lady, affordable childcare in the Senate.

We teach our kids the value of being a team player, which is what Hillary exemplified when she lost the 2008 election and actually agreed to work for her opponent as our secretary of state—earning sky-high approval ratings serving her country once again.

We also teach our kids that you don't take shortcuts in life, and you strive for meaningful success in whatever job you do. Well, Hillary has been a lawyer, a law professor, first lady of Arkansas, first lady of the United States, a US senator, secretary of state. And she has been successful in every role, gaining more experience and exposure to the presidency than any candidate in our lifetime—more than Barack, more than Bill. And, yes, she happens to be a woman.

And finally, we teach our kids that when you hit challenges in life, you don't give up, you stick with it. Well, during her four years as secretary of state alone, Hillary has faced her share of challenges. She's traveled to 112 countries, negotiated a ceasefire, a peace agreement, a release of dissidents. She spent 11 hours testifying before a congressional committee. We know that when things get tough, Hillary doesn't complain. She doesn't blame others. She doesn't abandon ship for something easier. No, Hillary Clinton has never quit on anything in her life.

So in Hillary, we have a candidate who has dedicated her life to public service, someone who has waited her turn and helped out while waiting. She is an outstanding mother. She has raised a phenomenal young woman. She is a loving, loyal wife. She's a devoted daughter who cared for her mother until her final days. And if any of us had raised a daughter like Hillary Clinton, we would be so proud. We would be proud.

And regardless of who her opponent might be, no one could be more qualified for this job than Hillary—no one. And in this election, if we turn away from her, if we just stand by and allow her opponent to be elected, then what are we teaching our children about the values they should hold, about the kind of life they should lead? What are we saying?

In our hearts, we all know that if we let Hillary's opponent win this election, then we are sending a clear message to our kids that everything they're seeing and hearing is perfectly OK. We are validating it. We are endorsing it. We're telling our sons that it's OK to humiliate women. We're telling our daughters that this is how they deserve to be treated. We're telling all our kids that bigotry and bullying are perfectly acceptable in the leader of their country. Is that what we want for our children?

And remember, we won't just be setting a bad example for our kids, but for our entire world. Because for so long, America has been a model for countries across the globe, pushing them to educate their girls, insisting that they give more rights to their women. But if we have a president who routinely degrades women, who brags about sexually assaulting women, then how can we maintain our moral authority in the world? How can we continue to be a beacon of freedom and justice and human dignity?

Well, fortunately, New Hampshire, here's the beauty: we have everything we need to stop this madness. You see, while our mothers and grandmothers were often powerless to change their circumstances, today, we as women have all the power we need to determine the outcome of this election.

We have knowledge. We have a voice. We have a vote. And on November the 8th, we as women, we as Americans, we as decent human beings can come together and declare that enough is enough, and we do not tolerate this kind of behavior in this country.

Remember this: in 2012, women's votes were the difference between Barack winning and losing in key swing states, including right here in New Hampshire. So for anyone who might be thinking that your one vote doesn't really matter, or that one person can't really make a difference, consider this: back in 2012, Barack won New Hampshire by about 40,000 votes, which sounds like a lot. But when you break that number down, the difference between winning and losing this state was only 66 votes per precinct. Just take that in.

If 66 people in each precinct had gone the other way, Barack would have lost.

So each of you right here today could help swing an entire precinct and win this election for Hillary just by getting yourselves, your families, and your friends and neighbors out to vote. You can do it right here. But you could also help swing an entire precinct for Hillary's opponent with a protest vote or by staying home out of frustration.

Because here's the truth: either Hillary Clinton or her opponent will be elected president this year. And if you vote for someone other than Hillary, or if you don't vote at all, then you are helping to elect her opponent. And just think about how you will feel if that happens. Imagine waking up on November the 9th and looking into the eyes of your daughter or son, or looking into your own eyes as you stare into the mirror. Imagine how you'll feel if you stayed home, or if you didn't do everything possible to elect Hillary.

We simply cannot let that happen. We cannot allow ourselves to be so disgusted that we just shut off the TV and walk away. And we can't just sit around wringing our hands. Now, we need to recover from our shock and depression and do what women have always done in this country. We need you to roll up your sleeves. We need to get to work. Because remember this: When they go low, we go …

Audience: High!

Yes, we do.

And voting ourselves is a great start, but we also have to step up and start organizing. So we need you to make calls and knock on doors and get folks to the polls on election day and sign up to volunteer with one of the Hillary campaign folks who are here today just waiting for you to step up.

And, young people and not-so-young people, get on social media. Share your own story of why this election matters, why it should matter for all people of conscience in this country. There is so much at stake in this election.

See, the choice you make November 8 could determine whether we have a president who treats people with respect—or not. A president who will fight for kids, for good schools, for good jobs for our families—or not. A president who thinks that women deserve the right to make our own choices about our bodies and our health – or not. That's just a little bit of what's at stake.

So we cannot afford to be tired or turned off. And we cannot afford to stay home on election day. Because on November the 8th, we have the power to show our children that America's greatness comes from recognizing the innate dignity and worth of all our people. On November the 8th, we can show our children that this country is big enough to have a place for us all—men and women, folks of every background and walk of life – and that each of us is a precious part of this great American story, and we are always stronger together.

On November 8, we can show our children that here in America, we reject hatred and fear and in difficult times, we don't discard our highest ideals. No, we rise up to meet them. We rise up to perfect our union. We rise up to defend our blessings of liberty. We rise up to embody the values of equality and opportunity and sacrifice that have always made this country the greatest nation on Earth.

That is who we are. And don't ever let anyone tell you differently. Hope is important. Hope is important for our young people. And we deserve a president who can see those truths in us – a president who can bring us together and bring out the very best in us. Hillary Clinton will be that president.

So for the next 26 days, we need to do everything we can to help her and Tim Kaine win this election. I know I'm going to be doing it. Are you with me? Are you all with me? You ready to roll up your sleeves? Get to work knocking on doors?

All right, let's get to work. Thank you all. God bless.

Nobel Lecture

Bob Dylan

(4 June 2017)

Bob Dylan, originally Robert Allen Zimmerman, is considered the most influential singer-songwriter of the 20th century, renowned for incorporating social and political issues in his lyrics. Dylan rose to fame as a folk singer who eventually infused rock and roll in his songs, he has sold tens of millions album till date. In 2012, Dylan was awarded the Presidential Medal of Freedom for his invaluable contribution to American culture, and in 2016, he was awarded the Nobel Prize in Literature.

Dylan finally delivered his Nobel Lecture in 2017, in which he talks about his music influences as well as books that have inspired him to make his songs more meaningful and 'unlike anything anybody ever heard'.

When I first received this Nobel Prize for Literature, I got to wondering exactly how my songs related to literature. I wanted to reflect on it and see where the connection was. I'm going to try to articulate that to you. And most likely it will go in a roundabout way, but I hope what I say will be worthwhile and purposeful.

If I was to go back to the dawning of it all, I guess I'd have to start with Buddy Holly. Buddy died when I was about eighteen and he was 22. From the moment I first heard him, I felt akin. I felt related, like he was an older brother. I even thought I resembled him. Buddy played the music that I loved—the music I grew up on: country western, rock 'n' roll, and rhythm and blues. Three separate strands of music that he intertwined and infused into one genre

One brand. And Buddy wrote songs—songs that had beautiful melodies and imaginative verses. And he sang great—sang in more than a few voices. He was the archetype. Everything I wasn't and wanted to be. I saw him only but once, and that was a few days before he was gone. I had to travel a hundred miles to get to see him play, and I wasn't disappointed.

He was powerful and electrifying and had a commanding presence. I was only six feet away. He was mesmerizing. I watched his face, his hands, the way he tapped his foot, his big black glasses, the eyes behind the glasses, the way he held his guitar, the way he stood, his neat suit. Everything about him. He looked older than twenty-two. Something about him seemed permanent, and he filled me with conviction. Then, out of the blue, the most uncanny thing happened. He looked me right straight dead in the eye, and he transmitted something. Something I didn't know what. And it gave me the chills.

I think it was a day or two after that that his plane went down. And somebody— somebody I'd never seen before—handed me a Leadbelly record with the song 'Cottonfields' on it. And that record changed my life right then and there. Transported me into a world I'd never known. It was like an explosion went off. Like I'd been walking in darkness and all of the sudden the darkness was illuminated. It was like somebody laid hands on me. I must have played that record a hundred times.

It was on a label I'd never heard of with a booklet inside with advertisements for other artists on the label: Sonny Terry and Brownie McGhee, the New Lost City Ramblers, Jean Ritchie, string bands. I'd never heard of any of them. But I reckoned if they were on this label with Leadbelly, they had to be good, so I needed to hear them. I wanted to know all about it and play that kind of music. I still had a feeling for the music I'd grown up with, but for right now, I forgot about it. Didn't even think about it. For the time being, it was long gone.

I hadn't left home yet, but I couldn't wait to. I wanted to learn this music and meet the people who played it. Eventually, I did leave, and I did learn to play those songs. They were different than the radio songs that I'd been listening to all along. They were more vibrant and truthful to life. With radio songs, a performer might get a hit with a roll of the dice or a fall of the cards, but that didn't matter in the folk world. Everything was a hit. All you had to do was be well versed and be able to play the melody. Some of these songs were easy, some not. I had a natural feeling for the ancient ballads and country blues, but everything else I had to learn from scratch. I was playing for small crowds, sometimes no more than four or five people in a room or on a street corner. You had to have a wide repertoire, and you had to know what to play and when. Some songs were intimate, some you had to shout to be heard.

By listening to all the early folk artists and singing the songs yourself, you pick up the vernacular. You internalize it. You sing it in the ragtime blues, work songs, Georgia sea shanties, Appalachian ballads and cowboy songs. You hear all the finer points, and you learn the details.

You know what it's all about. Takin' the pistol out and puttin' it back in your pocket. Whippin' your way through traffic, talkin' in the dark. You know that Stagger Lee was a bad man and that Frankie was a good girl. You know that Washington is a bourgeois town and you've heard the deep-pitched voice of John the Revelator and you saw the Titanic sink in a boggy creek. And you're pals with the wild Irish rover and the wild colonial boy. You heard the muffled drums and the fifes that played lowly. You've seen the lusty Lord Donald stick a knife in his wife, and a lot of your comrades have been wrapped in white linen.

I had all the vernacular down. I knew the rhetoric. None of it went over my head—the devices, the techniques, the secrets, the mysteries—and I knew all the deserted roads that it traveled on, too. I could make it all connect and move with the current of the day. When I started writing my own songs, the folk lingo was the only vocabulary that I knew, and I used it.

But I had something else as well. I had principles and sensibilities and an informed view of the world. And I had had that for a while. Learned it all in grammar school. *Don Quixote*, *Ivanhoe*, *Robinson Crusoe*, *Gulliver's Travels*, *Tale of Two Cities,* all the rest—typical grammar school reading that gave you a way of looking at life, an understanding of human nature, and a standard to measure things by. I took all that with me when I started composing lyrics. And the themes from those books worked their way into many of my songs, either knowingly or unintentionally. I wanted to write songs unlike anything anybody ever heard, and these themes were fundamental.

Specific books that have stuck with me ever since I read them way back in grammar school—I want to tell you about three of them: *Moby Dick, All Quiet on the Western Front* and *The Odyssey.*

Moby Dick is a fascinating book, a book that's filled with scenes of high drama and dramatic dialogue. The book makes demands on you. The plot is straightforward. The mysterious Captain Ahab—captain of a ship called the *Pequod*— an egomaniac with a peg leg pursuing his nemesis, the great white whale Moby Dick who took his leg. And he pursues him all the way from the Atlantic around the tip of Africa and into the Indian Ocean. He pursues the whale around both sides of the earth. It's an abstract goal, nothing concrete or definite. He calls Moby the emperor, sees him as the embodiment of evil. Ahab's got a wife and child back in Nantucket that he reminisces about now and again. You can anticipate what will happen.

The ship's crew is made up of men of different races, and any one of them who sights the whale will be given the reward of a gold coin. A lot of Zodiac symbols, religious allegory, stereotypes. Ahab encounters other whaling vessels, presses the captains for details about Moby. Have they seen him? There's a crazy prophet, Gabriel, on one of the vessels, and he predicts Ahab's doom. Says Moby is the incarnate of a Shaker god, and that any dealings with him will lead to disaster. He says that to Captain Ahab. Another ship's captain—Captain Boomer—he lost an arm to Moby. But he tolerates that, and he's happy to have survived. He can't accept Ahab's lust for vengeance.

This book tells how different men react in different ways to the same experience. A lot of Old Testament, biblical allegory: Gabriel, Rachel, Jeroboam, Bildah, Elijah. Pagan names as well: Tashtego, Flask, Daggoo, Fleece, Starbuck, Stubb, Martha's Vineyard. The Pagans are idol worshippers. Some worship little wax figures, some wooden figures. Some worship fire. The *Pequod* is the name of an Indian tribe.

Moby Dick is a seafaring tale. One of the men, the narrator, says, 'Call me Ishmael.' Somebody asks him where he's from, and he says, 'It's not down on any map. True places never are.' Stubb gives no significance to anything, says everything is predestined. Ishmael's been on a sailing ship his entire life. Calls the sailing ships his Harvard and Yale. He keeps his distance from people.

A typhoon hits the *Pequod*. Captain Ahab thinks it's a good omen. Starbuck thinks it's a bad omen, considers killing Ahab. As soon as the storm ends, a crew member falls from the ship's mast and drowns, foreshadowing what's to come. A Quaker pacifist priest, who is actually a bloodthirsty businessman, tells Flask, 'Some men who receive injuries are led to God, others are led to bitterness.'

Everything is mixed in. All the myths: the Judeo Christian Bible, Hindu myths, British legends, Saint George, Perseus, Hercules—they're all whalers. Greek mythology, the gory business of cutting up a whale. Lots of facts in this book, geographical knowledge, whale oil—good for coronation of royalty—noble families in the whaling industry. Whale oil is used to anoint the kings. History of the whale, phrenology, classical philosophy, pseudo-scientific theories, justification for discrimination—everything thrown in and none of it hardly rational. Highbrow, lowbrow, chasing illusion, chasing death, the great white whale, white as polar bear, white as a white man, the emperor, the nemesis, the embodiment of evil. The demented captain who actually lost his leg years ago trying to attack Moby with a knife.

We see only the surface of things. We can interpret what lies below any way we see fit. Crewmen walk around on deck listening for mermaids, and sharks and vultures follow the ship. Reading skulls and faces like you read a book. Here's a face. I'll put it in front of you. Read it if you can.

Tashtego says that he died and was reborn. His extra days are a gift. He wasn't saved by Christ, though, he says he was saved by a fellow man and a non-Christian at that. He parodies the resurrection.

When Starbuck tells Ahab that he should let bygones be bygones, the angry captain snaps back, 'Speak not to me of blasphemy, man, I'd strike the sun if it insulted me.' Ahab, too, is a poet of eloquence. He says, 'The path to my fixed purpose is laid with iron rails whereon my soul is grooved to run.' Or these lines, 'All visible objects are but pasteboard masks.' Quotable poetic phrases that can't be beat.

Finally, Ahab spots Moby, and the harpoons come out. Boats are lowered. Ahab's harpoon has been baptized in blood. Moby attacks Ahab's boat and destroys it. Next day, he cites Moby again. Boats are lowered again. Moby attacks Ahab's boat again. On the third day, another boat goes in. More religious allegory. He has risen. Moby attacks one more time, ramming the *Pequod* and sinking it. Ahab gets tangled up in the harpoon lines and is thrown out of his boat into a watery grave.

Ishmael survives. He's in the sea floating on a coffin. And that's about it. That's the whole story. That theme and all that it implies would work its way into more than a few of my songs.

All Quiet on the Western Front was another book that did. *All Quiet on the Western Front* is a horror story. This is a book where you lose your childhood, your faith in a meaningful world, and your concern for individuals. You're stuck in a nightmare. Sucked up into a mysterious whirlpool of death and pain. You're defending yourself from elimination. You're being wiped off the face of the map. Once upon a time you were an innocent youth with big dreams about being a concert pianist. Once you loved life and the world, and now you're shooting it to pieces.

Day after day, the hornets bite you and worms lap your blood. You're a cornered animal. You don't fit anywhere. The falling rain is monotonous. There's endless assaults, poison gas, nerve gas, morphine, burning streams of gasoline, scavenging and scabbing for food, influenza, typhus, dysentery. Life is breaking down all around you, and the shells are whistling. This is the lower region of hell. Mud, barbed wire, rat-filled trenches, rats eating the intestines of dead men, trenches filled with filth and excrement. Someone shouts, 'Hey, you there. Stand and fight.'

Who knows how long this mess will go on? Warfare has no limits. You're being annihilated, and that leg of yours is bleeding too much. You killed a man yesterday, and you spoke to his corpse. You told him after this is over, you'll spend the rest of your life looking after his family. Who's profiting here? The leaders and the generals gain fame, and many others profit financially. But you're doing the dirty work. One of your comrades says, 'Wait a minute, where are you going?' And you say, 'Leave me alone, I'll be back in a minute.' Then you walk out into the woods of death hunting for a piece of sausage. You can't see how anybody in civilian life has any kind of purpose at all. All their worries, all their desires—you can't comprehend it.

More machine guns rattle, more parts of bodies hanging from wires, more pieces of arms and legs and skulls where butterflies perch on teeth, more hideous wounds, pus coming out of every pore, lung wounds, wounds too big for the body, gas-blowing cadavers, and dead bodies making retching noises. Death is everywhere. Nothing else is possible. Someone will kill you and use your dead body for target practice. Boots, too. They're your prized possession. But soon they'll be on somebody else's feet.

There's Froggies coming through the trees. Merciless bastards. Your shells are running out. 'It's not fair to come at us again so soon,' you say. One of your companions is laying in the dirt, and you want to take him to the field hospital. Someone else says, 'You might save yourself a trip.' 'What do you mean?' 'Turn him over, you'll see what I mean.'

You wait to hear the news. You don't understand why the war isn't over. The army is so strapped for replacement troops that they're drafting young boys who are of little military use, but they're draftin' 'em anyway because they're running out of men. Sickness and humiliation have broken your heart. You were betrayed by your parents, your schoolmasters, your ministers, and even your own government.

The general with the slowly smoked cigar betrayed you too—turned you into a thug and a murderer. If you could, you'd put a bullet in his face. The commander as well. You fantasize that if you had the money, you'd put up a reward for any man who would take his life by any means necessary. And if he should lose his life by doing that, then let the money go to his heirs. The colonel, too, with his caviar and his coffee—he's another one. Spends all his time in the officers' brothel. You'd like to see him stoned dead too. More

Tommies and Johnnies with their whack fo' me daddy-o and their whiskey in the jars. You kill 20 of 'em and 20 more will spring up in their place. It just stinks in your nostrils.

You've come to despise that older generation that sent you out into this madness, into this torture chamber. All around you, your comrades are dying. Dying from abdominal wounds, double amputations, shattered hipbones, and you think, 'I'm only twenty years old, but I'm capable of killing anybody. Even my father if he came at me.'

Yesterday, you tried to save a wounded messenger dog, and somebody shouted, 'Don't be a fool.' One Froggy is laying gurgling at your feet. You stuck him with a dagger in his stomach, but the man still lives. You know you should finish the job, but you can't. You're on the real iron cross, and a Roman soldier's putting a sponge of vinegar to your lips.

Months pass by. You go home on leave. You can't communicate with your father. He said, 'You'd be a coward if you don't enlist.' Your mother, too, on your way back out the door, she says, 'You be careful of those French girls now.' More madness. You fight for a week or a month, and you gain ten yards. And then the next month it gets taken back.

All that culture from a thousand years ago, that philosophy, that wisdom—Plato, Aristotle, Socrates—what happened to it? It should have prevented this. Your thoughts turn homeward. And once again you're a schoolboy walking through the tall poplar trees. It's a pleasant memory. More bombs dropping on you from blimps. You got to get it together now. You can't even look at anybody for fear of some miscalculable thing that might happen. The common grave. There are no other possibilities.

Then you notice the cherry blossoms, and you see that nature is unaffected by all this. Poplar trees, the red butterflies, the fragile beauty of flowers, the sun—you see how nature is indifferent to it all. All the violence and suffering of all mankind. Nature doesn't even notice it.

You're so alone. Then a piece of shrapnel hits the side of your head and you're dead.

You've been ruled out, crossed out. You've been exterminated. I put this book down and closed it up. I never wanted to read another war novel again, and I never did.

Charlie Poole from North Carolina had a song that connected to all this. It's called 'You Ain't Talkin' to Me,' and the lyrics go like this:

I saw a sign in a window walking up town one day.
Join the army, see the world is what it had to say.
You'll see exciting places with a jolly crew,
You'll meet interesting people, and learn to kill them too.
Oh you ain't talkin' to me, you ain't talking to me.
I may be crazy and all that, but I got good sense you see.
You ain't talkin' to me, you ain't talkin' to me.
Killin' with a gun don't sound like fun.
You ain't talkin' to me.

The Odyssey is a great book whose themes have worked its way into the ballads of a lot of songwriters: 'Homeward Bound, 'Green, Green Grass of Home,' 'Home on the Range,' and my songs as well.

The Odyssey is a strange, adventurous tale of a grown man trying to get home after fighting in a war. He's on that long journey home, and it's filled with traps and pitfalls. He's cursed to wander. He's always getting carried out to sea, always having close calls. Huge chunks of boulders rock his boat. He angers people he shouldn't. There's troublemakers in his crew. Treachery. His men are turned into pigs and then are turned back into younger, more handsome men. He's always trying to rescue somebody. He's a travelin' man, but he's making a lot of stops.

He's stranded on a desert island. He finds deserted caves, and he hides in them. He meets giants that say, 'I'll eat you last.' And he escapes from giants. He's trying to get back home, but he's tossed and turned by the winds. Restless winds, chilly winds, unfriendly winds. He travels far, and then he gets blown back.

He's always being warned of things to come. Touching things he's told not to. There's two roads to take, and they're both bad. Both hazardous. On one you could drown and on the other you could starve. He goes into the narrow straits with foaming whirlpools that swallow him. Meets six-headed monsters with sharp fangs. Thunderbolts strike at him. Overhanging branches that he makes a leap to reach for to save himself from a raging river. Goddesses and gods protect him, but some others want to kill him. He changes identities. He's exhausted. He falls asleep, and he's woken up by the sound of laughter. He tells his story to strangers. He's been gone twenty years. He was carried off somewhere and left there. Drugs have been dropped into his wine. It's been a hard road to travel.

In a lot of ways, some of these same things have happened to you. You too have had drugs dropped into your wine. You too have shared a bed with the wrong woman. You too have been spellbound by magical voices, sweet voices with strange melodies. You too have come so far and have been so far blown back. And you've had close calls as well. You have angered people you should not have. And you too have rambled this country all around. And you've also felt that ill wind, the one that blows you no good. And that's still not all of it.

When he gets back home, things aren't any better. Scoundrels have moved in and are taking advantage of his wife's hospitality. And there's too many of 'em. And though he's greater than them all and the best at everything—best carpenter, best hunter, best expert on animals, best seaman—his courage won't save him, but his trickery will.

All these stragglers will have to pay for desecrating his palace. He'll disguise himself as a filthy beggar, and a lowly servant kicks him down the steps with arrogance and stupidity. The servant's arrogance revolts him, but he controls his anger. He's one against a hundred, but they'll all fall, even the strongest. He was nobody. And when it's all said and done, when he's home at last, he sits with his wife, and he tells her the stories.

So what does it all mean? Myself and a lot of other songwriters have been influenced by these very same themes. And they can mean a lot of different things. If a song moves you, that's all that's important. I don't have to know what a song means. I've written all kinds of things into my songs. And I'm not going to worry about it— what it all means. When Melville put all his old testament, biblical references, scientific theories, Protestant doctrines, and all that knowledge of the sea and sailing ships and whales into one story, I don't think he would have worried about it either—what it all means.

John Donne as well, the poet-priest who lived in the time of Shakespeare, wrote these words, 'The Sestos and Abydos of her breasts. Not of two lovers, but two loves, the nests.' I don't know what it means, either. But it sounds good. And you want your songs to sound good.

When Odysseus in *The Odyssey* visits the famed warrior Achilles in the underworld—Achilles, who traded a long life full of peace and contentment for a short one full of honor and glory—tells Odysseus it was all a mistake. 'I just died, that's all.' There was no honor. No immortality. And that if he could, he would choose to go back and be a lowly slave to a tenant farmer on Earth rather than be what he is—a king in the land of the dead—that whatever his struggles of life were, they were preferable to being here in this dead place.

That's what songs are too. Our songs are alive in the land of the living. But songs are unlike literature. They're meant to be sung, not read. The words in Shakespeare's plays were meant to be acted on the stage. Just as lyrics in songs are meant to be sung, not read on a page. And I hope some of you get the chance to listen to these lyrics the way they were intended to be heard: in concert or on record or however people are listening to songs these days. I return once again to Homer, who says, 'Sing in me, oh Muse, and through me tell the story.'

Women's March Speech

Gloria Steinem

Washington DC (21 January 2017)

Gloria Steinem is an American feminist, scholar, lecturer, journalist and author who is well-known for being an outspoken activist for equality. She was widely recognised as the leader of the American feminist movement in the 1960s and '70s. Steinem was awarded the Presidential Medal of Freedom in 2013 for her activism and for being an important participant in the women's liberation movement.

In her rousing 'Women's March Speech', Steinem stresses the need to continually oppose violence against women and denounces Trump's inaugural speech, stressing on the need for unity, now more than ever.

Friends, sisters and brothers, all of you who are before me today and in 370 marches in every state in this country and on six continents and those who will be communing with us in one at 1 [p.m.] in a silent minute for equality in offices, in kitchens, in factories, in prisons, all over the world. I thank each of you, and I especially want to thank the hardworking visionary organizers of this women-led, inclusive march, one of whom managed to give birth while she was organizing this march. Who else can say that?

Thank you for understanding that sometimes we must put our bodies where our beliefs are. Sometimes pressing send is not enough. And this also unifies us with the many in this world who do not have computers or electricity or literacy, but do have the same hopes and the same dreams.

I think that because I and my beloved co-chairs, the Golden oldies right? —Harry Belafonte, Dolores Huerta, LaDonna Harris—all these great people, we may be the oldest marchers here today, so I've been thinking about the uses of a long life, and one of them is you remember when things were worse.

We remember the death of the future, with Martin Luther King, with Jack Kennedy, with Bobby Kennedy, with Malcom X. Without those deaths for instance, Nixon would not have been elected, and there would not have been many of the wars that we had. Now, our great leaders like Barack Obama and Michelle Obama are still with us and remember how much we feared they might not be, and how much threat there was, in fact, on their lives. And they are with us.

And now, our honored Bernie Sanders is still with us. And not only with us but he's focusing on economic justice and achieving free universal college education in my state of New York. And now Hillary Clinton is alive and definitely not in jail. She who told the whole world that women's rights are human rights and human rights are women's rights. So crucial, when collectively violence against females in the world has produced a world in which for the first time there are fewer females than males.

I'm not trying to deny the danger that this day initiates. Trump and his handlers have found a fox for every chicken coop in Washington, and a Twitter finger must not become a trigger finger. Some very experienced doctors of the American Psychiatric Association have publicly written to warn us that, and I quote, 'His widely reported symptoms of mental instability, including grandiosity, impulsivity, hyper-sensitivity to slights or criticisms, and an apparent inability to distinguish between fantasy and reality, lead us to question his fitness for the immense responsibilities of the office.' Unquote.

This was on full display in his inaugural address yesterday. Everything that happened before him was a disaster. And everything that he would do would be fantastic, the best ever, miracles, and all the superlatives. He also said he was with the people. Indeed, he was the people. To paraphrase a famous quote, I just have to say, 'I have met the people, and you are not them.' We are the people

Just this march in Washington today required 1,000 more buses than the entire Inauguration. A 1000 more buses. And I was just talking with people from our many sister marches, including the one in Berlin, and they asked me to send a special message: 'We in Berlin know that walls don't work.'

And remember Poland where last month the government passed an anti-abortion law and six million women turned out in the streets and they had to change it. We are the people. We have people power and we will use it. All the power that you tried to eliminate. For instance, you tried to eliminate the Congressional Ethics Committee. You had to reinstate it, right? Because of people power. Because this, *this*, is the other side of the downside. This is an outpouring of energy and true democracy like I have never seen in my very long life. It is wide in age. It is deep in diversity. And remember the constitution does not begin with 'I, the president.' It begins with 'We, the people.'

So don't try to divide us. Do not try to divide us. If you force Muslims to register, we will all register as Muslims. I know that there are women here from corporations and media and all kinds of places that make it kind of risky for you to say what you care about, what you feel, and what you support. And there are women here, I know, who have survived a national and global sex industry that profiteers from body invasion. We are united here for bodily integrity. If you cannot control your body from the skin in, you cannot control it from the skin out, you cannot control your lives, our lives. And that means that the right to decide whether and when to give birth without government interference.

We are here and around the world for a deep democracy that says we will not be quiet, we will not be controlled, we will work for a world in which all countries are connected. God may be in the details, but the goddess is in connections. We are at one with each other, we are looking at each other, not up. No more asking daddy.

We are linked. We are not ranked. And this is a day that will change us forever because we are together. Each of us individually and collectively will never be the same again. When we elect a possible president we too often go home. We've elected an impossible president, we're never going home. We're staying together. And we're taking over. I thank you from the bottom of my heart. Make sure you introduce yourselves to each other and decide what we're gonna do tomorrow and tomorrow and tomorrow and we're never turning back. Thank you.'

Cecil B. DeMille Award Acceptance Speech

Oprah Winfrey

(2018)

Oprah Winfrey is an American television personality, actor, entrepreneur and philanthropist known as a media giant due to her widely successful talk show 'The Oprah Winfrey Show', which ran for 25 seasons from 1986 to 2011. The show earned Winfrey several Emmy Awards and other accolades. Winfrey was also awarded the Presidential Medal of Freedom in 2013.

Winfrey became the first black woman to accept the Cecil B. DeMille Award, and in her moving acceptance speech, she called for racial and gender equality.

Ah! Thank you. Thank you all. O.K., O.K. Thank you, Reese. In 1964, I was a little girl sitting on the linoleum floor of my mother's house in Milwaukee, watching Anne Bancroft present the Oscar for best actor at the 36th Academy Awards. She opened the envelope and said five words that literally made history: 'The winner is Sidney Poitier.' Up to the stage came the most elegant man I had ever seen. I remember his tie was white, and of course his skin was black. And I'd never seen a black man being celebrated like that. And I've tried many, many, many times to explain what a moment like that means to a little girl—a kid watching from the cheap seats, as my mom came through the door bone-tired from cleaning other people's houses. But all I can do is quote and say that the explanation's in Sidney's performance in 'Lilies of the Field': 'Amen, amen. Amen,

amen.' In 1982, Sidney received the Cecil B. DeMille Award right here at the Golden Globes, and it is not lost on me that at this moment there are some little girls watching as I become the first black woman to be given this same award.

It is an honor, and it is a privilege to share the evening with all of them, and also with the incredible men and women who've inspired me, who've challenged me, who've sustained me and made my journey to this stage possible. Dennis Swanson, who took a chance on me for 'A.M. Chicago'; Quincy Jones, who saw me on that show and said to Steven Spielberg, 'Yes, she is Sophia in 'The Color Purple''; Gayle, who's been the definition of what a friend is; and Stedman, who's been my rock—just a few to name. I'd like to thank the Hollywood Foreign Press Association, because we all know that the press is under siege these days.

But we also know that it is the insatiable dedication to uncovering the absolute truth that keeps us from turning a blind eye to corruption and to injustice. To tyrants and victims and secrets and lies. I want to say that I value the press more than ever before, as we try to navigate these complicated times. Which brings me to this: What I know for sure is that speaking your truth is the most powerful tool we all have. And I'm especially proud and inspired by all the women who have felt strong enough and empowered enough to speak up and share their personal stories. Each of us in this room are celebrated because of the stories that we tell. And this year we became the story. But it's not just a story affecting the entertainment industry. It's one that transcends any culture, geography, race, religion, politics or workplace.

So I want tonight to express gratitude to all the women who have endured years of abuse and assault, because they —like my mother—had children to feed and bills to pay and dreams to pursue. They're the women whose names we'll never know. They are domestic workers and farm workers; they are working in factories and they work in restaurants, and they're in academia and engineering and medicine and science; they're part of the world of tech and politics and business; they're our athletes in the Olympics and they're our soldiers in the military.

And they're someone else: Recy Taylor, a name I know and I think you should know, too. In 1944, Recy Taylor was a young wife and a mother. She was just walking home from a church service she'd attended in Abbeville, Ala., when she was abducted by six armed white men, raped and left blindfolded by the side of the road, coming home from church. They threatened to kill her if she ever told anyone, but her story was reported to the N.A.A.C.P., where a young worker by the name of Rosa Parks became the lead investigator on her case and together they sought justice. But justice wasn't an option in the era of Jim Crow. The men who tried to destroy her were never persecuted. Recy Taylor died 10 days ago, just shy of her 98th birthday. She lived, as we all have lived, too many years in a culture broken by brutally powerful men. And for too long, women have not been heard or believed if they dared to speak their truth to the power of those men. But their time is up. Their time is up. Their time is up.

And I just hope that Recy Taylor died knowing that her truth—like the truth of so many other women who were tormented in those years, and even now tormented—goes marching on. It was somewhere in Rosa Parks's heart almost 11 years later, when she made the decision to stay seated on that bus in Montgomery. And it's here with every woman who chooses to say, 'Me too.' And every man—every man—who chooses to listen. In my career, what I've always tried my best to do, whether on television or through film, is to say something about how men and women really behave: to say how we experience shame, how we love and how we rage, how we fail, how we retreat, persevere, and how we overcome. And I've interviewed and portrayed people who've withstood some of the ugliest things life can throw at you, but the one quality all of them seem to share is an ability to maintain hope for a brighter morning—even during our darkest nights.

So I want all the girls watching here and now to know that a new day is on the horizon! And when that new day finally dawns, it will be because of a lot of magnificent women, many of whom are right here in this room tonight, and some pretty phenomenal men, fighting hard to make sure that they become the leaders who take us to the time when nobody ever has to say, 'Me too' again. Thank you.